Learn Office 2016 for Mac

Second Edition

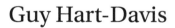

Guy Hart-Davis

Apress®

Special Edition **Using**

The One Source for Comprehensive Solutions™

The one stop shop for serious users, *Special Edition Using* offers readers a thorough understanding of software and technologies. Intermediate to advanced users get detailed coverage that is clearly presented and to the point.

Special Edition Using Visual Basic 6
Brian Siler & Jeff Spots
ISBN: 0-7897-1542-2
$39.99 US/
$57.95 CAN

Other Special Edition Using Titles

Special Edition Using Visual InterDev 6
Michael Morrison
ISBN: 0-7897-1549-x
$39.99 US/$57.95 CAN

Special Edition Using Windows NT Server 4
Roger Jennings
ISBN: 0-7897-1388-8
$49.99 US/$71.95 CAN

Special Edition Using Microsoft SQL Server 7
Steven Wynkoop
ISBN: 0-7897-1523-6
$39.99 US/$57.95 CAN

Special Edition Using Visual C++ 6
Kate Gregory
ISBN: 0-7897-1539-2
$39.99 US/
$57.95 CAN

Special Edition Using Access 97
Roger Jennings
ISBN: 0-7897-1452-3
$49.99 US/
$71.95 CAN

www.quecorp.com

All prices are subject to change.

Learn Office 2016 for Mac: Second Edition

Guy Hart-Davis
Barnard Castle, County Durham, UK

ISBN-13 (pbk): 978-1-4842-2001-6   ISBN-13 (electronic): 978-1-4842-2002-3
DOI 10.1007/978-1-4842-2002-3

Library of Congress Control Number: 2016947717

Managing Director: Welmoed Spahr
Acquisitions Editor: Louise Corrigan
Development Editor: Jim Markham
Technical Reviewers: Charlie Cruz and Brandon Scott
Editorial Board: Steve Anglin, Aaron Black, Pramila Balen, Laura Berendson, Louise Corrigan, Jonathan Gennick, Robert Hutchinson, Celestin Suresh John, Nikhil Karkal, James Markham, Susan McDermott, Matthew Moodie, Natalie Pao, Ben Renow-Clarke, Gwenan Spearing
Coordinating Editor: Nancy Chen
Copy Editor: Mary Behr
Compositor: SPi Global
Indexer: SPi Global
Cover Image:

Distributed to the book trade worldwide by Springer Science+Business Media New York, 233 Spring Street, 6th Floor, New York, NY 10013. Phone 1-800-SPRINGER, fax (201) 348-4505, e-mail orders-ny@springer-sbm.com, or visit www.springer.com. Apress Media, LLC is a California LLC and the sole member (owner) is Springer Science + Business Media Finance Inc (SSBM Finance Inc). SSBM Finance Inc is a Delaware corporation.

For information on translations, please e-mail rights@apress.com, or visit www.apress.com.

Apress and friends of ED books may be purchased in bulk for academic, corporate, or promotional use. eBook versions and licenses are also available for most titles. For more information, reference our Special Bulk Sales–eBook Licensing web page at www.apress.com/bulk-sales.

Any source code or other supplementary materials referenced by the author in this text is available to readers at www.apress.com. For detailed information about how to locate your book's source code, go to www.apress.com/source-code/.

Printed on acid-free paper

Contents at a Glance

Contents

About the Author

Guy Hart-Davis is the author of more than 100 computer books, including *Learn Excel 2016 for Mac* and *Pro Office for iPad*.

About the Technical Reviewers

Charlie Cruz is a mobile application developer for the iOS, Windows Phone, and Android platforms. He graduated from Stanford University with B.S. and M.S. degrees in engineering. He lives in Southern California and runs a photography business with his wife (www.bellalentestudios.com). When not doing technical things, he plays lead guitar in an original metal band (www.taintedsociety.com). Charles can be reached at codingandpicking@gmail.com and @CodingNPicking on Twitter.

Brandon Scott specializes in software engineering for desktop applications, software development kits, and distributed systems. He currently leads development efforts for AspiraCloud Ltd., focusing on Microsoft SharePoint and Azure workstreams. Additionally, Brandon also partners with Razer Inc., aiding with the design of SDK products and open source libraries. He has built experience working for a variety of companies in different industries, such as JP Morgan Chase & Co. and Microsoft.

Acknowledgments

My thanks go to the many people who helped create this book:

- Louise Corrigan for signing me to write the book
- James Markham for developing the manuscript
- Charles Cruz and Brandon Scott for reviewing the manuscript for technical accuracy and contributing helpful suggestions
- Mary Behr for editing the manuscript with care
- Nancy Chen for coordinating the book project and keeping things running
- SPi Global for laying out the chapters of the book
- SPi Global for creating the index

Introduction

Do you need to get your work done with the Office 2016 for Mac apps—smoothly, easily, and quickly?

Good! You've picked up the right book.

Who Is This Book For?

This book is designed to help beginning and intermediate users get up to speed quickly with the Office 2016 for Mac apps and immediately become productive with them.

If you need to learn to use Word, Excel, PowerPoint, and Outlook to get everyday tasks done, at work or at home, you will benefit from this book's focused approach and detailed advice. You can either start from the beginning of the book and work through it, or use the Table of Contents or the Index to find the topic you need immediately, and then jump right in there.

What Does This Book Cover?

This book contains five parts that cover the shared Office features and the four apps.

Part 1 of the book brings you up to speed with the common features that the Office apps share:

- Chapter 1 introduces you to Office's four apps—Word, Excel, PowerPoint, and Outlook—and what you can do with them. You learn how to open and close the apps; you meet key features such as the Ribbon interface; and you create, save, close, and reopen documents.

- Chapter 2 shows you how to control the Office apps using the menus, the Quick Access Toolbar, and the Ribbon, and how to use the Format pane. This chapter also explains Office's common ways of sharing a document with others, how to save time and effort by using the AutoCorrect and AutoFormat features the smart way, and how to use the spelling and grammar checkers. You also learn how to print documents.

- Chapter 3 shows you how to do everything from entering text (using the keyboard or other means) to creating tables and hyperlinks. Along the way, you learn how to work with the Cut, Copy, and Paste features, and how to use the Find and Replace features.

- Chapter 4 teaches you how to add visual interest to your Office document by adding pictures and shapes. You learn how to insert clip art, pictures (such as photos), and shapes; how to rotate and position graphical objects; and how to use Office's tools for making pictures look the way you want them to. This chapter also covers inserting SmartArt diagrams and arranging graphical objects to control which is visible.

- Chapter 5 walks you through the customization options the apps offer. You also learn how to set essential preferences in the apps, such as the General preferences and the Save preferences.

Part 2 of the book covers using Microsoft Word, the powerful word processing app:

- Chapter 6 shows you how to enter text quickly in Word documents. You learn how to select text in advanced ways with the pointing device and the keyboard, how to move around your documents, and how to tell Word where to find your custom templates. You also learn to create backup documents automatically, and to make the most of Word's many different views of a document.

- Chapter 7 teaches you the right way to format a document quickly and consistently by using styles rather than applying direct formatting bit by bit. It also shows you how to get around your documents by using the Sidebar and the Find feature, and how to harness the power of the Replace feature.

- Chapter 8 starts by showing you how to use Word's extra features for creating tables. The chapter then explains how to break a document into multiple sections; how to add headers, footers, and page numbers; and how to create newspaper-style columns of text. You learn how to use bookmarks and cross-references, develop your documents using Word's powerful Outline view, and add footnotes and endnotes to your documents.

- Chapter 9 shows you how to use Word to create business documents swiftly and efficiently. You learn to set up mail merge documents (such as letters or labels), connect them to data sources, and save or print the results.

- Chapter 10 covers how to use Word's features for working with your colleagues on documents. You learn how to edit a document either simultaneously or separately, how to use the Track Changes feature to mark revisions, and how to integrate changes into a document. You also see how to add comments to a document and compare two document versions that contain untracked changes.

- Chapter 11 explains how to print an entire document or just parts of it, with or without markup, and how to print markup without the document. You also learn how to remove sensitive information from documents, create a document you can open with earlier versions of Word, and create PDF files from documents.

Part 3 teaches you to create spreadsheets and charts with Excel:

- Chapter 12 covers creating different types of workbooks in Excel and entering data in them. You learn how to navigate the Excel interface, use workbooks and worksheets, and use Excel's views and features to see the data you need.

- Chapter 13 explains how to insert, delete, and format rows and columns in worksheets; how to format cells and ranges; and how to use the advanced conditional formatting and data validation features to identify unusual values or erratic input. This chapter also shows you how to format quickly and consistently with styles, how to add headers and footers to worksheets, and how to share workbooks effectively with your colleagues.

- Chapter 14 teaches you how Excel's charts work and how to add them to your workbooks. You learn how to lay out a chart effectively, how to make it look good, and how to hide any components you don't want to display. You even learn how to save time by reusing the custom chart formats you create.

- Chapter 15 makes clear the difference between a formula and a function, and shows you first how to create custom formulas and then how to use Excel's built-in functions.

- Chapter 16 shows you how to use Excel to create databases for storing and manipulating your information. You learn how to enter information into a database, how to sort the information, and how to filter it to find only the results you want. You also learn how to use the Goal Seek feature and scenarios to work out solutions to business problems.

- Chapter 17 explains how to use Excel's powerful PivotTable feature to manipulate your data so that you can discover the information you need. PivotTables take a few minutes to grasp, but you'll be surprised how easy they are to use.

Part 4 of the book takes you through creating good-looking, persuasive presentations with PowerPoint:

■   Chapter 18 gets you started by creating a presentation document using either a design template or a content template. The chapter then shows you how to add, delete, and rearrange slides; how to use PowerPoint's views effectively; how to develop the outline of a presentation; and how to break a presentation into separate sections. You also learn how to collaborate with your colleagues on creating a presentation.

■   Chapter 19 guides you through the toughest part of creating a good presentation: creating slides that convey your meaning clearly and powerfully. This chapter shows you how to plan a presentation, choose suitable layouts (or create your own), and add text and other content to your slides.

■   Chapter 20 shows you ways of spicing up a presentation by using graphics, movies, sounds, animations, and transitions. You also learn how to hide slides to keep them up your sleeve and how to build custom slide shows that enable you to reveal only part of a larger presentation.

■   Chapter 21 explains how to deliver the presentation you've created. You can deliver the presentation live in person or create a version of the presentation that you can share via e-mail or in other ways. You also learn how to use PowerPoint's Presenter view and how to create a handout for a presentation.

Part 5 of the book shows you how to manage your e-mail, schedule, contacts, and tasks with Outlook:

■   Chapter 22 first shows you how to set up Outlook to work with your ISP or e-mail provider's servers. Once Outlook is working, you learn how to get around its complex user interface, how to send and receive e-mail, and how to manage your messages.

■   Chapter 23 covers creating contacts either from scratch or importing them from your address books, spreadsheets, or other sources. The chapter also shows you how to view and sort your contacts, add or update their contact information, and quickly create communications to your contacts.

■   Chapter 24 brings you up to speed with Outlook's Calendar interface, shows you how to customize it, and teaches you to use its views. After that, it explains how to create one-shot appointments and repeating appointments, schedule meetings, and respond to meeting requests.

■   Chapter 25 shows you how to use Outlook to define the tasks you need to complete and track your progress on completing them. This chapter also explains how to use Outlook's Notes feature to jot down information as you work.

Conventions Used in This Book

This book uses several conventions to make its meaning clear without wasting words:

- Ribbon commands and menu commands: The ➤ sign shows the sequence for choosing an item from the Ribbon or a command from the menu bar. For example, "Choose Home ➤ Paragraph ➤ Decrease Indent from the Ribbon" means that you click the Home tab of the Ribbon (displaying the tab's contents), go to the Paragraph group, and then click the Decrease Indent button. Similarly, the ➤ sign indicates a menu sequence. For example, "Choose Insert ➤ Picture ➤ Picture from File from the menu bar" means that you click the Insert menu on the menu bar to open the menu, click the Picture item to open the Picture submenu, and then click the Picture from File item on the Picture submenu.

- Special paragraphs: Special paragraphs present information that you may want to pay extra attention to. Note paragraphs contain information you may want to know; Tip paragraphs present techniques you may benefit from using; and Caution paragraphs warn you of potential problems.

- Check boxes: The Office apps use many check boxes—the square boxes that can either have a check mark in them (indicating that the option is turned on) or not (indicating that the option is turned off). This book tells you to "select" a check box when you need to put a check mark in the check box, and to "clear" a check box when you need to remove the check mark from it. If the check box is already selected or cleared, you don't need to change it.

- Keyboard shortcuts: In the Office apps, you can often save time and effort by using a keyboard shortcut rather than a Ribbon command. This book uses + signs to represent keyboard shortcuts. For example, "press Cmd+S" means that you hold down the Cmd key, press the S key, and then release the Cmd key. "Press Cmd+Option+T" means that you hold down the Cmd key and the Option key, press the T key, and then release the Cmd key and the Option key.

Building Essential Office Skills

To save you time and effort, the Office 2016 for Mac apps share many common features. This part of the book shows you how to get started quickly with the applications and learn to use these common features.

In Chapter 1, you'll quickly meet Office's four main apps—Word, Excel, PowerPoint, and Outlook—and learn what you can do with them. You'll grasp essential moves, such as opening and closing the apps; and you'll create, save, close, and reopen documents.

In Chapter 2, you'll take control of the apps using the menus, the Quick Access Toolbar, and the Ribbon. You'll learn how to share a document with others, how to save time and effort by using the AutoCorrect and AutoFormat features the smart way, and how to use the spelling and grammar checkers. You'll also learn how to print documents.

In Chapter 3, you'll study how to work with text—everything from entering text using the keyboard to creating tables and hyperlinks. By the end of the chapter, you'll also know how to work with the Cut, Copy, and Paste tools, and how to use the Find and Replace features.

In Chapter 4, you'll add visual interest to your Office documents by inserting pictures and shapes. You'll learn how to insert clip art, pictures (such as photos), and shapes; how to rotate and position graphical objects; and how to use Office's tools for making pictures look the way you want them. When you need more complex illustrations, you can add SmartArt diagrams and arrange graphical objects to overlap each other, with fine control over which object is visible.

In Chapter 5, you'll make the Office apps easier and faster to use by customizing them. You'll also learn how to set essential preferences in the apps, such as the General preferences and the Save preferences.

Building Essential Office Skills

Chapter 1

Getting Up to Speed with the Office Apps

You're probably in a hurry to start being productive using Office 2016, so this chapter gets you moving quickly. First, you'll meet each of the apps, find out what you can do with them, and master key features such as the Ribbon and the Gallery dialog box. Then, I'll show you how to launch the apps or make them launch themselves. Finally, you'll look at how to create, save, and close documents, as well as how to reopen them when you need to work on them again.

Meeting the Office Apps and Learning What You Can Do with Them

Microsoft Office 2016 comes in several versions aimed at different but overlapping markets, so if you don't yet have Office, your first challenge is to decide which version to get. Table 1-1 summarizes the five Office versions that either include Mac versions or are exclusive to the Mac, what each costs, and which apps each includes.

G. Hart-Davis, *Learn Office 2016 for Mac*, DOI 10.1007/978-1-4842-2002-3_1

Table 1-1. Microsoft Office Versions with Mac Support or for the Mac

Version	Type	Cost	Installations	Includes
Office 365 Home	Subscription	$9.99 per month or $99.99 per year	Five PCs or Macs, five tablets, five phones	Word, Excel, PowerPoint, OneNote, Outlook, Publisher (PC only), Access (PC only)
Office 365 Personal	Subscription	$6.99 per month or $69.99 per year	One PC or Mac, one tablet, one phone	Word, Excel, PowerPoint, OneNote, Outlook, Publisher (PC only), Access (PC only)
Office Home & Student 2016 for Mac	Purchase	$149.99	One Mac	Word, Excel, PowerPoint, OneNote
Office Home & Business 2016 for Mac	Purchase	$229.99	One Mac	Word, Excel, PowerPoint, OneNote, Outlook
Office 365 University	Subscription	$79.99 per year for four years	Two PCs, Macs, or tablets; and two phones	Word, Excel, PowerPoint, OneNote, Outlook, Publisher (PC only), Access (PC only)

As you can see from Table 1-1, you can choose between buying Office outright or paying a yearly or monthly subscription. The Office 365 Home subscription is by far the best deal because it allows you to install Office on five PCs or Macs plus five tablets and five phones, so a single subscription can fully cover the Office needs of a nuclear family with its 2.4 children. As its name suggests, Office 365 Home is intended for home use rather than business use; for business use, you're supposed to buy Office Home & Business 2016 for Mac instead.

> **Tip** The numbers of PCs or Macs shown for the subscription versions of Office are the number of PCs or Macs on which you can have this version of Office active at the same time. You can install Office on more PCs or Macs than this and use the activation and deactivation features on the Office 365 web site (www.office365.com) to activate and deactivate computers as necessary.

For ease of use and to save time, the four main apps share many features, from the ways in which you create, save, and open documents to common actions you perform in them, such as copying text from one part of a document and pasting it in at another part.

Part 1 of this book discusses these common features. Parts 2 through 5 of the book then examine each of the apps in turn.

Microsoft Word

Microsoft Word (see Figure 1-1) is a word processing app that you can use to create everything from a single-page letter to a 1,000-page book complete with a table of contents, an index, and cross-references between different parts of the book.

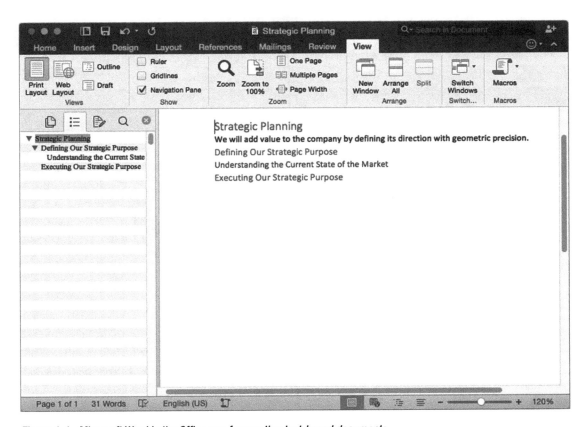

Figure 1-1. Microsoft Word is the Office app for creating text-based documents

Part 2 of this book explains how to make the most of Microsoft Word.

Microsoft Excel

Microsoft Excel (see Figure 1-2) is a spreadsheet app that you can use to record, calculate, and analyze data. Excel includes features for creating many different types of charts for presenting your data clearly and effectively.

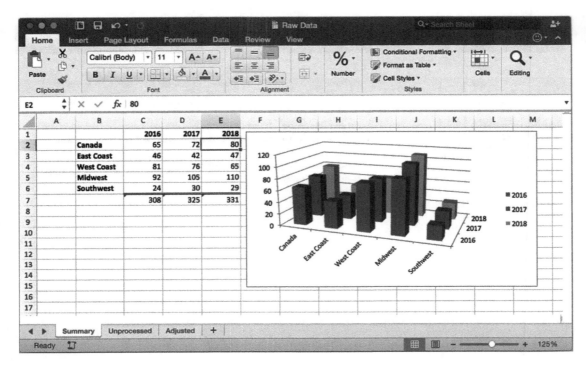

Figure 1-2. *Each Microsoft Excel workbook contains as many worksheets as you need for entering and analyzing your data*

Part 3 of this book shows you how to work quickly and effectively in Microsoft Excel.

Microsoft PowerPoint

Microsoft PowerPoint (see Figure 1-3) is an app for creating and delivering presentations. Each presentation consists of slides, to which you can add any data, from straightforward text to charts and movies. You can also add animations and transition effects to provide visual interest.

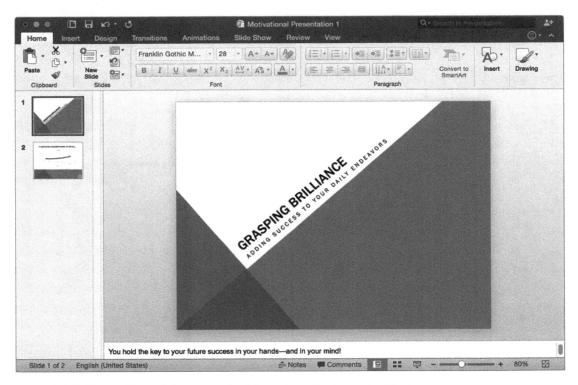

Figure 1-3. In Microsoft PowerPoint, you create slides and organize them into slide shows

Part 4 of this book covers creating persuasive presentations in PowerPoint and delivering them to your audience either in person or online.

Microsoft Outlook

Microsoft Outlook (see Figure 1-4) is an app for e-mail and managing your contacts, calendar, task list, and notes. If you have multiple e-mail accounts, you can manage them all within the single app, saving time and effort.

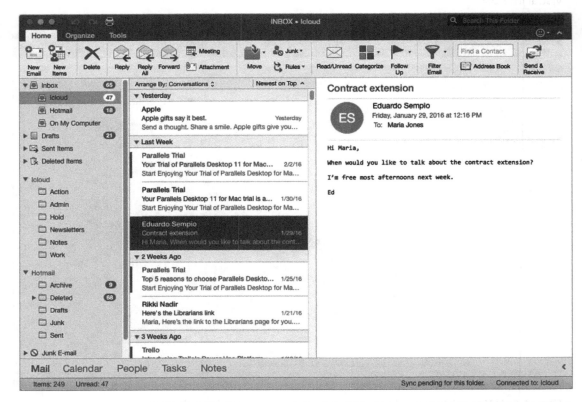

Figure 1-4. Microsoft Outlook makes it easy to work with multiple e-mail accounts and to schedule your business and home life

Part 5 of this book shows you how to send e-mail and organize your life with Outlook.

Understanding the Common Features of the Apps

As you can see from the figures on the past few pages, the Office apps share a common look and several common features. Some of the features are standard for OS X apps, but others are specific to the Office apps.

Figure 1-5 shows the OS X menu bar and a Word window with a document open and the major features labeled. The following sections explain what the features are and what you use them for.

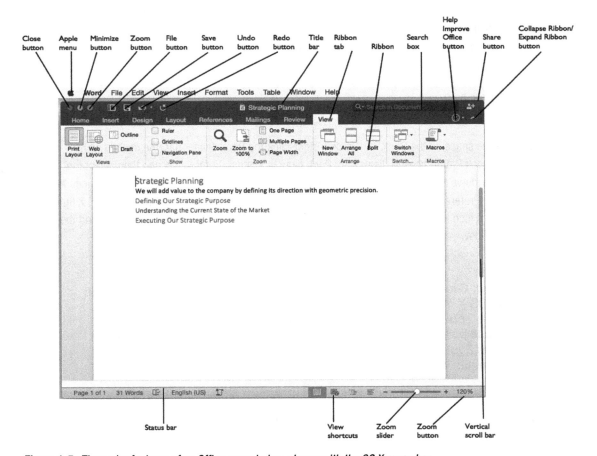

Figure 1-5. The major features of an Office app window, shown with the OS X menu bar

The Title Bar and the Close, Minimize, and Zoom Buttons

The title bar at the top of the window shows the name of the open document, such as Strategic Planning. The title bar may also show the document's file extension, such as .docx for a Word document.

> **Note** To control whether the title bar shows the document's file extension, click the app's menu (such as the Word menu for Word) and then Preferences to open the Preferences window. Click the General button to display the General pane. Select the Show file extensions check box, and then close the Preferences window by clicking the Close button (the red button at the left end of the window's title bar).

At the left end of the title bar are the following three buttons:

- *Close*: Click this button to close the window. The app stays open even if you close the last window; to close the app, quit it by pressing Cmd+Q or by clicking the app's menu and then clicking the Quit command (for example, choose Word ➤ Quit Word).

- *Minimize*: Click this button to minimize the window to the Dock. By default, OS X displays each minimized window as an icon on the right side of the Dock divider bar; click this icon to restore the window to its former size.

Tip   To save space on the Dock, Ctrl-click or right-click the Dock divider bar (the dashed white line), click Dock Preferences to display the Dock pane in System Preferences, and then select the Minimize windows into application icon check box. Press Cmd+Q or choose System Preferences ➤ Quit System Preferences to quit System Preferences. Now, when you minimize a window, OS X puts it in the app's icon in the Dock. To restore a window, Ctrl-click or right-click the app's icon, and then click the window you want.

- *Zoom*: Click this button to switch the app's window to full screen, hiding the OS X menu bar. Full screen is great when you want to focus on a single app. To switch back from full screen to a window, move the mouse pointer to the upper-left corner of the screen, and then click the green Zoom Back button that appears. The amount of space OS X estimates will make the contents fit just right.

Tip   You can also press Cmd+Ctrl+F to switch between a window and full screen.

To the right of the Close, Minimize, and Zoom buttons are four standard buttons in Word, Excel, and PowerPoint:

- *File*: Click this button to display the Gallery dialog box, which enables you to create new documents, open existing documents, and connect to services such as OneDrive. The Gallery dialog box shows the app's name rather than the word "Gallery" in its title bar.

- *Save*: Click this button to save the active document. If you've never saved the document before, the Save As sheet opens so that you can specify the name and folder for the document. If you have saved the document before, the app simply saves any unsaved changes.

- *Undo*: Click this button to undo the last action. You can continue to click the button to undo further actions as needed. Alternatively, click the pop-up arrow to display a pop-up menu that lists the changes you can undo, and then click the change you want to undo. The latest changes are at the top of the pop-up menu, so when you click a change on it, you're undoing all the changes down to the one you click.

- *Redo*: Click this button to redo the last action you've undone or to repeat the last action you've taken. You can click multiple times as needed.

The Ribbon

Below the title bar, the Ribbon runs across the top of the window. The Ribbon is a control bar that contains multiple tabs. You can display one tab's contents at a time by clicking the tab at the top.

Each Office app has a Home tab that contains some of the most useful commands, such as applying the most popular types of formatting. Beyond this tab, each app has other tabs to cover its needs. For example, PowerPoint's tabs include the Slide Show tab, the Transitions tab, and the Animations tab—none of which Word, Excel, or Outlook need.

> **Note**   When you need as much space as possible for working in a document, you can minimize the Ribbon by clicking the tab that's currently active, clicking the Collapse Ribbon button (the ^ button) at the right end of the Ribbon, choosing View ➤ Ribbon, or pressing Cmd+Option+R. To display the Ribbon again, click the tab you want to see, click the Show Ribbon button (the ^ button) at the right end of the Ribbon, choose View ➤ Ribbon, or press Cmd+Option+R.

In Word, Excel, and PowerPoint, each tab contains several groups of controls, divided into different types of actions. For example, the Home tab in PowerPoint contains a Slides group for creating and laying out slides, a Font group for applying font formatting, a Paragraph group for applying paragraph formatting, and several other groups. Unlike the other three apps, Outlook's tabs don't use groups.

> **Note**   You can choose whether to show the titles of the Ribbon groups. I recommend showing the group names because this book uses the groups to help make clear where to find commands on the Ribbon. For example, the instruction "choose Data ➤ Sort & Filter ➤ Advanced" means that you should click the Data tab of the Ribbon in Excel, go to the Sort & Filter group, and then click the Advanced button. If you don't have the group titles displayed, the instructions will seem to have an unnecessary second step.
>
> To control whether the group titles appear, click the app's menu (such as the Excel menu) and then click Preferences. In the Preferences window, click View to display the View pane. In the "In Ribbon, Show" area, select the Group Titles check box, and then close the Preferences window by clicking the Close button (the red button at the left end of the window's title bar).

You'll look at the details of how to use the Ribbon in Chapter 2, but the basic method is straightforward. You click the tab for the type of action you want to take and then click the button or control for the action you want to take. For example, to insert a picture in a Word document, you click the Home tab to display its contents, go to the Insert group, and then click the Picture button.

The Status Bar

At the bottom of the app window is the status bar, which shows information about the document and what you're currently working on, and provides controls for changing the view and zooming in or out. For example, in Word, the status bar shows the view the document is using, the current page number, the number of words in the document, and the proofing status (whether the document contains spelling or grammar errors).

Opening Apps

To get anything done in the Office apps, you need to open and close the apps. You can open an app from the Dock or the Applications folder or by opening a document associated with that app. You may also want to open one or more apps when you log in to your Mac.

Opening an App from Launchpad or the Dock

Usually, the easiest ways to open one of the Office apps are by using Launchpad or by using the Dock. Click the Launchpad icon on the Dock to display the Launchpad screen, and then click the appropriate app icon.

> **Tip**   You can also display the Launchpad screen by pressing F4 on many Mac keyboards or by pinching inward with four or five fingers on a Mac's trackpad.

If the app's icon already appears on the Dock, you can simply click the icon to launch the app. If the app's icon doesn't appear in the Dock, but you want to add it, open the app from Launchpad. The app's icon appears in the Dock because the app is running. Now Ctrl-click the app's icon, click or highlight Options on the context menu, and then click Keep in Dock on the Options submenu (see Figure 1-6).

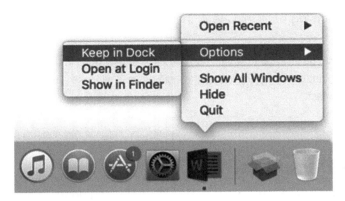

Figure 1-6. To keep an app's icon in the Dock, Ctrl-click the icon, click or highlight Options, and then click Keep in Dock

Opening an App from the Applications Folder

Another way to run an app is from the Applications folder. To do so, follow these steps:

1. Click the Finder icon on the Dock to activate the Finder.

2. Choose Go ➤ Applications from the menu bar to display the Applications folder.

3. Double-click the app you want to launch.

Making a App Launch Automatically

If you work in one or more of the Office apps every time you use your Mac, you can set the app to run automatically when you log in. For example, you may want to run Word, Excel, and Outlook each computing session so that you can work on documents, update your spreadsheets, and check your e-mail.

To make OS X launch an app automatically when you log in, follow these steps:

1. If the app's icon doesn't appear on the Dock, launch the app from Launchpad. OS X adds the app's icon to the Dock.

2. Ctrl-click or right-click the app's icon on the Dock to display the context menu.

3. Click or highlight the Options item to display the Options submenu.

4. Click the Open at Login item on the submenu to place a check mark next to this item.

Now log out and then log back in. Check that OS X automatically starts the apps you chose.

> **Note**   You can set up any app to launch automatically as described in this section. The more apps you set to launch automatically, the longer the login process will take—but once it is finished, you'll be ready to work fast.

Creating a Document

In Word, Excel, and PowerPoint, you create individual documents and save them in separate files. For example, in Word, you create word processing documents such as reports or letters. In Excel, you create workbooks containing worksheets of data. In PowerPoint, you create presentation documents containing slides.

> **Note**   Documents work differently in Outlook. While you create individual messages and other items (such as tasks and appointments) in Outlook, the app automatically stores most of your data for you.

Word, Excel, and PowerPoint come with *templates*, which are files that contain the basic structures of different kinds of documents. For example, Word includes templates for letters, reports, faxes, and other types of documents. A template can contain anything from the paper size, margins, and layout of a document up to an almost complete document in which you need to fill in only a few pieces of information to get a complete document. For example, in a customer letter template, you may need to fill in only the customer's name, address, and product type to produce a complete document.

When you want to work from a blank slate, you can create a new Word document, Excel workbook, or PowerPoint presentation that has no content and no special formatting.

To create a new document based on a template, follow these steps:

1.   Open the Gallery dialog box in one of the following ways:

   - *Launch the app*: The app displays the Gallery dialog box automatically by default. Word displays the Microsoft Word Gallery dialog box (see Figure 1-7), Excel displays the Microsoft Excel Gallery dialog box, and PowerPoint displays the Microsoft PowerPoint Gallery dialog box.

- *Choose File ➤ New from Template*: If the app is already running, click the File menu on the menu bar, and then click New from Template. Alternatively, press Cmd+Shift+P.

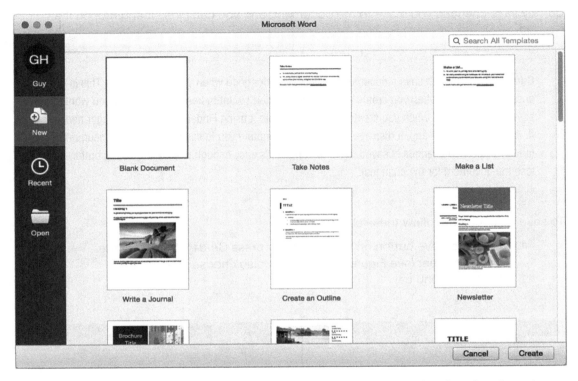

Figure 1-7. Use the app's Gallery dialog box, such as the Microsoft Word Gallery dialog box shown here, to create a new document. You can choose between having the document be blank or basing it on a template

2. Click the template or design. For a blank document, click the Blank Document icon in Word, the Blank Workbook icon in Excel, or the Blank Presentation icon in PowerPoint.

3. Click the Create button. The app closes the Gallery dialog box and creates the document.

Note   You can create a new blank document in Word, Excel, or PowerPoint by pressing the Cmd+N keyboard shortcut.

Saving a Document

As soon as you've created a document, save it. When you save a document, you choose the folder in which to store it and specify the file name to give the document. After that, you can quickly save changes you make to the document, and you can close it and reopen it as needed.

Caution   If you don't save a document, it disappears for good when you close the app. This is occasionally useful when you create a document you don't want to keep, but normally you want to save each document when you create it and then delete it using Finder when you no longer need it. When you close an app, it displays a dialog box prompting you to save any unsaved documents (and any unsaved changes in saved documents), but it's easy enough to click the wrong button and lose the document (or the changes).

To save a document, follow these steps:

1. Click the Save button on the title bar, or press Cmd+S to display the Save As sheet (see Figure 1-8). You can also choose File ➤ Save from the menu bar.

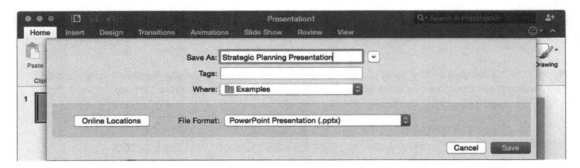

Figure 1-8. The Save As sheet at first appears as its smaller size, with the folder area hidden. To change folders, either pick a folder from the Where pop-up menu or click the button to the right of the Save As box to expand the dialog box

---

Note   A *sheet* is a kind of dialog box that's attached to a particular window rather than being freely movable. In Figure 1-8, the Save As sheet is attached to the Presentation1 window.

---

2. Choose the folder in which you want to store the document:

    ■ You can move quickly to one of the main folders on your Mac (such as the Desktop folder or the Documents folder) or a recent folder by opening the Where pop-up menu and then clicking the folder.

    ■ To display the folder area, click the button to the right of the Save As box. The Save As sheet expands, as shown in Figure 1-9. You can then navigate through your Mac's drives and folders using the same techniques as in a Finder window. If you need to create a new folder to save the document in, click the New Folder button, type the folder name in the New Folder dialog box, and then click the Create button.

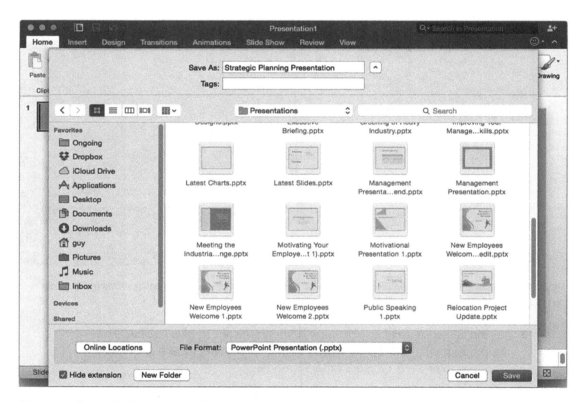

Figure 1-9. Expand the Save As sheet if you need to use the folder pane to navigate to a different folder. You can drag the left, right, or bottom border of the expanded Save As sheet to resize the sheet

Note   The Office apps come configured to save your documents in your Documents folder. You can switch to any other folder needed for any document, but you can also change the default location. Chapter 5 explains how to do this.

■ To switch to an online folder, click the Online Locations button to the left of the File Format pop-up menu. The Save As sheet switches to show the online drives and services you've configured Office to use, such as OneDrive (see Figure 1-10). You can then navigate to the appropriate folder.

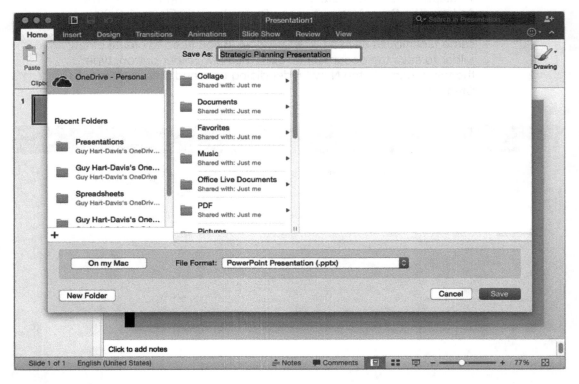

Figure 1-10. Clicking the Online Locations button makes the Save As sheet display the online drives and services you've configured. You can click the On my Mac button to switch back to your local drives

3. In the Save As text box, type the name you want to give the file. The app suggests the first few words of the document (if there are any), but you may want to use a different name.

4. In the Format pop-up menu, choose the file type you want the document to have.

   ■ The Format pop-up menu suggests the app's default format at first: Word suggests the Word Document (.docx) format, Excel suggests the Excel Workbook (.xlsx) format, and PowerPoint suggests the PowerPoint Presentation (.pptx) format.

- You may need to use a different format for sharing a document with people using earlier versions of Office or other apps. I'll discuss this in more detail in the chapters on the individual apps.

- You can change the default format as discussed in Chapter 5.

5. If you want to display the file extension (for example, .docx for a Word document) in the Save As box, clear the Hide extension check box.

6. Click the Save button. The app closes the Save As sheet and saves the document. The document's name appears in the app window's title bar so that you can easily identify it.

After saving a document as described here, you can save it again at any point by clicking the Save button on the title bar, by pressing Cmd+S, or by choosing File ➤ Save from the menu bar.

> **Tip**   Save your documents frequently. Any time you've made changes that you don't want to have to make again, press Cmd+S or click the Save button on the title bar.

Closing a Document

When you finish working on a document, close it. Use one of these methods:

- Click the Close button (the red button) at the left end of the window's title bar.

- Open the File menu and click Close.

- Press Cmd+W.

If the document contains unsaved changes, the app displays a sheet prompting you to save them (see Figure 1-11). Click the Save button to save the changes, the Don't Save button to jettison them, or the Cancel button to return to the document to remind yourself what you've changed.

Figure 1-11. *When you close a document that contains unsaved changes, the app checks whether you want to save them*

> **Note** Even though the apps prompt you to save unsaved changes when you close a document, it's a good idea to save the document before closing it. This eliminates the possibility of clicking the Don't Save button by mistake.

Opening a Document

You can open a document in the Office apps in various ways. The following list shows you the four most useful ways:

- *Open a recent document from the Apple menu*: Click the Apple menu at the left end of the menu bar, and then click or highlight Recent Items to display the list of recent items (see Figure 1-12). In the Documents list, click the document you want to open. If the app associated with the document isn't already running, OS X launches it automatically.

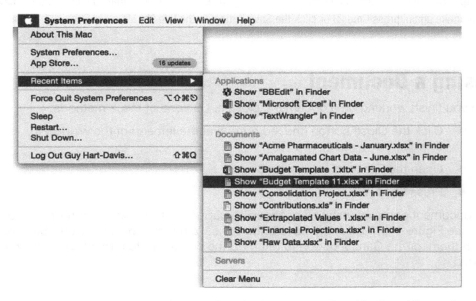

Figure 1-12. You can quickly open a recent document from the Documents section of the Recent Items submenu

> **Tip** Because the Documents list in the Recent Items submenu contains all kinds of documents, other recent documents may have knocked your recent Office documents off the list. You can improve matters by increasing the number of items in the Recent Items list. Click the Apple menu, and then click System Preferences to display the System Preferences window. Click the General icon to display the General pane, click the Recent items pop-up menu, and then click the appropriate number: None (if you don't want to use the Recent Items submenu), 5, 10, 15, 20, 30, or 50. When you've made your choice, click the Close button (the red button at the left end of the title bar), press Cmd+Q, or choose System Preferences ➤ Quit System Preferences.

- *Open a document from Finder*: Open a Finder window to the folder that contains the document, and then double-click the document. OS X opens the document in the app associated with the document type. For example, if you double-click an Excel workbook document in a Finder window, OS X opens the document in Excel. OS X launches the app if it's not currently running.

> **Note** You can also open a document that you've received as an attachment to an e-mail message in Outlook. Chapter 23 explains how to do this.

- *Open a recent document with the Gallery dialog box*: When you launch Word, Excel, or PowerPoint, the Gallery dialog box opens automatically by default. You can also open the Gallery dialog box at any time by choosing File ➤ New from Template. You can click the Recent button in the left pane to display the Recent pane (see Figure 1-13), which lists the documents you've worked with recently. Click the document you want to open and then click the Open button; alternatively, simply double-click the document.

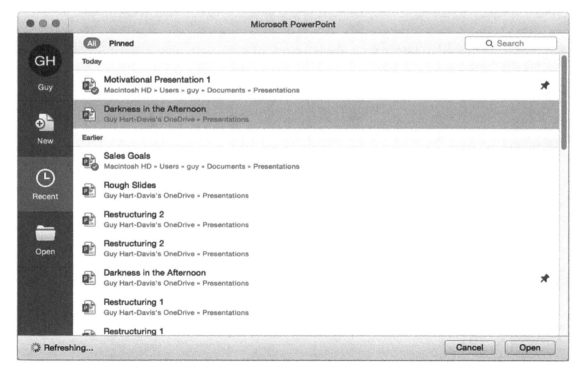

Figure 1-13. The Recent pane in the Gallery dialog box enables you to browse your recent documents in both local and online storage

Note   The Recent pane and the Open pane in the Gallery dialog box show both local documents and online documents. If you use both local storage and online storage, you may find that this feature gives the Gallery dialog box an advantage over the Open dialog box in Microsoft Word, which shows you local storage and online storage separately.

Tip   In either the Recent pane or the Open pane in the Gallery dialog box, you can click a document to pin it in place so that you can find it easily. You can then click the Pinned button in the upper-left corner of the Recent pane to display only the items you've pinned; click the All button when you want to view all items again.

- *Open any document with the Gallery dialog box*: You can open any document by using the Open pane in the Gallery dialog box, the dialog box that opens automatically by default when you launch Word, Excel, or PowerPoint. Click the Open button in the left pane to display the Open pane (see Figure 1-14). You can then click the document and click the Open button; alternatively, double-click the document.

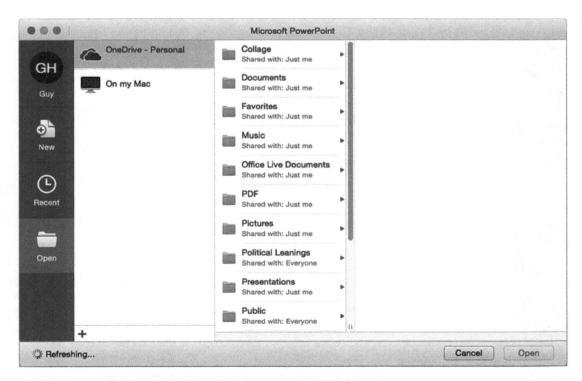

Figure 1-14. The Open pane in the Gallery dialog box lets you open any document

- *Open a document with the Open dialog box (Word only)*: With Word running, press Cmd+O or choose File ➤ Open from the menu bar. Word displays the Open dialog box (see Figure 1-15). Navigate to the folder that contains the document, click the document, and then click the Open button.

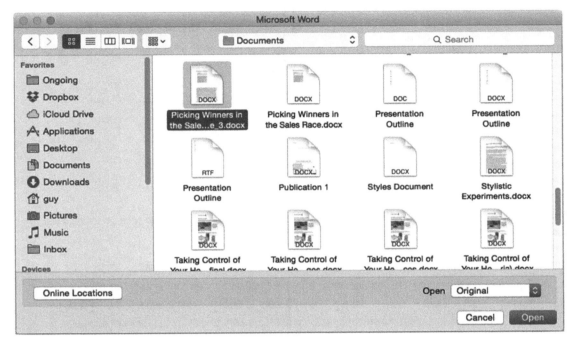

Figure 1-15. Use the Open dialog box to open a document from within Word. Click the Online Locations button to display your online locations in the Gallery dialog box

- *Open a document from the File ➤ Recent submenu*: With the app running, open the File menu, and then click or highlight the Recent item. On the submenu (see Figure 1-16), click the document you want to open. If the document doesn't appear on the menu, you can click the More item to display the Gallery dialog box with the Recent pane open in the lower-left corner.

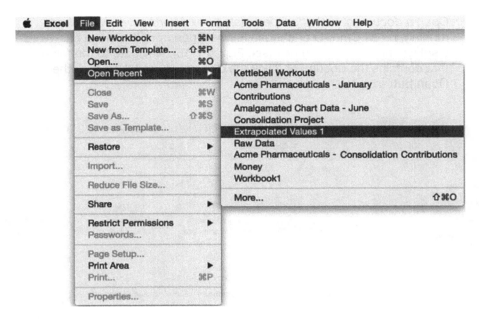

Figure 1-16. When you're working in a app, you can use the File ➤ Open Recent menu to open a document you've worked on recently

---

Tip You can also open a recent document from the Dock icon for a running app. Ctrl-click or right-click the Dock icon, click or highlight Open Recent to display the submenu, and then click the document. If the document doesn't appear, click the More item to display the Gallery dialog box.

Closing an App

When you have finished using an app, close it by quitting it. Quitting the app removes it from your Mac's memory so your Mac can use the memory to run other apps.

The standard way of quitting an app is to press Cmd+Q or open the app's menu and then click the Quit command. This command includes the app's name—for example, Quit Excel. The app closes any documents that are open, prompting you to save any unsaved changes, and then closes.

You can also quit an app by Ctrl-clicking or right-clicking its Dock icon and then clicking Quit on the context menu.

Note If you plan to use an app again later, you can simply hide the app until you need it rather than close it and restart it. To hide the app, open its application menu and then click the Hide command (for example, choose Word ➤ Hide Word, or Excel ➤ Hide Excel) or press Cmd+H. When you need to see the app again, click its Dock icon.

Summary

In this chapter, you met each of the Office apps—Microsoft Word, Microsoft Excel, Microsoft PowerPoint, and Microsoft Outlook. You learned what you can do with the apps, and you met several of their key features, such as the Ribbon and the Gallery dialog box. You now know how to launch the apps; create, save, and close documents; and reopen documents as needed.

In the next chapter, you'll learn how to work quickly and smartly with common tools in the Office apps.

Chapter **2**

Learning Common Tools Across the Office Suite

To save you time and effort, the Office apps have many common features, starting with the three elements you use to give most commands: the menu bar, the Ribbon control interface, and the Quick Access Toolbar.

In this chapter, you'll learn how to control the apps using the menus and the Ribbon. Next, you'll learn how to use the Format pane, a formatting tool that appears automatically when you go to apply formatting to an object. Then you'll explore the common ways of sharing a document with others, how to save time and effort with the AutoCorrect feature, and how to turn off AutoFormat features that can cause surprises and waste time. Lastly, you'll learn how to check spelling and grammar, customize the spelling checker and grammar checker for better results, and print your documents.

Using the Menus and the Ribbon

To give most commands in the Office apps, you use three main forms of control interface:

- *Menus*: Like most OS X apps, each Office app uses the menu bar that appears across the top of the screen. The menus provide access to most of the commands in the apps.

- *Ribbon*: Each app uses this Office-specific control strip that appears across the top of each document window. The Ribbon lets you give many (but not all) of the commands that the app offers.

- *Quick Access Toolbar*: The Quick Access Toolbar appears toward the left end of the title bar, just to the right of the Zoom button. The Quick Access Toolbar contains a handful of essential buttons by default, such as the Save button and the Undo button, but you can customize it with other buttons from a small selection.

© Guy Hart-Davis 2016
G. Hart-Davis, *Learn Office 2016 for Mac*, DOI 10.1007/978-1-4842-2002-3_2

> **Note**   Earlier versions of the Office apps for OS X included toolbars that you could display either docked above the Ribbon or floating freely. The Office 2016 apps for OS X have only the Quick Access Toolbar.

Figure 2-1 shows the menu bar, the Ribbon, and the standard Quick Access Toolbar buttons in a Word document window.

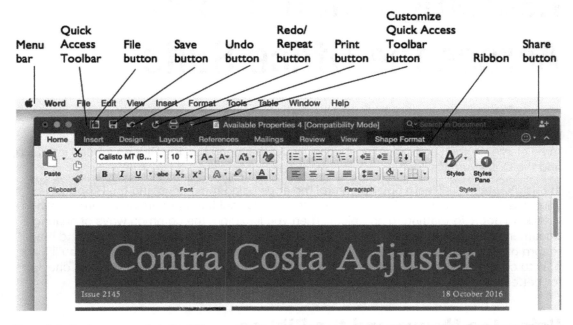

Figure 2-1. To give commands in the Office apps, you use the OS X menu bar, the Ribbon, and the Quick Access Toolbar

There's a considerable amount of overlap between the menus and the Ribbon. Here are some examples:

- To open a document (in Word, Excel, or PowerPoint), you can choose File ➤ Open from the menu bar or click the File button on the title bar.

- To apply formatting to cells in an Excel workbook, you can use the controls on the Home tab of the Ribbon or choose Format ➤ Cells from the menu bar and work in the Format Cells dialog box.

- To insert a slide in a PowerPoint presentation, you can use the New Slide command in the Slides group of the Home tab on the Ribbon or choose Insert ➤ New Slide from the menu bar.

As its name suggests, the Quick Access Toolbar provides a quick way to access certain key commands. Most of these commands are available on the menu bar or the Ribbon as well.

You can use whichever method of giving a command you find most convenient. The underlying commands are the same—it's just a question of how you give them.

Using the Menus

If you've used most any other OS X app, you know how to use the menus. If not, follow these steps:

1.   Make sure the app is active so that the menu bar shows its menus. If it's not, click the document window to make the app active.

2.   Click the menu you want to open. For example, click the View menu to reveal its commands.

3.   If the command you need is on a submenu, click or highlight the submenu. Figure 2-2 shows the Edit menu and its Find submenu open in PowerPoint.

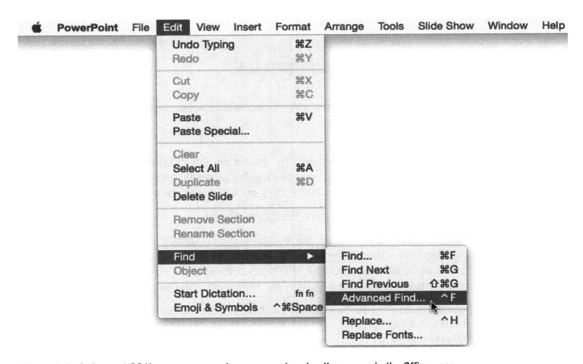

Figure 2-2. As in most OS X apps, you can give commands using the menus in the Office apps

4.   Click the command. The app closes the menu and performs the command.

Using and Customizing the Quick Access Toolbar

The Quick Access Toolbar, which appears toward the left end of the title bar of each Office app, contains a small number of buttons for frequently used commands. In Word, Excel, and PowerPoint, you can customize the buttons on the Quick Access Toolbar to make it more useful; in Outlook, you cannot customize the Quick Access Toolbar as of this writing.

To customize the Quick Access Toolbar, click the Customize Quick Access Toolbar pop-up menu button at the right end, and then click the appropriate item on the pop-up menu (see Figure 2-3). Clicking either places a check mark on the item, making the associated icon appear on the Quick Access Toolbar, or removes the existing check mark, removing the icon from the Quick Access Toolbar.

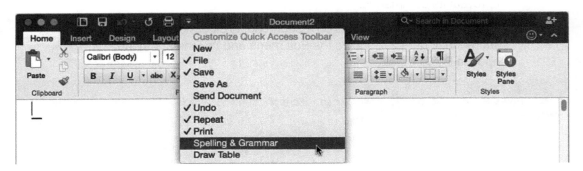

Figure 2-3. To customize the Quick Access Toolbar, click the Customize Quick Access Toolbar pop-up menu button, and then click the appropriate item on the pop-up menu

The selection of buttons on the Quick Access Toolbar is similar in Word, Excel, and PowerPoint. Outlook has only three buttons—Undo, Redo, and Print—in its main window, but the Save button appears in windows such as outgoing messages and calendar items.

The following list explains the Quick Access Toolbar buttons:

- *File (Word, Excel, PowerPoint)*: Click this button to display the app's Gallery dialog box—for example, the Microsoft Word Gallery dialog box for Word or the Microsoft Excel Gallery dialog box for Excel—so that you can configure connected services, create new files, and open existing files.

- *Save (Word, Excel, PowerPoint)*: Click this button either to save a file for the first time (in which case the Save As dialog box opens so that you can specify the filename and location) or to save any unsaved changes in the file.

- *Save As (Word, Excel, PowerPoint)*: Click this button to save the active document under a different name, in a different location, or both.

- *Send Document/Send Workbook/Send Presentation (Word, Excel, PowerPoint, respectively)*: Click this button to start a new message in your default e-mail app (such as Outlook) with the document, workbook, or presentation attached.

- *Undo (Word, Excel, PowerPoint, Outlook)*: Click this button to undo the previous action. Click the pop-up menu to display a list of actions you can undo.

- *Repeat/Redo (Word, Excel, PowerPoint, Outlook)*: Click this button to repeat the previous action, if it is one you can repeat. Otherwise, click this button to redo the action you last undid using the Undo feature.

- *Print (Word, Excel, PowerPoint, Outlook)*: Click this button to display the Print dialog box, in which you can choose parameters for printing.

- *Spelling & Grammar/Spelling/Spelling (Word, Excel, PowerPoint, respectively)*: Click this button to start a spelling and grammar check in Word or a spelling check in either Excel or PowerPoint.

- *Draw Table (Word only)*: Click this button to turn on the Draw Table feature, in which you drag a pen-like pointer to draw the type of table you want. Word switches the document to Print Layout view if it is in any other view.

- *Sort Ascending (Excel only)*: Click this button to sort the active column or the selected columns in ascending order

- *Sort Descending (Excel only)*: Click this button to sort the active column or the selected columns in descending order.

- *Start from Beginning (PowerPoint only)*: Click this button to start the slideshow playing from the beginning.

Tip   To control the order in which the buttons appear on the Quick Access Toolbar, remove all the buttons, and then put them back on in the order in which you want them. For example, if you want the Save button to appear first on the Quick Access Toolbar, click the Customize Quick Access Toolbar pop-up menu button and then click Save in the pop-up menu.

At the right end of the title bar, but not part of the Quick Access Toolbar, is the Share button. You can click this button to display the Sharing Options panel, which lets you share the active document by inviting people to view it online, sharing a link to the document, or sending the document as an attachment. I'll go through how to use these options in the "Sharing a Document with Other People" section later in this chapter.

Using the Ribbon

As you learned in Chapter 1, the Ribbon is the control strip that appears across the top of each document window, below any toolbars the window is displaying. The Ribbon contains tabs, groups, and controls.

■ *Tab*: A tab is one of the major groups of controls on the Ribbon and takes the whole width of the Ribbon. The Ribbon displays only one tab at a time; this tab is the *active tab*. You switch from tab to tab by clicking the small named tab at the top. For example, to display the Home tab of the Ribbon, you click the Home tab at the left end. Figure 2-4 shows the Home tab in Word.

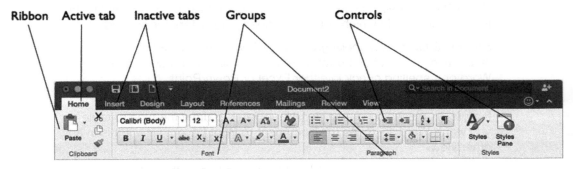

Figure 2-4. The Ribbon contains tabs, groups, and controls

Note   Unlike Word, Excel, and PowerPoint, Outlook doesn't divide its Ribbon tabs into groups.

■ *Group*: Each tab consists of several groups of controls. Each group is a vertical division of the Ribbon, with the group's name appearing at the top. For example, the Home tab in Word contains the Font group, the Paragraph group, and the Styles group.

Note   To follow the Ribbon commands easily, please display the group titles on the Ribbon. To do so, click the app's menu (such as the Word menu) and then click Preferences. In the Preferences window, click View to display the View pane. In the "In Ribbon, Show" area, select the Group Titles check box, and then close the Preferences window by clicking the Close button (the red button at the left end of the window's title bar).

■ *Controls*: Each group consists of one or more controls—buttons, control boxes, or pop-up menus that you click to give commands. For example, the Page Setup group on the Layout tab in Word (see Figure 2-5) contains several pop-up menus, including the Margins pop-up menu, the Orientation pop-up menu, and the Size pop-up menu; the Paragraph group contains four control boxes for adjusting indents and spacing; and the Arrange group (on the right, its name obscured by the open pop-up menu) includes pop-up menus for actions including positioning, wrapping text (the open pop-up menu), and aligning text.

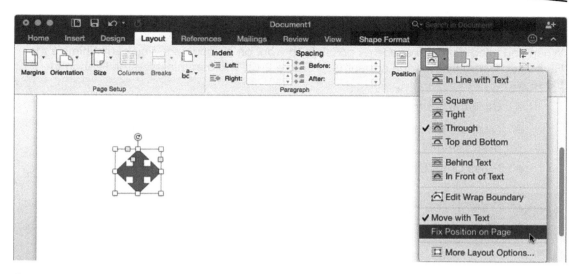

Figure 2-5. The controls on the Ribbon include buttons, pop-up menus, and boxes for entering quantities or measurements

Note   The Ribbon automatically resizes its groups and their controls to make the best use of the space available in the app window. For example, if you make the window narrower, the Ribbon hides the names of buttons to make them fit in the space. If you make the window narrower still, the Ribbon can collapse an entire group into a single button that you click to produce a pop-up panel containing the group's buttons.

Giving Commands from the Ribbon

To give commands from the Ribbon, click the tab that contains the command, go to the group, and then click the control. For example, to adjust hyphenation in Word, click the Layout tab (if it's not already displayed), go to the Page Setup group, click the Hyphenation button, and then click the appropriate command on it (such as the Automatic command or the Manual command).

To see information about what a button does, hold the pointer over the button for a moment until a tooltip appears. Move the pointer away when you no longer need to see the tooltip.

Note   This book presents Ribbon commands by tab, group, and command name. For example, "choose Review ➤ Comments ➤ New Comment" means that you click the Review tab to display it, go to the Comments group (you don't need to click it), and then click the New Comment button.

Minimizing the Ribbon

When you need as much space as possible to work on a document, you can minimize the Ribbon so that only the tabs appear (see Figure 2-6). You can minimize the Ribbon in these ways:

- Click the tab that's currently active.
- Click the Minimize the Ribbon button to the right of the tab bar (the ^ button).
- Press Cmd+Option+R.

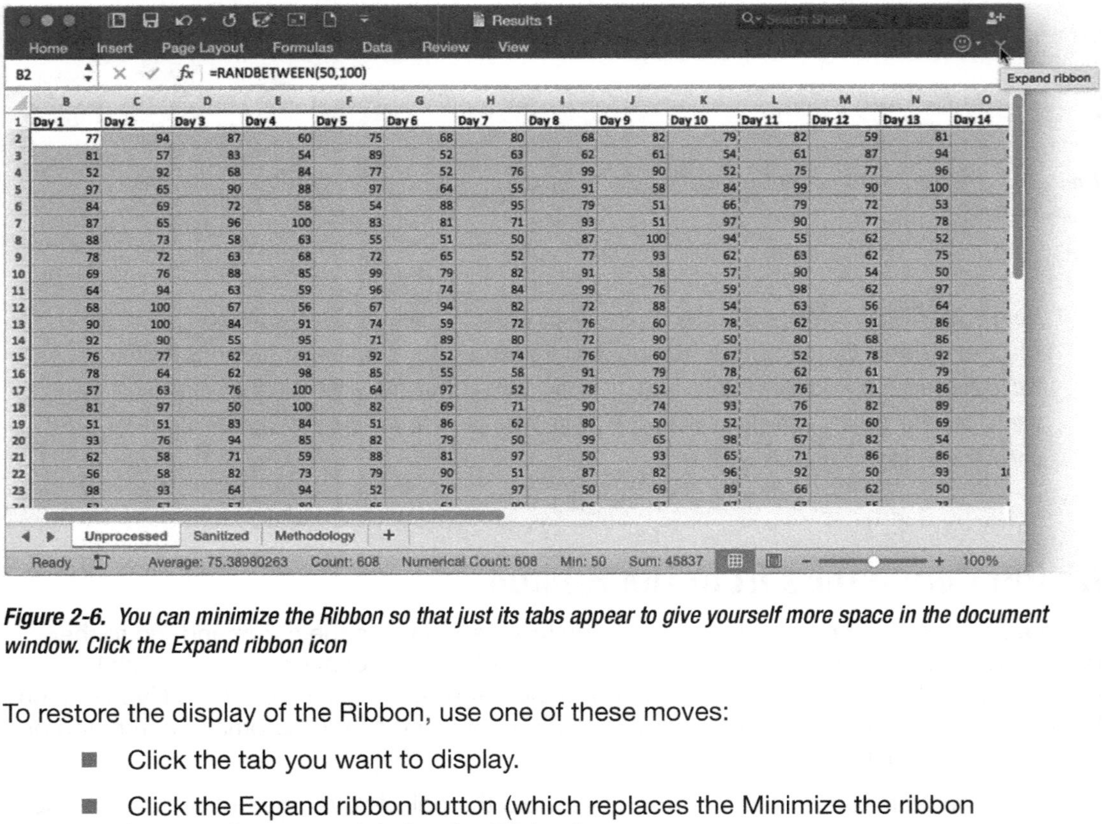

	Day 1	Day 2	Day 3	Day 4	Day 5	Day 6	Day 7	Day 8	Day 9	Day 10	Day 11	Day 12	Day 13	Day 14
1	Day 1	Day 2	Day 3	Day 4	Day 5	Day 6	Day 7	Day 8	Day 9	Day 10	Day 11	Day 12	Day 13	Day 14
2	77	94	87	60	75	68	80	68	82	79	82	59	81	
3	81	57	83	54	89	52	63	62	61	54	61	87	94	
4	52	92	68	84	77	52	76	99	90	52	75	77	96	
5	97	65	90	88	97	64	55	91	58	84	99	90	100	
6	84	69	72	58	54	88	95	79	51	66	79	72	53	
7	87	65	96	100	83	81	71	93	51	97	90	77	78	
8	88	73	58	63	55	51	50	87	100	94	55	62	52	
9	78	72	63	68	72	65	52	77	93	62	63	62	75	
10	69	76	88	85	99	79	82	91	58	57	90	54	50	
11	64	94	63	59	96	74	84	99	76	59	98	62	97	
12	68	100	67	56	67	94	82	72	88	54	63	56	64	
13	90	100	84	91	74	59	72	76	60	78	62	91	86	
14	92	90	55	95	71	89	80	72	90	50	80	68	86	
15	76	77	62	91	92	52	74	76	60	67	52	78	92	
16	78	64	62	98	85	55	58	91	79	78	62	61	79	
17	57	63	76	100	64	97	52	78	52	92	76	71	86	
18	81	97	50	100	82	69	71	90	74	93	76	82	89	
19	51	51	83	84	51	86	62	80	50	52	72	60	69	
20	93	76	94	85	82	79	50	99	65	98	67	82	54	
21	62	58	71	59	88	81	97	50	93	65	71	86	86	
22	56	58	82	73	79	90	51	87	82	96	92	50	93	
23	98	93	64	94	52	76	97	50	69	89	66	62	50	

B2   =RANDBETWEEN(50,100)   Expand ribbon

Unprocessed   Sanitized   Methodology   +

Ready   Average: 75.38980263   Count: 608   Numerical Count: 608   Min: 50   Sum: 45837   100%

Figure 2-6. You can minimize the Ribbon so that just its tabs appear to give yourself more space in the document window. Click the Expand ribbon icon

To restore the display of the Ribbon, use one of these moves:

- Click the tab you want to display.
- Click the Expand ribbon button (which replaces the Minimize the ribbon button when you minimize the Ribbon).
- Press Cmd+Option+R.

Using the Format Pane

Word, Excel, and PowerPoint use a feature called the Format pane to make available commands for formatting the selected object. The title and contents of the Format pane vary to suit the object; for example, the Format Shape pane (see the left screen in Figure 2-7) contains different controls than the Format Picture pane (see the right screen in Figure 2-7).

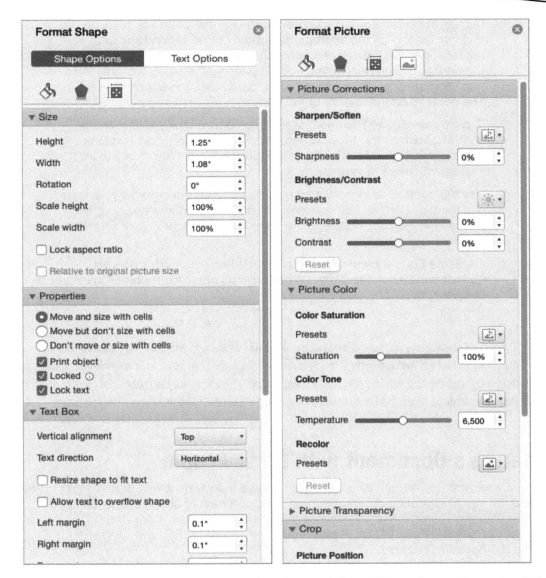

Figure 2-7. Use the Format pane to format objects such as shapes and pictures. The pane's name changes to reflect the object type, such as the Format Shape pane (left) and the Format Picture pane (right)

Whichever object's version of the Format pane you're using, you'll find it easy enough.

- *Display the tab you need*: If the Format pane you're using has multiple tabs, click the appropriate tab. For example, in the Format Shape pane, click the Shape Options tab or the Text Options tab, as needed. The tab's subtabs appear.

- *Display the subtab or tab you need*: If the Format pane you're using has multiple tabs, click the appropriate subtab on the second line of tabs, the tabs identified with icons rather than text, such as those you see in the Format Shape pane. If the Format pane you're using has only the icon tabs, as does the Format Picture pane, click the appropriate tab. The controls on the subtab or tab appear.

- *Expand the section you need*: Most tabs contain multiple sections of controls, such as the Size section, Properties section, and Text Box section you see in the left screen in Figure 2-7. Click the heading for the section you need to expand.

- *Use the controls as normal*: Once you've located the controls you need, use them as normal. For example, adjust the values in a text box, such as those in the Size section in the left screen in Figure 2-7, or select or deselect check boxes.

- *Close the Format pane when you finish*: When you finish using the Format pane, click the Close (X) button in its upper-right corner to close the pane.

Tip   The Format pane appears docked at the right side of the app window. You can undock it by grabbing its title bar and dragging it in any direction. Once the Format pane is undocked, you can drag it outside the app window and resize it as needed. There's no way to redock the Format pane manually; instead, close the Format pane. When you reopen the pane, it appears docked again.

Sharing a Document with Other People

Word, Excel, and PowerPoint all enable you to share a document with other people in several different ways. This section covers the three ways common to all three of these apps:

- Send using e-mail
- Save to OneDrive
- Save to SharePoint

Note   For coverage of the other ways of sharing documents that the individual apps offer, see the chapters on those apps.

Sending a Document via E-mail

You can send a document via e-mail by starting a message in Outlook (or another e-mail app) and then attaching the document's file. But if you're working from one of the other Office apps and have the document open, you can start a message directly from the app. This saves a bit of time and effort, because you use the app to identify the document—you don't have to navigate to the document in your Mac's file system like you usually must when attaching a file to a message.

> **Caution**   Before sending a document via e-mail, make sure you've saved it. The apps will let you send an unsaved document, but doing so isn't a good idea.

To send a document using e-mail, follow these steps:

1.   Make the document the active document. If the document is already open, click in its window; if the document isn't open, open it.

2.   Click the Share button at the right end of the title bar, click the Send Attachment submenu, and then click the item for the appropriate type of attachment. For example, in Excel, you can choose the Workbook item or the PDF item (see Figure 2-8). The app launches your default e-mail app (for example, Outlook) if it's not running, or activates it if it is running, and creates a new message with the document attached.

Figure 2-8. Click the Share button at the right end of the title bar when you need to send a file via e-mail or share it online

3.   Address and complete the message, and then send it as usual.

> **Note**   You can also choose File ➤ Share and then click the appropriate Send item on the Share submenu. For example, for an Excel workbook, you can choose File ➤ Share ➤ Send Workbook or File ➤ Share ➤ Send PDF.
>
> If you're sharing a document saved on OneDrive or a SharePoint site and you want to send the recipient only a link to the document rather than sending the document itself, click the Share button at the right end of the title bar, click the Copy Link item to display the Copy Link submenu, and then click the View-Only item or the View and Edit item, depending on whether you want to allow the person to edit the document. The app copies the link to the Clipboard. You can then paste it into an e-mail message or an instant message to share it with the recipient.

Setting Up Connected Services and SharePoint Servers

Word, Excel, and PowerPoint can save files to online services such as Microsoft's OneDrive service and those provided by SharePoint servers. To use such services, you need to set up an account for each service.

While setting up Office on your Mac, or while running the first Office app after installing Office, you likely set up an account to connect to OneDrive or a SharePoint server. If so, you may need to set up another account now—for example, so that you have a business account and a personal account. If not, you can set up an account now.

Setting Up Your First Connected Services

To set up your first connected service, follow these steps in Word, Excel, or PowerPoint:

1. If you have no document active, press Cmd+N to create a new blank document (in Word), blank workbook (in Excel), or blank presentation (in PowerPoint).

2. Click the File button near the left end of the title bar to display the app's Gallery dialog box (the Microsoft Word Gallery dialog box, the Microsoft Excel Gallery dialog box, or the Microsoft PowerPoint Gallery dialog box).

3. Click the Sign In button at the top of the left pane to display the first Sign In dialog box.

4. Type the e-mail address or phone number for your account.

5. Click the Next button. The Sign In dialog box prompts you for your password.

6. Type your password.

7. Click the Sign In button. One or more dialog boxes may open in sequence, each prompting you to allow other Office apps to use confidential information about your Microsoft identity that you have stored in your OS X keychain (see Figure 2-9).

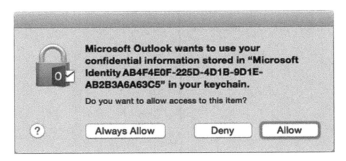

Figure 2-9. *If Office prompts you to allow an app access to confidential information stored in your Microsoft identity, click the Always Allow button*

8. Click the Always Allow button to allow the app access to the Microsoft identity information it needs to sign in to the service. The app sets up your account, and your initials and first name appear in place of the Sign In button.

You can now start using the service to which you have connected.

Setting Up Another Connected Service or a SharePoint Connection

To set up another connected service or a SharePoint connection, follow these steps in Word, Excel, or PowerPoint:

1. If you have no document active, press Cmd+N to create a new blank document (in Word), blank workbook (in Excel), or blank presentation (in PowerPoint).

2. Click the File button near the left end of the title bar to display the app's Gallery dialog box (the Microsoft Word Gallery dialog box, the Microsoft Excel Gallery dialog box, or the Microsoft PowerPoint Gallery dialog box). Figure 2-10 shows the Microsoft Excel Gallery dialog box.

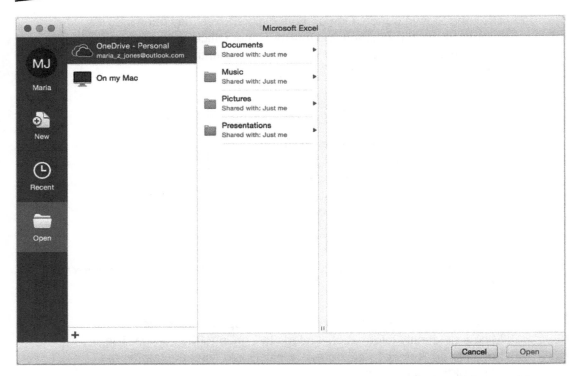

Figure 2-10. To add another connected service to Office, click the Add (+) button near the lower-left corner of the Gallery dialog box

3. Click the Add (+) button near the lower-left corner of the dialog box to display the first Add a Service dialog box (see Figure 2-11).

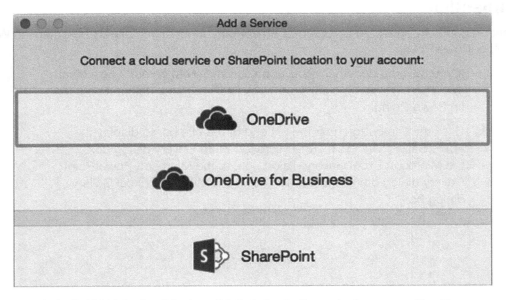

Figure 2-11. In the first Add A Service dialog box, click the button for the service type you want to add

4. Click the button for the service type you want to add, such as the OneDrive button, the OneDrive for Business button, or the SharePoint button. A second Add a Service dialog box opens, prompting you for further information.

5. Enter the appropriate information:

    ■   *OneDrive.* Type the e-mail address for the account.

    ■   *SharePoint.* Type the URL of the SharePoint server.

> **Note** For a SharePoint site, you must enter **https://** at the beginning of the SharePoint server's URL. The Add a Service routine doesn't automatically supply https:// if you enter only the remaining part of the address.

6. Click the Next button. The Sign In dialog box opens, prompting you for the password for your OneDrive account and for both your e-mail address and password for a SharePoint server.

7. Type your password or your e-mail address and password.

8. Click the Sign In button. One or more dialog boxes may open in sequence, each prompting you to allow other Office apps to use confidential information about your Microsoft identity that you have stored in your OS X keychain. (Look back to Figure 2-8, earlier in this chapter.)

9. Click the Always Allow button to allow the app access to the Microsoft identity information it needs to sign in to the service. The app sets up your account, and you can start using it.

Switching Among and Managing Your Services and Servers

After adding multiple services and servers, you can switch quickly among them by using the second-from-left pane in the Gallery dialog box for the app. Follow these steps:

1. If you have no document active, press Cmd+N to create a new blank document (in Word), blank workbook (in Excel), or blank presentation (in PowerPoint).

2. Click the File button near the left end of the title bar to display the app's Gallery dialog box (the Microsoft Word Gallery dialog box, the Microsoft Excel Gallery dialog box, or the Microsoft PowerPoint Gallery dialog box). Figure 2-12 shows the Microsoft PowerPoint Gallery dialog box.

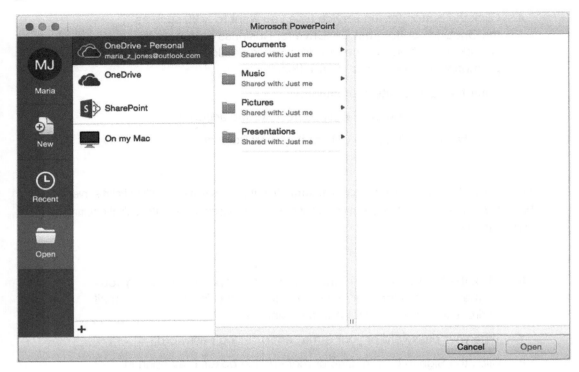

Figure 2-12. Use the second-from-left pane in the Gallery dialog box for an Office app to switch among your connected services and SharePoint servers

3. In the second-from-left pane, click the connected service or SharePoint server you want to use. The folders and files then appear in the third pane, and you can navigate to the item you need.

You can also manage your connected services and SharePoint servers from the Gallery dialog box.

   ■ *View your connected services and SharePoint servers*: Click the button that shows your initials and first name at the top of the left pane to display the pop-up panel (see Figure 2-13).

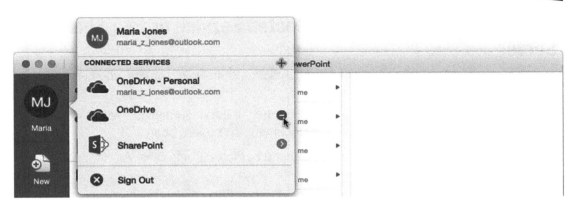

Figure 2-13. *Click the button that shows your initials and first name at the top of the left pane in the Gallery dialog box to view and manage your connected services and SharePoint servers*

- *Sign out of your main connected service*: To sign out of your main connected service (the one that appears at the top of the Connected Services list), click the button that shows your initials and first name at the top of the left pane to display the pop-up panel, and then click the Sign Out button. In the confirmation dialog box that opens (see Figure 2-14), click the Sign Out button.

Figure 2-14. *Click the Sign Out button in the confirmation dialog box to sign out of a connected service*

- *Remove a connected service other than your default (first) connected service*: Click the button that shows your initials and first name at the top of the left pane to display the pop-up panel. Move the pointer over the service so that a gray button with a white minus (–) sign appears on its right, and then click that button. In the "Are you sure you want to remove this service?" dialog box that opens, click the Sign Out button.

- *Remove a SharePoint server*: Click the button that shows your initials and first name at the top of the left pane to display the pop-up panel. Click the > icon on the right side of the button for the SharePoint server to display a further pop-up panel. Move the pointer over the second pop-up panel so that a gray button with a white minus (–) sign appears on its right, and then click that button. In the "Are you sure you want to remove this SharePoint URL?" dialog box that opens, click the OK button.

Saving a Document to a Connected Service or to a SharePoint Server

Once you have set up your connected accounts and SharePoint servers, you can easily save documents to them. Follow these steps:

1. Make the document the active document. If the document is already open, click in its window. If the document isn't open, open it.

2. Choose File ➤ Save As from the menu bar to open the Save As dialog box (see Figure 2-15).

> **Note**   If the Save As dialog box opens showing your Mac's file system, click the Online Locations button to switch to displaying online locations.

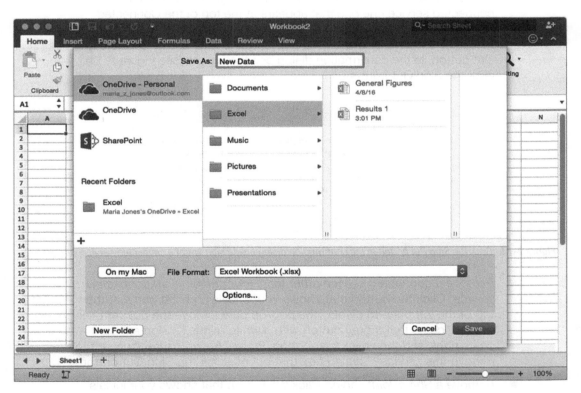

Figure 2-15.   In the Save As dialog box, select the connected service or SharePoint server on which to save the document

> **Note**   If the document you're saving to an online destination has never been saved before, you can open the Save As dialog box by giving the Save command—for example, click the Save button on the title bar or press Cmd+S.

3. In the Save As box at the top, type a new name for the document or edit the existing name as needed.

4. In the left pane, select the connected service or SharePoint server on which you want to save the document.

5. In the second-from-left pane, select the destination folder. If necessary, select a subfolder in the next pane.

6. Click the Save button. The app saves the document to the connected service or SharePoint server.

Saving Time and Effort with AutoCorrect

As you work in a document, the AutoCorrect feature watches the characters you type and springs into action if it detects a mistake it can fix or some formatting it can apply. This feature can save you a lot of time and effort, and can speed up your typing substantially, so it's well worth using—but you need to set it up to meet your needs. AutoCorrect also has some features that can cause surprises, so you will want to choose settings that suit the way you work.

To set up AutoCorrect, first open the AutoCorrect preferences pane:

- *Word*: Choose Tools ➤ AutoCorrect from the menu bar to display the AutoCorrect preferences pane in the Word Preferences window.

- *Excel*: Choose Tools ➤ AutoCorrect from the menu bar to display the AutoCorrect preferences pane in the Excel Preferences window.

- *PowerPoint*: Choose Tools ➤ AutoCorrect from the menu bar to display the AutoCorrect preferences pane in the PowerPoint Preferences window.

- *Outlook*: Choose Outlook ➤ Preferences from the menu bar (or press Cmd+,) to display the Outlook Preferences window. Then click the AutoCorrect icon in the Personal Settings area to display the AutoCorrect preferences pane.

The AutoCorrect preferences pane has different contents in each of the Office apps:

- *Word*: Word's AutoCorrect preferences pane (see Figure 2-16) has four tabs: one for standard AutoCorrect, one for Math AutoCorrect, one for AutoFormat as You Type, and one for AutoText.

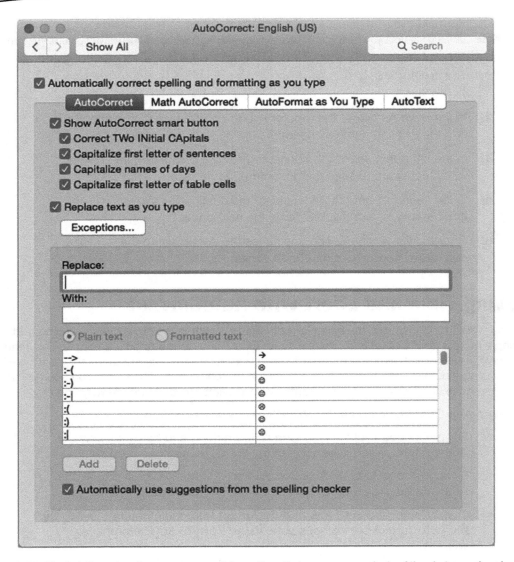

Figure 2-16. The AutoCorrect preferences pane contains options that can save you plenty of time but may also give you surprises. Word's AutoCorrect preferences pane (shown here) contains more options than the preferences panes in the other apps

- *Excel*: Excel's AutoCorrect preferences pane has no tabs because Excel has only the standard AutoCorrect feature.

- *PowerPoint*: The AutoCorrect preferences pane has two tabs: one for standard AutoCorrect and one for AutoFormat as You Type.

- *Outlook*: The AutoCorrect preferences pane has two tabs: one for standard AutoCorrect and one for AutoFormat (which includes options for applying formatting as you type and replacing characters with formatting as you type).

> **Tip**   In Outlook, you can leave the AutoCorrect preferences pane open as you work in the app. Doing this can save you time when you need to create multiple AutoCorrect entries at the same time or test different settings.

The details vary depending on what each app needs, but the basic part of AutoCorrect is the same for each app: AutoCorrect watches as you type and makes changes that are supposed to be helpful. To get the most out of AutoCorrect, you need to configure it carefully, as discussed in the following sections.

Choosing Standard AutoCorrect Options

Let's start by looking at what you might call the standard AutoCorrect options—those that appear on the AutoCorrect tab for Word, PowerPoint, and Outlook, and in the tab-free AutoCorrect preferences pane in Excel.

> **Note**   Word has a master control for turning off AutoCorrect as a whole. This is the "Automatically correct spelling and formatting as you type" check box that appears at the top of the AutoCorrect preferences pane. Clear this check box if you want to turn off AutoCorrect.

These are the options you can choose:

- *Show AutoCorrect smart button (Word and PowerPoint only)*: Select this check box to have the app display a small button under each item AutoCorrect changes. You can hold the pointer over this button to make the app display a menu of AutoCorrect-related choices, such as stopping making this change. These buttons are usually helpful.

- *Correct TWo INitial CApitals*: Select this check box to have AutoCorrect apply lowercase to a second initial capital, such as changing "THree" to "Three." This option is usually helpful.

- *Capitalize first letter of sentences*: Select this check box if you want AutoCorrect to automatically start each sentence (and paragraph) with a capital letter. Clear this check box if you prefer to write in fragments and then fix them afterward.

- *Capitalize names of days*: Select this check box to have AutoCorrect automatically capitalize the first letter of the day names (for example, Sunday). This option is usually helpful.

- *Capitalize first letter of table cell (Word only)*: Select this check box if you want AutoCorrect to automatically capitalize the first letter of each entry in a table cell. Some people find this option helpful; others don't.

- *Replace text as you type*: Select this check box to use AutoCorrect's main feature, replacing misspellings and contractions with their designated replacement text. You will want to use this feature to make the most of AutoCorrect.

- *Automatically use suggestions from the spelling checker (Word only)*: Select this check box to let the "Replace text as you type" feature use suggestions from the spelling checker as well as the entries in the list. This option is usually helpful too.

Choosing AutoFormat as You Type Options

The AutoFormat as You Type options are the ones that cause most surprises to Office users. These features try to apply necessary formatting as you work—without consulting you. You may well want to turn some or most of them off.

All four apps have AutoFormat as You Type options, but they put them in different places. Here are the details:

- *Word*: Word has the most AutoFormat as You Type options. They appear on the AutoFormat as You Type tab of the AutoCorrect preferences pane (see Figure 2-17).

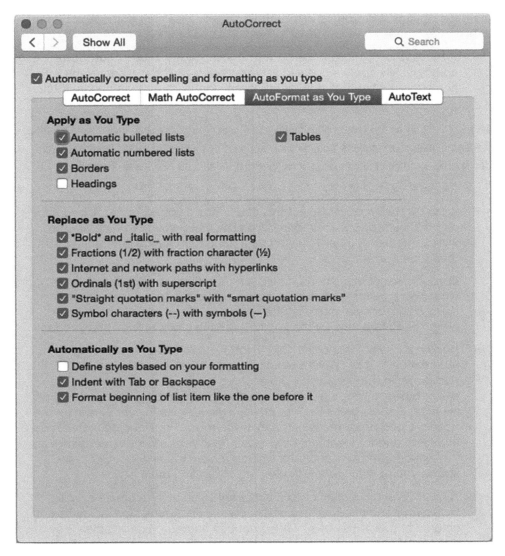

Figure 2-17. *You may want to turn off some of the AutoFormat as You Type options to avoid surprises. This is the AutoFormat as You Type tab in the AutoCorrect preferences pane for Word*

- *Excel*: Excel's only AutoFormat as You Type option is the "Replace Internet and network paths with hyperlinks" check box, which appears in the AutoCorrect preferences pane (rather than on a tab).

- *PowerPoint*: The AutoFormat as You Type tab in PowerPoint's AutoCorrect preferences pane has two Replace as You Type options and two Apply as You Type Options.

- *Outlook*: The AutoFormat as You Type tab in the AutoCorrect preferences pane contains two AutoFormat as You Type options and five Replace as You Type options.

These are the options Word offers in the Apply as You Type area of the AutoFormat as You Type tab:

- *Automatic bulleted lists*: Select this check box if you want AutoCorrect to automatically apply a bulleted list style when you start a paragraph with an asterisk, a hyphen, or a greater-than sign followed by a space or tab.

> **Note**   The Apply as You Type options can be useful once you know what they do and how they work. Until then, these options tend to cause surprises by making unwanted changes in your documents. If you don't find these options helpful, turn them off, like many people do.

- *Automatic numbered lists*: Select this check box if you want AutoCorrect to automatically apply a numbered list style when you start a paragraph with a number or letter followed by a period or closing parenthesis and then type a space or tab.

- *Borders*: Select this check box to have AutoCorrect apply border lines when you type three or more hyphens, underscores, asterisks, tildes, equal signs, or hash marks at the beginning of a paragraph and then press the Return key. Try these out to see the types of lines they produce.

- *Headings*: Select this check box if you want AutoCorrect to automatically apply Word's heading styles when you create a short paragraph in the right way. For Heading 1 style, press the Return key twice, type the heading, and then press the Return key twice more. For Heading 2 style, press the Return key twice, press the Tab key, type the heading, and press the Return key twice more. For Heading 3 style, use two tabs, and for Heading 4 style, use three tabs. AutoCorrect removes the extra paragraphs and tabs when it makes the change. Chapter 6 shows you how to work with heading styles and other styles.

- *Tables*: Select this check box if you want to be able to create a table by typing a line of plus signs and hyphens. Each plus sign indicates a column border, so +--+----+--+ produces a three-column table. The number of hyphens indicates the relative width of the columns—in the previous example, the left column and right column are narrow (two hyphens each), while the middle column is wider (four hyphens).

These are the options that Word offers in the Replace as You Type area:

- **Bold* and _italic_ with real formatting*: Select this check box if you want to be able to apply bold by typing an asterisk before and after a word and to apply italics by typing an underscore before and after a word. These are long-standing Internet conventions for designating formatting in plain text, but usually it's easier to use keyboard shortcuts to apply the bold or italics.

- *Fractions (1/2) with fraction character (½)*: Select this check box to have AutoCorrect insert real fraction characters in place of fractions you type. This too is usually helpful.

- *Internet and network paths with hyperlinks*: Select this check box to have AutoCorrect insert a hyperlink when you type a URL (for example, `www.microsoft.com`) or a network path (for example, `\\server1\users`). This option is helpful only if you want live hyperlinks in your documents.

- *Ordinals (1st) with superscript*: Select this check box to have AutoCorrect apply superscript to the letters of ordinals (for example, 1st, 2nd). This option is useful when you need fully formatted documents. If you don't need superscripted ordinals, clear this check box.

- *Straight quotation marks with smart quotation marks*: Select this check box to have AutoCorrect replace straight-up-and-down quotation marks with smart, or "curly," quotation marks. This is usually helpful.

- *Symbol characters (--) with symbols (—)*: Select this check box to have AutoCorrect insert en dashes (–) in place of a hyphen preceded and followed by spaces and to have AutoCorrect insert em dashes (—) for two hyphens typed between words. This option is usually helpful.

These are the options Word offers in the Automatically as You Type area:

- *Define styles based on your formatting*: Select this check box only if you want AutoCorrect to automatically create styles when it thinks you need them. This feature is a recipe for confusion, so you'll probably want to clear this check box.

- *Indent with tab or backspace*: Select this check box to have AutoCorrect automatically move the left indent to the left when you press the Backspace key at the beginning of a blank paragraph and to move it to the right when you press the Tab key. This feature tends to cause formatting surprises, so you may want to turn it off. For example, in most word processing apps and text editors, you can press Backspace from the beginning of a paragraph to delete the previous paragraph mark, joining the two paragraphs. When this check box is selected, that Backspace press moves the left indent instead.

- *Format beginning of list item like the one before it*: Select this check box to have AutoCorrect format the second and subsequent items in a list using the same formatting you added to the beginning of the first item, such as italic or bold. This setting can be useful when you override the standard formatting of the list, but you may find it easier to apply the formatting overrides yourself.

In PowerPoint, the AutoFormat as You Type tab contains four options divided into two sets. The first set, Apply as You Type, contains these two options:

- *AutoFit body text to placeholder*: Select this check box if you want PowerPoint to automatically reduce the point size of text when it becomes too long to fit in a body placeholder. This option is often helpful, but you may prefer to edit the text down to size to keep it readable.

■ *Automatic bulleted and numbered lists*: As discussed earlier, select this check box to have PowerPoint automatically create bulleted lists when you start a paragraph with a bullet-like character (such as *) and to create numbered lists when you start a paragraph with a numbering character (such as 1. or A.).

The second set of options on the AutoFormat as You Type tab of the AutoCorrect preferences pane in PowerPoint, the Replace as You Type set, contains these two options:

■ *Internet and network paths with hyperlinks*: As discussed earlier, select this check box to have PowerPoint automatically create links from Internet addresses and network paths.

■ *Straight quotes with smart quotes*: Select this check box to have AutoCorrect replace straight-up-and-down quotation marks with smart quotation marks.

In Outlook, the AutoFormat tab of the AutoCorrect preferences pane contains two sets of options. The first set, Apply as You Type, has two options:

■ *Automatic bulleted lists*: Select this check box to make Outlook automatically create a bulleted list when you start a paragraph with a bullet-like character (such as *).

■ *Automatic numbered lists*: Select this check box to make Outlook automatically create a numbered list when you start a paragraph with a numbering character (such as 1. or A.).

The second set of options on the AutoFormat tab of the AutoCorrect preferences pane in Outlook is the Replace as You Type set, which contains the following options:

■ *Dashes with n-dashes and m-dashes*: Select this check box to make AutoCorrect insert en dashes (–) in place of a hyphen preceded and followed by spaces and to make AutoCorrect insert em dashes (—) for two hyphens typed between words.

■ *"…" with ellipses*: Select this check box to make Outlook replace three periods with an ellipsis character (…).

■ **Bold* and _italic_ with real formatting*: Select this check box if you want to be able to apply bold by typing an asterisk before and after a word and if you want to apply italics by typing an underscore before and after a word. Usually, it's easier to apply bold or italics manually as needed—for example, press Cmd+B for bold or Cmd+I for italics.

- *Replace *** or —— with horizontal line (3 or more characters)*: Select this check box to have Outlook create a decorative line when you type three asterisks (***) or three underscores (___) and then press the Return key.

- *Internet and network paths with hyperlinks*: Select this check box to have AutoCorrect insert a hyperlink when you type a URL (for example, www.microsoft.com) or a network path (for example, \\server1\users). This can be helpful when you need to enter hyperlinks in your messages.

> **Note** In Word, the AutoCorrect preferences pane also includes an AutoText tab. This tab contains options for creating AutoText entries, blocks of text, or other content that you can insert quickly in your documents. Chapter 6 shows you how to save time and effort by using AutoText.

Choosing Math AutoCorrect Options in Word

Math AutoCorrect makes it easy to enter characters and symbols used in math in your Word documents. For example, you can type **\theta** to enter a lowercase theta character (θ) without visiting the Symbol dialog box. Math AutoCorrect comes with a long list of entries for math characters and symbols.

The Math AutoCorrect tab of the AutoCorrect preferences pane in Word (see Figure 2-18) lets you control whether and where to have AutoCorrect replace math terms with math symbols. If you use math in your documents, Math AutoCorrect can be a great time-saver; if you don't use math, turn it off by clearing the Replace text as you type check box on the Math AutoCorrect tab.

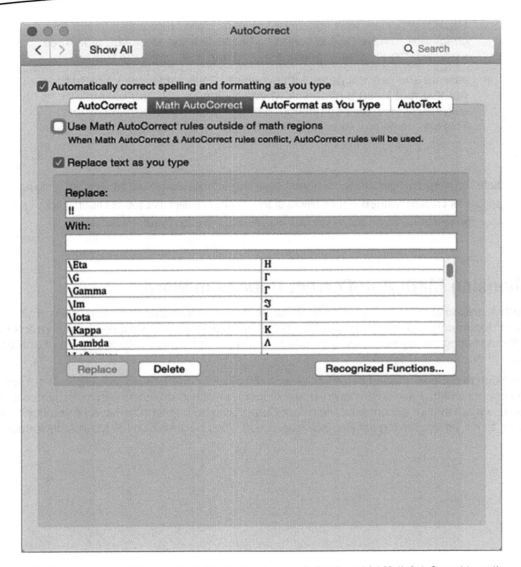

Figure 2-18. If you include math in your Word documents, choose whether to restrict Math AutoCorrect to math regions—areas in which you've inserted equations—and decide which items to replace as you type

These are the options you can choose on the Math AutoCorrect tab:

- *Use Math AutoCorrect rules outside of math regions check box*: Select this check box if you want to use Math AutoCorrect anywhere in your documents. If you want to use Math AutoCorrect only in math areas, clear this check box.

- *Replace text as you type*: Enables Word to replace the text items listed in the main box with their math replacements.

- *AutoCorrect items*: To add an item, type the abbreviation or text version in the Replace box, type or paste the replacement text in the With box, and then click the Add button.

- *Recognized functions*: To change the list of math expressions that Word recognizes and doesn't automatically italicize, click the Recognized Functions button, and then work in the Recognized Math Functions dialog box that opens.

Creating AutoCorrect Entries

The Replace Text as You Type feature in AutoCorrect can save you a large amount of time and typing. To make the most of this powerful feature, you need to spend some time creating a list of entries that will fix your typing mistakes and expand abbreviations you define.

> **Tip**   You can create standard AutoCorrect entries up to 255 characters long—enough for several sentences. Long AutoCorrect entries are great for quickly entering boilerplate text, such as addresses, company names, set phrases, or standard text for documents such as business letters or contracts. If you need to create longer AutoCorrect entries in Word, you can do so by creating formatted AutoCorrect entries, as you'll see shortly.

The basic way to create an entry is to type the error or short version in the Replace text box and the replacement text in the With text box and then click the Add button. You can create an entry faster by pasting in the replacement text, which is especially handy if it's long.

> **Note**   The quickest way of creating an AutoCorrect entry for a typo is by using the AutoCorrect option when checking spelling, as discussed in the "Checking Spelling and Grammar" section later in this chapter.

Regular AutoCorrect entries are plain text, but in Word, you can create formatted AutoCorrect entries as well. A formatted AutoCorrect entry can contain not only formatted text but also other objects, such as tables, graphics, or equations. To create a formatted AutoCorrect entry, follow these steps:

1. In a document, create the replacement text and other items exactly as you want them to appear in the document after the AutoCorrect replacement. For example, type text and format it, add a graphic, or add a table.

2. Select everything you want to include in the AutoCorrect entry.

3. Choose Tools ➤ AutoCorrect from the menu bar to open the AutoCorrect dialog box. The first part of your selection appears in the With text box.

4.   Make sure the Formatted text option button is selected. (If not, click it.)

5.   Click the Add button to add the entry.

> **Note**   Word stores formatted AutoCorrect entries in the Normal template (`Normal.dotm`), which it loads each time you launch the app. Depending on the options you've chosen for Word, you may see a prompt to save Normal when exiting Word after creating a formatted AutoCorrect entry. If you receive this prompt, click the Yes button to save the changes to Normal.

Creating AutoCorrect Exceptions

As well as AutoCorrect entries, you can create *AutoCorrect exceptions*—specific terms when you don't want AutoCorrect to replace text when it normally would. You can create AutoCorrect exceptions in Word, PowerPoint, and Outlook, but not in Excel.

To create AutoCorrect exceptions, follow these steps:

1.   Open the AutoCorrect Exceptions dialog box by clicking the Exceptions button on the AutoCorrect tab of the AutoCorrect preferences pane.

2.   Click the tab for the type of exception you want to work with:

   ■   *First Letter*: On this tab, list the terms that end with periods but after which you don't want the next word to start with a capital letter. Office starts you off with a list of built-in terms, such as vol. and wk. Figure 2-19 shows the First Letter tab of the AutoCorrect Exceptions dialog box in Word.

   ■   *INitial CAps*: On this tab, list the terms that start with two initial capital letters that you don't want AutoCorrect to reduce to a single capital—for example, IPv6.

   ■   *Other Corrections*: This tab appears only in Word. On it, list other terms that you don't want AutoCorrect to fix.

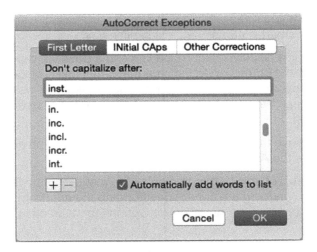

Figure 2-19. In the AutoCorrect Exceptions dialog box, you can create lists of terms that you want AutoCorrect to ignore

3. Add and delete exceptions as needed:

    ■ *Add an exception*: Type it in the "Don't capitalize after" box or the "Don't correct" box (depending on the tab), and then click the Add (+) button.

    ■ *Delete an exception*: Click it in the list box, and then click the Remove (–) button.

4. In Word, select the "Automatically add words to list" check box if you want Word to automatically add exceptions when you undo a correction it has made.

5. When you have finished working with exceptions, click the OK button in Word or PowerPoint to close the AutoCorrect Exceptions dialog box. In Outlook, click the Close button.

Working with Smart Buttons

A *smart button* is a little button that an Office app inserts automatically in a document to indicate that you can take actions with a particular type of material. The smart button provides a pop-up menu of actions tailored to that type of content.

For example, Word and PowerPoint can display a smart button after replacing an AutoCorrect entry with its replacement text, in case you need to undo the correction or stop the app from using it in the future. And when you paste in text or other options, Word, Excel, and PowerPoint display a Paste Options smart button that provides different ways of pasting the text, such as with or without formatting.

Figure 2-20 shows what you'll see when a smart button is available. This example is for AutoCorrect, but other smart buttons work in a similar way.

- At first, the app displays a light-blue line and a downward-pointing arrow below the correction to indicate that it has taken place. This line and arrow appear momentarily when the app makes the correction and then disappear. When you move the pointer near the correction, they appear again.

- When you move the pointer over the correction or the line and arrow, the app displays the AutoCorrect Options button.

- You can then click this button to display the menu of options—for AutoCorrect, undoing the correction, stopping the app from correcting it in future, or opening the AutoCorrect Options to make other changes.

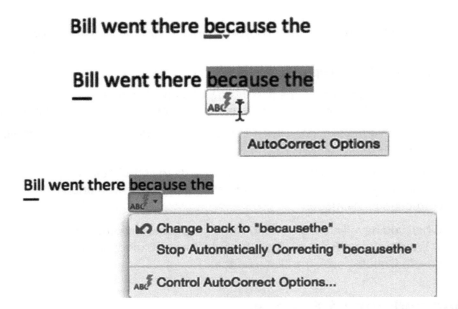

Figure 2-20. A smart button pops up when you move the pointer over text on which you can perform specific actions. For example, the AutoCorrect Options button appears first as a blue line (top). When you move the pointer over it, the full button appears (middle). You can click the button to display the actions (bottom)

Checking Spelling and Grammar

To check that your documents are as correct as possible, you can check the spelling in them. Each of the Office apps lets you use the spelling checker, which is shared among the apps. Word and Outlook also have a grammar checker.

Note   Computers are great at checking spelling because in most cases each word is spelled either correctly or incorrectly—there are few gray areas, and the spelling checker doesn't need to understand what the text means to evaluate the spelling. So, in most cases, it's a good idea to use the spelling checker to remove spelling mistakes from your documents. You still need to make sure that any suggested replacement is the right word—the spelling checker has minimal understanding of context, so don't accept its suggestions blindly.

Checking Spelling

In Word, PowerPoint, and Outlook, you can have the spelling checker check spelling either as you type or when you're ready to check the whole document. Excel doesn't offer on-the-fly checking, only full checking.

Checking Spelling as You Type

Word, PowerPoint, and Outlook can all check your spelling as you type. If you leave this checking turned on, the spelling checker puts a wavy red underline beneath any word whose spelling it thinks is wrong.

To check the spelling of a queried word, Ctrl-click or right-click the word, and then make one of the following choices from the context menu (see Figure 2-21):

- *Replace the word*: Click one of the suggested words at the top of the context menu.

- *Ignore All*: Ignore all instances of the apparently misspelled word in this document.

- *Add to Dictionary*: Add this word to your custom dictionary so that the spelling checker never queries it again.

- *Hyperlink*: Display the Insert Hyperlink dialog box so that you can create a hyperlink from the text.

- *New Comment*: Create a new comment that refers to the word—for example, you might query what the word should be.

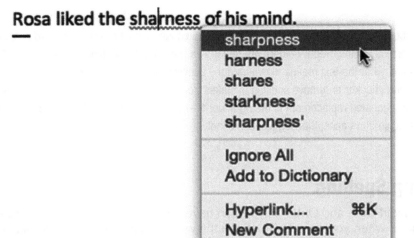

Figure 2-21. Ctrl-click or right-click a queried word and then click the appropriate item on the context menu

Checking Spelling in the Whole Document

Instead of checking spelling as you type (or in addition to doing so), you can run a spell check at any time. Before you start, position the insertion point or selection where you want to start the check.

Here are some examples:

- *Word*: Press Cmd+Home to move the insertion point to the start of the document.

- *Excel*: Click the cell in which you want to start the spell-check.

- *PowerPoint*: Click the slide at which you want to start the spell-check.

Open the Spelling and Grammar checker by pressing Cmd+Option+L or giving the appropriate command:

- *Word*: Choose Review ➤ Proofing ➤ Spelling & Grammar from the Ribbon or Tools ➤ Spelling & Grammar from the menu bar.

- *Excel*: Choose Review ➤ Proofing ➤ Spelling from the Ribbon or Tools ➤ Spelling from the menu bar.

- *PowerPoint*: Choose Review ➤ Proofing ➤ Spelling from the Ribbon or Tools ➤ Spelling from the menu bar.

- *Outlook*: In a message window, choose Options ➤ Spelling & Grammar from the Ribbon or Edit ➤ Spelling & Grammar ➤ Show Spelling and Grammar from the menu bar.

The spelling checker displays its first query.

Figure 2-22 shows the Spelling and Grammar dialog box in Word. The Spelling dialog box in Excel and PowerPoint has most of the same features.

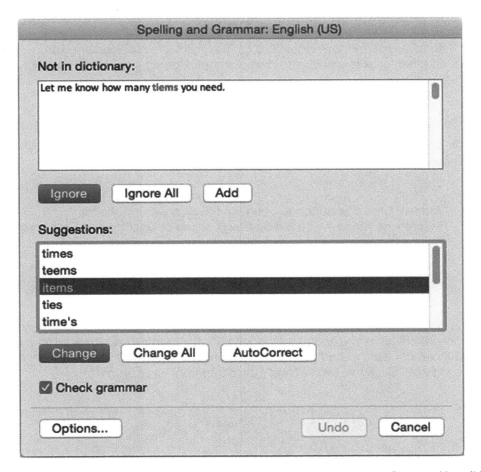

Figure 2-22. The Spelling dialog box or Spelling and Grammar dialog box suggests ways to fix any problems it finds

Note   If the spelling checker finds nothing to query, it displays a dialog box telling you that the check is complete. Click the OK button to dismiss the dialog box.

You can now choose how to deal with each query. These are your options:

- *Ignore*: Click this button to ignore this instance of the word.

- *Ignore All*: Click this button to ignore all instances of the word in this document (but query it in other documents).

- *Add*: Click this button to add the word to your custom dictionary so that the spelling checker never queries it again.

- *Change*: In the Suggestions list box, click the word with which to replace the queried word, and then click this button to change this instance.

- *Change All*: In the Suggestions list box, click the replacement word, and then click this button to change all instances in the document.

- *AutoCorrect*: In the Suggestions list box, click the replacement word, and then click this button to create an AutoCorrect entry and to correct this instance.

> **Tip**   When you check spelling, create an AutoCorrect entry for any misspelling you think you may repeat. Each AutoCorrect entry may help only a little, but taken together, they can make a huge improvement in your typing speed and accuracy.

- *Options*: Click this button to open the Proofing pane in the app's Preferences window with the Spelling options or Spelling and Grammar options displayed.

- *Undo*: Click this button to undo the last spelling change you made.

- *Cancel*: Click this button to end the spelling check before you've dealt with all the queries.

When you've dealt with one query, the spelling checker displays the next query. When the spelling checker reaches the end of the document after starting anywhere but the beginning, it asks whether you want to continue at the beginning. Figure 2-23 shows the dialog box you'll see in Excel. Click the Yes button or the No button, as appropriate.

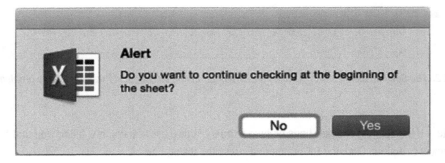

Figure 2-23. If you start checking from the middle of a document, the spelling checker prompts you to continue at the beginning

When you have dealt with every spelling query, the spelling checker lets you know that the check is complete (see Figure 2-24).

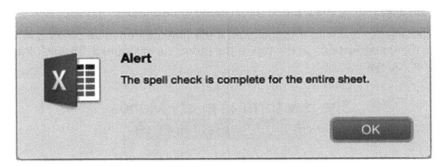

Alert

The spell check is complete for the entire sheet.

OK

Figure 2-24. The spelling checker confirms that the check is complete

Checking Grammar in Word and Outlook

For documents you create in Word or outgoing messages you write in Outlook, you can check the grammar as well as the spelling. As with spelling, you can check grammar either as you type or in a separate operation when you're ready to review your document.

> **Caution**   Before using the grammar checker, make sure you understand how severe its limitations are. The grammar checker doesn't understand the meaning of the text, but it tries to identify the different parts of speech (nouns, verbs, and so on) and their relationship to each other. Many of the grammar checker's suggestions will not improve your documents. Its best features are identifying minor problems such as unsuitable words or missing punctuation. It is particularly unsuited for creative writing that bends the rules of grammar.

If you choose to use on-the-fly grammar checking, the grammar checker puts a wavy green underline under any text that it queries. This may be a word, a phrase, or an entire sentence or more, depending on the query. You can then Ctrl-click or right-click the underlined text and choose an action from the context menu (see Figure 2-25):

■ *Replace the text with a suggestion*: If the grammar checker offers one or more suggestions at the top of the menu, as in Figure 2-25, click the one you want to use.

Figure 2-25. When using on-the-fly grammar checking, Ctrl-click or right-click a query to see what the problem is and whether the grammar checker has a suitable solution

■ *Grammar*: Click this item to open the Spelling and Grammar dialog box.

■ *Ignore*: Click this item to ignore this instance of the issue.

■ *Hyperlink*: Display the Insert Hyperlink dialog box so that you can create a hyperlink from the text.

■ *New Comment*: Create a new comment that refers to the word or phrase—for example, you might query what the word or phrase should be.

When you check grammar along with spelling, the grammar checker runs in tandem with the spelling checker, so you see queries from both of them in the Spelling and Grammar dialog box. Figure 2-26 shows an example of a grammar query.

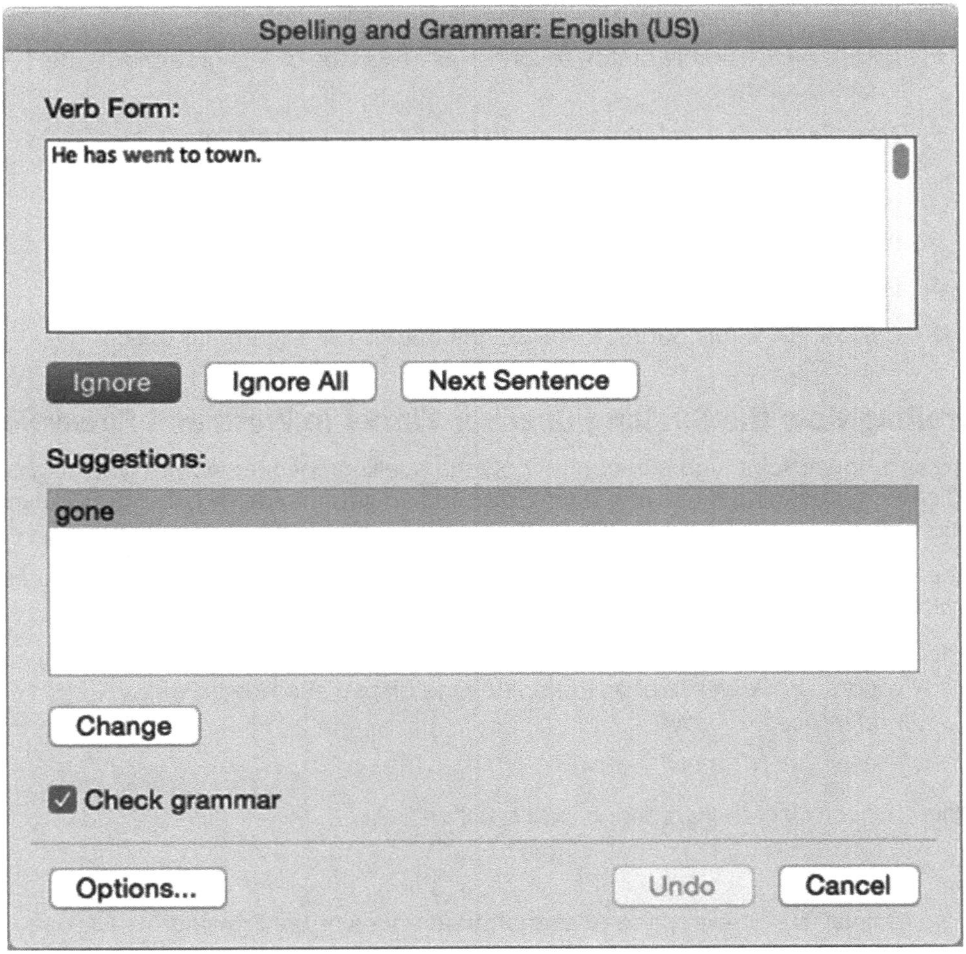

Figure 2-26. *If you choose to check grammar, the grammar checker runs alongside the spelling checker and displays queries in the Spelling and Grammar dialog box*

From the Spelling and Grammar dialog box, you can take the following actions:

- *Edit the text*: Click in the upper-left text box, and then type your fix for the problem. Click the Change button to apply the change in the document.

- *Ignore*: Click this button to ignore this grammar issue once.

- *Ignore All*: Click this button to ignore all instances of this grammar issue in this document.

- *Next Sentence*: Click this button to move to the next sentence, even if you haven't dealt with the current query.

- *Change*: If the Suggestions box contains a suitable suggestion, click it, and then click this button to replace the offending text with the suggestion.

- *Undo*: Click this button to undo the last change you made.

- *Cancel*: Click this button to cancel the spelling and grammar check.

Controlling How the Spelling Checker Works in Word and PowerPoint

In Word and PowerPoint, you can control how the spelling checker works by setting options for it. It's worth spending a few moments doing this to get the spelling checker working the way you prefer.

To make the most of the spelling checker in Word or PowerPoint, spend a few minutes customizing its settings. Follow these steps:

1. Choose Word ➤ Preferences to display the Word Preferences window or PowerPoint ➤ Preferences to display the PowerPoint Preferences window.

Note   You can't set spelling options in Excel or Outlook.

---

2. Display the Spelling and Grammar preferences or the Spelling preferences:

   - *Word*: Click the Spelling and Grammar icon in the Authoring and Proofing Tools section. Figure 2-27 shows the Spelling & Grammar preferences pane for Word.

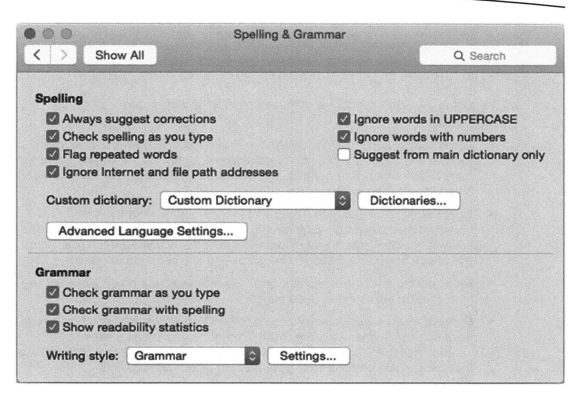

Figure 2-27. You can choose custom settings for the spelling checker and grammar checker in the Spelling & Grammar pane in the Word Preferences window

- *PowerPoint*: Click the Spelling button on the toolbar. Figure 2-28 shows the Spelling pane in the PowerPoint Preferences window. As you can see, it contains fewer options than Word offers.

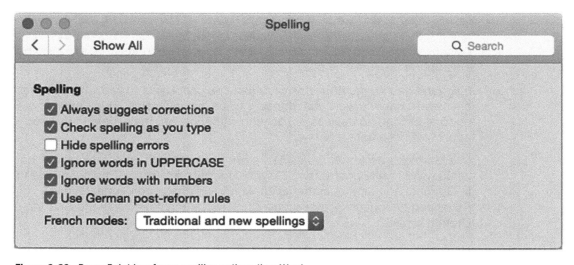

Figure 2-28. PowerPoint has fewer spelling options than Word

> **Tip** You can also open the Spelling preferences by clicking the Options button in the Spelling and Grammar dialog box in Word or the Spelling dialog box in PowerPoint.

3. To control the spelling checker, choose common options in the Spelling area:

- *Always suggest corrections (Word and PowerPoint)*: Select this check box to have the Spelling and Grammar dialog box or Spelling dialog box suggest corrections for spelling queries. This is usually helpful but may slow down an aging Mac that's struggling to run Office.

- *Check spelling as you type (Word and PowerPoint)*: Select this check box if you want the spelling checker to check spelling continually as you type. The spelling checker puts a wavy red underline under any word it queries. Clear this check box if you prefer to check spelling in a separate operation.

- *Hide spelling errors (PowerPoint only)*: Select this check box if you want to hide spelling errors in the document.

- *Suggest from main dictionary only (Word only)*: Select this check box if you want spelling suggestions only from Office's main dictionary file, not from custom dictionaries you create. Usually, you'll want to clear this check box so that the spelling checker uses your custom dictionaries as well.

- *Ignore words in UPPERCASE (Word and PowerPoint)*: Select this check box if you want the spelling checker to skip words that appear in uppercase. This is usually helpful because it helps you avoid queries on technical terms.

- *Ignore words with numbers (Word and PowerPoint)*: Select this check box to have the spelling checker skip any word that includes numbers (for example, IPv6). Clear this check box if you tend to get number typos in words and need the spelling checker to help root them out.

- *Ignore Internet and file path addresses (Word and PowerPoint)*: Select this check box to make the spelling checker ignore any URLs (for example, www.apress.com) and file addresses (for example, \\server2\reference\manual.pdf). This option is usually helpful.

- *Flag repeated words (Word only)*: Select this check box to allow the spelling checker to query a word that appears twice in succession. This option is good at picking up useless duplication, although you may sometimes need to approve a deliberate repetition.

- *Use German post-reform rules (Word and PowerPoint)*: Select this check box if you need to use post-reform German spelling rather than traditional spelling in German-language documents. In Word, this check box appears in the Advanced Language Settings dialog box rather than directly in the Spelling & Grammar pane.

- *French modes (Word and PowerPoint)*: In this pop-up menu, choose which spelling type you want the spelling checker to use: traditional and new spellings, traditional spelling, or new spelling. In Word, this pop-up menu appears in the Advanced Language Settings dialog box.

- *Custom dictionary (Word only)*: In this pop-up menu, select the custom dictionary you want to add words to when you use the Add command when checking spelling. For information on how to use custom dictionaries, see the "Taking Control over Spelling Checks with Custom Dictionaries" section later in this chapter.

4. To control grammar checking in Word, choose settings for the following options:

- *Check grammar as you type*: Select this check box if you want the grammar checker to raise queries as you work. The grammar checker puts a wavy green underline under items it queries. On-the-fly grammar checking tends to be distracting, so you'll probably want to clear this check box.

- *Check grammar with spelling*: Select this check box if you want to use the grammar checker. Otherwise, clear it.

- *Show readability statistics*: Select this check box if you want the spelling checker to display the Readability Statistics dialog box when it finishes a spelling check.

Tip   Don't bother with the readability statistics. The counts of words, characters, paragraphs, and sentences can be useful, but you can get the first three more easily in the Word Count dialog box (click the Words readout on the status bar or choose Tools ➤ Word Count from the menu bar). The averages of sentences per paragraph, words per sentence, and characters per word have little relevance. The Passive Sentences, Flesch Reading Ease, and Flesch-Kincaid Grade Level are computed statistics that don't accurately assess how easy or hard the document is to read. If you want to know whether a document is hard to understand, ask a colleague to read it.

---

5. For Word, you can also choose advanced language settings and grammar and style options. See the next two sections for details.

6. When you've finished choosing options for the spelling checker, close the Preferences window by clicking the Close button (the red button at the left end of the title bar) or pressing Cmd+W.

Choosing Advanced Language Settings for Word

In Word, you can choose further language settings by clicking the Advanced Language Settings button and making your choices in the Advanced Language Settings dialog box (see Figure 2-29). Apart from the "Use German post-reform rules" check box and the French modes pop-up menu mentioned in the previous section, the Advanced Language Settings dialog box contains the following controls:

■ *Enforce accented uppercase in French*: Select this check box if your documents use a French dialect (such as Canadian French) that retains accents on uppercase letters rather than removing the accents (as in standard French).

Figure 2-29. Word's Advanced Language Settings dialog box includes advanced settings for German, French, Russian, Spanish, and Portuguese

■ *Russian: Enforce strict ë in Russian*: Select this check box to make the spelling checker enforce the use of the ë character in Russian-language documents.

■ *Spanish modes*: In this pop-up menu, choose whether to use the Tuteo verb forms, the Voseo verb forms, or both for the second person. The choices are Tuteo verb forms only, Tuteo and Voseo verb forms, and Voseo verb forms only.

- *Portuguese modes*: In this pop-up menu, choose whether to use post-reform rules, pre-reform rules, or both in Portuguese-language documents.

- *Brazilian modes*: In this pop-up menu, choose whether to use post-reform rules, pre-reform rules, or both in documents that use Brazilian Portuguese.

Choosing Grammar and Style Options for Word and Outlook

When choosing proofing options for Word in the Spelling and Grammar dialog box, you can also choose options for the grammar checker.

If you turn on the grammar checker by selecting the "Check grammar with spelling" check box (and the "Check grammar as you type" check box if you want ongoing error checking as well), click the Settings button to display the Grammar Settings dialog box (see Figure 2-30), which enables you to choose the settings you need.

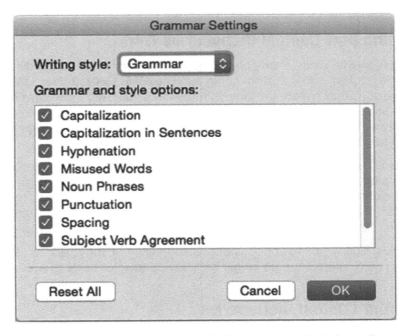

Figure 2-30. Use the Grammar Settings dialog box to control which grammar and style issues the grammar checker raises when checking your documents

At the top of the Grammar Settings dialog box is the Writing style pop-up menu. As of this writing, this pop-up menu offers only one choice: Grammar. In Word 2011, this pop-up menu offered five settings—Casual, Standard, Formal, Technical, and Custom—for different checking needs, plus Grammar Only and Grammar & Style settings.

It is not clear whether Microsoft intends to restore this grammar-checking flexibility to Word 2016. As it is, you can choose which specific items to check by selecting the check boxes in the Grammar and Style options box. For example, if you want the Spelling and Grammar checker to check for commonly misused words but leave punctuation and its positioning to you, select the Misused Words check box but clear the Punctuation check box.

When you have finished choosing grammar and style options, click the OK button to close the Grammar Settings dialog box.

Taking Control of Spelling Checks with Custom Dictionaries

The spelling checker uses a dictionary file for the language you've chosen (for example, U.S. English). The dictionary file consists of a list of words that are spelled correctly; unlike a conventional dictionary, the file doesn't contain definitions for the words.

You can't change the main dictionary file, but you can add to it by creating custom dictionaries containing words you don't want the spelling checker to query. For example, you may need to include technical terms in your documents that the main dictionary file doesn't contain.

Understanding How Custom Dictionaries Work

Office starts you off with a custom dictionary named Custom Dictionary. Office stores this dictionary inside a folder with a custom name such as `UBF8T346G3.Office` in your `~/Library/Group Containers folder` (where the tilde, ~, represents your home folder). Office sets the Office apps to add words to the custom dictionary automatically during spelling checks. So when you give the Add command as described earlier in this chapter, the spelling checker adds the word to your custom dictionary.

You can stick with using just this Custom Dictionary file if you want, but it's often useful to create extra custom dictionaries that contain different types of terms. You can then choose which custom dictionaries to load for a particular project. For example, you may work on some technical documents that need the spelling checker to accept various technical terms, but you may want the spelling checker to query the same terms in your other documents.

Normally, you just add words to your custom dictionaries, but you may sometimes need to remove words you've added and no longer want the spelling checker to accept.

Managing Your Custom Dictionaries

Office provides the Custom Dictionaries dialog box for creating, editing, and managing custom dictionaries. Here's how to open the Custom Dictionaries dialog box:

1. In Word, choose Word ➤ Preferences to display the Word Preferences window.

2. Click the Spelling & Grammar icon in the Authoring and Proofing Tools section to display the Spelling & Grammar preferences pane.

3. Click the Dictionaries button to display the Custom Dictionaries dialog box (shown in Figure 2-31 with several dictionaries already added).

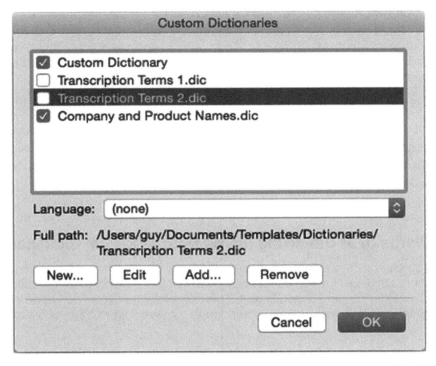

Figure 2-31. Use the Custom Dictionaries dialog box in Word to create, edit, and manage your custom dictionaries

Creating a Custom Dictionary

To create a new custom dictionary, follow these steps in the Custom Dictionaries dialog box:

1. Click the New button to open the Save dialog box.

2. In the Save As text box, type the name you want to give the new dictionary. You can use pretty much any name you want as long as there's no file of that name in the folder you use.

3. Select the folder in which you want to store the dictionary. If the dictionary is solely for your own use, you might save it in a folder in your user account. If you need to share the dictionary with others, use a network folder.

4. Click the Save button. The app closes the New Dictionary dialog box and creates the dictionary. The dictionary appears in the list box in the Custom Dictionaries dialog box.

5. Select the check box next to the dictionary.

The dictionary is now ready for use, but you may need to change its language. Word chooses the (none) setting in the Language pop-up menu, which sets the dictionary for use with all languages (by not restricting it to a particular language). If you want to restrict the dictionary to a particular language, click the dictionary in the list box, and then choose the language from the Language pop-up menu.

> **Note**   If you already have a custom dictionary file (for example, one your company has created), click the Add button in the Custom Dictionaries dialog box. In the Add Dictionary dialog box, select the dictionary file, and then click the Open button. The dictionary then appears in the list box in the Custom Dictionaries dialog box, and you can select its check box to make it active.

Adding Words to or Removing Words from a Custom Dictionary

Normally, you build a custom dictionary one word at a time by using the Add command when checking spelling. But you can also open a custom dictionary file for editing so that you can make wider-ranging changes to it. This is useful when you need to add a whole list of words to the dictionary or when you need to remove a word that you've added by mistake.

To edit a custom dictionary, follow these steps from the Custom Dictionaries dialog box:

1.   Click the custom dictionary in the list box.

2.   Click the Edit button to open the dictionary for editing. Word opens the dictionary in a document window, just like any other document (see Figure 2-32).

> **Note**   If you're using automatic spell checking, when you open a dictionary for editing, Word displays a dialog box warning you that it will turn off automatic spell checking. Click the OK button to proceed. After editing the dictionary, you need to turn automatic spell checking back on—if you don't, Word will leave it turned off.

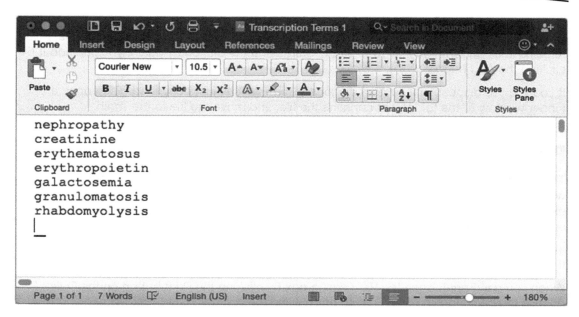

Figure 2-32. When you open a dictionary file for editing, Word uses a regular document window rather than a special dialog box. Word turns off as-you-type spelling checking for the dictionary

3. Change the list of words by using standard editing techniques. Type each entry in a separate paragraph, pressing the Return key to create a new paragraph.

4. Click the Save button on the title bar (or choose File ➤ Save or press Cmd+S) to save the dictionary.

5. Click the Close button on the title bar to close the dictionary file.

> **Note** If Word turned off automatic spell checking when you opened the dictionary for editing, turn it back on when you finish editing. Choose Word ➤ Preferences to open the Preferences window, and then click the Spelling and Grammar icon to display the Spelling and Grammar preferences pane. Select the Check spelling as you type check box, and then close the Preferences window by clicking the Close button (the red button at the left end of the title bar) or pressing Cmd+W.

Turning Off, Removing, or Deleting a Custom Dictionary

When you want to stop using a custom dictionary for the time being, clear its check box in the list box in the Custom Dictionaries dialog box. The dictionary remains in the list, and you can start using it again at any point by selecting its check box.

If you want to remove a custom dictionary from the list, click it in the list box, and then click the Remove button. The app removes the dictionary from the list, but its dictionary file remains in its current folder. If you need to start using the dictionary again, you can add it by clicking the Add button.

If you want to dispose of a custom dictionary, remove it as just described. Then open a Finder window to the folder that contains the file, and move the file to the Trash.

Printing Documents

These days, you probably share documents with others via e-mail frequently, but there will still be times when you need to print out hard copies of documents to share. For example, you may need to print letters or papers you write in Word, print a page of an Excel spreadsheet, or print a handout for a PowerPoint presentation.

In each of the Office apps, you can choose from a wide range of printing options to make the printout look the way you want.

When you need print, open the Print dialog box by clicking the Print button on the Quick Access toolbar, choosing File ➤ Print, or pressing the standard Cmd+P keyboard shortcut.

At first, Excel, PowerPoint, and Outlook usually display the Print dialog box with the details hidden (see Figure 2-33). From here, you can take essential actions such as changing the printer, choosing a preset set of printing options, or previewing the document. You can expand the dialog box by clicking the Show Details button at the bottom of the Print dialog box in order to see the quick preview and all the available options.

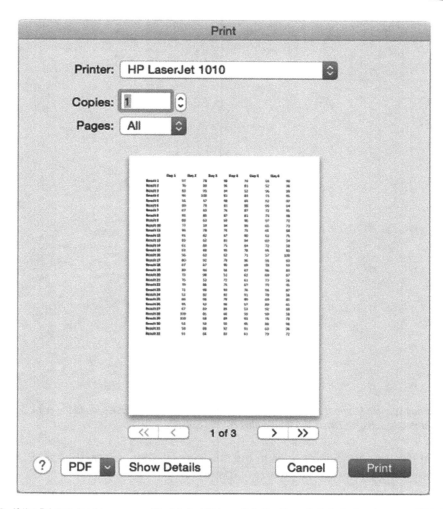

Figure 2-33. *If the Print dialog box opens with details hidden, click the Show Details button to expand it to its full size*

Figure 2-34 shows the Print dialog box for Excel with details displayed. The Print dialog box in each app is different because it contains controls suited to the document type that app produces. For example, in Word you can choose which pages to print and whether to include comments and tracked changes, while in PowerPoint you can choose which slides to print and whether to frame the slides. But in each case the basics are the same.

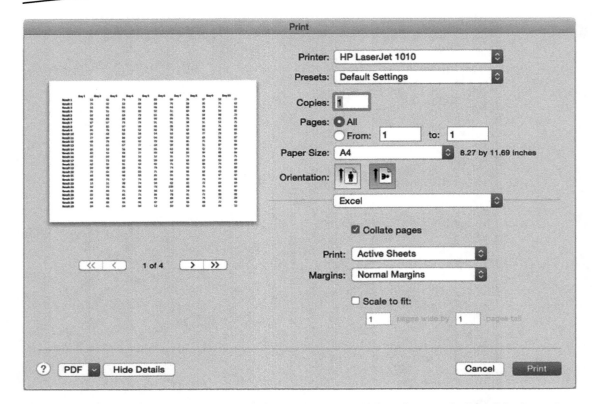

Figure 2-34. When you need to print only part of a document or print multiple copies, open the Print dialog box and choose the appropriate settings. This is the Print dialog box for Excel

You'll look at the app-specific options in the chapters on the individual apps. But these are the basic moves that you can use in any of the apps:

- *Choose the printer*: Open the Printer pop-up menu and choose the printer to use. If you need to add a printer, click the Add Printer item on this menu.

> **Tip**   OS X lets you either set a particular printer as your default printer or print to whichever printer you last used. To adjust this setting, open the Printer pop-up menu in the Print dialog box, and then click Printers & Scanners Preferences to display the Printers & Scanners preferences pane in System Preferences. Open the Default Printer pop-up menu, and then choose either the printer you want or the Last Printer Used setting. Click the Close button (the red button at the left end of the title bar), choose System Preferences ➤ Quit System Preferences, or press Cmd+Q to quit System Preferences.

■ *Choose a preset*: Open the Presets pop-up menu and choose the preset group of settings to use. Normally, the Presets pop-up menu contains only the Standard preset and the Last Used Settings preset until you define your own presets.

Tip   When you've chosen a group of printing settings you'd like to use again, create a preset for them. Open the Presets pop-up menu and click Save Current Settings as Preset to display the Save Current Settings as Preset dialog box. Type the name for the preset in the Preset Name box. In the Preset Available For area, select the Only this printer option button or the All printers option button. Then click the OK button to close the dialog box. The app adds the preset to the Presets pop-up menu, and it's ready for use.

■ *Change the number of copies*: To print more than one copy, type the number in the Copies box. If you want the sheets of each copy in order (1,2,3), select the Collated check box; clear this check box if you want all the copies of each page together.

■ *Create a PDF of the document*: To create a file in the widely used Portable Document Format (PDF), click the PDF button, and then click Save as PDF in the pop-up menu. In the Save dialog box (see Figure 2-35), specify the file name in the Save As box and the folder either in the Where pop-up menu or in the navigation pane. Then enter any metadata the document needs: the title, author, subject, and keywords (press the Return key after each keyword to create a keyword button). If you want to secure the PDF with a password for opening or printing it, click the Security Options button, and then work in the PDF Security Options dialog box. When you're ready to save the PDF, click the Save button. The app automatically closes the Print dialog box for you.

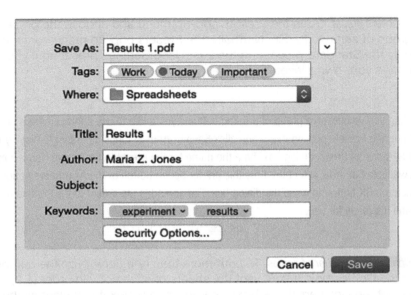

Figure 2-35. *In the Save dialog box, you can add a title, author, subject, and any keywords needed to a PDF file you're creating from an Office document*

Tip   If you just need to e-mail a PDF version of the document without adding metadata or applying a password, you can save a step by choosing the Mail PDF command from the PDF pop-up menu in the Print dialog box. The app creates a new message in your default e-mail app (for example, Outlook) and attaches a PDF file of the document to the message. Similarly, you can send a PDF version of the document quickly via Messages by choosing the Send PDF via Messages command from the PDF pop-up menu.

- *Preview the document*: In Word, Excel, and PowerPoint, the Print dialog box displays a quick preview of the document. You can click the First (<<), Previous (<), Next (>), and Last (>>) buttons below the preview to change the page displayed.

- *Print the document*: When you've chosen the settings you want, click the Print button. The app closes the Print dialog box and sends the details of the print job to the print queue for the printer.

Summary

In this chapter, you learned how to use several common features of the Office apps. You now know how to control apps using the menus, the Quick Access Toolbar, and the Ribbon; how to use the common palettes in the Toolbox; and how to share your documents quickly and easily with other people in formats they can read.

You also looked at ways to save time and effort by using the AutoCorrect feature and those AutoFormat options that you find helpful (while turning off any options that cause unpleasant surprises as you work). You can now choose settings for the spelling checker and grammar checker, run one or both, and choose which of its suggestions to accept and which to reject. And you know how to preview your documents and print them.

In the next chapter, I'll show you further vital skills for making the most of the Office apps: how to work with text; use Cut, Copy, and Paste; and create tables and hyperlinks.

Working with Text

In this chapter, I'll show you how to work with text in the Office apps. As you'll see, the operations are almost the same for each app, so once you learn to work with text in one app, you'll be able to work with text in each of the other apps too.

You'll start with entering text itself by using the keyboard or other means. Then you'll move to navigating with the keyboard and selecting objects. You'll then learn to apply direct formatting to text and objects; use the Cut, Copy, and Paste features; and use the core Find and Replace features that the apps share. Next, I'll show you how to create tables, enter text in them, and format them to look good. Finally, you'll learn to add to your Office documents hyperlinks that lead the user to another document, take them to a web site, or start a new e-mail message automatically.

Note To follow the Ribbon commands easily, please display the group titles on the Ribbon. To do so, click the app's menu (such as the Word menu) and then click Preferences. In the Preferences window, click View to display the View pane. In the "In Ribbon, Show" area, select the Group Titles check box, and then close the Preferences window by clicking the Close button (the red button at the left end of the window's title bar).

Entering Text in Your Documents

The main way to enter text in your Office documents is to type it with the keyboard, but you can also paste text from other documents, scan documents and use optical character recognition (OCR) to identify the text in them, or use dictation. Beyond the regular characters that appear on the keyboard, some documents will likely need symbols that don't appear on it, so you need to know how to enter those as well.

Entering Text in Documents Using Copy and Paste

To enter text using Copy and Paste, copy the text from the document that contains it, and then paste it into the Office document. See the section "Using Cut, Copy, and Paste" later in this chapter.

Entering Text by Scanning a Document and Using Optical Character Recognition

If you have a document that contains the text you want to use in an Office document, you can scan the text using a scanner and then use optical character recognition to get the text out of the picture file that the scanner produces.

To perform the scanning, you need a scanner and third-party OCR software such as OmniPage Pro X (www.nuance.com) or Readiris Pro (www.irislink.com). And to use the text from a hard-copy document in a document of your own, you will typically need to get permission from the copyright holder.

Caution   When you use OCR to recognize a document, always read through the resulting text and compare it to the original. Although OCR does its best to recognize the text accurately, it often introduces errors—sometimes surprising ones.

Entering Text by Using Dictation

You can use OS X's built-in Dictation feature to insert text in documents in the Office apps. If your work (or play) conditions are conducive to dictation, this can be a great way to enter text quickly and accurately. If you're in an open environment and don't want your immediate neighbors or colleagues to know what you're writing, dictation has obvious drawbacks.

Enabling Dictation on Your Mac

Follow these steps to enable the Dictation feature on your Mac:

1. Ctrl-click or right-click the System Preferences icon on the Dock. The context menu opens.

2. Click the Dictation & Speech item on the context menu. The System Preferences app opens, showing the Dictation & Speech preferences pane.

3. Click the Dictation tab button if necessary to display the Dictation pane (see Figure 3-1).

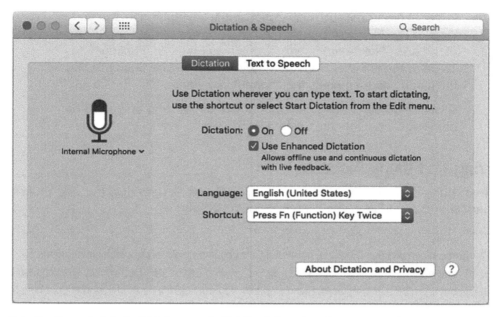

Figure 3-1. Use the controls in the Dictation pane in Dictation & Speech preferences to enable Dictation, activate the Enhanced Dictation feature, and choose your language and keyboard shortcut

4. On the left side of the Dictation pane, click the pop-up menu, and then click the microphone you want to use.

Tip   Use a headset microphone for dictation if possible because you will get much better results from having the microphone positioned consistently close to your mouth to pick up your voice clearly. Place the microphone to the side of your mouth rather than in front of it so that it doesn't pick up your breath stream.

---

5. On the Dictation line, select the On option button.

6. Select the Use Enhanced Dictation check box.

Note   Enhanced Dictation enables you to use dictation while your Mac is offline. It also lets you dictate continuously instead of having to pause while your Mac communicates with Apple's speech-recognition servers. The only disadvantage to Enhanced Dictation is that your Mac must download and install a large (1.2GB) file before you can start using the feature.

---

7. Make sure that the Language pop-up menu is showing the language you want to use, such as English (United States). If not, open the menu and select the right language.

8. In the Shortcut pop-up menu, choose the keyboard shortcut you want to use to toggle Dictation on and off. You can either choose one of the preset keyboard shortcuts, such as Press Fn (Function) Key Twice or Press Either Command Key Twice, or click Customize on the menu and then press the shortcut you want.

9. Click the Close button (the red button at the left end of the title bar) or press Cmd+Q to quit System Preferences.

Entering Text Using Dictation

Now that you've enabled Dictation, you can dictate text by activating the app, pressing your keyboard shortcut, and then speaking into your microphone.

> **Caution**   When you use Dictation, proofread your documents closely to catch substitutions of words and phrases. Simple mistakes such as substituting *can* for *can't* are usually easy enough to catch, but if the Dictation replaces a whole phrase, you may have a hard time working out how the text should actually read.

Inserting Symbols in a Document

By typing, you can easily insert any characters that appear on your keyboard—but many documents need other symbols, such as letters with dieresis marks over them (for example, Ä or ë) or ligatures that bind two characters (for example, Æ).

You can quickly insert one or more symbols in a Word document, Excel workbook, PowerPoint presentation, or Outlook item (such as a message) by using the Emoji & Symbols pane. In Word, you can also use the Symbol dialog box, which gives you access to a wider range of symbols.

> **Note**   When you insert a symbol using the Emoji & Symbols pane, the app inserts the symbol character in the same font you're currently using—if that font contains that character. If not, the app substitutes a font that does have the character. By contrast, when you use the Symbol dialog box, you can see exactly which symbols are available for a specific font.

Inserting a Symbol Using the Emoji & Symbols Panel

You can use the Emoji & Symbols panel to insert a symbol in Word, Excel, PowerPoint, or Outlook. To insert a symbol, follow these steps:

1. In the document, position the insertion point where you want the symbol to appear.

2. Open the Emoji & Symbols panel (see Figure 3-2) in one of these ways:

   ■ *Word, Excel, PowerPoint, or Outlook*: Choose Edit ➤ Emoji & Symbols from the menu bar or press Cmd+Ctrl+Space.

   ■ *Excel or PowerPoint*: Choose Insert ➤ Symbols ➤ Symbol from the Ribbon or Insert ➤ Symbol from the menu bar.

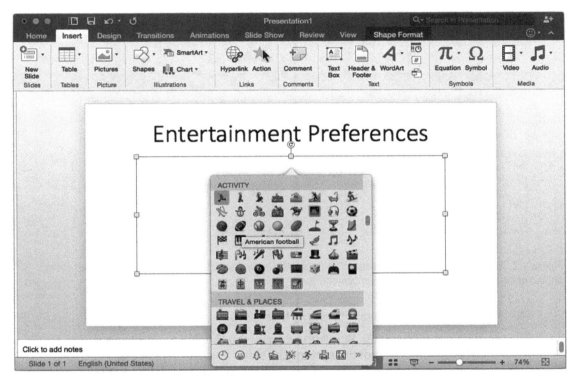

Figure 3-2. To insert a symbol in a document, open the Emoji & Symbols panel In PowerPoint (shown here) and Excel, you can choose Insert ➤ Symbols ➤ Symbol from the Ribbon to open the Emoji & Symbols panel

3. Explore the Emoji & Symbols panel to find the symbol you need. The left screen in Figure 3-3 shows the top part of the pop-up panel, with labels on the first several tabs at the bottom, and the right screen in Figure 3-3 shows a lower part of the panel, with labels on the remaining tabs.

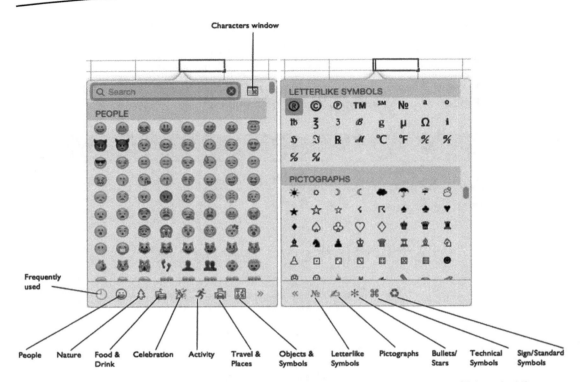

Figure 3-3. To insert a symbol in a workbook, click the symbol in the Characters pop-up panel. Click a tab at the bottom of the panel to display the set of symbols you want

4. Find the symbol you want in one of these ways:

    ■ *Browse all symbols*: Scroll up or down the Emoji & Symbols panel. The different sets of characters appear in a vertical stack that corresponds to the tabs: People at the top, Nature next, then Food & Drink, and so on.

    ■ *Display only a particular set of symbols*: Click the tab for the set of characters you want to view. For example, click the Travel & Places tab to display symbols showing taxis, trucks, planes, and the like.

    ■ *Search for a symbol*: Click the Search box at the top and type your search term.

5. Click the symbol to insert it in the document. The Emoji & Symbols panel closes automatically.

When you need to insert multiple symbols in sequence, open the Emoji & Symbols panel and then click the Characters window button in the upper-right corner. (You need to be scrolled up to the top of the Characters panel for this button to be visible.) The Characters window opens (see Figure 3-4), giving you different options for browsing symbol, and staying open after you insert a symbol, so you can continue inserting other symbols.

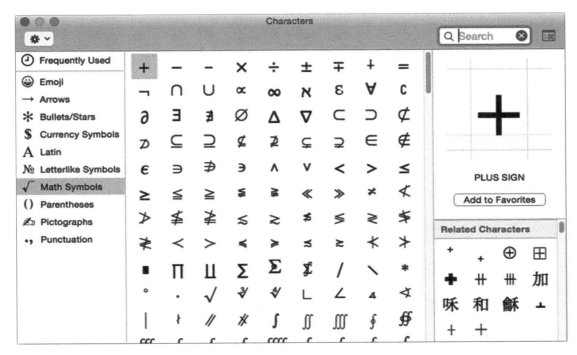

Figure 3-4. Use the Character window when you need to insert multiple symbols in sequence. Click the Add to Favorites button on the right side to add the selected character to your Frequently Used list

When you finish using the Characters window, close it by clicking the Close button (the red button) at the left end of its title bar.

Inserting a Symbol or Special Character Using the Symbol Dialog Box in Word

When you want to reach the full range of symbols that Word has to offer, use the Symbol dialog box instead of the Emoji & Symbols panel. The Symbol dialog box also contains a pane called Special Characters that lets you quickly insert widely used symbols such as dashes and copyright characters.

To insert a symbol using the Symbol dialog box, follow these steps:

1. Choose Insert ➤ Symbol ➤ Advanced Symbol from the Ribbon or Insert ➤ Advanced Symbol from the menu bar to display the Symbol dialog box (see Figure 3-5).

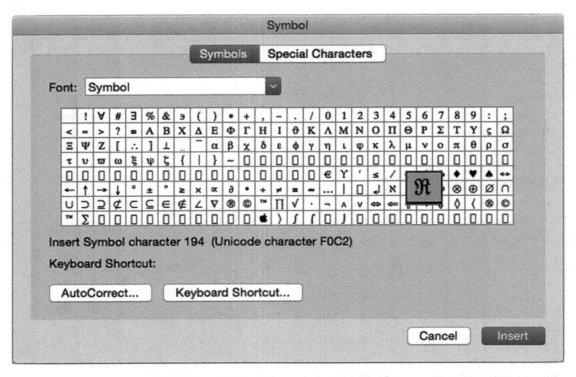

Figure 3-5. The Symbol dialog box in Word gives you access to a wide range of symbols and special characters. Click a character to display a larger preview, as shown here

2. Open the Font pop-up menu, and then click the font you want to use. The item named "(normal text)" that appears at the top of the list shows the symbol characters in the font you're using.

3. If you need to see a larger version of a symbol, click it to display a preview box.

Tip   After clicking a symbol to display its preview, you can continue to hold down the button on your pointing device and drag in any direction to preview other symbols. Alternatively, release the button on your overworked pointing device and then press the arrow keys to move the preview to other characters. This move is useful when you're looking for a symbol that's hard to distinguish from similar symbols around it.

4. To insert a symbol, click it, and then click the Insert button; you can also simply double-click the symbol. When you insert a symbol, the Symbol dialog box remains open, but the Cancel button changes to a Close button.

5. Insert other symbols as needed.

> **Tip** You can leave the Symbol box open and click in the Word document to resume work in the document. For example, you can type some text in the document, or reposition the insertion point, and then click in the Symbol dialog box and use it to insert another symbol character.

6. Click the Close button to close the Symbol dialog box.

To insert a special character, open the Symbol dialog box by choosing Insert ➤ Symbol ➤ Advanced Symbol from the Ribbon or Insert ➤ Advanced Symbol from the menu bar, and then click the Special Characters tab (see Figure 3-6). Click the character you want to insert, and then click the Insert button—or, as before, double-click the character you want to insert. Click the Close button to close the Symbol dialog box.

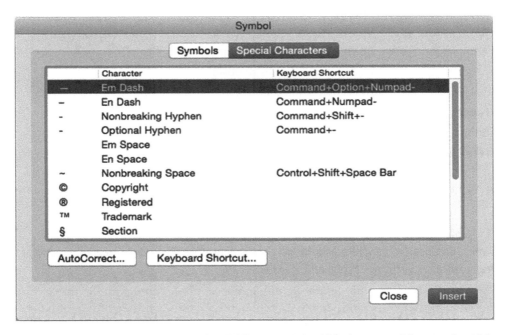

Figure 3-6. The Symbol dialog box includes the Special Characters tab, which gives you quick access to widely used symbols such as em dashes and en dashes, optional hyphens, and fixed-width spaces

When you've selected a symbol or special character in the Symbol dialog box, you can click the AutoCorrect button to start creating an AutoCorrect entry for that character or the Keyboard Shortcut button to start creating a keyboard shortcut for it.

> **Tip** If you often use the same words that include symbols or special characters, create an AutoCorrect entry for each of those words. This is usually much easier than using an AutoCorrect entry to enter a particular character within a word.

Navigating with the Keyboard and Selecting Objects

In OS X, the main means of moving around in a document is by using the pointing device. For example, you can click an object to select it, drag the scroll box down the scroll bar to move down the document, or click to place the insertion point where you want to type text.

When you're typing in a document, you may find it handier to use the keyboard to move the insertion point. Table 3-1 explains the standard keyboard shortcuts you can use to move the insertion point in the Office apps.

Table 3-1. Keyboard Shortcuts for Moving the Insertion Point in the Office Apps

Press These Keys	To Move the Insertion Point Like This
Left arrow	One character to the left
Right arrow	One character to the right
Up arrow	Up one line, paragraph, or cell
Down arrow	Down one line, paragraph, or cell
Home	To the start of the line or object
End	To the end of the line or object
Cmd+Home	To the start of the document
Cmd+End	To the end
Option+Left arrow	To the beginning of the current word (if the insertion point is in a word) or to the beginning of the previous word
Option+Right arrow	To the beginning of the next word

> **Note**   Because Excel's worksheets consist of cells rather than containing paragraphs, many of the keyboard shortcuts have different effects in Excel.

To work with text or an object in a document, you select that text or object by using the pointing device or the keyboard:

- *Select with the pointing device*: Click at the beginning of what you want to select, hold down the button, and then drag to the end of the selection.

- *Select with the pointing device and keyboard*: Click to place the insertion point at the beginning of what you want to select. Hold down the Shift key, and click at the end of the selection.

- *Select with the keyboard*: Move the insertion point to the beginning of the selection, hold down the Shift key, and then move the insertion point to the end of the selection (for example, by pressing the arrow keys).

Tip   In Word, you can also select multiple items at once. Select the first item as usual, using either the pointing device or the keyboard. Then hold down the Cmd key as you select each of the other items with the pointing device. Similarly, in Excel, you can press Cmd and click cells or ranges to add them to what you have already selected.

Applying Direct Formatting to Text and Objects

Each of the Office apps lets you apply a wide range of formatting to the text and objects you add to your documents. Each app has different types of formatting suited to its needs, but all the apps support direct formatting—formatting that you apply directly to text or to an object, such as bold and italic.

Note   Direct formatting is easy to use, but in Word and Excel, you can save time by formatting with styles instead. A *style* is a collection of formatting that you can apply in a single click. Not only can you apply formatting more quickly with styles, but you can also change the style's formatting and have the app automatically apply the change to the text that uses the style. This saves even more time and keeps your documents consistent.

The easiest way of applying most direct formatting is by using the controls and buttons on the Home tab of the Ribbon. Word, Excel, and PowerPoint all have a Font group on the Home tab, and Outlook has a similar but unnamed group. Word and PowerPoint also have a Paragraph group for applying paragraph formatting. Figure 3-7 shows the Home tab in PowerPoint with the Font group labeled.

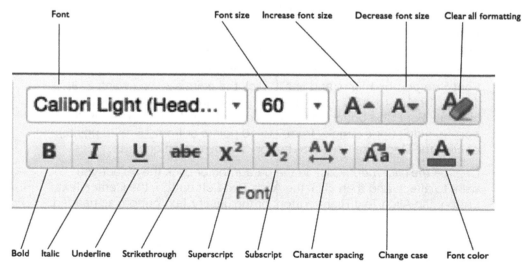

Figure 3-7. The Font group on the Home tab of the Ribbon includes widely used formatting tools. This is the Font group in PowerPoint

The Paragraph group on the Home tab of the Ribbon in Word and PowerPoint contains controls for formatting paragraphs. Figure 3-8 shows the Paragraph group in Word.

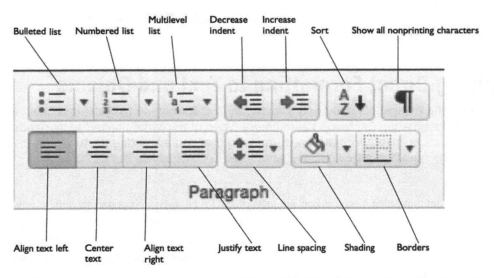

Figure 3-8. The Paragraph group on the Home tab of the Ribbon in Word (shown here) and PowerPoint provides essential commands for applying direct formatting to paragraphs

With a few exceptions, the controls in these groups are for applying direct formatting. And they're easy to use. In most cases, you select the text or other object you want to affect and then click the button. Here are some examples:

- *Apply bold*: Select the text you want to affect, or click in a single word. Then click the Bold button to apply bold. Click again to remove bold.

- *Change the font*: Select the text you want to affect. Click the Font pop-up menu, and then click the font name you want.

- *Change the font size*: Select the text you want to affect, then click the Font Size pop-up menu, and finally click the point size you want: 8, 9, 10, 11, 12, 14, 16, 18, 20, or whatever. For a quick change, click the Increase Font Size button to move up one of the steps in the Font Size pop-up menu (for example, from 9 to 10 points or from 18 to 20 points), or click the Decrease Font Size button to move down one size.

- *Change the alignment*: Click in the paragraph or click the object you want to affect, and then click the Align Text Left button, the Center Text button, the Align Text Right button, or the Justify Text button, as needed.

You can also apply widely used direct formatting by using keyboard shortcuts. Table 3-2 lists the most useful keyboard shortcuts for applying direct formatting.

Table 3-2. *Keyboard Shortcuts for Applying Direct Formatting*

Formatting Type	Keyboard Shortcut
Bold	Cmd+B
Italic	Cmd+I
Underline	Cmd+U
Subscript	Cmd+=
Superscript	Cmd++ (in other words, Cmd+Shift+=)
Grow font by one increment	Cmd+Shift+>
Shrink font by one increment	Cmd+Shift+<
Align left	Cmd+L
Align right	Cmd+R
Center	Cmd+E

Using Cut, Copy, and Paste

If you've worked with OS X apps before, you're almost certainly familiar with the Cut, Copy, and Paste features. You can use these features as usual in the Office apps by using either keyboard shortcuts or the buttons in the Clipboard group on the Home tab of the Ribbon (see Figure 3-9):

- *Cut*: Click the Cut button or press Cmd+X.
- *Copy*: Click the Copy button or press Cmd+C.
- *Paste*: Click the Paste button or press Cmd+V.

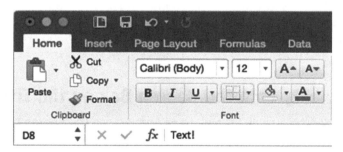

Figure 3-9. *You can perform Cut, Copy, and Paste operations by using the Cut, Copy, and Paste buttons in the Clipboard group on the Home tab of the Ribbon*

After you paste text or an object, you can use the Paste Options button that the app displays to change the way in which you pasted it. For example, in Word, the Paste Options button's pop-up menu (see Figure 3-10) frequently offers these choices:

- *Keep source formatting*: Click this item to maintain the formatting of the item you've pasted.

- *Use destination theme*: Click this item to apply the theme of the destination document to what you've pasted in.

- *Match destination formatting*: Click this item to make the pasted item take on the formatting of the paragraph or object into which you've pasted it. This formatting may or may not be different from the destination theme formatting.

- *Keep text only*: Click this item to keep only the text of the pasted item, discarding all formatting and any nontext objects (such as graphics).

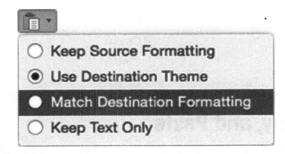

Figure 3-10. After pasting an item, you can use the Paste Options button to change the formatting used. This is the Paste Options menu you often see in Word

Using Find and Replace

When you need to locate specific text quickly in an Office document, use the Find feature. And when you need to replace specific text with other text, use the Replace feature.

Word, Excel, PowerPoint, and Outlook implement Find and Replace in different ways suited to their needs. This section introduces you to the basics of Find and Replace. The chapters on the individual apps provide further details on advanced Find and Replace features you may need to use.

Searching Quickly with the Search Box on the Title Bar

When you need to search quickly for a word or phrase, use the Search box at the right end of the title bar. Follow these steps:

1. Click in the Search box to place the insertion point there.

2. If necessary, click the Search pop-up menu button (click the Search icon itself or the downward arrow just to the right of the Search icon), and choose options as discussed next. Figure 3-11 shows the Search pop-up menu for Excel, which has the most choices.

   - *Word*: Click the List Matches in Sidebar item if you want to display the Sidebar containing all the matches for the search term. Click the Replace item if you want to display the Find and Replace pane in the Sidebar.

- *Excel*: Click the Search in Sheet item if you want to search just the displayed worksheet, or click the Search in Workbook item to search the whole workbook (including the displayed worksheet). Excel displays a check mark next to the item you chose so that you can see what you're searching. Click the Advanced Search item to display the Find dialog box (which you'll meet shortly). Click the Replace item to display the Replace dialog box (which you'll also meet shortly).

- *PowerPoint*: Click the Advanced Find item to display the Advanced Find dialog box, in which you can choose to match the case on searches or find only whole words rather than partial matches. Click the Replace item to display the Replace dialog box. Click the Replace Fonts item to display the Replace Font dialog box, which enables you to replace one font with another through a presentation.

- *Outlook*: Outlook has no pop-up menu button.

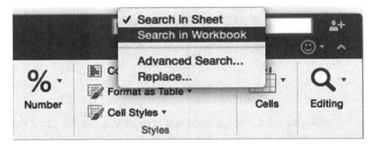

Figure 3-11. From the Search box on the Standard toolbar, you can search quickly or access search options. These are the search options for Excel

3. Type the search term in the Search box.

4. In Excel or PowerPoint, press the Return key to run the search. Word and Outlook search automatically as you enter the search term.

5. Click the Next button (the gray triangle pointing to the right) to move to the next instance of the term, or click the Previous button (the gray triangle pointing to the left) to move to the previous instance.

When you need to clear the Search box so that you can search for another term, click the × button at its right end.

Locating Text with the Find Dialog Box or Advanced Find Dialog Box

The Search box is easy to use, but often you'll want to locate text with more precision—for example, by matching the case used (rather than using non-case-sensitive matching) or by finding only whole-word matches rather than partial-word matches. To get these extra features, you need to use the Find dialog box or the Advanced Find dialog box, depending on the app you're using.

To open and use the Find dialog box or the Advanced Find dialog box, follow these steps:

1. Open the Find dialog box or the Advanced Find dialog box by using the appropriate command or keyboard shortcut:

    ■ *Word*: Choose Edit ➤ Find ➤ Advanced Find and Replace from the menu bar to display the Find and Replace dialog box with the Find tab at the front (see Figure 3-12).

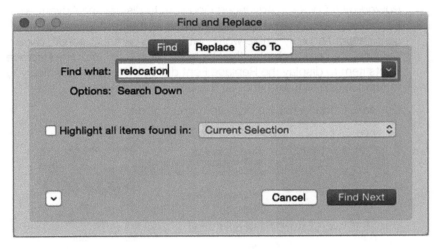

Figure 3-12. Word's Find and Replace dialog box at first opens at its smaller size. You can display further options by clicking the arrow button in the lower-left corner. To find single instances of the search term, clear the Highlight all items found in check box

    ■ *Excel*: Choose Edit ➤ Find from the menu bar, or click the Search pop-up menu at the right end of the toolbar and then click Advanced Find, to display the Find dialog box (see Figure 3-13).

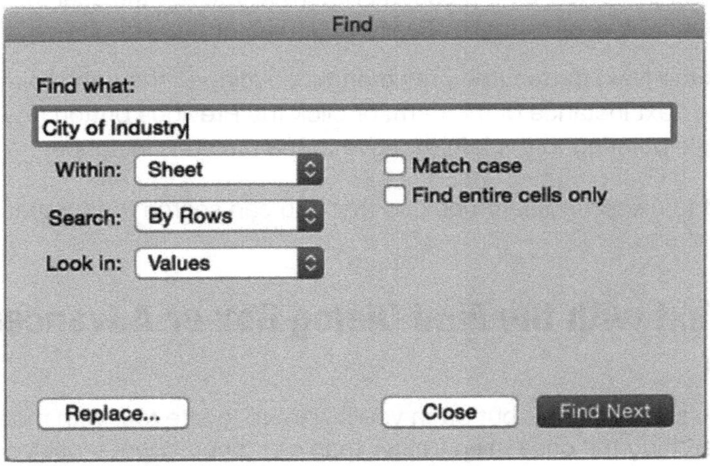

Figure 3-13. Excel's Find dialog box lets you choose whether to search the current worksheet or the whole workbook; whether to search by rows or columns; and whether to search in formulas, values, or comments

■ *PowerPoint*: Choose Edit ➤ Find ➤ Advanced Find from the menu bar, or click the Search pop-up menu at the right end of the toolbar and then click Advanced Find, to display the Advanced Find dialog box (see Figure 3-14).

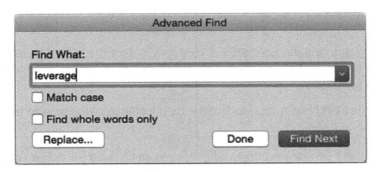

Figure 3-14. PowerPoint's Advanced Find dialog box includes options for matching the case on searches and finding only whole-word matches

■ *Outlook*: In a message window, choose Edit ➤ Find ➤ Find to display the Find dialog box (see Figure 3-15). When you need greater search power, choose Edit ➤ Find ➤ Advanced Find to display the Search tab of the Ribbon (see Figure 3-16), which enables you to specify exactly what you're searching for and where to look for it.

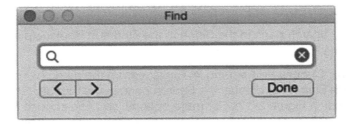

Figure 3-15. Outlook's Find dialog box contains no extra options. The right-arrow button finds the next instance of the search term, while the left-arrow button finds the previous instance

Figure 3-16. You can use the Search tab in Outlook to perform more focused searches. For example, you can search a particular mailbox, restricting the search to the From field and finding only unread messages marked Important

2.   In the Find What box, type or paste the text you want to find.

Tip   If you've performed a search earlier in this session of working with this app, you can open the pop-up menu on the Find What box and select the term again.

---

3.   Choose any options needed. For example, select the Match case check box to make the search find only items that use the same case as the text you've typed.

4.   Click the Find Next button to find the next instance of the search term.

Note   In Word, you can select the "Highlight all items found in" check box to make Word highlight all the instances of the search term in the main document (or the other area you choose in the pop-up menu). This is helpful when you need to get an overview of where the search term appears in the document. When this check box is selected, the Find and Replace dialog box contains a Find All button rather than a Find Next button.

---

5.   Click the Close button when you finish finding items.

Replacing Text with Replace

To replace text in Word, Excel, or PowerPoint, follow these steps:

1.   Open the Search pane in the Sidebar, the Find and Replace dialog box, or the Replace dialog box:

   ■   *Word*: Choose Edit ➤ Find ➤ Replace from the menu bar or press Cmd+Shift+H to display the Search pane in the Sidebar (shown on the left in Figure 3-17). For more options, you can choose Edit ➤ Find ➤ Advanced Find and Replace to display the Find and Replace dialog box and then click the Replace tab (shown on the right in Figure 3-17).

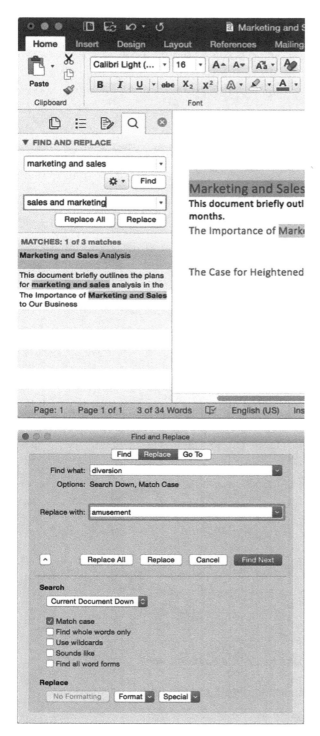

Figure 3-17. Word provides two tools for replacing text. The Search pane in the Sidebar (top) shows you all the matches for the search term and lets you quickly move among them. The Replace tab of the Find and Replace dialog box (bottom) provides more search options when you need them

- *Excel*: Choose Edit ➤ Replace from the menu bar, or click the Search pop-up menu at the right end of the toolbar and then click Replace, to display the Replace dialog box (see Figure 3-18).

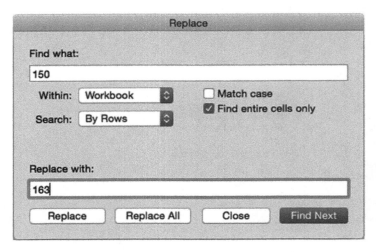

Figure 3-18. Excel's Replace dialog box includes options for matching case and limiting the replacement to the entire contents of cells rather than partial contents

- *PowerPoint*: Choose Edit ➤ Find ➤ Replace or press Cmd+Shift+H to display the Replace dialog box (see Figure 3-19).

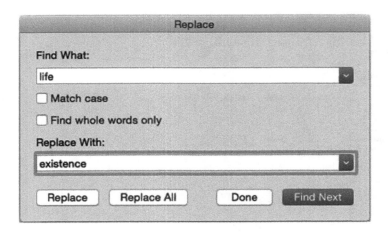

Figure 3-19. PowerPoint's Replace dialog box lets you match case or find only whole words

2.   In the Find What box, type or paste the text you want to find.

3.   In the Replace With box, type or paste the replacement text.

> **Tip**   In Word and PowerPoint, if you've performed a search earlier in this session of working with this app, you can open the pop-up menu on the Find What box and select the term again. If you've performed a replacement, you can open the pop-up menu on the Replace With box and select the term again.

4. If you need to use any other options, select them. For example, select the "Find whole words only" check box in Word or PowerPoint to find only whole-word matches rather than partial-word matches (for instance, you may need to replace *hand* without replacing *beforehand* or *underhand*).

5. Click the button for the operation you want to perform:

   ■ *Find Next*: Click this button to find the next instance of the search term.

> **Note**   In Word's Search pane, click the Find button to find all the instances of the search term.

   ■ *Replace*: Click this button to replace the current instance of the search term with the replacement term and find the next instance of the search term.

   ■ *Replace All*: Click this button to replace every instance of the search term with the replacement term.

6. When you have finished searching, click the Close button to close the Find and Replace dialog box or the Replace dialog box, or click the Close button (the × button) to close the Search pane in Word. The Close button replaces the Cancel button when you start replacing items.

Creating Tables

When you need to lay out data in a regular grid, create a table. A table consists of cells, which are rectangular areas formed by the intersection of rows and columns. Each table can contain one or more rows and one or more columns.

> **Note**   You can use tables in Word and PowerPoint. Excel's worksheets already have a grid structure, so you don't need to create tables for layout in Excel; instead, Excel uses the term *table* to mean a database laid out on a worksheet (see Chapter 16 for details).

Inserting a Table

The most straightforward way of adding a table to a Word document or a PowerPoint slide is to insert it. Inserting a table gives you a regular table with the number of rows and columns you choose. You can insert a table either using the Table panel on the Ribbon or using the Insert Table dialog box.

Inserting a Table Using the Table Panel on the Ribbon

To insert a table using the Table panel on the Ribbon, follow these steps:

1. Position the insertion point where you want the table to appear.

2. Choose Insert ➤ Tables ➤ Table, opening the Table panel
    (see Figure 3-20).

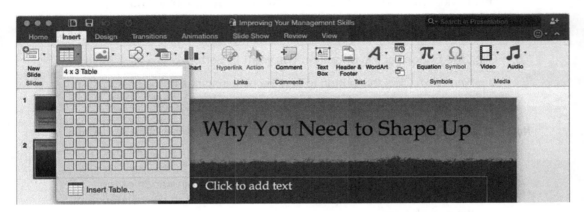

Figure 3-20. To insert a table, choose Insert ➤ Tables ➤ Table, and then click the square for the table configuration you want

3. Click the square for the table configuration you want—for example, a
    2×3 table is two columns wide and three rows deep.

Inserting a Table Using the Insert Table Dialog Box

When you need more control over a table's behavior in Word, use the Insert Table dialog box to insert the table. You can also use the Insert Table dialog box in PowerPoint, but it has no discernible advantage over using the Table panel on the Ribbon.

To insert a table using the Insert Table dialog box, follow these steps:

1. Place the insertion point where you want the table to appear.

2. Give the appropriate command:

    ▪ *Word*: From the Ribbon, choose Insert ➤ Tables ➤ Table, and then
      click the Insert Table command near the bottom of the Table panel to
      display the Insert Table dialog box (shown on the left in Figure 3-21).
      You can also choose Table ➤ Insert ➤ Table from the menu bar.

    ▪ *PowerPoint*: From the menu bar, choose Insert ➤ Table to display
      the Insert Table dialog box (shown on the right in Figure 3-21).

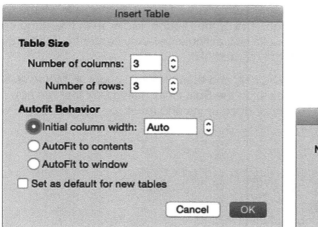
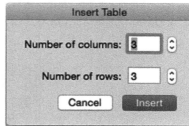

Figure 3-21. Word's Insert Table dialog box (left) lets you control AutoFit behavior and create default settings for new tables. PowerPoint's Insert Table dialog box (right) lets you set only the numbers of columns and rows

3. Use the Number of columns box and the Number of rows box to set the dimensions of the table.

4. In Word, select the appropriate option button in the AutoFit Behavior area:

    ■ *Initial column width*: Select this option button to have Word set the width of each column. In the pop-up menu, choose Auto to have Word automatically set the width, or set the precise width you want (for example, 1.25").

    ■ *AutoFit to contents*: Select this option button to make Word automatically adjust each column's width to fit its contents. This is often a good choice.

    ■ *AutoFit to window*: Select this option button to make Word automatically adjust each column's width to suit the document window. This option is useful for tables you expect people to view on the screen at different window widths.

5. Also in Word, select the "Set as default for new tables" check box if you want Word to store these settings for future use.

6. Click the OK button to close the Insert Table dialog box, and insert the table in the document or slide.

Merging and Splitting Cells in a Table

To change the layout of the table, you can merge cells together to form a larger cell or split a cell into several smaller cells.

To merge cells together, select the cells, and then choose Layout ➤ Merge ➤ Merge Cells (that's the Layout tab for tables, at the right end of the Ribbon, rather than the standard Layout tab). The app turns the selected cells into a single cell. Any contents of the previous cells appear as separate paragraphs in the merged cell.

To split a cell into multiple cells, click in the cell, and then choose Layout ➤ Merge ➤ Split Cells (again, that's the Layout tab for tables). In the Split Cells dialog box that the app displays (see Figure 3-22), enter the number of columns and rows you want to create within the cell, and then click the OK button.

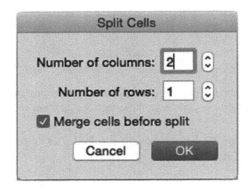

Figure 3-22. Use the Split Cells dialog box to split one existing cell into two or more new cells

Note   In Word, if you select multiple cells for splitting, select the "Merge cells before split" check box to make Word treat all the selected cells as one cell. For example, if you select two cells, select the "Merge cells before split" check box, and specify four columns, you get four columns total. By contrast, if you select two cells, clear the "Merge cells before split" check box, and specify four columns, you get four columns from each cell, giving eight columns altogether.

Adding Content to a Table

The most straightforward way to add content to a table is by clicking in the destination cell and then typing the text. Press the Tab key the insertion point to the next cell, or press Shift+Tab to move the insertion point to the previous cell.

You can also paste text into a table you've created. Simply click in the cell, and then paste the text (for example, click the Paste button on the Standard toolbar or press Cmd+V).

Tip   In Word, you can copy text that's laid out with a tab between each separate item and then paste it into multiple cells at once. Copy the text from the source, switch to the destination document in Word, select the appropriate number of cells in the table, and then give the Paste command.

Formatting a Table

To make a table look the way you want, you format it. You can apply formatting either quickly by using a table style or manually by applying only the formatting the table needs.

To apply a table style, click anywhere in the table, and then choose Table Design ➤ Table Styles ➤ Quick Styles, choosing the style you want either from the Quick Styles box or from the Quick Styles panel (see Figure 3-23). You can browse the table styles in the box by clicking the left arrow button and the right arrow button, but usually it's easier to use the panel. Move the pointer over the box so that the panel's button appears below it, as shown in the figure, and then click the button to open the panel.

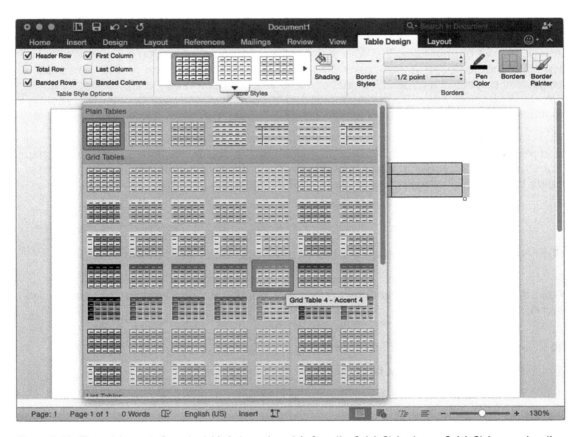

Figure 3-23. The quick way to format a table is to apply a style from the Quick Styles box or Quick Styles panel on the Table Design tab of the Ribbon

After applying a table style, you can customize it by selecting or clearing the check boxes in the Table Style Options group on the Table Design tab of the Ribbon. For example, select the Header Row check box to apply different formatting to the table's first row so that it looks like a header, or select the First Column check box to apply different formatting to the first column if it contains headings.

If you prefer not to use a table style, you can format a table manually. These are the main techniques you need:

- *Borders*: Select the table or the cells you want to affect, choose Table Design ➤Borders ➤Borders, and then click the border style you want.

- *Shading*: Select the table or the cells you want to affect, choose Table Design ➤Table Styles ➤ Shading, and then click the shading color.

- *Font formatting*: Select the cell or cells you want to format, and then use the controls in the Font group of the Home tab of the Ribbon, as for other text.

Creating Hyperlinks

As you know from browsing the Web, a *hyperlink* is text or an object on a web page that's linked to another location, such as another web page or another place on the same web page. You can insert a hyperlink in just about any Office document—a Word document, an Excel workbook, a PowerPoint presentation, or an e-mail message or task you're creating in Outlook. This section shows you how to create a hyperlink in Word, Excel, or PowerPoint.

You can create both text hyperlinks and object hyperlinks. A text hyperlink appears as underlined text. An object hyperlink appears as just the object, such as a picture or a shape. For either type of hyperlink, you can choose whether to display a ScreenTip when the user holds the pointer over the hyperlink, as in the text hyperlink shown in Figure 3-24.

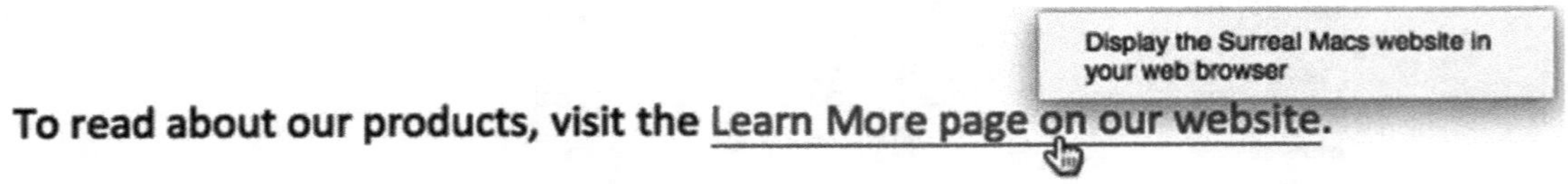

> Display the Surreal Macs website in your web browser

To read about our products, visit the Learn More page on our website.

Figure 3-24. When you create a hyperlink, you can include a ScreenTip that appears when the user holds the pointer over the hyperlink

To insert a hyperlink, follow these steps:

1. Choose the type of hyperlink you want to insert:

    - *New text hyperlink*: Position the insertion point where you want the hyperlink to appear.

    - *Hyperlink that displays existing text*: If the document already contains text that you want to use as the display text for the hyperlink, select that text.

    - *Object hyperlink*: Insert the object in the document, and then select it. For example, you can insert a graphic, which will be explained in Chapter 4.

2. Choose Insert ➤ Links ➤ Hyperlink from the Ribbon or Insert ➤ Hyperlink from the menu bar or press Cmd+K to display the Insert Hyperlink dialog box (see Figure 3-25).

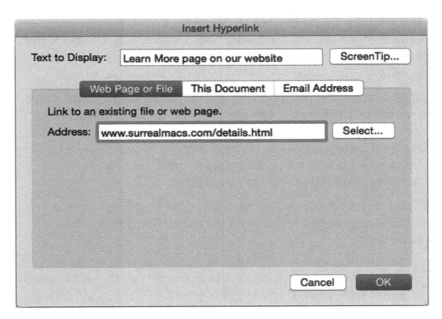

Figure 3-25. *Use the Insert Hyperlink dialog box to quickly create a link to a file, a web page, an e-mail address, or a document*

3. In the Text to Display box, enter the text that you want the document to display for the hyperlink:

   ■ If you selected text in the document in step 1, that text appears here.

   ■ If you selected an object in step 1, the Text to display box shows <<Selection in Document>> and is not available for change.

4. To add to the hyperlink a ScreenTip that appears when the user holds the pointer over it, click the ScreenTip button. In the Set Hyperlink ScreenTip dialog box (see Figure 3-26) that opens, type the ScreenTip text, and then click the OK button.

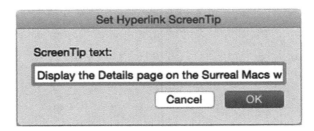

Figure 3-26. *You can add a ScreenTip to a hyperlink to provide a more detailed explanation of where the link goes or why the user may want to click it*

5. On the tab bar below the Text to Display box, click the tab button for the type of link you want to create: Web Page or File, This Document, or Email Address. The appropriate tab of the Insert Hyperlink box appears.

6. If you selected the Web Page or File tab, click the Address box and enter the URL (the web address) or network address to which you want to link. You can type in the address (which is tricky unless it's short and sweet), paste it in (always easy), or click the Select button and use the Choose a File dialog box to enter the address of a file on your Mac's file system or an attached drive.

7. If you selected the This Document tab, go to the Select a place in this document box and choose the appropriate place in the document:

    ■ *Top of the document*: To make the hyperlink point to the top of the document, click the Top of the Document item. This is the default location for a hyperlink to the document.

    ■ *Headings*: Click the disclosure triangle to the left of the Headings item to display the next level of headings. You can then click another disclosure triangle to expand further headings as needed. When you can see the heading to which you want to point the hyperlink, click it. Figure 3-27 shows an example of selecting a heading for a hyperlink.

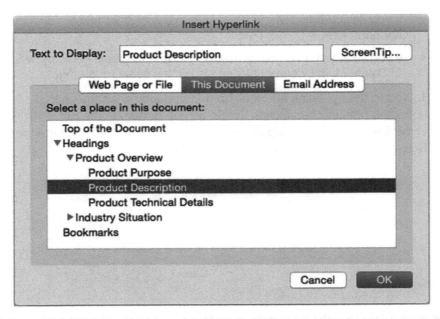

Figure 3-27. To create a hyperlink to the open document, click the This Document tab, and then select the destination in the "Select a place in this document" box

- *Bookmarks*: Click the disclosure triangle to the left of the Bookmarks item to display the list of bookmarks in the document, and then click the bookmark at which you want to point the hyperlink.

8. If you selected the Email Address tab, type or paste the address in the Email address box, and then type the default subject for the message in the Subject box (see Figure 3-28).

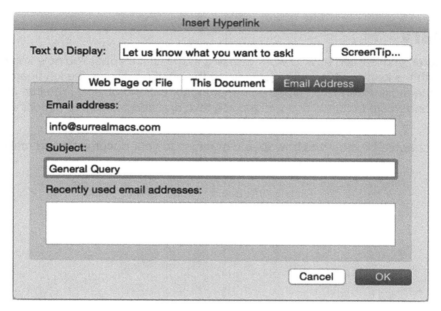

Figure 3-28. To create a hyperlink that automatically starts an e-mail message, enter the address and subject line on the E-mail Address tab of the Insert Hyperlink dialog box

9. In the Text to Display box, enter the text that you want the document to display for the hyperlink:

- If you selected text in the document in step 1, that text appears here.

- If you selected an object in step 1, the Text to Display box shows <<Selection in Document>> and is not available for change.

10. When you finish specifying the details of the hyperlink, click the OK button to insert it in the document.

You can now test your hyperlink by clicking it.

> **Note**   To edit a hyperlink, Ctrl-click or right-click the text or object, click or highlight Hyperlink on the context menu, and then click Edit Hyperlink. The Office app opens the Edit Hyperlink dialog box, which is the Insert Hyperlink dialog box with a different name. To remove a hyperlink, Ctrl-click or right-click the text or object, click or highlight Hyperlink on the context menu, and then click Remove Hyperlink.

Summary

In this chapter, you learned how to work with text in the Office apps. You now know how to navigate with the keyboard; select objects using the pointing device, the keyboard, or both; and apply the most widely used types of formatting to text and objects. You can also use the Cut, Copy, and Paste features; find and replace text; and add tables and hyperlinks to your documents.

In the next chapter, I'll show you how to add graphics to your documents and make them look good.

Chapter 4

Using Pictures and Shapes in Your Documents

To give your documents visual interest, you can add various types of graphical content to them—graphics themselves (I'll use this term to cover all kinds of pictures and images), shapes (anything from a simple arrow or circle to a complex shape), charts, and even movies.

This chapter shows you how to insert, crop, and resize pictures; how to insert shapes and format them; and how to position graphical objects where you want them. You'll learn how to wrap text around a graphical object in Word, how to make a picture look the way you want it, and how to illustrate your documents by adding SmartArt diagrams.

I'll start by going over how the Office apps handle graphical objects because understanding this is essential to mastering how to place objects.

> **Note**   To follow the Ribbon commands easily, please display the group titles on the Ribbon. To do so, click the app's menu (such as the Excel menu) and then click Preferences. In the Preferences window, click View to display the View pane. In the "In Ribbon, Show" area, select the Group Titles check box, and then close the Preferences window by clicking the Close button (the red button at the left end of the window's title bar).
>
> See Chapter 14 for instructions on creating charts in Excel.

Understanding How to Position Graphical Objects

Even though an Office document appears to be flat, it actually consists of multiple separate layers. Until you add objects to a layer, the layer is transparent, so you see through the layer to whatever is underneath. One layer contains the text; the other layers contain graphical objects.

Having these multiple layers enables you to position one graphical object in front of another graphical object—for example, to superimpose one graphical object on another. Word also enables you to position graphical objects either in front of the text layer or behind the text layer.

Word, Excel, and PowerPoint let you position graphical objects in the graphics layers, where you can move them freely. Word also lets you position graphical objects as inline characters in the text layer. When you do this, Word places the graphical object just like a character in the document's text. If you then insert text before the graphical object, it moves further down the document.

Outlook gives you far less control over graphical objects. You can add pictures to a message or attach an audio or video file, but that's about all. You'll look at how to do this in Chapter 22.

Choosing Where to Insert a Graphical Object

Before inserting a graphical object, you need to place the insertion point or selection where you want to insert the object. Place the insertion point or selection like this:

- *Word*: Place the insertion point where you want to insert the object.

- *Excel*: Click the cell where you want to place the upper-left corner of the object.

- *PowerPoint*: Click the slide on which you want to insert the object, or select the placeholder in which you want to place the object. If the placeholder is a standard placeholder, you can click either of the Picture from File icons or the Insert Movie from File icon (see Figure 4-1) to start inserting a graphical object.

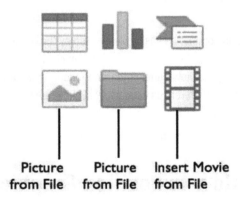

Picture   Picture   Insert Movie
from File   from File   from File

Figure 4-1. Click either Picture from File icon in a standard placeholder on a PowerPoint slide to start inserting an image in that placeholder

Inserting Pictures into Documents

You can easily insert pictures, such as your own photos, in your Office documents. You can either insert pictures you've added to the Photos app or insert pictures that are in your Mac's file system but not in the Photos app.

GETTING CLIP ART

Earlier versions of Office for Mac, including Office 2011, included a selection of clip art images that you could use freely in your documents, plus tools—such as the Clip Art Browser and Clip Art Gallery—for browsing and managing the images. You could also download extra clip art images from Microsoft's web site; these would show up in the Clip Art Browser and Clip Art Gallery too.

Microsoft has removed the clip art selection and clip art tools from Office 2016. Instead, you need to find images yourself, either among your own photos or by searching online.

If you need images that you can use freely in your documents, search for images that have the right sort of license (the license specifies the types of usage permitted by the copyright holder, if there is one; if the image is in the public domain, you can use it freely). Here is how to find such images on Microsoft's Bing search engine:

1. Click the Safari icon on the Dock or on the Launchpad screen to launch Safari (if it's not running) or to switch to it (if it is running).

2. Click the address box, type bing.com, and press Return. The Bing home page appears.

3. Click the Images tab at the top to specify that you want to search for images.

4. Click in the Search box and start typing your search term. A list of suggested searches appears.

5. Click the best match. Bing displays thumbnails of images matching the search.

6. Click the License pop-up menu above the thumbnails and then click the type of license needed: Public domain; Free to share and use; Free to share and use commercially; Free to modify, share, and use; or Free to modify, share, and use commercially. Bing narrows down the selection of thumbnails to those with the type of license you chose.

7. When you find a file you want to download, Cmd-click or right-click it, and then click Save Image As to display the Save Image As sheet. Specify the folder and filename, and then click the Save button.

Once you have saved an image to your Mac, you can insert it in a document by using the method explained in the "Inserting Pictures from Your Mac's File System" section later in this chapter.

Inserting Pictures from the Photos App

To insert a picture from the Photos app, follow these steps:

1. Give the appropriate command to open the Photo Browser (see Figure 4-2):

   ■ *Word*: Choose Insert ➤ Illustrations ➤ Pictures ➤ Photo Browser from the Ribbon or Insert ➤ Pictures ➤ Photo Browser from the menu bar.

   ■ *Excel*: Choose Insert ➤ Illustrations ➤ Pictures ➤ Photo Browser from the Ribbon or Insert ➤ Picture ➤ Photo Browser from the menu bar.

   ■ *PowerPoint*: Choose Insert ➤ Picture ➤ Pictures ➤ Photo Browser from the Ribbon or Insert ➤ Picture ➤ Photo Browser from the menu bar.

   ■ *Outlook*: Choose Message ➤ Pictures ➤ Photo Browser from the Ribbon or View ➤ Media Browser ➤ Photo Browser from the menu bar.

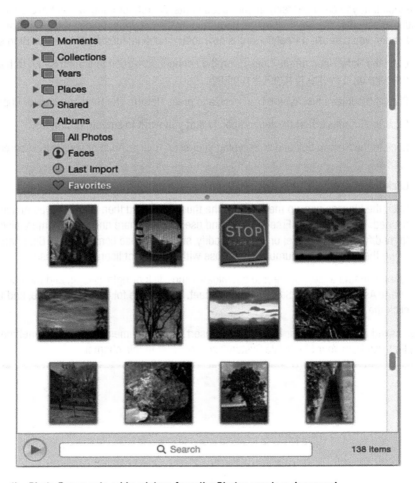

Figure 4-2. Use the Photo Browser to add a picture from the Photos app to a document

2. Use the upper pane to navigate to the source of the pictures, such as the Albums list. Click a category's name to display the pictures the category contains, or click the disclosure triangle to the left of the category's name to expand the category, showing its contents. For example, in the figure, the Albums category is expanded, and the Favorites album is selected.

Tip   You can use the Search feature to search for photos. Click in the Search box to activate it, then click the Search pop-up menu and click what you want to search: All, Faces, Places, Keyword, or Rating. Once you've done that, specify your search term or rating in the Search box, and the Photo Browser displays matching results.

Note   Searching by keyword works best if you have assigned keywords to photos in the Photos app. To assign keywords in Photos, choose Window ➤ Keyword Manager from the menu bar to display the Keywords window. Select the picture to which you want to assign keywords, and then click the button in the Keywords window for each keyword you want to assign. You can click the Edit Keywords button in the Keywords window to edit the list of keywords, adding ones you need and changing any you don't need.

---

3. Click the photo you want, and then drag it to the document window, dropping it where you want it to appear.

4. Leave the Photo Browser window open if you want to use it further. Otherwise, click the Close button (the red button in its upper-left corner) to close it.

Inserting Pictures from Your Mac's File System

To insert a picture that's not in the Photos app but is stored in your Mac's file system or on a network drive, follow these steps:

1. Position the inserstion point or selection where you want the picture to appear.

2. Give the appropriate command to open the Choose a Picture dialog box (see Figure 4-3).

   ■ *Word*: Choose Insert ➤ Illustrations ➤ Pictures ➤ Picture from File from the Ribbon or Insert ➤ Pictures ➤ Picture from File from the menu bar.

   ■ *Excel*: Choose Insert ➤ Illustrations ➤ Pictures ➤ Picture from File from the Ribbon or Insert ➤ Picture ➤ Picture from File from the menu bar.

- *PowerPoint*: Choose Insert ➤ Picture ➤ Pictures ➤ Picture from File from the Ribbon or Insert ➤ Picture ➤ Picture from File from the menu bar.

- *Outlook*: Choose Message ➤ Pictures ➤ Picture from File from the Ribbon.

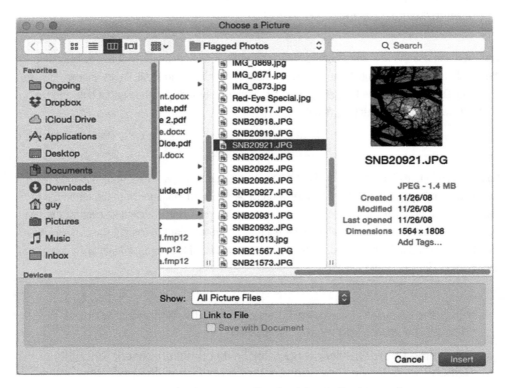

Figure 4-3. From the Choose a Picture dialog box, you can link the picture to the document

3. Navigate to the folder that contains the file, and then click the file.

4. If you want to link the picture file to the document rather than insert it, select the Link to File check box. When you do this, you can select the Save with Document check box to store the latest version of the picture file in the document. See the sidebar "Linking a Picture to a Document" for advice about linking.

5. Click the Insert button. The app closes the Choose a Picture dialog box and inserts the picture in the document.

Tip   You can also insert a picture file by dragging it from a Finder window to an Office document window.

```
LINKING A PICTURE TO A DOCUMENT
```

When you add a picture to a document from your Mac's file system, you can either insert it or link it. Inserting the picture adds a copy of the picture to the document. The app saves the picture in the document, so even if you move the document, the picture stays in it.

If you need to keep the document's file size down or if you need to be able to update the picture easily, you can link the picture instead. Linking makes the app add to the document a link to the picture file. When you open the document, the app loads the current version of the picture from the file. But if you move the document to a different computer, the link will no longer work because the app will be unable to find the picture file.

To solve the problem of broken links, you can link a picture but also save the latest version of it. To do this, select the Link to File check box and the Save with Document check box in the Choose a Picture dialog box. When you open the document, the app checks to see whether the linked version is available. If so, the app loads the linked picture; if not, it displays the version saved in the document.

Adding and Formatting a Shape

If a document needs a drawing, you can create it from scratch by using Office's shapes. Office provides a wide variety of shapes, from arrows and basic shapes to stars, banners, and callouts.

To insert a shape, follow these steps:

1. Display the area of the document where you want to add the shape. When adding a shape, you don't need to position the insertion point or make a selection.

2. Choose Insert ➤ Illustrations ➤ Shapes to display the Shapes panel (see Figure 4-4).

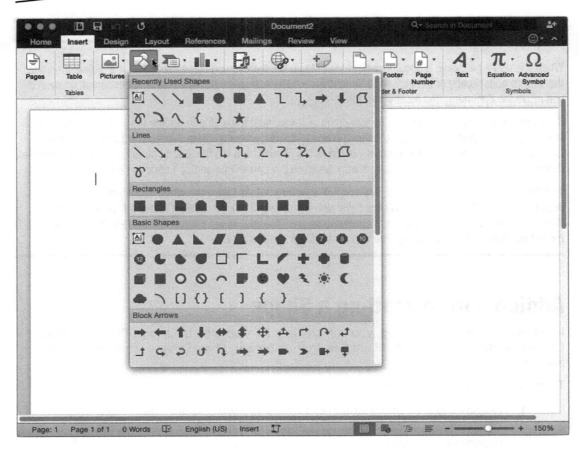

Figure 4-4. Choose the type of shape from the Shapes pane. Hold the pointer over a shape to see a ScreenTip showing its description

3. Scroll down the Shapes pane as needed to locate the category of shapes you want to see: Recently used shapes, Lines, Rectangles, Basic shapes, Block arrows, Equation shapes, Flowchart, Stars and banners, or Callouts.

4. Click the shape you want. The app changes the pointer to a crosshair.

5. With this crosshair, click where you want to place one corner of the shape, and then drag to the opposite corner (see Figure 4-5). It doesn't matter which corner you place first, because you can drag in any direction, but placing the upper-left corner first is usually easiest.

Width: 3.75"
Height: 3.75"

Figure 4-5. Click and drag with the crosshair to place and size the shape you're inserting

When you release the button, the shape appears with selection handles around it so you can work with it as described in the following sections. When the shape is selected, the app adds the Shape Format tab to the Ribbon, which provides controls for formatting the shape.

Applying a Style to a Shape

After inserting a shape, you can apply a style to it from the Shape Styles box or panel in the Shape Styles group on the Shape Format tab of the Ribbon. If the style you want appears in the Shape Styles box, click it; otherwise, move the pointer over the Shape Styles box so that the panel button appears, and then click the button to display the Shape Styles panel (see Figure 4-6). You can then click the style you want.

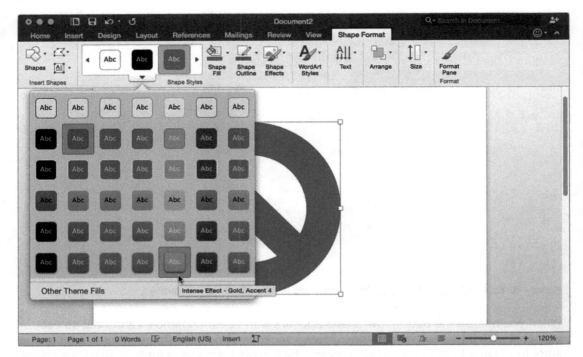

Figure 4-6. *To change a shape's style, open the Shape Styles panel on the Format tab of the Ribbon, and then click the style you want*

To refine the shape, open the Shape Fill panel, the Shape Outline panel, or the Shape Effects panel in the Shape Styles group, and then click the option you want. For example, choose Shape Format ➤ Shape Styles ➤ Shape Effects ➤ 3-D Rotation, and then click one of the 3-D rotation effects (see Figure 4-7).

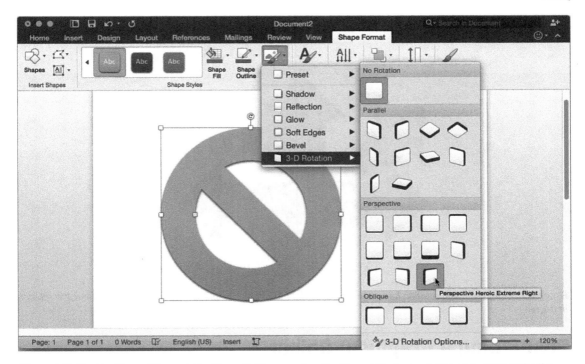

Figure 4-7. Use the Shape Fill panel, the Shape Outline panel, or the Shape Effects panel (shown here) to make the shape look the way you want it to look

Rotating a Graphical Object

After inserting a graphical object, you can rotate it as needed. Click to select the object, and then drag the round handle that shows a clockwise arrow to the left to rotate counterclockwise (see Figure 4-8) or to the right to rotate clockwise.

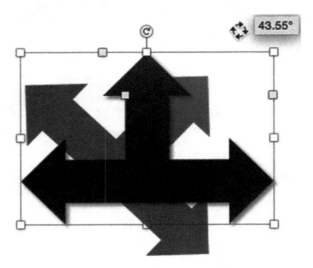

Figure 4-8. Drag the round rotation handle to the left or right to rotate a graphical object. The tooltip shows the rotation in degrees

Positioning a Graphical Object

If you don't get a graphical object in precisely the right position when you insert it, you can easily move it afterward.

The quick way to reposition a graphical object is to click it and then drag it to where you want it. This works well most of the time, but for more precision you can also click the object to select it and then press an arrow key (such as the Left arrow key or the Up arrow key) to nudge it a small distance in the arrow's direction.

When you need to control exactly where the object appears, Cmd-click or right-click the object, and then click the Format command on the context menu (for example, the Format Shape command for a shape) to display the Format pane for the object. The name of this pane shows the type of object—for example, the Format Shape pane in PowerPoint (shown on the left in Figure 4-9) for a shape or the Format Picture pane in Excel (shown on the right in Figure 4-9) for a picture.

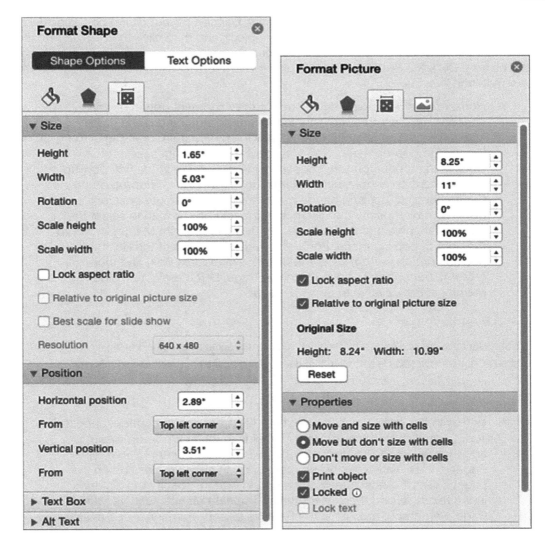

Figure 4-9. Use the controls in the Size category of the Format pane for an object to resize and position the object precisely. The selection of controls and their layout depends on the object and its properties. The Format Shape pane shown on the left here is from PowerPoint. The Format Picture pane shown on the right is from Excel

You may need to do some exploring in the Format pane to find the Position controls. For example, in PowerPoint, you click the Shape Options tab button at the top of the Format Shape pane, then click the Size & Properties tab button (the blue square with white arrows pointing north, south, east, and west). You then expand the Position head to find the Horizontal position box and the Vertical position box. By contrast, in Excel, you click the Size & Properties tab button (again, the blue square with white arrows pointing to the four points of the compass), expand the Properties head, and then select the "Move and size with cells" option button, the "Move but don't size with cells" option button, or the "Don't move or size with cells" option button.

In Word, you can also use the Position tab of the Advanced Layout dialog box to position an object precisely. Cmd-click or right-click the object, and then click the Size and Position item or the More Layout Options item on the context menu (the command varies depending on the object). Click the Position tab to display its contents (see Figure 4-10). You can then choose settings like this:

- *Horizontal*: In this area, you can select the Alignment option button; choose Left, Centered, or Right in the first pop-up menu; and then select the appropriate object (such as Column, Margin, or Page) in the Relative to pop-up menu. For a layout with facing pages, select the Book layout option button, choose Inside or Outside in the first pop-up menu, and then choose either Margin or Page in the Of pop-up menu. For an absolute position on the page, select the Absolute position option button, specify the distance in the text box, and then select the appropriate object (such as Page, Left Margin, or Right Margin) in the To the right of pop-up menu. For a relative position, select the Relative position option button, enter the distance in the text box, and then select the appropriate object (such as Page, Left Margin, or Inside Margin) in the Relative to pop-up menu.

> **Note**   An *absolute position* is a position that remains the same as the other contents of the page change. A *relative position* is a position that does change as the page's other contents change.

- *Vertical*: In this area, you can select the Alignment option button; choose Top, Centered, Bottom, Inside, or Outside in the first pop-up menu; and then select the appropriate object (such as Column, Margin, or Page) in the Relative to pop-up menu. For an absolute position on the page, select the Absolute position option button, specify the distance in the text box, and then select the appropriate object (such as Margin, Page, Paragraph, or Line) in the Relative to pop-up menu. For a relative position, select the Relative position option button, enter the distance in the text box, and then select the appropriate object (such as Page, Top Margin, or Bottom Margin) in the Relative to pop-up menu.

- *Options*: In this area, select the Allow overlap check box if you want to allow this object to overlap other objects (or other objects to overlap this object). For an object positioned in a table, select the Layout in a table cell check box if you want Word to shoehorn the object into the nearest cell; if not, clear this check box. Select the Lock anchor check box if you want to lock this object's anchor to the same position on the page even when you move the object. Select the "Move object with text" check box if you want Word to move the object down the document as you enter more text before the object or back up the document as you delete text before it. Select the Placeholder check box if you want to display a placeholder box instead of the object; as of this writing, this setting does not work consistently.

Tip   Selecting the Lock anchor check box for an object locks only the anchor, not the object itself. The advantage to locking the anchor is that you'll be able to find the anchor in the same position on the page even after you move the object to another position. To see object anchors, choose Home ➤ Paragraph ➤ Show all nonprinting characters from the Ribbon or press Cmd+8.

When you finish making your choices in the Advanced Layout dialog box, click the OK button to apply them to the object.

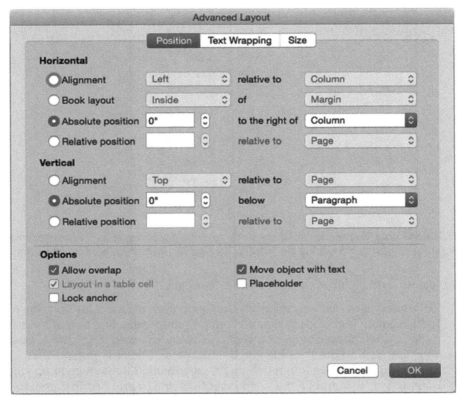

Figure 4-10. In Word, you can use the controls on the Position tab of the Advanced Layout dialog box to specify exactly where you want to position an object

Choosing Text Wrapping in Word

In Word, you can place a graphical object either inline with the text or in the graphics layers. It can be hard to tell just by looking at a graphical object how it's positioned, but if you find you can't move a graphical object freely, it's most likely because it's inline.

The quick way to set text wrapping for an object is to use the Wrap Text panel in the Arrange group on the Format tab of the Ribbon. The Format tab's name varies depending on the object, so you need to choose Picture Format ➤ Arrange ➤ Wrap Text for a picture (or a movie, or an audio file), choose Shape Format ➤ Arrange ➤ Wrap Text for a shape, and so on. Figure 4-11 shows the Wrap Text panel open.

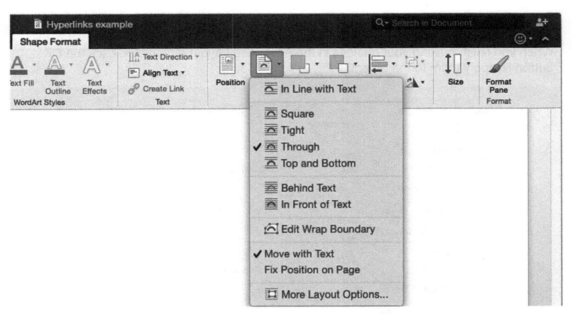

Figure 4-11. Use the Wrap Text panel to quickly specify the type of text wrapping to use for the selected object in Word. Click the More Layout Options item at the bottom of the Wrap Text menu if you need more flexibility

You can make three main choices on the Wrap Text panel:

- *Document layer and wrapping*: All the items from In Line with Text down to In Front of Text work as a single option group: selecting one of them deselects whichever other one was previously selected. Click the In Line with Text item to put the object in the text layer. Click the Behind Text item to put the object into a document layer behind the text layer so you can put text in front of it if you choose. Click the In Front of Text item to put the object into a document layer in front of the text layer so you can use the object to obscure text. Otherwise, choose the type of wrapping you want: Square, Tight, Through, or Top and Bottom. Figure 4-12 shows an example of the Square wrapping style.

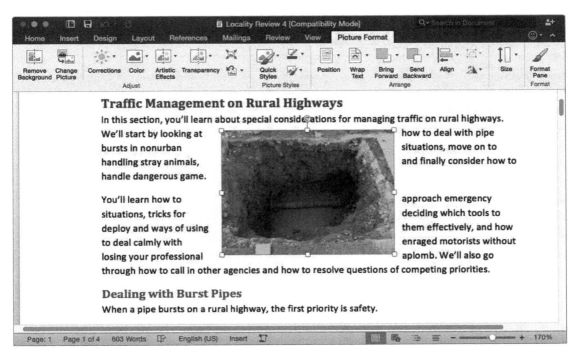

Figure 4-12. Text wrapped around a picture in Word using the Square wrapping style

- *Fix in place or allow movement*: Click the Move with Text item if you want the object to move with the document's text. Click the Fix Position on Page item if you want to keep the object exactly where you've positioned it. These menu items are another option group, so selecting one of them deselects the other.

- *Edit the wrap boundary*: Click the Edit Wrap Boundary item to display black handles that you can drag to create a custom wrapping boundary (see Figure 4-13). You can place another handle by clicking and dragging the appropriate point on the blue borders.

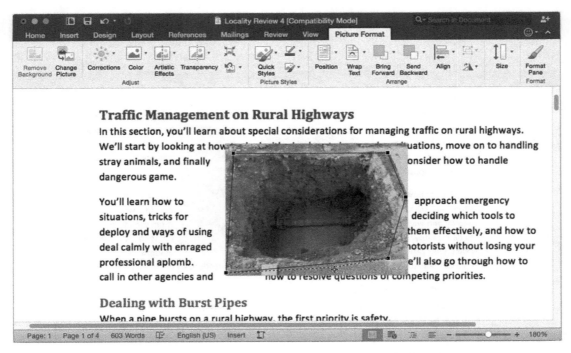

Figure 4-13. Drag the black handles or the blue borders to create a custom wrapping boundary

For greater control over the wrapping style and distance, click the More Layout Options item on the Wrap Text panel to display the Text Wrapping pane in the Advanced Layout dialog box (see Figure 4-14).

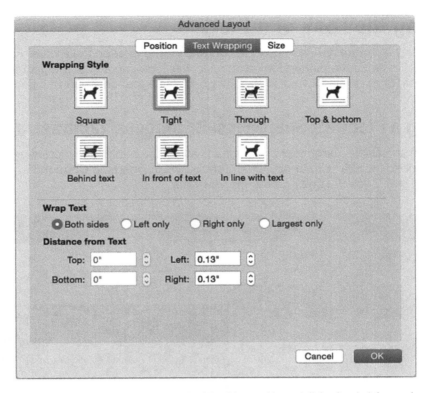

Figure 4-14. Use the options on the Text Wrapping tab of the Advanced Layout dialog box to take precise control over the way Word wraps text around an object

You can then work like this:

- In the Wrapping Style area, click the wrapping style you want: Square, Tight, Through, Top and Bottom, Behind text, In front of text, or In line with text.

- For the Square style, Tight style, or Through style, select the appropriate option button in the Wrap text area: Both sides, Left only, Right only, or Largest only.

- For the Square style, Tight style, Through style, or Top and Bottom style, use the Top box, Bottom box, Left box, and Right box in the Distance from text area to specify how much space to leave between the object and the text.

- Click the OK button to close the Advanced Layout dialog box. Word applies the wrapping to the object, and you can see how well it works.

> **Note**   You can also Cmd-click or right-click a picture or shape, click the Wrap Text submenu, and then click the appropriate command: In Line with Text, Square, Tight, Through, Top and Bottom, None, or Edit Wrap Boundary.

Changing the Look of a Picture

After you insert a picture, you can use the controls that appear on the Picture Format tab of the Ribbon to make the picture look a specific way. You can adjust the picture's colors, apply a picture style to the picture, or crop the picture so that only part of it shows.

Adjusting a Picture's Sharpness, Brightness, Contrast, and Colors

To adjust the sharpness, brightness, or contrast in a picture, click the picture to select it, and then choose Picture Format Adjust ➤ Corrections to open the Corrections panel (see Figure 4-15). Click the color correction you want.

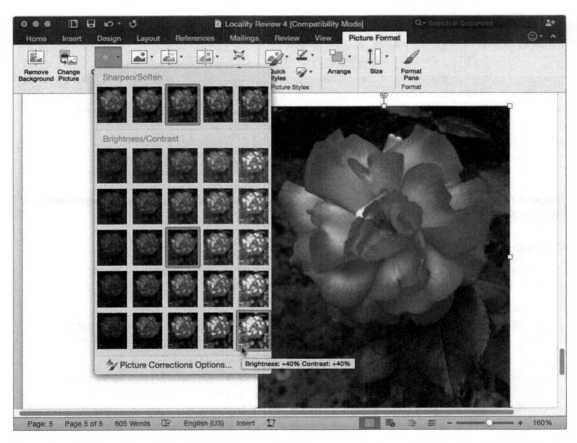

Figure 4-15. To fix problems with a picture's sharpness, brightness, or contrast, open the Corrections panel and choose the look you want

To change the colors in a picture, click it, choose Picture Format ➤ Adjust ➤ Color, and then click the effect you want. The Color drop-down panel has different sections for Color Saturation, Color Tone, and Recolor (for example, Grayscale or Sepia).

To apply an artistic effect such as paint strokes or a light screen to a picture, click the picture, choose Picture Format ➤ Adjust ➤ Artistic Effects, and then click the effect you want.

To reset a picture to its original look, choose Picture Format ➤ Adjust ➤ Reset Picture ➤ Reset Picture. To reset a picture to its original look and size, choose Picture Format ➤ Adjust ➤ Reset Picture ➤ Reset Picture & Size.

Applying a Picture Style

To apply a picture style to a picture, click the picture, click the Picture Format tab of the Ribbon to display it, and then click the picture style you want. If the picture style appears in the Quick Styles box in the Picture Styles group, click it there; otherwise, move the pointer over the Quick Styles box so that the panel button appears, click the panel button, and then click the picture style on the panel (see Figure 4-16).

Note   The Quick Styles box appears only when the app window is relatively wide. When the window is narrower, click the Quick Styles button to display the Quick Styles panel, and then click the style you want.

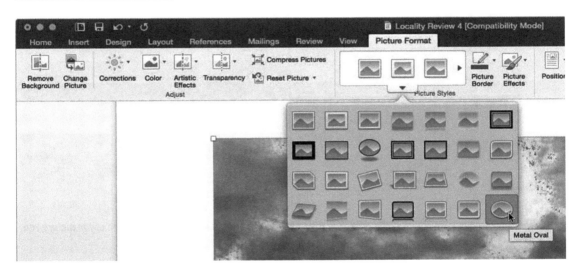

Figure 4-16. Choose the picture style from the Quick Styles box or panel in the Picture Styles group of the Picture Format tab on the Ribbon

Cropping a Picture

If you need the document to show only part of a picture rather than the whole picture, you can crop off the parts you don't want. The Office apps let you crop a picture in several ways, but this way is usually the easiest:

1. Click the picture to select it. The app adds the Picture Format tab to the Ribbon.

2. Click the Picture Format tab if the app has not displayed it.

3. Choose Picture Format ➤ Size ➤ Crop, clicking the main part of the Crop button rather than the drop-down button. The app displays crop handles on the picture (see Figure 4-17).

Figure 4-17. The quick way of cropping is to drag the crop handles until they encompass the part of the picture you want to keep

4. Drag the crop handles to make the cropping area contain the part of the picture you want to show:

    ■ Shift-drag to crop the image proportionally.

    ■ Option-drag to crop the image evenly around its center point.

    ■ Option-Shift-drag to crop the image proportionally around its center point.

    ■ Cmd-drag to crop the image in increments of Word's underlying drawing grid or Excel's worksheet cells.

Tip   If you make the crop area exactly the size you need, you can click and drag within the crop area to make a different part of the picture appear in it. You move the picture, not the crop area—much as if you were to reach through a window and move the landscape until the window displayed the part you wanted to see.

5. Click the Crop button again to turn off the Crop tool, or click elsewhere in the document to deselect the picture. The app applies the cropping to the picture.

> **Note**   You can also crop a picture to fit into a shape. To do this, choose Picture Format ➤ Size ➤ Crop, clicking the Crop pop-up arrow button rather than the top part of the button. On the pop-up menu that appears, choose Crop to Shape, and then click the shape you want.

Saving Space by Compressing Pictures in a Document

When you insert pictures in a document (rather than linking them, as discussed earlier in this chapter), the app saves a copy of each picture in the document. Saving the pictures in the document is good in that the pictures travel with the document when you move or share it, but it can greatly increase the file size of the document.

To keep the document's file size down, you can compress the pictures and delete the cropped areas of them. To do so, follow these steps:

1. Click a picture to make the app add the Format Picture tab to the Ribbon.

2. Choose Picture Format ➤ Adjust ➤ Compress to display the Compress Pictures dialog box (see Figure 4-18).

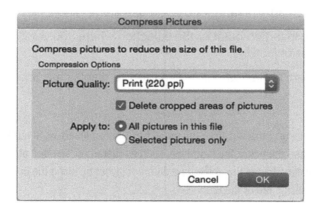

Figure 4-18. Use the Compress Pictures dialog box when you want to reduce the file size of one or more pictures or when you want to delete the cropped areas of pictures

3. In the Picture Quality pop-up menu, select the picture quality you want:

    ■ *Print (220 ppi)*: Compresses the pictures only a bit, maintaining a high-enough quality for most purposes, including printing the document.

■ *On-screen (150 ppi)*: Compresses the pictures a bit further but leaves them looking good enough for use on the screen.

■ *Email (96 ppi)*: Compresses the pictures to the extent that they start to look bad but are OK for viewing on the screen at small sizes.

■ *Use original quality*: Keeps the pictures at their current resolution. Use this setting for removing the cropped parts of pictures without changing the resolution.

4. Select the "Delete cropped areas of pictures" check box if you want to get rid of the areas you've cropped off. This is a good security measure provided you don't need to adjust the cropping of any pictures in the document to reveal more.

5. In the Apply to area, select the "Selected pictures only" option button if you want to affect only the picture (or pictures) you've selected. Normally, you want to select the "All pictures in this file" option button to make the app compress all the pictures in the document.

6. Click the OK button. The app closes the Compress Pictures dialog box and changes the quality or cropping as you specified.

Inserting SmartArt

When you need to create an illustration such as an organization chart, a flow chart, or a Venn diagram, use Office's SmartArt feature. Follow these steps:

1. Position the insertion point or the selection where you want to insert the SmartArt object.

2. Choose Insert ➤ Illustrations ➤ SmartArt to display the SmartArt panel.

Note   You can also insert SmartArt from the menu bar. Choose Insert ➤ SmartArt to display the SmartArt submenu, and then click the item type, such as Hierarchy. The app places a default object of that type, but you can change the object to a different layout by using the controls in the Layouts group on the SmartDesign tab of the Ribbon.

3. Click or highlight the item for the category of SmartArt graphic you want to create: List, Process, Cycle, Hierarchy, Relationship, Matrix, Pyramid, or Picture. A panel opens showing the available types. Figure 4-19 shows the Hierarchy panel, which includes various kinds of organization charts.

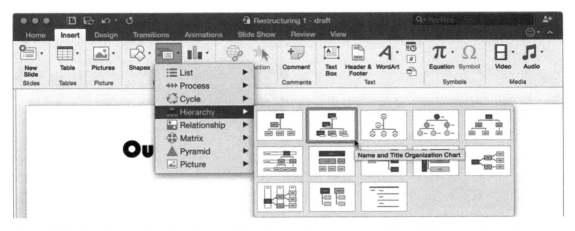

Figure 4-19. Open the panel for the category of SmartArt graphics you want and then click the type of graphic

Tip   In PowerPoint, if you're inserting the SmartArt on a slide that has a standard placeholder, you can click the Insert SmartArt Graphic icon in the placeholder to display the SmartArt pop-up menu, click the appropriate category, and then click the type of SmartArt you want to insert.

4. Click the type of graphic you want. The app inserts in the document, displays the Text pane (see Figure 4-20), and adds the SmartArt Design tab and the Format tab to the Ribbon, with the SmartArt Design tab selected.

Figure 4-20. When you insert a SmartArt graphic, the app displays the SmartArt Text next to it

Note If the app doesn't display the SmartArt Text panes, choose SmartArt Design ➤ Create Graphic ➤ Text Pane from the Ribbon to display the SmartArt Text pane. You can also click the SmartArt Text Pane button (the button at the upper-left corner of the SmartArt graphic, showing an arrow pointing to the left) to display the SmartArt Text pane. When the SmartArt Text pane is open, you can click the SmartArt Text pane (which now shows an arrow pointing to the right) to hide the SmartArt Text pane when you don't need it.

5. In the SmartArt Text pane, type the text for each item. As you do, the app adds the text to the SmartArt graphic (see Figure 4-21).

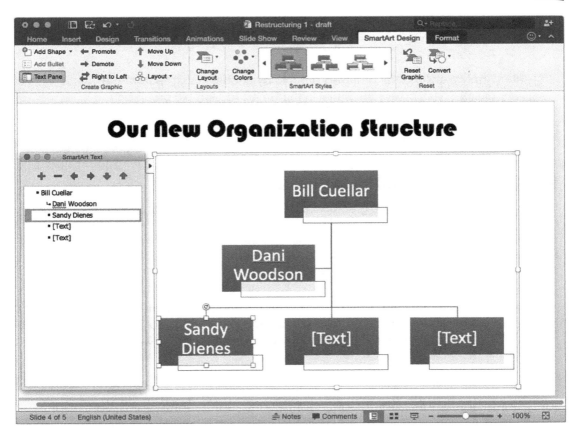

Figure 4-21. Add the text to the SmartArt graphic by typing in the Text pane

6. Add any other items the SmartArt graphic needs. For example, to add titles to the org chart shown, click in each title placeholder and then type the title.

7. Resize the SmartArt graphic to suit the document best. For example, in a PowerPoint presentation, you may want to make the graphic as big as will fit on the slide to enable the audience to read it easily.

8. Use the controls in the Create Graphic group on the SmartArt Design tab of the Ribbon to change the SmartArt graphic as needed. For example, click a box and choose SmartArt Design ➤ Create Graphic ➤ Move Up to move it up the graphic or choose SmartArt Design ➤ Create Graphic ➤ Move Down to move it down.

9. If you need to change the layout of the SmartArt graphic, choose another layout from the Layouts group on the SmartArt tab of the Ribbon.

10. Apply a style to the SmartArt graphic by choosing a style from the Quick Styles box or the panel in the SmartArt Graphic group on the SmartArt Design tab.

When you have finished creating the SmartArt graphic, save the document as usual.

Arranging Graphical Objects

When you have placed multiple graphical objects in the same area of a document, you may need to arrange the order in which they appear in the document's layers to control how they appear in relation to each other. For example, you may need to move a particular object to the front of the stack of document layers so that it appears on top of the other objects, or move another object back so that it appears behind one of its companion objects.

In Word, Excel, or PowerPoint, you can rearrange objects by using either the Arrange commands or the context menu for the object. The Arrange commands appear on the Format tab of the Ribbon when you select an object—for example, on the Shape Format tab when you select a shape or the Picture Format tab when you select a picture.

> **Tip**   In Word, the Arrange commands also appear in the Arrange group on the Layout tab of the Ribbon, so you can use either the Layout tab or the Format tab to arrange objects. Because the Arrange group on the Format tab is often collapsed to a button, it is usually easier to use the Layout group.

Excel and PowerPoint also let you drag the objects into a different order, which can be quicker and easier.

Arranging Graphical Objects Using the Arrange Commands

In Word, Excel, and PowerPoint, you can arrange objects by using the Arrange commands. Click an object to display the appropriate Format tab of the Ribbon, such as the Shape Format tab for the shapes shown in an Excel worksheet in Figure 4-22. Go to the Arrange group, and then click the appropriate button to change where the object appears in the document's layers.

- *Bring Forward*: Click this command to bring the object forward by one layer. Give the command again as many times as necessary to bring the object up the stack to where you need it.

- *Bring to Front*: Click the Bring Forward pop-up button and then click Bring to Front to bring the item to the very front of the stack.

- *Send Backward*: Click this command to send the object backward by one layer. As with the Bring Forward command, you may need to give this command multiple times to get the object to where you need it.

- *Send to Back*: Click the Send Backward pop-up button and then click Send to Back to send the item right to the back of the stack.

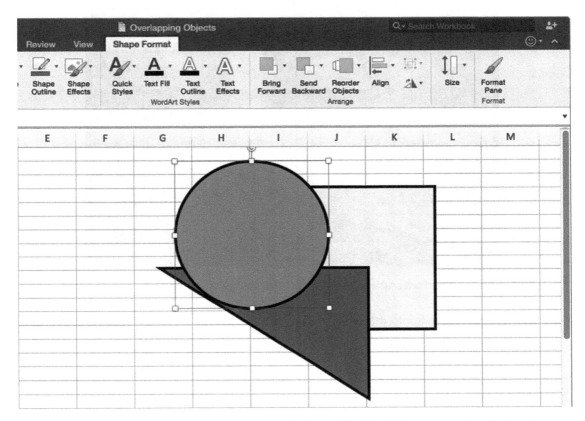

Figure 4-22. Use the commands in the Arrange group on the Format tab of the Ribbon to move the selected object up or down the layers in the document. In this example, you can use the Bring Forward command to bring the square in front of the triangle but still keep it behind the circle

Rearranging Graphical Objects by Dragging

Excel and PowerPoint enable you to drag objects into the order you want. Follow these steps:

1. Click one of the objects whose order you want to change. The appropriate Format tab appears on the Ribbon, with its contents displayed.

2. In the Arrange group on the Format tab of the Ribbon, click the Reorder Objects button. The app displays the objects as a sequence of layers (see Figure 4-23).

Note   If you want to view only the objects that overlap each other, click the pop-up button on the Reorder Objects button, and then click Reorder Overlapping Objects.

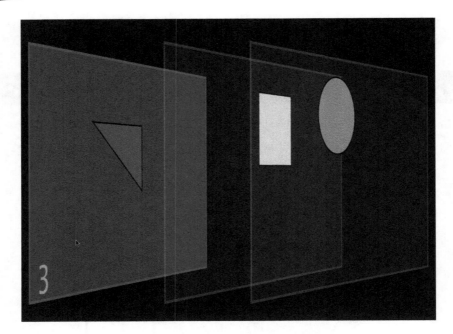

Figure 4-23. Excel and PowerPoint enable you to drag objects into the order you want

3.   Drag the layers into the order you want.

4.   Click the OK button in the lower-right corner of the screen when you finish.

Summary

In this chapter, you learned how to work with graphical objects in the Office apps. You now know how to insert your own pictures from the Photos app or from your Mac's file system, how to insert shapes and format them, and how to position graphical objects where you want them. You also learned how to control text wrapping in Word; how to recolor, crop, and compress pictures; and how to create SmartArt graphics to illustrate your documents.

In the next chapter, I'll show you how to customize the Office apps to suit your needs.

Chapter 5

Customizing Office to Suit You

Microsoft has put a lot of work into making the Office apps easy to use, but only you know exactly how you work and what you need. To make the Office apps suit you better, you can customize their user interface a little and their behavior a lot.

Earlier versions of Office for Mac, such as Office 2011, enabled you to customize the user interface extensively. Office 2016 lets you customize the status bar in Word, Excel, and PowerPoint, but it removes the capability to customize the menu bar and the Ribbon (not to mention the toolbars, which are no longer in the interface). However, you can still create custom keyboard shortcuts so that you can give commands without moving your fingers from the keyboard.

Beyond these direct customizations to the user interface, each app has hundreds of settings you can use to change how the apps work. In the second half of this chapter, you'll look at two key areas of options common to the apps: the General preferences, which control vital aspects of the apps' looks and behavior, and the Save preferences, which control the default formats that the apps use to store your documents.

Customizing the Status Bar

Word, Excel, and PowerPoint enable you to customize the status bar at the bottom of the window by choosing which of a preset selection of controls to display on it. Ctrl-click or right-click the status bar to display the Customize Status Bar context menu, and then click an item to either place a check mark next to it (making it appear on the status bar) or to remove the existing check mark.

The following sections explain the items you can display on the status bar.

> **Note** Some items appear on the status bar only when they are available, such as when a particular feature is active.

© Guy Hart-Davis 2016
G. Hart-Davis, *Learn Office 2016 for Mac*, DOI 10.1007/978-1-4842-2002-3_5

Customizing the Status Bar in Word

In Word, the Customize Status Bar context menu (see Figure 5-1) contains a wide variety of items. Table 5-1 explains these items and what they do.

Table 5-1. *Items on the Customize Status Bar Context Menu in Word*

Item Name	What It Displays	Click It To
Formatted Page Number	The current page number in its formatted state. This may be different from the actual page number represented by the Page Number readout.	Display the Go To tab of the Find and Replace dialog box.
Section	The section number of the current section.	Display the Go To tab of the Find and Replace dialog box.
Page Number	The current page number and the total number of pages in the document—for example, Page 1 of 20.	Toggle the display of the Navigation pane.
Vertical Page Position	A readout showing "At:" and the position, such as At: 1.5". You may find this readout useful when working on layouts.	Display the Go To tab of the Find and Replace dialog box.
Line Number	A readout showing the line number of the current line.	Display the Go To tab of the Find and Replace dialog box.
Column	A readout showing the "column" number, an ordinal number showing this character's position from the left margin. For example, if the column number is 5, the character is the fifth character on the current line.	Display the Go To tab of the Find and Replace dialog box.
Word Count	A readout showing the word count for the current selection (if there is one) or the whole document (if there is no selection).	Display the Word Count dialog box.
Spelling and Grammar Check	The current spelling and grammar check status—a book icon showing either a check mark (indicating no issues) or a cross (indicating one or more issues).	Run a spelling and grammar check.
Language	A readout showing the current language.	Open the Language dialog box.
Signatures	The name of any digital signature applied to the document.	N/A
Permissions	Any permission restrictions applied to the document.	N/A
Track Changes	A readout showing "Track Changes: On" or "Track Changes: Off."	Toggle Track Changes on or off.
Caps Lock	A readout showing "Caps Lock" if Caps Lock is on.	Turn Caps Lock off.
Overtype	A readout showing "Overtype" if Overtype mode is on, or "Insert" if Overtype mode is not on.	Toggle between Overtype mode and Insert mode.
Selection Mode	A readout showing "Extend Selection" if Extend Selection mode is on, or nothing if Extend Selection mode is off.	Turn Extend Selection mode off.

(continued)

Table 5-1. *(continued)*

Item Name	What It Displays	Click It To
Macro Recording	A Record Macro icon when you are not recording a macro and a Stop Recording icon when you are recording a macro.	Display the Record Macro dialog box. Click the Stop Recording icon to stop recording.
Upload Status	The document's status, such as "Uploading to OneDrive," while activity is taking place.	N/A
Document Updates Available	An icon indicating whether the document is up to date or whether updates are available.	Display choices for getting the updates.
View Shortcuts	The Print Layout button, Web Layout button, Outline button, and Draft button.	Switch to the corresponding view. For example, click the Print Layout button to switch to Print Layout view.
Zoom Slider	The Zoom slider.	Zoom quickly to the point you clicked. Click the – button and + button to zoom in increments.
Zoom	The current zoom percentage.	Open the Zoom dialog box.

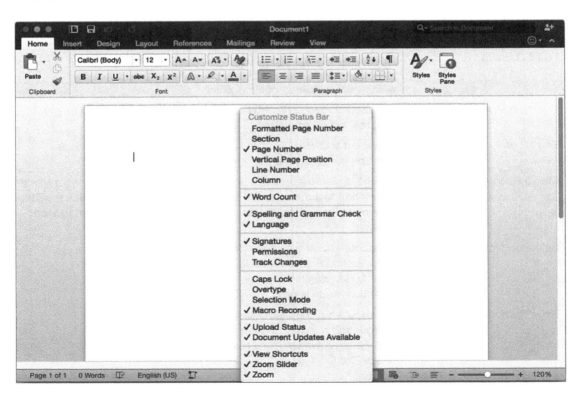

Figure 5-1. *The Customize Status Bar context menu for Word contains a wide range of items, from information such as the page number and section to whether updates are available for a document stored online*

Customizing the Status Bar in Excel

In Excel, the Customize Status Bar context menu (see Figure 5-2) contains a wide variety of items. Table 5-2 explains these items and what they do.

Table 5-2. Items on the Customize Status Bar Context Menu in Excel

Item Name	What It Displays	Click It To
Cell Mode	A readout showing the editing mode for the current cell, such as Ready (the default state), Enter (when the cell is open for entering content), Edit (when the cell is open for editing), or Point (when you're creating a formula and pointing at cells).	N/A
Fill by Example Blank Cells	A readout showing the number of cells left blank after a Fill operation.	N/A
Fill by Example Changed Cells	A readout showing the number of cells changed during a Fill operation.	N/A
Signatures	Information about a digital signature applied to the workbook.	N/A
Caps Lock	A readout showing "Caps Lock" when Caps Lock is on.	Turn off Caps Lock.
Fixed Decimal	A readout showing "Fixed Decimal" when the worksheet is set to automatically insert a decimal point.	N/A
Overtype Mode	A readout showing "Overtype" to indicate that Overtype mode is enabled.	Disable Overtype mode.
End Mode	A readout showing "End" to indicate that End mode is enabled.	Disable End mode.
Macro Recording	A Record Macro icon when you are not recording a macro and a Stop Recording icon when you are recording a macro.	Display the Record Macro dialog box. Click the Stop Recording icon to stop recording.
Selection Mode	A readout showing "Extend Selection" when Extend Selection mode is on and "Add to Selection" when Add to Selection mode is on.	N/A
Page Number	A readout showing the active page number and the total number of pages in Page Layout view—for example, "Page 2 of 8."	N/A
Average	The average value (for example, "Average: 2.5") when you select multiple cells containing values.	N/A

(continued)

Table 5-2. (continued)

Item Name	What It Displays	Click It To
Count	The number of cells selected (for example, "Count: 4").	N/A
Numerical Count	The number of selected cells that contain numerical values (for example, "Numerical Count: 12").	N/A
Minimum	The minimum numerical value in the selected cells (for example, "Minimum: 2").	N/A
Maximum	The maximum numerical value in the selected cells (for example, "Maximum: 100").	N/A
Sum	The sum of the numerical values in the selected cells (for example, "Sum: 250").	N/A
Upload Status	The document's status, such as "Uploading to OneDrive," while activity is taking place.	N/A
View Shortcuts	The Normal button and the Page Layout button.	Switch to the corresponding view. For example, click the Page Layout button to switch to Page Layout view.
Zoom Slider	The Zoom slider.	Zoom quickly to the point you clicked. Click the – button and + button to zoom in increments.
Zoom	The current zoom percentage.	Open the Zoom dialog box.

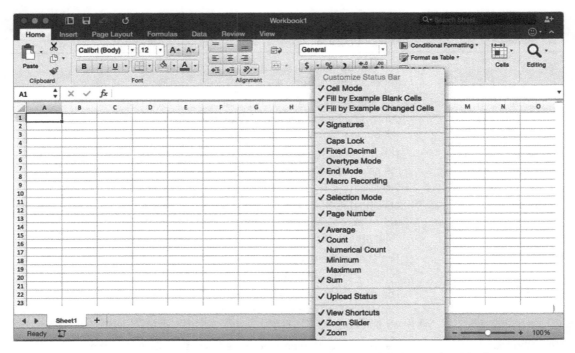

Figure 5-2. The Customize Status Bar context menu for Excel lets you put key functions on the status bar

Customizing the Status Bar in PowerPoint

In PowerPoint, the Customize Status Bar context menu (see Figure 5-3) is more limited than its siblings in Word and Excel, but it still enables you to choose which information you want to have displayed. Table 5-3 explains the items you can display on the status bar.

Table 5-3. Items on the Customize Status Bar Context Menu in PowerPoint

Item Name	What It Displays	Click It To
View Indicator	A readout showing the name of the item you are viewing, such as "Slide 1 of 253" for a slide, "Slide Master" for a slide master, or "Handout Master" for a handout master.	N/A
Theme	The theme name, such as "Office Theme."	N/A
Language	The current language.	Open the Language dialog box.
Upload Status	The document's status, such as "Uploading to OneDrive," while activity is taking place.	N/A
Document Updates Available	An icon indicating whether the document is up to date or whether updates are available.	Display choices for getting the updates.

(continued)

Table 5-3. (continued)

Item Name	What It Displays	Click It To
Notes	The Notes icon, including the text "Notes."	Toggle the display of the Notes pane.
Comments	The Comments icon, including the text "Comments."	Toggle the display of the Comments pane.
View Shortcuts	The Normal button, the Slide Sorter button, and the Slide Show button.	Switch to the associated view. For example, click the Slide Sorter button to switch to Slide Sorter view.
Zoom Slider	The Zoom slider.	Zoom quickly to the point you clicked. Click the – button and + button to zoom in increments.
Zoom	The current zoom percentage.	Open the Zoom dialog box.
Zoom to Fit	The Zoom to Fit button.	Zoom to display the current slide as large as possible in the window.

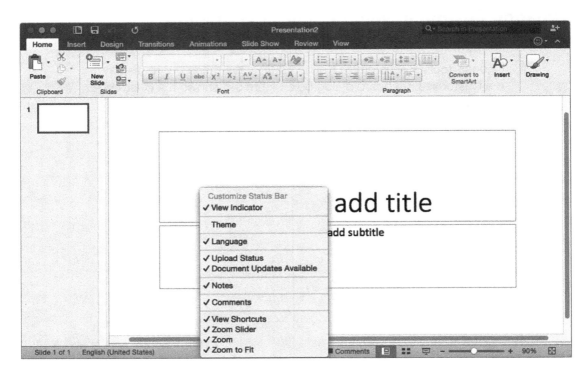

Figure 5-3. The Customize Status Bar context menu for PowerPoint enables you to choose whether to see the theme, notes, and comments on the status bar

Creating Custom Keyboard Shortcuts

The Ribbon and the menus on the menu bar can be great for giving commands with the pointing device, but if you prefer to keep your hands on the keyboard, you can give commands by pressing keyboard shortcuts instead. Each of the apps comes with many keyboard shortcuts built in, but you can also create custom keyboard shortcuts of your own.

Word has a custom tool that enables you to create exactly the keyboard shortcuts you need. For Excel, PowerPoint, and Outlook, you can use OS X's Shortcuts feature, which lets you create keyboard shortcuts for existing menu items.

> **Note**   Keyboard shortcuts can save you time and effort, so it's well worth learning the ones you'll find most useful. The easiest way to learn the keyboard shortcuts for the most widely used commands is to look at the shortcuts listed on the Office apps' menus. For example, the File menu shows you shortcuts such as Cmd+O for the File ➤ Open command, Cmd+W for the File ➤ Close command, and Cmd+P for the File ➤ Print command. You can also find impressively long lists of keyboard shortcuts in the Help files (search for *keyboard shortcuts*).

Creating Custom Keyboard Shortcuts in Word

To create a custom keyboard shortcut in Word, follow these steps:

1. Choose Tools ➤ Customize Keyboard from the menu bar to display the Customize Keyboard dialog box. Figure 5-4 shows the Customize Keyboard dialog box with settings chosen.

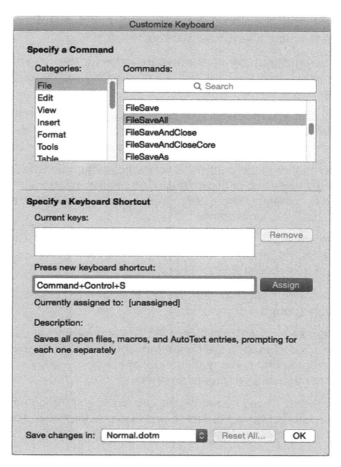

Figure 5-4. In Word, use the Customize Keyboard to set up custom keyboard shortcuts for the commands you need to give most often

2. At the bottom of the Customize Keyboard dialog box, make sure the Save changes in pop-up menu is showing Normal.dotm (see the nearby Note). Choose another template or document only if you want to save the keyboard shortcuts in that template or document rather than have them available for general use.

> **Note**   Normal.dotm, usually called "the Normal template," is a template that Word opens automatically each time you launch the app and keeps open until you quit the app. The Normal template contains settings for blank documents and also Word-wide settings, such as macros and keyboard shortcuts. By saving your keyboard shortcuts in the Normal template, you make them available to all documents and templates except those containing their own keyboard shortcuts (which override those in the Normal template). Any keyboard shortcuts you save in a template are available when that template itself is active or when a document attached to the template is active. Any keyboard shortcuts you save in a document are available only when that document is active.

3. In the Categories list box, click the category of command for which
    you want to create a keyboard shortcut.

    ■ The beginning of the list shows categories for the main menus that appear on
      the menu bar all the time: the File menu, the Edit menu, the View menu, and
      so on.

    ■ You'll also find a category for each menu or Ribbon tab that becomes
      available only when you work with particular objects. For example, the
      Drawing category gives you access to commands for manipulating drawing.

    ■ If you can't find the command you want, either click the Search box and start
      typing a keyword, or click the All Commands category to see the full list of
      Word commands. There are more than 1,000 in All Commands, so working
      with this list is slow going.

    ■ There are also categories for Macros, Fonts, AutoText, Styles, and Common
      Symbols. For example, click Styles to display the list of styles so that you can
      assign a keyboard shortcut to one.

4. In the Commands list box, click the command. Word displays
    information about the command:

    ■ *Current keys*: The Current keys list box shows any keyboard shortcuts
      currently assigned to the command (some commands have several shortcuts).
      If this command has any shortcuts, check that you know them and decide
      whether you need to create another.

    ■ *Description*: This area shows the description of the command. Read it to
      make sure you've picked the command you intended. Some command names
      are clear, but others can be confusing.

5. Click in the "Press new shortcut key" text box.

6. Press the keyboard shortcut you want to assign:

    ■ You can create keyboard shortcuts that start with the Cmd and Ctrl keys:
      Cmd, Cmd+Option, Cmd+Ctrl, Cmd+Option+Shift, Cmd+Option+Ctrl,
      Cmd+Option+Ctrl+Shift, Cmd+Ctrl+Shift, Ctrl, Ctrl+Option, Ctrl+Shift,
      Ctrl+Option+Shift are all possible.

    ■ You can use pretty much any key on the keyboard—letters, numbers, function
      keys, and so on.

    ■ A normal shortcut consists of a modifier or modifiers plus one key, such
      as Cmd+Option+T. But you can also create modifiers that use two keys in
      sequence—for example, Cmd+Option+T, S—by pressing the extra key after
      the key combination. This lets you create many more keyboard shortcuts and
      is good for related commands—for example, using the Cmd+Option+S, 1
      keyboard shortcut for one style, the Cmd+Option+S, 2 keyboard shortcut for
      another, and the Cmd+Option+S, 3 keyboard shortcut for a third.

7. Check the Currently assigned to readout to see whether the keyboard shortcut is currently used. If so, press another keyboard shortcut if you don't want to overwrite it.

8. Click the Assign button. Word assigns the keyboard shortcut to the command.

9. When you've finished assigning keyboard shortcuts, click the Close button to close the Customize Keyboard dialog box.

Caution   To save your keyboard customizations, you need to save the changes you've made to the Normal template (or to the template or document you've customized). The best way to do this is to Shift-click the File menu and then click Save All. If Word displays a dialog box asking whether you want to save changes that affect the global template, Normal.dotm, click the Save button; similarly, if Word prompts you to save changes to the template, click the Save button. While it's possible to leave your changes unsaved until you quit Word, it's not usually a good idea, because you will lose the changes if Word crashes.

Creating Keyboard Shortcuts for Excel, PowerPoint, and Outlook

For Excel, PowerPoint, and Outlook, you can create keyboard shortcuts for menu commands by using the OS X Shortcuts feature. Follow these steps:

1. Ctrl-click or right-click the System Preferences icon on the Dock to display the context menu, and then click Keyboard to display the Keyboard preferences pane in System Preferences.

2. Click the Shortcuts tab button to display the Shortcuts pane.

Note   If the System Preferences icon doesn't appear on the Dock, choose Apple ➤ System Preferences from the menu bar to open the System Preferences window. Then click the Keyboard icon to display the Keyboard pane.

---

3. In the left pane, click the App Shortcuts item. The current list of shortcuts set for apps appears in the right pane (see Figure 5-5).

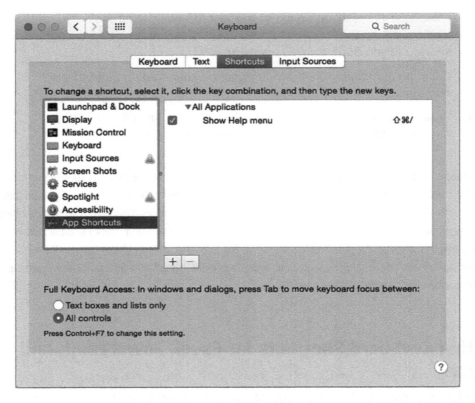

Figure 5-5. In the Keyboard pane in System Preferences, click the Shortcuts button to display the Shortcuts pane, and then click App Shortcuts in the left pane

4. Click the Add (+) button to start creating a new shortcut. The Add dialog box opens (see Figure 5-6).

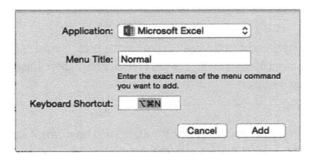

Figure 5-6. In the Add dialog box, choose the app, type the command's name, and press the keyboard shortcut

5. Open the Application pop-up menu and click the app's name, such as Microsoft Excel.

6. Click the Menu Title box and then type the command's name as it appears on the menu. You don't need to type the menu name.

7. Click the Keyboard Shortcut box and press the keys for the keyboard shortcut you want to assign.

8. Click the Add button to close the Add dialog box and add the shortcut.

Choosing Essential Preferences in Word, Excel, and PowerPoint

Each of the Office apps includes several hundred preferences that you can set to make the app behave the way you prefer. That's many more than I can cover in detail here. So, this section concentrates on those settings that are common to Word, Excel, and PowerPoint and make a big difference in the way that the apps behave.

> **Note**   You'll find information on important preferences peculiar to individual apps in the app-specific chapters later in the book.

Opening the Preferences Window

To work through this section, open the app's Preferences window by choosing Word ➤ Preferences, Excel ➤ Preferences, PowerPoint ➤ Preferences, or Outlook ➤ Preferences.

> **Tip**   You can also press Cmd+, (Cmd and the comma key) to display the Preferences window. This keyboard shortcut works in most Mac apps.

Figure 5-7 shows the Preferences window for Word. Each app not only has different preferences but also divides them up differently among the panes in the Preferences window.

> **Note**   You can leave Outlook's Preferences window open as you work, which can be handy for seeing the effect of settings you change. By contrast, in Word, Excel, and PowerPoint, you must close the Preferences window before you can continue working in the app.

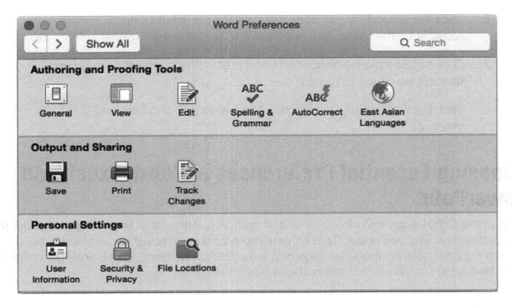

Figure 5-7. *Each Preferences window divides the preferences into different categories, such as the Authoring and Proofing Tools category, the Output and Sharing category, and the Personal Settings category in the Word Preferences window*

In Word, Excel, and PowerPoint, you can navigate the Preferences window in these ways:

- *Display a category of preferences*: Click the category you want to display—for example, the General category. The app displays the corresponding preferences pane.

- *Return to the main preferences screen*: Click the Show All button on the toolbar. Alternatively, click the Back button on the toolbar.

- *Search for a preference*: Click in the Search box, and then type the term to search for. Click the search result you want to see; alternatively, press the up arrow or the down arrow to highlight the search result that matches, and then press the Return key. The Preferences window displays the pane that contains the match.

- *Retrace your path through the preferences panes*: Click the Back button on the toolbar to display the previous pane. Keep clicking the Back button as many times as needed to go back as far as you need.

- *Go forward again through the preferences panes*: After going back, you can click the Forward button on the toolbar to display the next pane. Again, keep clicking to keep going forward.

The Outlook Preferences window doesn't have the Search box or the Forward button and Back button, so you click the icon for the Preferences pane you want and then simply click the Show All button on the toolbar to return to the main Preferences screen.

Setting Your User Name, Initials, and Address

If you installed Office yourself, you probably set your user name and initials during setup. If not, you may find that the Office apps think you're called Authorized User or some other generic name. Either way, you may need to add or change your address information.

To change your name, initials, or address information, use Word. In the Word Preferences window, click the User Information icon in the Personal Settings area to display the User Information pane (see Figure 5-8). You can then fill in as many fields as you want: your names and initials; your company name, the city, state, and ZIP code; and the phone number and e-mail address you want to have associated with the Office apps.

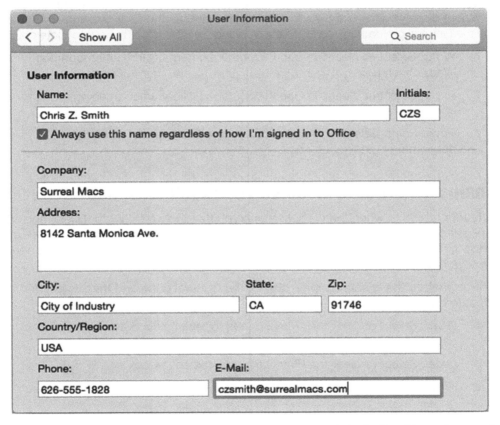

Figure 5-8. Word is the best app for entering your details because it provides fields for the address, phone number, and e-mail address as well as your name and initials

> **Note**   Select the "Always use this name regardless of how I'm signed in to Office" check box if you want Office to use the name entered in the Name box no matter which of your Office accounts you're using. For example, your personal Office 365 account may use a different spelling of your name than your corporate account. By selecting this check box, you can apply a standard version of your name.

Word makes the information you enter available to Excel and PowerPoint, so you don't need to enter your name and initials separately in them. You'll find your user name in the General preferences pane in Excel, and you'll find your name and initials in the User Information preferences pane in PowerPoint.

Choosing Whether to Display the Gallery Dialog Box When the App Opens

By default, Word, Excel, and PowerPoint display the Gallery dialog box automatically when you launch the app. The Gallery dialog box can be helpful when you need to create a new document or open a recent document (as discussed in Chapter 2), but you may prefer to have the app open without displaying the extra window. To control whether the Gallery dialog box opens, display the General preferences pane for the app and select or clear the appropriate check box:

- *Word*: Select or clear the Show Word Document Gallery when opening Word check box.
- *Excel*: Select or clear the Open Workbook Gallery when opening Excel check box.
- *PowerPoint*: Select or clear the "Show the Start screen when this application starts" check box.

Choosing Whether to Receive Feedback with Sound

To grab your attention when there's something you need to know, Word, Excel, and PowerPoint can all provide feedback using sound. For example, the app plays a sound to let you know it has finished saving or printing a document. Whether this is helpful depends on how you work and where, such as whether you're in a cubicle or your own office.

To control whether these sounds play, display the General pane and then select or clear the appropriate check box:

- *Word*: Select or clear the "Play sounds for events such as opening, saving, or printing" check box.
- *Excel*: Select or clear the Play Office sounds check box.
- *PowerPoint*: Select or clear the Provide feedback with sound check box.

Choosing Whether to Confirm Launching Other Apps

Mostly, when you're working in an app, you create or open files created in that app or ones compatible with it. For example, when you're working in Excel, you normally create or open workbook files or open text files that Excel can display.

But sometimes you may take an action that creates or opens a type of file that requires a different app. When you do this, the app can warn you that it needs to use a different app. You can then click the Open button, such as an Open in Word button for a Word document, or click the Cancel button to cancel the action.

This prompting is usually helpful. To turn it on in Word, select the "Confirm before opening different applications" check box in the General preferences pane. In Excel, select the "Confirm before opening other applications" check box in the General preferences pane. As of this writing, PowerPoint doesn't offer this setting.

Choosing the Default Format for Saving Documents

Word, Excel, and PowerPoint can each save documents in several different formats. Each application comes set to save documents in its preferred format. For example, Word uses the latest Word Document format by default. But to make sure other people can open the documents you share with them, you may need to change the format. For example, you may need to use a Word document format that colleagues using an older version of Office (such as Office 2004 for Mac or Office 2003 for Windows) or a different word processing app can open.

When saving a document for the first time, you can save it in any of the formats the application supports. You can also use the File ➤ Save As command to save a new copy of an existing document in a different format. But it's a good idea to set the default format for the documents you create in the application.

> **Note** Word and Excel enable you to set the default file format, but PowerPoint does not.

Setting the Default Document Format in Word

To set the default format Word uses to save documents, display the Save preferences pane in the Word Preferences window (see Figure 5-9), open the Save Word files as pop-up menu, and click the format you want.

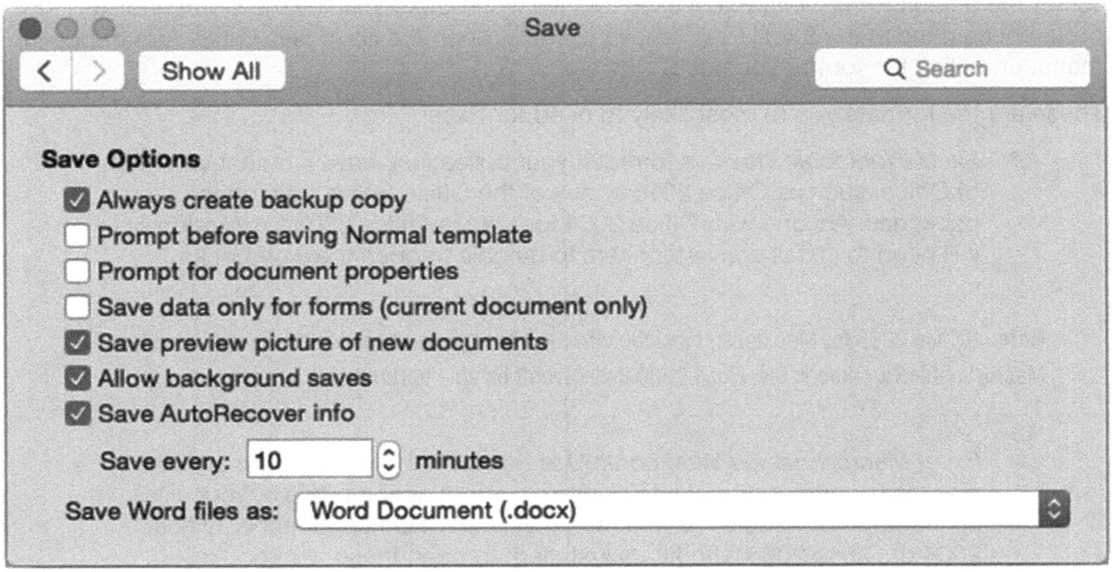

Figure 5-9. In the Save preferences pane for Word, you can set the default format for saving files, set up AutoRecover backups, and choose other save-related options

These are the formats you're most likely to need for Word:

- *Word Document*: Use this format if your colleagues have a recent version of Office, such as Office 2016 or any of the Office 365 subscription packages. Anyone with Office 2004 for Mac or Office 2003 for Windows will need to install converter filters to be able to open the documents.

- *Word 97–2004 Document*: Use this format if your colleagues have Office 2004 for Mac, Office 2003 for Windows, or an earlier version of Office. You can also use this format for greater compatibility with other word processors, such as OpenOffice.org Writer or Google Docs.

- *Rich Text Format*: Use this format if you're creating text-based documents that you need to ensure are fully readable in almost any word processor.

Tip   While you're on the Save preferences pane in Word, you may want to set a couple of other preferences. First, select the "Always create backup copy" check box if you want to keep a quick backup each time you save a document after the first. When you do this, Word renames the previously saved version of the document, making it the backup file, and saves the current document under the document's name. You may also want to select the "Save preview picture of new documents" check box to create a thumbnail preview of each document, which can help you to identify it visually.

Setting the Default Workbook Format in Excel

To set the default format that Excel uses to save workbooks, display the Compatibility preferences pane in the Excel Preferences window, open the Save files in this format pop-up menu, and click the format you need.

These are the formats you're most likely to need for Excel:

- *Excel Workbook*: Use this format if your colleagues have a recent version of Office, such as Office 2016 or any of the Office 365 subscription packages. Anyone with Office 2004 for Mac or Office 2003 for Windows will need to install converter filters to be able to open the workbooks.

Note   Office 2008 for Mac doesn't include VBA. So although you can include macros in an Excel Macro-Enabled Workbook file, Excel 2008 users won't be able to run them.

- *Excel Macro-Enabled Workbook*: Use this format if you need to include macros in your workbooks to perform custom actions. Again, your colleagues will need to have a recent version of Office, or either Office 2004 or Office 2003 with filters installed, to open these workbooks.

■ *Excel Binary Workbook*: Use this format if you create large and complex workbooks and need to improve performance. Once more, your colleagues will need to have a recent version of Office, or either Office 2004 or Office 2003 with filters, installed to work with these workbooks.

■ *Excel 97–2004 Workbook*: Use this format if your colleagues have Office 2004 for Mac, Office 2003 for Windows, or an earlier version of Office. You can also use this format for greater compatibility with other spreadsheet apps, such as OpenOffice.org Calc or Google Docs.

Setting AutoRecover to Keep Backups of Your Documents for Safety

Word, Excel, and PowerPoint also let you choose whether to keep AutoRecover files. AutoRecover is a safety net that automatically saves a copy of each open document every few minutes in case the app closes unexpectedly and loses the changes you've made. After the app restarts automatically or you restart it manually, the app opens the latest AutoRecover files for you so that you can choose which versions to keep. If you save your documents and then exit the app, it gets rid of the saved AutoRecover files.

> **Caution**   Never rely on AutoRecover as protection against disasters. When AutoRecover works, it can save your bacon, but sometimes it doesn't save everything. So, you should always save your documents frequently while working on them and use AutoRecover only if disaster strikes. You can save a document at any time by pressing Cmd+S, clicking the Save button on the title bar of the app, or choosing File ➤ Save from the menu bar.

To choose AutoRecover settings, follow these steps:

1. Display the Save preferences pane.

2. Select or clear the Save AutoRecover info check box (in Word and PowerPoint) or the Save AutoRecover information in every *NN* minutes check box (in Excel).

3. If you select the check box, enter the number of minutes in the text box. You can set any interval from 1 minute to 120 minutes. An interval of around 3 minutes usually works well, because it saves information frequently enough to avoid disasters but doesn't overly interrupt your work by saving constantly.

> **Note**   You can use different AutoRecover settings in each app if you want. For example, you may want AutoRecover to save your Word documents every 2 minutes, your Excel workbooks every 15 minutes, and your PowerPoint presentations not at all.

Summary

In this chapter, you learned essential techniques for making the Office apps work your way. You now know how to customize the status bar in Word, Excel, or PowerPoint so that it displays the tools and information you need, and you've learned how to create custom keyboard shortcuts to speed up your work.

You also learned how to open the Preferences window and access the hundreds of settings you can choose in each app. And you went through a handful of essential settings, including those for setting your name, initials, and address; for choosing the default formats for saving Word documents and Excel workbooks; and for setting AutoRecover to create automatic backups of your open documents.

This is the end of the first part of the book. You're now familiar with the most important tools and techniques that the apps share, so it's time to dig into using the individual apps. We'll start with Microsoft Word.

Part 2

Creating Documents with Microsoft Word

In this part of the book, you'll learn how to harness the power of Microsoft Word to create whichever kinds of documents you need—anything from a short memo or letter to a full-scale book that makes this tome look puny.

In Chapter 6, you'll first learn ways to enter text quickly in Word documents. Next up is selecting text in advanced ways with the pointing device and the keyboard, moving around your documents swiftly and smoothly, and pointing Word at the folder that contains your custom templates. You'll also learn to create backup documents automatically, and to make the most of Word's various views of a document.

In Chapter 7, I show you the right way to format a document quickly and consistently by using styles rather than by applying direct formatting bit by bit. In this chapter, you'll also learn how to get around your documents by using the Sidebar and the Find feature, and how to harness the power of the Replace feature.

In Chapter 8, you'll first study Word's extra features for creating complex tables—for example, creating a table from existing text. You'll then learn how to break a document into multiple sections; how to add headers, footers, and page numbers; and how to create newspaper-style columns of text. You'll also learn to use bookmarks and cross-references, develop your documents using Word's powerful Outline view, and add footnotes and endnotes to your documents.

In Chapter 9, you'll use Word's Mail Merge feature to create business documents swiftly and efficiently. You'll learn to set up mail merge documents (such as letters or labels), connect them to data sources, and save or print the results.

In Chapter 10, you'll use Word's features for working with your colleagues on documents. You'll learn how to edit a document either simultaneously or separately, how to use the Track Changes feature to mark revisions, and how to integrate changes into a document. You'll also see how to add comments to a document and compare two document versions that contain untracked changes.

In Chapter 11, you'll put your documents to use. First, you'll learn to print an entire document or just parts of it, print a document with or without markup, and even print markup without the document. You'll also learn how to remove sensitive information from documents, create a document you can open with earlier versions of Word, and create PDF files from documents.

Chapter 6

Entering Text and Using Views

In this chapter, I'll show you how to enter text quickly in Word documents by using the extra features that Word provides, which go beyond those in the other apps. You'll see how to select text in advanced ways with the pointing device and the keyboard, how to move around your documents using keyboard shortcuts and the Go To feature, and how to tell Word where to find your custom templates.

You'll also learn how to make Word automatically create backup documents so that you can recover from disastrous edits or other mishaps and how to exploit the possibilities offered by Word's various views of a document.

Entering Text in Your Word Documents

In Word, you can enter text in your documents by typing it in as usual, but you can often save time by entering text in other ways:

- *Paste*: If you have the text in another document or e-mail, you can copy it and then paste it into the Word document.

- *Scan*: If you have the text in a hard-copy document, you can scan it with a scanner and use an optical character recognition (OCR) app such as Prizmo 3 ($49.99 from the App Store) or PDFpen 6 ($79.99 from the App Store) to get the text from the scanned image. You can export or copy the text to Word.

> **Tip** If you don't mind waiting for OCR on your documents, you can upload them as images to the Evernote note-syncing service. Evernote automatically scans each image for text and adds it to your note. At busy times, Evernote may take a day or two to get around to scanning your images, but if you're not in a hurry, this can be a great solution for occasional OCR.

© Guy Hart-Davis 2016
G. Hart-Davis, *Learn Office 2016 for Mac*, DOI 10.1007/978-1-4842-2002-3_6

- *Inserting a file*: If you have the text in a Word document or a text file, you can insert it quickly in a Word document. See the "Inserting Text from One Document to Another" section for details.

- *Using AutoCorrect*: After creating AutoCorrect entries as described in the "Saving Time and Effort with AutoCorrect" section in Chapter 3, you can insert their contents by just typing their names. AutoCorrect is great for entering sections of boilerplate text with just a few keystrokes.

- *Using AutoText*: As well as AutoCorrect, Word provides AutoText, which is another easy way of inserting preexisting blocks of text. See the "Inserting Prebuilt Blocks of Text with AutoText" section for details.

Inserting Text from One Document to Another

When you need to put all the text from one document into another document, you can use the Insert File feature instead of opening the document, copying the content, closing the document, and then pasting the content. You can also use this command to insert a defined part of a file, such as the section marked by a bookmark.

To use the Insert File feature, follow these steps:

1. Place the insertion point where you want to insert the text.

2. Choose Insert ➤ Text ➤ Object ➤ Text from File from the Ribbon or Insert ➤ File from the menu bar to display the Insert File dialog box (see Figure 6-1).

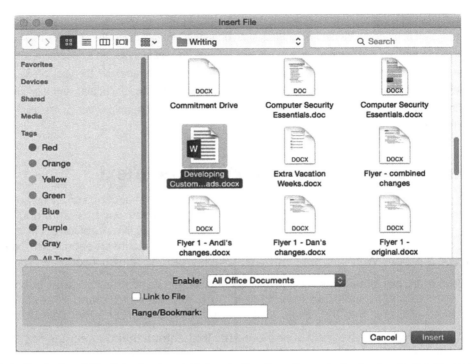

Figure 6-1. Use the Insert File dialog box to quickly insert either the entire contents of a document or the contents marked by a bookmark or range in it

3. Navigate to the document you want to insert, and then click it.

Note   You can also use the Insert File dialog box to insert the contents of a range of cells in an Excel worksheet into a Word document. In the Enable pop-up menu, choose All Office Documents. Then select the workbook, type the appropriate range in the Range/Bookmark text box, and click the Insert button.

4. Make sure the Link to File check box is cleared. (If this check box is selected, Word creates a link to the file's data rather than inserting the data itself, which is what you usually want.)

5. Click the Insert button. Word inserts the document's text.

> **Tip**   Instead of inserting the entire contents of a document, you can insert the contents of a single bookmark, an electronic marker that you set. To use this feature, set up a document with bookmarks containing the chunks of text you want to use separately, and give the bookmarks names you can remember. Then, in the Insert File dialog box, select the document, and then click in the Range/Bookmark box and type the bookmark's name. Once you've made your choice, click the Insert button in the Insert File dialog box as usual.

Inserting Prebuilt Blocks of Text with AutoText

If some or many of your documents will include some of the same sections of text, you may be able to save time by using AutoText. This feature gives you an easy way to store prebuilt sections of text so that you can reuse them in your documents. AutoText is like AutoCorrect in a way, but it doesn't replace text automatically—instead, you choose when to insert each AutoText entry, although you can have Word prompt you with available AutoText entries if you like.

An AutoText entry consists of as much text as needed, plus any other objects, such as graphics or tables. Word includes some built-in AutoText entries for standard text items such as "Dear Sir or Madam" and the "Page X of Y" numbering used for headers and footers.

To use AutoText, you first create one or more AutoText entries that contain the text and elements you want. You can then insert these entries as needed in your documents.

To create a new AutoText entry, follow these steps:

1.   In your document, enter the material that you want to include in the AutoText entry:

     ■   Type in the text, and apply any formatting it needs.

     ■   Add other elements such as graphics or tables.

> **Tip**   Unless you're highly organized, you may find it easier to create AutoText entries when you realize that part of a document you've created would be useful again in the future. If you need to modify the material before creating an AutoText entry from it, copy that part of the document, paste it into a new document, and then change it—for example, remove specific information that you will fill in each time you reuse it. When the material is ready, select it, and then create an AutoText entry.

2.   Select the material.

3.   Choose Insert ➤ AutoText ➤ New from the menu bar to open the Create New AutoText dialog box (see Figure 6-2).

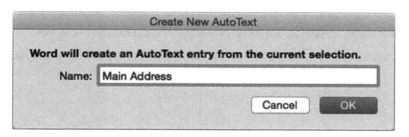

Figure 6-2. Use the Create New AutoText dialog box to create a new AutoText entry from the text or other material you've selected in the document

4. In the Name text box, type the name you want to give the AutoText entry.

> **Tip** As you'll see in a moment, the easiest way to insert an AutoText entry is by typing enough of its name to identify it. It is best to give your AutoText entries distinctive names that describe their contents so that you can type the names without having to look up the entries.

5. Click the OK button. Word closes the Create New AutoText Entry dialog box and adds the AutoText entry to the list Word maintains.

After creating an AutoText entry, you can insert it quickly at the position of the insertion point by typing the first four characters of the name or enough to identify it uniquely among your AutoText entries. When Word displays a ScreenTip containing the name of the AutoText entry (see Figure 6-3), press Return to insert it.

main

Figure 6-3. Word displays a ScreenTip containing the first part of the AutoText entry when you type enough of the name to identify it uniquely. Press Return to insert the entry

Typing is usually the easiest way to insert your AutoText entries, but you can also browse them by using the AutoText submenu on the Insert menu and the AutoText tab of the AutoCorrect dialog box.

To insert a built-in AutoText entry from the menu bar, choose Insert ➤ AutoText from the menu bar and then click the appropriate entry on the AutoText submenu.

To insert either a built-in AutoText entry or an entry you've created, use the AutoText tab of the AutoCorrect pane of Word's Preferences dialog box. Follow these steps:

1. Choose Insert ➤ AutoText ➤ AutoText from the menu bar to display the AutoCorrect preferences pane with the AutoText tab at the front (see Figure 6-4).

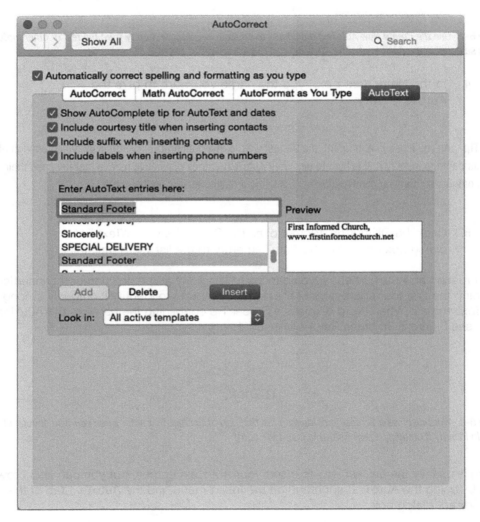

Figure 6-4. *From the AutoText tab of the AutoCorrect preferences pane in Word's Preferences dialog box, you can insert AutoText entries, delete existing entries, or create new entries*

2. You can then scroll down the list of entries and click the entry you want to see in the Preview box.

3. When you've selected the entry you want, click the Insert button.

From the AutoText tab of the AutoCorrect preferences pane, you can also delete an AutoText entry you no longer need: click the entry in the list, and then click the Delete button. You can also create a new AutoText entry from text and objects you've already selected in your document by typing a name and clicking the Add button, but usually it's easier to use the Create New AutoText dialog box, as described earlier in this section.

Selecting Text in Word-Specific Ways

Apart from the ways of selecting text that you learned in Chapter 3, you can use several shortcuts for selecting text in Word. You can use the pointing device, the keyboard, or both.

Selecting Text with the Pointing Device

When you're using the pointing device to move around a document, you can quickly select text by moving the pointer to the left of the text area so that the pointer changes to an arrow pointing up and to the right. You can then use this selection pointer like this:

- *Select a line*: Click next to the line you want to select.

- *Select multiple lines*: Click to place the insertion point anywhere in the line at which you want to begin the selection. Then Shift-click in the left margin at the line on which you want to end the selection.

- *Select a paragraph*: Double-click next to the paragraph you want to select.

- *Select the whole document*: Triple-click or Cmd-click. (Again, you click to the left of the text area, not in the text.)

- *Select a column of text*: Sometimes it's useful to select not whole lines but part of several lines—for example, to select the first few blank characters at the beginning of several lines of text you've pasted so that you can delete them all at once. You can do this by Option-dragging with the pointing device (see Figure 6-5). When you've selected the text you want, you can format it or delete it.

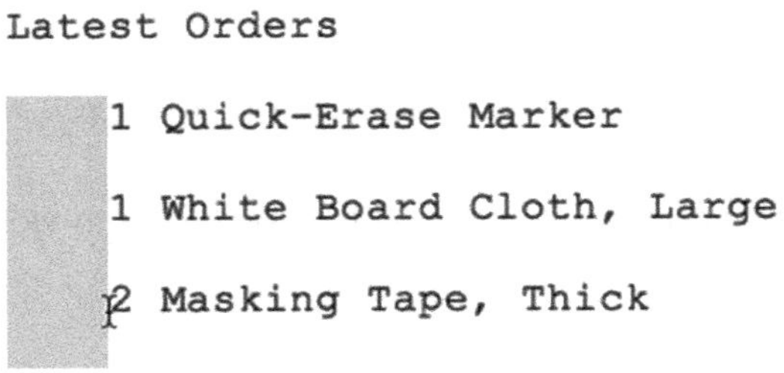

```
Latest Orders

1 Quick-Erase Marker

1 White Board Cloth, Large

2 Masking Tape, Thick
```

Figure 6-5. Option-drag when you need to select part of the text on each of several lines—for example, to delete unwanted blank space

Selecting Text with the Extend Selection Feature

You can select text in Word using the standard keyboard selection methods discussed in Chapter 4, but Word also provides an odd feature called Extend Selection. You put Word into Extend mode by pressing F8, which makes the Extend Selection readout appear on the status bar but otherwise has no visible effect. You can then continue selecting like this:

- Keep pressing F8. Press once more to select the current word. Press twice more to select the current sentence. Press three more times to select the current paragraph. Press four more times to select the whole document.

> **Note** Depending on how your Mac is configured, you may need to press Fn+F8 rather than F8 on its own to give the Extend Selection command. The setting that controls this is the "Use all F1, F2, etc. keys as standard function keys" check box on the Keyboard tab in Keyboard preferences in System Preferences. When this check box is cleared, as it is by default on most MacBook models, the function keys deliver the special functions printed on them; for example, F1 dims the display and F10 mutes sound. To get the standard function-key functions, you press Fn and the appropriate function key.

- Press the character to which you want to extend the selection. For example, press M to extend the selection to the next letter m, press . (the period key) to extend the selection to the end of the sentence, or press Return to extend the selection to the end of the paragraph. You can then press another key to extend the selection further, as needed.

- Press the right arrow key to extend the selection by a single character, or press the left arrow key to reduce the selection by a single character. Press the down arrow key to extend the selection by a line, or press the up arrow key to reduce the selection by a line.

> **Tip** You can also extend the selection by opening the Find and Replace dialog box and searching for particular text. Make sure the "Highlight all items found in" check box is cleared.

- With the pointing device, click at the point to which you want to extend the selection.

- Press Esc when you've finished selecting and want to work with the selection.

> **Note** The Extend Selection feature can be useful, but don't worry if you decide it's too bizarre to use. You should still know about Extend Selection because if Word starts behaving oddly and selecting sections of text you're not trying to select, you may have switched on Extend mode by accident. Look at the status bar to see if the Extend Selection readout appears. If so, press Esc to switch Extend mode off again.

Selecting Multiple Items at Once

Sometimes in Word it's useful to select multiple items at the same time. To do so, select the first item using the keyboard, the pointing device, or both. Then hold down Cmd and select the other items with the pointing device. After you've selected multiple objects, you can apply most types of formatting to them all at the same time.

Moving with Keyboard Shortcuts

As well as the standard keyboard shortcuts discussed in Chapter 3, you can move around a document by using the keyboard shortcuts listed in Table 6-1.

Table 6-1. Keyboard Shortcuts for Moving the Insertion Point in Word

Press These Keys	To Move the Insertion Point Like This
Cmd+Up arrow *or* Option+Up arrow	If the insertion point is in a paragraph, to the start of that paragraph. If the insertion point is at the start of a paragraph, to the start of the previous paragraph.
Cmd+Down arrow *or* Option+Down arrow	To the start of the next paragraph.
Cmd+Home *or* Cmd+Fn+Left arrow	To the start of the document.
Cmd+End *or* Cmd+Fn+Right arrow	To the end of the document.
Cmd+Page Down *or* Fn+Down arrow	To the next page.
Cmd+Page Up *or* Fn+Up arrow	To the previous page.

To move about a document with the pointing device, you can click the scroll arrows or drag the scroll box as usual.

Moving with the Go To Feature

Another way of moving about your documents is by using the Go To feature, which Word implements as a tab in the Find and Replace dialog box. The Go To feature enables you to move among various types of elements in your documents, such as from heading to heading or from one table to the previous table.

You can display the Go To tab of the Find and Replace dialog box (see Figure 6-6) in any of these ways:

- *Keyboard*: Press Cmd+Option+G.

- *Pointing device*: Click the Page readout (which shows the page position in the "Page 1 of 256" format) on the status bar.

> **Note**   You can also display the Go To tab of the Find and Replace dialog box by clicking other items on the status bar, if you have them displayed: the Formatted Page readout (which shows the page number, such as "Page 15"), the Section readout (which shows the section number, such as "Section 1"), the Vertical Page Position readout (which shows a position such as "At: 6.4""), the Line Number readout (which shows the line number, such as "Line: 63"), or the Column readout (which shows the character position, such as "Column: 12").

■   *Menu bar*: Choose Edit ➤ Find ➤ Go To.

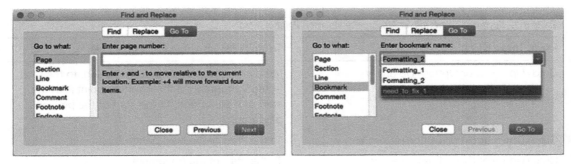

Figure 6-6. To browse through a document by pages (left), bookmarks (right), footnotes, tables or another object, display the Go To tab of the Find and Replace dialog box, and then click the object you want

In the "Go to what" box on the left side of the Go To tab, click the type of object you want to browse. Table 6-2 explains these items. Then click the Next button to go to the next instance or the Previous button to go to the previous instance.

To move in bigger jumps, type + and a number or – and a number in the text box on the right side, and then click the Go To button that appears. For example, type +5 and click the Go To button to move forward by five of whichever object you're using, or type –3 and click the Go To button to move backward by three of that object.

When you reach the object you want to work with, you can click the Close button to close the Find and Replace dialog box. Alternatively, you can click in the document, leaving the Find and Replace dialog box open so that you can quickly resume browsing by objects.

Table 6-2. Objects You Can Browse by Using the Go to Tab of the Find and Replace Dialog Box

Object	Explanation
Page	Browse from page to page in the document. This is the default setting until you change objects.
Section	Browse from one section to the next. See Chapter 8 for information on sections.
Line	Browse from one line to another. This is useful for very long documents, for documents that use line numbers, or both. For example, if you know the line number you want to go to, you can enter that number. Or if you want to move forward 1,000 lines, you can type **+1000** and press Return.

(continued)

Table 6-2. (*continued*)

Object	Explanation
Bookmark	Browse from one bookmark to another. A bookmark is an invisible marker you place to mark a particular point or range of text. See Chapter 8 for information on bookmarks.
Comment	Browse from one comment attached to text (or another object) to the next. See Chapter 10 for information on comments.
Footnote	Browse from one footnote to the next. A footnote is a note that appears at the foot of the page that refers to it. See Chapter 8 for information on footnotes.
Endnote	Browse from one endnote to the next. An endnote is a note that appears at the end of a section or document. See Chapter 8 for information on endnotes.
Field	Browse from one field to the next. See Chapter 8 for details on how to use fields.
Table	Browse from one table to the next. See Chapter 3 and Chapter 8 for information on creating tables.
Graphic	Browse from one graphic to the next.
Equation	Browse from one equation to another. You can insert an equation by choosing Insert ➤ Symbols ➤ Equation from the Ribbon or Insert ➤ Equation from the menu bar.
Object	Browse from one object to another. Open the Enter object name pop-up menu and choose the object type, such as Microsoft Excel Chart, or use the Any Object setting to browse all types of objects.
Heading	Browse from one heading to the next. This works with any paragraph you've given a Heading style (see Chapter 7 for details).

Tip   You can move the insertion point to your last four edits by pressing Shift+F5 once, twice, thrice, or four times.

Telling Word Where to Find Your Templates

If you have your own custom templates, you may need to tell Word where they're located, or you may need to move them into the Templates folder that Word is already using so that you can use them from the Word Document Gallery.

Note   Word uses two template folders, the User Templates folder and the Workgroup Templates folder. When you install Office, the installer automatically sets the User Templates folder for you to a folder on your Mac. For a normal installation, the installer does not set the Workgroup Templates folder; in a company network, an administrator may set this folder for you. If you share templates with others on your network, you can set the Workgroup Templates folder manually to point to this folder by using the technique described in this section.

To set your Templates folders or to check which folders Word is using for them, follow these steps:

1. Choose Word ➤ Preferences from the menu bar or press Cmd+, (Cmd and the comma key) to display the Word Preferences window.

2. In the Personal Settings area, click the File Locations icon to display the File Locations pane (see Figure 6-7).

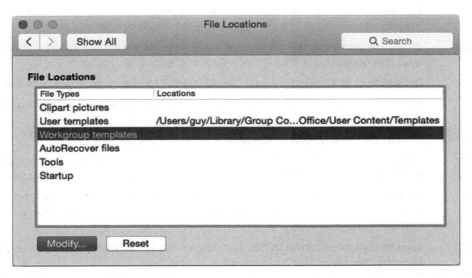

Figure 6-7. Use the File Locations pane in the Word Preferences window to check or change the folder in which Word stores your templates

3. In the File types list, click the type of file for which you want to see or change the path. For example, click the Workgroup templates item.

> **Tip** If the folder path is too long to appear fully in the Location column of the File Locations pane, click the Modify button to display the Open dialog box. You can then click the pop-up menu at the top of the dialog box to see the details of the path to the folder.

4. Click the Modify button to display the Open dialog box.

5. To choose or change the folder, navigate to the folder you want to use, click it, and then click the Open button. Word closes the Open dialog box and displays the new path (or as much of it as will fit) in the File Locations pane.

6. Choose or change any other file paths. For example, you may want to change the User Templates path.

7. Close the Preferences window by clicking the Close button (the red button at the left end of the title bar) or pressing Cmd+W.

Creating Backup Documents and Recovering from Disaster

Like the other Office apps, Word includes the AutoRecover feature that automatically saves versions of your documents as you work and offers you the chance to recover them when Word restarts after closing unexpectedly (see Chapter 5). But to keep your documents safe, it's a good idea to also turn on Word's feature for creating automatic backups. When you do so, you can also check that a couple of other important options are set correctly. Follow these steps:

1. Choose Word ➤ Preferences from the menu bar or press Cmd+, (Cmd and the comma key) to display the Word Preferences window.

2. In the Output and Sharing area, click the Save icon to display the Save preferences pane.

3. Select the "Always create backup copy" check box.

4. If you want Word to automatically save changes you make to the Normal template, such as AutoText entries or new keyboard shortcuts you've created, make sure the "Prompt to save Normal template" check box is cleared. Select this check box if you want Word to ask you to decide whether to save changes.

5. Close the Preferences window by clicking the Close button (the red button at the left end of the title bar) or pressing Cmd+W.

Now that you've selected the "Always create backup copy" check box, Word keeps one backup of each document. Here's how it does it:

- The first time you save, Word saves the document as normal. There's no backup.

- Each time you save the document after that, Word changes the name of the latest saved version of the document to the backup name and then saves the current version under the document name.

Word names the backup file *Backup of* and the document's name and keeps it in the same folder as the document. So if you create a document named `Merlot Tasting.docx`, Word names the backup file `Backup of Merlot Tasting.docx`.

Tip   Save your documents frequently to minimize the number of changes that are in the current version of the document but not in the backup version created from the previously saved version.

If a document becomes corrupted or if you delete a vital part of it and save the change, you can recover your work by opening the backup document.

Using Views and Windows to See What You Need

To work quickly and comfortably in your documents, you need to understand the five different views that Word provides and know when to use each of them. You may also need to open multiple windows on the same document so that you can work in different parts of it. Or you may want to split a single document window into two panes so that you can view the document differently in each.

Picking the Right View for What You're Doing

Each of Word's views has a distinct purpose, but you can use each view as much or as little as you want. Most likely, you will find some views much more useful than others for the types of documents you create and the Mac you work on.

You can switch from view to view in these ways:

- *Status bar*: Click the View buttons toward the right end of the status bar (see Figure 6-8) to switch to Print Layout view, Web Layout view, Outline view, or Draft view. You can't switch to Full Screen view this way.

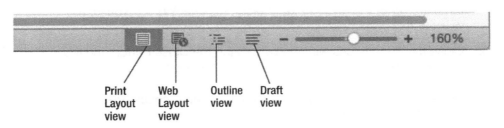

Print
Layout
view

Web
Layout
view

Outline
view

Draft
view

Figure 6-8. To change views quickly with the pointing device, click the view buttons near the right of the status bar. Hold the pointer over a view button to display a tooltip showing its name

- *Menu bar*: Choose View ➤ Print Layout, View ➤ Web Layout, View ➤ Outline, View ➤ Draft, or View ➤ Enter Full Screen.

- *Ribbon*: Choose View ➤ Views ➤ Print Layout, View ➤ Views ➤ Web Layout, View ➤ Views ➤ Outline, or View ➤ Views ➤ Draft.

- *Keyboard*: Press Cmd+Option+P for Print Layout view, Cmd+Option+O for Outline view, Cmd+Option+N for Draft view (which used to be called Normal view—hence the keystroke), or Cmd+Ctrl+F for Full Screen view. Web Layout view doesn't have a built-in keyboard shortcut, but you can create one as described in Chapter 5.

Using Print Layout View to See How a Document Will Look When Printed

For most documents, Word opens at first in Print Layout view (see Figure 6-9), which shows you the document as it will appear on paper. You can see each printable element in the document—text, tables, graphics, equations, and so on—in the positions they occupy on the page, along with the white space of the page margins. If you have added headers or footers to the document, you see them too.

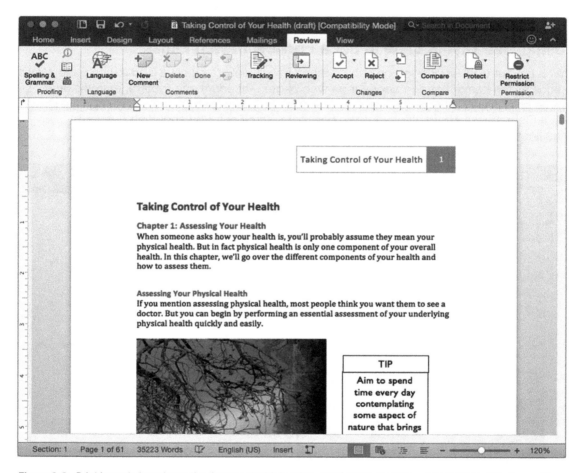

Figure 6-9. Print Layout view shows the document with headers and footers, margins, and graphics all in the positions they occupy on paper

Using Full Screen View to See More of a Document

Word uses the standard OS X version of Full Screen view, so when you choose View ➤ Enter Full Screen or press Cmd+Ctrl+F, your Mac expands the active Word window to fill the screen, hiding the OS X menu bar and the Word window's title bar. Beyond that, the view remains the same, so if you're using Print Layout view when you switch to Full Screen view, you'll see Print Layout view as big as it goes.

> **Note**   In Office 2011 for Mac, Word used a custom full-screen view that removed much of the
> Word interface in order to maximize your reading space. Word 2016 does not have this feature.

When you are ready to leave Full Screen view, you can move the pointer to the upper-left corner
of the screen, making the Word window's title bar and the OS X menu bar slide back into view,
and then either click the green Zoom button on the Word window or choose View ➤ Exit Full
Screen from the menu bar. Alternatively, press Cmd+Ctrl+F again, or simply press Esc.

Using Web Layout View to Get a Preview of Web Pages

Web Layout view shows you how the document will look if you save it as a web page. Word
hides all the items that don't appear on web pages—headers and footers, margins, and
page breaks—and wraps the lines to the width of the window, just as a web browser does
(see Figure 6-10). Word also hides the horizontal scroll bar; you shouldn't need it because
the lines are wrapped.

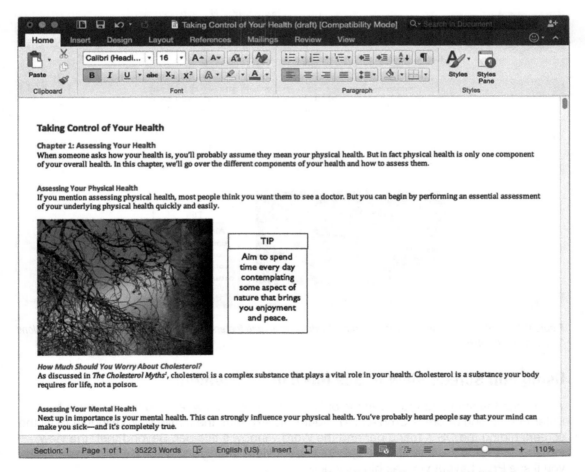

*Figure 6-10. Web Layout view displays the page as if it were in a web browser, with no headers and footers, margins,
or page breaks*

Developing a Document in Outline View

Outline view is a powerful tool for developing the outline and structure of a document. Outline view displays the document as a structure of headings, each of which you can collapse or expand as needed (see Figure 6-11). See Chapter 8 for instructions on using Outline view.

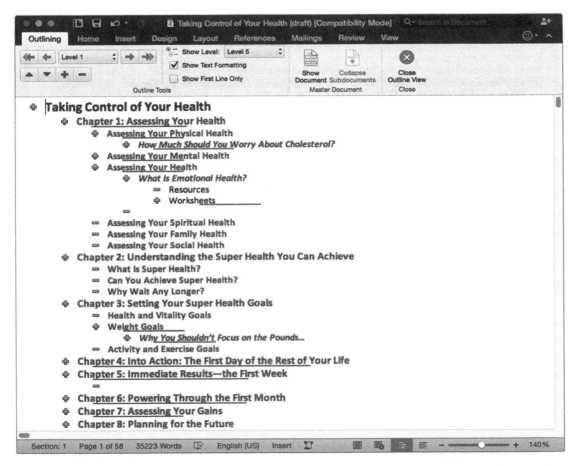

Figure 6-11. Outline view is a great tool for working on the structure of a document. You can expand different sections of the document to different levels as needed

Using Draft View

Draft view, which used to be called Normal view, is great for working with the body text of a document. You see all the text, but Word hides items such as headers and footers, margins, and objects. Figure 6-12 shows Draft view.

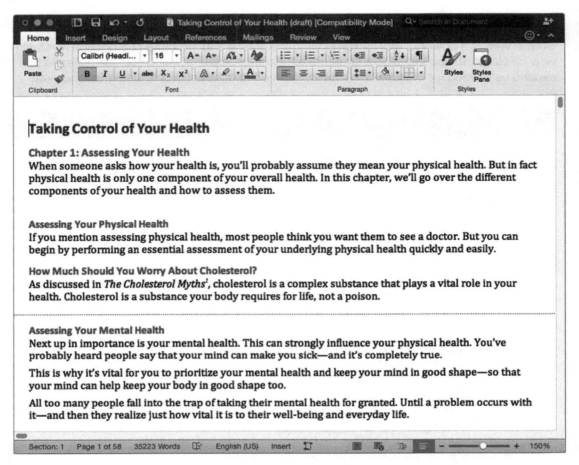

Figure 6-12. Draft view enables you to concentrate on the text of the document without worrying about layout elements such as headers and footers. To display as much text as possible and avoid having white space on the right side of the window (as shown here), turn on the Wrap to window feature

Tip   Draft view is usually easiest to use if you make Word wrap the text to the window so that the text fills the window—otherwise, you'll often get blank space on the right side of the window, or you may have to scroll horizontally to reach the end of the lines. Word doesn't do this by default. To make Word wrap the text, choose Word ➤ Preferences to display the Word Preferences window, and then click the View icon in the Authoring and Proofing Tools section. In the View preferences pane, select the Wrap to window check box in the Show Window Elements area. Close the Preferences window by clicking the Close button (the red button at the left end of the title bar) or pressing Cmd+W.

Opening Extra Windows

At first, Word displays a single window of each document. For short documents, this is all you need, but for long or complex documents, you may find it helpful to open extra windows so that you can see two or more parts of the document at once or use different views.

For example, when you're writing a lengthy report, you may benefit from seeing the introduction as you write the conclusion, to make sure you nail each of your main points. Or you may want to open a window showing the outline of a document so that you can add headings and change its structure even as you write regular text in one of its sections.

Here's how to open and work with extra windows:

- *Open a new window*: Choose View ➤ Arrange ➤ New Window from the Ribbon or Window ➤ New Window from the menu bar. Word adds ": 1" to the document's name in the title bar of the original window to indicate that it's now the first window of the document. The second window's name includes ": 2"—for example, Linguistics Report: 2.

- *Arrange your Word windows*: Click and drag the windows to where you need them.

> **Note**   Word includes an Arrange All command (choose View ➤ Arrange ➤ Arrange All from the Ribbon or Window ➤ Arrange All from the menu bar), but it tiles the Word windows horizontally, which usually isn't what you want. Normally it's best to arrange your windows manually, but you can also use a third-party utility such as Divvy (www.mizage.com/divvy/) or SizeUp (http://irradiatedsoftware.com/sizeup/) or create a macro using Visual Basic for Applications (VBA). If possible, try such a third-party utility before buying it because the Office apps appear to disagree with some of them.

- *Switch from window to window*: If you can see the window you want, click it. Otherwise, choose View ➤ Switch Windows ➤ Switch Windows from the Ribbon, or open the Window menu on the menu bar, and then click the window you want on the list at the bottom.

> **Tip**   Press Cmd+F6 or Option+F6 to display the next window (of any open Word document, not just the one that has multiple windows open). Press Cmd+Shift+F6 or Option+Shift+F6 to display the previous window.

- *Close a window*: Click the window's Close button (the red button at the left end of the title bar). The document remains open until you close its last window.

Splitting the Document Window into Two Panes

Sometimes it's useful to split the document window into two panes so that you can work in two different parts of the same document at once. Splitting the document window is like opening a new window except that you don't need more space. Figure 6-13 shows the document window split, with the upper pane showing Print Layout view and the lower pane showing Outline view.

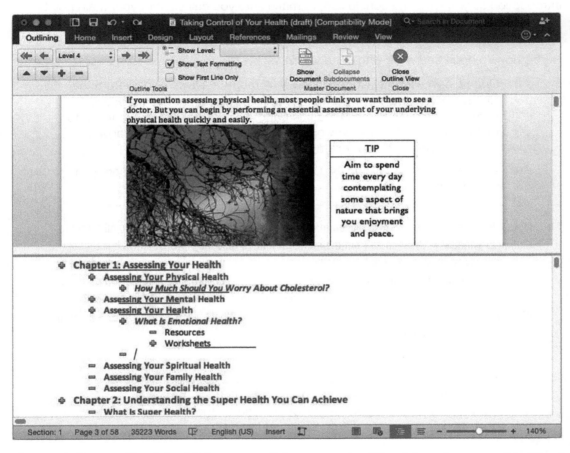

Figure 6-13. You can split a window into two panes so that you can use two different views at once or work in different parts of the document

To split the document window into two equal parts, choose View ➤ Arrange ➤ Split from the Ribbon or Window ➤ Split from the menu bar. You can also press Cmd+Option+S. You can then adjust the split by dragging the split bar up or down as needed.

Once you've split the window, you can scroll each pane separately so you can display a different part of the document in each pane. You can also use a different view in each pane; for example, you can display the document's outline in Outline view in one pane while you write the introduction or summary in Normal view in the other pane.

To switch to the other pane, click in it or press F6.

> **Tip**   You can also zoom out in one pane to get an overview of the document as a whole, and you can zoom in using the other pane so that you can see the detail of a section.

When you want to remove the split, take one of these actions:

- *Pointing device*: Drag the split bar to the top of the window (to keep the lower pane) or to the bottom (to keep the upper pane).

- *Keyboard*: Press Cmd+Option+S.

- *Ribbon*: Choose View ➤ Arrange ➤ Remove Split.

- *Menu bar*: Choose Window ➤ Remove Split.

Summary

In this chapter, you learned new tricks for inserting text quickly and easily in Word document, including how to insert the text from an existing document and how to create AutoText entries to reuse boilerplate text. You also grasped how to select blocks of text using the Option-drag maneuver and the Extend Selection feature, and learned new ways of navigating around a document using keyboard shortcuts and the browse object.

Better yet, you now know how to get Word to make automatic backups of your documents, how to make the most of Word's views, and how to open extra windows or split a single window into two panes.

In the next chapter, you'll learn how to save any amount of time by formatting your documents the right way—by using Word's powerful styles.

Chapter 7

Formatting Your Documents Swiftly and Easily

To make your documents look good, you must apply formatting to the text and other elements in them. That's probably obvious, but Word gives you such a wide range of formatting options that it's easy to use the wrong ones. This chapter teaches you the right way to format a document quickly and consistently by using styles—collections of formatting—rather than by applying direct formatting piece by piece. It also shows you how to use the Sidebar pane and the Find feature to navigate your documents and how to make the most of the versatile Replace feature.

Before we start, a word of warning: styles are an extremely powerful tool that can save you huge amounts of time—but you will need to invest some time and effort in understanding how they work before you can harness all their power. To complicate things, Word provides several different tools for working with styles, and the way these tools interact and overlap takes some getting used to. But once you get the hang of them, you'll find that you can work swiftly and effectively with them.

Understanding Word's Many Types of Formatting

Word gives you such a wide variety of formatting that it's easy to waste time by using the wrong ones for your needs. This section explains the different types of formatting and shows you the best and fastest way to use them.

Understanding Direct Formatting and When to Use It

Where most people start is by using direct formatting, the kind of formatting that you can apply by using the controls in the Font group and the Paragraph group on the Home tab of the Ribbon (see Figure 7-1). For example, you can create a heading paragraph by changing to a different font, increasing the font size, changing the font color, giving it an "outdent" so that it sticks out into the margin, and adding extra space before and after the paragraph.

© Guy Hart-Davis 2016
G. Hart-Davis, *Learn Office 2016 for Mac*, DOI 10.1007/978-1-4842-2002-3_7

Figure 7-1. *You can easily apply direct formatting such as font formatting and paragraph formatting using the Font group and Paragraph group controls on the Ribbon, but you can save time and effort by applying styles from the Styles group or the Quick Style panel first*

Each part of this formatting is easy enough to apply—click this, click that, click the other—but it takes time. And if you need to create another heading of the same type, you need to do it all over again. Or you can copy and paste the formatted paragraph and type the new heading over it (as many people do) or use Word's clever Format Painter feature (which you'll learn about later in this chapter).

Because direct formatting takes extra time and effort, it's best to apply it only when you have formatted your documents almost completely using better tools, as discussed next.

Understanding Styles and When to Use Them

To help you apply standard formatting quickly, Word includes a feature called styles. A *style* is a collection of formatting that you can apply all at once. So, once you've set up a style for the heading that contains exactly the formatting you want, you can apply it in a single click.

In fact, in many cases you don't even need to create the styles yourself. Word comes with many styles built in to its Normal template and other templates. As soon as you create a document based on one of these templates, you can start applying styles, formatting your documents swiftly and consistently.

Word gives you four different types of styles:

- *Paragraph style*: This is a style you apply to a whole paragraph at a time—you can't apply it to just part of a paragraph. A paragraph style contains a full range of formatting for that paragraph: everything from the font name, size, and color to the indentation and spacing for the paragraph, and the language used. For example, many documents use a Body Text style that gives a distinctive look to the body paragraphs.

- *Character style*: This is a style you apply to individual characters within a paragraph, usually to make it look different from the style of the rest of the paragraph. For example, within a paragraph that uses the Body Text style, you can apply an Emphasis character style to a word to make it stand out.

- *Table style*: This is a style you can apply to a Word table. Like a paragraph style, the style can contain font and paragraph formatting, but it can also contain table formatting such as borders and shading.

- *List style*: This is a style you can apply to one or more paragraphs to make them into a list—a numbered list, a bulleted list, or a multilevel list. A list style usually contains font formatting and numbering formatting.

Styles enable you not only to apply formatting quickly but also to change the formatting by modifying or replacing the style:

- *Modify the style*: If the style doesn't look right, you can modify it. Each paragraph to which you've applied the style takes on the changes you make immediately.

- *Replace one style with another style*: You can replace every instance of one style with another style in moments, making sweeping changes right through a document.

Formatting Your Documents the Best Way

Here's the best way to format your documents:

- First, format each paragraph with a paragraph style. This style gives the whole paragraph its overall look. If the paragraph is a heading, the Heading style tells Word to include the paragraph in the document's outline.

- Next, use character styles to add extra formatting within paragraphs. For example, use a character style such as Emphasis to add impact to a word or phrase that you want to stand out.

- If the document contains lists, apply the appropriate list style to each list. For example, apply a numbered list style to a list that needs numbers, or apply a bulleted list style to a list that needs bullets.

- If the document contains tables, apply a suitable table style to each table.

UNDERSTANDING WHERE WORD KEEPS STYLES

Word keeps styles in templates and documents. As you learned in Chapter 1, a template is a file that contains the basic structure of a document, such as the structure of a business letter. When you create a new document, you can choose whether to base it on a particular template or on the Normal template that Word uses for "blank" documents.

The styles available from the Styles group and the Styles panel when you first open Word are the ones stored in the Normal template. You can customize these styles as needed, but be aware that the changes carry through to all documents based on the Normal template.

When you create or open a document based on a template other than the Normal template, Word makes that template's styles available in the Styles group and the Styles panel. If the template is one that comes with Word or one that you've downloaded from the Web, it will most likely contain its own styles. You can modify these styles if you need to do so.

When you create a new template, you can create all the custom styles you need. You can also import styles from other templates or documents to save time.

Even though each document picks up the details of the styles from the attached template, the document itself contains information about the styles. This enables Word to display the document correctly when the template is not available.

When you're working in a document and modify a style, you can choose whether to save the changes in that document or in the template attached to the document. Normally you'll want to save the changes in the template, making them available to all existing documents based on the template and any new documents you create based on the template. By contrast, changes you save in the document are available only to that document (and to other documents you base on it).

Applying Styles to a Document

Word 2016 gives you three main ways of applying styles to a document:

- *Ribbon*: Use the Quick Style box and Quick Style panel on the Home tab. The Quick Style box and Quick Style panel together make up what Microsoft calls the Quick Style Gallery.

- *Styles pane*: Open the Styles pane and use it to apply styles or work with styles.

- *Styles dialog box*: Open the Style dialog box, and use it to apply a style.

Each method has its pros and cons. Let's look at each method in turn.

Applying Styles from the Quick Style Box and Quick Style Panel on the Ribbon

Usually, the easiest way to get started with styles is to apply styles by using the Quick Style box and Quick Style panel on the Home tab of the Ribbon. Follow these steps:

1. Click in the paragraph to which you want to apply the style. If you want to apply the style to several paragraphs at once, select all or part of each paragraph.

2. Apply the style:

    - If the style name is in the Quick Style box that appears in the Styles group, click it.

    - If the style name doesn't appear in the Styles group, hold the pointer over the Quick Style box to display the panel button, and then click the panel button to display the Quick Style panel (see Figure 7-2). Then click the style name.

> **Note** You can also click the left-arrow button on the left of the Quick Style box to scroll the list of displayed styles to the right or click the right-arrow button on the right of the Quick Style box to scroll the list to the left. But usually it's easier to simply display the Quick Style panel so that you can see all the styles in the Quick Style Gallery, and then click the style you want.

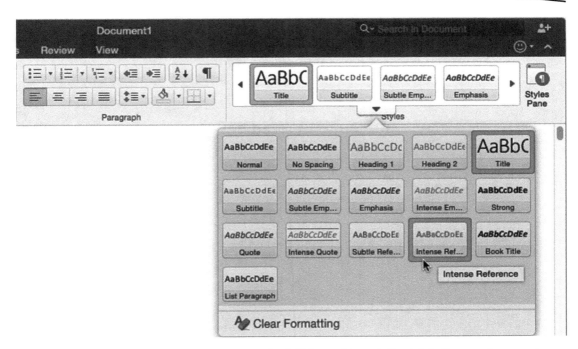

Figure 7-2. Click a style in the Quick Style box or the Quick Style panel to apply the style to the current paragraph or selected paragraphs

> **Tip**   Never use the Normal style as the formatting for the body of your documents. The problem is that Word uses the Normal style as the default, so it can be hard to tell whether you've applied the Normal style or Word has applied it because you haven't applied another style. For the body text in your documents, use a style such as Body Text instead, keeping the Normal style only for text you still need to give a style. You can then search (as described later in this chapter) for the Normal style and apply another style to each instance of it as needed.

Applying Styles with the Styles Pane

When you need to work extensively with styles, use the Styles pane. Choose Home ➤ Styles ➤ Styles Pane to display the Styles pane. As you can see in Figure 7-3, the Styles pane at first appears docked to the right side of the Word window; if you prefer, you can drag it by the title bar to undock it, and then move it freely either within the Word window or outside the Word window.

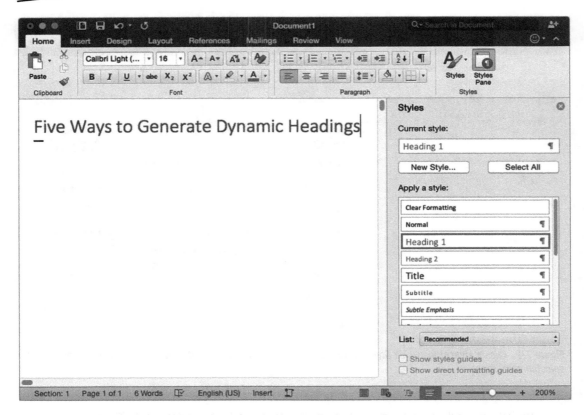

Figure 7-3. *The Styles pane is the best choice for extensive work with styles. The ¶ symbol to the right of a style's name indicates a paragraph style; the letter a indicates a character style*

In the Styles pane, you can take the following actions:

- *Check the current style*: The Current style box at the top of the pane shows the style of the current paragraph or selected text.

- *Start creating a new style*: Click the New Style button.

- *Select all instances of the current style*: Click the Select All button. By selecting all instances, you can then apply another style easily.

- *Apply another style*: In the Apply a style list box, click the style you want to apply.

- *Choose which styles to show in the list*: Many Word templates contain large numbers of styles, so you don't necessarily want all the styles to appear in the Styles pane. Use the List pop-up menu to control which styles do appear. Your choices are as follows:

  - *Recommended*: Click this item to display the styles that Word recommends for widespread use in documents of this type.

  - *Styles in Use*: Click this item to restrict the list to the styles you're currently using in the documents based on this template.

- *In Current Document*: Click this item to restrict the list to the styles the current document uses so far. This is often a good choice once you've applied most of the styles you intend to use for the document at least once.

- *All Styles*: Click this item to display the full list of styles. You'll need to scroll up and down to find the styles you need.

- *Toggle styles guides on and off*: Select the Show Styles Guides check box to display a color-coded number next to each paragraph in Print Layout view showing the style. The Styles pane shows the color-coded numbers next to their styles. For example, in Figure 7-4, the Heading 1 style has the number 1 and is applied to the top paragraph.

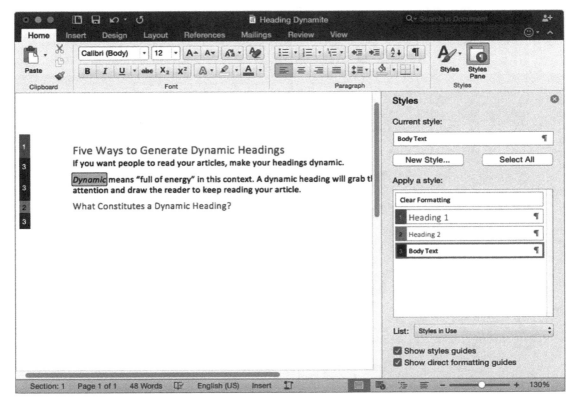

Figure 7-4. Select the Show Styles Guides check box in the Styles pane to display color-coded numbers showing the styles. Select the Show Direct Formatting Guides check box to display boxes around the text that has direct formatting applied, such as "Dynamic" in the second body paragraph

- *Toggle direct formatting guides on and off*: Select the Show Direct Formatting Guides check box to make Word display a box around each item that contains direct formatting. For example, in Figure 7-4, the word *Dynamic* in the second paragraph has direct italic formatting applied.

> **Tip**   After displaying the direct formatting guides, click one of the boxes to see the details of the formatting applied. The Current style box at the top of the Styles pane shows the details, such as Body Text + Italic. If you want to remove the direct formatting, hold the pointer over the Current style box, click the pop-up button to display the pop-up menu, and then click Clear Formatting.

- *Select all instances of a style*: Move the pointer over the style name in the Apply a style list so that a pop-up arrow appears, click the arrow to display the pop-up menu (see Figure 7-5), and then click the Select All item on the menu.

Figure 7-5. Use the pop-up menu for a style to access the Select All command, the Modify Style command, the Delete command, and the Update to Match Selection command

- *Open the Modify Style dialog box*: Open the pop-up menu for the style, and then click the Modify Style item.
- *Delete a style*: Open the pop-up menu for the style, and then click the Delete item. This item isn't available for key built-in styles such as Heading 1 and Normal.

- *Update a style to match the selection*: When you've applied a style but then changed it with direct formatting, you can update the style so that it takes on the direct formatting. To do this, select the paragraph, open the pop-up menu for the style, and then click the Update to Match Selection item.

Applying Styles Using the Style Dialog Box

The third way of applying styles is to use the Style dialog box. This method is sometimes useful, but generally it's more awkward than using the Styles pane.

To apply a style using the Style dialog box, follow these steps:

1. Click in the paragraph to which you want to apply the style, or select the text that'll receive the style.

2. Choose Format ➤ Style to open the Style dialog box (see Figure 7-6).

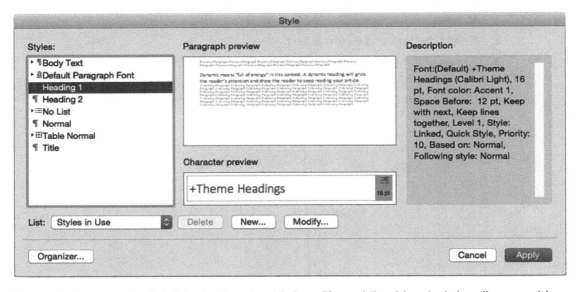

Figure 7-6. You can use the Style dialog box to apply a style, to modify an existing style, or to start creating a new style

3. In the Styles list box, click the style you want to apply.

Note   If the style you're looking for doesn't appear in the Styles list box, open the List pop-up menu and choose All Styles instead of Styles in Use or User-Defined Styles.

4. Click the Apply button. Word closes the Style dialog box and applies the style.

Changing the Styles in the Quick Style Gallery

The Quick Style Gallery on the Home tab of the Ribbon includes a selection of styles to get you started. But if you apply styles frequently from the Quick Style box or Quick Style panel, as is handy, you may want to customize the selection of styles in the Quick Style Gallery.

You can customize the Quick Style Gallery like this:

- *Remove an existing style*: In either the Quick Style box or the Quick Style panel, Ctrl-click or right-click the style, and then click Remove from Quick Style Gallery on the context menu.

- *Add an existing style*: In the Apply a style list in the Styles pane, hold the pointer over the style, click the pop-up button, and then click the Modify Style item. In the Modify Style dialog box, select the Add to Quick Style list, and then click the OK button.

- *Create a new style and add it*: Follow these steps:

    1. Format some text with the formatting you want the new style to have.

    2. Select the text you've formatted.

    3. Choose Home ➤ Styles ➤ Styles Pane to display the Styles pane if it's not already displayed.

    4. Click the New Style button to display the New Style dialog box (see Figure 7-7).

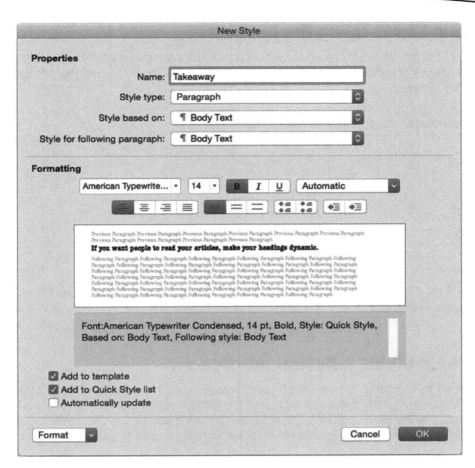

Figure 7-7. Select the Add to Quick Style list check box in the New Style dialog box to make Word add the new style to the Quick Style Gallery

5. In the Name box, type the name you want the style to have.

6. Choose other settings for the style as needed. You'll dig into these in the section "Creating Custom Styles" later in this chapter.

7. Select the Add to template check box if you want to add the style to the template. This is usually a good idea.

8. Make sure the "Add to Quick Style list" check box is selected.

9. Click the OK button. Word closes the New Style dialog box and adds the style to the Quick Style Gallery. You can then apply it like any other style.

Applying Styles Using the Keyboard

You can also apply styles by using keyboard shortcuts, which is useful when you're typing. Table 7-1 shows standard keyboard shortcuts, which work in Word's Normal template and in many other templates.

Table 7-1. Standard Keyboard Shortcuts for Applying Styles in Word

Style	Keyboard Shortcut
Normal	Cmd+Shift+N
Heading 1	Cmd+Option+1
Heading 2	Cmd+Option+2
Heading 3	Cmd+Option+3

> **Tip**   If you want to apply other styles from the keyboard, create keyboard shortcuts for them, as discussed in Chapter 5.

See Which Styles a Document Uses

To see which style a particular paragraph uses, you can click in the paragraph and look at the style selected in the Styles pane or the Quick Style Gallery controls on the Ribbon. In Print Layout view, you can also select the Show Styles Guides check box in the Styles pane to display the color-coded numbered boxes to the left of the text, as discussed earlier in this chapter.

To see the style applied to each paragraph in Draft view and Outline view, you can open the style area, which is a vertical strip at the left side of the Word window that displays the style applied to each paragraph (see Figure 7-8).

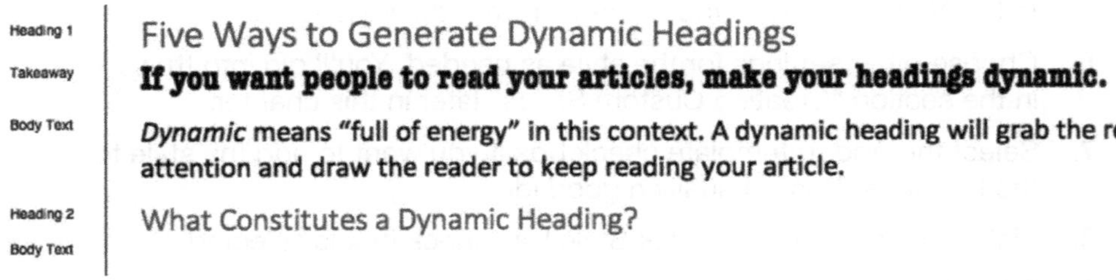

Heading 1	Five Ways to Generate Dynamic Headings
Takeaway	**If you want people to read your articles, make your headings dynamic.**
Body Text	*Dynamic* means "full of energy" in this context. A dynamic heading will grab the reader's attention and draw the reader to keep reading your article.
Heading 2	What Constitutes a Dynamic Heading?
Body Text	

Figure 7-8. In Draft view and Outline view, you can display the style area on the left side of the window to see the style applied to each paragraph

To display the style area, follow these steps:

1. Choose Word ➤ Preferences from the menu bar or press Cmd+, (Cmd and the comma key) to display the Word Preferences window.

2. In the Authoring and Proofing Tools area, click the View icon to display the View preferences pane.

3. In the Show Window Elements area, enter the measurement in the Style area width box. One inch is usually about right.

4. Close the Preferences window by clicking the Close button (the red button at the left end of the title bar) or pressing Cmd+W.

Now click the Draft button to the left of the zoom control on the status bar to switch to Draft view, or click the Outline button to switch to Outline view. The style area appears on the left of the screen, and you can easily see the style applied to each paragraph.

> **Tip**   To change the width of the style area, move the pointer over the line that divides the style area from the text. When the pointer changes to a double-headed arrow, click and drag the line to the width you want. Drag the line all the way to the left to close the style area.

Creating Custom Styles

If you find that Word's styles don't meet your needs, you can either create custom styles of your own or customize the built-in styles to make them suitable. The easiest way to create a custom style is by example, and that's the way you'll look at first. After that, you'll also see how to create a new style by specifying its formatting in the New Style dialog box.

Creating a Custom Style by Example

To create a custom style by example, you set up a paragraph or other object with the formatting you want. You then tell Word to create a style from that formatted text so you can reapply the style wherever you need it.

Type a paragraph of text to use as a sample, or pick an existing paragraph in the document. If Word has an existing style that's similar to the style you want to create, apply that style first so you don't need to make as many formatting changes.

Choosing the Font Formatting for a Style

Often, you'll want to start by choosing the font formatting for the style. You can do so by using any of the standard tools:

- *Font group*: Use the controls in the Font group of the Home tab of the Ribbon.

■ *Font dialog box*: Choose Format ➤ Font or press Cmd+D to open the Font dialog box. On the Font tab (see Figure 7-9), choose the font, font style, size, color, underline, and other effects you need (for example, small caps). Click the OK button when you've finished.

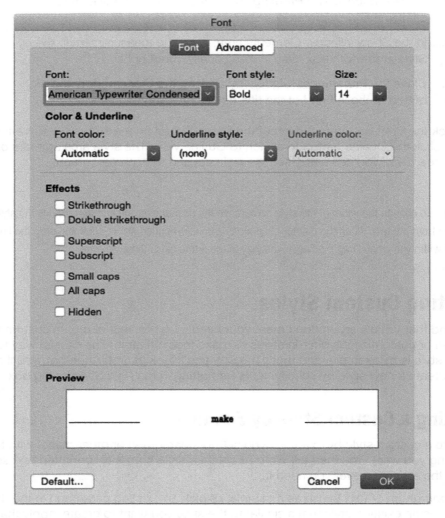

Figure 7-9. You can quickly choose font formatting on the Font tab of the Font dialog box

Note   On the Advanced tab of the Font dialog box, you can change the scaling, spacing, and position of fonts. For example, you can change the spacing to spread the letters farther apart, or you can choose the Raised position to create a superscript. You can also work with typography features such as ligatures (two letters joined together), which you normally need only if you're typesetting a document.

Choosing the Paragraph Formatting for the Style

You can set some paragraph formatting for your sample paragraph by using the controls in the Paragraph group on the Home tab of the Ribbon, but you'll usually want to open the Paragraph dialog box so you can reach all the most useful types of paragraph formatting.

To choose paragraph formatting, follow these steps:

1. Choose Format ➤ Paragraph on the menu bar, or press Cmd+Option+M to open the Paragraph dialog box.

2. On the Indents and Spacing tab (see Figure 7-10), choose settings like this:

   ■ *Alignment*: Choose Left, Centered, Right, or Justified, as needed. Justified text is aligned with both margins.

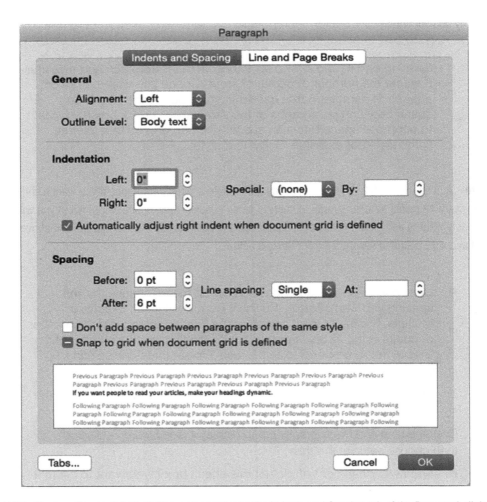

Figure 7-10. Choose alignment, indentation, and spacing on the Indents and Spacing tab of the Paragraph dialog box

- *Outline level*: If you want Word to treat this style as a type of heading, click the appropriate level, from Level 1 (a top-level item) down to Level 9. Choose Body Text (the default setting) if you want Word to treat paragraphs of this style as regular body text.

- *Indentation*: In the Left box and the Right box, set any indentation needed from the margins. To create a first-line indent, choose First line in the Special pop-up menu, and then set the distance in the By box. You can also create a hanging indent (also known as an *outdent*) by choosing Hanging in the Special pop-up menu.

> **Note**   Select the "Automatically adjust right indent when document grid is defined" check box If you want Word to automatically adjust the right indent when the document contains a custom grid. This grid is normally invisible and is used for placing graphical objects (such as images or shapes) quickly and accurately.

- *Spacing before and after paragraphs*: In the Before box and the After box, set the number of points of empty space you want before or after each paragraph that uses this style. Select the "Don't add space between paragraphs of the same style" check box if you want to suppress space between successive paragraphs that use the same style (for example, Body Text style).

> **Note**   A point (pt) is 1/72-inch. Try six points after single-spaced paragraphs if you want a small gap, or try 12 points for a larger gap. Body text doesn't usually need space before it, but you will probably want to add 12–24 points of space before a heading to separate it from the text above it, and about 12 points to separate it from the text below.

- *Line spacing*: In the Line Spacing pop-up menu, choose the line spacing you want: Single, 1.5 lines, Double, At least, Exactly, or Multiple. For the At least setting or the Exactly setting, set the number of points in the At box. For the Multiple setting, set the number of lines in the At box—for example, use **3** to set three-line spacing.

- *Snap to grid*: Select the "Snap to grid when document grid is defined" check box if you want objects to snap automatically to the document grid.

3. Click the Line and Page Breaks tab to display it (see Figure 7-11), and then choose settings like this:

- *Widow/Orphan control*: Select this check box if you want to avoid a single line appearing at the top of a page (a widow) and a single line appearing at the end of a page (an orphan), each separated from the rest of its paragraph. Normal typesetting practice is to suppress both widows and orphans.

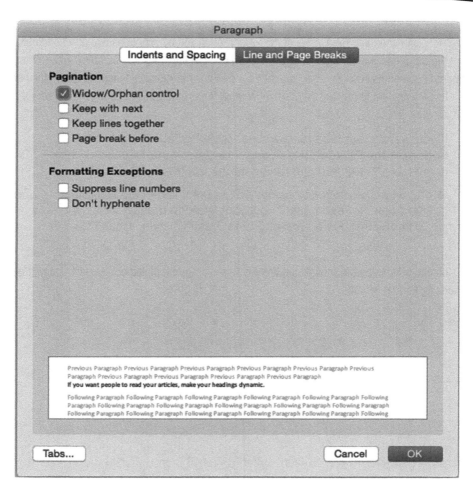

Figure 7-11. In the Line and Page Breaks tab of the Paragraph dialog box, you can tell Word whether to keep a paragraph with the next paragraph or add a page break before it

- *Keep with next*: Select this check box to make Word keep the paragraph on the same page as the next paragraph. Typically, you'll set this option for a heading style to prevent Word from putting it at the bottom of a page with the following paragraph on the next page. Don't use this option for body text paragraphs, or they'll end up bouncing from one page to the following page so that they can stay together.

- *Keep lines together*: Select this check box to make Word keep all the lines of a paragraph on the same page rather than breaking the paragraph across pages. This setting is useful for headings and display paragraphs, but not for body text.

- *Page break before*: Select this check box to have Word start a new page each time the style occurs. You normally use this only for styles such as chapter headings.

Note   The Line and Page Breaks tab of the Paragraph dialog box contains two other settings. Select the Suppress line numbers check box if you want to suppress line numbers (in automatically numbered documents such as legal papers) for a particular paragraph. Select the Don't hyphenate check box if you want to prevent Word's hyphenation feature from hyphenating the paragraph.

4. If you want to set tabs for the style, click the Tabs button at the bottom of the Paragraph dialog box to display the Tabs dialog box (see Figure 7-12). You can then set tabs like this:

    ■   *Change the default spacing*: Adjust the value in the Default tab stops text box. For example, if you want Word to move 1 inch each time you press Tab in a paragraph that has this style, enter **1"**.

Tip   Instead of opening the Tabs dialog box from the Paragraph dialog box, you can open it directly by choosing Format ➤ Tabs.

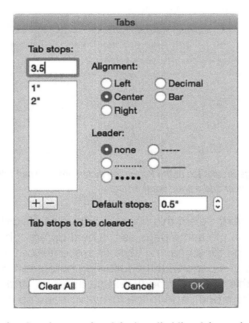

Figure 7-12. Use the Tabs dialog box to set any custom tab stops that the style needs

    ■   *Set a new tab stop*: In the Tab stop position text box, type the position for the tab, such as **1"**. Click the appropriate option button in the Alignment area, such as the Left option button. If you want to use tab leader characters, click the appropriate option button in the Leader area. Then click the Add (+) button.

> **Note**   A left tab is the usual kind: the text starts left-aligned at the position of the tab stop. A center tab centers the text around the tab stop and is widely used in headers and footers that have a left section (at the left margin), a center section (with a center tab), and a right section (with a right tab). A right tab makes the right part of the text align with the tab stop, so as you type, the text moves back to the left. A decimal tab aligns the text with the decimal point, enabling you to align numbers with different numbers of decimal places (for example, 123.45 and 678.9). A bar tab is a way of creating a vertical line but is little used these days.

- *Delete an existing tab stop*: Click the tab in the Tab stop position list box, and then click the Delete (–) button. Click the Clear All button if you want to delete all the tabs.

- *Move or change a tab stop*: Delete the tab stop you want to change, and create a new tab stop with the position and alignment you want.

5. When you've finished setting tabs for the style, click the OK button to close the Tabs dialog box.

Adding Bullets or Numbering to the Style

If you're creating a list style, add whichever bullets or numbering it needs. The quick way to add bullets or numbering is to use the first three controls in the Paragraph group on the Home tab of the Ribbon. Click the Bullets pop-up button, the Numbering pop-up button, or the Multilevel List pop-up button in the Paragraph group to open the panel, and then click the style you want to apply. Figure 7-13 shows the Numbering panel.

> **Note**   You can also apply the default style of bullets, numbering, or multilevel list by clicking the button itself (for example, the Bullets button) rather than the drop-down button. If you need to customize bulleted or numbered lists, choose Format ➤ Bullets and Numbering from the menu bar, and then work in the Bullets and Numbering dialog box.

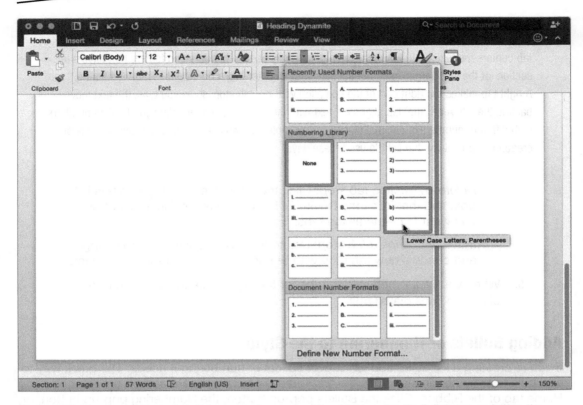

Figure 7-13. You can quickly apply bullets, numbering, or a multilevel list by using the Bullets pop-up button, the Numbering pop-up button, or the Multilevel List pop-up button in the Paragraph group of the Home tab

Adding Borders and Shading to the Style

Next, add any borders or shading that the style needs. You can apply individual borders by clicking the Home ➤ Paragraph ➤ Borders pop-up button and then clicking the border you want in the panel, but you can get greater control by choosing Format ➤ Borders and Shading from the menu bar to display the Borders and Shading dialog box.

To add borders, click the Borders tab of the Borders and Shading dialog box (see Figure 7-14), and then work like this:

1. In the Apply to pop-up menu, choose Paragraph if you want to apply the border to the whole paragraph. Choose Text if you want to put the border only around the text.

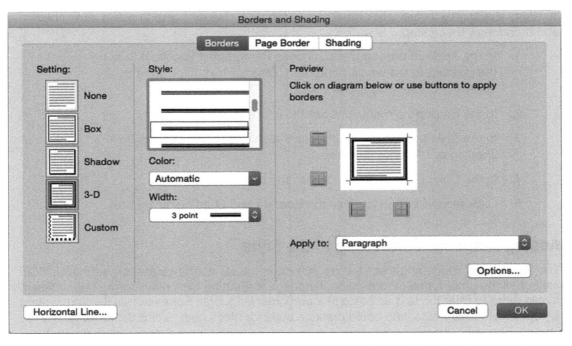

Figure 7-14. Use the Borders tab of the Borders and Shading dialog box to quickly apply borders to a paragraph

2. To apply a standard border, click Box, Shadow, or 3-D in the Setting area. To create a custom border, click the borders in the diagram in the Preview area to place borders where you want them. When you click a border in the diagram, Word selects the Custom item in the Setting area.

3. Change the border's appearance by using the Style list, the Color pop-up menu, and the Width pop-up menu.

> **Note**   To move the borders closer to the text or farther away from it, click the Options button. In the Borders and Shading Options dialog box that opens, adjust the Top, Bottom, Left, and Right measurements, and then click the OK button.

4. Click the OK button to close the Borders and Shading dialog box.

> **Note**   A paragraph border is usually the most useful kind of border for a style, but if you're creating a style that will occupy most (or all) of a page, you may want to create a page border in the style. In this case, click the Page Border tab in the Borders and Shading dialog box, select the appropriate document part in the Apply to pop-up menu (for example, select the This section item), and then work with the border controls in the same way as for applying a paragraph border.

To apply shading to a style, click the Shading tab in the Borders and Shading dialog box, and then follow these steps:

1. In the Apply to pop-up menu, choose Paragraph if you want to apply the shading to the whole paragraph. Choose Text if you want to apply the border only to the text.

2. In the Fill pop-up menu, choose the shading color you want.

3. In the Style pop-up menu, choose the shading style, such as 25% shading or Dk Trellis shading.

4. In the Color pop-up menu, choose the pattern color.

5. Click the OK button to close the Borders and Shading dialog box.

Adding Language Formatting to the Style

The final type of formatting that you can include in the style is language formatting. Unlike almost all the other types of formatting, language formatting isn't visual formatting. Instead, it tells Word to treat the text as being in a particular language. For example, if you're writing a paper on French poets, you could create a style for block quotes and set its language to French. The spell checker would then refrain from querying the words as not being in the English language.

> **Note**   When you apply language formatting, the text you format doesn't actually have to be in the language you specify, but you're telling Word to treat it as if it is.

To apply language formatting to text, follow these steps:

1. Choose Tools ➤ Language to display the Language dialog box (see Figure 7-15).

Figure 7-15. In the Language dialog box, you can specify the language used for the text. You can also turn off spelling and grammar checking for the style

2. In the "Mark selected text as" list box, select the language you want to use. Your current language appears at the top of the list to save you from having to scroll to find it.

3. If you want to tell the spell checker and grammar checker not to check the text, select the "Do not check spelling or grammar" check box. This setting is useful for styles you use for text that will contain apparent misspellings, such as computer code.

4. Click the OK button to close the Language dialog box.

Creating the Style

Once you have set up the paragraph with all the formatting it needs, you can create a style like this:

1. Select the paragraph.

2. Choose Home ➤ Styles ➤ Styles Pane from the Ribbon to open the Styles pane.

3. Click the New Style button to display the New Style dialog box (shown in Figure 7-7, earlier in this chapter).

4. Type the name for the style in the Name text box.

5. In the Style type pop-up menu, choose the style type: Paragraph, Character, Table, or List.

6. In the "Style for following paragraph" pop-up menu, choose the style you want Word to apply automatically to the next paragraph when you press the Return key at the end of a paragraph with this style. For a display style (such as a heading), you will normally want a body style next; for a body style, you will probably want to continue with the same body style.

7. Select the Add to template check box if you want Word to add this style to the document's template so that it will be available for other documents. Usually, this is helpful. If you clear this check box, Word stores the style in the document, where other documents can't use it.

8. Select the "Add to Quick Style list" check box if you want Word to include this style in the Quick Style Gallery. Otherwise, clear this check box.

9. Clear the Automatically update check box unless you want Word to update the style without consulting you when it thinks you've altered the style. Automatic updating is well intended but usually confusing.

10. Click the OK button to close the New Style dialog box.

> **Note**   If you need to make any other changes to the style's formatting after you've opened the New Style dialog box, use the formatting controls in the middle of the New Style dialog box or the Format pop-up menu in the lower-left corner. For example, to change the paragraph formatting, click the Format pop-up menu, and then click Paragraph to display the Paragraph dialog box.

Modifying an Existing Style

You can modify an existing style by opening it in the Modify Style dialog box and working from there. You can also change the formatting of a paragraph of text that uses the style and then make the style pick up your changes.

Changing a Style Using the Modify Style Dialog Box

The more formal way of modifying an existing style is to open the style in the Modify Style dialog box, which is a renamed version of the New Style dialog box. You can then use the formatting controls and the options on the Format pop-up menu to adjust the style exactly as you need it.

You can open the Modify Style dialog box from the Styles pane, the Quick Style Gallery, or the Style dialog box:

- *Styles pane*: Move the pointer over the style name, click the pop-up button, and then click Modify Style.

- *Quick Style Gallery*: Ctrl-click or right-click the style name, and then click Modify on the context menu.

- *Style dialog box*: Select the style in the Styles list box, and then click the Modify button.

Updating a Style with New Formatting

Instead of modifying an existing style as described in the previous section, you can apply a style, change its formatting, and then update the style to match the new formatting. This method can be useful when you're developing a template and you need to keep adjusting styles to make everything look and fit right.

To update a style with new formatting, follow these steps:

1. Apply the style using whichever tool you prefer (for example, the Styles pane).

2. Reformat the text as needed.

3. Update the style in one of these ways:

   - *Styles pane*: Hold the pointer over the style name, click the pop-up button, and then click Update to Match Selection on the pop-up menu.

   - *Quick Style Gallery*: Ctrl-click or right-click the style, and then click Update to Match Selection on the context menu.

Applying Direct Formatting on Top of Styles

After you've applied the style each paragraph needs and you've applied list styles and character styles as needed, you can finish off the formatting by applying direct formatting to any parts of the document that need it. For example, you may need to apply different font formatting to pick out special display elements or add more space before some paragraphs.

> **Note**   To get the most out of Word's automatic formatting features, use direct formatting as little as possible. If you need to apply the same direct formatting to several different items, consider creating a style with that formatting so you can apply it instantly in future. If you will need to use the same direct formatting and text, save it as an AutoText entry (see Chapter 6 for instructions).

To apply direct formatting, use the tools you met earlier in this chapter for setting up font formatting, paragraph formatting, bullets and numbering, and so on. Here are some examples:

- *Font formatting*: Use the controls in the Font group on the Home tab of the Ribbon or in the Font dialog box.

- *Paragraph formatting*: Use the controls in the Paragraph group on the Home tab of the Ribbon or in the Paragraph dialog box.

- *Bullets and numbering*: Use the controls in the Paragraph group on the Home tab of the Ribbon.

Tip   To remove direct formatting from text, select the text, and then press Ctrl-spacebar. If you find this keyboard shortcut doesn't work, it may be because another app is already using it. Choose Apple ➤ System Preferences, click the Keyboard icon, and then click the Keyboard Shortcuts tab. You can then click an app to see which keyboard shortcuts it's using.

Copying and Pasting Formatting Using the Format Painter

When you've painstakingly applied direct formatting to text or another object, you may want to reuse that direct formatting for other text or another object. The straightforward way to do so is to copy the text (or object), paste it in, and then type the new text over it. This works fine for new text items or objects (unless you forget to replace the pasted text), but it's not efficient if the text is already there.

Instead, you can use Word's Format Painter. This feature enables you to pick up the formatting for a selection and then "paint" it on other text or another object. Follow these steps:

1. Select the text or object that contains the formatting you want to copy.

2. Choose Home ➤ Clipboard ➤ Format Painter (the button with the paintbrush icon) on the Ribbon or press Cmd+Shift+C to copy the formatting. Word changes the pointer to an I-beam with a paint brush beside it.

Tip   If you want to apply the formatting to multiple items, double-click the Format button. The pointer becomes the Format Painter I-beam until you turn it off by clicking the Format button again or pressing the Esc key.

---

3. Drag the I-beam and paint brush over the text or object to which you want to apply the formatting. Word applies the formatting and then restores the pointer.

Navigating Quickly Around Your Documents

To help you navigate quickly around your documents, Word provides the Navigation pane, the Find and Replace feature, and the Go To feature. You met the Go To feature in Chapter 6; you'll meet the Navigation pane and the Find and Replace feature here.

Using the Sidebar

The Sidebar is a pane that appears at the left side of the Word window and contains four panes that you can switch among by clicking the four buttons at the top of the pane:

- *Thumbnails pane*: This pane (shown on the left in Figure 7-16) displays thumbnail pictures of your document's pages. Click the thumbnail for the page you want to display.

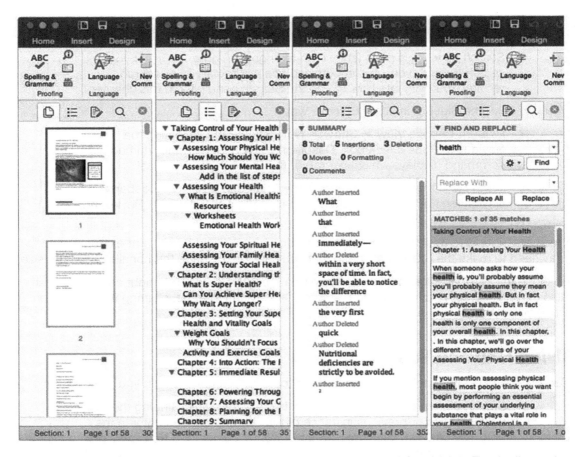

Figure 7-16. In the Sidebar on the left of the Word window, you can display (from left to right) the Thumbnail pane, the Document Map pane, the Reviewing pane, or the Search pane

- *Document Map pane*: This pane (shown second from left in Figure 7-16) displays your document as an outline of collapsible headings. Word also refers to this pane as the Navigation pane. If a heading contains subheadings, a triangle appears next to it. Click the triangle to display the headings or to hide them again. Click the heading you want to display in the main part of the window.

> **Tip**   To control which levels of headings appear in the Document Map pane, Ctrl-click or right-click any heading, and then click the heading level you want, such as Show Heading 3. From the context menu, you can also expand the section or collapse it, but usually it's easier to use the triangles in the Document Map pane.

- *Reviewing pane*: This pane (shown second from right in Figure 7-16) displays a summary of the tracked changes in the document. You'll learn how to use the Reviewing pane in Chapter 10.

- *Search pane*: This pane (shown on the right in Figure 7-16) lets you search through your documents and see a summary of all search results. You'll dig into how to use the Search pane later in this chapter.

You can open the Sidebar in either of these ways:

- *Ribbon*: Choose View ➤ Show ➤ Navigation Pane, selecting the Navigation Pane check box. Despite the "Navigation Pane" name, this command displays whichever tab of the Sidebar you used last.

- *Menu bar*: Choose View ➤ Sidebar ➤ Thumbnail, View ➤ Sidebar ➤ Navigation (for the Document Map pane), View ➤ Sidebar ➤ Reviewing, or View ➤ Sidebar ➤ Search.

Once the Sidebar is open, you can resize it by dragging its right border. For example, you may need to make the Sidebar wider so that you can see the page thumbnails at a larger size.

To close the Sidebar, click the Close button (the × button) in its upper-right corner. You can also close the Sidebar choosing View ➤ Show ➤ Navigation Pane, clearing the Navigation Pane check box.

Using Find and Replace

As you saw in Chapter 3, Word provides three tools for searching within your documents:

- *Search box on the title bar*: This box is good for quickly finding the next instance or previous instance of the search term you enter in the box. You can also click the pop-up button at the left end to display two options: click the List Matches in Sidebar item to open the Sidebar and show all matches for the search term, or click the Replace item to open the Sidebar ready for replacing items.

■ *Search pane in the Sidebar*: This pane lets you quickly search for text you enter in the Search Document box or replace that text with text you enter in the Replace With box. What's less obvious is that you can also search for and replace special characters (such as a paragraph mark or a tab character) by using the pop-up menu at the end of the Search Document box or the Replace With box (as shown on the right in Figure 7-17). And you can also set four search options—Whole Word Only, Ignore Case, Sounds Like, and All Work Forms—by clicking the Action button (the button bearing the cog icon) and then clicking the appropriate item on the Action pop-up menu (as shown on the left in Figure 7-17).

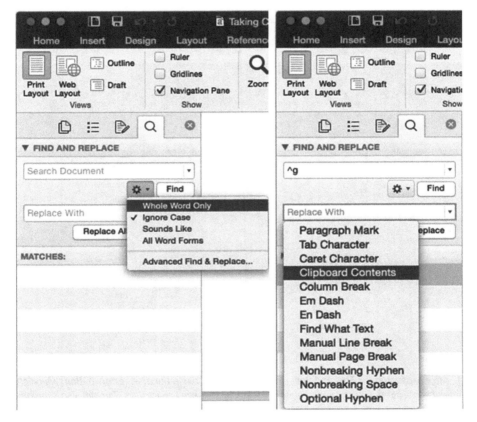

Figure 7-17. The Search pane in the Sidebar is good for straightforward searches, but you can also choose search options from the Action menu (left) or search for or replace special characters or elements (right)

■ *Find and Replace dialog box*: When you need to access Word's full Find and Replace capabilities, open the Find and Replace dialog box. In this section, you'll look at the extra features this dialog box provides.

You can open the Find and Replace dialog box in either of these ways:

- *From the menu bar*: Choose Edit ➤ Find ➤ Advanced Find and Replace.

- *From the Search pane in the Sidebar*: Click the Action button to display the Action pop-up menu, and then click Advanced Find & Replace.

With the Find and Replace dialog box open, you can search for regular text by using the techniques explained in Chapter 3. But you can also click the down arrow button to display the hidden part of the dialog box (see Figure 7-18) and then choose other search options as described here.

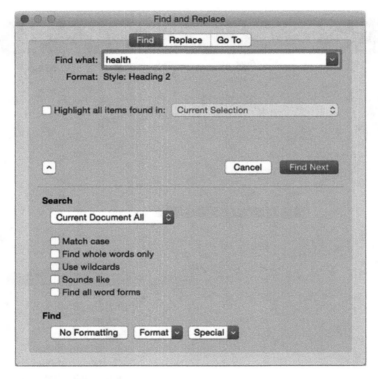

Figure 7-18. After expanding the Find and Replace dialog box by clicking the down arrow button (which changes to the up arrow button shown here), you can search with wildcards and special characters. You can also search for particular formatting or for styles. The area below the Find what box shows the search options you're using

---

Tip   You can work in the document while the Find and Replace dialog box is open—just click in the document and edit it as needed, and then click in the dialog box when you want to start using it again. This means you can leave the Find and Replace dialog box open until you've finished searching and making any changes needed to what you find.

Highlighting All Instances of a Search Term

To make Word highlight all the instances it has found, select the "Highlight all items found in" check box, and then choose the appropriate item in the pop-up menu. Normally, you want to choose Main Document to search in the main part of the document, but you can also search in other areas the document contains, such as Headers and Footers, Endnotes, Footnotes, or Text Boxes in Main Document.

Searching Only Part of the Document

When you need to search in just part of the document, select it. You can do this either before opening the Find and Replace dialog box or when the dialog box is open.

When Word finishes searching the selected part of the document, it asks whether you want to search the remainder of the document (see Figure 7-19).

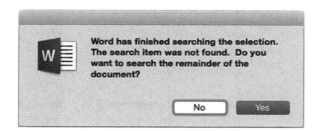

Figure 7-19. You can search only part of a document rather than the whole document. After searching that part, Word prompts you to search the remainder of the document

Changing the Search Direction

When you first search, Word searches from the position of the insertion point to the end of the document, wraps around automatically to the beginning, and continues until it gets back to the insertion point.

If you want to search upward rather than downward, open the Search pop-up menu, and choose Current Document Up; at the beginning of the document, Word asks if you want to continue. To search downward and have Word ask at the end of the document if you want to continue, choose Current Document Down. To search through the whole of the document without prompting, choose Current Document All.

Finding Search Terms That Match the Case You Type

Normally, Find ignores the case of characters, so it finds the search term no matter what capitalization it uses. If you want Find to find only results that match the case you type, select the Match case check box.

Restricting the Search to Whole Words

If you want to find your search term only as a whole word rather than as part of other words, select the Find whole words only check box. For example, you may need to find the word *any* rather than *many* or *anywhere*. This option works only for single words; as soon as you type a space in the Find what box, Word makes this check box unavailable.

Using Wildcards to Find Variable Text

To give your searches more flexibility, select the Use wildcards check box. A *wildcard* is a character or group of characters that represents other characters—a bit like your being able to use a joker as another card in some games or a blank tile in Scrabble. Table 7-2 explains the wildcards you can use for searching in Word.

Table 7-2. Wildcard Characters for Searching in Word

Use This Wildcard	To Find This Text	Example
?	Any character	**r?de** finds *rede*, *ride*, *rode*, and *rude*.
*	Any characters, or none	**force*** finds *force*, *forced*, *forceps*, and *forces*.
[*characters*]	Any one of the characters you've specified	**b[aeiou]ll** finds *ball*, *bell*, *bill*, and *bull*.
[*character1–character2*]	Any one of the characters in the alphabetical range you've entered	**b[a-j]t** finds words such as *bat*, *bet*, and *bit*. It does not find *but* because *u* is not in the range.
[!*character1–character2*]	Any one character that's not in the alphabetical range you've entered	**b[!a-jt]** finds *bot* and *but* but doesn't find *bat*, *bet*, and *bit*.
character{*number*}	The number of occurrences of the character	**20{4}** find *20000* because it has four zeroes.
character{*number1, number2*}	From *number1* instances to *number2* instances of the character	**20{1,4}** finds *20*, *200*, *2000*, *20000*, and similar numbers.
character@	One or more instances of the character	**0@in** finds *10in*, *100in*, and other text with one or more zeroes followed by *in*.

Finding Words That Sound Like Other Words

If you need to find words that sound like other words, select the Sounds like check box. This feature is worth trying if you work in documents that may have unintentional word substitutions (for example, documents entered using speech recognition), but overall it's too hit-and-miss to rely on.

Finding All Forms of a Word

Select the "Find all word forms" check box if you need to find each different form of the search text. For example, if you search for *go*, Find finds *went* and *gone* as well.

Searching for Special Characters

If you need to search for a character that you can't type with the keyboard, such as a paragraph mark (the normally hidden character that ends a paragraph) or an em dash (—), open the Special pop-up menu (see Figure 7-20), and then click the item you want. Word enters the appropriate code in the Find what text box, and you can then run the search.

Figure 7-20. Use the Special pop-up menu in the Find and Replace dialog box to enter a special character, such as the code for a paragraph mark or a graphic

Searching Only at the Start or End of a Word

To make Word search for your search text only at the start of words, select the Use wildcards check box, open the Special pop-up menu, and click Beginning of Word. (The Special menu's contents change to wildcard options when you select the Use wildcards check box.) For example, you can search for *after* at the beginning of words to find *afterward* and *afternoon*.

Similarly, you can select the Use wildcards check box and then choose the End of Word item on the Special menu to search for your search term only at the end of words, such as finding *after* in *hereafter* or *rafter*.

Finding Formatting

As well as finding text, Word enables you to find formatting—either formatting applied to particular text or formatting on its own. For example, you can search for instances of the word *industry* with the Subtle Emphasis style applied to it, or you can search for any text formatted with both bold and italic.

To search for formatting, follow these steps:

1. Type your search text in the Find what box like you've done before. If you want to search for just formatting, delete anything that's in the Find what box.

2. Click the Format pop-up menu, and then click the type of formatting (see Figure 7-21).

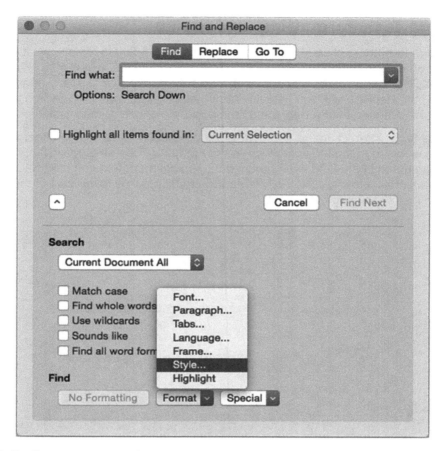

Figure 7-21. Use the commands on the Format pop-up menu in the Find and Replace dialog box to specify the formatting you want to find

3. In the dialog box that opens, set up the type of formatting. For example, in the Find Style dialog box, click the style name, and then click the OK button.

Note   The Highlight item on the Format pop-up menu doesn't display a dialog box—it just switches on searching for Highlight text. Choose Format ➤ Highlight again to search for Not Highlight; choose Format ➤ Highlight a third time to remove Highlight from the search.

Click the No Formatting button when you want to remove the formatting criteria from the search.

Replacing Text, Formatting, and Styles

Finding text or formatting is great, but what you often need to do is replace what you're finding with other text, other formatting, or both. To replace items, display the Replace tab of the Find and Replace dialog box by choosing Edit ➤ Find ➤ Advanced Find and Replace and then clicking the Replace tab. You can also click the Action button in the Search pane in the Sidebar, click Advanced Find & Replace on the pop-up menu, and then click the Replace tab.

The Replace tab (shown in Figure 7-22 with settings chosen for replacing direct formatting with a style) works in much the same way as the Find tab. For a straightforward replacement, type the search text in the Find what box and the replacement text in the Replace with box. For a complex replacement, click the More button to display the lower part of the dialog box, and then choose the options you want.

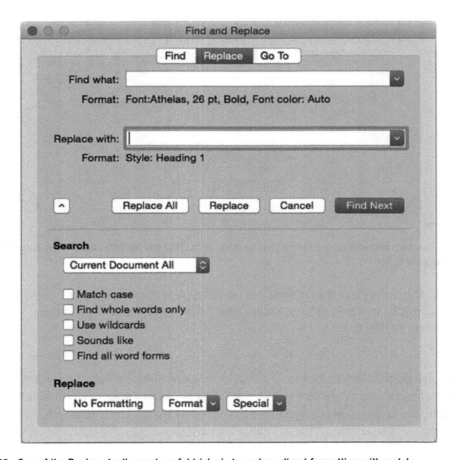

Figure 7-22. One of the Replace tool's most useful tricks is to replace direct formatting with a style

Once you've set up the replacement, use the Replace button, Replace All button, and Find Next button to run it:

- *Find Next*: Click this button to find the next instance of the search term.

- *Replace*: Click this button to replace the instance Word has found and to find the next instance.

- *Replace All*: Click this button to replace every instance. If you've chosen Current Document Up or Current Document Down rather than Current Document All in the Search pop-up menu, Word asks if you want to continue when it reaches the beginning or end of the document.

Replacing Text

To replace text, simply type the replacement in the Replace with box. But you can also make Word insert the contents of the Clipboard or the Find what box:

- *Insert the contents of the Clipboard*: Open the Special pop-up menu and click Clipboard Contents, or simply type ^c in the Replace with box, to make Word insert the contents of the Clipboard in place of whatever you're searching for. You can use this trick to insert a table, an image, or a section of text that you've copied to the Clipboard.

- *Insert the contents of the Find what box*: Open the Special pop-up menu and click Find What Text, or simply type ^& in the Replace with box, to make Word insert the contents of the Find what box (or what the contents represents). For example, you can type wildcards in the Find what box and then have the Replace with box insert text plus whatever expression matched the wildcards.

Replacing Formatting or Styles

When you need to reformat documents, you can use Replace to replace formatting. You can replace formatting in several ways:

- *Replace text and formatting*: Sometimes you may need to find given text that's formatted in a particular way and replace it with other text formatted differently. (You can also replace it with the same text formatted differently.)

- *Replace text with formatting*: You can find text that's formatted in a particular way and replace it with formatting, getting rid of the text. This approach is useful if you create documents in a text editor (for example, on a portable device) and need to apply formatting in Word. For example, you can replace the text *h1* with the Heading 1 style.

- *Replace formatting only*: You can replace one type of formatting with another type, such as replacing bold italic 20-point text with a Heading 2 style. Or you can replace one style with another style.

To replace formatting or styles, follow these steps:

1. Open the Replace tab of the Find and Replace dialog box. For example, choose Edit ➤ Find ➤ Advanced Find and Replace, and then click the Replace tab.

2. In the Find what box, enter any text you want to find. If you're searching for formatting only, delete anything in the Find what box.

3. With the insertion point in the Find what box, specify the formatting you want to find. Open the Format pop-up menu; click Font, Paragraph, Tabs, Language, Frame, or Style; and use the dialog box that opens to specify the details. When you click the OK button, the Format line under the Find what box shows your choices.

4. In the Replace with box, enter any replacement text. To replace only with formatting, delete anything in this box.

5. With the insertion point in the Replace with box, specify the replacement formatting. Use the same techniques as in step 3.

6. Run the replacement as usual. For example, click the Replace All button to replace all instances of the formatting.

Summary

In this chapter, you learned the best way to format your Word documents—by using styles from start to finish and then adding only such little direct formatting as is absolutely necessary. You saw how to apply Word's existing styles, how to create custom styles of your own, and how to modify a style either directly or by updating it to match an example.

You now also know how to navigate around your documents using the Sidebar and the Find feature. And you learned how to find any document item you need, from plain text to characters you can't type—and how to replace it if necessary.

In the next chapter, I'll show you how to create complex documents and complex layouts. Turn the page when you're ready to start.

Chapter 8

Creating Complex Documents and Layouts

Now that you've mastered the art of formatting your documents with styles (as explained in Chapter 7), you're ready to create long or complex documents in Word.

In this chapter, you'll learn first how to use the extra table features that Word provides over those that the Office apps share. Then I'll show you how to break a document into multiple sections; how to add headers, footers, and page numbers; and how to create newspaper-style columns of text.

After that, you'll see how to mark important parts of a document with bookmarks and how to insert cross-references back to these bookmarks or to other parts. Finally, you'll learn how to develop your documents using Word's powerful Outline view and how to add footnotes and endnotes to your documents.

Working with Word's Extra Table Features

In Word, you can create tables in the following three ways:

- *Insert a table*: As discussed in Chapter 3, choose Insert ➤ Table from the Ribbon, and then click the table arrangement you want on the Insert Table grid, such as five rows of three columns each. This is good for creating regular tables, ones that have the same number of cells in each row.

- *Draw a table*: Also as discussed in Chapter 3, choose Insert ➤ Table ➤ Draw Borders ➤ Draw, and then use the drawing cursor to draw the table layout you want. Drawing a table is good for creating irregular tables.

- *Convert existing text to a table*: If the document already contains the text you want to create the table from, you can convert the text into a table, as discussed next.

© Guy Hart-Davis 2016
G. Hart-Davis, *Learn Office 2016 for Mac*, DOI 10.1007/978-1-4842-2002-3_8

Converting Existing Text into a Table

Converting existing text to a table is usually faster than creating a table and moving existing data into it.

First, you need to make sure that the material is laid out regularly, with its contents separated using one of these four items:

- *Tabs*: This is usually the easiest way of separating material because you can see the different columns that the table will create. Figure 8-1 shows a table laid out with tabs. Notice that because the tab stops aren't optimally positioned, the columns don't align in each row. This doesn't matter as long as there's only one tab between each item destined for a cell.

Figure 8-1. When using tabs to lay out text you plan to turn into a table, use only one tab between the contents of each cell. Press Cmd+8 to display the invisible characters including the tabs and paragraph marks

> **Note** When converting tabbed material into a table, you must make sure of two things. First, check that each item is separated by only one tab, not by two or more tabs; otherwise, you'll get the wrong number of columns. (But if you need to leave a cell blank, do use two tabs in sequence.) Second, check that the material for each cell is not broken onto multiple lines; otherwise, you'll get the wrong number of rows.

- *Paragraphs*: If each cell's data appears in a separate paragraph, you can quickly convert it to a table. Make sure the data contains no unnecessary blank paragraphs.

- *Commas*: If you have data separated by commas, such as a comma-separated values exported from a spreadsheet, you can use a comma as the separator character for a table.

- *Other character*: If your data is separated consistently by another character (for example, * or |), you can specify that character as the separator character. You need to make sure that this character doesn't appear as part of the regular text, only as the separator character.

When your data is in good order, convert it to a table like this:

1. Select the paragraphs of data. Select right from the start up to the paragraph mark at the end of the last paragraph. (If Word is hiding paragraph marks, you'll appear to have selected a chunk of blank space at the end of the last paragraph.)

2. Choose Insert ➤ Table ➤ Convert Text to Table from the Ribbon, or choose Table ➤ Convert ➤ Convert Text to Table from the menu bar, to display the Convert Text to Table dialog box (see Figure 8-2).

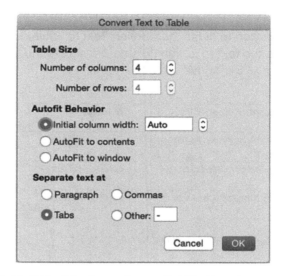

Figure 8-2. In the Convert Text to Table dialog box, make sure that Word has chosen the right separator character (for example, tabs), and choose the AutoFit behavior you want

3. In the Separate text at area, make sure that Word has picked the right separator character. If not, select the Paragraphs option button, the Commas option button, the Tabs option button, or the Other option button as appropriate; for the Other option button, type the separator character in the text box.

4. In the Table Size area, make sure that the number of columns is correct:

    ▪ If you're using tabs as the separator character and the number of columns is wrong, one or more of the paragraphs contains an extra tab (or is missing a tab). Click the Cancel button, find the extra tab or missing tab, and then start the conversion again.

    ▪ If you're using paragraphs as the separator character, you must tell Word how many paragraphs to use for each row. Enter this number in the Number of columns box.

5. In the AutoFit Behavior area, choose whether to fit the column widths automatically to their contents:

   ■ *Initial column width*: Select this option button to use a fixed width for each column. You can then choose Auto to have Word allocate the space equally among the columns or type the fixed width you want.

   ■ *AutoFit to contents*: Select this option button to let Word adjust each column's width to fit its contents. You may need to adjust the widths afterward.

   ■ *AutoFit to window*: Select this option button to have Word make the table automatically fit the window's width.

6. Click the OK button to close the Convert Text to Table dialog box. Word converts the text to a table. Figure 8-3 shows the text from the example in Figure 8-1 converted into a table.

Department¤	Position Needed¤	Manager¤	Target Hire Date¤	¤
Sales and Marketing¤	Administrative Assistant¤	Renee Williams¤	4 October 2016¤	¤
Operations¤	Director of Operations¤	Mauro Flaherty¤	11 October 2016¤	¤
HR¤	Administrative Support¤	[Hiring Manager]¤	11 October 2016¤	¤

Figure 8-3. The table that Word created from the tabbed text in Figure 8-1

Converting a Table to Text

Word also lets you convert a table back to text. This move is useful when you've received material in table form that you need to convert to a different layout.

To convert a table to text, follow these steps:

1. Click anywhere in the table. You don't need to select it.

2. Choose Table ➤ Convert ➤ Convert Table to Text from the menu bar to display the Convert Table to Text dialog box (see Figure 8-4).

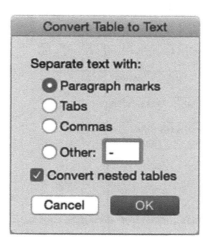

Figure 8-4. When converting a table back to text, you can separate the cells with paragraph marks, tabs, commas, or another character of your choice

3. In the Separate text with area, choose the character with which to separate the cell contents: select the Paragraph marks option button, the Tabs option button, the Commas option button, or the Other option button (and type the character in the text box).

4. Select the Convert nested tables check box if you want to convert nested tables as well. (The next section explains nested tables.) This check box is available only when you're using paragraphs as the separator character.

> **Note** Word converts a nested table to paragraphs of text like the rest of the table. The nested table's paragraphs appear in their cell order between the paragraphs for the table cells that surround them.

5. Click the OK button to close the Convert Table to Text dialog box and perform the conversion.

Nesting One Table Inside Another Table

When you need to create a complex layout, you can nest one table inside another so that one cell of the outer table contains however many cells the inner table has. Figure 8-5 shows an example of a nested table.

To nest a table, click in the cell in which you want to nest the table, and then insert the table as usual.

Department	Coverage		Contact Information
Anthropology	Biological Anthropology	1-8	
	Cultural Anthropology	1-4	
	Linguistic Anthropology	5-12	
	Social Anthropology	1-12	
Biology			
Chemistry			

Figure 8-5. You can nest one table inside another table to create complex layouts

> **Tip**   You can nest tables several levels deep if necessary, but the further you nest tables, the more confusing working with them tends to become. If you're considering several levels of nesting, see whether merging and splitting cells could give you a similar result with less fuss.

Creating Complex Documents with Multiple Sections

When you need to create documents that use multiple layouts, you have to put each layout in a separate section. Here are three examples of documents that use multiple layouts:

- A newsletter may need different numbers of columns on different pages.
- A report may require different headers and footers for different chapters.
- A business letter may need to contain an envelope page as well.

Word's sections are highly useful, but they're tricky both to see and to grasp. Word makes matters worse by automatically creating sections when your documents need them— for example, when you apply columns to part of a document, as discussed later in this chapter—but not making clear what it's doing.

Here is the essential information you need to know about sections:

- *Each new blank document has a single section at first*: When you create a new blank document, Word creates it as a single section until you add further sections. By contrast, documents you create based on a template contain however many sections that template has.
- *When you need to give part of the document a different layout, you create a new section*: For example, if you need to create a landscape page in a document that uses portrait orientation, you put the landscape page in a separate section so that you can change the layout.

- *A section can start on the same page or on a different page*: Word gives you four kinds of section breaks.

  - *Continuous*: The new section starts on the same page as the previous section. This type of break is useful for creating multicolumn layouts on part of a page.

  - *Next page*: The new section starts on the next page after the previous section ends. This is the kind of break you use for putting a new chapter on a new page or for changing the layout from portrait to landscape.

  - *Even page*: The new section starts on the next even page after the previous section ends. This may mean having a blank page in the printed document.

  - *Odd page*: The new section starts on the new odd page after the previous section ends. This too may mean a blank page appears in the printed document.

- *A section break divides one section from the next*: When you create a section (or Word creates one automatically for you), you add a section break to the document. A section break is normally hidden, but if you display paragraph marks and other invisible characters, it appears as a blue double line with the words Section Break and the type in the middle, such as Section Break (Continuous).

Once you know all this, inserting a section break is easy:

1. Place the insertion point where you want the new section to start. It's best to put the insertion point at the beginning of a paragraph.

2. On the Ribbon, choose Layout ➤ Page Setup ➤ Breaks to open the Breaks panel, and then click the section break type you want: Next Page, Continuous, Even Page, or Odd Page. Word inserts the break.

> **Note**   If you prefer to use the menus, you can choose Insert ➤ Break from the menu bar to display the Break submenu and then click Section Break (Next Page), Section Break (Continuous), Section Break (Odd Page), or Section Break (Even Page), as needed.

To see the break in Print Layout view or Web Layout view, choose Home ➤ Paragraph ➤ Show all nonprinting characters (the button with the pilcrow, the ¶ mark) or press Cmd+8 on the keyboard. In Draft view or Outline view, Word displays the break all the time.

When you start using sections in a document, Word adds the Section readout to the status bar to give you a heads-up on which section you're working in.

Adding Headers, Footers, and Page Numbers

If you're planning to print out a multipage document or to distribute it as a PDF or XPS file, it's often a good idea to add headers, footers, and page numbers to make the pages easy to identify.

Adding Headers and Footers to a Document

A *header* appears across the top of a page and a *footer* appears across the bottom of a page. You can use headers and footers to add information such as the document name and file name, author name, date, and page numbers—or any other information that you need to make available to the reader.

Word gives you plenty of flexibility with headers and footers. If a document needs the same header (or footer) all the way through, you can quickly add one. But you can also use different headers or footers on the odd pages of the document to the even pages, and you can use different headers and footers from one section of the document to the next. You can also prevent the header or footer from appearing on the first page of a document, which is useful for letters and various other documents.

Word's templates come with built-in headers and footers that you can quickly add to give your documents a standard look. These headers and footers range from the straightforward Blank one to stylish designs that can look good in a variety of documents. Many of the headers and footers come with odd-page and even-page versions so that you can create effective page spreads.

> **Note**   If you want to create a header or footer completely from scratch, choose Insert ➤ Header & Footer ➤ Header ➤ Edit Header from the Ribbon or View ➤ Header and Footer from the menu bar to open the Header area. In Print Layout view, you can also simply double-click in the header area at the top of the page.

To insert a built-in header or footer, follow these steps:

1. If the document has multiple sections, click in the section where you want to add the header or footer.

2. Choose Insert ➤ Header and Footer ➤ Header or Insert ➤ Header and Footer ➤ Footer to open the Header panel or the footer panel. Figure 8-6 shows the Header panel.

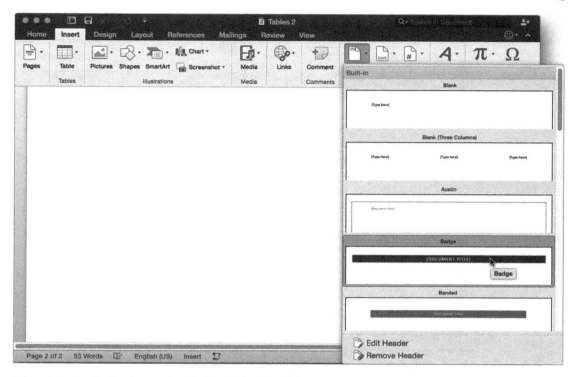

Figure 8-6. Use the Header panel on the Insert tab of the Ribbon to insert the type of header you want

3. Click the header or footer you want. Word then does the following:

■ Inserts the header or footer in the document.

■ Switches to Print Layout view if the document is in another view.

■ Displays the header or footer area with the header or footer ready for editing. Figure 8-7 shows a header added to a page. The Header tab shows that you're working in the header; if you're in a particular section of the document rather than the document as a whole, the tab shows that too.

■ Adds the Header and Footer tab to the Ribbon.

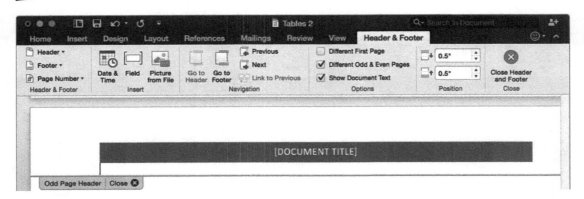

Figure 8-7. Word adds the Header and Footer tab to the Ribbon to give you access to the commands for working with the header or footer that you've inserted. Below the header in the document, Word displays a button identifying the header (here, Odd Page Header) and the Close button

4. Fill in the placeholders in the header or footer. For example,

    ■ If the header or footer shows a [Type here] placeholder, click it, and then type the text you want.

    ■ If the header or footer shows a placeholder for document information, such as the [Document Title] placeholder shown, choose File ➤ Properties from the menu bar to open the Properties dialog box for the document, and then click the Summary tab. Fill in the field information (in this example, the Title field) and then click the OK button to close the Properties dialog box. The contents of the field then appear in the placeholder.

    ■ If the header or footer includes a Year placeholder, click the pop-up button, and then click the date in the panel that opens.

5. If necessary, adjust the position or alignment of the header:

    ■ To change the header's position relative to the top of the page, alter the value in the Header from Top box in the Position group of the Header and Footer tab of the Ribbon. When you do this, you may also need to change the page margins.

Note When the Word window is too narrow for the labels to fit, the Header from Top box and the Footer from Bottom box appear unmarked. You can hold the pointer over the controls in the Position group to display tooltips identifying each button.

■ To change the footer's position relative to the bottom of the page, alter the value in the Footer from Bottom box in the Position group.

6. Click the Close button under the header area or above the footer area to close the header and footer area and return to the main document. You can also choose Header & Footer ➤ Close ➤ Close Header and Footer from the Ribbon, press Ctrl+Shift+C, or simply double-click in the main text area.

Creating Different Headers and Footers for Different Pages

Many documents either don't need a header (or footer) on the first page or need a different one there. Likewise, many documents need a different header or footer on their odd pages than on their even pages.

To set up different headers and footers for the first page or for odd and even pages, follow these steps:

1. Open the header area or footer area in one of these ways:

   ■ In Print Layout view, double-click in the header area or footer area.

   ■ Choose Insert ➤ Header & Footer ➤ Header ➤ Edit Header or Insert ➤ Header & Footer ➤ Footer ➤ Edit Footer from the Ribbon.

   ■ Choose View ➤ Header and Footer from the menu bar.

2. Click the Header and Footer tab on the Ribbon to display its contents.

3. To create a different first page header or footer, select the Different First Page check box in the Options group on the Header and Footer tab of the Ribbon.

4. To create different headers and footers for odd pages and even pages, select the Different Odd & Even check box in the Options group.

5. Use the Previous button and Next button in the Navigation group on the Header and Footer tab to move from one header or footer to another, entering the material you want each to have. If you're using Word's built-in headers or footers, try the Odd Page and Even Page ones for your odd and even pages.

Using Different Headers and Footers in Different Sections of a Document

If you break a document into separate sections, you can create different headers and footers in each section or continue headers and footers from one section to the next. As well as making each section's headers or footers different from the other sections, you can also create different first-page and odd- and even-page headers and footers within sections as needed.

Create your sections as described earlier in this chapter, and then go to the beginning of the document and open the header area or footer area. Give the first section the headers and footers it needs, and then go through the remaining sections.

Word automatically carries through the headers and footers from one section to the next until you tell it to stop. You'll see the Same as Previous indicator between the Section indicator and the Close button for the header or footer, as in Figure 8-8.

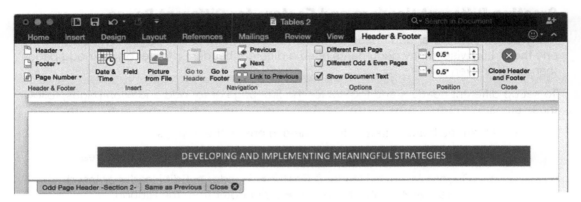

Figure 8-8. *Word displays the Same as Previous indicator to show that a header or footer is linked to the previous one. Choose Header & Footer ➤ Navigation ➤ Link to Previous, unpushing the Link to Previous button, to break the link*

To stop Word from continuing the headers and footers like this, move to the section you want to change, and then click the Link to Previous button in the Options group on the Header and Footer tab of the Ribbon. (The Link to Previous button appears pushed-in and darker when it is selected.) You can then create a different header or footer in this section.

Delete a Header or Footer

When you want to get rid of a header or footer, open it for editing, press Cmd+A to select all its contents, and then press Delete.

Inserting Page Numbers in a Document

To help your readers (or perhaps yourself) keep the pages of a document in the right order, it's often useful to add page numbers. The best way to add page numbers in Word is to put a page number field in the header or footer. Word then repeats the page number on each page, inserting the correct value.

> **Note**   If you need to insert in the body of a document a page number that's in fact a reference to another page, insert a cross-reference, as discussed later in this chapter. You can refer either to an item such as a heading, table caption, or graphic or to a bookmark that you place exactly where you need it.

To add page numbers to a header or footer, follow these steps:

1. Open the Page Numbers dialog box (see Figure 8-9) in one of these ways:

   ▪ *Ribbon*: Choose Insert ➤ Header & Footer ➤ Page Number ➤ Page Number.

   ▪ *Menu bar*: Choose Insert ➤ Page Numbers.

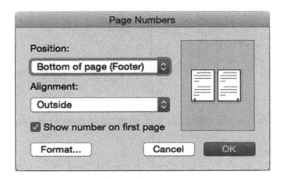

Figure 8-9. In the Page Numbers dialog box, choose the position and alignment for the page numbers. You can also choose whether to show the page number on the first page

2. In the Position pop-up menu, choose Top of page (Header) or Bottom of page (Footer), as needed.

3. In the Alignment pop-up menu, choose Left, Center, Right, Inside, or Outside. Inside and Outside are for facing-page designs; for example, using Inside in a header places the page number at the upper-right corner of the left page and the upper-left corner of the right page. The Preview box shows you where the page numbers will appear.

4. Select the "Show number on first page" check box if you want the first page to have a number too. To suppress the number on the first page, clear this check box.

5. If you want to set the formatting for the page numbers, follow these steps:

   ▪ Click the Format button to display the Page Number Format dialog box (see Figure 8-10).

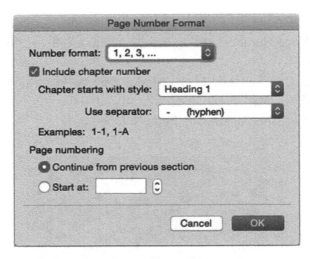

Figure 8-10. Use the Page Number Format dialog box to change the formatting of a page number, such as including a chapter number in it

■ Open the Number format pop-up menu, and click the number formatting you want, such as 1, 2, 3; A, B, C; or i, ii, iii.

■ If your document has chapters and you want to include the chapter number in the page numbering, select the Include chapter number check box. Then open the "Chapter starts with style" pop-up menu, and click the style that marks the beginning of each chapter, such as Heading 1 or a Chapter Title style you've added. Last, open the Use separator pop-up menu, and choose the separator character to use between the chapter number and the page number. Your choices are a hyphen, a period, a colon, an em dash (a long dash), or a en dash (a short dash but longer than a hyphen).

■ In the Page Numbering area, choose how to control the numbering. Click the "Continue from previous section" option button to have the page numbers follow those in the previous section. To start again or start at a specific number, click the Start at option button, and enter the number in the text box.

■ Click the OK button to close the Page Number Format dialog box and return to the Page Numbers dialog box.

6. Click the OK button to close the Page Numbers dialog box. Word inserts the page numbers.

Note   To remove the page numbers from a document, choose Insert ➤ Header & Footer ➤ Header ➤ Edit Header or Insert ➤ Header & Footer ➤ Footer ➤ Edit Footer from the Ribbon, or choose View ➤ Header and Footer from the menu bar. Select the page number in the header area or footer area, and then press the Delete key.

Creating Newspaper-Style Columns of Text

If you create newsletters or similar publications, you may want to create multicolumn layouts. Word can do this well, but there are a couple of tricks you need to learn.

> **Tip**   Only Print Layout view shows the columns on-screen, so it's best to use this view to work with columns.

To create simple columns, follow these steps:

1. If you want to turn only part of the document into columns, select that part. For example, select existing text, or select a blank paragraph at the point where you want to start the columns.

> **Note**   If you want to turn the whole document into columns (and the same number of columns throughout), click anywhere in the document.

2. Choose Layout ➤ Page Setup ➤ Columns to open the Columns panel, and then click the type of columns you want (see Figure 8-11). Word turns your selection into columns.

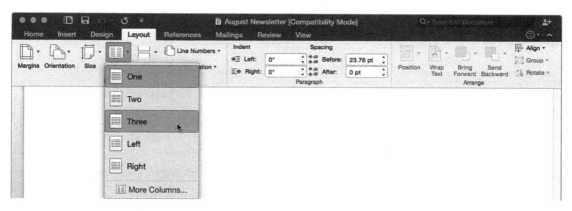

Figure 8-11. *From the Columns panel, choose One, Two, or Three columns. Choose Left for a narrow left column and a wide right column, and choose Right for wide left and narrow right. Click More Columns for literally more columns or for further options*

If you need to create other types of columns than appear on the Columns panel, such as four columns or columns with a vertical line between them, follow these steps:

1. Select the part of the document you want to apply the columns to.

2. Choose Format ➤ Columns from the menu bar or choose Layout ➤ Page Setup ➤ Columns from the Ribbon to display the Columns dialog box (see Figure 8-12).

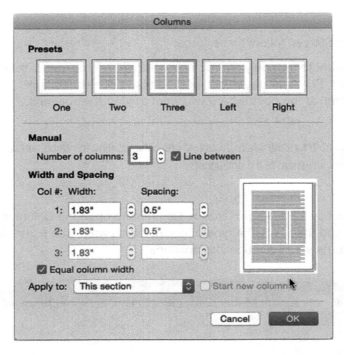

Figure 8-12. Use the options in the Columns dialog box to create more complex column layouts in your Word documents

3. Choose the type of columns you want:

   ■ To use one of the presets in the Presets area, click it.

   ■ To specify a different number of columns, enter it in the Number of columns box. Either type in the number or use the spin button to change the current number.

4. If you want a vertical line between the columns, select the Line between check box.

5. Set up the column width and spacing:

   ■ To make each column the same width, select the Equal column width check box. On the Col # 1 line of controls, set the width and spacing for the columns.

■ To set each column to the width you want, clear the Equal column width check box, and then set the width for each column in the Width box and the spacing in the Spacing box. If you have four or more columns, you'll need to scroll down to reach the last ones.

6. Make sure the Apply to pop-up menu shows the right part of the document—the "Selected text item to affect only the selection," the "This section item to affect only the current section," the "This point forward item to affect the rest of the document from here on," or the "Whole document item to affect the whole document" option.

7. If you chose the This point forward item, you can select the Start new column check box if you want to create a new column layout from the current position of the insertion point.

8. Click the OK button to close the Columns dialog box. Word creates the columns using your choices. Figure 8-13 shows a three-column layout with vertical lines between the columns.

The Bread Baking Newsletter¶

24 August 2016¶

Welcome to the *Bread Baking Newsletter* for August 2016! This issue gives you great new recipes, brings you up to date on all the latest improvements we've made to our website, and takes you on a visit to the best stoneground flour mill in Northern California. ¶ —————————— Section Break (Continuous) ——————————

• Breaking News¶

We have 20 places left in our bread-baking class for October. Sign up now using the form on page 4. ¶

The next class will take place in January. Put your name down on the list, and we'll send you details as soon as they're available. ¶

Raisin-Nut Bread¶

This delicious loaf takes only minutes to mix and will be a favorite with all of the family. ¶

• Ingredients¶
4 cups white flour↵
2 cups water↵
1 teaspoon salt↵
1 cup walnuts↵
1 cup raisins¶

The Importance of Stoneground¶

If you've decided to bake your own bread, take the next step and insist on stoneground flour for all your wholegrain breads. ¶

Most people think there's no great difference between stoneground and regular·

Figure 8-13. You can include vertical lines between the columns to make a multicolumn layout easier to read

Breaking Your Columns with Column Breaks

After you've created the columns, Word automatically flows the text down each column as you enter it. When the first column reaches the bottom of the text area on the page, Word flows it to the start of the second column, and so on.

To end a column early, you can insert a column break. Position the insertion point where you want the break, and then choose Layout ➤ Page Setup ➤ Breaks ➤ Column from the Ribbon. Word inserts the column break and moves the insertion point to the top of the next column.

> **Tip**   You can also insert a column break by choosing Insert ➤ Break ➤ Column Break from the menu bar or pressing Cmd+Shift+Return.

If you need to remove a column break, delete it. Choose Home ➤ Paragraph ➤ Show all nonprinting characters or press Cmd+8 to display invisible characters so that you can see the column break, which appears as a blue line with the words Column Break in the middle. Position the insertion point before the column break, and then press Delete to delete it.

Removing Multiple Columns from a Section or Document

If you want to change a multiple-column section or document back to a single column, click in the section or document, and then choose Layout ➤ Page Setup ➤ Columns ➤ One. Word restores the text to a single column.

Using Bookmarks, Fields, and References

In long documents, you often need to mark parts of the document so that you can find them easily or refer to them. You may also want to insert pieces of information that Word can automatically update for you, such as the date and time or the name of the last person to save a document. And you may find it useful to be able to refer easily to another part of the document and have Word keep its page number, name, or contents automatically updated.

Marking Important Parts of a Document with Bookmarks

To identify parts that you want to return to or refer to, you can place bookmarks in your Word documents. A bookmark is an electronic marker that you can place either at a single point in text (between two characters or other objects) or around text or an object.

> **Note**   Use a single-point bookmark when you need to move the insertion point to a particular point or refer to a page number. Use a bookmark with contents when you need to refer to the specific contents; for example, to make a reference automatically display the text that appears in the bookmark.

Insert a Bookmark to Mark Part of a Document

To insert a bookmark, follow these steps:

1. Click the point where you want to place the bookmark, or select the text or other object you want the bookmark to contain.

2. Choose Insert ➤ Bookmark from the menu bar to display the Bookmark dialog box (see Figure 8-14).

Figure 8-14. Create a bookmark when you need to mark a specific point or an area of content in a document

3. Type the name for the bookmark in the Bookmark name text box. You must start the name with a letter, but after that you can use any letters, numbers, and underscores as needed. You can't use spaces or symbols in the name.

4. Click the Add button. Word adds the bookmark and closes the dialog box.

> **Note**   If you need to move a bookmark to a different point in a document, position the insertion point or select the new location. Then open the Bookmark dialog box, click the bookmark name, and click the Add button. Word changes the bookmark to the new location without comment.

Navigating from Bookmark to Bookmark

After placing a bookmark, you can move the insertion point to the bookmark. Follow these steps:

1. Choose Insert Bookmark to display the Bookmark dialog box.

2. In the Bookmark name list box, click the bookmark.

3. Click the Go To button. If the bookmark is a single point, Word moves the insertion point to it; if the bookmark has contents, Word selects them.

4. Click the Close button to close the Bookmark dialog box.

Seeing Where Bookmarks Are in Your Documents

Word hides the bookmarks in your documents unless you set it to display them. When you're editing a document, it's often useful to display the bookmarks to avoid deleting them by accident. You may also need to display the bookmarks to make sure they're in the right place.

To display bookmarks, follow these steps:

1. Choose Word ➤ Preferences or press Cmd+, (Cmd and the comma key) to display the Word Preferences window.

2. In the Authoring and Proofing Tools section, click the View icon to display the View preferences pane.

3. In the Show in Document area, select the Bookmarks check box.

4. Close the Preferences window by clicking the Close button (the red button at the left end of the title bar) or pressing Cmd+W.

For a single-point bookmark, Word displays a black I-beam in the document. For a bookmark that contains text or another object, Word displays brackets around the contents. Figure 8-15 shows a single-point bookmark in the first paragraph and a bookmark with content in the second paragraph.

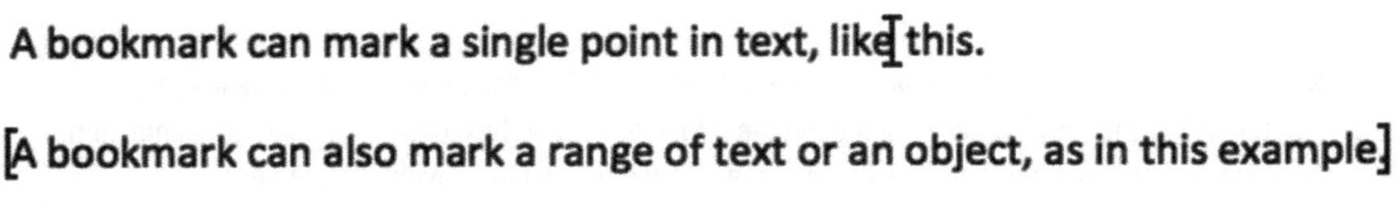

A bookmark can mark a single point in text, like this.

[A bookmark can also mark a range of text or an object, as in this example]

Figure 8-15. Word displays a black I-beam for a single-point bookmark marker and a pair of black brackets around the text or object in a bookmark that has contents

Deleting a Bookmark You No Longer Need

When you no longer need a bookmark, delete it like this:

1.   Choose Insert ➤ Bookmark to display the Bookmark dialog box.

2.   In the Bookmark name list box, click the bookmark.

3.   Click the Delete button.

4.   Click the Close button to close the Bookmark dialog box.

Inserting Automated Information with Fields

Many documents need automated items of information that Word can provide for you, such as the date or time, page numbers (discussed earlier in this chapter), or the file name. To add such information to your documents, you use fields, which are codes that tell Word to insert the information you want and whether to update it automatically.

Inserting a Field

To insert a field in a document, follow these steps:

1.   Choose Insert ➤ Field from the menu bar to display the Field dialog box (shown in Figure 8-16 with the Date and Time category selected in the Categories list box and the SaveDate field selected in the Field names list box).

Figure 8-16. The Field dialog box includes a wide range of fields. Normally, you start by choosing the type of fields in the Categories list box

2. In the Categories list box, choose the category of fields you want (see the following list). This example uses the Date and Time category:

    ■ *(All)*: Lists all the fields. This is useful when you know the field's name but not the category that contains it.

    ■ *Date and Time*: Contains fields for entering dates and times, such as the current date or the time the document was last saved, in various formats. You can also insert a date, time, or both more easily by choosing Insert Date & Time from the menu bar and using the Date and Time dialog box.

    ■ *Document Automation*: Contains fields for automating movement around the document, running macros, printing, and similar actions.

    ■ *Document Information*: Contains fields for inserting information contained in the document's properties, such as the author name or file name.

    ■ *Equations and Formulas*: Contains fields for inserting equations and formulas. Use them when the Insert ➤ Symbols ➤ Equation panel on the Ribbon doesn't contain what you need.

    ■ *Index and Tables*: Contains fields for creating indexes and content tables (such as tables of contents and tables of figures). The References tab of the Ribbon contains controls for inserting these fields more easily.

    ■ *Links and References*: Contains fields for inserting links (such as hyperlinks) or cross-references. The Insert ➤ Hyperlink, Insert ➤ Bookmark, and Insert ➤ Cross-reference commands on the menu bar provide easier access to these fields.

    ■ *Mail Merge*: Contains fields for creating mail-merge documents. Usually it's easier to work on the Mailings tab of the Ribbon, as discussed in Chapter 9.

    ■ *Numbering*: Contains fields for inserting automatic numbering in a document. For creating page numbers, it's easier to work in the header or footer, as described earlier in this chapter.

    ■ *User Information*: Contains fields for inserting the user's name, initials, or address.

3. In the Field names list box, click the field you want. In the example, I've clicked the SaveDate field, which inserts the date the document was last saved. The Field codes area shows the code format for the field, and the text box underneath it shows the current version of the field—at the moment, just SAVEDATE.

4. Select the "Preserve formatting during updates" check box if you want to keep the field's formatting when you update it. This behavior is normally useful.

5. You can insert the field at this point if you want, but you may prefer to choose options for the field first. To choose options, follow these steps:

    ■ Click the Options button to display the Field Options dialog box (see Figure 8-17). The contents of this dialog box vary depending on the field: some fields have many options, while others have few or none.

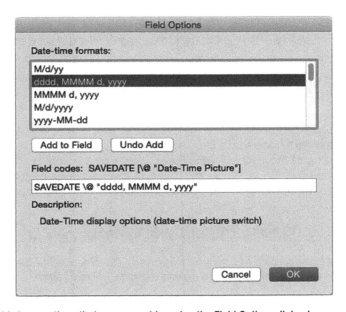

Figure 8-17. Most fields have options that you can set by using the Field Options dialog box

    ■ Click the option you want, and then click the Add to Field button. For example, in the Field Options dialog box for the SaveDate field, click the format you want in the Date-time formats list box, and then click the Add to Field button. Word adds the option's code to the Field codes text box.

    ■ Click the OK button to close the Field Options dialog box and return to the Field dialog box.

6. Click the OK button to close the Field dialog box and insert the field.

Examining and Updating a Field

Now that you've inserted a field, you can examine it. At first, the field displays the field results—the information that the field produces. For example, the SaveDate field displays a date in the format you chose.

Normally, the field result appears like normal text until you click in it or select it, at which point Word displays gray shading behind it to indicate that it's a field (see Figure 8-18). To update the field, Ctrl-click or right-click it, and then click Update Field on the context menu.

Last saved date: Thursday, March 3, 2016

Figure 8-18. When you click a field result, Word displays gray shading to indicate that it is a field

> **Note** If you want to see field shading all the time, choose Word ➤ Preferences to display the Word Preferences window. In the Authoring and Proofing Tools area, click the View icon to display the View preferences pane. In the Show in Document area, open the Field shading pop-up menu, and choose Always. You can also select the "Field codes instead of values" check box (also in the Show in Document area if you want to display field codes all the time. Close the Preferences window by clicking the Close button (the red button at the left end of the title bar) or pressing Cmd+W.

If you want to see the field code that's producing the field result, Ctrl-click or right-click anywhere in the field, and then click Toggle Field Codes on the context menu. Word displays the field code, as shown in Figure 8-19. You can edit the field code directly if you know which changes you want to make, but generally it's easier to use the Field Options dialog box.

Last saved date: { SAVEDATE \@ "dddd, MMMM d, yyyy" * MERGEFORMAT }

Figure 8-19. If you want to see the code that produces a field result, Ctrl-click or right-click in the field, and then click Toggle Field Codes on the context menu. Repeat this move to show the field result again

Adding Cross-References to Other Parts of a Document

When you create formal documents, you often need to refer from one part to another. To do so, you can create cross-references to any of several different types of items, including headings, bookmarks, figures, and tables.

To insert a cross-reference, follow these steps:

1. Position the insertion point where you want the reference.

2. Choose Insert ➤ Cross-reference from the menu bar to display the Cross-reference dialog box (shown in Figure 8-20 with settings chosen for referring to a bookmark).

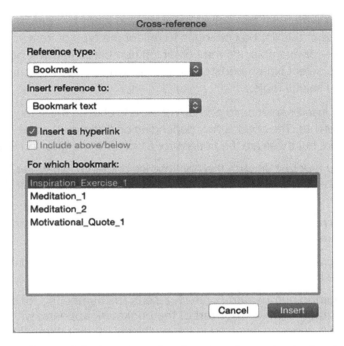

Figure 8-20. In the Cross-reference dialog box, you can insert a cross-reference to a bookmark, heading, table, or other item in the document

3. Open the Reference type pop-up menu and choose the type of item you want to refer to:

■ *Numbered item*: An item to which you have applied Word's automatic numbering, such as a paragraph in a numbered list.

■ *Heading*: A paragraph you have formatted with one of Word's Heading styles.

■ *Bookmark*: A bookmark you have inserted in the document (as described earlier in this chapter).

■ *Footnote*: A footnote you have created in the document, as discussed later in this chapter.

■ *Endnote*: An endnote you have created in the document, as discussed later in this chapter.

■ *Equation*: An equation you have inserted by choosing Insert ➤ Symbols ➤ Equation from the Ribbon or Insert ➤ Equation from the menu bar, or as a field.

■ *Figure*: A figure that you have marked with an automatically numbered caption using the Insert ➤ Caption command.

■ *Table*: A table that you have marked with an automatically numbered caption using the Insert ➤ Caption command.

4. In the For which list box, click the item you want to refer to. (The name of this list box changes to reflect the type of item you've selected—for example, it's the For which numbered item list box when you select Numbered item or the For which caption list box when you select Table.)

5. Open the Insert reference to pop-up menu, and choose the item you want to refer to. The options vary depending on the object you're referring to, but these are the options for a bookmark to give you an idea:

    -   *Bookmark text*: Inserts the bookmark's contents (whatever that may be). Use this for bookmarks that have contents rather than for single-point bookmarks.

    -   *Page number*: Inserts the page number on which the first part of the bookmark appears.

    -   *Paragraph number*: Inserts the paragraph number in which the start of the bookmark appears. Use this only with numbered paragraphs.

    -   *Paragraph number (no context)*: Inserts the numbering for the paragraph in which the start of the bookmark appears, without any other numbering involved in the multilevel list. For example, if you have a three-level list and the bookmark appears in paragraph 2. a. (ii), this choice inserts the (ii) part without the rest of the numbering.

    -   *Paragraph number (full context)*: Inserts the numbering for the paragraph in which the start of the bookmark appears, including the full number; for example, 2. a. (ii).

    -   *Above/below*: Inserts "above" if the start of the bookmark appears earlier in the document than the reference or "below" if it appears later in the document. This is occasionally useful, but see the next paragraph for a better alternative.

6. If you choose a page number or paragraph number in the Insert reference to pop-up menu, you can select the Include above/below check box if you want to add "above" or "below" to the end of the reference to indicate whether the item falls before or after the reference.

7. Select the Insert as hyperlink check box if you want the reference to appear as a hyperlink. The reader can click the hyperlink to jump to the referenced item.

8. Click the Insert button to insert the reference in the document. The Cancel button changes to a Close button.

9. Click the Close button to close the Cross-reference dialog box.

Note   A cross-reference is a field code, so you can update it by Ctrl-clicking or right-clicking in the field and then clicking Update Field on the context menu.

Creating Long Documents with Outline View

To plan, structure, and rearrange long documents, use Outline view. You met Outline view briefly in Chapter 6 when you looked at each of Word's main views in turn. In this section, you'll learn how Word handles outlines, how to create the outline of a document, and how to use Outline view to edit and rearrange a document quickly and easily.

How Outlines Work

Word creates outlines by assigning different outline levels to the paragraphs of a document. There are nine outline levels, with Level 1 being the highest and Level 9 the lowest. Below these is the body text level, which prevents a paragraph from appearing in the outline of the document.

Word's nine heading styles automatically map to the outline levels—Heading 1 to Level 1, Heading 2 to Level 2, and all the way down to Heading 9 mapping to Level 9. But you can also set the outline level of any style to the level you want, which allows you to make other styles appear in the outline as needed. For example, if you want your figure captions to appear at the fifth level of the outline, you can change the Caption style so that it has the Level 5 outline level.

> **Note** You can also set the outline level of an individual paragraph if you want, without assigning that paragraph a style that has an outline level. Promoting a paragraph manually like this can be useful sometimes, but using styles gives you greater consistency in your documents.

Developing the Outline of a Document

To develop the outline of a document, you work in Outline view. You can either start off in Outline view and work in it to structure your document at first, or you can switch to Outline view at any point when you need to work on the outline or get an overview of the structure of the document.

> **Tip** When you're working intensively on a document, it's often useful to open a second window on the document and keep that window in Outline view. If you prefer to work in a single window, you can either switch views or split the window into two panes and then use Outline view in one pane. To open a second window, choose View ➤ Arrange ➤ New Window from the Ribbon or Window ➤ New Window from the menu bar. To split a window in half, choose View ➤ Arrange ➤ Split from the Ribbon or Window ➤ Split from the menu bar.

Switching to Outline View

You can switch to Outline view in any of these ways:

- *Pointing device*: Click the Outline View button on the right side of the status bar.

- *Keyboard*: Press Cmd+Option+O.

- *Menu bar*: Choose View ➤ Outline.

When you switch to Outline view, Word automatically displays the Outlining tab of the Ribbon. You use the controls in the Outline Tools group (shown labeled in Figure 8-21) to create the outline and display the parts of it you want to see.

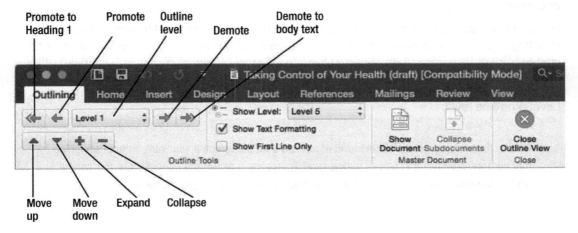

Figure 8-21. Use the controls on the Outlining tab of the Ribbon to develop your outline. Word displays the Outlining tab when you switch to Outline view

Creating Headings in Outline View

When you switch a document to Outline view, Word displays the document's headings (or more correctly, its outline levels). When you press Return at the end of a heading paragraph in Outline view, Word continues the heading style to the next paragraph rather than applying whichever style that paragraph's style specifies for the following paragraph. So when you type a heading, pressing Return creates another paragraph at the same level in the outline. This enables you to create multiple headings quickly without needing to apply a heading style as you would need to do in another view.

> **Note**   If you create a new blank document and switch it straight to Outline view, Word automatically applies Heading 1 style to the first paragraph. You can then start creating your outline immediately.

Promoting and Demoting Headings

You can quickly promote or demote headings by using the buttons in the Outline Tools group:

- To move the current paragraph down to the next heading level, click the Demote button.

- To change a paragraph to body text, click the Demote to Body Text button.

- To move the current paragraph up to the next heading level, click the Promote button.

- To promote the current paragraph to Heading 1, click the Promote to Heading 1 button.

Tip   From the keyboard, press Tab to demote the current paragraph or Shift+Tab to promote it. You can also select a section and then drag it to the left to promote it or to the left to demote it, but doing so sometimes requires a steady touch.

Expanding and Collapsing the Outline and Headings

One of Outline view's strongest features is that you can expand the outline to different levels so that you can see exactly what you need to see. Figure 8-22 shows a section of outline with three levels of heading displayed and some sections expanded.

✣ **Taking Control of Your Health**
    ✣ **Chapter 1: Assessing Your Health**
        ✣ **Assessing Your Physical Health**
        ✣ **Assessing Your Mental Health**
        ✣ **Assessing Your Health**
           • **Next up is emotional health**
              ✣ *What Is Emotional Health?*
                  ⬜ **Resources**
                  ✣ **Worksheets**
                      ⬜ *Emotional Health Worksheet*

              ⬜
        ⬜ **Assessing Your Spiritual Health**
        ⬜ **Assessing Your Family Health**
        ⬜ **Assessing Your Social Health**
    ✣ **Chapter 2: Understanding the Super Health You Can Achieve**
        ⬜ **What Is Super Health?**
        ⬜ **Can You Achieve Super Health?**
        ⬜ **Why Wait Any Longer?**
    ✣ **Chapter 3: Setting Your Super Health Goals**
        ⬜ **Health and Vitality Goals**
        ✣ **Weight Goals**
           • **Fill in your desired weight here: _____ pounds.**
              ✣ *Why You Shouldn't Focus on the Pounds...*
                  • **... But Still Use Them to Track Your Progress**
        ⬜ **Activity and Exercise Goals**
    ✣ **Chapter 4: Into Action: The First Day of the Rest of Your Life**
    ✣ **Chapter 5: Immediate Results—the First Week**

Figure 8-22. You can expand an outline to different levels so that you can see exactly what you need

To choose the overall level of outline levels displayed, open the Show Level pop-up menu, and then click the level you want. Your choices are from Level 1 to Level 9, or All Levels if you want to display every paragraph. For much of your work in Outline view, you'll likely want to show several levels of headings, such as Levels 1, 2, and 3.

Once you've chosen the outline level, you can double-click the + sign next to a heading to display or hide the headings and other contents below it. A - sign next to a heading indicates that it has no lower-level headings or body text below it, as is the case with the "Activity and Exercise Goals" heading in Chapter 3.

The dotted underline that appears under some headings indicates that the heading has collapsed subheadings under it. The underline starts at the indentation level of the first subheading so you can see which level this is at. For example, the Chapter 4 heading has an underline that starts at the first level of indentation, indicating that the first subheading is a Heading 3-level or Outline 3-level item (the next level below the Chapter heading, which is Heading 2-level).

If you want to expand or collapse multiple sections at once, select the sections, and then click the Expand button or the Collapse button.

> **Tip**   If you want to zero in on the text of your outline without distractions, clear the Show Text Formatting check box in the Outline Tools group on the Outlining tab of the Ribbon. Clearing this check box makes Word show all the text in a standard font that lets you see more of the outline at once. Select this check box when you want to see the formatting again.

When you display all of the text of the document, you may find you lose many of the advantages of Outline view. But you can select the Show First Line Only check box in the Outline Tools group on the Home tab to make Word display only the first line of each paragraph (ending with an ellipsis to show that the rest is hidden). This feature lets you follow the gist of the paragraphs in the document without displaying the full text.

> **Tip**   Select the Show First Line Only check box when you need to change the order of paragraphs within a long section.

Moving Paragraphs Up and Down the Document

When you have displayed the outline level you want, you can quickly move paragraphs up and down the outline.

Click a + sign to select that item and all its subordinate items, or click and drag in the selection bar to select multiple items. You can then move them up or down the outline in these ways:

- *Ribbon*: Click the Move Up button or the Move Down button in the Outline Tools group on the Outlining tab to move the selection up or down by one displayed paragraph at a time.

- *Keyboard*: Press Ctrl+Shift+Up arrow or Ctrl+Shift+Down arrow to move the selection up or down by one displayed paragraph at a time.

- *Pointing device*: Drag the selection up or down as far as necessary. Word displays a line between paragraphs to indicate where the selection will land when you drop it.

Switching from Outline View to Another View

When you've finished working on the outline, choose Outlining ➤ Close ➤ Close Outline View from the Ribbon to return to the view you were using before.

You can also switch to another view by clicking the appropriate View button on the right side of the status bar or by opening the View menu and clicking the view you want.

> **Tip**   If you need to create very long documents, look into Word's Master Document feature, which you access by choosing Outlining ➤ Master Document ➤ Show Document from the Ribbon or View ➤ Master Document from the menu bar. This feature, which is beyond the scope of this book, enables you to create a kind of super-document that consists of multiple subdocuments. You can work with the master document in Master Document view, which is similar to Outline view.

Adding Footnotes and Endnotes

If you create professional or academic documents, you may need to add footnotes or endnotes to provide extra information or show your sources. A *footnote* is a note that appears at the foot of the page that refers to it, while an *endnote* is a note that appears at the end of a section or document. Use footnotes when it's likely the reader will want to read the information and the chunks of information are short enough to fit at the bottom of pages. Use endnotes for information that you think only a few readers will need to consult or for longer pieces of information.

> **Tip**   You can convert footnotes to endnotes, or endnotes to footnotes, if necessary. So, it's not a disaster if you start with one type of note and then realize you need the other type.

Adding a Footnote

To add a footnote to a document, follow these steps:

1. Place the insertion point immediately after the last word of the text you want the footnote to refer to.

> **Note**   You can also insert a footnote or endnote using the Footnote or Endnote dialog box, which you'll meet later in this chapter. Normally, you use the Footnote or Endnote dialog box to insert a footnote (or endnote) only when you need choose specific settings for the note, such as changing the numbering.

2. Choose References ➤ Footnotes ➤ Insert Footnote to insert a superscript footnote number or mark and open the footnote area.

    ■   In Print Layout view, Word shows the footnote area at the bottom of the page, separated by a horizontal line, as shown in the upper part of Figure 8-23. The footnote area shows only the footnotes that appear on that page.

- In Draft view, Outline view, or Web Layout view, Word shows the footnote area as a separate pane, as shown in the lower part of Figure 8-23. The footnote pane shows a list of all the footnotes in the document.

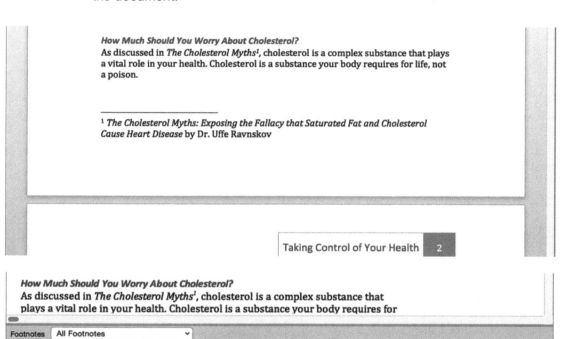

Figure 8-23. In Print Layout view, the footnote area appears at the bottom of the page (above). In other views, the footnote area appears as a separate pane (below)

3. Add the text or other material for the footnote by typing it in or pasting it.

4. Click in the main text of the document again to resume work in it. You can either leave the footnote pane open so that you can work with other footnotes in it or close it in one of these ways:

   - Drag the bar that separates the pane from the main window down to the bottom of the window.

   - Press Ctrl+Shift+C.

Adding an Endnote

To add an endnote to a document, follow these steps:

1. Place the insertion point immediately after the last word of the text you want the footnote to refer to.

2. Choose References ➤ Footnotes ➤ Insert Endnote from the Ribbon to insert a superscript endnote number or mark and open the endnote area.

   - In Print Layout view or Web Layout view, Word shows the endnote area on the last page of the document or section, separated by a horizontal line, as shown in the upper part of Figure 8-24.

   - In Draft view or Outline view, Word shows the endnote area as a separate pane, as shown in the lower part of Figure 8-24. The endnote pane shows a list of all the endnotes in the document.

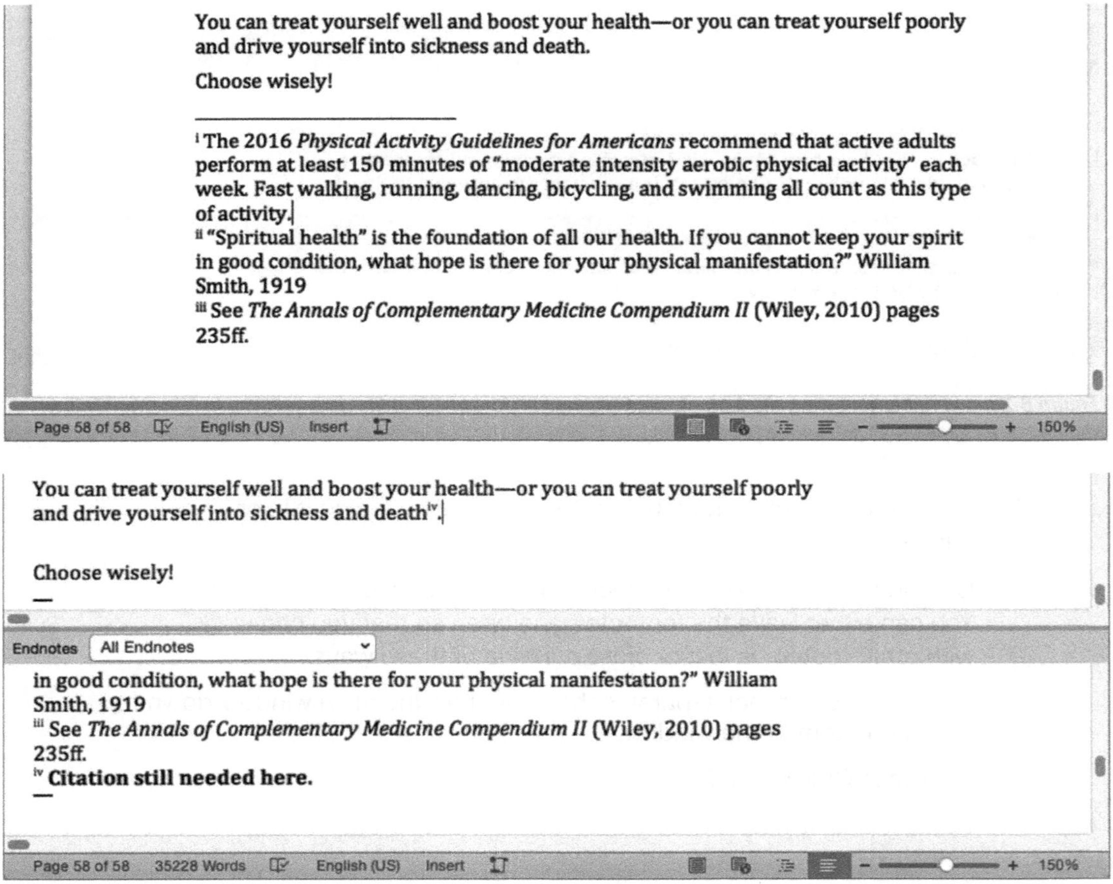

You can treat yourself well and boost your health—or you can treat yourself poorly and drive yourself into sickness and death.

Choose wisely!

---

[i] The 2016 *Physical Activity Guidelines for Americans* recommend that active adults perform at least 150 minutes of "moderate intensity aerobic physical activity" each week. Fast walking, running, dancing, bicycling, and swimming all count as this type of activity.
[ii] "Spiritual health" is the foundation of all our health. If you cannot keep your spirit in good condition, what hope is there for your physical manifestation?" William Smith, 1919
[iii] See *The Annals of Complementary Medicine Compendium II* (Wiley, 2010) pages 235ff.

Page 58 of 58   English (US)   Insert   150%

You can treat yourself well and boost your health—or you can treat yourself poorly and drive yourself into sickness and death[iv].

Choose wisely!

Endnotes All Endnotes

in good condition, what hope is there for your physical manifestation?" William Smith, 1919
[iii] See *The Annals of Complementary Medicine Compendium II* (Wiley, 2010) pages 235ff.
[iv] **Citation still needed here.**

Page 58 of 58   35228 Words   English (US)   Insert   150%

Figure 8-24. In Print Layout view and Web Layout view, the endnote area appears at the bottom of the final page of the document or section (above). In Draft view and Outline view, the endnote area appears as a separate pane (below)

3. Type or paste in the text or other material for the endnote.

4. Click in the main text of the document again to resume work in it. In Draft view or Outline view, you can either leave the endnote pane open for further use or close it in one of these ways:

   - Drag the bar that separates the pane from the main window down to the bottom of the window.

   - Press Cmd+Shift+C.

Customizing Footnotes and Endnotes to Suit Your Document

Word automatically numbers footnotes and endnotes and inserts them using its default placement: footnotes at the foot of the page and endnotes at the end of the document. The default settings work well for many documents, but for others, you may want to change the numbering or the placement. To do so, follow these steps:

1. Click in the section of the document for which you want to change the footnotes or endnotes. (If the document has only a single section, click anywhere in it.)

2. Choose Insert ➤ Footnote from the menu bar to display the Footnote and Endnote dialog box (see Figure 8-25).

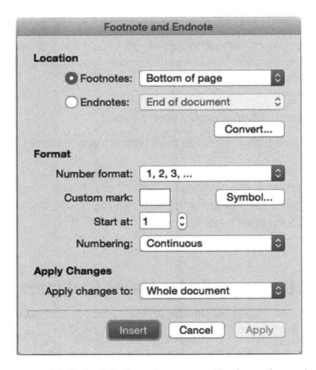

Figure 8-25. Open the Footnote and Endnote dialog box when you need to choose the numbering or symbols for footnotes or endnotes, change the position or numbering, or convert footnotes to endnotes or endnotes to footnotes

3.   In the Location area, select the Footnotes option button or the Endnotes option to tell Word which type of notes you want to affect.

4.   Choose where to place the notes in the document:

   - *Footnotes*: In the Footnotes pop-up menu, choose Bottom of page (the default) or Below text (which gives an odd look but helps make the footnotes more obvious to the reader).

   - *Endnotes*: In the Endnotes pop-up menu, choose End of document (the default setting) or End of section.

5.   In the Format area, choose the numbering you want for the notes whose option button you've selected:

   - *Number format*: In this pop-up menu, click the numbering format to use: 1, 2, 3; a, b, c; A, B, C; i, ii, iii; I, II, III; or a series of symbols.

   - *Custom mark*: To use a custom note mark, click the Symbol button. In the Symbol dialog box, click the symbol you want, and then click the OK button. The symbol appears in the Custom Mark box; delete it if you want to return to regular numbering.

   - *Start at*: In this box, enter the starting number to use for numbering. The default is the first character of the number format, such as 1, i, or A.

   - *Numbering*: In this pop-up menu, choose Continuous if you want to use the numbering sequence throughout the document. Choose Restart each section to start afresh with each section (this is useful for a document with endnotes at the end of each chapter). Choose Restart each page if you want to restart footnote numbering on each page (you can't use this option for endnotes because it wouldn't make sense).

6.   Click the Apply button to apply your choices.

7.   Click the Close button to close the Footnote and Endnote dialog box.

Note   To insert a footnote or endnote using the Footnote and Endnote dialog box, select the Footnotes option button or the Endnotes option button (as appropriate), choose any other options needed, and then click the Insert button.

Converting Footnotes to Endnotes or Endnotes to Footnotes

To convert footnotes to endnotes, endnotes to footnotes, or each kind of note to the other at the same time, follow these steps:

1.   Choose Insert ➤ Footnote to display the Footnote and Endnote dialog box.

Caution   Before converting the footnotes or endnotes in a long or complex document that contains many notes, create a fresh backup of the document. The conversion seldom goes wrong, but when it does, the notes can become severely scrambled.

2. Click the Convert button to display the Convert Notes dialog box (see Figure 8-26).

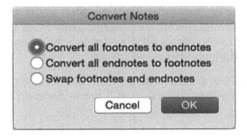

Figure 8-26. Use the Convert Notes dialog box to convert footnotes to endnotes, convert endnotes to footnotes, or switch each kind of note to the other

3. Click the Convert all footnotes to endnotes option button, the Convert all endnotes to footnotes option button, or the Swap footnotes and endnotes option button, as needed.

4. Click the OK button to close the Convert Notes dialog box and perform the conversion.

5. Click the OK button to close the Footnote and Endnote dialog box.

Navigating Among and Viewing Footnotes or Endnotes

You can navigate from one footnote or endnote to another by using the Go To tab of the Find and Replace dialog box. Click the Pages readout in the status bar to display the Go To tab of the Find and Replace dialog box. In the Go to what list box, click the Footnote item or the Endnote item, as needed. You can then move between footnotes or endnotes by clicking the Next button or the Previous button on the Go To tab.

Once you've located a footnote mark or endnote mark, you can preview the footnote or endnote by holding the pointer over the footnote mark or endnote mark until Word displays a tooltip containing the text of the footnote or endnote (see Figure 8-27).

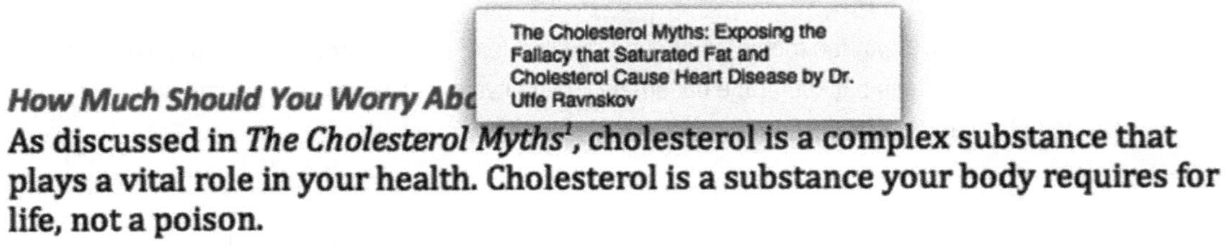

The Cholesterol Myths: Exposing the
Fallacy that Saturated Fat and
Cholesterol Cause Heart Disease by Dr.
Uffe Ravnskov

How Much Should You Worry Abo

As discussed in *The Cholesterol Myths*[1], cholesterol is a complex substance that plays a vital role in your health. Cholesterol is a substance your body requires for life, not a poison.

Figure 8-27. The quick way to view a footnote is to preview it in a tooltip

If the note is short and text only, this may be all you need to do. But if the note is longer or contains other types of contents (such as graphics, tables, or charts), double-click the footnote mark or endnote mark to display the footnote area or endnote area and jump directly to the note whose mark you double-clicked.

You can then move from note to note in the footnote area or endnote area. As you move the insertion point to another note, Word displays the corresponding part in the main document.

> **Note**   You can also display the footnote or endnote area by choosing View ➤ Footnotes. If Word displays the View Footnotes dialog box, click the View footnote area option button or the View endnote area option button as appropriate, and then click the OK button. (If the document contains only one kind of note, Word displays the area for that kind of note without opening the View Footnotes dialog box.)

Summary

In this chapter, you learned how to create complex documents and complex layouts. You now know how to convert existing text in a Word document into a table; how to add headers, footers, and page numbers to a document; and how to create a multicolumn, newsletter-style layout.

You also saw how to insert bookmarks to enable yourself to easily access and refer to parts of a document and how to insert cross-references to bookmarks or other document elements. And you learned to develop a document's outline swiftly and easily in Outline view, plus techniques for adding footnotes and endnotes to your documents.

In the next chapter, I'll show you how to create business documents and perform mail merge.

Chapter **9**

Creating Business Documents with Mail Merge

In this chapter, you will learn how to use Word's powerful mail merge feature to create business documents such as form letters, catalogs, mailing labels, and envelopes. Each of these types of documents is built around a common core, the main document, into which you merge variable data contained in records in a list, or data source, such as an Excel workbook or an address book.

Mail merge may initially seem daunting, but it's a great way of saving time and effort—so if you can invest some time learning how mail merge works, you'll soon reap the rewards.

I'll start by running through how mail merge works and the six separate steps Word uses to set up and execute mail merges. I'll then go through each step in turn so that you can get comfortable creating mail merge documents. Lastly, I'll show you how to turn a mail merge main document back into a regular Word document.

Understanding How Mail Merge Works

Mail merge works by using a standard document that contains data that remains constant and a list or data source that contains the records to be merged into the document.

- *Main document*: This is the document that contains the body of the merge documents you're creating. For example, when you use mail merge to create form letters, the main document is a letter that contains your address, the text that remains constant for each recipient, and fields into which the variable information (such as the recipient's name and address) is entered.

© Guy Hart-Davis 2016
G. Hart-Davis, *Learn Office 2016 for Mac*, DOI 10.1007/978-1-4842-2002-3_9

> **Note**   In mail merge, the main document is always a Word document. The list can also be a Word document that contains a table with the records for the mail merge, but it is more often a database-like file: an Excel workbook containing a table of records, your OS X Contacts file or Outlook's Contacts, or a query on a "real" database in an app such as FileMaker Pro.

- *List*: This is the file that contains the records or data that the merge places in the main document to create each merge document. For example, when you're creating a form letter, the list will contain each recipient's name and address, nickname or preferred greeting, and other items of information such as the product or query about which you're contacting the recipient. Each record consists of one or more *fields*, discrete items of information. For example, when you create a customer record, you usually have separate fields for the last name, first name, middle initial, e-mail address, all the separate components of the physical address, and so on.

> **Tip**   When you're creating a list, break up your records using a field for each item of data you may want to use separately. For example, instead of having a single field containing the street address, you may find it better to create a field for the street name and a separate field for the house number. This separation enables you to use the street name separately from the house number, which can be useful (for instance, if you need to identify all your customers in a particular street).

Word treats mail merge as a six-step process, during which it provides helpful prompts:

- *Step One: Select Document Type.* In this step, you choose the type of mail-merge document you want to create and create that document.

- *Step Two: Select Recipients List.* In this step, you choose the recipients list to use for the mail merge, such as a Word document containing a table or an Excel workbook.

- *Step Three: Insert Merge Fields.* In this step, you insert merge fields in the main document to mark the places where the merge will insert fields of information. For example, you insert the Last Name field where you want the recipient's last name to go.

- *Step Four: Filter Recipients.* In this step, you choose whether to merge all the records in the list or only some of them.

- *Step Five: Preview Results.* In this step, you preview how your merged documents will look so that you can make any changes needed before you proceed.

- *Step Six: Complete Merge.* In this step, you perform the merge, producing one of three end results: a document containing mail-merge letters (or labels or whatever) that you can use like any other document; multiple documents that Word sends directly to your printer; or e-mail messages.

In the rest of this chapter, you'll look at each step in turn.

Creating the Main Document for the Mail Merge

The first step in mail merge is to tell Word what kind of mail merge documents you want to create—form letters, e-mail messages, labels, envelopes, or a catalog-like list—and create a suitable main document. You can either create a new document from scratch or open an existing document.

To choose the merge document type and create the main document, follow these steps:

1. Open the existing document you want to use or create a new document:

   - *Open an existing document*: Click the File button on the title bar to display the Microsoft Word dialog box. Click the Recent tab for a recent document or the Open tab for any document. Navigate to and select the document, and then click the Open button.

   > **Tip** When creating form letters, you can often save time either by reusing an existing letter or by basing the main document on a letter template that has the sender address, recipient address, salutation, and so on, in suitable places. Similarly, if you already have the framework for a catalog-style list, you can reuse that. You can also reuse an existing document when creating envelopes or labels, but these are easy to create quickly from scratch using the Mailing tools.

   - *Create a new document*: Click the File button on the title bar, or choose File ➤ New from Template, to display the Word Document Gallery dialog box. Click the template on which to base the document, and then click the Create button. Click the Save button on the title bar (or press Cmd+S), specify the document name and folder in the Save As sheet, and then click the Save button.

2. Click the Mailings tab on the Ribbon to display its controls. Figure 9-1 shows the Mailings tab with the Start Mail Merge panel open.

Figure 9-1. The Mailings tab of the Ribbon contains controls for creating and running a mail merge

3. Choose Mailings ➤ Start Mail Merge ➤ Start Mail Merge to display the Start Mail Merge panel, and then click the item you want to create:

    ■ *Letters*: Click this item to create merged letters. This is the type of document I'll use in the examples. The documents don't have to be letters as such; you can create anything from party invitations to personalized storybooks.

    ■ *E-mail Messages*: Click this item to create e-mail messages ready to send in Outlook.

    ■ *Envelopes*: Click this item to create envelopes for printing on a printer. In the Envelope dialog box that Word displays, you then choose the size and shape of envelope you will use.

    ■ *Labels*: Click this item to create labels such as mailing labels for printing on a printer. In the Label Options dialog box that Word displays, you can choose from a wide variety of types of mailing labels.

    ■ *List*: Click this item to create a list containing mail merge data. For example, if you have a data-source list with records that contain details of machine parts, you can pull those records into a list to make them easily readable.

Once you've specified the document type, Word displays a prompt on the Information bar between the Ribbon and the document. Figure 9-2 shows an example. Click the X button at the left end of the Information bar if you don't want to see these prompts.

Figure 9-2. Word displays a prompt on the Information bar to let you know what to do next. You can click the X button at the left end of the Information bar to suppress the prompts

Selecting the Recipients for the Mail Merge

Once you've created the main document, the next step in the mail merge is to tell Word which list to use. To do so, choose Mailings ➤ Start Mail Merge ➤ Select Recipients to display the Select Recipients panel (see Figure 9-3), and then click the appropriate item:

■ *Create a New List*: Click this item to create a new list in Word.

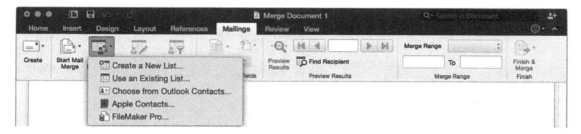

Figure 9-3. Choose your data source in the Select Recipients panel

■ *Use an Existing List*: Click this item to open an existing list in a Word document.

■ *Choose from Outlook Contacts*: Click this item to use data from your Outlook Contacts list.

■ *Apple Contacts*: Click this item to use data from your OS X Contacts list.

■ *FileMaker Pro*: Click this item to use data from a FileMaker Pro database.

How you use each of these list types varies, so I'll show each in a separate section.

Creating a New List in Word

The first option that Mail Merge offers you is to create a new list in Word. Word creates a list by inserting a table in a document and then storing the list items in the rows of the table.

> **Caution**   Creating a list in Word does work, but you should almost never do it. In many cases, you'll have the information you need in a more easily accessible format, such as a worksheet in an Excel workbook, your Outlook Contacts list, or your OS X Contacts list. And even if you don't have the information in such a format, it's better to put it in a spreadsheet, contacts list, or database because you'll be able to keep it updated and reuse it more easily there than if you create a list in Word.

If you decide to create a list in Word (see the nearby Caution), follow these steps:

1. Choose Mailings ➤ Start Mail Merge ➤ Select Recipients from the Ribbon, and then click Create a New List on the Select Recipients panel. The Edit List Fields dialog box opens (see Figure 9-4). This dialog box contains a list of standard fields for form letters, labels, and envelopes: Title, FirstName, LastName, JobTitle, Company, and so on.

Figure 9-4. Use the Edit List Fields dialog box to set up the fields for a new list stored in a Word document. Before you create such a data source, consider alternatives such as an Excel workbook, your Outlook Contacts, or your OS X Contacts list

2. Customize the list of fields as needed:

    ■ *Add a field*: Type the name in the New field name text box, and then click the Add (+) button. Word adds the field to the bottom of the Field names in header row list box. You can move it up by clicking the Move Up button (the button with the up arrow).

    ■ *Remove a field*: Click the field in the Field names list box, and then click the Remove (–) button. Word doesn't confirm the removal, but it places the field name in the Placeholder list text box in case you need to edit it and add it back to the list.

    ■ *Rearrange the fields*: To change the order in which the fields appear in the Field names list box, click the field, and then click the Move Up button (the button with the up arrow) or the Move Down button (the button with the down arrow).

3. When you've finished customizing the fields, click the Create button to close the Edit List Fields dialog box. Word displays the Save dialog box.

4. Type the name for the list document, and select the folder in which to save it.

5. Click the Save button to close the Save dialog box. Word saves the list document and then displays the Edit List Entries dialog box (see Figure 9-5).

Figure 9-5. Use the Edit List Entries dialog box to enter data in a new Word list quickly and easily

6. Type the information in each field, pressing Tab to move from one field to the next. (Press Shift+Tab if you need to move back to the previous field.)

7. When you've finished adding a record, click the Add (+) button to add a new record.

8. When you've finished adding records, click the OK button to close the Edit List Entries dialog box. Word automatically saves the data source document.

EDITING RECORDS IN THE EDIT LIST ENTRIES DIALOG BOX

When you create a new list, you mostly use the Add New button in the Edit List Entries dialog box. But when you open a list for updating or editing, you can also take other actions. To open a list for editing, choose Mailings ➤ Start Mail Merge ➤ Edit Recipient List.

These are the other actions you can take when editing records:

- *Navigate among records*: In the Record area in the lower-left corner of the Edit List Entries dialog box, click the First button to move to the first record, the Previous button to move to the previous record, the Next button to move to the next record, or the Last button to move to the last record. Or, if you know the number of the record you want, type it in the text box, and then press Return to display that record.

- *Delete the current record*: Click the Delete (–) button in the Edit List Entries dialog box.

- *Reset the record you're editing*: Click the Reset button to read the record again from the list document, and enter its data into the fields in the Edit List Entries dialog box. Resetting the record wipes out any changes you've made to the record.

- *Find a record*: Click the Find button to display the Find in Field dialog box (see Figure 9-6). Type the search term in the Find what box, entering all the text that will appear in the field (Word doesn't find matches for part of a field). Then open the In field pop-up menu, and click the field to search. Click the Find First button to locate the first matching record. Click the Find Next button (which replaces the Find First button after Word finds a match) to search again. Click the Close button when you've found the record you want to edit.

- *Open the list document*: Click the View Source button in the Edit List Entries dialog box. Normally you don't need to open the list document, because it's easier to add and edit records by using the Edit List Entries dialog box; Word keeps the list document hidden from view, even though it is open for editing. But you may sometimes need to open the list document so that you can make sweeping changes to it, for example, by using Word's Replace features to replace all instances of a particular term.

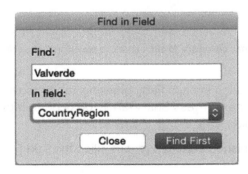

Figure 9-6. Use the Find in Field dialog box to quickly locate a particular record in a Word list

Opening an Existing List

If you already have your data in a Word document that you created previously, in an Excel workbook (for example, one that contains a database table), or in a text file, give the Use an Existing List command to connect the list to the main document. Follow these steps:

1. Choose Mailings ➤ Start Mail Merge ➤ Select Recipients ➤ Use an Existing List. Word displays the Choose a File dialog box, which works like any other Open dialog box.

2. Navigate to the folder that contains the list, and then click the file.

3. Click the Open button to close the Choose a File dialog box. Word connects the list to the main document.

Using Contacts from Your Outlook Contacts

If your version of Office for Mac includes Outlook, you probably store your contacts in Outlook's Contacts list. In this case, you can use your contacts easily in mail merges.

To use your Outlook Contacts list in a mail merge, choose Mailings ➤ Start Mail Merge ➤ Select Recipients ➤ Choose from Outlook Contacts. Word connects your Outlook Contacts list to the main document.

Using Contacts from Your OS X Contacts

If you keep your contacts' data in the OS X Contacts app rather than in Outlook, choose Mailings ➤ Start Mail Merge ➤ Select Recipients ➤ Apple Contacts. Word connects the OS X Contacts list to the main document.

Using Data from a FileMaker Pro Database

If the data you will use for the mail merge is in a FileMaker Pro database, follow these steps to connect the database to the main document:

1. Choose Mailings ➤ Start Mail Merge ➤ Select Recipients ➤ FileMaker Pro. Word displays the Choose a File dialog box, which works like any other Open dialog box.

2. Navigate to the folder that contains the list, and then click the file.

3. Click the Open button to close the Choose a File dialog box. Word connects the database to the main document.

Inserting Merge Fields in Your Main Document

Now that you've connected the data source to the main document, you're ready for the third step in the mail merge process. This step is to insert merge fields in your main document to tell Word where to place each field of information from the records.

Place the insertion point at the appropriate place in the document, choose Mailings ➤ Write & Insert Fields ➤ Insert Merge Field to display the Insert Merge Field panel, and then click the field you want to insert. Figure 9-7 shows an example of inserting fields to create a name-and-address block suitable for a letter.

> **Tip**   Remember to add all the necessary spaces and punctuation between the merge fields. It's easy to omit the spaces and punctuation when you're arranging the merge fields, but the resulting merged documents look unprofessional and unconvincing. You've probably received enough of them yourself to know how even a minor mistake in layout instantly destroys the illusion of care that the personalized letter is intended to give. If you can get the spaces and punctuation right when inserting the merge fields, you're ahead of the game; if not, you can catch errors at the preview stage.

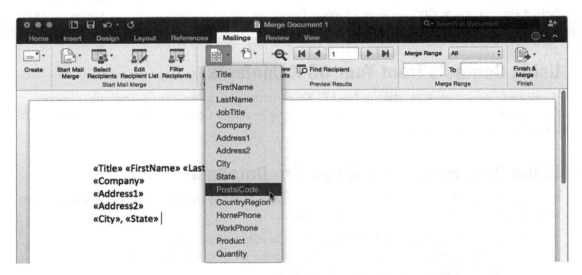

Figure 9-7. Add merge fields to your main document by from the Insert Merge Field panel in the Write & Insert Fields group on the Mailings tab of the Ribbon

> **Note**   The Rules button in the Write & Insert Fields group on the Mailings tab of the Ribbon enables you to insert *rules*, which are fields you can insert in the document to do things such as add information about the merge itself or insert data only if a condition is met. For example, the Merge Sequence # rule inserts the merge sequence number, and the If… Then… Else rule inserts one text string if the condition you specify is met and a different text string if it is not. Rules are beyond the scope of this book, but you can find information on how to use them online or in Word's Help file.

Filtering the Recipients of the Merge Document

The fourth step in the mail merge process is to filter the recipients of your data source to specify which of them should receive the merged documents.

> **Note**   If you want to use each item in your data source to produce a document or entry in the mail merge, you don't need to apply filtering.

To filter the recipients of the merge, follow these steps:

1. Choose Mailings ➤ Start Mail Merge ➤ Filter Recipients from the Ribbon to open the Query Options dialog box. The contents of the Query Options dialog box vary depending on the list you're using, so I'll show you a couple of examples.

2. Figure 9-8 shows the Query Options dialog box as it appears for Outlook Contacts. Figure 9-9 shows the Query Options dialog box as it appears for a list created in Word.

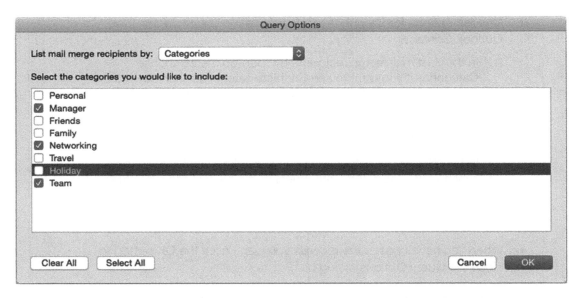

Figure 9-8. In the Query Options dialog box, set up any filtering needed to identify the records you want to use in the mail merge. This is the Query Options dialog box you see for Outlook Contacts

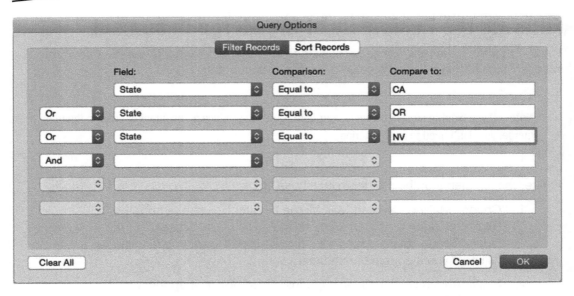

Figure 9-9. The Query Options dialog box for a list created in Word enables you not only to filter the records but also sort them into your preferred order

3. Choose options for filtering the data source. For example, for Outlook Contacts,

    ■ In the "List mail merge recipients by" pop-up menu, choose Categories if you want to see Contacts categories such as Personal, Work, Friends, and Family. Using a category is the quick and easy way to filter records, as long as you've arranged your contacts by categories. Choose Complete Record if you want to be able to choose individual contacts by name.

    ■ In the "Select the categories you would like to include" list box (when you've selected Categories) or the "Select the individual contacts you would like to include" list box (when you've selected Complete Record), select the check box for each category or for each contact you want to include.

4. When you have chosen the records you want, click the OK button to close the Query Options dialog box.

Previewing the Results of the Mail Merge

At this point, the merge is set up and ready to run—in theory. In practice, it's all too easy to waste paper or send embarrassing e-mail messages by getting merge fields and text in the wrong places. So, it's always wise to use the preview feature to make sure your merge works the way you intend it to work.

To preview the results, choose Mailings ➤ Preview Results ➤ Preview Results, clicking the Preview Results button so that it appears darker and pushed in. The first of the merged documents appears (see Figure 9-10), and you can see whether you've got the fields and text in the right places.

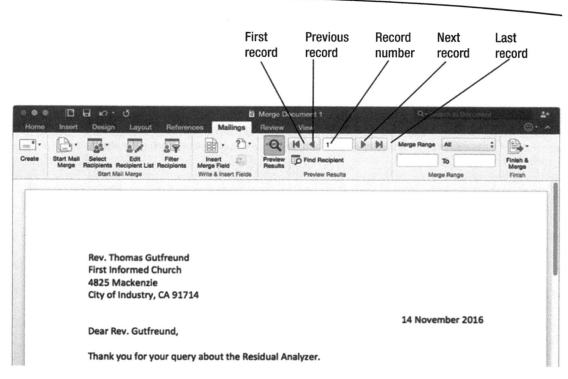

Figure 9-10. *Use the controls in the Preview Results group on the Mailings tab of the Ribbon to make sure the merged documents look correct before you create them*

You can then move through the records using the Next Record button, Last Record button, Previous Record button, and First Record button in the Preview Results group, looking to see whether data missing from or present in any of the records shows up problems with the document's merge fields and layout. With the data in place, it's much easier to see whether you're missing text, spaces, punctuation, or even paragraph marks.

If you need to move to a particular record by number, click the Record Number box to select its current contents, type the number, and then press Return to display it.

Click the Preview Results button again, unpushing it, when you want to display all the merge fields instead of the data. Showing the merge fields can be helpful when you need to see exactly what information is going where.

Completing the Mail Merge

After you've previewed the merge results and deemed them satisfactory, you're ready for the sixth and final step: completing the mail merge. In this step, you choose among sending the mail merge documents directly to your printer, creating a document that contains them all (and that you can edit and customize further if necessary), or creating e-mail messages to the recipients.

When you're ready to complete the mail merge, choose Mailings ➤ Merge Range ➤ Merge Range from the Ribbon to display the Merge Range pop-up menu, and then choose which records to merge:

- *All*: Select this item to merge all the records.

- *Current Record*: Select this item to merge just the record you've selected. This setting is useful for merging individual records you missed in your main merge or for running a test item to make sure everything's working okay.

- *Custom*: Select this item when you need to specify a range of records. Type the start number in the left text box (which has no label) and the end number in the To text box.

Once you've selected the records, follow the instructions in the next three subsections for the type of merge documents you want to create.

Merging to a New Document

To merge the records to a new document that contains all the documents together, choose Mailings ➤ Finish ➤ Finish & Merge ➤ Edit Individual Documents from the Ribbon. Word creates a new document that contains all the merged documents. You can then check through the document, add any extra information needed (for example, you may want to personalize some documents manually), and then save it or print it as needed.

Merging Individual Documents to a Printer

To merge the records to individual documents and send them directly to a printer, follow these steps:

1. Choose Mailings ➤ Finish ➤ Finish & Merge ➤ Print Documents from the Ribbon. The Print dialog box opens.

2. Make sure the correct printer is selected in the Printer pop-up menu.

3. Choose any other print options needed. For example, if you need to print two copies of each merged document, enter **2** in the Copies text box.

4. Make sure that the document in the Quick Preview box looks the way it should. Use the First Page button, Previous Page button, Next Page button, and Last Page button below the Quick Preview area to move from page to page, making sure that each page looks right.

5. Click the Print button to merge the documents to the printer and print them.

Merging to E-mail Messages

To merge the records and create e-mail messages, follow these steps:

1. Choose Mailings ➤ Finish ➤ Finish & Merge ➤ Merge to E-mail. Word displays the Mail Recipient dialog box (see Figure 9-11).

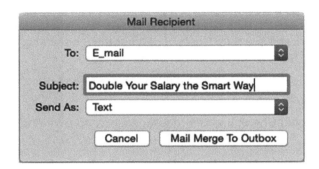

Figure 9-11. In the Mail Recipient dialog box, enter the subject line for the e-mail messages, and choose whether to send them as text, HTML, or attachments

> **Tip**   If the Merge to E-mail command on the Finish & Merge panel is dimmed and unavailable, you likely need to set Outlook as your default e-mail reader. Save your work and quit Word. Open the Mail app, choose Mail ➤ Preferences, and click the General tab button to display the General preferences. Open the Default email reader pop-up menu and choose Microsoft Outlook in it. Quit Mail, reopen Word, and then reopen your merge document and choose Mailings ➤ Finish ➤ Finish & Merge ➤ Merge to E-mail from the Ribbon again.

2. In the To pop-up menu, make sure the field containing the e-mail address is selected. Word suggests the E_mail field by default, but you may need to select a different field (for example, one with a home e-mail address rather than a work e-mail address).

3. In the Subject text box, type the subject line you want each message to use.

4. In the Send As pop-up menu, choose the format in which to send the e-mail messages:

   - *Text*: Choose this item to send the Word document's text without formatting. Using text makes sure the addressee receives the message, but the text loses any formatting. If you use plain text, test how the document looks in a text-only format before sending the merged documents. For example, you may need to add a blank line between paragraphs to make sure they don't appear as a single block.

- *Attachment*: Choose this item to send the Word document as an attachment to the e-mail message. Sending the document as an attachment ensures that the Word document retains all its formatting in transit, but recipients must have Word (or a compatible word-processing app) in order to read the attachment.

- *HTML Message*: Choose this item to send the Word document as a formatted e-mail message. This works well as long as the recipient's e-mail app can accept HTML-formatted messages; if not, the recipient will see a text-only version of the message and a version with HTML codes studded through it.

5. Click the Mail Merge To Outbox button to merge the documents to your e-mail outbox.

6. Go to Outlook. Check that the messages look correct, and then send them.

Restoring a Mail Merge Main Document to a Normal Document

Sometimes you may need to change a main document that you used for mail merge back to a normal document so that you can use it normally. To do so, follow these steps:

1. Open the document.

2. Choose Mailings ➤ Start Mail Merge ➤ Start Mail Merge ➤ Normal Word Document from the Ribbon. Word displays a confirmation dialog box (see Figure 9-12).

Figure 9-12. Click the Restore button in this confirmation dialog box to change a Word document back from a mail merge main document to a normal document

3. Click the Restore button. Word removes the link to the list.

4. Save the document. For example, click the Save button on the title bar or press Cmd+S.

Summary

In this chapter, you learned how to use Word's powerful mail merge feature to create business documents such as form letters, mailing labels, envelopes, and catalogs. You now know how Word's six-step process for creating mail merge documents works. You can create main documents, build new lists or connect existing lists, filter the records to use only those you need, and perform the merge.

In the next chapter, I'll show you how to revise, review, and finalize documents. Turn the page when you're ready to start.

Chapter 10

Revising and Reviewing Documents

Chances are that you'll create some documents on your own, but for other documents, you'll need to work with other people—either sharing the documents on a network or via the Internet or using e-mail to send the documents back and forth.

Word includes strong features for working together on documents. In this chapter, I'll start by reviewing the different options so that you're clear about the different choices. After that, I'll show you how to work on a document simultaneously with your colleagues—if you have the technology required—and how to share documents but work on them one person at a time.

Next, you'll learn how to use the Track Changes feature, also called revision marking, to track all the edits you and your colleagues make to a document so that you can keep an audit trail. You can then review the changes and decide which to keep and which to remove.

Last, I'll show you how to add comments to a document, how to compare two documents to identify their differences automatically, and how to incorporate changes from two or more copies of a document into a single file.

Working on Documents with Your Colleagues

In Word, you can work on documents with your colleagues either together or separately:

- *Work on the same copy of the document simultaneously*: If you have a SharePoint site or you store documents on OneDrive, you and your colleagues can store the document on the site, each open it at the same time, and work on it together. Microsoft calls this *coauthoring*.

© Guy Hart-Davis 2016
G. Hart-Davis, *Learn Office 2016 for Mac*, DOI 10.1007/978-1-4842-2002-3_10

- *Work on separate copies of the document*: If you don't have a SharePoint site or use OneDrive, and you open a document that somebody else is using, Word opens the document in a read-only state. If necessary, you can save the document under a new name so that you can edit it, and then integrate any changes you make back into the main copy.

- *Circulate a copy of the document, and each work on it in turn*: This method is easiest because you use only a single copy of a document, and each person has free rein when they're editing it—but it usually takes longer than the other methods. To see clearly which changes each person has made to the document, you normally use Word's Track Changes feature, as discussed in this chapter.

> **Note**   If you have a SharePoint site, chances are you will want to try simultaneous editing and see how well it works for you. But if you find that running into conflicting changes creates more problems than it solves, you may be better off using the older means of collaboration. Coauthoring is technically very impressive, and it can be great in the right situation, but it's not suitable for everyone.

Whichever way you work, you can use three main features for revising and reviewing documents with your colleagues:

- *Track Changes*: When you turn on this feature, Word tracks the insertions, deletions, formatting changes, and most other changes to the document. You can then view the changes, accept the changes you want to keep, and reject the others.

- *Comments*: You and your colleagues can attach comments to items in the document to offer opinions or suggest changes, without actually changing the text itself. You can then view the comments and remove them once you've dealt with them.

- *Compare*: This feature makes Word analyze and mark up the differences between two versions of the same document. Document Compare is useful when you need to amalgamate changes from two or more different versions in which you haven't tracked changes.

Editing a Document Simultaneously with Your Colleagues

Word's most advanced way of working on a document with your colleagues is for each of you to open the same copy of the document at the same time and all work on it together. Here's what happens:

- *Create the document*: You create the document as normal (for example, by using a template) and store it on your SharePoint site or on OneDrive.

> **Caution**   Unless you have a fast and reliable Internet connection, simultaneous editing of a large document stored on OneDrive can be slow enough to make collaboration difficult.

- *Open the document:* The first person opens the document as normal. When another person opens the document, they see a pop-up message (see Figure 10-1) telling them about the other people already editing the document. The first person also receives a pop-up message as soon as Word notices that other authors have joined in.

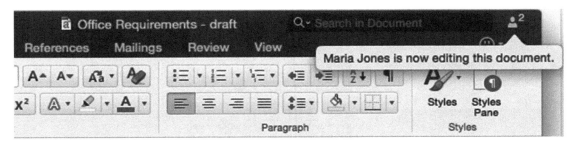

Figure 10-1. When you open a document that others are working on, Word displays a pop-up message to let you know they're editing it

- *See who's editing the document:* The status icon at the right end of the title bar displays an icon showing the number of people editing the document. (This number includes you.) You can click the icon to see who the people are (see Figure 10-2) and click a person's name to display information and contact buttons (for e-mail, instant messaging, and audio and video calls) for him or her.

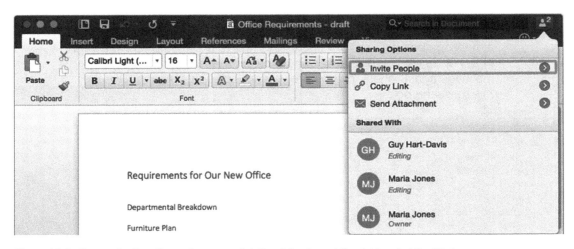

Figure 10-2. To see who the other authors are, click the status icon at the right end of the title bar

- *Edit the document*: You can work pretty much as normal in Word, except that only one person can edit a particular paragraph or other element at a time. As you work, Word shows you which parts of the document other authors are working on by placing a line to the left of the items and displaying a name box (see Figure 10-3). Word also displays an icon with the Update symbol (two arrows curling clockwise) to indicate when updates are available.

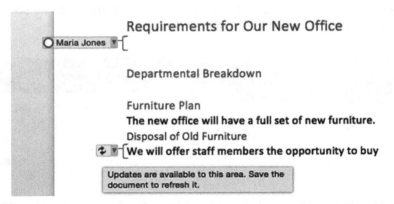

Figure 10-3. Word shows you which parts of the document your coauthors are working on at the moment and when updates are available

- *Update the document*: When you're ready to save changes and get any updates that are available, you press Cmd+S or click the Save button on the title bar as usual. The Save button displays the Update icon (those curving arrows) to indicate that it's acting as an Update button. Word then updates the copy of the document you're viewing with the changes the others have made (see Figure 10-4), applies shading to the changes to draw your attention to them, and makes your changes available to your coauthors. At first, when you update the document, Word displays a message box (Figure 10-4 shows this too) to make sure you're aware of the updates; you probably want to select the "Do not show this message again" check box before you click the OK button to dismiss this message box.

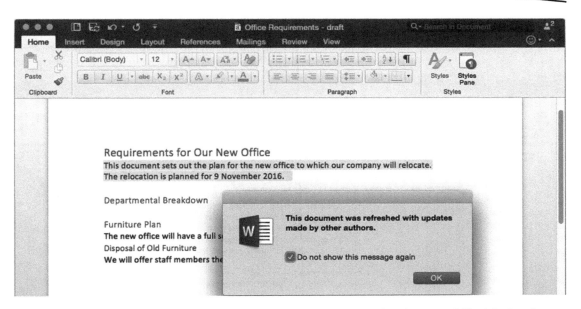

Figure 10-4. When you save your changes, Word merges in updates your coauthors have saved. Word displays the new items with shading (as in the highlighted paragraph here). Word also displays a message box about the updates, but you can suppress this by selecting the "Do not show this message again" check box before you click the OK button

- *Resolve conflicts*: Word does its best to show you and your coauthors who's working where, but sooner or later, two or more of you may change the same part of the document in the same cycles of saving and updating. When this happens, Word displays the Upload Failed message on the Information bar (see Figure 10-5) to the author who tried to save changes over the changes another author had already saved. Click the Resolve button at the right end of the Information bar to add the Conflicts tab to the Ribbon and display the Conflicts pane (see Figure 10-6). You can then use the controls in the Conflicting Changes group on the Conflicts tab of the Ribbon to resolve the conflicts by accepting or rejecting changes. When you have resolved all the conflicts, Word displays the Conflicts Resolved message on the Information bar. Click the Save button at the right end of the Information bar to save the changes and exit from Conflict Mode back to the normal editing mode.

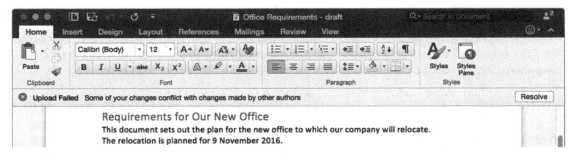

Figure 10-5. Word warns you of any conflicting changes when you try to save the document. Click the Resolve button on the Information bar to deal with the highlighted conflicts

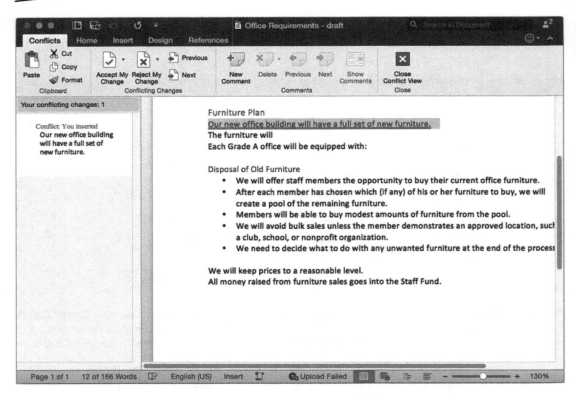

Figure 10-6. In the Conflict pane on the left, click the change you want to resolve. Use the controls in the Conflicting Changes group on the Conflict tab of the Ribbon to accept and reject changes and move among them

■ *Close the document*: When you have finished working with the document, save any unsaved changes, and then close it as usual.

Sharing Documents with Your Colleagues on a Network

You can also share documents with your colleagues on a network without using SharePoint. In this case, you save the document in a shared folder on the network. From there, anyone permitted to use the folder can open the document, edit it, and save it.

In previous versions of Word, only one person at a time could open a document in a shared folder. If you tried to open a document that somebody else had already opened, Word would display a message saying that the file was locked for editing and inviting you to open a read-only copy of the file. After opening the read-only copy, you could make changes to the document, but you could save them only by using a different file name, a different location, or (for bonus points) both.

As of this writing, Word no longer warns you that a file is locked for editing. Instead, Word opens the file and displays a Read Only message on the Information bar beneath the Ribbon (see Figure 10-7). You can click the Duplicate button at the right end of the Information bar to create a copy of the document in which you can save changes. If you want to integrate those changes into the network copy, you need to do so either manually or by using the Document Combine feature (discussed later in this chapter).

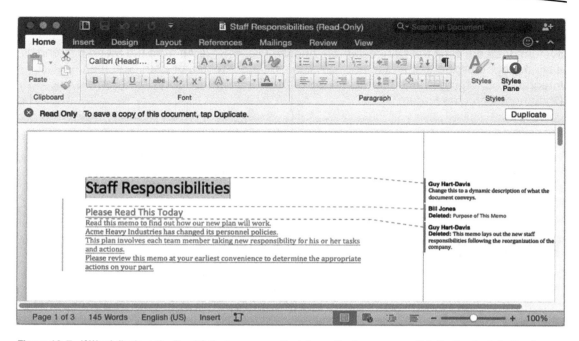

Figure 10-7. *If Word displays the Read Only message on the Information bar, you can click the Duplicate button to create a copy of the file in which you can save changes*

This arrangement works well most of the time, but Word seems sometimes to miss the fact that a document is open and locked for editing. When this happens, you appear to have the document open for editing, and all goes well until you try to save it. At this point, Word discovers the problem and displays the Grant File Access dialog box (see Figure 10-8), inviting you to grant Word access to the locking file, which has an automatically generated name such as .smbdeleteAAA184e75e. (The period at the beginning of the file name is correct.)

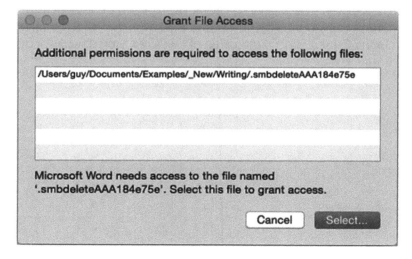

Figure 10-8. *If Word displays the Grant File Access dialog box, it means that someone else is already editing the document. Click the Cancel button, and then save your copy under a different name*

Don't click the Select button and use the resulting dialog box to try to locate the locking file—it's a hidden file, and you won't be able to see it unless you tinker with the OS X file system. Instead, click the Cancel button, choose File ➤ Save As from the menu bar, and save the document under a different name, in a different folder, or both. You then need to integrate your changes with the main copy of the document by using, for example, the Document Combine feature.

> **Tip** Save your changes to documents frequently. Not only does frequent saving help you avoid losing data if Word or your Mac crashes, but it can also prevent you from losing much time to the sharing bug explained in this section.

Tracking the Changes in a Document

When you need to work with other people on creating or revising a document, use Word's Track Changes feature. Track Changes can automatically track almost all the changes in the document so that you can review them, see who made which changes when, accept the changes you want to keep, and reject the rest.

You can choose which types of changes to track and which to ignore. For example, you may want to track only the edits to the text of a document and let your colleagues handle the formatting.

Choosing Which Changes to Track

To choose which types of changes Word tracks in a document, follow these steps:

1. From the Ribbon, choose Review ➤ Tracking ➤ Markup Options ➤ Preferences to display the Track Changes pane in the Word Preferences window (see Figure 10-9). You can also choose Word ➤ Preferences from the menu bar and then click the Track Changes icon in the Output and Sharing area of the Word Preferences window.

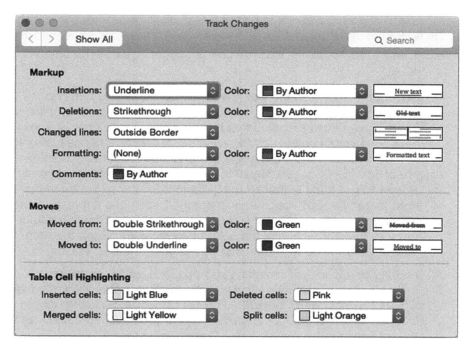

Figure 10-9. In the Track Changes preferences pane, choose how to show markup, track moves, and handle changes to table cells and formatting

2. In the Markup area, choose how to mark insertions, deletions, changed lines, and comments:

    ■ *Insertions*: Open the Insertions pop-up menu, and then click the type of markup you want for inserted text. Your choices are (None), Color Only, Bold, Italic, Underline, Double Underline, Strikethrough, or Double Strikethrough. Use the Color Only setting when you need a subtle indication of added text; use Underline or Double Underline when you need a stronger indication. Open the topmost Color pop-up menu, and choose By Author if you want Word to use a different color for each reviewer's additions; to use a specific color or shading for all added text, click that color or shading.

    ■ *Deletions*: Open the Deletions pop-up menu, and then click the type of markup to use for deleted text. Your choices are (None), Color Only, Bold, Italic, Underline, Double Underline, Strikethrough, Hidden, ^ (Word displays a single caret mark to show where text has been deleted), # (Word shows a single pound sign where text has been deleted), or Double Strikethrough. Open the second Color pop-up menu and choose By Author if you want Word to use a different color for each reviewer's deletions; to use a specific color or shading for all deletions, click that color or shading.

> **Tip**   The Hidden item can be a good choice for deletions because it makes the deleted items disappear from the document, leaving only the text that hasn't been deleted and the text that has been added.

- *Changed lines*: Open the Changed lines pop-up menu and choose whether (and, if so, where) you want Word to display a vertical line in the margin next to each line that has changed. These changed lines help you locate changes in documents that contain changes on only some lines, but if most every line has changed, the changed lines are of little use. Choose (None) to skip using changed lines, Left Border to put them in the left margin, Right Border to put them in the right margin, or Outside Border to put the lines in the left margin on left pages and the right margin on right pages. Open the third Color pop-up menu and choose the color or shading you want; the Auto item applies the default text color and is often the best choice.

- *Formatting*: Open the Formatting pop-up menu, and choose how to mark up items whose formatting has changed. Your choices are (None), Color Only, Bold, Italic, Underline, Double Underline, Strikethrough, or Double Strikethrough. Pick a formatting type you haven't yet used, and then choose the color in the fourth Color pop-up menu.

- *Comments*: Open the Comments pop-up menu, and choose the color or shading to give to each reviewer's comments. Choose the By Author item to have Word use different colors for each reviewer.

3. In the Moves area, select the Track moves check box if you want Word to track text you've moved within a document separately from insertions and deletions. If you select this check box, you can choose settings as follows:

   - *Moved from*: Open the Moved from pop-up menu and choose how to mark the text that is no longer there because it has been moved to a different location in the document. Your choices are the same as for Deletions, but you should use a different marking so that you can distinguish moved text from deletions. For example, use Strikethrough for Deletions and Double Strikethrough for Moved From text. Open the Color pop-up menu, and choose By Author or the color or shading you want.

   - *Moved to*: Open the Moved to pop-up menu, and choose how to mark the moved text in its new location. Your choices are the same as for Insertions, but you should use a different marking so that you can distinguish the moved text; for example, Underline for Insertions and Double Underline for Moved To text.

> **Note**   Word's feature for tracking moved text separately from insertions and deletions works only for documents that use the Word Document format (with the .docx file extension), not for documents that use the older Word 97–2004 Document format (on the Mac) or the Word 97–2003 Document format (on Windows).

4. In the Table Cell Highlighting area, choose the colors with which to shade cells that have been inserted, deleted, merged, or split in a table. Usually, you use a different color for each of these changes to a table's structure.

> **Caution** Word provides the By Author setting for the four pop-up menus in the Table cell highlighting area of the Track Changes Options dialog box, but it's best not to use this setting. Otherwise, although you can see who changed the table's structure, you need to dig deeper to see what the person did to the table. Usually, it's easier to see how the table has changed and then find out who made the changes only if you need to do so.

5. Close the Preferences window by clicking the Close button (the red button at the left end of the title bar) or pressing Cmd+W.

Turning On Track Changes for a Document

To turn on Track Changes for a document, choose Review ➤ Tracking ➤ Track Changes, moving the Track Changes switch from the Off position to the On position.

> **Tip** From the keyboard, press Cmd+Shift+E to toggle Track Changes on or off. This is usually the quickest way of toggling Track Changes.

You can also choose Tools ➤ Track Changes ➤ Highlight Changes from the menu bar to display the Highlight Changes dialog box (see Figure 10-10), select the "Track changes while editing" check box, and then click the OK button.

Figure 10-10. You can turn Track Changes on by selecting the "Track changes while editing" check box in the Highlight Changes dialog box and then clicking the OK button

When you need to turn Track Changes off again, choose Review ➤ Tracking ➤ Track Changes again, moving the Track Changes switch from the On position to the Off position.

Ensuring Your Colleagues Use the Track Changes Feature

Track Changes is a great feature, but anyone can turn off tracking and rampage through the document making untracked changes unless you force them to use Track Changes. You can do this by protecting the document. Follow these steps:

1. Choose Review ➤ Protect ➤ Protect Document from the Ribbon or Tools ➤ Protect Document from the menu bar to display the Password Protect dialog box (see Figure 10-11).

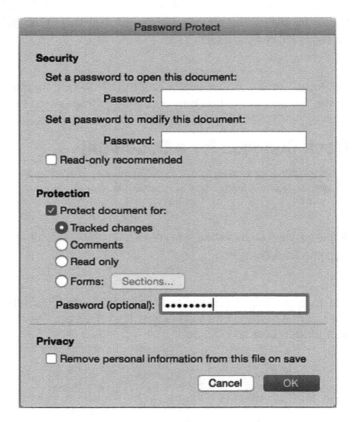

Figure 10-11. Use the Password Protect dialog box to ensure that your colleagues use Track Changes when editing the document

2. In the Protection area, select the Protect document for check box.

3. In the same area, select the Tracked changes option button.

4. In the Password (optional) box, type a password. You should make the password at least eight characters long, mix upper- and lowercase letters, and include numbers and symbols.

5. Click the OK button. Word displays a dialog box prompting you to re-enter the password.

6. Type the password in the Re-enter the password box, and then click the OK button. Word closes both the confirmation dialog box and the Password Protect dialog box and applies the protection to the document.

7. Save the document by clicking the Save button on the title bar or pressing Cmd+S.

Working in a Document with Track Changes On

After you turn on Track Changes for a document, you can work in it much as normal. Word tracks your insertions, deletions, and other changes, and displays such markup as you've chosen to show.

For example, in Print Layout view and Web Layout view, Word normally displays the markup area and balloons, as shown in Figure 10-12.

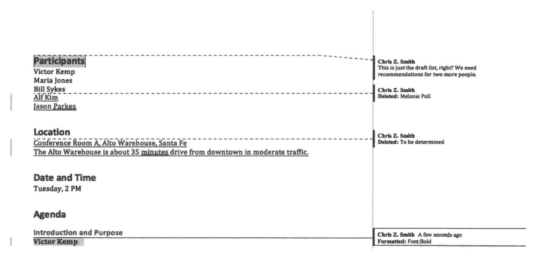

Figure 10-12. In Print Layout view and Web Layout view, Word displays the markup area with balloons detailing the changes

Tip To switch among the settings for markup balloons, choose Review ➤ Tracking ➤ Markup Options ➤ Balloons, and then click the command you want: Show Revisions in Balloons, Show All Revisions Inline, or Show Only Comments and Formatting in Balloons.

In Draft view and Outline view, Word shows the changes inline, using the markup specified in the Track Changes pane of the Word Preferences dialog box, such as applying an underscore to each insertion and strikethrough to each deletion, as shown in Figure 10-13.

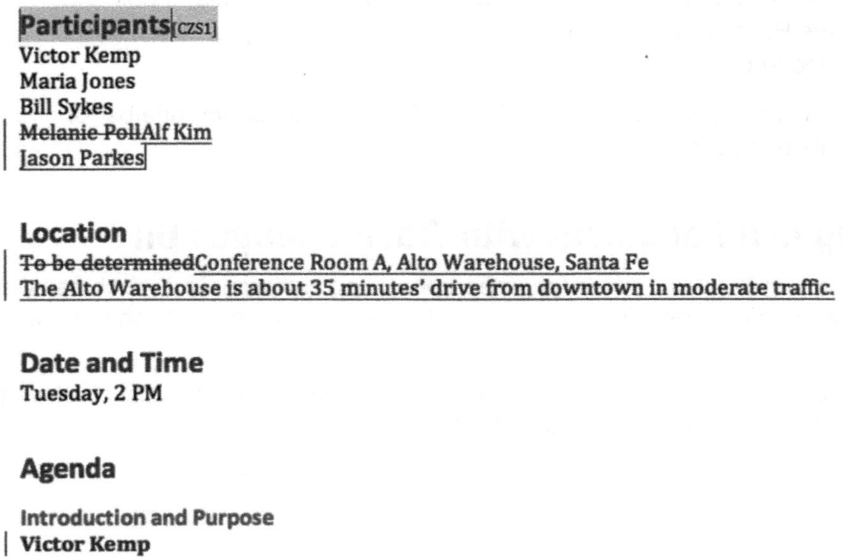

Participants[CZS1]
Victor Kemp
Maria Jones
Bill Sykes
~~Melanie Poll~~Alf Kim
Jason Parkes

Location
~~To be determined~~Conference Room A, Alto Warehouse, Santa Fe
The Alto Warehouse is about 35 minutes' drive from downtown in moderate traffic.

Date and Time
Tuesday, 2 PM

Agenda

Introduction and Purpose
Victor Kemp

Figure 10-13. Depending on the markup options you've chosen and the view you're using, Word can mark insertions and deletions inline

To see information about a change in Draft view or Outline view (or in one of the other views— for example, when you have chosen not to use the markup area), hold the pointer over the change. Word displays a tooltip showing the details of the change (see Figure 10-14).

Location
~~To be determined~~Conference Room A, Alto
The Alto Warehouse is about 35 minutes' drive from downtown in moderate traffic.

Chris Z. Smith, 3/17/16 9:54 AM: Inserted
The Alto Warehouse is about 35 minutes' drive from downtown in moderate traffic.

Figure 10-14. Hold the pointer over a tracked change to display a tooltip showing the details

Note   If Word doesn't display a tooltip when you hold the pointer over a tracked change, choose Word ➤ Preferences to display the Preferences window. In the Authoring and Proofing Tools area, click the View icon to display the View preferences pane. In the Show in Document area, select the Comments on rollover check box. Close the Preferences window by clicking the Close button (the red button at the left end of the title bar) or pressing Cmd+W. Word now displays the tooltips.

Choosing How to View the Document's Changes and Markup

As you work with Track Changes on, you may find it helpful to change how Word displays the markup for review. For example, you can show the document as it will appear with all the markup accepted or show the document's original version to see how it was before you or other editors let rip.

To choose how to view the document's markup, go to the Tracking group on the Review tab of the Ribbon. Open the Display for Review pop-up menu (this is the upper-right pop-up menu; its name doesn't appear), and then click the setting you want:

- *All Markup*: Choose this item to see the document's final text with all the markup displayed. This is the default setting and the one you probably want to use most of the time while marking up the document. In the layout views with balloons displayed, the insertions appear in the document's text without balloons; the deletions disappear from the document except from markers connected to balloons in the markup pane that show what was deleted.

- *Simple Markup*: Choose this item to see the document's final text with only change lines (the vertical bars in the margin) and comments. This view is useful for reading through the changed areas of the document for completeness without the detail of the changes to distract you.

- *No Markup*: Choose this item to see the document's final text with no markup appearing. Use this view when you want to read the document without the visual distraction of markup or when you want to see the true page count of the final document.

- *Original*: Choose this item to see the document's original text before any of the changes were made. Use this view when you need to remind yourself of how the document originally read.

Controlling Which Changes Word Displays

Word enables you to choose which tracked changes to display. To do so, go to the Tracking group on the Review tab of the Ribbon, open the Markup Options pop-up menu (see Figure 10-15), and then display an item by clicking to place a check mark next to it or hide a displayed item by clicking to remove its check mark.

> **Tip**   Which tracked changes you find helpful to display and the best way to display them will likely depend on the amount of changes in the document; the nature of those changes; and your role in creating, editing, or finalizing the document. For example, when cleaning up a document that contains only a few changes, you likely want to display all the tracked changes. By contrast, when reviewing edits on a document savaged by multiple colleagues, you may want to hide formatting changes so that you can concentrate on the text, view only one reviewer's changes at a time, or go through comments before looking at the actual changes. Experiment with different combinations of settings to find out what works best for you.

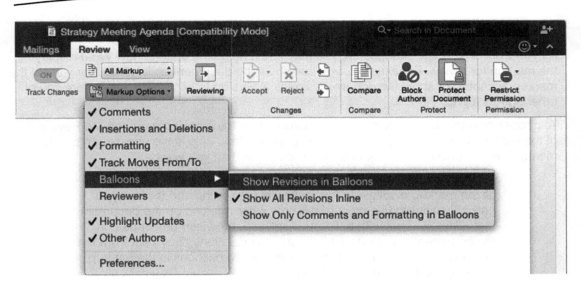

Figure 10-15. *Use the Markup Options pop-up menu to control which tracked changes appear on screen and how they appear. The Balloons submenu lets you choose whether to show revisions in balloons or show them inline*

These are the items you can display or hide:

- *Comments*: Choose whether to show comments inserted in the document (as discussed in the "Adding Comments to a Document" section later in this chapter).

- *Insertions and deletions*: Choose whether to show text and other items inserted in the document, deleted from it, or moved from one place in the document to another.

- *Formatting*: Choose whether to show changes to formatting, such as the application of a style or the addition of direct formatting.

- *Markup area highlight*: Choose whether to show shading on the markup area rather than displaying it as the document's normal background color. Usually it's helpful to show the shading so that you can easily see where the page ends and the markup area starts.

- *Balloons*: This submenu gives you a choice of three ways to use balloons; even though the submenu displays a check mark for your selection, its three items work as an option group, so you can select only one item at any given time. Choose the Show Revisions in Balloons item to display a balloon for each revision; choose the Show All Revisions Inline to force Word to display revisions inline even for Print Layout and Web Layout view; or choose Show Only Comments and Formatting in Balloons to display comments and formatting changes in balloons but other changes inline.

- *Reviewers*: In this submenu, choose All Reviewers to display comments from all reviewers. Otherwise, remove the All Reviewers check mark, and put a check mark next to each reviewer whose changes you want to see.

- *Highlight updates*: Choose whether to have Word highlight the latest updates to the document so that you can identify them more quickly.

- *Other authors*: Choose whether to mark updates by other authors.

> **Note**   Click the Preferences item at the bottom of the Show Markup pop-up menu to display the Track Changes pane in the Word Preferences window.

Integrating Tracked Changes into a Document

When everyone has made their edits to the document, you can go through the changes and accept those you want to keep and reject the others.

To go through the changes, use the controls in the Changes group on the Review tab of the Ribbon (see Figure 10-16). First, select a change by clicking the Next button or the Previous button, clicking the balloon in the markup area, or clicking the change in the Reviewing pane.

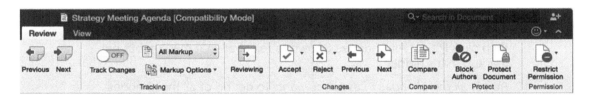

Figure 10-16. Click the Next button or the Previous button in the Changes group on the Review tab of the Ribbon to navigate from one revision to another

You can then accept changes by using the Accept button and its pop-up menu (see the left screen in Figure 10-17):

- *Accept the selected change and automatically select the next change*: Click the main part of the Accept button (or click the pop-up button and then click the Accept and Move to Next item).

- *Accept the selected change*: Click the Accept pop-up button, and then click Accept This Change.

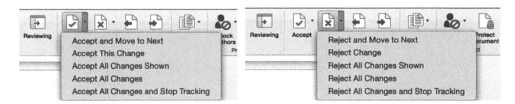

Figure 10-17. Use the Accept button and the options on the Accept pop-up menu (left) to accept tracked changes in the document; similarly, use the Reject button and the options on the Reject pop-up menu (right) to reject tracked changes

- *Accept all changes shown with your Markup Options settings*: When you've chosen to show only some markup, click the Accept pop-up button, and then click Accept All Changes Shown to accept all that markup but not markup that's hidden. For example, if you've chosen to show formatting but not show insertions and deletions, clicking Accept All Changes Shown accepts all formatting changes.

- *Accept all the changes in the document*: If the document contains changes light enough that you can review them all without dealing with individual changes along the way, click the Accept pop-up button, and then click Accept All Changes.

- *Accept all the changes and stop tracking changes*: Click the Accept pop-up button, and then click Accept All Changes and Stop Tracking.

Similarly, you can reject one or more changes at once by using the Reject button and its pop-up menu (see the right screen in Figure 10-17):

- *Reject the selected change and automatically select the next change*: Click the Reject button (or click the pop-up button and then click the Reject and Move to Next item).

- *Reject the selected change*: Click the Reject pop-up button, and then click Reject Change.

- *Reject all changes shown with your Show Markup options*: When you've chosen to show only some markup, click the Reject pop-up button, and then click Reject All Changes Shown to reject all that markup but not markup that's hidden.

- *Reject all the changes in the document*: To get rid of all the changes, click the Reject pop-up button, and then click Reject All Changes.

- *Reject all the changes and stop tracking changes*: Click the Reject pop-up button, and then click Reject All Changes and Stop Tracking.

When you've finished accepting or rejecting changes, save the document. You may want to save it under a different name (or in a different folder) if the document is now ready for another stage in its evolution.

Tip   You can also accept or reject a change by using the context menu. Ctrl-click or right-click the change in the text, in the markup area, or in the Reviewing pane, and then click the Accept item or the Reject item on the context menu. The name of the menu items varies depending on the change, such as Accept Insertion or Reject Deletion.

Adding Comments to a Document

When you need to give your input on a document without making changes to the text, use Word's comments. A *comment* appears in a floating balloon attached to a word or another object in text, enabling you to comment easily and clearly on a specific item.

> **Note**   If you want to ensure your colleagues use comments on a document rather than altering its text, protect the document for comments. Choose Review ➤ Protect ➤ Protect Document from the Ribbon or Tools ➤ Protect Document from the menu bar to display the Password Protect dialog box. In the Protection area, select the Protect document for check box, and then select the Comments option button. Type a password in the Password (optional) box, and then click the OK button. Confirm the password in the confirmation dialog box, click the OK button, and then save the document.

Adding a Comment

To add a comment to a document, select the text or object you're commenting on, and then give the appropriate command:

- *Ribbon*: Choose Review ➤ Comments ➤ New Comment.
- *Menu bar*: Choose Insert ➤ Comment.

> **Note**   If you want to attach a comment to a single word, just click in that word or immediately before it. When you insert the comment, Word automatically puts the comment parentheses around the word.

Word then adds colored parentheses around your selection to indicate that it has a comment attached. The way Word displays the comment depends on the view you're using:

- *Print Layout view or Web Layout view*: Word displays the markup area at the right side of the page and opens a comment balloon for you to type the comment in. The comment balloon is attached to the comment markers by a thin line, so you can see which part of the document each comment belongs to. Figure 10-18 shows the markup area open with two comments inserted.

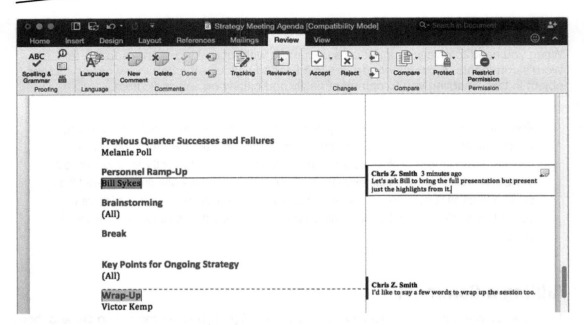

Figure 10-18. In Print Layout view and Web Layout view, Word displays comments in the markup area to the side of the document

- *Draft view or Outline view*: Word opens the Reviewing pane, which you use for reviewing comments and other markup. Figure 10-19 shows the Reviewing pane open in Draft view.

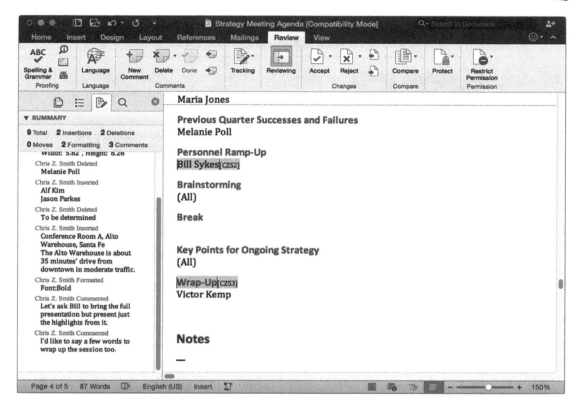

Figure 10-19. *In Draft view and Outline view, Word displays comments in the Reviewing pane and shows the comment number in brackets after the commented item*

Type (or paste) the text of the comment either in the comment balloon or in the comment's area in the Reviewing pane. Most people leave comments as plain text, but you can apply formatting to a comment if you want. For example, you can apply bold or a style to a word that you want to emphasize. You can also insert elements such as tables and graphics in comments.

If you're using the Reviewing pane, click the Close button (the × button) at the upper-right corner when you've finished using it. You can also choose Review ➤ Reviewing from the Ribbon to toggle the display of the Reviewing pane.

Viewing and Reviewing Comments

To review comments, you normally use the markup area and comment balloons (in Print Layout view or Web Layout view) or the Reviewing pane.

You can also hold the pointer over commented text or the comment mark to display a tooltip showing the text of the comment, as shown in Figure 10-20.

> Chris Z. Smith, 3/17/16 10:59 AM:
> Commented - I'd like to say a few words to wrap up the session too.

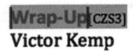

Victor Kemp

Figure 10-20. Hold the pointer over commented text or a comment mark to display a tooltip showing the text of the comment

> **Note**   If Word doesn't display a tooltip when you hold the pointer over a comment, choose Word ➤ Preferences to display the Preferences window. In the Authoring and Proofing Tools area, click the View icon to display the View preferences pane. In the Show in Document area, select the Comments on rollover check box, and then close the Preferences window by clicking the Close button (the red button at the left end of the title bar) or pressing Cmd+W.

Most people find the markup area and comment balloons easy unless a document has a huge number of comments, but if you find the balloons awkward, you can turn them off by choosing Review ➤ Tracking ➤ Markup Options ➤ Balloons ➤ Show All Revisions Inline.

Even when the markup area is open, you can display the Reviewing pane by choosing Review ➤ Reviewing from the Ribbon or View ➤ Sidebar ➤ Reviewing from the menu bar.

Deleting Comments

You can delete a comment by Ctrl-clicking or right-clicking it in the text, in the comments pane, or in the Reviewing pane, and then clicking Delete Comment on the context menu.

> **Note**   If you're using balloons, you can delete a comment by clicking the × button in its balloon.

Alternatively, click the comment in the text, in the comments pane, or in the Reviewing pane, and then choose Review ➤ Comments ➤ Delete (clicking the main part of the Delete button).

To delete only the comments currently displayed, choose Review ➤ Comments ➤ Delete ➤ Delete All Comments Shown (clicking the Delete pop-up button to display the pop-up menu, as shown in Figure 10-21).

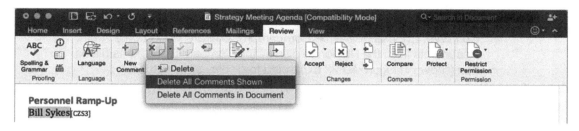

Figure 10-21. From the Delete pop-up menu in the Comments group of the Review tab of the Ribbon, you can delete all the comments shown or all the comments in the document

To delete all the comments from the document, choose Review ➤ Comments ➤ Delete ➤ Delete All Comments in Document. Word doesn't confirm the deletion, but you can use Undo if you give the command by accident.

Comparing or Combining Different Versions of the Same Document

When you need to follow and review the changes in a document, the best approach is to use Track Changes (as described earlier in this chapter) on a single document that each reviewer works on in turn. This way, Track Changes records all the information you need about the changes made to a document and gives you the tools to review the changes and incorporate them easily.

Other times, you may need to circulate a document to various colleagues at the same time, such as to get the review done more quickly. This method gives you multiple copies of the same document containing their different edits marked by Track Changes. To incorporate all the different edits into a single copy of the document, you can use Word's Document Combine feature.

You may also need to compare two copies of a document in which the changes haven't been tracked. For this, you can use the Document Compare feature. This feature isn't as good as Track Changes used consistently, but it's a huge improvement over spending hours poring over different document files and trying to integrate the best changes into a single version.

To use Document Compare to compare or combine two documents, follow these steps:

1. If either or both of the documents are open, close them. Starting with both documents closed is usually easier than starting with either or both open, because it avoids any confusion over similarly named documents you have open.

2. If you have no document open in Word, press Cmd+N to open a new blank document. You need to do this because Word makes the Compare Documents command and the Merge Documents command unavailable when no document is open.

3. Give the command for comparing or combining, as needed:

    ■ *Compare*: Choose Review ➤ Compare ➤ Compare ➤ Compare Documents from the Ribbon to display the Compare Documents dialog box (shown in Figure 10-22 expanded to display all its settings).

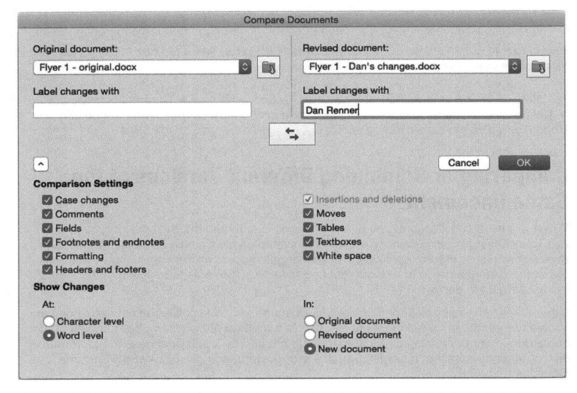

Figure 10-22. Use the Compare Documents dialog box or the related Combine Documents dialog box to identify the changes between two documents based on the same document

    ■ *Combine*: Choose Review ➤ Compare ➤ Compare ➤ Combine Documents from the Ribbon or Tools ➤ Combine Documents from the menu bar to display the Combine Documents dialog box, which is almost identical to the Compare Documents dialog box apart from the title.

4. Choose the documents you want to compare:

    ■ Either open the Original document pop-up menu and click the document in the list or click the Open button next to the pop-up menu, click the document in the Open dialog box, and then click the Open button.

    ■ Similarly, either open the Revised Document pop-up menu and click the document in the list or click the Open button next to the pop-up menu, click the document in the Open dialog box, and then click the Open button.

Tip If you get the original document and revised document on the wrong sides of the Compare Documents dialog box or the Combine Documents dialog box, click the Switch Documents button (the button showing left and right arrows) in the middle of the dialog box to switch the two documents.

5. Tell Word how to label the changes to the document:

   ■ The left "Label changes with" text box or the "Label unmarked changes with" text box shows the name of the original document's last reviewer who used Track Changes. Type a different name if necessary. If the text box is blank and unavailable, the document contains no tracked changes.

   ■ The right "Label changes with" text box or "Label unmarked changes with" text box shows the last reviewer of the revised document. Again, you may need to type a different name.

6. Click the arrow button to the left of the Cancel button to display the lower part of the dialog box so that you can choose comparison settings.

7. In the Comparison settings area, clear the check box for any items you don't want to integrate. For example, if you want to omit the changes to fields, clear the Fields check box. Usually, you want to leave most of the check boxes selected.

8. On the left side of the Show changes area (under the At heading), select the Word level option button to make Word analyze changes at the word level. If you need to dig deeper, you can select the Character level option button instead, but for many documents this produces more detail than is helpful.

9. On the right side of the Show changes area (under the In heading), select the New document option button if you want to merge the changes into a new document. This is usually clearest, but you can select the Original document option button or the Revised document option button instead if you prefer.

10. Click the OK button to close the dialog box and make Word analyze the changes.

11. If Word displays the dialog box shown in Figure 10-23, warning you that the new document already has changes and that Word may ignore some existing changes, click the Yes button. What this means is that the revised document contains tracked changes; to make the comparison, Word will accept these changes. (The alternative is to click the No button, go back into the documents, and accept or reject the revisions before you compare or combine the documents.)

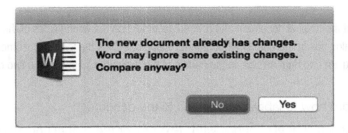

Figure 10-23. If Word displays this dialog box when you're comparing or combining documents, click the Yes button to proceed

Word then displays the result of the comparison or combination, for example a new document containing tracked changes shown in balloons. You can then review the tracked changes as discussed earlier in this chapter. If you've created a new document that you want to keep, save it.

Summary

In this chapter, you learned essential techniques and tools for revising and reviewing documents. You learned how to edit a document simultaneously with your colleagues and how to share documents via a network. You now know how to set up Track Changes to mark the changes you want to track, how to make your colleagues use Track Changes, and how to accept or reject the changes that Word records. You can use comments to add suggestions or requests to documents, and you can use the Document Compare feature and Document Combine feature to analyze documents and automatically incorporate different edits in them.

In the next chapter, I'll show you how to finalize, print, and share your Word documents.

Printing, Securing, and Sharing Documents

In this chapter, you'll look at how to share your documents with other people. You'll start by seeing how to print an entire document or the relevant pages or sections of it, how to choose whether to include markup, and how to print other parts of the document, such as markup and document properties. After that, I'll show you how to secure your Word documents by removing sensitive information, locking the documents with passwords, and marking the documents as read-only.

Next, you'll learn how to deal with issues in making a Word 2016 document compatible with earlier versions of Word. Last, I'll show you how to create an electronic version of a document suitable for distributing online or sending to a print shop for specialist printing.

Using Word's Features for Printing Documents

You can print your Word documents by using the standard techniques discussed in Chapter 2, but Word also offers extra features that you may want to use, such as printing a custom range of pages; printing markup with its document or without its document; or printing a document's properties, styles, or custom key assignments.

Printing a Custom Range of Pages

After correcting a document, you may need to print a custom range of pages, such as pages 1, 3, 5, 8–10, 15, and 30. To do so, follow these steps:

1. Choose File ➤ Print or press Cmd+P to display the Print dialog box.

2. Make sure the Copies & Pages category is selected in the nameless pop-up menu below the Presets pop-up menu (see Figure 11-1).

© Guy Hart-Davis 2016
G. Hart-Davis, *Learn Office 2016 for Mac*, DOI 10.1007/978-1-4842-2002-3_11

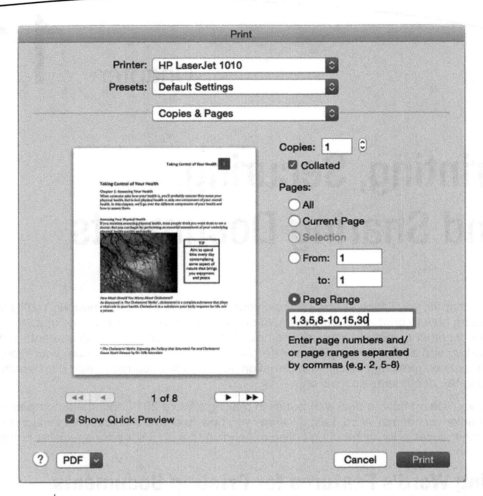

Figure 11-1. *Use the Page Range option button and text box in the Copies & Pages pane of the Print dialog box to print a custom range of pages*

3. Select the Page Range option button.

4. In the text box below the Page Range option button, type the details of the range you want to print, using the conventions shown in Table 11-1. For example, **1,3,5,8-10,15,30** prints the pages mentioned at the beginning of this section.

Table 11-1. Specifying a Custom Range of Pages to Print

To Print These Pages	Type This	Example
Consecutive pages	Starting page number, hyphen, ending page number	**8-10**
Individual pages	Page number, comma, page number	**7,11,15**
Sections	**s** and section number	**s1, s3**
Range of sections	**s** and starting section number, hyphen, **s** and ending section number	**s1-s3**
Pages within sections	**p** and page number, **s** and section number	**p3s5-p8s7**

5. Choose any other print options needed.

6. Click the Print button to print the pages.

> **Note** Printing by sections is most useful if you've split up a document into sections, each of which starts on a new page.

Printing Markup and Other Items

To print items such as markup and document properties, you use the Print What pop-up menu in the Microsoft Word pane of the Print dialog box. To display the Microsoft Word pane, follow these steps:

1. Choose File ➤ Print or press Cmd+P to display the Print dialog box.

2. Open the pop-up menu below the Presets box, and then click the Microsoft Word item to display the Print What pop-up menu and Print option buttons in the Microsoft Word pane (see Figure 11-2).

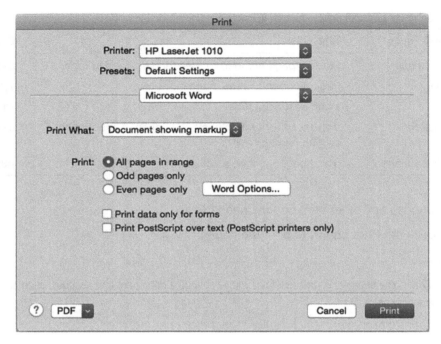

Figure 11-2. Choose the Microsoft Word item in the pop-up menu below the Presets pop-up menu to display the Microsoft Word pane, which contains the Print What pop-up menu and the Print option buttons

Choosing Whether to Print Markup—or Only Markup

When you print a document, you can choose either to print any markup and comments it contains or to print the document as it appears without the markup and comments.

To tell Word which you want, open the Print What pop-up menu in the Microsoft Word pane in the Print dialog box. Click the Document item on the menu to print the document without markup. Click the Document showing markup item on the menu to include the markup in the printout.

> **Note**   Sometimes it's useful to print only the markup for a document. To do so, open the Print What pop-up menu in the Microsoft Word pane in the Print dialog box, click the List of markup item, and then click the Print button.

Printing Document Properties, Styles, AutoText Entries, and Key Assignments

In the same way that you can print only the markup in a document, you can also print four other items by choosing them on the Print What pop-up menu in the Microsoft Word pane in the Print dialog box:

- *Document properties*: Select this item to print a page showing the document's properties: the file name, directory (folder), template, title, subject, author, and so on.

- *Styles*: Select this item to print pages listing the styles used in the document and their formatting.

- *AutoText entries*: Select this item to print a list of the AutoText entries stored in the document's template.

- *Key assignments*: Select this item to print a list of the custom key assignments in the document (there may not be any).

> **Note**   Depending on the printer model you have, you may be able to choose other settings, such as controlling layout or paper handling.

Securing a Document

When you are ready to share a document with others, you may need to secure it. Word gives you several tools for securing a document:

- You can set Word to warn you before you print, close, or send a file that contains tracked changes or comments.

- You can protect the document with a password to prevent unauthorized people from opening it or modifying it.

- You can remove sensitive information from the document automatically.

- You can mark a document with a read-only recommendation.

- You can restrict access to the document to only specific people. This topic is beyond the scope of this book.

In this section, you'll look at the first four of these five tools.

Setting Word to Warn You About Tracked Changes or Comments

As you saw in Chapter 10, Word's Track Changes feature and Comments feature are great for collaborating on documents with your colleagues. But tracked changes and comments often contain information not intended for a document's final audience, so it's vital to remove them before distributing a document.

Word includes a setting to warn you that a document contains tracked changes or comments before you distribute it. Follow these steps to turn on this setting:

1. Open the document you want to affect. If the document is already open, click it to make it active.

2. Choose Word ➤ Preferences or press Cmd+, (Cmd and the comma key) to display the Word Preferences window.

3. In the Personal Settings area, click the Security & Privacy icon to display the Security & Privacy pane (see Figure 11-3).

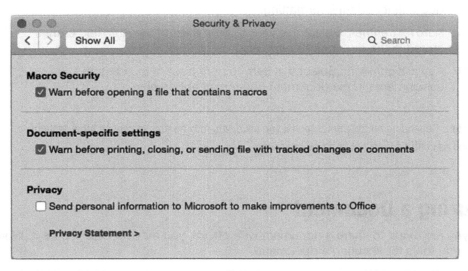

Figure 11-3. To turn on Word's features for helping you avoid distributing documents containing sensitive metadata, select the two check boxes in the Privacy options area of the Security pane in the Word Preferences dialog box

4. In the Document-specific settings area, select the "Warn before printing, closing, or sending a file that contains tracked changes or comments" check box. This makes Word display a warning dialog box (Figure 11-4 shows an example) when you go to print, close, or send a file that contains tracked changes, comments, or both.

> **Note**   The "Warn before printing, closing, or sending a file that contains tracked changes or comments" setting tends to give a lot of false-positive warnings because when you save a document, Word doesn't know whether you're about to attach it to an e-mail message from your e-mail application or distribute it another way. But if your documents contain comments or tracked changes you need to remove before distributing the documents, these extra warnings should be only a minor irritant.

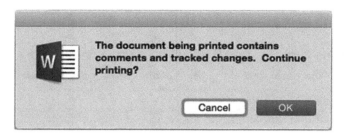

Figure 11-4. You can set Word to warn you that a document you're about to print, close, or send contains comments or tracked changes

5. Close the Preferences window by clicking the Close button (the red button at the left end of the title bar) or pressing Cmd+W.

6. Click the Save button on the title bar or press Cmd+S to save the document with its new settings.

Protecting a Document with a Password

If you need to keep other people out of a document or let only approved people open it, you can protect the document with a password. Word lets you use two types of password:

■ *Password to open*: This is a password required to open the document at all. Word prompts you to enter this password when you try to open the document (see Figure 11-5).

Figure 11-5. When you set a password to open a document, Word prompts you for the password before you can open the document

■ *Password to modify*: This is a password required to open a document in write mode, in which you can save changes to the document. Word prompts you for this password when you open the document (see Figure 11-6). If you don't have the password, you can click the Read Only button to open the document in read-only mode, in which you cannot save changes under the current file name and folder. (You can save a copy of the document using a different file name, folder, or both.)

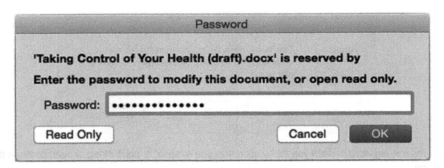

Figure 11-6. When you set a password to modify a document, Word prompts you for the password when you open the document. You can open the document in read-only mode by clicking the Read Only button

Use a password to open when you need to protect the contents of the document against people who shouldn't see them. Use a password to modify when you want to protect this particular copy of the document against unwanted changes. Use both when you need to implement both forms of protection; Word displays the Password dialog box for the password to open first and then (if the user gets that password right) the Password dialog box for the password to modify.

Caution   Word's password protection is effective only against casual snoopers. An attacker who uses a password-cracking program (such programs are widely available on the Internet) can open a password-protected document with minimal effort.

To encrypt a document with a password, follow these steps:

1. Choose Review ➤ Protect ➤ Protect Document from the Ribbon or Tools ➤ Protect Document from the menu bar to open the Password Protect dialog box (shown in Figure 11-7 with settings chosen).

Figure 11-7. Use the Password Protect dialog box to apply a password to open, a password to modify, or both to the active document

2. In the Security area, click in the Password box under the Set a password to open this document heading if you want to set a password to open.

3. Type the password.

4. Press the Tab key. Word displays a sheet prompting you to enter the password again.

5. Type the password again in the Re-enter the password box, and then click the OK button. The sheet closes, returning you to the Password Protect dialog box.

6. In the Security area, click in the Password box under the Set a password to modify this document heading if you want to set a password to modify.

7. Type the password.

8. Press the Tab key. Word displays a sheet prompting you to enter the password again.

9. Type the password again in the Re-enter the password box, and then click the OK button. The sheet closes, returning you to the Password Protect dialog box.

10. Click the OK button to close the Password Protect dialog box.

11. Now that the protection is in place, save the document. For example, click the Save button on the title bar or press Cmd+S.

> **Note**   You (or anyone else who knows the password) can remove it easily. Choose Review ➤ Protect ➤ Protect Document from the Ribbon or Tools ➤ Protect Document from the menu bar to open the Password Protect dialog box. Select the password in the Password to open text box or the Password to modify text box, and then press Delete to delete it. Click the OK button to close the Password Protect dialog box, and then save the document (for example, press Cmd+S).

Removing Sensitive Information from a Document

Quite apart from any confidential contents, a Word document can include sensitive information about who worked on it, who last saved it, and who added and deleted which parts of it. This information is often helpful while you're developing a document, but you may want to remove it before you distribute the document.

You can set Word to remove the sensitive information—Word calls it "personal" information—automatically. To do so, open the Password Protect dialog box as explained in the previous section and select the "Remove personal information from this file on save" check box. Close the Password Protect dialog box and save the document as usual.

Marking a Document As Read-Only

As well as providing password protection, the Password Protect dialog box also contains the Read-only recommended check box. By selecting this check box (and then saving the document), you can make Word display a dialog box (see Figure 11-8) to anyone who opens the document. The dialog box recommends that the user open the document as read-only, but the user is free to click the No button and open it for editing.

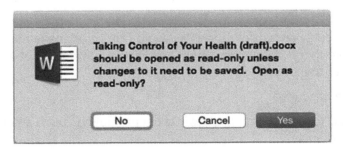

Figure 11-8. When you mark a document as read-only, Word displays this dialog box to recommend that the user open the document as read-only. The user can easily ignore the recommendation

> **Caution**   Marking a document as read-only is a feeble security measure that is seldom helpful. If you want to force your colleagues to treat a particular document as read-only, apply a password to modify to the document, and share the password with nobody but yourself.

Making a Document You Can Open with Earlier Versions of Word

If you work with people who use versions of Word earlier than Word 2008 for Mac or Word 2007 for Windows or with people who use other word processing programs, you may need to make versions of your documents that will open in earlier versions of Word. This is because earlier versions of Word used a different file format than the recent versions; Word 2003 for Windows and Word 2004 for Mac can open the new file format only if you install file converters (see the nearby Note), and many other word processing programs can open only files in the older format, which is generally referred to as Word 97–2003 on Windows or Word 98–2004 on the Mac.

> **Note**   If you need to get the file converters, steer your browser to the Microsoft Download Center (www.microsoft.com/downloads/). For Windows, download the Microsoft Office Compatibility Pack for Word, Excel, and PowerPoint File Formats file. For the Mac, download the Open XML File Format Converter.

To save a document in a format compatible with earlier versions of Word, follow these steps:

1. If the document contains unsaved changes, save them.

2. Choose File ➤ Save As or press Cmd+Shift+S to display the Save As sheet.

3. Open the Format pop-up menu (see Figure 11-9), and click the format you want. These are the file types you're most likely to need:

    ■ *Word 97–2004 Document (.doc)*: Use this format to create a document readable by older versions of Word and by compatible word processing programs.

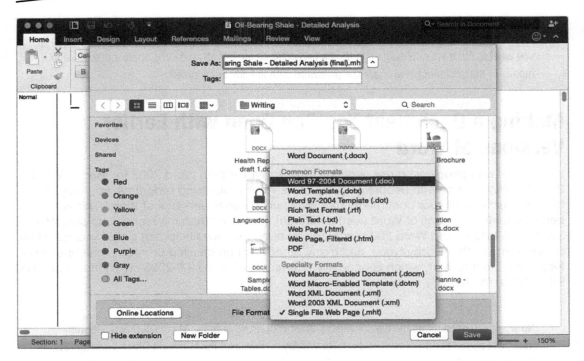

Figure 11-9. Use the Format pop-up menu in the Save As sheet to save a Word document in a format that's compatible with other word processors

---

Note   The format listed as "Word Document (.docx)" in the Format pop-up menu is the latest Word format. This is the format in which Word 2016 saves documents unless you specify another format—so in most cases you will be changing the document from this format to another format.

■ *Word Template (.dotx)*: Use this format to create a Word template on which you can base new documents.

■ *Rich Text Format (.rtf)*: Use this format to create a document with formatting that most word processing programs and text editors can open successfully.

4. Choose any other settings needed for the new document. For example, you may want to give it a different file name or save it in a different folder.

5. Click the Save button to save the document.

6. If you have finished working with the document, close it.

Creating PDF Documents for Digital Distribution

When you want to distribute a Word document digitally (as opposed to printing it and distributing the hard copy), you can choose between sending the document in Word format and sending an electronic file that shows the Word document's contents and layout.

Normally, you send the Word document only when the recipient needs to edit the document in Word or a compatible word processor. For other purposes, sending a file of the laid-out document is usually better. Word makes it easy to create a file in the widely used Portable Document Format (PDF).

To create a PDF file from a document, follow these steps:

1. If the document contains unsaved changes, save them.

2. Choose File ➤ Save As or press Cmd+Shift+S to display the Save As sheet.

3. Open the Format pop-up menu, and click the PDF item.

4. Choose any other settings needed for the PDF file. For example, you may want to give it a different file name or save it in a different folder.

5. Click the Save button. Word creates a PDF file with the name and folder you specified and then returns you to the document you were working in.

Now open a Finder window to the folder in which you created the PDF file. Double-click the PDF file to open it in Preview (or your default PDF viewer), and make sure all the content appears correctly.

> **Note**   You can also create a PDF of the active document and send it in a single move by using the Share button at the right end of the title bar. See Chapter 2 for coverage of this feature.

Summary

In this chapter, you learned how to use Word's extra features for printing documents or parts of them, such as document properties or details of the styles they contain. You now know how to secure your documents with passwords, remove sensitive information from them, and mark them as read-only.

You also learned how to save a Word 2016 document so that it's usable with earlier versions of Word and how to create documents in the widely used PDF format that you can take to specialist printing services or distribute across the Internet.

Part **3**

Analyzing Data with Microsoft Excel

In this part of the book, you'll learn how to use Microsoft Excel to build powerful spreadsheets and analyze your data.

In Chapter 12, you'll learn how to create different types of workbooks in Excel and enter data in them. You'll navigate the Excel interface, work with workbooks and worksheets, and use Excel's views and features to see the data you need.

In Chapter 13, you'll insert, delete, and format rows and columns in worksheets; format cells and ranges; and use the advanced conditional formatting and data validation features to identify unusual values or erratic input. You'll also learn how to format quickly and consistently with styles, how to add headers and footers to worksheets, and how to share workbooks with your colleagues.

In Chapter 14, you'll grasp how Excel's charts work and start adding them to your workbooks. You'll learn how to lay out a chart effectively, how to make it look good, and how to hide any components you don't want to display. You'll even learn how to save time by reusing the custom chart formatting you create.

In Chapter 15, you'll first learn the difference between a formula and a function. You'll then grasp how to create custom formulas and how to use Excel's built-in functions to perform preset calculations.

In Chapter 16, you'll start using Excel to create databases for storing and manipulating your information. You'll learn how to enter information in a database, how to sort the information, and how to filter it to find only the results you want. You'll also learn how to use the Goal Seek feature and scenarios to work out solutions to business problems.

In Chapter 17, you'll meet Excel's powerful PivotTable feature and start using it to manipulate your data so that you can discover the information you need. You'll learn to build a PivotTable from a spreadsheet, sort and filter the PivotTable, and make it show the data you're looking for.

Part

3

Analyzing Data with
Microsoft Excel

Creating Workbooks and Entering Data

In this chapter, you'll get started quickly with Excel by creating and saving a new workbook. You'll then look at how to navigate the Excel interface and work with worksheets and workbooks. You'll also learn how to enter data in worksheets, how to select and manipulate cells, and how to use Excel's various view features to see the worksheet data you need so that you can work easily with it.

Creating and Saving a New Workbook

When you launch Excel, the application by default displays the New pane in the Microsoft Excel Gallery dialog box automatically so that you can create a new workbook or open an existing workbook. In this section, you'll look at how to create a new workbook and how to save it.

> **Note**   To follow the Ribbon commands easily, please display the group titles on the Ribbon. To do so, choose Excel ➤ Preferences from the menu bar. In the Excel Preferences window, click View to display the View pane. In the "In Ribbon, Show" area, select the Group Titles check box, and then close the Excel Preferences window by clicking the Close button (the red button at the left end of the window's title bar).

Creating a New Workbook

To create a new workbook, you use the Microsoft Excel Gallery dialog box (see Figure 12-1). By default, the Microsoft Excel Gallery dialog box opens when you launch Excel, but you can also display it at any other time by choosing File ➤ New from Template from the menu bar or pressing Cmd+Shift+P.

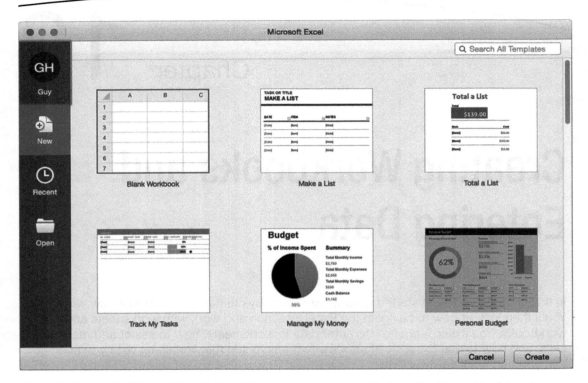

Figure 12-1. *From the Microsoft Excel Gallery dialog box, you can create a blank workbook, a workbook based on a template on your Mac, or a workbook based on an online template. You can also open a workbook you've used recently by using the Recent pane or any workbook by using the Open pane*

> **Note**   If you don't want the Microsoft Excel Gallery dialog box to open when you launch Excel, you can turn it off. With Excel open, choose Excel ➤ Preferences or press Cmd+, (Cmd and the comma key) to display the Excel Preferences window. In the Authoring area, click the General icon to display the General preferences pane. Clear the Open Workbook Gallery when opening Excel check box, and then click the Close button at the left end of the title bar to close the Excel Preferences window.

From here, you have three ways to create a new workbook:

- *Blank workbook*: To create a blank workbook, click the Blank Workbook item, and then click the Create button. You can also simply double-click the Blank Workbook item.

- *Template on your Mac*: To create a new workbook based on a template that's stored on your Mac, click the template in the list in the New pane, and then click the Create button. Again, you can double-click the template instead of clicking it and then clicking the Create button.

■ *Online template*: To create a workbook based on a template from Microsoft's Office.com site, click the Search All Templates box in the upper-right corner of the New tab and type your search term or terms. You don't need to press Return because Excel searches as you type. Click the result that seems most suitable and then click the Create button. Alternatively, double-click the result.

> **Note** If you need to base a new workbook on an existing workbook, open the workbook in whichever way you find most convenient, and then use the File ➤ Save As command to save the workbook under a different name, in a different folder, or both.

Saving a Workbook

To save a workbook for the first time, give the Save command in any of the usual ways: by clicking the Save button on the title bar, by choosing File ➤ Save from the menu bar, or by pressing Cmd+S. In the Save As sheet that opens, select the folder in which to save the workbook, type the workbook name, and then click the Save button.

When you save a workbook, Excel uses the file type that's set in the Save files in this format pop-up menu in the Compatibility preferences pane in Excel Preferences. If you've chosen the format you want, as discussed in the "Setting the Default Workbook Format in Excel" section in Chapter 5, you're all set. If you haven't chosen a different format, Excel uses the format called Excel Workbook, which works well for recent versions of Excel but may cause problems for versions before Excel 2008 for Mac or Excel 2007 for Windows.

> **Tip** If you start recording or writing macros to automate your work in Excel, you need to use a workbook format that can contain macros because the Excel Workbook format cannot contain macros or other VBA code. Use the Excel Macro-Enabled Workbook format for recent versions of Excel, or use the Excel 97–2004 format if the workbook is for Excel 2004, Excel 2003, or an earlier version. Excel 2008 for Mac doesn't run macros.

If you need to save the workbook in a different format than the default one, open the File Format pop-up menu and click the format you want to use. For example, if you will share the workbook with people who use Excel 2004 for Mac or Excel 2003 for Windows (or even older versions of Excel), choose the Excel 97–2004 Workbook format.

> **Note** The latest Excel file format (the one called simply Excel Workbook) is technically superior to the earlier file format (Excel 97–2004 Workbook or Excel 97–2003 Workbook). Using the Excel Workbook format, you can create workbooks containing more worksheets, and each worksheet can have many more rows and columns. The file format is also more resilient to data corruption. But for normal-size spreadsheets, such as those that most business users and home users create, the earlier file format still works just fine.

Navigating the Excel Interface, Worksheets, and Workbooks

When you create a new workbook or open an existing one, you see the worksheets in the workbook. Figure 12-2 shows a new workbook with some data entered.

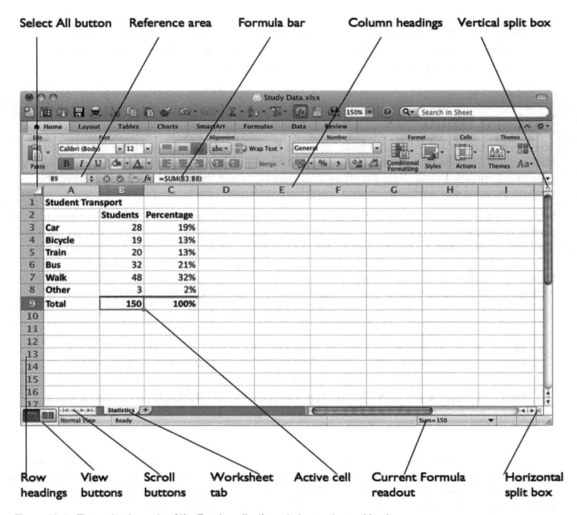

Figure 12-2. The main elements of the Excel application window and a workbook

Apart from regular Office application elements such as the Ribbon, the scroll bars, and the status bar, these are the main elements of the Excel application window and workbooks:

- *Formula bar*: This is the bar below the Ribbon. This area shows the data or formula in the active cell and gives you an easy place to enter and edit data.

- *Reference area*: This area appears at the left end of the formula bar. It shows the active cell's address (for example, A1) or name.

- *Row headings*: These are the numbers at the left side of the screen that identify each row. The first row is 1, the second row 2, and so on. The last row is 1048576.

- *Column headings*: These are the letters at the top of the worksheet grid that identify the columns:

  - The first column is A, the second column B, and so on up to Z.

  - Excel then uses two letters: AA to AZ, BA to BZ, and so forth until ZZ.

  - After that, Excel uses three letters: AAA, AAB, and so on up to the last column, XFD.

- *Cells*: These are the boxes formed by the intersections of the rows and columns. Each cell is identified by its column letter and row number. For example, the first cell in column A is cell A1, and the second cell in column B is cell B2. The last cell in the worksheet is XFD1048576.

- *Active cell*: This is the cell you're working in—the cell that receives the input from the keyboard. Excel displays a green rectangle around the active cell.

- *Select All button*: Click this button at the intersection of the row headings and column headings to select all the cells in the worksheet.

- *Worksheet tabs*: Each worksheet has a tab at the bottom that bears its name. To display a worksheet, you click its tab in the worksheet tabs area.

- *Insert Sheet button*: Click this button to insert a new worksheet after the active sheet.

- *Scroll buttons*: Click these buttons to scroll the worksheet tabs so that you can see the ones you need. Click the leftmost button to scroll all the way back to the first tab, or click the rightmost button to scroll to the last tab. Click the two middle buttons to scroll back or forward by one tab.

- *View buttons*: Click these buttons to switch between Normal view and Page Layout view. You'll learn how to use these views later in this chapter.

- *Split boxes*: Use these boxes when you need to split the worksheet window into two or four areas. You'll learn how to do this in the "Splitting the Window to View Separate Parts of a Worksheet" section later in this chapter.

- *Record Macro button*: Click this button to start recording a macro. A *macro* is a sequence of commands that you can record to automate actions you need to take consistently.

- *Zoom control*: Drag the slider to zoom in or out on the worksheet. Click the – button to decrease the zoom by 10% increments. Click the + button to increase the zoom by 10% increments.

Understanding Workbooks, Worksheets, Columns, and Rows

Each workbook consists of one or more worksheets or other sheets, such as chart sheets or macro sheets. To display the worksheet you want to use, click its tab in the worksheet tab bar (see Figure 12-3); if the worksheet's tab isn't visible in the worksheet tab bar, click the scroll buttons to display it (unless you've hidden the worksheet).

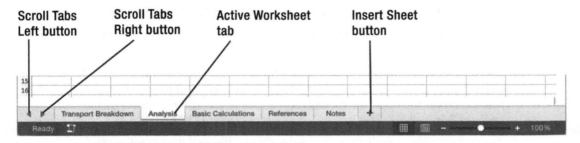

Figure 12-3. *Use the worksheet tab bar to display the worksheet you want or to insert a new worksheet*

Each worksheet contains 16,384 columns and 1,048,576 rows, giving a grand total of 17,179,869,184 cells. (This is a worksheet in the Excel Workbook format; the older format uses smaller worksheets.) Normally, you use only a small number of these cells—perhaps a few hundred or a few thousand—but there's plenty of space should you need it for large data sets.

> **Tip**   You can quickly move to the next worksheet by pressing Cmd+Page Down or Fn+Right arrow, or to the previous worksheet by pressing Cmd+Page Up or Fn+Left arrow.

Moving the Active Cell

In Excel, you usually work in a single cell at a time. That cell is called the *active cell* and receives the input from the keyboard.

You can move the active cell easily using either the pointing device (such as a mouse or a trackpad) or the keyboard:

- *Pointing device*: Click the cell you want to make active.

- *Keyboard*: Press the arrow keys to move the active cell up or down by one row or left or right by one column at a time. You can also press the keyboard shortcuts shown in Table 12-1 to move the active cell further.

Table 12-1. Keyboard Shortcuts for Moving the Active Cell

To Move the Active Cell Like This	Press This Keyboard Shortcut
First cell in the row	Home *or* Fn+Left arrow
First cell in the active worksheet	Cmd+Home *or* Cmd+Fn+Left arrow
Last cell used in the worksheet	Cmd+End *or* Cmd+Fn+Right arrow
Down one screen	Page Down *or* Fn+Down arrow
Up one screen	Page Up *or* Fn+Up arrow
Right one screen	Option+Page Down *or* Option+Fn+Down arrow
Left one screen	Option+Page Up *or* Option+Fn+Up arrow
To the last row in the worksheet	Cmd+Down arrow
To the last column in the worksheet	Cmd+Right arrow
To the first row in the worksheet	Cmd+Up arrow
To the first column in the worksheet	Cmd+Left arrow *or* Home
To the next corner cell clockwise in a selected range	Ctrl+. (Ctrl and the period key)

Selecting and Manipulating Cells

To work with a single cell, you simply click it or use the keyboard to move the active cell to it. When you need to affect multiple cells at once, you select the cells using the pointing device or keyboard, as described below.

Excel calls a selection of cells a *range*. A range can consist of either a rectangle of contiguous cells or various cells that aren't next to each other. The left illustration in Figure 12-4 shows a range of contiguous cells and the right illustration shows a range of separate cells.

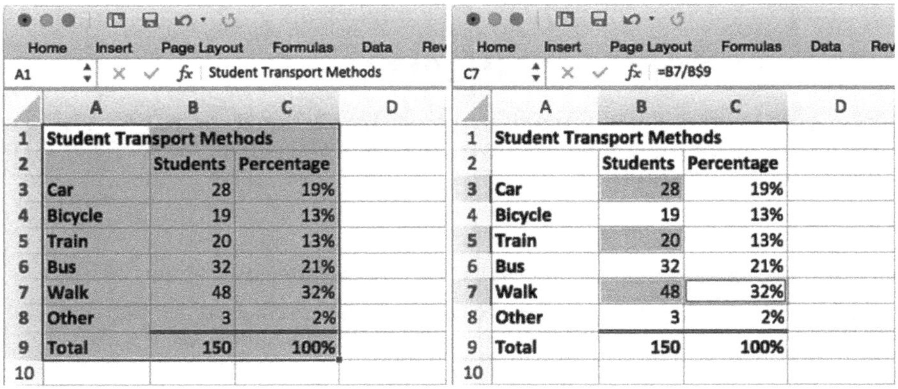

Figure 12-4. You can select either a range of contiguous cells (left) or a range of individual cells (right)

You can select a range of contiguous cells in any of these three ways:

- *Click and drag*: Click the first cell in the range, and then drag to select all the others. For example, if you click cell B2 and then drag to cell E7, you select a range that's four columns wide and six rows deep. Excel uses the notation B2:E7 to describe this range (the starting cell address, a colon, and then the ending cell address).

- *Click and then Shift-click*: Click the first cell in the range, and then Shift-click the last cell. Excel selects all the cells in between. This technique tends to be the easiest to use when the first cell and last cell are widely separated; for example, when they don't appear in the same window.

- *Hold down Shift and use the arrow keys.* Use the arrow keys to move the active cell to where you want to start the range; then hold down Shift and use the arrow keys to extend the selection for the rest of the range. This method is good if you prefer using the keyboard to the pointing device.

You can select a range of noncontiguous cells by clicking the first cell (or dragging through a range of contiguous cells) and then holding down Cmd while you click other individual cells or drag through ranges of contiguous cells. Excel uses commas to separate the individual cells in this type of range. For example, the range D3,E5,F7,G1:G13 consists of three individual cells (D3, E5, and F7) and one range of contiguous cells (G1 through G13).

> **Note** You can quickly select an entire row by clicking its row heading or pressing Shift+spacebar when the active cell is in that row. Likewise, you can select an entire column by clicking its column heading or pressing Ctrl+spacebar. To select all the cells in the active worksheet, click the Select All button (where the row headings and column headings meet). You can also either press Cmd+A or press Shift+spacebar followed by Ctrl+spacebar (or vice versa).

To deselect a range you've selected, click anywhere outside the range or press an arrow key.

Enter Data in Your Worksheets

You can enter data in your worksheets by typing it, by pasting it, or by using drag and drop to move or copy it. Excel also includes a feature called AutoFill that automatically fills in series data for you based on the input you've provided.

> **Note** Excel also includes features for importing existing data from sources such as comma-separated values (CSV) files and FileMaker Pro databases. See *Learn Excel 2016 for Mac*, also from Apress, for details.

Typing Data in a Cell

The most straightforward way to enter data is to type it into a cell. Once you make a cell the active cell by clicking it or moving the selection rectangle to it, you can start typing in it. When you start typing, Excel displays an insertion point in the cell.

When you've finished typing the contents of the cell, move to another cell in any of these ways:

- *Press Return*: Excel moves the active cell to the next cell below the current cell (but see the next Tip). If you select a range of cells, Excel moves the active cell down until it reaches the bottom of the range and then moves it up to the first cell in the range's next column.

- *Click another cell*: Excel moves the active cell to the cell you click.

- *Press an arrow key*: Excel moves the active cell to the next cell in the direction of the arrow. For example, press the right arrow key to move the active cell to the next cell to the right.

> **Tip**   To change the direction Excel moves the active cell when you press Return, choose Excel ➤ Preferences or press Cmd+, (Cmd and the comma key). In the Excel Preferences window, click the Edit icon in the Authoring area to display the Edit preferences pane. Make sure the "After pressing Return, move selection" check box is selected, then open the pop-up menu and click Down, Right, Up, or Left, as needed. (If you don't want Excel to move the active cell when you press Return, clear the "After pressing Return, move selection" check box.) Close the Excel Preferences window by clicking the Close button (the red circle at the left end of the title bar) or pressing Cmd+W.

Editing a Cell

When you need to edit the existing contents of a cell, open it for editing in one of these ways:

- Double-click the cell. Excel displays an insertion point in the cell.

- Move the active cell to the cell, and then press Ctrl+U. Excel displays an insertion point in the cell. Figure 12-5 shows an example of editing in a cell.

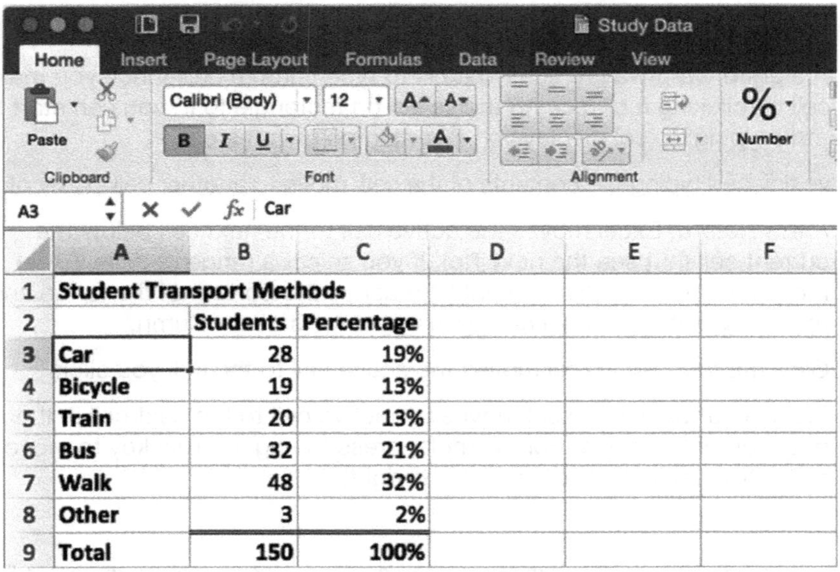

Figure 12-5. Double-click in a cell or press Ctrl+U to edit its contents in place. In this example, cell A3 is open for editing

- Click the cell (or move the active cell to it), and then click the cell's contents in the formula bar. Excel displays an insertion point in the formula bar (see Figure 12-6).

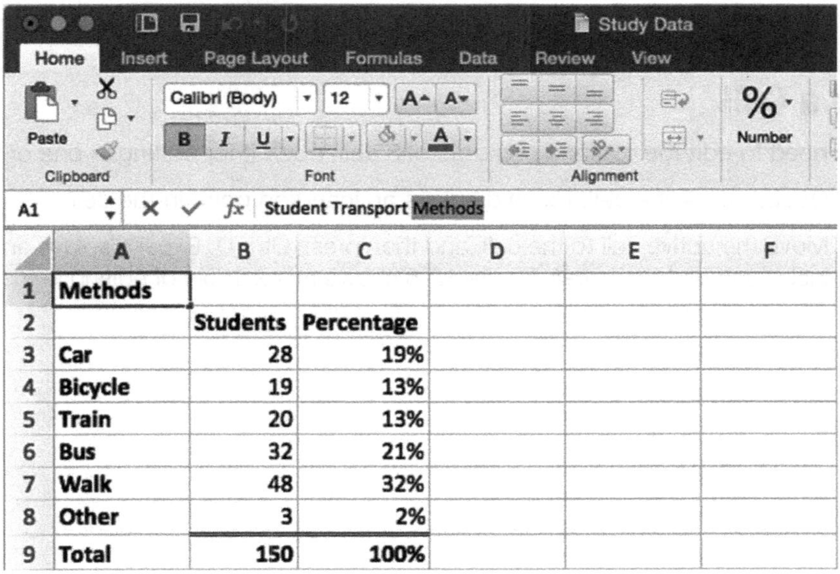

Figure 12-6. You can also edit a cell by clicking in the formula bar. This method is often easier for editing entries longer than their cells

When you're editing a cell, pressing an arrow key moves the insertion point within the cell's contents rather than finishing the entry and moving to another cell:

- *Left arrow key*: Press this key to move left by one character.

- *Right arrow key*: Press this key to move right by one character.

- *Down arrow key*: Press this key to move to the end of the cell's contents.

- *Up arrow key*: Press this key to move the insertion point back to where it was before you moved to the end of the cell's contents by pressing the down arrow key.

To finish editing a cell, press Return, click the check-mark button on the formula bar, or click another cell. To cancel editing a cell and restore its previous contents, press Esc or click the cross button on the formula bar.

> **Tip**   Instead of editing a cell's existing contents, you can simply replace them by making the cell active and then typing new contents. Replacing tends to be faster than editing when a cell needs a short entry that you can easily type.

Entering Data Quickly Using AutoFill

When you need to fill in a series of data, see whether Excel's AutoFill feature can do the trick. To use AutoFill, you enter the base data for the series in one or more cells and then select them and drag the AutoFill handle in the direction you want to fill. AutoFill checks your base data, works out what the other cells should contain, and fills in the data for you. For example, you can fill in a series of numbers or a range of days, months, or years.

Using AutoFill's Built-in Capabilities

Open a test workbook, or add a test worksheet to your current workbook by clicking the Insert Sheet button, and then try using AutoFill.

> **Tip**   You can also insert a new worksheet by pressing Excel's Shift+F11 keyboard shortcut—but only if your Mac isn't set to use F11 as the keyboard shortcut for the Show Desktop command in Mission Control. This is a standard setting in OS X so if you want to be able to insert new worksheets from the keyboard, you must either change the Show Desktop keyboard shortcut (in the Mission Control pane in System Preferences) or assign a new keyboard shortcut in Excel (see Chapter 5 for instructions).

Type **Monday** in cell A1, press Return to enter the data, and then click cell A1 again. Then drag the AutoFill handle—the green square that appears at the lower-right corner of the selection—down to cell A7. As you drag past each cell, AutoFill displays a ScreenTip showing the data it will fill in that cell (see Figure 12-7). When you release the button on cell A7, AutoFill fills in the days Tuesday through Sunday.

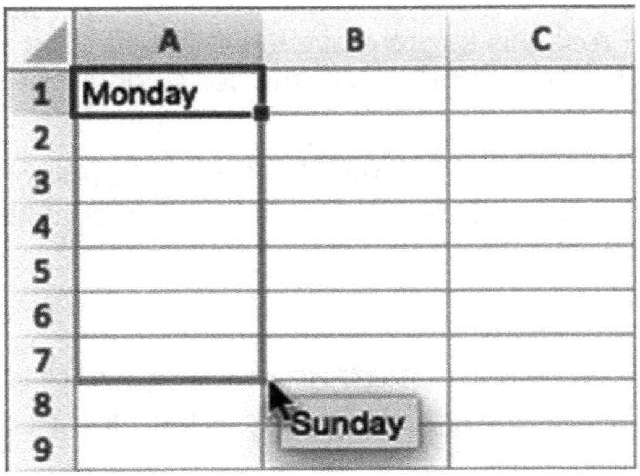

Figure 12-7. Drag the AutoFill handle down or across to fill in a series of data derived from one or more existing entries. In this case, AutoFill fills in the days of the week and repeats the series if you drag farther

Now drag through the range to select it, and then press Delete to clear it. Then follow these steps:

1. Click cell B2, and type a date such as **5-15-16** in it.

2. Press Return, and you'll see that Excel changes it to a full date, such as 2/15/2016.

3. Click cell B2 again to select it once more.

4. Ctrl-click or right-click the AutoFill handle and drag it to cell G2. As you drag, AutoFill displays dates incremented by one day for each column (5/16/2016, 5/17/2016, and so on), but when you release the button on the pointing device, AutoFill displays a context menu (see Figure 12-8).

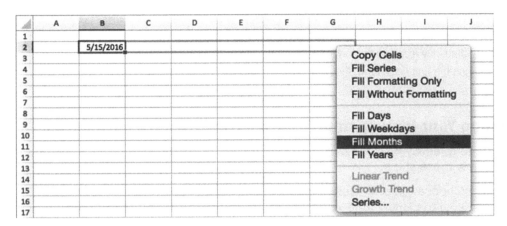

Figure 12-8. *To reach more AutoFill options, Ctrl-drag or right-drag the AutoFill handle, and then choose the option you want from the context menu*

5. Click the Fill Months item, and Excel fills in a separate month for each column: 6/15/2016, 7/15/2016, and so on.

Now clear your data again, and then follow these steps:

1. Click cell A1, and type **5** in it.

2. Press Return to move to cell A2, type **25** in it, and press the up arrow to move back to cell A1.

3. Press Shift+down arrow to select cells A1 and A2.

4. Click the AutoFill handle, and drag downward. AutoFill fills in a series with intervals of 20—cell A3 gets 45, cell A4 gets 65, and so on—using a linear trend.

Delete the data that AutoFill entered, leaving 5 in cell A1 and 25 in cell A2. Then follow these steps:

1. Select cells A1 and A2.

2. Ctrl-click or right-click the AutoFill handle, and drag downward. As you drag, you'll see ScreenTips for the same values as in the previous list.

3. Release the button on the pointing device, and then click Growth Trend on the context menu. AutoFill enters a growth trend instead of the linear trend: because the second value (25) is 5 times the first value (5), Excel multiplies each value by 5, giving the sequence 5, 25, 125, 625, 3125, and so on.

> **Note** The AutoFill context menu also contains items for copying the cells, filling the cells with formatting only (copying the formatting from the first cell), filling the cells without formatting (ignoring the first cell's formatting), and filling in days, weekdays, months, and years.

Creating Your Own Custom AutoFill Lists

If you need to enter the same series of data frequently, you can create your own AutoFill lists. Follow these steps:

1. Choose Excel ➤ Preferences or press Cmd+, (Cmd and the comma key) to display the Excel Preferences window.

2. In the Formulas and Lists area, click the Custom Lists item to display the Custom Lists pane (shown in Figure 12-9 with settings chosen).

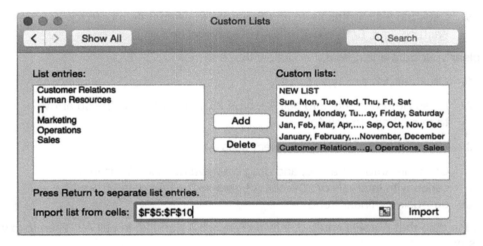

Figure 12-9. You can supplement Excel's built-in AutoFill lists by creating your own data series that you need to enter frequently in your worksheets

3. In the Custom lists box, click the NEW LIST item.

4. Enter the items for your list in one of these ways:

   ■ Click in the List entries box, and then type your list, putting one item on each line.

   ■ Click the Collapse Dialog button at the right end of the Import list from cells box, select the range containing the list entries in the worksheet, and then click the Collapse Dialog button again to restore the dialog.

5. If you've just entered a list, click the Add button to add the list to the Custom lists box. If you imported a list from a worksheet, click the Import button.

6. Click the Close button (the red button at the left end of the title bar) to close the Excel Preferences window.

Pasting Data into a Worksheet

If the data you need to add to a worksheet is already in another document, you can copy it and paste it into the worksheet using the techniques explained in Chapter 3. You can also use Excel's Paste Special command to paste only some of the data—for example, the values of formulas rather than formulas themselves.

Using Paste and Paste Options

To paste data, position the active cell at the upper-left corner of where you want the data to land. In most cases, you don't need to select the right number of cells for the data because Excel does that for you automatically; if you find Excel prompts you to select the destination range, do so.

After positioning the active cell, you can either simply give the Paste command or choose one of the available Paste Options:

■ *Paste*: Press Cmd+V, choose Home ➤ Clipboard ➤ Paste from the Ribbon (clicking the main part of the Paste button rather than the pop-up button), or choose Edit ➤ Paste from the menu bar. If you don't get the result you want, click the Paste Options button that appears near the lower-right corner of what you pasted, and then click the option button you want on the Paste Options menu (shown on the left in Figure 12-10).

- *Paste Options*: Choose Home ➤ Clipboard ➤ Paste (clicking the Paste pop-up button), and then click the appropriate item on the Paste pop-up menu (shown on the right in Figure 12-10).

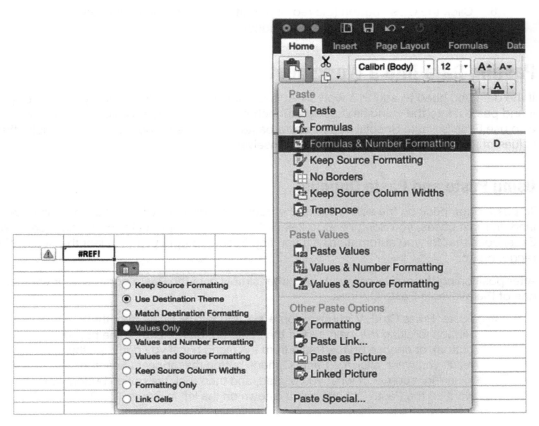

Figure 12-10. If pasted data arrives in the wrong format, click the Paste Options button, and then choose a different option from the Paste Options menu (left). You can also use the Paste pop-up menu on the Home tab of the Ribbon to choose the format while pasting (right)

Which Paste Options are available depends on the data you're pasting, but in most cases you have at least the choice of Keep Source Formatting (retaining the formatting the data had wherever you copied it from) and Match Destination Formatting (making it look like the worksheet you're pasting it on).

Controlling Pasted Data with the Paste Special Command

Sometimes you want to paste less than all of the data you've copied. For example, you may need to paste all the data and formatting except for cell borders, or you may want to retain only the values and number formats rather than other information.

For these needs, Excel provides the Paste Special command. You can access most of these options from either the Paste pop-up menu in the Edit group of the Home tab or from the Paste Options pop-up menu, but in most cases it's clearest to use the Paste Special dialog box.

To display the Paste Special dialog box (see Figure 12-11), use one of these commands:

■ *Ribbon*: Choose Home ➤ Clipboard ➤ Paste ➤ Paste Special.

■ *Menu bar*: Choose Edit ➤ Paste Special.

■ *Context menu*: Ctrl-click or right-click the destination cell, and then click Paste Special.

■ *Keyboard*: Press Cmd+Ctrl+V.

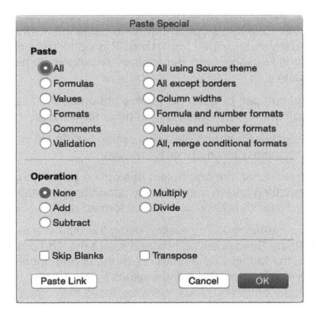

Figure 12-11. *Use the Paste Special dialog box when you need to paste only some of the data, when you need to perform an operation on the data, or when you need to transpose its rows and columns*

You then select the option button you want in the Paste area:

■ *All*: Select this option button to paste all the data and all its formatting. Normally, you only do this if you're using the Skip blanks check box, the Transpose check box, or the Paste Link button; otherwise, it's easier to use the Paste command.

■ *Formulas*: Select this option button to paste in all the formulas and constants without formatting.

■ *Values*: Select this option button to paste in formula values instead of pasting in the formulas themselves. Excel removes the formatting from the values.

■ *Formats*: Select this option button to paste in the formatting without the data. This option is surprisingly useful once you know it's there.

- *Comments*: Select this option button to paste in only comments. This option is handy when you're integrating different colleagues' takes on the same worksheet.

- *Validation*: Select this option button to paste in data-validation criteria.

- *All using Source theme*: Select this option button to paste in all the data using the theme from the workbook the data came from.

- *All except borders*: Select this option button to paste in all the data and formatting but to strip out the cell borders.

- *Column widths*: Select this option button to paste in only the column widths—no data and no other formatting. This option is useful when you need to lay one worksheet out like another existing worksheet but put all different data in it.

- *Formulas and number formats*: Select this option button to paste in formulas and number formatting but no other formatting.

- *Values and number formats*: Select this option button to paste in values (rather than formulas) and number formatting.

- *All, merge conditional formats*: Select this option button to copy all data and formatting and to merge in any conditional formatting. See Chapter 13 for details on conditional formatting.

If you need to perform a mathematical operation using the data you're pasting, go to the Operation area of the Paste Special dialog box and select the Add option button, the Subtract option button, the Multiply option button, or the Divide option button, as needed. For example, if you want to multiply the current values in the cells by the values you're pasting, select the Multiply option button. Otherwise, leave the None option button selected to paste the data without performing math with it.

In the bottom section of the Paste Special dialog box, you can select or clear the two check boxes as needed:

- *Skip blanks*: Select this check box to prevent Excel from pasting blank cells.

- *Transpose*: Select this check box to transpose columns to rows and rows to columns. This option is much quicker than retyping data that you (or someone else) have laid out the wrong way.

When you've chosen the options you want, click the OK button. Excel closes the Paste Special dialog box and pastes the data or formatting you chose.

> **Note** If you need to link the data you're pasting back to its source, click the Paste Link button in the Paste Special dialog box instead of the OK button. This makes Excel create a link to the source data so that when the source data changes, the linked data changes too. If the source data is in the same workbook, Excel updates the links automatically. If the source data is in another workbook, Excel updates the data when you open the workbook that contains the links.

Copying and Moving Data with Drag and Drop

When you need to copy or move data within Excel, you can use drag and drop. Follow these steps:

1. Select the data you want to move or copy.

2. Move the pointer over an edge of the section so that the pointer turns to a hand icon (see Figure 12-12).

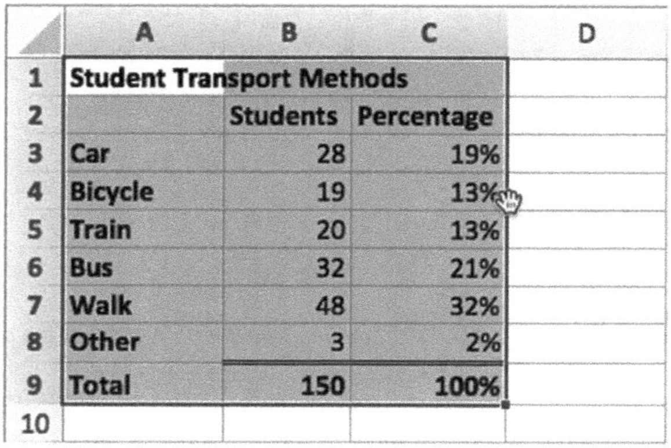

	A	B	C	D
1	Student Transport Methods			
2		Students	Percentage	
3	Car	28	19%	
4	Bicycle	19	13%	
5	Train	20	13%	
6	Bus	32	21%	
7	Walk	48	32%	
8	Other	3	2%	
9	Total	150	100%	
10				

Figure 12-12. To move data using drag and drop, select the data, and then move the pointer over one of its edges to display the drag-and-drop pointer, which is the hand icon that appears on the right border of cell C4 here

3. Click and drag the data to where you want it to appear. If you want to copy the data rather than move it, Option-drag rather than drag; the hand icon shows a plus (+) sign to indicate you're making a copy. Release the button on your pointing device before releasing the Option key.

Normal drag and drop moves or copies all of the data and all of its formatting, much like pasting the material. To reach more options, such as copying only the values or the formats or creating a link or a hyperlink to the source, Ctrl-click or right-click and drag instead of left-clicking and dragging. When you release the button, Excel displays a context menu of choices together with the address of the destination range (see Figure 12-13). Click the choice you want.

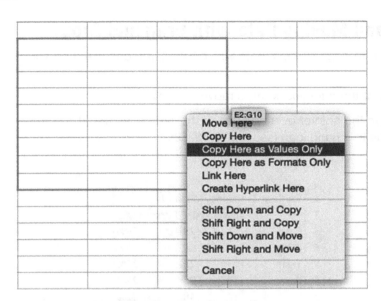

Figure 12-13. Use the Ctrl-drag or right-drag context menu to transfer only some of the data or to create a link

Inserting, Deleting, and Rearranging Worksheets

When you create a workbook, Excel puts a single worksheet in it by default. For many workbooks, this may be all you need, but for other workbooks, you need to insert further worksheets to give yourself space to work in.

For most workbooks, give the worksheets custom names instead of the default names. You may also need to rearrange the worksheets into a different order.

Tip To change the number of worksheets that Excel includes in a blank workbook, choose Excel ➤ Preferences or press Cmd+, (Cmd and the comma key) to display the Excel Preferences window. In the Authoring area, click the General icon to display the General preferences pane. Change the number in the "Sheets in new workbook" box to the number of worksheets you want, and then close the Excel Preferences window by clicking the Close button (the red button at the left end of its title bar).

Inserting and Deleting Worksheets

You can easily insert a new worksheet in a workbook in either of these ways:

- *Insert a new worksheet after the last existing worksheet*: Click the Insert Sheet button that appears on the tab bar after the last worksheet tab.

- *Insert a new worksheet after a particular worksheet*: Ctrl-click or right-click the existing worksheet tab, and then click Insert Sheet on the context menu.

> **Tip**   You can also press Shift+F11 to insert a new worksheet after the worksheet that's currently selected—as long as OS X isn't using F11 for a different purpose, such as the Show Desktop feature in Mission Control. If OS X is already using F11, you can map the Insert Sheet command to a different keyboard shortcut using the technique explained in the "Creating Custom Keyboard Shortcuts in Word and Excel" section in Chapter 5.

After inserting a worksheet, double-click its tab to select the default name, type the name you want, and then press Return. You can use up to 31 characters in the name. If you want to make the tab stand out, Ctrl-click or right-click the tab, click Tab Color to display the Tab Color panel, and then click the color for the tab.

To delete a worksheet, Ctrl-click or right-click its tab, and then click Delete on the context menu. Excel displays an Alert dialog box (see Figure 12-14) to double-check that you're prepared to delete it; click the Delete button to go ahead.

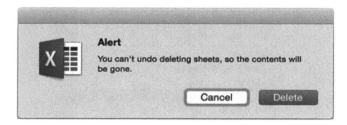

Figure 12-14.   Excel confirms the deletion of one or more worksheets in case you've given the Delete command by accident

> **Note**   If the worksheet contains no data, Excel deletes it without displaying the Alert dialog box.

Rearranging the Worksheets in a Workbook

You can rearrange the worksheets in a workbook into the order you need. The quick way to move a worksheet is to click its tab, drag it left or right until Excel displays a downward arrow between the worksheets where you want to place it, and then drop it.

> **Tip**   To move two or more worksheets, select them first. To select a range of worksheets that appear next to each other, click the first worksheet's tab, and then Shift-click the tab for the worksheet at the other end of the range. To select worksheets that aren't next to each other, click the first worksheet's tab, and then Cmd-click each other worksheet's tab in turn.

This method works well for moving a worksheet a short distance along the tab bar, but for moving larger distances, you may prefer to use the Move or Copy dialog box. You can also use the Move or Copy dialog box to move or copy worksheets to a different workbook. Follow these steps:

1. If you want to move or copy the worksheets to a different workbook, open that workbook.

2. In the source workbook, Ctrl-click or right-click the worksheet's tab to display the context menu. To move multiple worksheets, select them, and then Ctrl-click or right-click one of the selected tabs.

3. On the context menu, click the Move or Copy item to display the Move or Copy dialog box (see Figure 12-15).

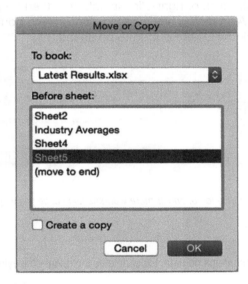

Figure 12-15. *Use the Move or Copy dialog box to move one or more worksheets farther than you can comfortably drag within a workbook or to move or copy worksheets to another open workbook*

4. In the To book pop-up menu, make sure the current workbook is selected unless you want to move the worksheet to another workbook—in which case, select that workbook.

5. In the Before sheet list box, click the worksheet before which you want to position the worksheet you're moving. If you want to put the worksheets at the end of the workbook, select the (move to end) item.

6. Select the Create a copy check box if you want to copy the worksheet to the destination rather than move it. Copying tends to be most useful when the destination is another workbook, but you can copy within a workbook as well.

7. Click the OK button to close the dialog box. Excel moves or copies the worksheet to the destination you chose.

Making Excel Display Worksheets the Way You Need

To work quickly and easily in your workbooks, you need to know how to make the most of Excel's two views and how to use Full Screen view. You also need to know how to split the window into two or four parts, how to hide windows when you don't need to see them, and how to use Excel's features for freezing parts of a window that you need to keep in sight.

Understanding Excel's Views

Excel gives you two views for working in your workbooks:

- *Normal view*: This is the view in which workbooks normally open and is the view in which you do most of your data entry, formatting, and reviewing. Normal view is the view in which you've seen Excel so far in this chapter.

- *Page Layout view*: This view shows your worksheets as they will look when laid out on paper. You use it to adjust the page setup. You'll learn how to do this in Chapter 13.

To switch the view, click the Normal View button or the Page Layout View button in the lower-right corner of the Excel window (see Figure 12-16) or choose View ➤ Normal or View ➤ Page Layout from the menu bar. If you prefer to use the Ribbon, choose View ➤ Workbook Views ➤ Normal or View ➤ Workbook Views ➤ Page Layout.

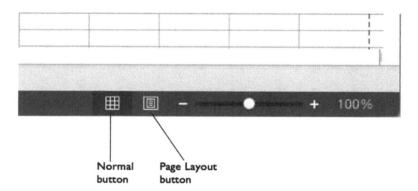

Normal   Page Layout
button   button

Figure 12-16. Use the View buttons in the lower-right corner of the Excel window to change views quickly

> **Tip**   When you want to see as much of a worksheet as possible, choose View ➤ Enter Full Screen from the menu bar or press Cmd+Ctrl+F. When you want to leave Full Screen view, you can press Esc (the simplest way), press Cmd+Ctrl+F, or move the mouse pointer up to the top of the screen (making the menu bar appear) and choose View ➤ Exit Full Screen.

Splitting the Window to View Separate Parts of a Worksheet

Often, it's useful to be able to see two parts of a worksheet at the same time as you work in it—for example, to make sure that your notes correctly describe your data, or when you're copying information from one part to another.

When you need to see two parts of the worksheet in the same window, you can split the window either horizontally or vertically. To do so, use the horizontal split box at the right end of the horizontal scroll bar, the vertical split box at the top end of the vertical scroll bar, or the Split button in the Window group of the View tab of the Ribbon.

Double-click the horizontal split box to split the window horizontally above the active cell, or double-click the vertical split box to split the window vertically to the left of the active cell. If the active cell isn't in the right place for splitting, click the horizontal split box or the vertical split box, and then drag it until the split bar appears where you want the split.

If you want to split the window into four panes, split it in the other dimension as well. For example, if you've already split the window horizontally, split it vertically as well. Figure 12-17 shows the Excel window split into four panes.

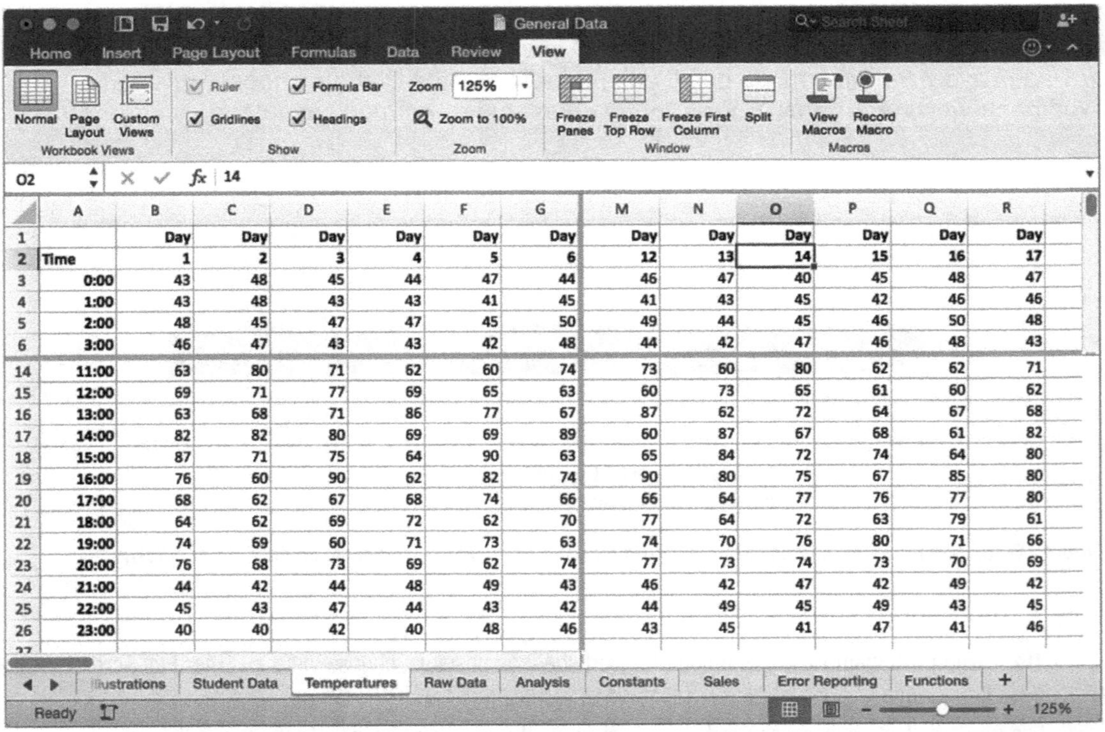

Figure 12-17. Split the Excel window into two or four panes when you need to work in separate areas of the worksheet at the same time

> **Note**   You can also split the window into four panes by choosing View ➤ Window ➤ Split from the Ribbon or Window ➤ Split from the menu bar.

Once you split the window, you get a separate scroll bar in each part, so you can scroll the panes separately to display whichever areas of the worksheet you need.

> **Note**   When you split the window, you may find it helpful to freeze certain rows and columns, as discussed later in this chapter, to keep them visible even when you scroll to other areas of the worksheet.

To reposition the split, click the split bar, and drag it to where you want it. If you've split the window into four panes, you can resize all four panes at once by clicking where the split bars cross and then dragging.

To remove the split, either double-click the split bar or click the split bar and drag it all the way to the left of the screen or all the way to the top. You can also choose View ➤ Window ➤ Split from the Ribbon or Window ➤ Remove Split from the menu bar.

Opening Extra Windows to Show Other Parts of a Workbook

Instead of splitting a window, you can open one or more extra windows to show other parts of the workbook. Choose Window ➤ New Window from the menu bar to open a new window on the active workbook. Excel distinguishes the windows by adding :1 to the name of the first and :2 to the name of the second; for example, General Data:1 and General Data:2 (or General Data.xlsx:1 and General Data.xlsx:2 if you have set Excel to display file extensions).

> **Note**   Opening extra windows has two advantages over splitting a window. First, you can display other worksheets in the windows if you want rather than just other parts of the same worksheet. Second, you can zoom each window by a different amount as needed or use a different view in each window.

Changing the Window and Arranging Open Windows

The easiest way to change the window you're working in is to click the window you want to use—either click the window itself (if you can see it) or click its button on the Dock. You can also choose Open from the Window menu on the menu bar and then click the window in the list at the bottom.

> **Note**   If you've selected the "Minimize windows into application icon" check box in the Dock
> preferences pane in the System Preferences app, your open Excel windows appear under the Excel
> app's icon on the Dock rather than as separate windows. To switch to a window via the Dock, first
> open the app's context menu by clicking and holding, or Ctrl-clicking, or right-clicking the Excel icon
> on the Dock. Then click the window you want to view.

When you've opened several windows, you can arrange them by using standard OS X
techniques, such as by dragging them to the size and position you want or using the Split
Screen mode in OS X El Capitan (click and hold the green Zoom button at the left end of the
title bar, drag the window to the left or right side of the screen, and then click the thumbnail
of the window you want to position on the other side of the screen). You can also use Excel's
Arrange Windows dialog box or Arrange pop-up menu to arrange Excel's windows.

To arrange windows using the Arrange Windows dialog box, follow these steps:

1. Choose Window ➤ Arrange from the menu bar to display the Arrange
   Windows dialog box (see Figure 12-18).

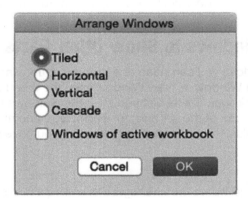

*Figure 12-18. Use the Arrange Windows dialog box to tile or otherwise arrange all the Excel windows or only those
from the active workbook*

2. Click the option button for the arrangement you want:

   - *Tiled*: Select this option button to make Excel resize all the
     nonminimized windows to roughly even sizes so that they fit in
     the Excel window. If you have several windows open, tiling tends
     to make them too small for working in, but it's good for seeing
     which windows are open and closing those you don't need.

   - *Horizontal*: Select this option button to arrange all the windows
     horizontally in the Excel window. This arrangement works well
     for two windows in which the data is laid out in rows rather than
     columns.

- ■ *Vertical*: Select this option button to arrange all the windows vertically in the Excel window. This arrangement works well for two windows in which the data is laid out in columns rather than rows.

- ■ *Cascade*: Select this option button to arrange the windows in a stack so that you can see each one's title bar. This arrangement is useful for picking the window you want out of many open windows.

3. To arrange only the windows of the active workbook, select the "Windows of active workbook" check box. This option is good for the Horizontal and Vertical arrangements.

4. Click the OK button to close the Arrange Windows dialog box. Excel arranges the windows as you chose.

Tip   When you don't need to see a particular window, you can hide it to get it out of the way. Click the window, and then choose Window ➤ Hide from the menu bar. To display the window again, choose Window ➤ Unhide, click the window in the Unhide dialog box, and then click the OK button.

Zooming to Show the Data You Need to See

You can zoom in or out on your worksheets to make the data easier to read or to display more of a worksheet at once.

The easiest way to zoom in or out is by using the Zoom slider at the right end of the status bar on the Excel window. Click the – button to zoom out by 10% increments; click the + button to zoom in by 10% increments; or drag the slider to zoom quickly.

If you want to zoom to a different percentage, click the current percentage readout to the right of the + button to display the Zoom dialog box (see Figure 12-19); alternatively, choose View ➤ Zoom from the menu bar to open this dialog box. Select the appropriate option button for your needs, and then click the OK button. You can undo the zoom if necessary by clicking the Undo button on the title bar or by pressing Cmd+Z.

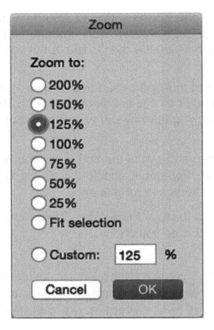

Figure 12-19. When you need to zoom to a specific percentage, or to fit the selection, open the Zoom dialog box, click the appropriate option button, and then click the OK button

Note   The Fit Selection option button in the Zoom dialog box enables you to zoom to the right percentage to fit a particular selection. Make the selection before you open the Zoom dialog box, then click the Fit Selection option button, and click the OK button.

Freezing Rows and Columns So That They Stay On-Screen

To keep your data headings on-screen when you scroll down or to the right on a large worksheet, you can freeze the heading rows and columns in place. For example, if you have headings in column A and row 1, you can freeze column A and row 1 so that they remain on-screen.

You can quickly freeze the first column, the top row, or your choice of rows and columns:

- *Freeze the first column*: Choose View ➤ Window ➤ Freeze Panes ➤ Freeze First Column from the Ribbon.

- *Freeze the first row*: Choose View ➤ Window ➤ Freeze Panes ➤ Freeze Top Row from the Ribbon.

- *Freeze your choice of rows and columns*: Click the cell below the row and to the right of the column you want to freeze. For example, to freeze the top two rows and column A, select cell B3. Then choose View ➤ Window ➤ Freeze Panes ➤ Freeze Panes from the Ribbon or Window ➤ Freeze Panes from the menu bar.

Excel displays a gray line along the gridlines of the frozen cells. Once you've applied the freeze, the frozen columns and rows don't move when you scroll down or to the right. Figure 12-20 shows a worksheet with rows 1 and 2 and column A frozen.

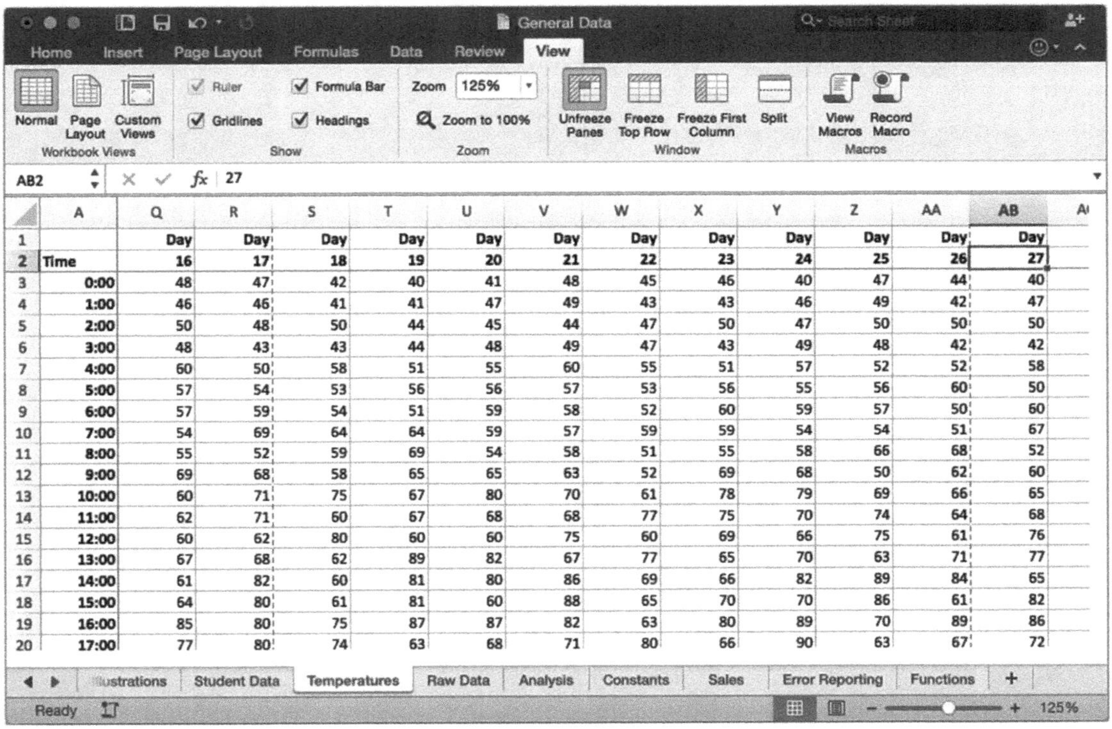

Figure 12-20. Freeze the heading rows and columns to keep them in place when you scroll down or across the worksheet

When you no longer need the freezing, choose View ➤ Window ➤ Unfreeze Panes from the Ribbon or Window ➤ Unfreeze Panes to remove the freezing.

Summary

In this chapter, you learned how to create and save a workbook and start entering data in it. You explored the Excel interface, and you now know how to add, delete, and rearrange the worksheets in a workbook. You also learned how to select cells and ranges, plus essential techniques for making Excel display worksheets the way you need them—everything from splitting a window into separate parts to opening and arranging multiple windows and freezing any heading rows and columns you want to keep on-screen when you scroll.

Chapter 13

Formatting Your Worksheets

In this chapter, you'll learn how to format your worksheets so that they show the information you need and present it clearly. You'll start by looking at how to work with rows and columns—inserting, deleting, and formatting them so that your worksheet is the right shape. Then you'll learn how to format cells and ranges, how to apply conditional formatting to quickly flag values that need attention, and how to use data validation to check for invalid entries.

After that, you'll look at how to format worksheets quickly using table formatting or Excel's styles, how to add headers and footers to worksheets, and how to print worksheets and workbooks.

Lastly, you'll learn to use Excel's features for sharing workbooks with your colleagues. You can protect a workbook against unwelcome changes, and even share a workbook so that both you and your colleagues can edit it at the same time.

> **Note** To follow the Ribbon commands easily, please display the group titles on the Ribbon. To do so, choose Excel ➤ Preferences from the menu bar. In the Excel Preferences window, click View to display the View pane. In the "In Ribbon, Show" area, select the Group Titles check box, and then close the Excel Preferences window by clicking the Close button (the red button at the left end of the window's title bar).

Working with Rows and Columns

In this section, you'll learn how to insert and delete rows, columns, and cells; change the width of columns and the height of rows; and hide rows or columns when you don't need to see them.

Inserting and Deleting Rows, Columns, and Cells

To accommodate the data in your worksheets, you often need to insert or delete entire columns or rows. Sometimes you may also need to delete a block of cells without deleting an entire column or row.

© Guy Hart-Davis 2016
G. Hart-Davis, *Learn Office 2016 for Mac*, DOI 10.1007/978-1-4842-2002-3_13

The easiest way to insert a column or row is to Ctrl-click or right-click the heading of the existing column or row before which you want to insert the new one and then click Insert on the context menu.

To insert more than one column or row, select the same number of columns or rows first. For example, to insert three columns before column F, drag through the headings of columns F, G, and H to select those columns; then Ctrl-click or right-click anywhere in the selected headings, and click Insert on the context menu.

You can also insert a column by selecting a cell in the column before which you want to add the new column, and then giving either of these commands:

- *Ribbon*: Choose Home ➤ Cells ➤ Insert ➤ Insert Sheet Columns.

> **Note**   If the Excel window isn't wide enough for the Insert button, Delete button, and Format button to appear in the Cells group, the Cells pop-up button appears instead. Click this button to display a pop-up menu with an Insert submenu, a Delete submenu, and a Format submenu. Click the appropriate menu, and then make your choice from it.

- *Menu bar*: Choose Insert ➤ Columns.

Similarly, you can insert a row by selecting a cell in the row before which you want to add the new row and then giving either of these commands:

- *Ribbon*: Choose Home ➤ Cells ➤ Insert ➤ Insert Sheet Rows.
- *Menu bar*: Choose Insert ➤ Rows.

As before, if you want to insert multiple columns or rows, select cells in the corresponding number of columns or rows first.

> **Note**   What the Insert button in the Cells group on the Home tab of the Ribbon inserts depends on what you've selected. Select one or more columns to make the Insert button insert columns; select one or more rows to make the Insert button insert rows; or select one or more cells to make the Insert button insert cells. If you haven't selected the appropriate item, click the Insert pop-up button rather than the main Insert button, and then choose the item you want from the pop-up menu.

To insert an individual cell or multiple cells (but not an entire row or column), follow these steps:

1. Select the range before which you want to insert the cells.

2. Choose Home ➤ Cells ➤ Insert ➤ Insert Cells from the Ribbon to display the Insert dialog box (see Figure 13-1).

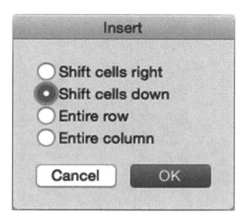

Figure 13-1. When you insert a block of cells, click the Shift cells right option button or the Shift cells down option button in the Insert dialog box to tell Excel which way to move the existing cells

3. Select the Shift cells right option button to move the existing cells to the right. Select the Shift cells down option button to move the existing cells down the worksheet. You can also select the Entire row option button to insert a whole row or select the Entire column option button to insert a whole column, but it's usually easier to insert a row or column by using the methods described earlier.

4. Click the OK button to close the Insert dialog box. Excel inserts the cells.

The easiest way to delete a column or row is to Ctrl-click or right-click its heading, and then click Delete on the context menu. Alternatively, you can select the row or column and then choose Edit ➤ Delete from the menu bar or Home ➤ Cells ➤ Delete (clicking the main part of the Delete button) from the Ribbon.

Instead of selecting the column or row, you can click a cell in it, choose Home ➤ Cells ➤ Delete from the Ribbon (clicking the Delete pop-up button), and then click Delete Columns or Delete Rows, as needed. Usually, it's easier to select the row or column first.

To delete an individual cell or multiple cells (but not an entire row or column), select them, and then choose Home ➤ Cells ➤ Delete ➤ Delete Cells from the Ribbon or Edit ➤ Delete from the menu bar. In the Delete dialog box (see Figure 13-2) that Excel displays, select the Shift cells left option button or the Shift cells up option button, as appropriate, and then click the OK button.

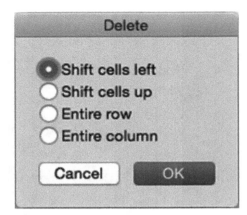

Figure 13-2. When you delete a block of cells, click the Shift cells left option button or the Shift cells up option button in the Delete dialog box to tell Excel how to fill the gap in the worksheet

> **Note**   In the Delete dialog box, you can select the Entire row option button to delete the row the selected cell is in, or select the Entire column option button to delete the column. This is useful when you realize you need to delete entire rows or columns rather than just a block of cells. Otherwise, you don't need to open the Delete dialog box to delete rows or columns.

Setting Row Height

Excel normally sets the row height automatically to accommodate the tallest character or object in the row. For example, if you type an entry in a cell, select the cell, and click the Increase Font Size button in the Font group of the Home tab a few times, then Excel automatically increases the row height so that there's enough space for the tallest characters.

If Excel doesn't set the row height automatically, select the rows you want to affect, and then choose Home ➤ Cells ➤ Format ➤ AutoFit Row Height from the Ribbon or Format ➤ Row ➤ AutoFit from the menu bar to force automatic fitting.

You can also set row height manually in either of these ways:

- *Drag the lower border of the row heading*: Move the pointer over the lower border of the row heading so that the pointer changes to an arrow pointing up and down, and then click and drag the border up (to make the row shallower) or down (to make the row deeper).

- *Use the Row Height dialog box*: Ctrl-click or right-click the row heading, and then click Row Height on the context menu to display the Row Height dialog box (see Figure 13-3). Type the row height you want, and then click the OK button.

Figure 13-3. Use the Row Height dialog box when you need to set a row's height precisely

Note   You can also display the Row Height dialog box by choosing Home ➤ Cells ➤ Format ➤
Row Height from the Ribbon or Format ➤ Row ➤ Height from the menu bar.

Setting Column Width

Unlike with row height, Excel doesn't automatically adjust column width as you enter data in
a worksheet. This is because the cells in many columns contain entries of varying lengths so
automatic adjustment would likely make constant changes.

You can quickly set column width in any of these ways:

- *AutoFit a column*: Double-click the right border of the column heading.
  Excel automatically changes the column's width so that it's wide enough
  to contain the widest entry in the column.

- *AutoFit several columns*: Select cells in all the columns you want to
  affect, and then double-click the right border of any of the selected
  column headings. Excel automatically fits each column's width to suit its
  contents. You can also select the cells and then choose Home ➤ Cells
  ➤ Format ➤ AutoFormat Column Width from the Ribbon or Format ➤
  Column ➤ AutoFit Selection from the menu bar.

Tip   AutoFit is usually the best way to resize a worksheet's columns. But if some cells have such
long contents that AutoFit will create huge columns, set the column widths manually and hide parts
of the longest contents. You can also wrap the text within a cell so that it occupies as many lines as
it needs; you'll learn how to do this in the section "Setting Alignment" later in this chapter.

- *Resize a column by hand*: Drag the right border of the column heading
  as far as needed.

- *Resize a column precisely*: Ctrl-click or right-click the column heading,
  and then click Column Width on the context menu to display the
  Column Width dialog box (see Figure 13-4). Type the cell width, and
  then click the OK button.

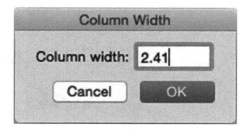

Figure 13-4. Use the Column Width dialog box when you need to set column width precisely

- *Resize several columns precisely*: Select the columns by dragging through their column headings or by selecting cells in each column. Ctrl-click or right-click in the selected column headings, and then click Column Width on the context menu to display the Column Width dialog box. Type the column width, and then click the OK button.

> **Note**   You can also display the Column Width dialog box by choosing Home ➤ Cells ➤ Format ➤ Column Width from the Ribbon or Format ➤ Column ➤ Width from the menu bar.

Hiding Rows and Columns

Sometimes it's helpful to hide particular columns and rows so that they're not visible in the worksheet. You may want to do this to hide sensitive data from your printouts or simply to make the part of the worksheet you're actually using fit on the screen all at once.

To hide a column or row, Ctrl-click or right-click its column heading or row heading, and then click Hide on the context menu. You can also click a cell in the row or column and choose Home ➤ Cells ➤ Format ➤ Hide & Unhide ➤ Hide Rows or Home ➤ Cells ➤ Format ➤ Hide & Unhide ➤ Hide Columns from the Ribbon or Format ➤ Row ➤ Hide or Format ➤ Column ➤ Hide from the menu bar.

> **Tip**   You can also use keyboard shortcuts to hide and unhide rows and columns. To quickly hide the active row or selected rows, press Ctrl+9. To hide the active column or selected columns, press Ctrl+0. To unhide a row, select the rows above and below the hidden row, and then press Ctrl+Shift+9. To unhide a column, select the columns before and after the hidden column, and then press Ctrl+Shift+0.

To unhide a row or column, select the rows above and below it or the columns on either side of it. Then Ctrl-click or right-click the selected row headings or column headings and click Unhide on the context menu.

> **Note**   You can also hide and unhide items by choosing Home ➤ Cells ➤ Format ➤ Hide & Unhide ➤ Unhide Rows or Home ➤ Cells ➤ Format ➤ Hide & Unhide ➤ Unhide Columns from the Ribbon or by choosing Format ➤ Row ➤ Unhide or Format ➤ Column ➤ Unhide from the menu bar.

Formatting Cells and Ranges

In Excel, you can format cells in a wide variety of ways—everything from choosing how to display the borders and background to controlling how Excel represents the text you enter in the cell. This section shows you the most useful kinds of formatting work and how to apply them.

Each cell comes with essential formatting applied to it: the font and font size to use and usually the General number format, which you'll meet shortly. So when you create a new workbook and start entering data in it, Excel displays the data in a normal-size font.

> **Tip** To control the font and font size Excel uses for new workbooks, choose Excel ➤ Preferences or press Cmd+, (Cmd and the comma key). Click the General icon in the Authoring area of the Excel Preferences window to display the General preferences pane. Open the Default font pop-up menu, and click the font you want. The Body Font choice at the top of the list gives you the body font set in the workbook's template; if you change this font, you change the font used in all the styles except the Title style (which uses the Heading font). Then choose the size in the Size pop-up menu. Close the Preferences window by clicking the Close button (the red button at the left end of the title bar) or pressing Cmd+W.

Understanding the Two Main Tools for Applying Formatting

Excel gives you two main tools for applying formatting to cells and ranges:

- *Home tab of the Ribbon*: The Font group provides widely used font formatting; the Alignment group offers horizontal and vertical alignment, orientation, indentation, wrapping, and merging; and the Number group gives you a quick way to apply essential number formatting. Figure 13-5 shows the Font group with its controls labeled. Figure 13-6 shows the Alignment group and Number group with their controls labeled.

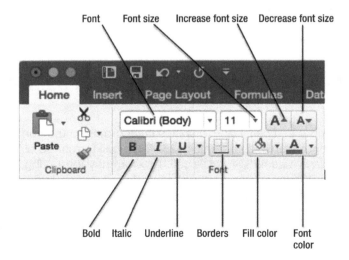

Figure 13-5. You can quickly apply essential font formatting, borders, and fills from the Font group on the Home tab of the Ribbon

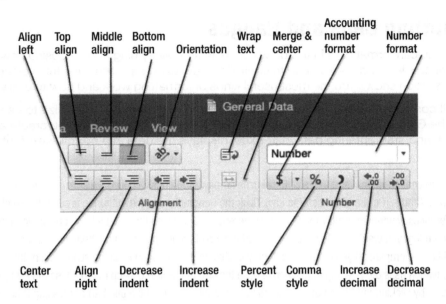

Figure 13-6. From the Alignment group on the Home tab of the Ribbon, you can set horizontal and vertical alignment, orientation, and wrapping. From the Number group, you can apply number formatting

> **Note**   When the Excel window is small, the buttons in the Alignment group appear in three rows rather than the two rows shown here.

■   *Format Cells dialog box*: When you need to apply formatting types that don't appear on the Home tab of the Ribbon, open the Format Cells dialog box and work on its six tabs, which you'll meet later in this chapter. The easiest way to display the Format Cells dialog box is to Ctrl-click or right-click a cell or a selection and then click Format Cells on the context menu. You can also open the Format Cells dialog box by pressing Cmd+1 or choosing Format ➤ Cells from the menu bar.

Controlling How Data Appears by Applying Number Formatting

When you enter a number in a cell, Excel displays it according to the number formatting applied to that cell. For example, if you enter **42524** in a cell formatted with General formatting, Excel displays it as 42524. If the cell has Currency formatting, Excel displays a value such as $42,524.00 (depending on the details of the format). And if the cell has Date formatting, Excel displays a date such as 3 June 2016 (again, depending on the details of the format). In each case, the number stored in the cell remains the same—so if you change the cell's formatting to a different type, the way that Excel displays the data changes to match.

Table 13-1 explains Excel's number formats and tells you the keyboard shortcuts for applying them. You can also apply number formatting by using the buttons on the Number Format pop-up menu and buttons in the Number group of the Home tab of the Ribbon and by using the controls on the Number tab of the Format Cells dialog box (see Figure 13-7).

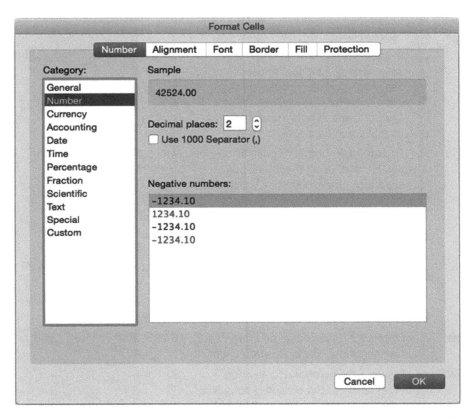

Figure 13-7. Use the Number tab of the Format Cells dialog box when you need access to the full range of number formatting

Table 13-1. Excel's Number Formats

Number Format	Explanation	Examples	Keyboard Shortcut
General	Excel's default format for all cells in new worksheets.	1234567 Industry	Ctrl+Shift+~ (tilde)
	No specific format, but displays up to 11 digits per cell and uses no thousands separator. For any entry longer than 11 digits, General format uses scientific notation (see the "Scientific" entry later in this table).		

(continued)

Table 13-1. (continued)

Number Format	Explanation	Examples	Keyboard Shortcut
Number	Displays the number of decimal places you choose. You can choose whether to use the thousands separator and how to display negative numbers.	1000 1,000 1,000.00	Ctrl+Shift+!
Currency	Displays the number of decimal places you choose, using the thousands separator. You can choose which currency symbol to display (for example, $) and how to display negative numbers.	$2,345.67 –$2,345.67	Ctrl+Shift+$
Accounting	Displays the number of decimal places you choose, using the thousands separator. You can choose which currency symbol to use. The symbol appears aligned at the left edge of the cell. Negative numbers appear with parentheses around them.	$1,000,000 $(99.999.00)	—
Date	Displays any of a variety of date formats.	2/24/2017 Friday, February 24, 2017	Ctrl+Shift+#
Time	Displays any of a variety of time formats.	11:59:59 PM 23:59:59	Ctrl+Shift+@
Percentage	Displays a percent sign and the number of decimal places you choose.	78.79% 200%	Ctrl+Shift+%
Fraction	Displays the number as a fraction. Fractions tend to be visually confusing in spreadsheets, so use them only if you must, such as in betting charts.	1/2 1 1/4	—
Scientific	Displays the number in exponential form, with E and the power to which to raise the number. You can choose how many decimal places to use.	1.2346E+08 –9.8765E+07	Ctrl+Shift+^
Text	Displays and treats the data as text, even when it appears to be another type of data (for example, a number or date).	Champions of Breakfast 18	—
Special	Displays the data in the format you choose: ZIP code, ZIP code + 4, phone number, or social security number.	10013 10013–8295 (212) 555-9753 722-86-8261	—
Custom	Displays the data in the custom format you choose. Excel provides dozens of custom formats, but you can also create your own formats.	[Various]	—

Understanding How Excel Stores Dates and Times

Excel stores dates as serial numbers starting from 1 (Sunday, January 1, 1900) and running way into the future. To give you a couple of points of reference, Sunday, January 1, 2017 is 42736, and Monday, January 1, 2018 is 43101.

You can enter a date by typing the serial number (if you know it or care to work it out), but it's much easier to type a date in a conventional format because Excel recognizes most of them. For example, if you type **1/1/2017**, Excel converts it to 42736 and displays the date in whichever format you've chosen.

Excel stores times as decimal parts of a day. For example, 42736.25 is 6 a.m. (one quarter of the way through the day) on January 1, 2017.

Older versions of Excel used the starting date January 2, 1904, by default for workbooks. Excel 2016 doesn't do this, but you can set the 1904 starting date manually if necessary (for example, if you're using an older workbook with 1904-based dates). To switch to 1904-based dates, choose Excel ➤ Preferences or press Cmd+, (Cmd and the comma key). In the Excel Preferences window, click the Calculation icon in the Formulas and Lists area to display the Calculation preferences pane. In the When Calculating Workbooks area, select the "Use the 1904 date system" check box, and then click the Close button at the left end of the title bar or press Cmd+W to close the Excel Preferences window.

Setting the Workbook's Overall Look by Applying a Theme

To control the overall look of a workbook, apply a suitable theme to it by choosing Page Layout ➤ Themes ➤ Themes from the Ribbon and then clicking the theme you want on the Themes panel.

The theme applies a set of colors and a pair of fonts to the workbook. After applying the theme, you can change the colors or fonts by using the Colors pop-up menu or the Fonts pop-up menu in the Themes group on the Page Layout tab of the Ribbon.

Setting Alignment

You can quickly align the contents of cells by using the buttons in the Alignment group on the Home tab of the Ribbon or the controls on the Alignment tab of the Format Cells dialog box (see Figure 13-8):

- *Horizontal alignment*: You can align the text Left (Indent), Center, Right, or Justify; apply General alignment, which depends on the data type (left for text, right for numbers); choose Center Across Selection to center the text across multiple cells; or choose Distributed to distribute the text across the cell (using wider spaces between words).

> **Note** The Fill horizontal alignment fills the cell with the character you specify.

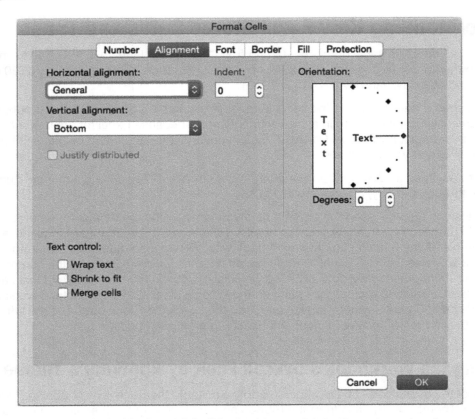

Figure 13-8. The Alignment tab of the Format Cells dialog box lets you rotate text to precise angles when needed

- *Vertical alignment*: You can align text as Top, Center, Bottom, or Justify. You can also choose Distributed to distribute the text vertically, which can be useful when you rotate the text so that it runs vertically.

- *Indent*: You can indent the text as far as is needed. Either enter the indentation amount in the Indent box on the Alignment tab of the Format Cells dialog box or choose Home ➤ Alignment ➤ Increase Indent from the Ribbon. Excel uses a standard character width (about the width of a lowercase *n* character) for each indent increment.

- *Change text orientation*: In the Orientation box on the Alignment tab of the Format Cells dialog box, you can click the left box to apply vertical orientation, click the appropriate point on the dotted arc to apply approximate orientation, or type the exact number of degrees in the Degrees box. Alternatively, use the Orientation pop-up menu in the Alignment group.

- *Wrap text*: In the Text control area, select the Wrap text check box. You can wrap the text to make a long entry appear on several lines in a cell rather than disappear where the next cell's contents start. The disadvantage to wrapping text is that the row height increases automatically to accommodate the wrapped text. (If you set a specific row height that's less than the height needed to display all the wrapped text, only the text that fits appears in the cell.)

■ *Shrink to fit*: Also in the Text control area, select this check box to shrink the text so that it fits in the cell. Shrinking works well when the text is only a bit too big for the cell. If the text is much too big, shrinking makes it unreadably small.

■ *Merge cells*: Use the Merge & Center pop-up menu in the Alignment group to merge selected cells together into a single cell. You can also center an entry across a merged cell. In the Format Cells dialog box, you can merge cells by selecting the Merge cells check box in the Text control area on the Alignment tab.

Choosing Font Formatting

You can quickly format the contents of a cell (or the selected part of a cell's contents) by using the controls in the Font group on the Home tab of the Ribbon or the Font tab of the Format Cells dialog box (see Figure 13-9). See the "Applying Direct Formatting to Text and Objects" section in Chapter 3 for information on this type of formatting.

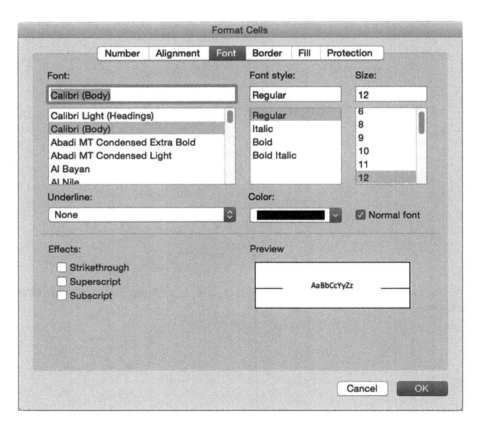

Figure 13-9. The Font tab of the Format Cells dialog box gives you a full range of font formatting for the current selection

Applying Borders and Fills

To apply borders to a cell, open the Borders pop-up menu in the Font group on the Home tab of the Ribbon, and then click the border type you want (see Figure 13-10).

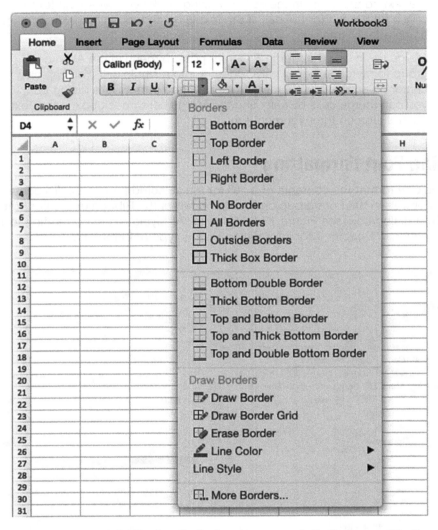

Figure 13-10. *You can quickly apply borders from the Borders pop-up menu in the Font group of the Home tab. You can also draw a border or a border grid with the pointer*

Note   The options in the Draw Borders section of the Borders pop-up menu enable you to draw
borders on and around cells by dragging the pointer across the worksheet. For example, you can
open the Borders pop-up menu, click Draw Border Grid, and then drag across the cells to which you
want to apply the grid. You can then open the Borders pop-up menu again, click Erase Border, and
use the pointer to erase any borders you don't need within the grid you've applied. Press Esc to turn
off the current tool. Depending on the type of table you need to create, this can be a quicker way of
working than selecting the cells and then applying the border formatting.

For more border options, click the More Borders item at the bottom of the Borders pop-up
menu to display the Border tab of the Format Cells dialog box (see Figure 13-11). You
can also choose Format ➤ Cells from the menu bar (or press Cmd+1) and then click the
Border tab. Use the controls on the Border tab to set up the borders you want. For example,
to apply a heavy bottom border, click a dark line in the Line Style box, and then click the
Bottom Border button in the Border box. Then click the OK button.

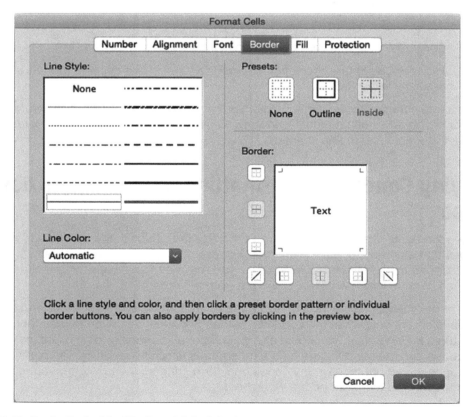

Figure 13-11. Use the Border tab of the Format Cells dialog box when you need to change the line style or color of borders

To apply a fill, use the Fill Colors pop-up menu in the Font group on the Home tab of the Ribbon or work on the Fill tab of the Format Cells dialog box. The controls on the Fill tab are straightforward to use:

- *Background color*: To apply a background color to the cell or the selection, open this pop-up menu and select the color.

- *Pattern color*: To apply a pattern to the cell or the selection, open this pop-up menu and select the color for the pattern.

- *Pattern style*: After selecting the pattern color you want, open this pop-up menu and select the style for the pattern. The Sample area in the lower half of the Fill tab shows how the pattern looks with the color and style you've selected.

When you've made your choices on the Fill tab, click the OK button to close the Format Cells dialog box and apply them.

Applying Protection to Cells

The Protection tab of the Format Cells dialog box contains only two controls:

- *Locked*: Select this check box to lock a cell against changes.

- *Hidden*: Select this check box to hide the formula in a cell (the formula's result remains visible).

After selecting either of these check boxes, you must protect the worksheet before the locking or hiding takes effect. You'll learn how to protect a worksheet in the "Protecting a Worksheet" section later in this chapter.

Applying Conditional Formatting to Identify Particular Values

In many worksheets, it's useful to be able to monitor the values in the cells and to pick out values that stand out in particular ways. For example, you may want to see which ten products are bringing in the most revenue, or you may need an easy way to make unusually high values or unusually low values stand out from the others.

To monitor the values in a cell or a range, you can apply *conditional formatting*—formatting that Excel displays only when the condition is met. For example, if you're monitoring temperatures in Fahrenheit, you could apply conditional formatting to highlight low temperatures (say, below 20F) and high temperatures (say, above 100F). Temperatures in the normal range would not receive any conditional formatting so the low temperatures and high temperatures would jump out on the worksheet.

Understanding Excel's Preset Types of Conditional Formatting

Excel provides five kinds of preset conditional formatting, which you can apply from the Conditional Formatting panel in the Styles group of the Home tab of the Ribbon. Figure 13-12 shows the Conditional Formatting panel with the Icon Sets panel displayed.

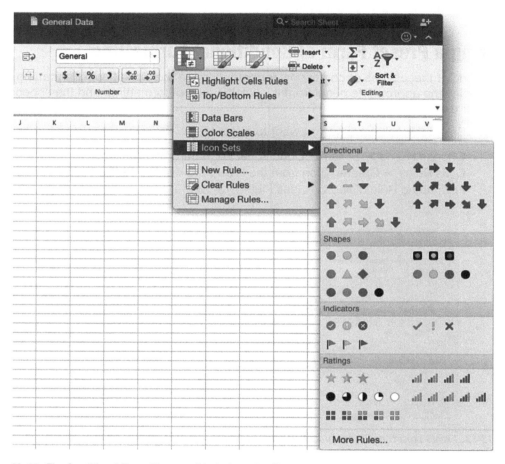

Figure 13-12. The Conditional Formatting panel includes sets of icons you can apply to indicate data trends

- *Highlight cells rules*: This panel gives you an easy way to set up conditional formatting using Greater Than, Less Than, Between, Equal To, Text that Contains, A Date Occurring, or Duplicate Values criteria.

- *Top/bottom rules*: This panel lets you apply conditional formatting for Top 10 Items, Top 10 %, Bottom 10 Items, Bottom 10 %, Above Average, and Below Average criteria.

- *Data bars*: This panel enables you to apply different gradient fills and solid fills.

- *Color scales*: This panel lets you set up color scales using two or three colors; for example, using green, amber, and red to indicate different levels of risk associated with activities.

- *Icon sets*: This panel provides different sets of icons, such as directional arrows (up, sideways, down) or a checkmark/exclamation point/cross set for indicating data trends.

Applying a Preset Form of Conditional Formatting

To apply one of these types of conditional formatting, open the Conditional Formatting panel, display the appropriate panel from it, click the type of formatting, and then specify the details. For example,

1. Select the cell or range you want to affect.

2. Choose Home ➤ Styles ➤ Conditional Formatting ➤ Highlight Cells Rules ➤ Greater Than from the Ribbon to display the New Formatting Rule dialog box (see Figure 13-13).

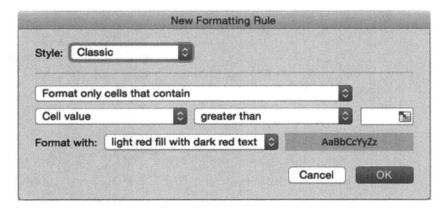

Figure 13-13. Excel's preset conditional formatting types make it easy to apply conditional formatting to cells quickly

3. In the Style pop-up menu, you can choose a different style for the conditional formatting if you want. Excel automatically selects the style that suits the type of conditional formatting you chose; in the example, it's Classic.

4. The Comparison pop-up menu below the Style pop-up menu shows the comparison for the type of conditional formatting; in the example, it's "Format only cells that contain." You can choose a different comparison if necessary, but you won't normally need to do so.

5. On the next line of controls, set up the comparison. In the example, the first pop-up menu is set to Cell value, and the second pop-up menu is set to "greater than" because this is a Greater Than rule. In the third box, you enter the comparison. You can either type in the value or collapse the dialog box, click the cell that contains the value, and then restore the dialog box.

6. In the Format with pop-up menu, choose the formatting you want. Excel provides various canned options, but you can also create custom formatting by clicking the custom format item at the bottom of the list and working in the Format Cells dialog box that opens. (This is a cut-down version of the Format Cells dialog box you met earlier in the chapter; it has only the Font tab, the Border tab, and the Fill tab.)

7. Click the OK button to close the New Formatting Rule dialog box. Excel applies the conditional formatting.

> **Note**   If none of the preset conditional formatting rules meets your needs, you can define conditional formatting rules of your own. To do so, choose Home ➤ Styles ➤ Conditional Formatting ➤ New Rule, and then work in the New Formatting Rule dialog box that opens.

Using Data Validation to Check for Invalid Entries

When you're entering large amounts of data, it's easy to type an incorrect value by mistake. To help avoid errors in your data, you can use Excel's data validation feature to check entries automatically and flag those that may be wrong. For example, if every entry in a range of cells should be between 250 and 1000 (inclusive), you can validate the data to flag any entry that is not in that range.

> **Caution**   Data validation works only when the user types in a value. If the user pastes in a value, Excel doesn't check it.

To apply validation to cells, follow these steps:

1. Click the cell or select the range you want to validate.

2. Choose Data ➤ Data Tools ➤ Data Validation (clicking the main part of the Validate button) from the Ribbon or Data ➤ Validation from the menu bar to display the Data Validation dialog box.

3. Click the Settings tab (shown in Figure 13-14 with settings chosen) to bring it to the front of the dialog box if it's not already there.

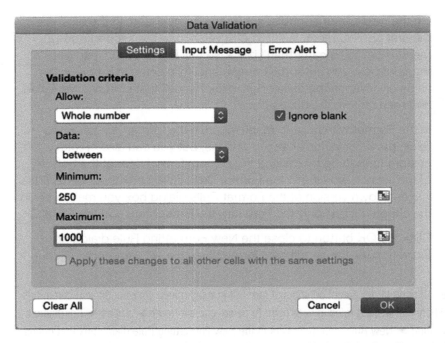

Figure 13-14. Set up the validation criteria on the Settings tab of the Data Validation dialog box. The controls that appear depend on the data type you choose in the Allow pop-up menu

4.   In the Allow pop-up menu, choose the type of data you want to validate, and then use the controls that appear to set the details.

■   *Any value*: Select this item when you want to turn off validation for the cell or range. Even with this setting, you can use the Input Message tab (discussed later in this list) to display a message about the cell or range.

> **Tip**   When setting the criteria for your data validation, you can either type in a value or click the Collapse Dialog button and then click the cell that contains the value. Using a value in a cell enables you to change the value easily without editing the conditional formatting.

■   *Whole number*: Select this item to set criteria for a whole number: one with no decimal places. For example, in the Data pop-up menu, click the between item, and then set the minimum value in the Minimum box and the maximum value in the Maximum box.

■   *Decimal*: Select this item to set criteria for a number with decimal places. For example, in the Data pop-up menu, click the greater than or equal to item, and then set the minimum value in the Minimum box.

- *List*: Select this item when you need to restrict the cell to a list of valid entries that you specify. You can enter this list in two ways: either type it in the Source box, separating each entry with a comma, or click the Collapse Dialog button at the right end of the Source box, select the worksheet range that contains the data, and then click the Collapse Dialog button again to restore the dialog box. Select the In-cell drop-down check box to make Excel display a pop-up menu with the valid entries in the cell so that the user can enter one of those valid entries easily.

- *Date*: Select this item to set criteria for a date. For example, click the Greater than item in the Data pop-up menu, and then enter the start date in the Start date box.

- *Time*: Select this item to set criteria for a time. For example, click the Not between item in the Data pop-up menu, and then enter the start time in the Start time box and the end time in the End time box.

- *Text length*: Select this item to set criteria for a text entry or formula. For example, click the Less than or equal to item in the Data pop-up menu, and then enter the maximum length in the Maximum box.

- *Custom*: Select this item when you need to enter a formula that returns a logical value of TRUE or FALSE.

5. Select the Ignore blank check box if you want to let the user leave the cell blank. Clear this check box to make the user fill in the cell with valid data.

6. Click the Input Message tab to display it. The left screen in Figure 13-15 shows the Input Message tab with settings chosen.

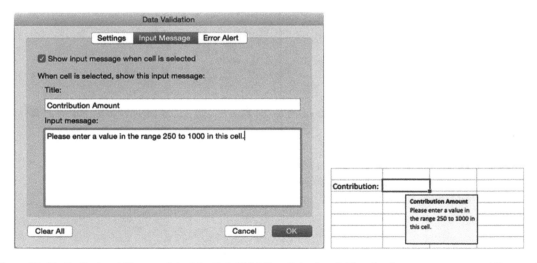

Figure 13-15. On the Input Message tab of the Data Validation dialog box (left), enter the message you want the user to see when the cell is active (right)

7. To display a message when the user makes the cell active, select the "Show input message when cell is selected" check box. Type the title in the Title box and the message in the Input message box. The right screen in Figure 13-15 shows how the message appears.

8. Click the Error Alert tab to bring it to the front. The left screen in Figure 13-16 shows the Error Alert tab with settings chosen; the right screen in Figure 13-16 shows how the error message appears.

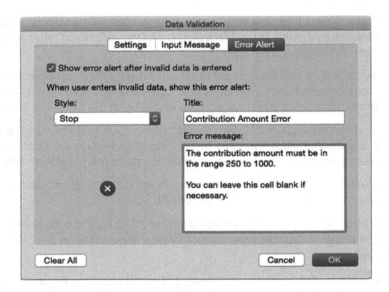

Figure 13-16. On the Error Alert tab of the Data Validation dialog box (top), set up the error to display when the user enters invalid data in the cell (bottom)

9. Select the "Show error alert after invalid data is entered" check box if you want Excel to display an error message box when the user enters invalid data. This is usually helpful.

10. In the Style pop-up menu, choose the icon type for the behavior
     you want:

     ■ *Stop*: The error dialog box has a Retry button and a Cancel button.
        If the user clicks the Retry button, Excel selects the entry that failed
        validation so that the user can change it. If the user clicks the
        Cancel button, Excel restores the cell's previous entry.

> **Note** On Windows, the Stop, Warning, and Information settings in the Style pop-up menu make
> the error message box show the different icons that appear under the Style pop-up menu when you
> make your choice. For example, the Stop style shows the red circle bearing a white cross that you
> see on the left in Figure 13-16. On OS X, the error message box displays the same Excel icon (shown
> on the right in Figure 13-16) for each style, but with different command buttons and behavior.

     ■ *Warning*: The error dialog box ends with a "Continue?" prompt after
        your message. On Windows, the error dialog box has a Yes button,
        a No button, and a Cancel button; on OS X, the error dialog box has
        a Yes button and a No button. If the user clicks the Yes button, Excel
        accepts the value, even though it has failed validation. If the user
        clicks the No button, Excel selects the entry that failed validation
        so that the user can change it. If the user clicks the Cancel button,
        Excel restores the cell's previous entry.

     ■ *Information*: The error dialog box has an OK button and a Cancel
        button on Windows and only an OK button on OS X. If the user
        clicks the OK button, Excel accepts the value, even though it has
        failed validation. On Windows, if the user clicks the Cancel button,
        Excel restores the cell's previous entry.

> **Tip** To force the user to enter valid data, choose the Stop item in the Style pop-up menu on the
> Error Alert tab of the Data Validation dialog box. The Warning style and the Information style can be
> useful for when you're providing gentler guidance on how to use the worksheet and the conformity
> of the data is less critical.

11. Enter the title and error message for the message box.

12. Click the OK button to close the Data Validation dialog box. Excel
     applies the validation.

Formatting Quickly with Table Formatting and Styles

To save you time with formatting, Excel provides preset formatting that you can apply to a
table to give it an overall look. And to save you the effort of applying many different types of
formatting over and over again to different cells, Excel includes styles, which are collections
of formatting that you can apply all at once.

Formatting with Table Formatting

When you need to format a table quickly, see if Excel's preset table formatting will do the trick. Select the table, choose Table ➤ Table Styles ➤ Table Styles from the Ribbon, and then click the style you want.

Note See Chapter 16 for instructions on creating and working with Excel tables.

Formatting with Styles

As you saw earlier in this chapter, you can give any cell exactly the formatting you want by using the controls in the Font group, Alignment group, and Number group of the Home tab of the Ribbon or by opening the Format Cells dialog box and working on its tabs. But applying formatting one aspect at a time—font, font size, alignment, and so on—takes ages, and it's easy to apply formatting inconsistently.

To save time and ensure your formatting is consistent, you can use Excel's styles. If you're familiar with Word's styles (discussed in Chapter 7), you'll find Excel's styles a snap because they work in much the same way.

Each style is a collection of formatting that you can apply to one or more cells. The style contains six types of formatting, one for each tab of the Format Cells dialog box:

- *Number*: For example, General, Currency, or Percentage.
- *Alignment*: Horizontal alignment (for example, General, Center, or Justify), vertical alignment (for example, Top, Center, or Bottom), and any trimmings (such as wrapping the text inside the cell).
- *Font*: The font, font size, font color, and so on.
- *Border*: Any borders you've applied to the style, or No Borders if it has no borders.
- *Fill*: Any fill you've applied to the style, or No Shading if it's plain.
- *Protection*: Locked, Hidden, both, or No Protection.

Most Excel templates contain plenty of styles to get you started, but you can create your own custom styles as well if necessary.

Meeting Excel's Styles

To see which styles are available in a workbook, choose Home ➤ Styles ➤ Cell Styles and look at the Cell Styles panel (see Figure 13-17). This panel lists the styles in the following categories:

- *Custom*: This category appears only when you have created one or more custom styles in the workbook.

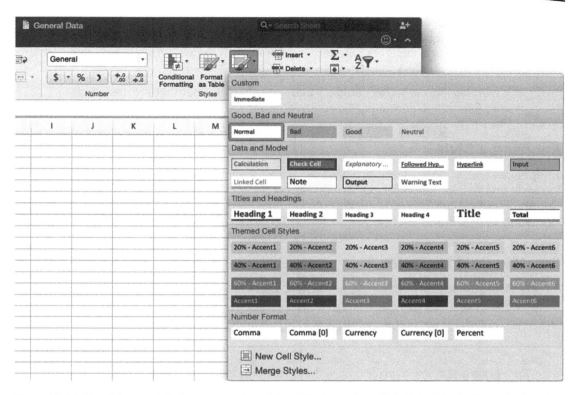

Figure 13-17. The Styles panel displays your custom styles at the top and Excel's built-in styles in different categories

- *Good, Bad, and Neutral*: This category contains Good, Bad, and Neutral styles that you can use to apply color coding to cells. Here is also where you will find the Normal style that Excel applies to any cell that doesn't have another style.

- *Data and Model*: This category contains the Calculation, Check Cell, Explanatory, Followed Hyperlink, Hyperlink, Input, Linked Cell, Note, Output, and Warning Text styles. Most of these styles are used for data modeling. Excel automatically applies the Hyperlink style to cells containing hyperlinks you have not clicked yet, changing their style to Followed Hyperlink once you have clicked them.

> **Note**   The Hyperlink style appears in the Data and Model category in the Styles panel only if the workbook contains hyperlinks. Similarly, the Followed Hyperlink style appears only if the workbook contains hyperlinks you've followed.

- *Titles and Headings*: This category contains four styles for descending levels of headings (Heading 1, Heading 2, Heading 3, and Heading 4), the Title style for giving a worksheet a title, and the Total style for easily formatting cells that contain totals.

- *Themed Cell Styles*: This category contains six Accent styles (Accent 1 through Accent 6) featuring six of the theme colors, with four degrees of shading for each. This category appears only if the workbook's template contains themed cell styles.

- *Number Format*: This category contains styles for number formats such as Comma, Comma [0], Currency, Currency [0], and Percent.

Applying a Style

To apply a style, choose Home ➤ Styles ➤ Cell Styles from the Ribbon, and then click the style on the Styles panel. You can also apply the various Number styles (such as the Currency styles, the Percent style, and the Comma style) from the Number group on the Home tab of the Ribbon.

Creating Custom Styles

If none of Excel's styles meets your needs, you can create your own styles. To create a style, follow these steps:

1. Format a cell with the formatting you want the style to have.

Tip   To jump-start your formatting, apply the existing style that's nearest to the look and formatting you want. Then change the formatting so that it looks the way you want.

---

2. Select the cell you've formatted.

3. Choose Home ➤ Styles ➤ Cell Styles ➤ New Cell Style from the Ribbon to display the New Cell Style dialog box (shown in Figure 13-18 with settings chosen).

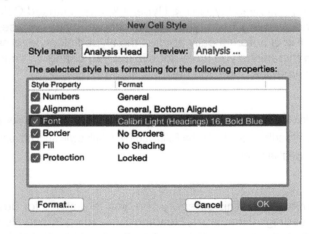

Figure 13-18. In the New Cell Style dialog box, you can quickly create a new style based on the formatting of the selected cell. You can change the formatting as needed by clicking the Format button and working in the Format Cells dialog box

4. In the Style name box, type the name you want to give the style.

5. In the "The selected style has formatting for the following properties" area, clear the check boxes for any formatting the cell has that you want to omit from the style. For example, clear the Protection check box to leave out the Locked or Hidden formatting.

Note   If you need to alter the formatting, click the Format button to display the Format Cells dialog box. Make the changes needed, and then click the OK button to return to the New Cell Style dialog box.

---

6. Click the OK button to close the New Cell Style dialog box and create the style. Excel adds the style to the Custom area at the top of the Styles panel.

Tip   Instead of creating a new style, you can modify one of the built-in styles. Choose Home ➤ Styles ➤ Cell Styles from the Ribbon to display the Styles panel, Ctrl-click or right-click the style you want to change, and then click the Modify item on the context menu. In the Modify Cell Style dialog box, select or clear the check boxes in the "The selected style has formatting for the following properties" area, or click the Format button to display the Format Cells dialog box, and make the changes you need. When you have finished, click the OK button to return to the Modify Cell Style dialog box, and then click the OK button.

Copying Styles from One Workbook to Another

If you have styles in one workbook that you want to use in another workbook, you can copy the styles across. Excel calls this *merging styles* or *importing styles*. When you merge the styles, the destination workbook receives all the styles from the source workbook—you can't pick and choose (but see the nearby Tip).

To import the styles, follow these steps:

1. Open the source workbook (the workbook that contains the styles) and the destination workbook.

2. Switch to the destination workbook by clicking in it.

3. Choose Home ➤ Styles ➤ Cell Styles ➤ Merge Styles from the Ribbon to display the Import Cell Styles dialog box (see Figure 13-19).

Figure 13-19. Use the Import Cell Styles dialog box to copy all the styles from one workbook into another workbook

4.   In the Copy cell styles from an open workbook list box, click the source workbook.

5.   Click the OK button to close the import Cell Styles dialog box. Excel copies the styles into the destination workbook, and you can then start using them.

Tip   If you need to copy just one style from one workbook to another, apply that style to a cell. Then copy that cell and switch back to the destination workbook. Ctrl-click or right-click a cell you don't mind changing, and then click Paste Special to display the Paste Special dialog box. In the Paste area, select the Formats option button, and then click the OK button. Excel pastes the style onto the cell, and you can then use the style in the workbook.

Deleting Styles You Don't Need

If you no longer need a style, you can delete it. Choose Home ➤ Styles ➤ Cell Styles from the Ribbon, Ctrl-click or right-click the style in the Cell Styles panel, and then click Delete on the context menu.

Note   Excel prevents you from deleting the Normal style because it uses this style for any cell that doesn't have another style applied.

Adding Headers and Footers to Your Worksheets

Before printing a worksheet or creating a PDF file from it, you probably want to add headers, footers, or both to identify the pages. Excel gives each worksheet a separate header and footer, which you can fill with either preset text or custom text. Each header and footer area consists of a left section, a center section, and a right section, so you can easily add several different pieces of information.

> **Note**   Apart from the method shown here, you can also add headers and footers by choosing File
> ➤ Page Setup from the menu bar and then working on the Header/Footer tab of the Page Setup
> dialog box. Here, you can create a header either by opening the Header pop-up menu and choosing
> a preset header or by clicking the Custom Header button and working in the Header dialog box.
> Similarly, you can create a footer either by opening the Footer pop-up menu and clicking a preset
> footer or by clicking the Custom Footer button and working in the Footer dialog box. You can also
> select or clear the Different odd and even pages check box, the Different first page check box, the
> Scale with document check box, and the Align with page margins check box, as needed. Click the
> OK button when you're ready to close the Page Setup dialog box.

Excel's main way to add or edit headers or footers is by working directly on the worksheet. To do so, follow these steps:

1. Choose Insert ➤ Text ➤ Header & Footer from the Ribbon. If the worksheet is in Normal view, Excel switches automatically to Page Layout view. Excel adds the Header & Footer tab to the Ribbon, displays its controls, and selects the center section of the header (see Figure 13-20).

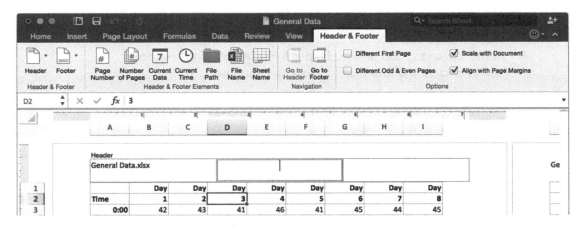

Figure 13-20. After giving the Insert ➤ Text ➤ Header & Footer command, you can use the controls on the Header & Footer tab of the Ribbon to create the header or footer a worksheet needs

> **Tip**   You can also start editing a header or footer in Page Layout view. Scroll so that you can see the "Click to add header" prompt or "Click to add footer" prompt on the sheet you want to change, and then click the prompt. Excel adds the Header & Footer tab to the Ribbon, but you need to click the tab to display its controls.

> **Note**   If you switch to another workbook, Excel closes the header or footer you were editing.

2. Click the section of the header you want to change. (If you want to start in the center section, you're all set.) If you want to work in the footer, choose Header & Footer ➤ Navigation ➤ Go to Footer to display the footer.

> **Tip**   You can insert a preset header by choosing Header & Footer ➤ Header & Footer ➤ Header and then clicking the appropriate preset header on the pop-up menu. Similarly, you can insert a preset footer by choosing Header & Footer ➤ Header & Footer ➤ Footer and then clicking the appropriate preset footer on the pop-up menu.

3. Add the header or footer by following these techniques:
    - Click a button in the Header & Footer Elements group to insert a field code (such as &[Date] for the date) or a piece of information (such as the sheet name).
    - Type in any text needed.
    - Format the text as needed by selecting it and applying formatting from either the Home tab of the Ribbon or the Font tab of the Format Cells dialog box.

4. In the Options group on the Header & Footer tab of the Ribbon, select or clear the four check boxes as needed:
    - *Different first page*: Select this check box to give the worksheet a different header or footer on the first page, or to have no header or footer on the first page.
    - *Different odd & even pages*: Select this check box to use different headers and footers on the odd pages and the even pages, as you might do in in a facing-pages layout.
    - *Scale with document*: Select this check box (which is normally selected by default) to have Excel scale the header and footer with the document. This setting is mostly useful for making sure that the headers and footers you create for portrait pages don't look absurdly big when you switch the pages to landscape orientation. If you scale down a worksheet to make it fit on a sheet of paper, you may prefer to keep the headers and footers full size.

- *Align with page margins*: Select this check box (which also is normally selected by default) to have Excel align the headers and footers with the page margins. This type of alignment works well for many worksheets; if not, you can override it easily.

5. When you have finished creating or editing the header or footer, click a cell in the worksheet to close the header or footer. You can then click the Normal View button on the status bar if you want to switch back to Normal view.

Printing Your Excel Worksheets and Workbooks

To print from Excel, you use the Print dialog box, as with the other applications. But before you print, you need to tell Excel which part of the workbook to print. You may also want to check the page setup to make sure the page breaks fall where you want them to fall.

Telling Excel Which Part of the Worksheet to Print

As you learned earlier in this chapter, each worksheet contains billions of cells, so normally you don't want to print the whole worksheet; you want to print only the range of cells you've used, or perhaps only a small subset of that range. So when you're printing, the first thing to do is tell Excel which part of the worksheet you want to print. Excel calls this setting the print area. You can set a separate print area for each worksheet.

Caution   Until you set the print area, Excel assumes you want to print all the cells you've used on the worksheet—even if there are huge amounts of blank space between them. So, it's a good idea always to set the print area before printing.

To set the print area, follow these steps:

1. Click the worksheet whose print area you want to set.

2. Select the range of cells you want to print.

3. Choose File ➤ Page Layout ➤ Page Setup ➤ Print Area ➤ Set Print Area from the Ribbon or File ➤ Print Area ➤ Set Print Area from the menu bar. Excel displays a dotted blue line around the print area to indicate that it is set.

Note   When you create a print area that consists of multiple ranges of cells, the ranges don't need to be contiguous. Excel prints each separate range on a separate page.

If you need to change the print area altogether, select a new range of cells, and then choose File ➤ Page Layout ➤ Page Setup ➤ Print Area ➤ Set Print Area from the Ribbon or File ➤ Print Area ➤ Set Print Area again from the menu bar.

If you need to clear the print area so that the worksheet has no print area set, click the worksheet, and then choose File ➤ Page Layout ➤ Page Setup ➤ Print Area ➤ Clear Print Area from the Ribbon or File ➤ Print Area ➤ Clear Print Area from the menu bar.

Checking the Page Layout and Where the Page Breaks Fall

After setting the print area, check the page layout of the worksheet and adjust it as needed. Follow these steps:

1. Switch to Page Layout view by clicking the Page Layout View button toward the right end of the status bar or choosing View ➤ Page Layout from the menu bar.

2. Click the Page Layout tab of the Ribbon to show its controls. Figure 13-21 shows a worksheet in Page Layout view with the Page Layout tab displayed.

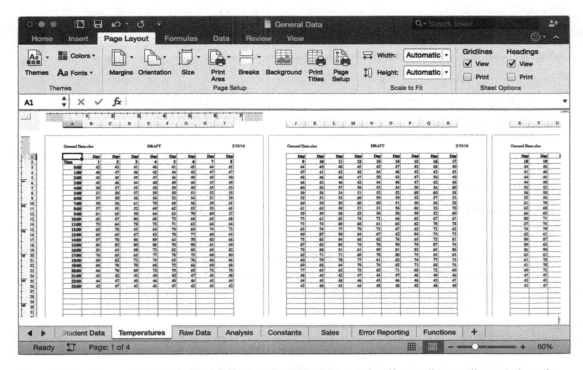

Figure 13-21. To see a worksheet's pages laid out, switch to Page Layout view. You can then use the controls on the Page Layout tab of the Ribbon to refine the layout

3. Use the controls in the Page Setup group to change the page setup as needed:

   ■ *Change the margins*: Open the Margins pop-up menu, and then click Normal, Wide, or Narrow. For greater control, click Custom Margins, work on the Margins tab of the Page Setup dialog box, and then click the OK button.

   ■ *Change the orientation*: Open the Orientation pop-up menu, and then click Portrait or Landscape.

   ■ *Change the paper size*: Open the Size pop-up menu, and then click the paper size.

   ■ *Set or clear the print area*: Open the Print Area pop-up menu, and then click Set Print Area or Clear Print Area.

   ■ *Insert a page break*: Click the column before which you want to insert a manual page break. Open the Breaks pop-up menu, and then click Insert Page Break.

Note   If you put a page break in the wrong place, click the column after it, and then choose Page Layout ➤ Page Setup ➤ Breaks ➤ Remove Page Break from the Ribbon. To restore all page breaks to where Excel had placed them, choose Page Layout ➤ Page Setup ➤ Breaks ➤ Reset All Page Breaks from the Ribbon.

When you have finished laying out the pages, it's a good idea to save the workbook—for example, click the Save button on the Quick Access Toolbar, or press Cmd+S—to store the print settings.

Printing a Worksheet or Workbook

After you've set the print area for each worksheet you want to print, you can print a worksheet or workbook like this:

1. If you want to print anything less than a whole workbook, choose what you want to print:

   ■ *Print a worksheet*: Make that worksheet active. For example, click its worksheet tab.

   ■ *Print multiple worksheets*: Make all those worksheets active by selecting their worksheet tabs.

   ■ *Selection of cells*: Select the cells.

2. Choose File ➤ Print from the menu bar or press Cmd+P to display the Print dialog box. If the Print dialog box opens at its smaller size, click the Show Details button to expand the dialog box to its larger size.

Tip   If you need to print frequently, put the Print icon on the Quick Access Toolbar for instant access.

---

3. In the Print pop-up menu, choose what to print:

    ■ *Selection*: Select this option to print only the cells you've selected. This option is useful for printing smaller amounts without resetting the print area.

    ■ *Active sheets*: Select this option to print the active worksheet (if you've selected only one) or active worksheets (if you selected more than one).

    ■ *Entire workbook*: Select this option to print every worksheet in the workbook. Normally, you use this option only for small workbooks.

4. Check that the preview of the printout looks right. If you need to change the scaling to make the printout fit the paper better, select the Scale to fit check box, and then set the number of pages in the *N* page(s) wide box and the by *N* page(s) tall box. For example, you might choose 1 page(s) wide by 2 page(s) tall.

5. Click the Print button to print your selection.

Sharing Your Workbooks with Your Colleagues

You may create some workbooks on your own, but for others, you probably need to work with colleagues to collect, enter, and analyze data. You can either share a workbook on the network so that one person can work on it at a time or turn on Excel's sharing features that enable you and your colleagues to work on the workbook at the same time.

Before sharing a workbook, you may choose to protect it with a password or to allow your colleagues to make only some types of changes to it.

Protecting a Workbook or Some of Its Worksheets

Before sharing a workbook with your colleagues for editing individually on a network, you may want to restrict the changes your colleagues can make in the workbook or on some of its worksheets. Excel calls this *protecting* the workbook or worksheets.

Protecting a Workbook

To protect a workbook, follow these steps:

1. Choose Review ➤ Changes ➤ Protect Workbook from the Ribbon or Tools ➤ Protection ➤ Protect Workbook from the menu bar to display the dialog box shown in Figure 13-22.

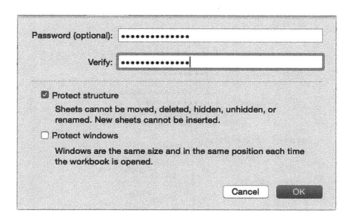

Password (optional): ••••••••••••••

Verify: ••••••••••••••|

☑ Protect structure

Sheets cannot be moved, deleted, hidden, unhidden, or renamed. New sheets cannot be inserted.

☐ Protect windows

Windows are the same size and in the same position each time the workbook is opened.

Cancel   OK

Figure 13-22. When protecting a workbook, you normally want to protect the structure but not the windows

2. Select the Structure check box to prevent your colleagues from inserting, deleting, or otherwise changing whole worksheets.

3. Select the Windows check box only if you need to prevent your colleagues from changing the number or sizes of windows that you're using for the workbook. Normally, you don't need to do this if your colleagues will work conventionally in the workbook.

4. Type a password in the Password text box and in the Verify text box.

5. Click the OK button to close the dialog box.

6. Save the workbook. For example, click the Save button on the Quick Access Toolbar or press Cmd+S.

Note   To unprotect a workbook, choose Review ➤ Changes ➤ Protect Workbook from the Ribbon or Tools ➤ Protection ➤ Unprotect Workbook from the menu bar. Excel displays a dialog box prompting you for the password. Type it, and then click the OK button. Save the changes to the workbook.

Protecting a Worksheet

When you need to limit the changes your colleagues can make to a particular worksheet, apply protection to it. Follow these steps:

1. Click the worksheet to activate it.

2. Choose Review ➤ Changes ➤ Protect Sheet from the Ribbon or Tools ➤ Protection ➤ Protect Sheet from the menu bar to display the Protect the sheet and contents of locked cells sheet (shown in Figure 13-23 with settings chosen).

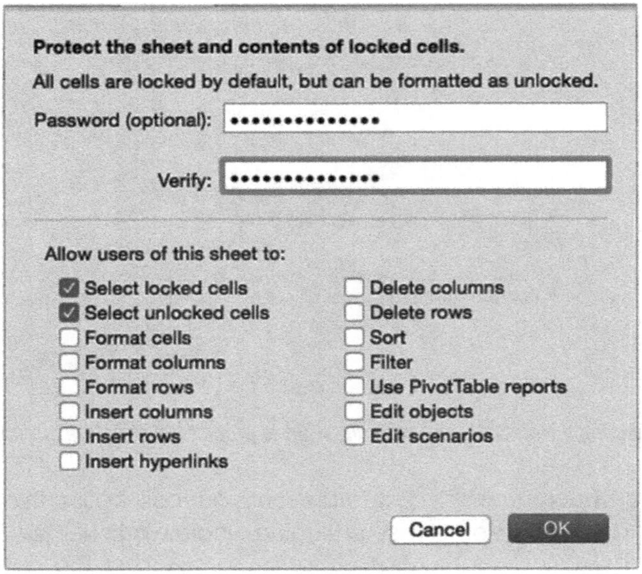

Figure 13-23. *Protect a worksheet when you need to prevent your colleagues from making specific types of changes to it*

3. Type a password in the Password text box and the Verify text box.

4. In the Allow users of this sheet to box, select each check box for actions you want your colleagues to be able to take. Clear each other check box.

5. Click the OK button. Excel closes the sheet and applies the protection.

6. Save the workbook. For example, press Cmd+S or click the Save button on the Quick Access Toolbar.

Sharing a Workbook So That Your Colleagues Can Edit It

When you need to be able to share a workbook with your colleagues, follow these steps:

1. Open the workbook.

2. Choose Review ➤ Changes ➤ Share Workbook from the Ribbon or Tools ➤ Share Workbook from the menu bar to display the Share Workbook dialog box. The left screen in Figure 13-24 shows the Editing tab of the Share Workbook dialog box, which is where you start the sharing process.

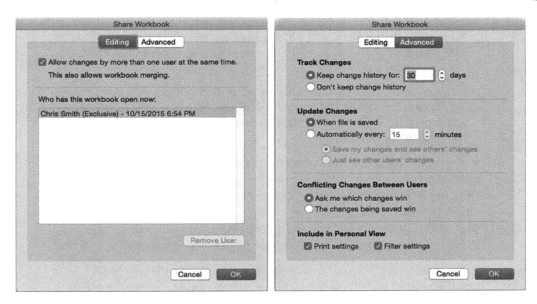

Figure 13-24. On the Editing tab (left) of the Share Workbook dialog box, select the "Allow changes by more than one user at the same time" check box. You can then choose options on the Advanced tab (right)

3. Select the "Allow changes by more than one user at the same time" check box on the Editing tab.

4. Check the "Who has this workbook open now" list box. It should show only your name and should include the word *Exclusive* to indicate that you've got sole access to the workbook.

5. Click the Advanced tab to display its contents (shown on the right in Figure 13-24).

6. In the Track Changes area, choose how long to keep the change history for the workbook:

    ▪ Normally, you want to select the "Keep change history for option button and set the number of days in the days" check box.

    ▪ The default setting is 30 days, but if you develop your workbooks quickly, you may want to reduce the interval to 7 days or 14 days to prevent Excel from keeping large amounts of history you don't need.

    ▪ The alternative is to select the "Don't keep change history" option button, but usually it's best to keep change history so that you can unravel any mysterious changes.

7. In the Update changes area, choose when to update the changes to the workbook:

    ▪ The default setting is the "When file is saved" option button, which generally works pretty well.

- The alternative is to select the Automatically every option button and set the number of minutes in the minutes box. The default setting is 15 minutes; if you work fast, you may want to shorten the interval to 5 or 10 minutes.

- If you select the Automatically every option button, you can choose between the "Save my changes and see others' changes" option button (usually the better choice) and the "Just see other users' changes" option button.

8. In the "Conflicting change between users" area, choose how to handle conflicting changes to the workbook. Normally, you want to select the "Ask me which changes win" option button so that you can decide which of the conflicting changes to keep. The alternative is to select the option button called "The changes being saved win," which tells Excel to overwrite the conflicting changes with the latest changes.

9. In the Include in Personal View area, select the Print settings check box if you want to include print settings in your view of the workbook. Select the Filter settings check box if you want to include filter settings. (See Chapter 16 for instructions on filtering an Excel database table.)

10. Click the OK button to close the Share Workbook dialog box. Excel sets up the sharing and adds "[Shared]" to the workbook's title bar so that you can easily see it's shared.

Working in a Shared Workbook

Once you've shared a workbook or someone else has shared it, you can perform basic editing in it much as normal. You can enter data and formulas in cells or edit their existing contents, format cells, and use both drag and drop and cut, copy, and paste. You can also insert rows, columns, and even whole worksheets.

Beyond these basics, Excel prevents you from making changes that may cause problems with the sharing. These are the main restrictions:

- *Apply conditional formatting*: If your workbook needs conditional formatting, apply it before sharing the workbook.

- *Insert objects*: You can't insert pictures, SmartArt, charts, hyperlinks, or various other objects.

- *Insert or delete blocks of cells*: You can insert or delete a whole row or column, but you can't insert or delete a block of cells. You also can't merge cells together.

- *Delete a worksheet*: You can't delete a worksheet from the shared workbook.

- *Protect a sheet with a password*: Any protection you've applied before sharing the workbook remains in force, but you can't apply protection to a sheet in a shared workbook.

■ *Outline the workbook*: Excel's advanced capabilities include creating a collapsible outline from a worksheet. (This book does not cover outlining.) You can't create an outline in a shared workbook.

Resolving Conflicts in a Shared Workbook

If you chose the "Ask me which changes win" option button when sharing the workbook, Excel prompts you to deal with conflicts that arise between the changes you're saving and the changes that your colleagues have already saved. The Resolve Conflicts dialog box (see Figure 13-25) takes you through each of the changes in turn, showing the change you made and the conflicting change.

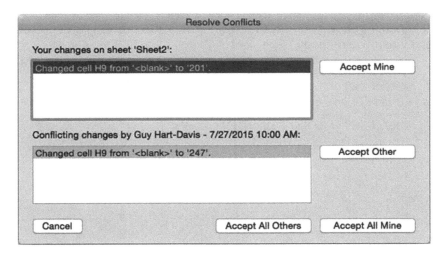

Figure 13-25. When you and another user have changed the same cells, the Resolve Conflicts dialog box walks you through each change in turn. You can accept all your changes, all your colleagues' changes, or some of each

For each change, you can click the Accept Mine button to accept your change or click the Accept Other button to accept your colleague's change. To clear all the changes at once, click the Accept All Mine button or the Accept All Others button. Excel closes the Resolve Conflicts dialog box automatically when you've finished reviewing the conflicts.

Summary

In this chapter, you learned how to apply all of Excel's most useful types of formatting to a worksheet. You now know how to manipulate the worksheet's rows and columns to make it fit your data, how to format cells and ranges, and how to save time and worry by using conditional formatting and data validation.

You also went through how to format quickly with table formatting and styles, how to give your worksheets the headers and footers that printouts need, and how to use page breaks to divide a spreadsheet across pages so that they come out right when you print. You also know how to control Excel-specific printing features.

Finally, you learned to protect worksheets and workbooks against changes, and you now know how to share your worksheets with colleagues—and how to resolve the conflicts that often occur.

In the next chapter, I'll show you how to turn your data into powerful and persuasive charts. Turn the page when you're ready.

Creating Powerful and Persuasive Charts

In this chapter, you'll learn how to create powerful charts that present your data clearly and persuasively. You'll also learn how to use sparklines, which are miniature charts that fit inside individual cells.

We'll start by going over the essentials of charts, such as the different ways you can place them in your workbooks, which components charts have, and which types of charts you can create. We'll then spend most of the chapter looking in detail at how you create a chart from your data, lay it out the way you want, and then give it the look it needs—everything from displaying or hiding components to formatting components for impact.

After that, I'll show you how to reuse your custom chart formatting by either pasting it onto an existing chart or by creating a custom chart template from it. Finally, I'll show you sparklines—what they are, how they work, and how you can make them look them the way you want them to.

Learning the Essentials of Charts in Excel

Before you start creating charts, let's look at the two ways you can place charts in your workbooks, what the different components of charts are called and what they show, and the many different types of charts that Excel offers you.

© Guy Hart-Davis 2016
G. Hart-Davis, *Learn Office 2016 for Mac*, DOI 10.1007/978-1-4842-2002-3_14

Understanding Embedded Charts and Chart Sheets

In Excel, you can place a chart either on a worksheet (for example, with its data) or on its own chart sheet:

- *Chart on a worksheet*: Excel calls a chart on a worksheet an *embedded chart* because the chart object is embedded in the worksheet. Usually, the worksheet is the one that contains the chart's data, but you can embed a chart on a different worksheet if necessary. Create an embedded chart when you want to look at the chart alongside its data or alongside other information. Figure 14-1 shows an embedded chart.

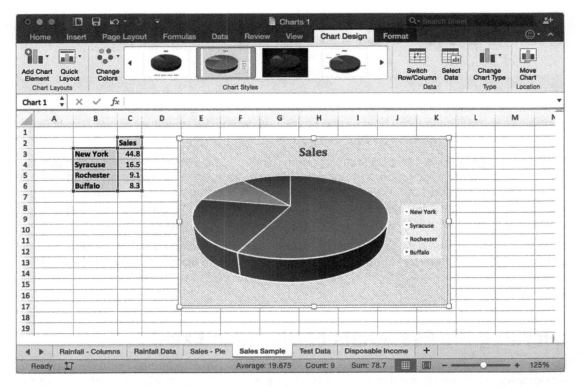

Figure 14-1. Create an embedded chart on a worksheet when you want to work on or view the chart alongside its data

- *Chart on chart sheet*: Instead of creating an embedded chart, you can create a chart on a *chart sheet*, which is a separate page in the workbook that contains only a chart. Using a chart sheet gives you more space to lay out the chart and view it. The chart sheet doesn't contain the source data, but you can add a data table showing the source data if you don't mind sacrificing some of the chart sheet's space for the table. Figure 14-2 shows a chart on a chart sheet without a data table.

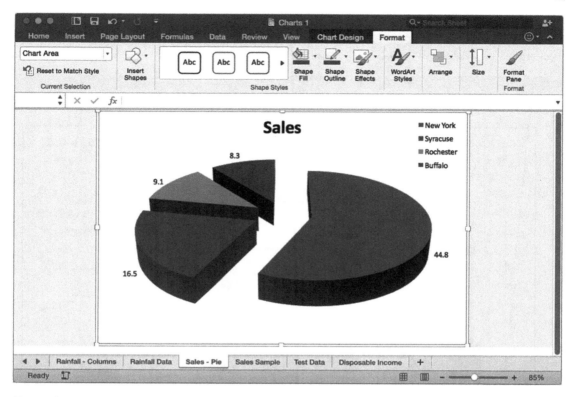

Figure 14-2. Place a chart on its own chart sheet when you want to give it plenty of space

> **Note**   You can change an embedded chart to a chart on its own chart sheet, or a chart on a chart sheet to an embedded chart, as needed. You may find it easiest to develop a chart as an embedded chart, where you can see the data and modify it as needed, and then move the chart to a chart sheet when it's ready for deployment.

Understanding the Components of a Chart

Excel's charts vary widely in looks and use, but most of them use the same set of components. Figure 14-3 shows a typical type of chart—a 3-D column chart—of rainfall data for six months for seven weather stations, with the main parts of the chart labeled.

> **Note**   If you have some sample data you're ready to try turning into a chart, select the data and choose Insert ➤ Charts ➤ Column from the Ribbon, and then click a chart type on the Column panel. This will give you a quick column chart that you can experiment with as we go through the components of charts.

The following sections discuss the individual components of charts.

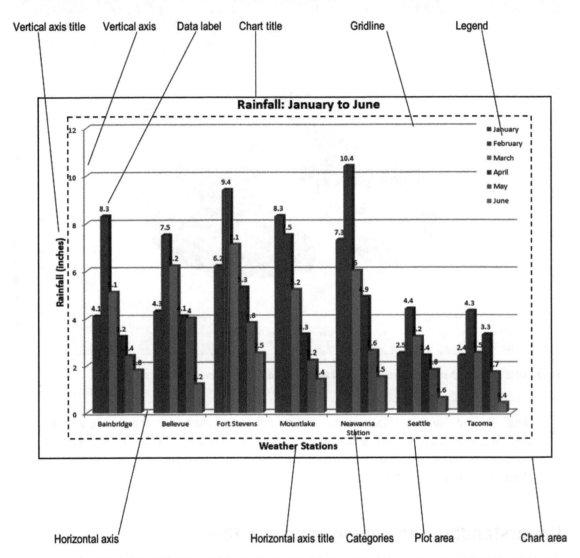

Figure 14-3. This column chart contains most of the typical elements of Excel charts. The chart area is the whole area occupied by the chart, and the plot area is where the data series are plotted.

Chart Area and Plot Area

The *chart area* is the whole area occupied by the chart. If the chart has a white background, the easiest way to see the extent of the chart area is to click the chart so that Excel displays a border around it.

The *plot area* is the area of the chart that contains the plotted data—in other words, the main part of the chart area, excluding the areas occupied by the chart title, the axis titles, and the legend (if it appears outside the plot area).

Chart Axes

Most charts have one, two, or three axes:

- *Horizontal axis*: This is the axis along which the data categories are laid out, such as the weather stations in the sample chart. This axis is also called the *category axis* or the x-*axis*.

- *Vertical axis*: This is the axis along which the data series are laid out. This axis is also called the y-*axis*.

- *Depth axis*: In 3-D charts, this is the axis that provides the third dimension. This axis is also called the z-*axis*.

Each axis has tick marks that show where the values appear on it.

Categories and Data Series

The *categories* are the subdivisions of data that appear on the horizontal axis. For example, in the sample chart, each weather station is a category. Each month appears in a different color for each category, making the difference clearly visible. The legend (which I'll cover a little later in this chapter) shows which color represents which month.

The *data series* are the sets of data used to create the chart. For example, in the sample chart, the data series contain the rainfall measurements.

Chart Title and Axis Titles

The *chart title* is text that identifies the chart as a whole. Normally, you put the chart title at the top of the chart, but you can place it elsewhere if you want.

The *horizontal axis title* is text that explains what is shown on the horizontal axis, such as the weather stations in the sample chart.

The *vertical axis title* is text that explains what the vertical axis shows, such as the amount of rainfall in the sample chart.

A 3-D chart can also have a *depth axis title* that explains what the depth axis shows.

Note   Chart titles and axis titles are optional, so you can include only those your chart needs. Generally, people viewing your charts will benefit from having clear chart titles and axis titles. But don't feel obliged to include any element that seems to complicate your charts. Remember the saying "if in doubt, leave it out."

Data Markers, Gridlines, and Data Labels

The *data markers* are the points on the chart that show where each data point appears. Each series typically contains several data markers. Depending on the chart type, the data markers may appear as separate points, or they may be linked together.

To make it easy to see how the data markers relate to the axes, you can add *gridlines* to the chart, which are lines that run across or up from the data markers.

Data labels are text items that display the exact value of data points. You can display data labels when viewers need to see the exact figure for each data point rather than judging the value from the chart.

Legend

The legend is a key to the data series in the chart. For example, in the sample chart, the legend shows which color represents which month: dark blue for January, red for February, green for March, and so on.

The legend is an optional element that you may choose to omit when you feel it is not needed. Many charts and chart types benefit from having a legend, but others are abundantly clear without a legend.

Understanding Excel's Chart Types and Choosing Which to Use

Excel enables you to create an impressive variety of different types of charts. Some of the charts are widely useful, whereas others are highly specialized. Table 14-1 describes the types of charts that Excel provides and suggests typical uses for them. The table lists the charts in the same order as Excel's Insert ➤ Chart submenu on the menu bar; the order in the Charts group on the Insert tab of the Ribbon is a little different.

Table 14-1. Excel's Chart Types and Suggested Uses

Chart Category	Description	Suggested Uses
Column	Displays data in vertical bars.	Comparing equivalent items (such as sales results) or sets of data that change over time (such as rainfall).
Line	Displays each series in a line.	Showing evenly spaced values that change over time, such as temperatures.
Pie	Displays a single data series as a pie divided up by the contribution of each data point.	Showing how much each item contributes to the whole, such as breaking down expenses by department.
Bar	Displays data in horizontal bars.	Comparing similar items or indicating progress.
Area	Displays data as lines but with the areas between them shaded.	Showing how values have changed over time, especially the contribution of different data points in the series.
XY (Scatter)	Displays each data point as a point (or cross, or similar marker) on the plot area.	Showing values sampled at different times or that are not directly related to each other.

(continued)

Table 14-1. (*continued*)

Chart Category	Description	Suggested Uses
Stock	Displays each data series as a vertical line or bar indicating three or more prices or measurements (for example, high, low, and closing prices).	Showing the daily prices of stocks. Also suitable for some scientific data.
Surface	Displays the data points as a three-dimensional surface.	Comparing two sets of data to find a suitable combination of them.
Radar	Displays the combined values of different data series.	Showing how the combined values of separate data series compare to each other; for example, the sales contributions of several different products over several periods of time.

Note   Earlier versions of Excel, such as Excel 2011 for Mac, offered two other chart categories: the Doughnut category and the Bubble category. Excel 2016 brings the Doughnut chart type into the Pie category, perhaps because they share a round shape and belong to the same food group, and adds the Bubble chart type and the 3D Bubble chart type to the XY (Scatter) category.

Creating, Laying Out, and Formatting a Chart

In this section, you'll look at how to create a chart from your data, lay it out with the components and arrangement you want, and apply the most useful types of formatting.

Creating a Chart

To create a chart, you use the commands on the Charts tab of the Ribbon. Follow these steps:

1. Select the data you want to chart, including any row or column headings needed. For example, click the first cell in the data range, and then Shift-click the last cell.

Tip   You can create a chart from either a block range or from a range of separate cells. To use separate cells, select them as usual—for example, click the first, and then Cmd-click each of the others.

2. Click the Insert tab of the Ribbon to display its contents, and then click the appropriate button in the Insert Chart group: Column; Bar; Pie; Line; XY (Scatter); Area; or Insert Area, Stock, Surface or Radar Chart (the button that shows assorted chart types). For the sample chart, you would click the Column button.

3. On the panel that opens, click the chart type you want. Figure 14-4 shows the Column panel, which is one of the most widely useful. For the sample chart, you click the 3-D Clustered Column chart type.

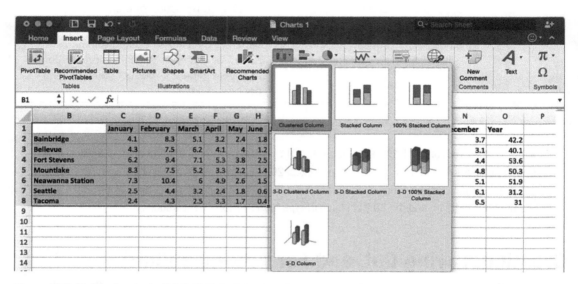

Figure 14-4. *To insert a chart, click the appropriate pop-up button in the Charts group on the Insert tab of the Ribbon, and then click the chart type you want*

Excel creates the chart as an embedded chart in the current worksheet, as shown in Figure 14-1. You can then reposition it, resize it, or move it to a chart sheet as follows:

- *Reposition the chart*: If you want to keep the chart as an embedded chart, move the pointer over the chart border so that it turns into a four-headed arrow, and then drag the chart to where you want it.

- *Resize the chart*: Click to select the chart, and then drag one of the handles that appear. Drag a corner handle to resize the chart in both dimensions; you can Shift-drag to resize the chart proportionally. Drag a side handle to resize the chart in only that dimension; for example, drag the bottom handle to resize the chart only vertically.

- *Move the chart to a chart sheet*: If you want to move the chart to a chart sheet, follow the instructions in the next section.

When a chart is active, as it is immediately after you insert it, the Chart Design tab and the Format tab appear on the Ribbon, as you'll see later in this chapter. The Chart Design tab is active at first.

Changing a Chart from an Embedded Chart to a Chart Sheet

You can change a chart from being embedded in a worksheet to being on its own chart sheet like this:

1. Click the chart on the worksheet it's embedded in.

2. Choose Chart Design ➤ Location ➤ Move Chart from the Ribbon to display the Move Chart dialog box (see Figure 14-5).

> **Tip**   You can also display the Move Chart dialog box by Ctrl-clicking or right-clicking the chart and then clicking Move Chart on the context menu. You need to Ctrl-click or right-click the chart itself rather than one of its components.

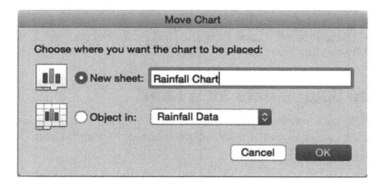

Figure 14-5. Use the Move Chart dialog box to change a chart from being embedded to being on its own chart sheet

3. Select the New sheet option button.

4. Type the name for the new chart sheet in the New sheet text box.

5. Click the OK button. Excel creates the new chart sheet and moves the chart to it. The chart is still attached to its source data, so if you change the data, Excel changes the chart too.

> **Note**   You can also use the Move Chart dialog box to move a chart from a chart sheet to an embedded chart on a worksheet or to move an embedded chart from one worksheet to another.

Changing the Chart Type

If you find the chart type you've chosen doesn't work for your data, you can change the chart type easily without having to create the chart again from scratch. Follow these steps:

1. Click the chart to select it.

2. Click the Chart Design tab of the Ribbon to display its contents.

3. In the Type group, click Change Chart Type to display the Change Chart Type panel, click the chart category to display the category's pop-up panel, and then click the chart type.

Switching the Rows and Columns in a Chart

When Excel displays the chart, you may realize that the data series are in the wrong place; for example, the chart is displaying months by rainfall instead of rainfall by months.

When this happens, there's a quick fix: switch the rows and columns by choosing Chart Design ➤ Data ➤ Switch Row/Column from the Ribbon. Excel displays the chart with the series the other way around.

Changing the Source Data for a Chart

Sometimes you may find that your chart doesn't work well with the source data you've chosen. For example, you may have selected so much data that the chart is crowded, or you may have missed a vital row or column.

When this happens, you don't need to delete the chart and start again from scratch. Instead, follow these steps:

1. Choose Chart Design ➤ Data ➤ Select Data from the Ribbon to display the Select Data Source dialog box (see Figure 14-6).

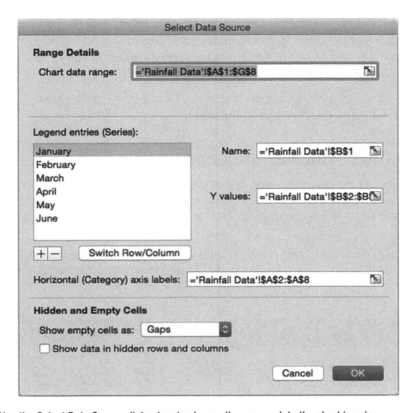

Figure 14-6. Use the Select Data Source dialog box to change the source data the chart is using

2. In the Chart data range box, enter the data range you want to use:

    ■ If your Mac has a small screen, it's easiest to click the Collapse Dialog button to collapse the Select Data Source dialog box, drag on the worksheet to select the right data range, and then click the Collapse Dialog button again to restore the dialog box. (If you have plenty of space on screen, you can just work around the Select Data Source dialog box instead.)

    ■ You can also type the data range in the Chart data range box. This is easy when you just need to change a column letter or row number to fix the data range.

3. If you need to switch the rows and columns as well, click the Switch Row/Column button.

4. If your chart data contains empty cells, open the "Show empty cells as" pop-up menu and choose how to represent them. Your choices are Gaps (the default setting for most charts) or Zero.

5.   Select the "Show data in hidden rows and columns" check box only if you want the chart to include data in hidden rows and columns within the source range. Normally, you should keep these hidden, but it's sometimes useful to show them.

6.   Click the OK button to close the Select Data Source dialog box. Excel applies the changes to the chart.

Choosing the Layout for the Chart

When you've sorted out the chart type and the source data, it's time to choose the layout for the chart. For each chart type, Excel provides various preset layouts that control where the title, legend, and other elements appear. After applying a layout, you can customize it further as needed.

To apply a layout, click the chart, choose Chart Design ➤ Chart Layouts ➤ Quick Layout to display the Quick Layout panel (see Figure 14-7), and then click the layout you want to apply to the chart.

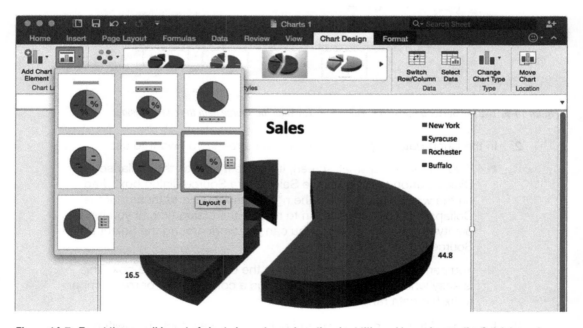

Figure 14-7. To set the overall layout of chart elements, such as the chart title and legend, open the Quick Layouts panel, and then click the layout you want

Adding a Separate Data Series to a Chart

Sometimes you may need to add to a chart a data series that doesn't appear in the chart's source data; for example, to add projections of future success to your current data.

To add a data series, work from the Select Data Source dialog box. Follow these steps:

1. Click the chart to select it.

2. Choose Chart Design ➤ Data ➤ Select Data from the Ribbon to display the Select Data Source dialog box. You can also Ctrl-click or right-click the chart and then click Select Data on the context menu.

3. Click the Add button below the Series list box. Excel adds a new item to the series box, giving it a default name such as Series3 or Series4.

4. Click in the Name text box, and then type the name you want to give the series. If the name appears in a cell on the worksheet, you can click it. When you move the focus out of the Name text box, Excel changes the default name to the name you type.

5. In the Y values text box, type the values for the series inside the braces, putting a comma between the values; for example, **{4.5,8.3,6.2,5.1,4.8,10.2}**. If the values appear in cells on the worksheet, you can enter them by selecting the range.

> **Note**   When adding a new data series, you don't normally need to change the contents of the Category (X) axis labels text box. This text box contains the range of cells that provide the labels for the horizontal axis.

6. Click the OK button to close the Select Data Source dialog box.

Applying a Style to a Chart

To control the overall graphical look of a chart, apply one of Excel's styles to it from the Styles box or the Styles panel in the Chart Styles group on the Charts tab of the Ribbon. Click the chart to select it, and then click the Chart Design tab of the Ribbon to display its controls. Either click a style in the Chart Styles box in the Chart Styles group or hold the pointer over the Chart Styles box until the panel button appears, click the panel button to display the Chart Styles panel (see Figure 14-8), and then click the style.

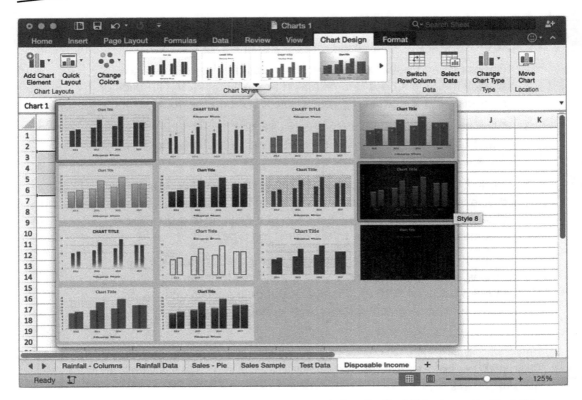

Figure 14-8. To give the chart an overall graphical look, apply a style from the Chart Styles box or the Chart Styles panel in the Chart Styles group of the Chart Design tab of the Ribbon. You can hold the pointer over a style to display a ScreenTip showing the style's name

Adding a Title to a Chart

To let viewers know what a chart is about, you should add a title to it. To do so, follow these steps:

1. Click the chart to select it.

2. Choose Chart Design ➤ Chart Layouts ➤ Add Chart Element ➤ Chart Title from the Ribbon, and then choose the title type you want:

   ■ *None*: Choose this item to remove the existing title. You can also click the title and press Delete to delete it.

   ■ *Above Chart*: Choose this item to place the title above the chart, making the chart smaller to provide space for the title. Use this placement when you want to keep the title clearly separated from the chart; for example, because the chart is busy.

   ■ *Centered Overlay*: Choose this item to place the title on the chart, centered over the top. Placing the title on the chart lets you keep the chart as large as possible. If the title lands on top of data, you can click it and drag it to a different position.

- *More Title Options*: Choose this item to display the Format Chart Title pane. Here, you can click the Title Options tab to work on the title area or the Text Options tab to work on the text itself. On the Title Options tab, you can use the controls in the Fill & Line pane (shown on the left in Figure 14-9), the Effects pane (shown in the center), or the Size & Properties pane (shown on the right) to apply exactly the formatting you want to the title. On the Text Options tab, you can use the controls in the Text Fill & Outline pane, the Text Effects pane, and the Textbox pane to format the text.

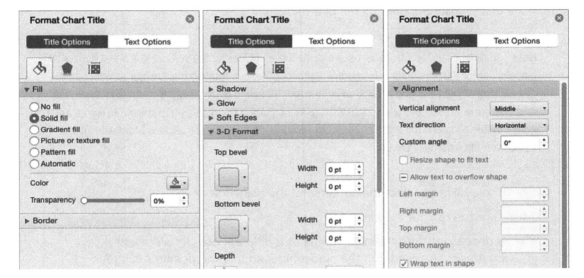

Figure 14-9. You can create a custom chart title by working in the Format Chart Title pane. Click the Title Options tab, and then work on the Fill & Line pane (left), the Effects pane (center), and the Size & Properties pane (right), as needed

3. Triple-click to select the contents of the Chart Title placeholder that Excel adds for you.

4. Type the title for the chart over the default text.

5. If necessary, drag the chart title placeholder to a different position. Move the pointer over a border of the chart title placeholder so that the pointer changes to a four-headed arrow, and then click and drag.

6. Click elsewhere to deselect the chart title.

Tip   You can also display the Format Chart Title pane by Ctrl-clicking or right-clicking the chart title and then clicking Format Chart Title on the context menu.

Adding Axis Titles to the Chart

To make clear what the chart shows, you should add titles to the axes. To do so, follow these steps:

1. Click the chart to select it.

2. Choose Chart Design ➤ Chart Layouts ➤ Add Chart Element ➤ Axis Titles to display the Axis Titles panel, and then click to select the appropriate axis, such as Primary Horizontal or Primary Vertical. A check mark appears next to the axis you clicked, and the placeholder appears on the chart.

Note   In most chart layouts, Excel uses a vertical placeholder for the vertical axis and a horizontal placeholder for the horizontal axis and the depth axis. You can rotate a placeholder as needed by Ctrl-clicking or right-clicking it, clicking Format Axis Title, and then using the controls in the Format Axis Title pane. These controls work like those in the Format Chart Title pane (shown in Figure 14-9, earlier in this chapter). You can also open the Format Axis Title pane by clicking More Axis Title Options on the Axis Titles panel.

---

3. Triple-click to select the contents of the placeholder.

4. Type the text for the axis title.

5. If necessary, drag the placeholder to a different position. Move the pointer over a border of the placeholder so that the pointer changes to a four-headed arrow, and then click and drag.

Changing the Scale or Numbering of an Axis

When you insert a chart, Excel automatically numbers the axes to suit the data range the chart uses. This automatic numbering works well for many charts, but for other charts, you may need to change the scale or numbering of an axis.

The options for formatting an axis vary depending on the chart type and the axis type. In this section, you'll explore the formatting options for first the horizontal axis and then the vertical axis of a column chart, which are fairly typical and will put you in a good position to format other chart types.

Changing the Scale or Numbering of a Horizontal Axis

If you need to change the scale or numbering of the horizontal axis of a chart, follow these steps:

1. Double-click the horizontal axis, or Ctrl-click or right-click in the horizontal axis titles area, and then click Format Axis on the context menu to display the Format Axis pane. (You can also choose Chart Design ➤ Chart Layouts ➤ Add Chart Element ➤ Axis ➤ More Axis Options.)

The Axis Options pane appears at the front. This pane contains four sections: the Axis Options section and the Tick Marks section (shown on the left in Figure 14-10) and the Labels section and the Number section (shown on the right in Figure 14-10). You can expand or collapse each section as needed by clicking its heading.

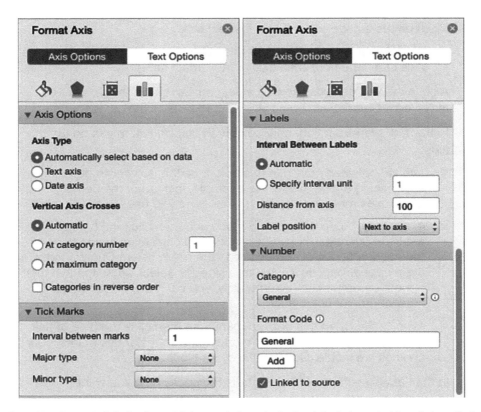

Figure 14-10. Use the controls in the Format Axis pane to format a horizontal axis to control its axis type, its tick marks, its labels, and its number format

2. In the Axis Type area, select the appropriate option button:

    ■ *Automatically select based on data*: Select this option button to have Excel automatically determine the axis type based on the data the chart uses. This setting often works well, but if you need to make changes, select one of the other option buttons.

    ■ *Text axis*: Select this option button to specify that the axis uses text (even if that text looks like dates).

    ■ *Date axis*: Select this option button if the axis uses dates.

3. In the Vertical Axis Crosses area, select the appropriate option button to control where the vertical axis crosses the horizontal axis:

    ■ *Automatic*: Select this option button to have Excel decide where the vertical axis crosses.

    ■ *At category number*: To make the vertical axis cross the horizontal axis at a particular category number, select this option button and type the category number in the text box.

    ■ *At maximum category*: Select this option button to make the vertical axis cross the horizontal axis at the largest category.

4. Also in the Vertical Axis Crosses area, you can select the Categories in Reverse Order check box if you want to reverse the category order.

5. In the Tick Marks section, choose how to display tick marks on the axis:

    ■ *Interval between marks*: In this box, type the number to determine the spacing of tick marks. For example, instead of the default 1 that Excel uses for many charts, you can type 5 to use fewer tick marks.

    ■ *Major type*: Open this pop-up menu and then click the type of tick mark you want for major tick marks. You can select Inside to have the major tick marks appear inside the chart, select Outside to have them appear outside (on the axis side), or select Cross to have them appear on both sides. Alternatively, you can select None if you do not want major tick marks.

    ■ *Minor type*: Open this pop-up menu and then click the type of tick mark you want for minor tick marks. As with major tick marks, your choices are Inside, Outside, Cross, or None.

6. In the Labels section, set the controls to specify how you want Excel to label the axis:

    ■ *Automatic*: Select this option button to have Excel automatically determine the interval between labels.

    ■ *Specify interval unit*: To control the interval between labels, select this option button and type the value in the text box.

    ■ *Distance from axis.* In this text box, type a number between 0 and 1000 to specify how far the labels should appear from the axis. Using 0 puts the labels very close to the axis; using 1000 puts the labels a fair distance away.

    ■ *Label position*: Open this pop-up menu and then click Next to axis, High, Low, or None. Choosing High puts the labels above the chart, whereas choosing Low puts the labels below the chart (which may have the same effect as choosing Next to axis). Choosing None suppresses the labels.

7. In the Number section, choose how to format the numbers on the axis:

- *Category*: Open this pop-up menu and choose the number category, such as General, Currency, or Date. These are the same formats you use for controlling how data appears in cells; depending on the format you choose, the Number section may display other options you can set for the format. For example, if you choose the Number category, you can set the number of decimal places, choose whether to use the thousands separator, and specify how to display negative numbers.

- *Format code*: In this text box, you can specify formatting codes for the category. For example, for the Date category, you can specify codes such as m/d/yy or mm/dd/yyyy to control how the dates appear. Click the Add button to add the formatting code you've entered.

- *Linked to source*: Select this check box if the data is linked to its source in the worksheet.

8. When you finish choose formatting for the axis, click the Close button (the X button in the upper-right corner) to close the Format Axis pane.

Changing the Scale or Numbering of a Vertical Axis

When you need to change the scale or numbering of the vertical axis of a chart, follow these steps:

1. Double-click the vertical axis, or Ctrl-click or right-click in the vertical axis titles area, and then click Format Axis on the context menu to display the Format Axis pane. The Axis Options pane appears at the front. As for a horizontal axis, this pane contains four sections: the Axis Options section (shown on the left in Figure 14-11) and the Tick Marks section, the Labels section, and the Number section (shown on the right in Figure 14-11). You can expand or collapse each section as needed by clicking its heading.

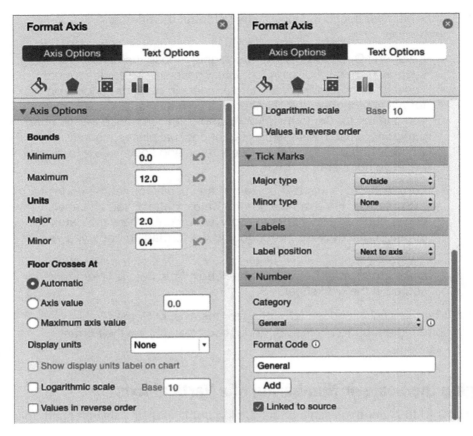

Figure 14-11. Use the controls in the Format Axis pane to format a vertical axis to control its axis type, its tick marks, its labels, and its number format.

2. Use the controls in the Bounds area of the Axis Options section to set the minimum and maximum bounds for the axis:

   ■ *Minimum*: Type the value for the minimum bound over the value that Excel has set.

   ■ *Maximum*: Type the value for the maximum bound over the value that Excel has set.

3. Use the controls in the Units area to set the major and minor units:

   ■ *Major*: Type the value for the major units over the value that Excel has set. Depending on how big your chart is, you probably want between five and ten major units on the scale you've set by choosing the Minimum value and Maximum value.

   ■ *Minor*: Type the value for the minor units over the value that Excel has set. You normally want between four and ten minor units per major unit, depending on what the chart shows.

4. In the Floor Crosses At area, choose where the horizontal axis should cross the vertical axis:

   ■ *Automatic*: Select this option button to have Excel place the crossing point automatically, such as at 0.

   ■ *Axis value*: To have the horizontal axis cross at a specific value of the vertical axis, select this option button and type the value in the text box.

   ■ *Maximum axis value*: Select this option button to have Excel place the crossing point at the maximum value of the vertical axis.

5. If you want to display the units the chart uses, open the Display units pop-up menu and click the appropriate item, such as the Hundreds item, the Thousands item, or the Millions item. If you choose to display units, make sure the Show display units label on chart check box is selected, making Excel display a label showing the units. If you don't want to show the units, choose None in the Display units pop-up menu.

6. If you need the chart to use a logarithmic scale rather than an arithmetic scale, select the Logarithmic scale check box, then enter the logarithm base in the Base box. For example, enter 10 to have the scale use the values 1, 10, 100, 1000, 10000, and so on, at regular intervals.

7. If you need the chart to show the values in reverse order, select the "Values in reverse order" check box. For example, you might need a chart to show the lowest value at the top instead of the highest values.

8. In the Tick Marks section, choose how to display tick marks on the axis:

   ■ *Major type*: Open this pop-up menu and then click the type of tick mark you want for major tick marks. You can select Inside to have the major tick marks appear inside the chart, select Outside to have them appear outside (on the axis side), or select Cross to have them appear on both sides. Alternatively, you can select None if you do not want major tick marks.

   ■ *Minor type*: Open this pop-up menu and then click the type of tick mark you want for minor tick marks. As with major tick marks, your choices are Inside, Outside, Cross, or None.

9. In the Labels section, open the Label position pop-up menu and then click Next to axis, High, Low, or None. Choosing High puts the labels above the chart, whereas choosing Low puts the labels below the chart (which may have the same effect as choosing Next to axis). Choosing None suppresses the labels.

10. In the Number section, choose how to format the numbers on the axis:

   ■ *Category*: Open this pop-up menu and choose the number category, such as General, Currency, or Date. These are the same formats you use for controlling how data appears in cells; depending on the format you choose, the Number section may display other options you can set for the format. For example, if you choose the Number category, you can set the number of decimal places, choose whether to use the thousands separator, and specify how to display negative numbers.

   ■ *Format code*: In this text box, you can specify formatting codes for the category. For example, for the Date category, you can specify codes such as m/d/yy or mm/dd/yyyy to control how the dates appear. Click the Add button to add the formatting code you've entered.

   ■ *Linked to source*: Select this check box if the data is linked to its source in the worksheet.

11. When you're satisfied with the axis, click the Close button (the X button in the upper-right corner) to close the Format Axis pane.

Adding a Legend to a Chart

Many charts benefit from having a legend that summarizes the colors used for different data series. You can add a legend by selecting the chart, choosing Chart Design ➤ Chart Layouts ➤ Add Chart Element ➤ Legend, then clicking the placement you want: Right, Top, Left, or Bottom.

To control whether the legend appears outside the chart area (which reduces the available chart area) or overlaps the chart area, choose Chart Design ➤ Chart Layouts ➤ Add Chart Element ➤ Legend ➤ More Legend Options. The Format Legend pane opens, showing the Legend Options pane in the Legend Options tab (yes, this gets recursive). You can then select or clear the "Show the legend without overlapping the chart" check box, as needed.

Whichever placement you use for the legend, you can drag it to a better position as needed. You can also resize the legend by clicking it and then dragging one of the handles that appears around it.

If you need to remove a legend from a chart, simply click the legend and then press Delete. If you're feeling more formal, choose Chart Design ➤ Chart Layouts ➤ Add Chart Element ➤ Legend ➤ None.

Adding Axis Labels from a Range Separate from the Chart Data

Depending on how the worksheet containing the source data is laid out, you may need to add axis labels that are in separate cells from the chart data. This move is often useful when you're creating a chart that uses only some of the available data.

To add axis labels from a separate range, follow these steps:

1. Click the chart to select it.

2. Choose Chart Design ➤ Data ➤ Select Data from the Ribbon to display the Select Data Source dialog box.

3. If necessary, click the Collapse Dialog button to the right of the Horizontal (Category) axis labels text box to collapse the dialog box. If you've got plenty of space to work in, just click the Horizontal (Category) axis labels box to tell Excel what you want to affect.

4. Drag through the cells in the work sheet that contain the axis labels. Excel enters them in the Horizontal (Category) axis labels text box.

5. If you collapsed the Select Data Source dialog box, click the Collapse Dialog button again to restore it.

6. Click the OK button to close the Select Data Source dialog box. Excel applies the labels to the axis.

Adding Data Labels to the Chart

If viewers will need to see the precise value of data points rather than just getting a general idea of their value, add data labels to the chart. To do so, click the chart, then choose Chart Design ➤ Chart Layouts ➤ Add Chart Element ➤ Data Labels and then click the placement you want on the Data Labels submenu. The Data Labels submenu offers different options, depending on the chart type. For example, for a column chart, you choose among Center, Inside End, Inside Base, and Outside End.

To control the data that appears in the data labels, choose Chart Design ➤ Chart Layouts ➤ Add Chart Element ➤ Data Labels ➤ More Data Label Options and then make your choices in the Format Data Labels pane. Your choices here too vary depending on the chart type. The left screen in Figure 14-12 shows the options for a column chart; the right screen in Figure 14-12 shows the options for a pie chart.

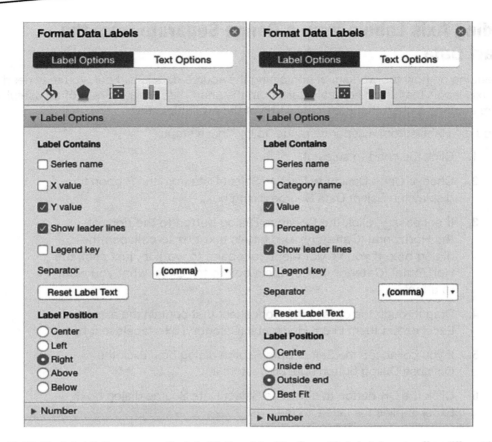

Figure 14-12. The Label Options pane on the Label Options tab of the Format Data Labels pane offers different label contents and label position options for different chart types. The left screen shows the options for a column chart. The right screen shows the options for a pie chart.

> **Caution**   Use data labels sparingly. Only some charts benefit from data labels—other charts may become too busy, or the details may distract the audience from the overall thrust of the chart.

When you add data labels to a chart, Excel displays a data label for each data marker. If you want to display only some data labels, delete the ones you don't need. To delete a data label, click it once to select all data labels, then click it again to select just the one label. Then either press Delete or Ctrl-click or right-click the selection and click Delete on the context menu.

> **Tip**   You can edit the text of data labels if necessary. Click a data label once to select all data labels, then click again to select just the data label you want to change. You can then double-click the data label to select its contents and type in your text. For example, you might want to add text explaining the figure, write the figure in a more accessible format (such as "One MILLION dollars!" instead of $1,000,000), or simply falsify the figure. Editing a data label changes only the label displayed on the chart—the value in the source data remains the same.

Choosing Which Gridlines to Display

On many types of charts, you can choose whether to display horizontal and vertical gridlines to help the viewer judge how the data points relate to each other and to the axes. The left screen in Figure 14-13 shows a chart with both major and minor gridlines. The right screen in Figure 14-13 shows the same chart with just minor gridlines.

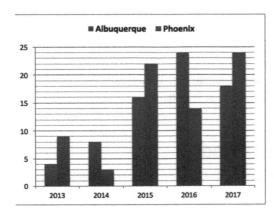 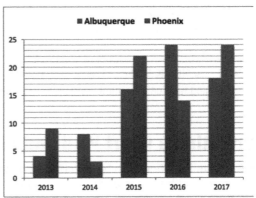

Figure 14-13. Using both major and minor gridlines (left) usually makes a chart easier to read than using only minor gridlines (right)

To control which gridlines appear, follow these steps:

1. Select the chart.

2. Choose Chart Design ➤ Chart Layouts ➤ Add Chart Element ➤ Gridlines to display the Gridlines submenu.

3. Click the menu item for the type of gridlines you want to display, placing a check mark next to it. The menu items available depend on the chart type, but these options (for a column chart) are fairly typical:

    ■ *Primary major horizontal*: Click this item to display horizontal gridlines at the major divisions in the data series. For example, if your data is in the range 0–25, major gridlines normally appear at 5, 10, 15, 20, and 25.

    ■ *Primary major vertical*: Click this item to display vertical gridlines at the major divisions.

    ■ *Primary minor horizontal*: Click this item to display horizontal gridlines at the minor divisions in the data series. For example, if your data is in the range 0–25, minor gridlines normally appear at each integer—1, 2, 3, and so on up to 25.

    ■ *Primary minor vertical*: Click this item to display vertical gridlines at the minor divisions.

Tip   When the viewer needs to see clearly where each value falls, use either data labels or major and minor gridlines. If using minor gridlines (with or without major gridlines) makes the chart look cluttered, use only major gridlines. Normally, it's best not to use both horizontal and vertical minor gridlines because they tend to make charts look confusingly busy, but sometimes your charts may need them.

4.   Repeat steps 2 and 3 for each set of gridlines the chart needs. You can display multiple sets of gridlines.

Note   To change the values at which the gridlines appear, format the axis, as described in the "Changing the Scale or Numbering of an Axis" section earlier in this chapter.

Formatting a Chart Wall and Chart Floor

Some charts look fine with a plain background, but for 3-D charts, you may want to decorate the chart walls (the areas at the back and the side of the chart) and the chart floor (the area at the bottom of the chart). You can add a solid color, a gradient, a picture, or a texture to the walls, the floor, or both. Figure 14-14 shows a chart that uses a picture for the walls.

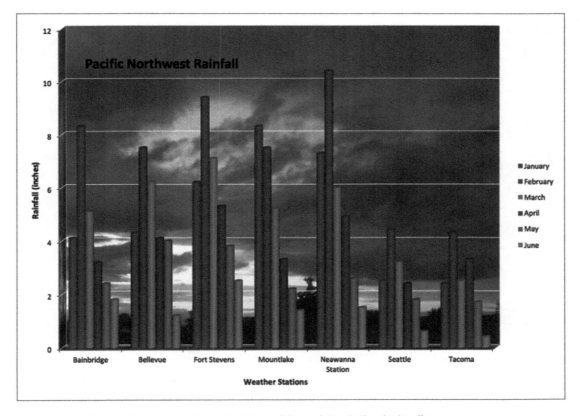

Figure 14-14. You can give a chart a themed look by applying a picture to the chart walls

Tip   Usually, the chart walls and floors are the elements that look best with a custom fill (such as a picture). But you can apply a custom fill to many other chart elements as well. To do so, display the Format dialog box for the element, click the Fill category in the left pane, and then make your choices.

To format the chart wall or the chart floor, follow these steps:

1. Click the chart to select it.

2. Choose Format ➤ Current Selection ➤ Chart Elements to open the Chart Elements pop-up menu. (The Chart Elements pop-up menu is the pop-up menu at the top of the Current Selection group; it shows the currently selected element.) Then click the item you want to format: back wall, floor, side wall, or walls (to format both the back wall and the side wall).

3. Still on the Format tab, go to the Format group and click the Format Pane button to display the Format pane for the item you selected. Figure 14-15 shows the Format Walls pane with the controls for inserting a picture fill displayed.

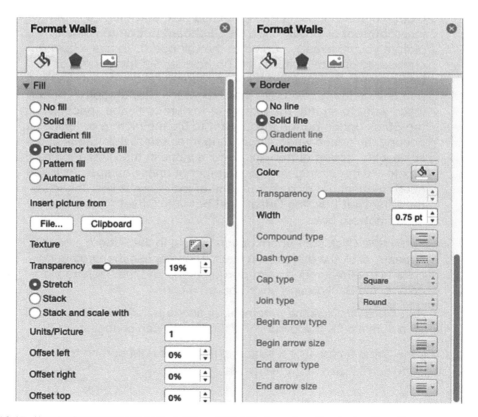

Figure 14-15. Use the Format pane to apply a picture fill to objects such as the chart walls or floor

4. Make sure the Fill tab is displayed. If not, click the Fill Tab button (the one that shows a tipping paint can).

5. In the Fill section, set up the fill you want:

    ■ *No fill:* Click the No fill option button.

    ■ *Solid fill*: Click the Solid fill option button. Open the Color pop-up menu, and then click the color you want. Drag the Transparency slider or type a value in the text box to choose how transparent the fill is.

    ■ *Gradient fill*: Click the Gradient fill option button. Open the Preset Gradients pop-up menu and select the style, then open the Type pop-up menu and choose the gradient style you want: linear, radial, rectangular, or path. Use the Direction pop-up menu and the Angle knob to set the angle and direction of the gradient if applicable. Use the Gradient stops bar to adjust the points at which the color gradient changes, and then use the Color, Position, Transparency, and Brightness controls to tweak the gradient as needed.

    ■ *Picture or texture fill*: Click the Picture or texture fill option button. To use a picture, you can either click the File button, click the picture in the Choose a Picture dialog box, and then click the Insert button; or simply click the Clipboard button to paste in a picture you've already copied to the Clipboard. To use a texture, choose it from the Texture pop-up palette. Set the degree of transparency by dragging the Transparency slider or entering a percentage in the text box. Then select the Stretch option button if you want to stretch the picture or texture to fill the space, select the Stack option button if you want to tile the picture or texture to occupy the space without distorting it, or select the "Stack and scale with" option button and enter a value in the Units/Picture box to tile the picture with the number of units you specify. If you need to offset the picture from one of the sides, adjust the value in the Offset left box, the Offset right box, the Offset top box, or the Offset bottom box.

    ■ *Pattern fill*: Click the Pattern option button. In the Pattern area that appears, click the pattern you want. Then choose the foreground color in the Foreground color pop-up menu and the background color in the Background color pop-up menu.

    ■ *Automatic fill*: Click the Automatic option button to have Excel apply an automatic fill. If you don't like the fill, you can change it.

6. Click the Close button (the X button in the upper-right corner) to close the Format pane for the element you chose.

Formatting Individual Chart Elements

You can format any of the individual elements of a chart—such as the legend, the gridlines, or the data labels—by selecting the element and then using its Format pane. This pane includes the name of the element it affects: the Format Data Labels pane, the Format Plot Area pane, and so on.

You can display the Format pane in either of these ways:

- Ctrl-click or right-click the element, and then click the Format item on the context menu. This is usually the easiest way of opening the Format pane.

- Select the element in the Chart Elements pop-up menu, and then click the Format Selection button. If it's hard to Ctrl-click or right-click the element on the chart (for example, because the chart is busy), choose Format section ➤ Current Selection ➤ Chart Elements from the Ribbon, and then click the element you want on the pop-up menu. You can then choose Format ➤ Format ➤ Format Pane from the Ribbon to display the Format pane for the element.

The contents of the Format pane vary depending on the object you've selected, but for most objects, you'll find categories such as these:

- *Fill.* You can fill in a solid shape with a solid color, color gradient, picture, or texture. See the "Formatting a Chart Wall and Chart Floor" section earlier in this chapter for instructions on creating fills.

- *Line*: You can give a shape a color border, gradient border, or no line. You can also choose among different border styles, change the border width, and pick a suitable line type.

- *Shadow*: You can add a shadow to the shape, set its color, and adjust its transparency, width, and other properties.

- *Glow and soft edges*: You can make an object stand out by giving it a glow, choosing a color that contrasts with the object's surroundings, and choosing how wide the glow should be. You can also apply soft edges to a shape.

- *3-D format*: You can apply a 3-D format to different aspects of a shape; for example, setting a different bevel for the top and bottom of the shape.

- *3-D rotation*: You can apply a 3-D rotation to the object.

- *Font*: For objects that use text, you can control how the text looks.

Tip   If the chart element contains text, you can also format it by using the controls on the Home tab of the Ribbon or keyboard shortcuts. For example, to apply boldface to the data labels, click the data labels, and then choose Home ➤ Font ➤ Bold (or press Ctrl+B). This is often easier than using the Font controls in the Format pane for the element.

Copying a Chart's Formatting to Another Chart

After you set up a chart with all the formatting you need, you can apply that formatting to another chart by using Copy and Paste. Follow these steps:

1. Click the formatted chart to select its chart area.

2. Right-click the border of the chart, and then click Copy on the context menu to copy the chart and its formatting to the Clipboard.

3. Go to the sheet that contains the chart onto which you want to paste the formatting.

4. Choose Home ➤ Clipboard ➤ Paste ➤ Paste Special to display the Paste Special dialog box shown in Figure 14-16.

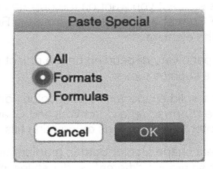

Figure 14-16. *In the Paste Special dialog box, select the Formats option button to paste just the formatting from one chart onto another chart*

5. Select the Formats option button.

6. Click the OK button to close the Paste Special dialog box. Excel applies the formatting to the chart.

Reusing Your Own Designs by Creating Custom Chart Types

If you want to be able to reuse a chart design you've created, you can turn it into a custom chart type. Follow these steps:

1. Select the formatted chart either on a chart sheet or on a worksheet.

2. Choose Chart Design ➤ Change Chart Type ➤ Save As Template from the Ribbon to display the Save as Template dialog box. This is a standard Save As dialog box.

3. If you want, change the folder in which to save the chart type. Excel suggests using the `~/Library/Application Support/Microsoft/Office/Chart Templates/` folder (where ~ represents your home folder). This is a good location for a template that only you will use, but if your colleagues will need to use the template too, you may need to store it in a shared folder on the network.

4. Type a descriptive name for the template in the Save As text box.

5. Click the Save button to close the Save Chart Template dialog box. Excel saves the template in the folder you chose.

To create a chart based on your template, follow these steps:

1. Select the source data for the chart.

2. Choose Insert ➤ Charts ➤ Insert Area, Stock, Surface, or Radar Chart ➤ Templates to display the Templates pop-up panel.

3. Click the template.

Adding Sparklines to Your Worksheets

Charts are great for illustrating medium to large quantities of information, but sometimes you need something smaller, like a chart that fits inside a single cell, giving a quick visual indication of a trend. Excel calls such charts *sparklines*.

Excel provides three kinds of sparklines:

- *Sparkline*: A sparkline is a straightforward line that runs through the data points, as in the top part of Figure 14-17. Excel uses the term "sparkline," but I'll refer to them as "plain sparklines" to distinguish them from column sparklines and win/loss sparklines. A plain sparkline is good for showing data that flows from one data point to the next, such as temperatures.

- *Column*: A column sparkline shows the data as a series of columns, as in a column chart. The middle part of Figure 14-17 shows an example. A column sparkline is good for comparing data points that are separate from each other, such as sales results by month.

- *Win/Loss*: A win/loss sparkline shows results as either a win (a positive result) or a loss (a negative result). The lower part of Figure 14-17 shows an example of win/loss sparklines. A win/loss sparkline is good for when you want to take a black-and-white view of results, such as whether your investments are up or down in a particular month. In a win/loss sparkline, a zero value appears as a blank, as in the second Sacramento result.

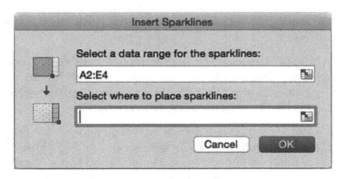

	2013	2014	2015	2016	
Albuquerque	10	12	13	15	
Phoenix	11	17	19	15	
Little Rock	23	21	18	10	
	2013	2014	2015	2016	
Albuquerque	10	12	13	15	
Phoenix	11	17	19	15	
Little Rock	23	21	18	10	
	Q1	Q2	Q3	Q4	
Sacramento	-1	0	-2	3	
Oakland	1	2	3	-3	
Redding	4	-5	2	18	

Figure 14-17. Sparklines are single-cell charts that you can use to indicate trends or results visually

Inserting Sparklines

To insert one or more sparklines in a worksheet, follow these steps:

1. Select the range that contains the data you will use for the sparklines.

2. Click the Insert tab to display its contents, click the Sparklines button to display the pop-up panel, and then click Sparklines, Column, or Win/Loss, as needed. Whichever button you click, Excel displays the Insert Sparklines dialog box (see Figure 14-18).

Insert Sparklines

Select a data range for the sparklines:

A2:E4

Select where to place sparklines:

Cancel   OK

Figure 14-18. In the Insert Sparklines dialog box, choose the data range for the sparklines and the cells in which to place them

3. Make sure the Select a data range for the sparklines text box contains the source range for the sparklines. If you chose the range before displaying the Insert Sparklines dialog box, it'll be correct. Otherwise, click in this text box, then drag in the worksheet to select the range.

4. Click the Select where to place sparklines text box, and then drag in the worksheet to select the range. Or, if you prefer, type in the range.

5. Click the OK button to close the Insert Sparklines dialog box. Excel inserts the sparklines in the cells.

Formatting Your Sparklines

After inserting sparklines, you can format them by using the controls on the Sparkline Design tab of the Ribbon. Click a cell in the sparklines to select the group of sparklines and make Excel add the Sparklines tab to the Ribbon. If Excel doesn't display the Sparkline Design tab automatically, click the tab to display it (see Figure 14-19).

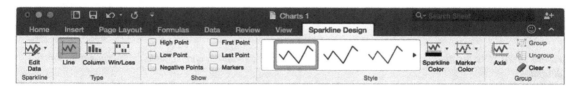

Figure 14-19. Use the controls on the Sparkline Design tab of the Ribbon to format sparklines to look the way you want them to

These are the main moves for formatting your sparklines:

■ *Change the source data for a group of sparklines*: Click a cell in the group of sparklines, and then choose Sparkline Design ➤ Data ➤ Edit Data from the Ribbon (clicking the main part of the Edit button). Excel displays the Edit Sparklines dialog box, which has the same controls as the Insert Sparklines dialog box.

■ *Change the source data for a single sparkline*: Click the sparkline cell, and then choose Sparkline Design ➤ Data ➤ Edit ➤ Edit Selected Sparkline. Excel displays the Edit Sparkline dialog box, which works like the Insert Sparklines dialog box, but affects only the cell you chose.

■ *Change a sparkline to a different type*: Click the sparkline cell, and then click the Line button, the Column button, or the Win/Loss button in the Change Type group on the Sparkline Design tab of the Ribbon.

■ *Add markers to the sparklines*: In the Markers group on the Sparkline Design tab of the Ribbon, select the High Point check box, the Low Point check box, the Negative Points check box, the First Point check box, or the Last Point check box as needed—or select the All check box to select all the others. To change the marker color, choose Sparkline Design ➤ Format ➤ Marker Color, and then click the appropriate color in the Markers panel (see Figure 14-20).

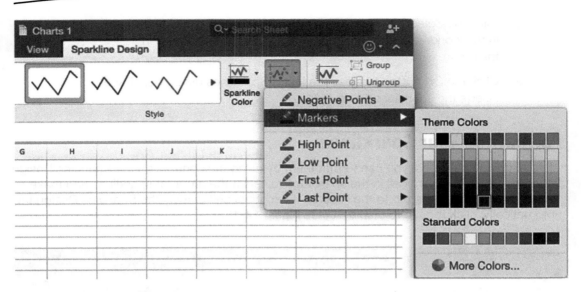

Figure 14-20. Use the Markers panel to change the colors of markers and to choose which ones appear on the sparklines

Tip   For many kinds of data, the High Point marker and the Low Point marker are the most useful. Win/loss sparklines use the Negative Points marker by default, while plain sparklines and column sparklines don't use any markers by default.

- *Apply a style to the sparklines*: In the Format group on the Sparkline Design tab of the Ribbon, either click a style in the Styles box or hold the pointer over the Styles box to display the panel button; then click the panel button to display the Styles panel. Click the style you want.

- *Change the color of the sparklines*: Choose Sparkline Design ➤ Style ➤ Sparkline Color to display the Sparkline Color panel, and then click the color you want.

- *Change the weight of plain sparklines*: Choose Sparkline Design ➤ Style ➤ Sparkline Color ➤ Weight, and then click the line weight. If you need a custom weight, click Custom Weight to display the Sparkline Weight dialog, enter the weight, and then click the OK button.

- *Change the axes for the sparklines*: Choose Sparkline Design ➤ Group ➤ Axis to display the Axes dialog box (see Figure 14-21), and then make your choices in it.

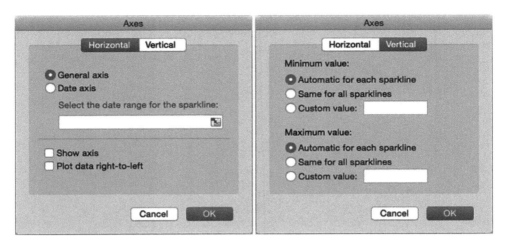

Figure 14-21. You can use the Axes dialog box to choose settings for the horizontal and vertical axes of the sparklines

- *Group sparklines together*: If you need to format separate sets of sparklines quickly, group them together. Select each set of sparklines, and then choose Sparkline Design ➤ Group ➤ Group from the Ribbon to group them.

- *Clear sparklines*: When you no longer need sparklines, clear them from the cells. Select the sparkline cells you want to clear, and then choose Sparkline Design ➤ Group ➤ Clear, clicking the main part of the Clear button. You can also click a single cell and then choose Sparklines ➤ Group ➤ Clear ➤ Clear Selected Sparkline Groups to clear all the cells in the group.

Summary

In this chapter, you learned how to create powerful and persuasive charts from your data. You now know what the separate components of charts are called, how to create a chart, and how to position it either on a worksheet or on its own chart sheet. You can also make Excel show the components you want for a chart and format them as needed. To save time and effort, you also learned to reuse your custom chart formatting either by pasting it onto an existing chart or by creating a custom chart template from it.

You also learned about sparklines and can now use them to illustrate results and trends in your worksheets.

In the next chapter, I'll show you to create custom formulas and harness the power of Excel's functions to perform calculations.

Chapter 15

Crunching Numbers with Formulas and Functions

To make your worksheets deliver the information you want, you'll probably need to perform calculations with your data. To perform calculations, you enter formulas and functions in cells, as you'll learn to do in this chapter.

I'll start by going over what functions and formulas are so that you're clear on the difference between them. Then I'll show you how to create your own formulas using Excel's calculation operators. You'll find it easy to get started because Excel provides plenty of help, but you'll also look at how to troubleshoot common problems that occur with formulas.

In the second half of the chapter, you'll dig into functions: how to insert them in your worksheets using the various tools that Excel provides, how to find the ones you want, and how to point the functions to the data they need for the calculations.

Understanding the Difference Between Formulas and Functions

In Excel, you can perform calculations in two main ways:

- *By using a formula*: A *formula* is a custom calculation that you create when none of Excel's functions (discussed next) do what you need. The word *formula* may sound imposing, but a formula can be a simple calculation; for example, to subtract 50 from 100, you can type **=100-50** in a cell (the equal sign tells Excel you're starting a formula). Formulas can also be more complex. For example, say you need to add the contents of the cells in the range A1:A6 and then divide them by the contents of cell B1. Excel doesn't have a built-in function for doing this because it's not a standard calculation. So instead, you create a formula such as this: **=SUM(A1:A6)/B1**. (In this example, the / is the keyboard equivalent of the ÷ symbol.)

© Guy Hart-Davis 2016
G. Hart-Davis, *Learn Office 2016 for Mac*, DOI 10.1007/978-1-4842-2002-3_15

■ *By using a function*: A *function* is a preset formula that performs a standard calculation. For example, when you need to add several values together, you use the SUM( ) function, such as **=SUM(1,2,3,4,5,6)**, which is simpler than **=1+2+3+4+5+6** but has the same effect.

In the following sections, I'll show you how to use each of these methods. But before I do that, let's go over the ways of referring to cells and ranges in formulas and functions.

Referring to Cells and Ranges in Formulas and Functions

To make your formulas and functions work correctly, you need to refer to the cells and ranges you want. This section makes sure you know how to refer to cells and ranges, both when they're on the same worksheet as the formula and when they're on a different worksheet. You can even refer to cells and ranges in another workbook—as long as it will remain in the same place in your Mac's file system.

Referring to a Cell

To refer to a cell on the same worksheet, simply use its column lettering and its row number. For example, use **=A10** to refer to cell A10.

To refer to a cell on a different worksheet, enter the worksheet's name followed by an exclamation point and the cell reference. For example, use **=Supplies!A10** to refer to cell A10 on the worksheet named Supplies. The easiest way to set up such a reference is like this:

1. Start creating the formula. For example, type = in the cell.

2. Click the worksheet tab for the worksheet that contains the cell you want to refer to.

3. Click the cell.

4. Click the Enter button on the formula bar to enter the reference. Excel returns you to the worksheet on which you're creating the formula. You'll see that the cell displays the result of the formula— whatever value was in the cell you clicked in step 3—rather than the formula itself.

> **Note**   Instead of clicking the Enter button on the formula bar in step 4, you can press Return to enter the cell reference. When you do this, Excel returns you to the cell below the formula on the worksheet on which you're creating the formula. You then need to press the Up arrow key before taking Step 5.

5. Press Ctrl+U to resume editing the cell. Alternatively, click in the formula bar, and continue editing there. Either way, Excel displays the formula, such as **='Sales Results'!A10**.

6. Finish creating the formula as usual.

> **Note** If the worksheet's name contains any spaces, you must put the name inside single quotes; for example, **='Sales Results'!A10** rather than **=Sales Results!A10**. You can also use the single quotes on worksheet names that don't have spaces if you find it easier to be consistent. If you omit the single quotes when they're needed, Excel either displays the Open dialog, with a message such as "Cannot find 'Results'. Copy from:", inviting you to find the right workbook, or displays an error message.

To refer to a cell in a different workbook, put the workbook's path and file name in brackets, then the worksheet's name, and then the cell reference. For example, the reference **=[Shared:Spreads:Results.xlsx]'Area Sales'!AB12** refers to cell AB12 on the worksheet named Area Sales in the workbook `Results.xlsx` in the `Shared:Spreads` folder.

Unless you happen to know the path, file name, worksheet name, and cell, it's usually easiest to set up the reference by using the pointing device. Follow these steps:

1. Open the workbook you want to refer to.

2. In the workbook that will contain the reference, start creating the formula. For example, type = in the cell.

3. Switch to the other workbook. If you can see the other workbook, click it. If you can't see the other workbook, open the Window menu on the menu bar, and then click the appropriate window.

4. Navigate to the worksheet that contains the cell, and then click the cell.

5. Switch back to the workbook in which you're creating the reference, and then complete the formula.

Referring to Ranges

To refer to a range that consists of a block of cells, give the cell addresses of the first cell and the last cell, separating them with a colon. For example, to refer to the range from cell P10 to cell Q12, use **=P10:Q12**.

To refer to a range that consists of individual cells, give the address of each cell, separating the addresses with commas. For example, to refer to cell J14, cell K18, and cell Z20, use **=J14,K18,Z20**.

To refer to a range on a different worksheet or in a different workbook, use the techniques explained in the previous section. For example, if you need to refer to the range P10 to Q12 on the worksheet named Stock Listing, use **='Stock Listing'!P10:Q12**.

> **Tip**   Sometimes you may need to make the contents of one row or column refer to another row or column. For example, say you need to make each cell in row 25 refer to the corresponding cell in row 4, so that cell A25 refers to cell A4, cell B25 to cell B4, and so on. To do this, click the row heading for row 25, selecting the row. Then type **=4:4** to create the reference to row 4, and press Cmd+Return to enter it in all the cells of the selection. Similarly, you can refer to a whole column by entering its letter designation, a colon, and the letter designation again; for example, **E:E**.

UNDERSTANDING ABSOLUTE REFERENCES, RELATIVE REFERENCES, AND MIXED REFERENCES

Using cell addresses or range addresses is straightforward enough, but when you start using formulas, there's a complication: if you copy a formula and paste it, you need to tell Excel whether the pasted formula should refer to the cells it originally referred to, or the cells in the same relative positions to the cell where the formula now is, or a mixture of the two. (If you move a formula rather than copy it, Excel keeps the formula as it is.)

To make references clear, Excel uses three types of references:

- *Absolute reference*: A reference that always refers to the same cell, no matter where you copy it. Excel uses a dollar sign ($) to indicate that each part of the reference is absolute. For example, B3 is an absolute reference to cell B3.

- *Relative reference*: A reference that refers to the cell by its position relative to the cell that holds the reference. For example, if you select cell A3 and enter **=B5** in it, the reference means "the cell one column to the right and two rows down." So if you copy the formula to cell C4, Excel changes the cell reference to cell D6, which is one column to the right and two rows down from cell C4. To indicate a relative reference, Excel uses a plain reference without any dollar signs; for example, B4.

- *Mixed reference*: A reference that is absolute for either the column or the row and relative for the other. For example, $B4 is absolute for the column (B) and relative for the row (4), while B$4 is relative for the column and absolute for the row. When you copy and paste a mixed reference, the absolute part stays the same, but the relative part changes to reflect the new location.

If you're typing a reference, you can type the $ signs into the reference to make it absolute or mixed. If you're entering references by selecting cells, click in the reference in the cell you're editing or in the Formula bar, and then press F4 one or more times to cycle a reference through its absolute, relative, column-absolute, and row-absolute versions.

Referring to Named Cells and Ranges

To make your references easier to enter and recognize, you can give a name to any cell or range. You can then refer to the cell or range by the name.

To create a named range, follow these steps:

1. Select the cell or range you want to name.

2. Choose Insert ➤ Name ➤ Define from the menu bar to display the Define Name dialog box (shown in Figure 15-1 with settings chosen).

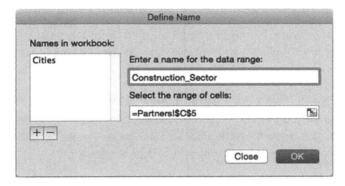

Figure 15-1. *Use the Define Name dialog box to give a cell or range a name by which you can easily refer to it*

3. In the Enter a name for the data range text box, type the name for the range. Follow these rules:

   ■ The name must start with a letter or an underscore.

   ■ The name can contain only letters, numbers, and underscores. It can't contain spaces or symbols.

   ■ The name must be unique in the workbook.

4. Make sure that the "Select the range of cells" box shows the right cell or range. If not, select the cell or range you want. If you need to get the Define Name dialog box out of the way, you can click the Collapse Dialog button, but most likely you won't need to.

5. If you want to create only this one name, click the OK button to apply the name to the range and close the Define Name dialog box. If you want to create more names before you close the Define Name dialog box, click the Add button (the + button).

> **Note**   You can also name the selected cell or range by clicking in the Reference area (to the left of the Formula bar), typing the name you want to assign, and then pressing Return. This method can be handy, but there's one complication you need to watch out for: if you type an existing name (instead of a new name) into the Reference area and press Return, Excel selects the cell or range to which the name refers. If you're working fast, this can be confusing because you may not spot that you have moved the active cell to an existing named cell or range rather than defining a new named cell or range.

After you've named a range, you can use the name in your formulas instead of the cell reference or range reference. Named ranges can be a great time-saver because the names are much easier to remember and to type than the cell references or range references.

> **Note**   To delete a name from a range, choose Insert ➤ Name ➤ Define from the menu bar to display the Define Name dialog box. In the Names in workbook list, click the name. Click the Delete button (the – button) to delete the name. Click the Close button to close the Define Name dialog box. If you find you've deleted the wrong name, use Undo to restore it.

Performing Custom Calculations by Creating Formulas

When you need to perform a custom calculation in a cell, use a formula rather than a function. All you need to do is type in a simple formula using the appropriate calculation operators, such as + signs for addition and – signs for subtraction. In this section, you'll meet the calculation operators, try using them in a worksheet, and learn the order in which Excel applies them—and how to change that order when you need to.

Meeting Excel's Calculation Operators

To perform calculations in Excel, you need to know the operators for the different operations: addition, division, comparison, and so on. Table 15-1 explains the full set of calculation operators you can use in your formulas in Excel.

Table 15-1. Calculation Operators You Can Use in Excel

Calculation Operator	Operation	Explanation or Example
Arithmetic Operators		
+	Addition	=1+2 adds 2 to 1.
–	Subtraction	=1–2 subtracts 2 from 1.
*	Multiplication	=2*2 multiplies 2 by 2.
/	Division	=A1/4 divides the value in cell A1 by 4.
%	Percentage	=B1% returns the value in cell B1 expressed as a percentage. Excel displays the value as a decimal unless you format the cell with the Percentage style.
^	Exponentiation	=B1^2 raises the value in cell B1 to the power 2.
Comparison Operators		
=	Equal to	=B2=15000 returns TRUE if cell B2 contains the value 15000. Otherwise, it returns FALSE.
<>	Not equal to	=B2<>15000 returns TRUE if cell B2 does not contain the value 15000. Otherwise, it returns FALSE.
>	Greater than	=B2>15000 returns TRUE if cell B2 contains a value greater than 15000. Otherwise, it returns FALSE.
>=	Greater than or equal to	=B2>=15000 returns TRUE if cell B2 contains a value greater than or equal to 15000. Otherwise, it returns FALSE.
<	Less than	=B2<15000 returns TRUE if cell B2 contains a value less than 15000. Otherwise, it returns FALSE.
<=	Less than or equal to	=B2<=15000 returns TRUE if cell B2 contains a value less than or equal to 15000. Otherwise, it returns FALSE.
Reference Operators		
[cell reference]:[cell reference]	The range of cells between the two cell references	A1:G5 returns the range of cells whose upper-left cell is cell A1 and whose lower-right cell is cell G5.
[cell reference],[cell reference]	The range of cells listed	A1,C3,E5 returns three cells: A1, C3, and E5.
[cell or range reference] [space][cell or range reference]	The range (or cell) that appears in both cells or ranges given	=A7:G10 B10:B12 returns the cell B10 because this is the only cell that appears in both the ranges given. If more than one cell appears in the range, this returns a #VALUE! error.
Text Operator		
&	Concatenation (joining values as text)	=A1&B1 returns the values from cells A1 and B1 joined together as a text string. For example, if A1 contains "New York " (including a trailing space) and B1 contains "Sales", this formula returns "New York Sales." If A1 contains 100 and B1 contains 50, this formula returns 10050.

Using the Calculation Operators

Now that you know what the calculation operators are, try the following example of creating a simple worksheet (see Figure 15-2) that uses the four most straightforward operators: addition, subtraction, multiplication, and division.

	A	B
1	Gross	$84,000.00
2	Expenses	$30,000.00
3	Tax Rate	18%
4	Tax Amount	$15,120.00
5	Net	$38,880.00
6	Months	12
7	Monthly Net	$3,240.00

Figure 15-2. Create this simple worksheet to try using Excel's addition, subtraction, multiplication, and division operators

To create the worksheet, follow these steps:

1. Create a new workbook. The quickest way to do this is to press Cmd+N.

2. Type the following text in cells A1 through A7:

   ■ *A1.* Gross

   ■ *A2.* Expenses

   ■ *A3.* Tax Rate

   ■ *A4.* Tax Amount

   ■ *A5.* Net

   ■ *A6.* Months

   ■ *A7.* Monthly Net

3. Apply boldface to column A by clicking the column heading and then choosing Home ➤ Font ➤ Bold.

4. Apply Currency format to column B by clicking the column heading and then choosing Home ➤ Number ➤ Number Format ➤ Currency.

5. Type the following text in cells B1 through B3:

   ■ *B1.* 84000

   ■ *B2.* 30000

   ■ *B3.* 0.18

6. Apply Percent style to cell B3 by clicking the cell and then choosing Home ➤ Number ➤ Percent Style.

Note You can also enter the percentage in Step 6 by typing **18%** and pressing Return. Excel automatically changes the number format to Percentage.

---

7. Now enter the formula **=B1*B3** in cell B4, like this:

   ■ Click cell B4 to select it.

   ■ Type = to start creating a formula in the cell.

   ■ Click cell B1 to enter it in the formula. Excel displays a shimmering dotted blue outline around the cell and adds it to the formula in the cell and to the Formula bar (see Figure 15-3).

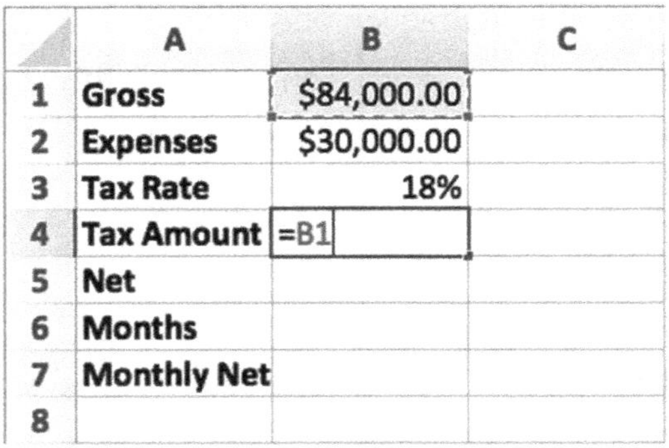

	A	B	C
1	Gross	$84,000.00	
2	Expenses	$30,000.00	
3	Tax Rate	18%	
4	Tax Amount	=B1	
5	Net		
6	Months		
7	Monthly Net		
8			

Figure 15-3. When you click cell B1, Excel adds it to the formula in both the cell and the Formula bar and displays a dotted blue outline around it

   ■ Type * to tell Excel you want to multiply the value in cell B1. Excel enters the asterisk in the formula and changes the outline around cell B1 to solid blue.

   ■ Click cell B3 to enter it in the formula. Excel displays a shimmering dotted outline (green this time) around the cell and adds it to the formula in the cell and in the formula bar (see Figure 15-4).

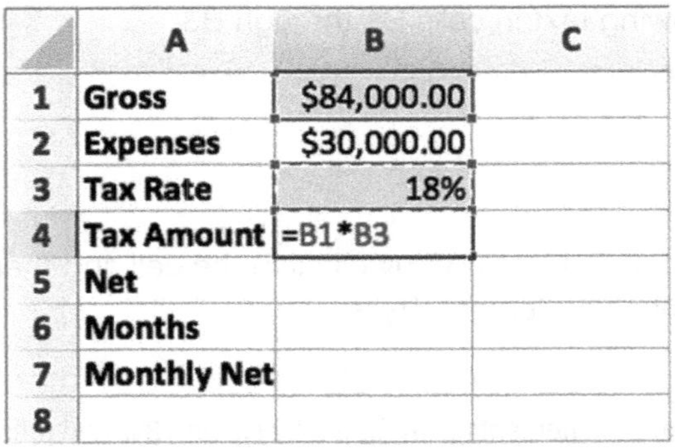

	A	B	C
1	Gross	$84,000.00	
2	Expenses	$30,000.00	
3	Tax Rate	18%	
4	Tax Amount	=B1*B3	
5	Net		
6	Months		
7	Monthly Net		
8			

Figure 15-4. Click cell B3 to add it to the formula

- Press Return or click the Enter button (the check-mark button in the Formula bar) to finish entering the formula in cell B4.

8. Enter the formula **=B1-(B2+B4)** in cell B5. Follow these steps:

- Click cell B5 to select it. If you pressed Return to enter the previous formula, Excel may have selected this cell already.

- Type = to start creating a formula in the cell.

- Click cell B1 to add it to the formula.

- Type – to enter the subtraction operator.

- Type **(** to start a nested expression. (More on this shortly.)

- Click cell B2 to add it to the formula.

- Type + to enter the addition operator.

- Click cell B4 to add it to the formula.

- Type **)** to end the nested expression.

- Click the Enter button to finish entering the formula.

9. Enter **12** in cell B6 and apply General formatting to it. Follow these steps:

- Click cell B6.

- Choose Home ➤ Number ➤ Number Format ➤ General.

- Type **12**.

- Press the down arrow to enter the value and move the active cell to cell B7.

10. Enter the formula **=B5/B6** in cell B7. This time, simply type the formula in—lowercase is fine—and then press Return. You'll notice that when you type **b5**, Excel selects cell B5 to let you check visually that you have the right cell.

Now that you've created the worksheet, try changing the figures in cells B1, B2, and B3. You'll see the results of the formulas in cells B4, B5, and B7 change accordingly. Excel recalculates the formulas each time you change a value in a cell, so the formula results remain up to date.

TURNING OFF AUTOMATIC RECALCULATION FOR LARGE WORKBOOKS

If you create a workbook with huge amounts of data, automatic recalculation may make Excel run slowly, especially when one recalculated value causes many other values to need recalculation.

If you find Excel struggling to recalculate a workbook, turn off automatic calculation by choosing Formulas ➤ Calculation ➤ Calculation Options ➤ Manual from the Ribbon. If recalculation was the problem, you'll notice the difference immediately.

You can recalculate manually when necessary by choosing Formulas ➤ Calculation ➤ Calculate Sheet from the Ribbon (to recalculate just the active worksheet) or choosing Formulas ➤ Calculation ➤ Calculate Now from the Ribbon to recalculate the whole workbook.

Understanding the Order in Which Excel Evaluates Operators

In the previous example, you entered the formula **=B1-(B2+B4)** in cell B5. The parentheses are necessary because the calculation has two separate stages—one stage of subtraction and one stage of addition—and you need to control the order in which they occur.

Try changing the formula in cell B5 to **=B1-B2+B4** and see what happens. Follow these steps:

1. Click cell B5.

2. Click in the Formula bar to start editing the formula there. (You can also edit in the cell by double-clicking the cell or pressing Ctrl+U, but editing in the Formula bar gives you more space, so it's often easier.)

3. Delete the opening and closing parentheses.

4. Click the Enter button on the Formula bar.

You'll notice that the Net amount (cell B5) jumps substantially. This is because you've changed the meaning of the formula:

■ =B1-(B2+B4). This formula means "add the value in cell B2 to the value in cell B4, and then subtract the result from the value in cell B1."

■ =B1-B2+B4. This formula means "subtract the value in cell B2 from the value in cell B1, and then add the value in cell B4 to the result."

To restore the formula, click cell B5 and press Ctrl+U to open the cell for editing. Position the insertion point before **B2** and type **(** and then position the insertion point after **B4** and type **)**. Then press Return to enter the formula in the cell.

> **Note**   When you use nested parentheses in a formula, Excel uses a different color for each pair of parentheses to help you see which closing parenthesis and opening parenthesis go together.

The order in which Excel evaluates the operators is called *operator precedence*, and it can make a huge difference in your formulas—so it's vital to know both how it works and how to override it. Table 15-2 shows you the order in which Excel evaluates the operators in formulas.

Table 15-2. Excel's Operator Precedence in Descending Order

Precedence	Operators	Explanation
1	−	Negation
2	%	Percentage
3	^	Exponentiation
4	* and /	Multiplication and division
5	+ and −	Addition and subtraction
6	&	Concatenation
7	=, <>, <, <=, >, and >=	Comparison operators

When two operators are at the same level, Excel performs the operator that appears earlier in the formula first.

Nesting Parts of Formulas to Control Operator Precedence

You can control operator precedence in any formula by nesting one or more parts of the formula in parentheses. For example, as you just saw, using **=B1-(B2+B4)** makes Excel evaluate **B2+B4** before the subtraction.

You can nest parts of the formula several levels deep if necessary. For example, the following formula uses three levels of nesting and returns 180:

$$=10*(5*(4/(1+1))+8)$$

Breaking Up a Complex Formula into Separate Steps

A cell can accept more or less as complex a formula as you care to create—and some people enjoy creating formulas that are so complex that it takes an expert to figure them out.

Unless you like to work this way, when you have to create a complex formula, consider breaking it up into separate steps, putting each step in its own cell or row. For example, you could break up that =10*(5*(4/(1+1))+8) formula like this:

- *Cell B1.* =1+1

- *Cell B2.* =4/B1

- *Cell B3.* =5*B2

- *Cell B4.* =B3+8

- *Cell B5.* =10*B4

Broken up like this, each formula is easy to read, and you can easily see if any of the steps gives the wrong result. You can type a text description of each step in the next cell for reference, or (more discreetly) insert a comment describing the step.

When you've checked that the formula works, you have the option of creating a new version of the formula that goes into a single cell. But if you want to keep the worksheet easy to read and easy to audit, leave the formula in its step-by-step form.

Entering Formulas Quickly by Copying and Using AutoFill

In many worksheets, you may need to enter related formulas in several or many cells. For example, say you have the worksheet shown in Figure 15-5, which lists a range of products with their prices and sales. Column D needs to show the total revenue derived by multiplying the Units figure by the Price value.

D2		fx =B2*C2			
	A	B	C	D	E
2	Emulator	915	$39.99	$36,590.85	
3	Virtualizer	638	$4.99		
4	Video Mule	18	$189.99		
5	Q Leader	1827	$19.99		
6					

Figure 15-5. When a worksheet needs similar formulas in a column or row, you can enter one formula manually and then use AutoFill or Copy and Paste to enter it quickly in the other cells

Each cell in column D needs a different formula: Cell D2 needs =B2*C2, Cell D3 needs =B3*C3, and so on. Because the formula is the same except for the row number, you can use either AutoFill or Copy and Paste to enter the formula from cell D2 into the other cells as well.

To enter the formula using AutoFill, click the cell that contains the formula (here, cell D2), and then drag the AutoFill handle (the green square at the lower-right corner of the active cell) down through cell D5. Excel automatically fills in the formulas, adjusting each for the change in row.

To enter the formula using Copy and Paste, click the cell that contains the formula, and then give the Copy command (Cmd+C.). Select the destination cells, and then give the Paste command (Cmd+V).

Note   If you need to copy a formula to a different row or column but have it refer to the original location, create the formula using mixed references. If you need to keep the column the same, make the column absolute (for example, **=$B2**); if you need to keep the row the same, make the row absolute (for example, **=B$2**). If you need the formula to refer to the same cell or range always, create it as an absolute reference.

Choosing Preferences for Error Checking

Excel can automatically identify various errors in your formulas. To choose which errors Excel marks, you set the error-checking preferences. Choose Excel ➤ Preferences or press Cmd+, (Cmd and the comma key) to display the Excel Preferences window, and then click the Error Checking icon in the Formulas and Lists area to display the Error Checking preferences pane (see Figure 15-6).

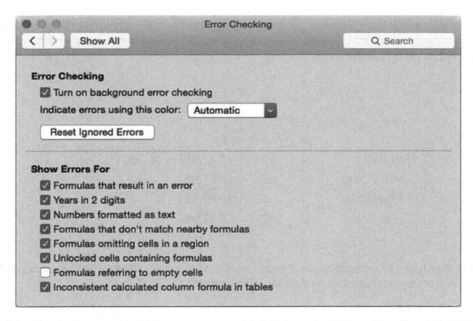

Figure 15-6. *In the Error Checking preferences pane of the Excel Preferences window, choose whether to use background error checking and decide which errors to show*

You can then choose the following settings in the upper box:

- *Turn on background error checking*: Select this check box to turn on error checking in the background. Background error checking is a good idea for small and medium-size workbooks, but you may want to turn it off for larger workbooks because it can slow Excel down. If you do turn off background error checking, be sure to check for errors manually (choose Formulas ➤ Formula Auditing ➤ Error Checking from the Ribbon, clicking the main part of the Error Checking button).

- *Indicate errors using this color*: In this pop-up menu, choose the color to use for indicating errors. The default setting is Automatic, which lets Excel choose the color. You might prefer to choose a garish color to make errors stand out.

- *Reset ignored errors*: Click this button to reset all the errors in the active workbook that you've told Excel to ignore. You may find it helpful to ignore errors when you're building a worksheet and the errors occur because the data isn't in place. When the worksheet is finished, you can click the Reset Ignored Errors button to see any remaining errors.

In the Show Errors For box, you can select or clear the following check boxes to control which errors (or apparent errors) Excel indicates by putting a green triangle at the upper-left corner of the cell:

- *Formulas that result in an error*: Select this check box to make Excel mark cells whose formulas produce errors. This is normally helpful.

- *Years in 2 digits*: Select this check box to make Excel mark cells that contain years represented by two digits rather than four digits (for example, 16 instead of 2016). Using four-digit years helps avoid confusion in your spreadsheets.

- *Numbers formatted as text*: Select this check box to make Excel mark numbers that have text formatting rather than number formatting or that you've preceded with an apostrophe to force Excel to treat them as text. This option can be helpful, but it's likely to mark cells you've deliberately formatted as text.

- *Formulas that don't match nearby formulas*: Select this check box to make Excel mark formulas that appear wrong because they're different from formulas in adjoining cells. For example, if you have a row of eight cells, and six contain SUM( ) formulas adding the cells above them but two contain SUM( ) formulas adding the three cells to their left, this setting makes Excel mark those two cells because they contain formulas different from their neighbors. This can be helpful, but if the two oddball cells are summarizing the fiscal year quarters, you may want the formulas to be different.

■ *Formulas omitting cells in a region*: Select this check box to make Excel mark formulas that are apparently intended to cover a whole region of a worksheet but omit particular cells in it. If these omissions are intentional, you can suppress the warnings.

■ *Unlocked cells containing formulas*: Select this check box to make Excel mark unlocked cells that contain formulas. This setting can help you track down cells you need to lock to prevent your colleagues taking liberties with your calculations.

■ *Formulas referring to empty cells*: Select this check box to make Excel mark formulas that try to use empty cells. Empty cells can cause plenty of problems in your formulas, including division-by-zero errors, so having Excel identify formulas that use empty cells is usually a good idea.

■ *Inconsistent calculated column formula in tables*: Select this check box to make Excel mark formulas in tables that differ from the other formulas in their columns. (Chapter 16 shows you how to create tables.)

When you've finished choosing error-checking preferences, click the Close button (the red button at the left end of the title bar) to close the Preferences window.

Troubleshooting Common Problems with Formulas

Formulas are great when they work, but a single-letter typo or a wrong reference can prevent a formula from working correctly. This section shows you how to deal with common problems with formulas, starting with solutions to the error messages you're most likely to produce.

Understanding Common Errors—and Resolving Them

Excel includes an impressive arsenal of error messages, but some of them appear far more frequently than others. Table 15-3 shows you eight errors you're likely to encounter, explains what they mean, and tells you how to solve them.

Table 15-3. How to Solve Excel's Eight Most Common Errors

Error	What the Problem Is	How to Solve It
#####	The formula result is too wide to fit in the cell.	Make the column wider by double-clicking the column head's right border to AutoFit the column width.
#NAME?	A function name is misspelled, or the formula refers to a range that doesn't exist.	Check the spelling of all functions; correct any mistakes. If the formula uses a named range, check that the name is right and that you haven't deleted the range.
#NUM!	The formula tries to use a value that is not valid for it; for example, returning the square root of a negative number.	Give the function a suitable value.
#VALUE!	The function uses an invalid argument; for example, using =FACT( ) to return the factorial of text rather than a number.	Give the function the right type of data.
#N/A	The function does not have a valid value available.	Make sure the function's arguments provide values of the right type.
#DIV/0	The function is trying to divide by zero (which is mathematically impossible).	Change the divisor value from zero. Often, you'll find that the function is using a blank cell (which has a zero value) as the argument for the divisor; in this case, enter a value in the cell.
#REF!	The formula uses a cell reference or a range reference that's not valid because, for example, you've deleted a worksheet.	Edit the formula and provide a valid reference.
#NULL!	There is no intersection between the two ranges specified.	Change the ranges to produce an intersection.

> **Caution**   The =SUM( ) function is smart enough to ignore text values that you feed it. For example, if cell A1 contains the value 1 and cell A2 contains the text Dog, the function =SUM(A1:A2) returns 1 even though the formula =A1+A2 returns a #VALUE! error. The =SUM( ) function's smartness here is a mixed blessing: you get a usable result, which is presumably what you want—but this hides the mistake you've made in trying to add text instead of a numerical value.

Seeing the Details of an Error in a Formula

When Excel identifies an error in a formula, it displays a green triangle at the upper-left corner of the cell that contains the formula. Click the cell to display an action button that you can hold the pointer over to display a ScreenTip explaining the problem (as shown on the left in Figure 15-7) or click to display a menu of actions you can take to resolve the problem (as shown on the right in Figure 15-7).

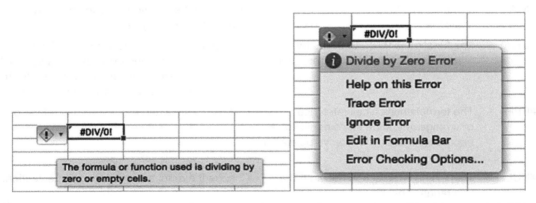

Figure 15-7. Hold the pointer over the action button for an error cell to display a ScreenTip explaining what's wrong (left). Click the button to display details of the error (right)

Tracing an Error Back to Its Source

To see which cell is causing an error, click the error cell, then choose Formulas ➤ Formula Auditing ➤ Error Checking ➤ Trace Error from the Ribbon. Excel displays an arrow from the guilty cell or cells to the error cell. The left screen in Figure 15-8 shows a simple example of tracing an error; the more complex the worksheet, the more helpful this feature is. Excel displays a worksheet symbol (see the right screen in Figure 15-8) if the cell reference is on another worksheet or in another workbook.

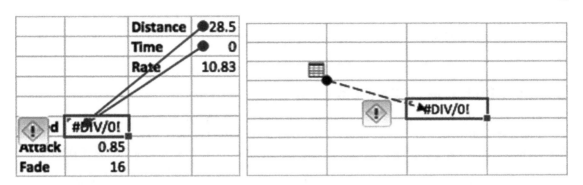

Figure 15-8. Choose Formulas ➤ Formula Auditing ➤ Error Checking ➤ Trace Error from the Ribbon to identify the cell or cells causing an error. If the cell reference is on another worksheet or in another workbook, Excel displays a worksheet symbol, as shown on the right

> **Note**   If you've turned off background error checking in the Error Checking preferences pane, choose Formulas ➤ Formula Auditing ➤ Error Checking (clicking the main part of the Error Checking button) from the Ribbon or Tools ➤ Error Checking from the menu bar to check for errors.

Displaying All the Formulas in a Worksheet

When you need to review or check all the formulas in a worksheet, choose Formulas ➤ Auditing ➤ Show Formulas from the Ribbon. Excel displays the formulas and automatically widens the worksheet columns to give you more space (see Figure 15-9).

	A	B	C	D	E
2	Emulator	915	39.99	=B2*C2	
3	Virtualizer	638	4.99	=B3*C3	
4	Video Mule	18	189.99	=B4*C4	
5	Q Leader	1827	19.99	=B5*C5	
6				=SUM(D2:D5)	
7					

Figure 15-9. Choose Formulas ➤ Formula Auditing ➤ Show Formulas from the Ribbon when you need to see all the formulas in a worksheet

When you've finished viewing the formulas, choose Formulas ➤ Formula Auditing ➤ Show Formulas from the Ribbon again. Excel automatically restores the columns to their former widths.

Seeing Which Cells a Formula Uses

To see which cells a formula uses, click the cell that contains the formula, and then choose Formulas ➤ Formula Auditing ➤ Trace Precedents from the Ribbon. Excel displays an arrow showing the formula back to its roots. If one of the cells the formula uses contains a formula itself, you can click that cell and click the Trace Precedents button again to display its precedents in turn. Figure 15-10 shows the precedents of cell D6 and one of the cells that it uses, cell D2.

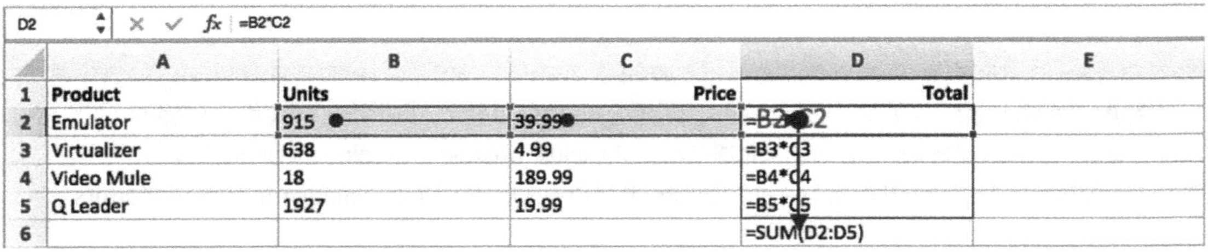

| D2 | ▲▼ | × | ✓ | fx | =B2*C2 | | | |

	A	B	C	Price	D	E
1	Product	Units		Price	Total	
2	Emulator	915 ●	39.99●		=B2●2	
3	Virtualizer	638	4.99		=B3*C3	
4	Video Mule	18	189.99		=B4*C4	
5	Q Leader	1927	19.99		=B5*C5	
6					=SUM(D2:D5)	

Figure 15-10. Use the Trace Precedents command to see which cells you're using to produce a formula result. In this example, cells B2 and C2 go to make up the formula in cell D2, which in turn appears in the =SUM(D2:D5) formula in cell D6.

When you need to look at the problem the other way and see which formulas use a particular cell, click the cell, and then choose Formulas ➤ Formula Auditing ➤ Trace Dependents from the Ribbon. Again, Excel displays arrows, this time from the cell going to each of the formulas that use it. Figure 15-11 shows an example of tracing dependent cells.

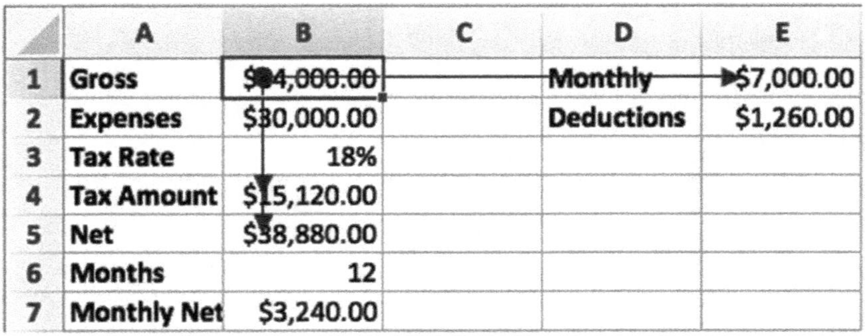

	A	B	C	D	E
1	Gross	$94,000.00		Monthly	▶$7,000.00
2	Expenses	$30,000.00		Deductions	$1,260.00
3	Tax Rate	18%			
4	Tax Amount	$15,120.00			
5	Net	$38,880.00			
6	Months	12			
7	Monthly Net	$3,240.00			

Figure 15-11. Use the Trace Dependents command to see which formulas use a particular cell's value to produce their results

> **Note**   You can use the Trace Precedents command and the Trace Dependents command either with formulas displayed or with formula results displayed, whichever you find most useful.

When you've finished tracing precedents and dependents, choose Formulas ➤ Formula Auditing ➤ Remove Arrows from the Ribbon (clicking the main part of the Remove Arrows button) to remove the arrows from the screen. If you want to remove just precedent arrows or dependent arrows, click the Remove Arrows pop-up button, and then click the Remove Precedent Arrows item or the Remove Dependent Arrows item on the pop-up menu.

Removing Circular References

Even if you're careful, it's easy enough to create a *circular reference*, one that refers to itself.

Circular references most often occur when you enter a formula that refers to a cell that itself refers to the cell in which you're entering the formula. For example, say cell A1 contains the formula **=B1**. If you enter the formula **=A1** in cell B1, you've created a circular reference: cell B1 gets its value from cell A1, which gets its value from cell B1, and so on.

You can also enter a circular reference by making a cell refer to itself. For example, if you enter **=A1/B1** in cell A1, you've created a circular reference in that cell because cell A1 refers to itself. This type of circular reference is usually easier to avoid than the previous type.

Circular references can be useful in some specialized circumstances, such as when you need to perform iterations of a calculation, but normally you don't want them in your worksheets, so Excel helps you to get rid of them.

When you create a circular reference that Excel cannot calculate, Excel displays the Excel Cannot Calculate a Formula dialog box shown in Figure 15-12. Click the OK button if you want to open a Help window showing information on how to deal with circular references, or click the Cancel button if you want to go ahead and enter the circular reference in the cell (for example, because you can tell what the problem is and will be able to fix it easily).

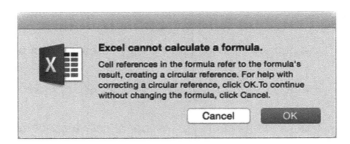

Figure 15-12. Circular references can cause problems in worksheets so Excel warns you when you enter one. You can click the Cancel button if you're sure you want to create the circular reference

> **Note** If you leave circular references in a worksheet, use the Circular References readout toward the left end of the status bar to identify them. This readout shows the location of the most recent circular reference that Excel has identified. When you've dealt with that circular reference, the Circular References readout shows the next one, and so on, until there are none left.

Performing Standard Calculations by Inserting Functions

When you need to perform standard calculations in your worksheets, use Excel's built-in functions, which are predefined formulas that you simply insert in a cell and provide with the data they need.

You can enter functions in three ways:

- *Use the AutoSum button or AutoSum pop-up menu*: The AutoSum button and pop-up menu appear in the Function Library group on the Formulas tab of the Ribbon and in the Editing group on the Home tab of the Ribbon and give quick access to five widely used functions.

- *Use the Formula Builder*: The Formula Builder is a pane that walks you through putting together the formula you need. You can open the Formula Builder in various ways, such as by clicking the fx button on the formula bar, clicking the Insert Function button in the Function Library group on the Formulas tab of the Ribbon, or choosing Insert ➤ Function from the menu bar.

- *Type the function in manually*: When you know which function you want, you can type it straight into a cell.

Understanding Function Names and Arguments

In Excel, a function has a name written in capitals followed by a pair of parentheses. Here are three examples:

- *SUM( )*: This widely used function adds together two or more values that you specify.

- *COUNT( )*: This function counts the number of cells that contain numbers (as opposed to text, blanks, or other data types) in the range you specify.

- *TODAY( )*: This function enters the current date in the cell.

Most functions take *arguments*, which are pieces of information that tell the function what you want it to work on. Excel prompts you to provide the arguments each function needs. For example, when you enter the function in a cell, Excel displays a ScreenTip showing the arguments needed. Figure 15-13 shows an example using the SUM( ) function.

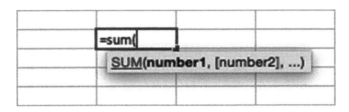

Figure 15-13. When you enter a function in a cell, Excel prompts you to supply the arguments it needs. The current argument appears in bold, such as the number1 argument here. An argument that appears in brackets is optional

The ScreenTip shows that the SUM( ) function has one required argument and one optional argument, and you can add further arguments as needed:

- *Required argument*: Each required argument appears without brackets, like the argument *number1* in the ScreenTip. You separate the arguments with commas. For example, you can use SUM( ) to add the values of cells in a range: SUM(C1:C10). Here, C1:C10 is a single argument, the required argument.

- *Optional argument*: Each optional argument appears in brackets, like the argument *[number2]* in the ScreenTip. For example, you can use SUM( ) to add the values of two cells: SUM(C1,C3). Here, C1 is the required argument, and C3 is the first optional argument.

- *Extra arguments*: The ellipsis (…) shows that you can enter extra arguments of the same type. For example, you can use SUM( ) to add the values of many cells: SUM(C1,C3,D4,D8,E1,XF202). Here, C1 is the required argument, and all the other cell references are optional arguments.

> **Note**   A few functions take no arguments. For example, you don't need to tell the TODAY( ) function which day you're talking about. Similarly, the NOW( ) function needs no arguments to return the current date and time, and the NA( ) function simply enters #(N/A) in a cell to indicate that the information is not available.

Inserting Functions with the AutoSum Pop-up Menu

The quickest and easiest way to enter any of five widely used functions—SUM( ), AVERAGE( ), COUNT( ), MAX( ), or MIN( )—in your worksheets is to use the AutoSum pop-up menu in the Function Library group on the Formulas tab of the Ribbon. Follow these steps:

1. Click the cell you want to enter the function in.

2. If you want to create a SUM( ) function for the cells immediately above or to the left of the selected cell, click the AutoSum button itself, either in the Function Library group on the Formulas tab of the Ribbon or in the Editing group on the Home tab of the Ribbon. Otherwise, click the AutoSum pop-up button, and then click the function (see Figure 15-14).

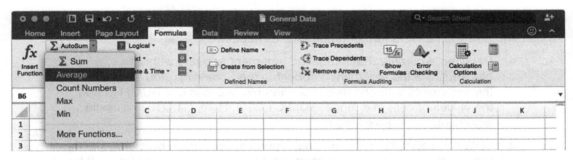

Figure 15-14. Use the AutoSum pop-up menu on the Formulas tab of the Ribbon when you need to insert the SUM( ), AVERAGE( ), COUNT( ), MAX( ), or MIN( ) function quickly

3. Excel inserts the function in the cell you chose and selects the range it thinks you may want to use as the argument. Figure 15-15 shows an example with the AVERAGE( ) function.

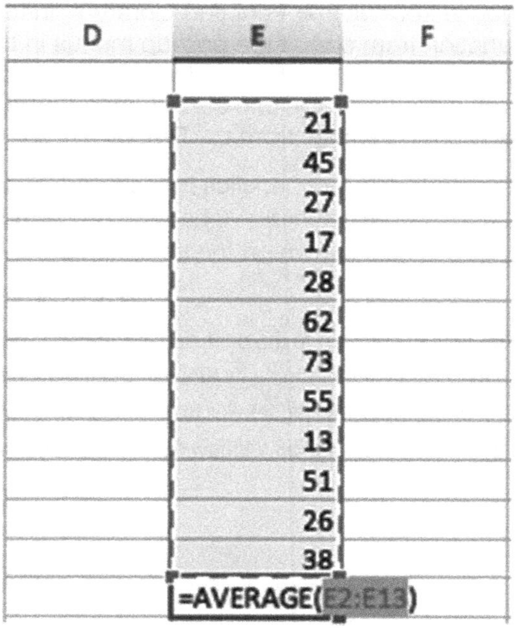

D	E	F
	21	
	45	
	27	
	17	
	28	
	62	
	73	
	55	
	13	
	51	
	26	
	38	
	=AVERAGE(E2:E13)	

Figure 15-15. When you insert a function from the AutoSum pop-up menu, Excel selects a range of data it thinks may be suitable

4. If you need to change the range, do so in one of these ways:

   ■ Click and drag to select the right range.

   ■ Type the range over the range selected within the parentheses.

5. Add another argument to the formula if needed. For example, type a comma, and then click and drag to select another range.

6. When the formula is as you want it, press Return to enter it in the cell. Excel displays the result of the formula.

Inserting Functions with the Formula Builder

When you need to find the right function to insert or when you need to learn about the arguments for a function, use the Formula Builder to insert the function. The Formula Builder is a pane that gives you access to a complete list of Excel's functions, together with descriptions and details of the arguments they use.

To insert a function with the Formula Builder, follow these steps:

1. Select the cell in which you want to enter the function.

2. Open the Formula Builder in one of these ways:

   ■ *Formula bar*: Click the fx button.

   ■ *Menu bar*: Choose View ➤ Formula Builder or Insert ➤ Function.

■ *Ribbon*: Choose Formulas ➤ Function Library ➤ Insert Function or choose a function from one of the pop-up menus in the Function Library group. For example, click the Date & Time pop-up menu and then click a function. You can also choose Home ➤ Editing ➤ AutoSum ➤ More Functions from the Ribbon.

3. If you want to search for a function, click in the Search box at the top, and then start typing the function's name. The Formula Builder displays a list of results, as shown on the left in Figure 15-16.

> **Note**   The Formula Builder appears docked to the right side of the Excel window at first. You can undock it and reposition it by clicking and dragging its title bar. You can then resize the Formula Builder window as needed; for example, making it taller to give yourself a better view of the function information. You can position the Formula Builder window outside the Excel window if you want.

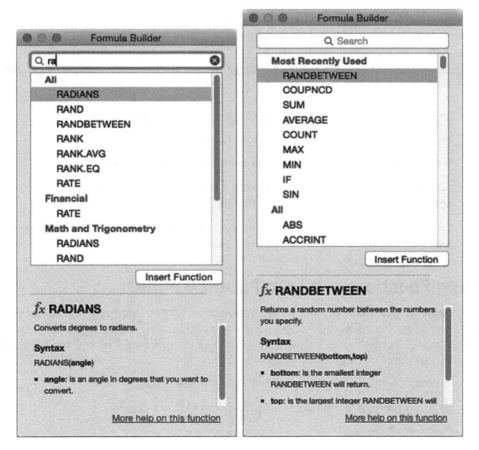

Figure 15-16. To find a function, start typing its name in the Search pane of the Formula Builder; the Formula Builder shows a list of results (left). Otherwise, browse the full list of functions, and click the function you want to see information on (right)

4. Otherwise, browse through the list of functions to find the function you need, as shown on the right in Figure 15-16. The Formula Builder breaks the functions up into the following categories:

    ■ *Most Recently Used*: This category provides quick access to the functions you've used most recently, so if you're looking for a function you've used before, start by looking here.

    ■ *All*: This category contains the full list of functions.

    ■ *Financial*: This category contains functions for financial calculations, such as calculating the payments on your mortgage or the depreciation on an asset.

    ■ *Date and Time*: This category contains functions ranging from returning the current date with the TODAY( ) function to using the WEEKDAY( ) function to return the day of the week for a particular date.

    ■ *Math and Trigonometry*: This category contains mathematical functions, such as the SQRT( ) function for returning a square root, and trigonometric functions, such as the COS( ) function for calculating the cosine of an angle.

    ■ *Statistical*: This category contains functions for performing statistical calculations, such as working out standard deviations based on a population or a sample.

    ■ *Lookup and Reference*: This category contains functions for looking up data from other parts of a worksheet or referring to other cells in it.

    ■ *Database*: This category contains functions for working with databases; for example, returning the average of values in a column or list or the count of cells containing numbers in a field.

    ■ *Text*: This category contains functions for manipulating text, such as the TRIM( ) function (for trimming off leading and trailing spaces) and the LEFT( ) function, which returns the leftmost part of the value.

    ■ *Logical*: This category contains functions for performing logical tests, such as testing whether a particular cell contains an error.

    ■ *Information*: This category contains functions for returning information about data, such as whether it is text or a number.

    ■ *Engineering*: This category contains functions including the DEC2HEX( ) function (for converting a decimal number to hexadecimal, base 16) and the HEX2OCT( ) function (for converting a hexadecimal number to octal, base 8).

    ■ *Cube*: This category contains functions for manipulating data cubes, which are multi-dimensional sets of values.

■ *Compatibility*: This category contains functions included for compatibility with older versions of Excel. It's best to use these functions only for compatibility with these older versions. If you're developing worksheets for Excel 2015 or Excel 2013 (Windows), use the newer functions that these versions support; for example, use the new POISSON.DIST( ) function rather than the old POISSON( ) function.

5. To learn more about a function, click it. The Formula Builder shows its details at the bottom of the window, as shown on the left in Figure 15-17.

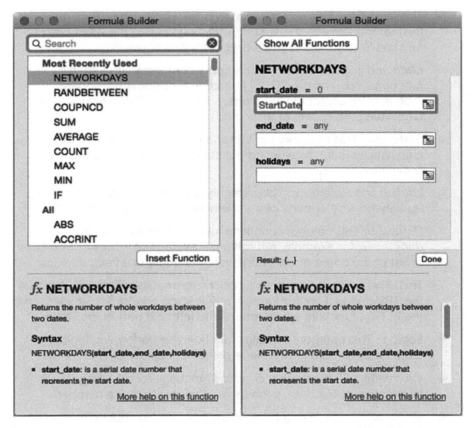

Figure 15-17. Use the description at the bottom of the Formula Builder to identify the function you want (left). When you double-click the function to insert it, the Formula Builder displays the Arguments pane (right)

6. When you've found the function you want to insert, click the Insert Function button. The Formula Builder displays the Arguments pane for the function, as shown on the right in Figure 15-15 (with one argument already entered).

7. Click in the box for the first argument, and then enter the data. You can type in a value or range name, type in a cell reference or range, or use the pointing device to choose a cell reference or range in the worksheet (or in another worksheet or workbook).

8. Fill in each of the other arguments for the function. When you have entered all the required arguments, the Result readout to the left of the Done button in the Function Builder window shows the result of the function.

9. Click the Done button or press Return to enter the function in the worksheet.

If you have finished using the Function Builder, close it by clicking its Close button (the button at the left end of its title bar) or by choosing View ➤ Formula Builder from the menu bar.

Inserting Functions with the Function Library Pop-up Menus

When you know which function you want to insert, the easiest way to insert it (unless it's one of the five functions on the AutoSum pop-up menu) is to use the pop-up menus in the Function Library group on the Formulas tab of the Ribbon. These pop-up menus help you pick the function by category and insert it directly in the cell.

To insert a function using the pop-up menus, follow these steps:

1. Select the cell in which you want to enter the function.

2. Click the Formulas tab of the Ribbon to display its contents.

3. Go to the Function Library group at the left end of the Ribbon and locate the function category for the function you want to insert. There are nine categories: AutoSum (which we've discussed already), Recently Used, Financial, Logical, Text, Date & Time, Lookup & Reference, Math & Trig, and More Functions (which displays a submenu showing Statistical, Engineering, Cube, Information, Compatibility, and Web). As you'll notice, these categories are similar to those that appear in the Formula Builder, discussed earlier in this chapter.

4. Click the function category's button to display the pop-up menu containing the functions. Figure 15-18 shows the Date and time submenu open.

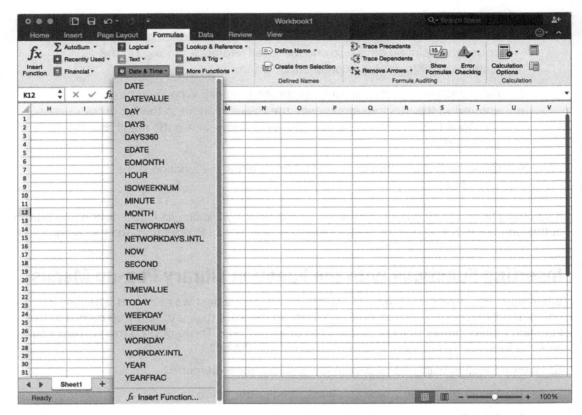

Figure 15-18. Use the pop-up menus in the Function Library group on the Formulas tab of the Ribbon when you want to insert a function by category

5. Click the function you want to insert. Excel inserts it in the cell and displays the Formula Builder.

6. Enter the arguments for the function as usual.

7. Press Return or click the Enter button on the Formula bar to enter the formula in the cell.

Inserting Functions by Typing Them into a Worksheet

You can also enter functions in your worksheets by typing them into cells. Follow these general steps:

1. Click the cell to select it.

2. Type = to tell Excel that you're creating a formula.

3. Start typing the function's name. Excel displays a list of matching functions (see Figure 15-19).

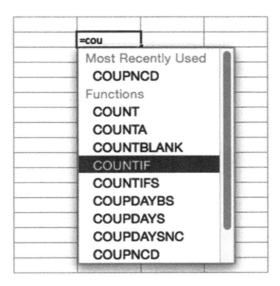

Figure 15-19. When you start typing a function name into a cell, Excel lists matching functions. Click the function you want to insert

> **Note**   You can also keep typing until you've typed enough to identify the function uniquely or type the whole of the function name if you prefer.

4. To enter a function, double-click it, or move the highlight to it by pressing down arrow or up arrow, and then press Return.

5. Specify the arguments for the function. You can either type in a value or a reference or use the pointing device to select a cell or range.

Summary

In this chapter, you learned how to use formulas and functions to perform calculations in your workbooks. You now know that a formula is the recipe for a calculation, and you know how to assemble it from its various components—an equal sign, cell or range references, operators, and more. You also now know how to create the formulas you need and how to troubleshoot them when they go wrong.

You're now also familiar with functions. You know that a function is a preset formula built into Excel, how to insert functions using the various tools Excel provides, and how to furnish functions with the arguments they need to work.

In the next chapter, I'll show you how to create databases and solve business problems.

Creating Simple Databases and Solving Business Problems

Packed with more than 16,000 columns and more than 1 million rows, each Excel worksheet has enough space to contain serious amounts of data—so it's great for creating a database to store information and quickly find the items you need.

In this chapter, you'll learn first to use Excel to create databases for storing information, sorting it, and filtering it to show the information you need. You'll then learn to use Excel's scenarios feature and its Goal Seek tool to solve business problems by performing what-if analysis.

Creating Databases in Excel

When you need to store a lot of the same type of information in a worksheet, you can create a database. For example, if you run a business, you can make a database of your customers and their orders.

> **Note**   Excel refers to databases as *tables*, which can be confusing if you're used to that word's normal meaning in the Office applications. So, this chapter refers to these databases as *database tables* for clarity.

The first step is to set up the database table and to tell Excel that you're creating a database table rather than a regular worksheet. The next step is to add your data to the database. Once the data is in the database table, you can sort the table to reveal different aspects of its contents or filter it to identify items that match the criteria you specify.

© Guy Hart-Davis 2016
G. Hart-Davis, *Learn Office 2016 for Mac*, DOI 10.1007/978-1-4842-2002-3_16

Understanding What You Can and Can't Do with Excel Database Tables

Before you start creating a database table in Excel, it's important to be clear on what you can and can't do with Excel database tables.

As you know, an Excel worksheet consists of rows and columns. To create a database table on a worksheet, you make each row into a *record*, an item that holds all the details of a single entry. For example, in a database table that records your sales to customers, a record would contain the details of a purchase. You make each column a *field* in the database table—a column for the purchase number, a column for the date, a column for the customer's last name, and so on. Figure 16-1 shows part of an Excel database table for tracking sales to customers.

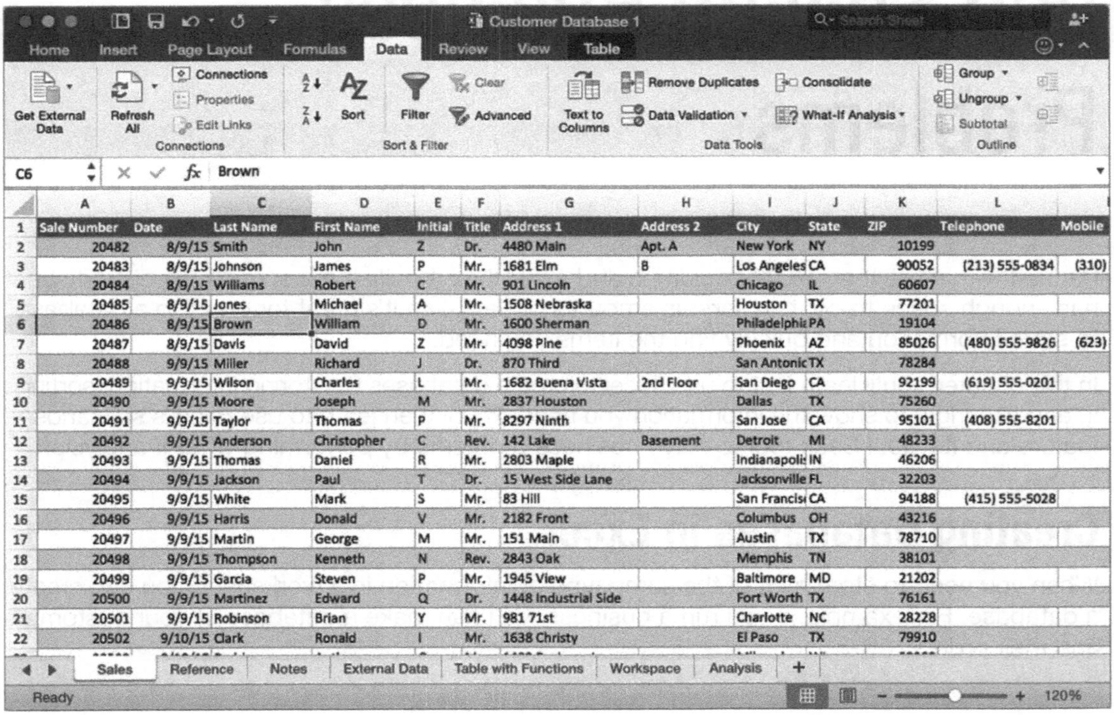

	A	B	C	D	E	F	G	H	I	J	K	L	M
1	Sale Number	Date	Last Name	First Name	Initial	Title	Address 1	Address 2	City	State	ZIP	Telephone	Mobile
2	20482	8/9/15	Smith	John	Z	Dr.	4480 Main	Apt. A	New York	NY	10199		
3	20483	8/9/15	Johnson	James	P	Mr.	1681 Elm	B	Los Angeles	CA	90052	(213) 555-0834	(310)
4	20484	8/9/15	Williams	Robert	C	Mr.	901 Lincoln		Chicago	IL	60607		
5	20485	8/9/15	Jones	Michael	A	Mr.	1508 Nebraska		Houston	TX	77201		
6	20486	8/9/15	Brown	William	D	Mr.	1600 Sherman		Philadelphia	PA	19104		
7	20487	8/9/15	Davis	David	Z	Mr.	4098 Pine		Phoenix	AZ	85026	(480) 555-9826	(623)
8	20488	9/9/15	Miller	Richard	J	Dr.	870 Third		San Antonio	TX	78284		
9	20489	9/9/15	Wilson	Charles	L	Mr.	1682 Buena Vista	2nd Floor	San Diego	CA	92199	(619) 555-0201	
10	20490	9/9/15	Moore	Joseph	M	Mr.	2837 Houston		Dallas	TX	75260		
11	20491	9/9/15	Taylor	Thomas	P	Mr.	8297 Ninth		San Jose	CA	95101	(408) 555-8201	
12	20492	9/9/15	Anderson	Christopher	C	Rev.	142 Lake	Basement	Detroit	MI	48233		
13	20493	9/9/15	Thomas	Daniel	R	Mr.	2803 Maple		Indianapolis	IN	46206		
14	20494	9/9/15	Jackson	Paul	T	Dr.	15 West Side Lane		Jacksonville	FL	32203		
15	20495	9/9/15	White	Mark	S	Mr.	83 Hill		San Francisco	CA	94188	(415) 555-5028	
16	20496	9/9/15	Harris	Donald	V	Mr.	2182 Front		Columbus	OH	43216		
17	20497	9/9/15	Martin	George	M	Mr.	151 Main		Austin	TX	78710		
18	20498	9/9/15	Thompson	Kenneth	N	Rev.	2843 Oak		Memphis	TN	38101		
19	20499	9/9/15	Garcia	Steven	P	Mr.	1945 View		Baltimore	MD	21202		
20	20500	9/9/15	Martinez	Edward	Q	Dr.	1448 Industrial Side		Fort Worth	TX	76161		
21	20501	9/9/15	Robinson	Brian	Y	Mr.	981 71st		Charlotte	NC	28228		
22	20502	9/10/15	Clark	Ronald	I	Mr.	1638 Christy		El Paso	TX	79910		

***Figure 16-1.** An Excel database consists of a table, with each row forming a record and each column containing a field*

This is what's called a *flat-file* database: all the data in the database is stored in a single table rather than in separate tables that are linked to each other.

This means you can use Excel to create any database for which you can store all the data for a record in a single row. Because you have a million rows at your disposal, you can create large databases if necessary, but they may make Excel run slowly.

What you can't do with Excel is create *relational databases*—ones that store the data in linked tables. A relational database is the kind of database you create with full-bore database applications such as FileMaker or Microsoft Access (on Windows). In a relational database, every record has a unique ID number or field that the application uses to link the data in the different tables.

Creating a Database Table and Entering Data

In this section, you'll look at how to create a database table and enter data in it.

Creating a Database Table

To create a database table, follow these steps:

1. Create a workbook as usual. For example, you can

    ■ *Create a new blank workbook*: Press Cmd+N or choose File ➤ New Workbook from the menu bar. You can also click File toward the left end of the title bar, click Blank Workbook on the New tab of the Microsoft Excel dialog box, and then click Create.

    ■ *Create a workbook based on a template or an existing workbook*: Open the Microsoft Excel dialog box by clicking File toward the left end of the title bar, pressing Cmd+Shift+P, or choosing File ➤ New from Template. You can then click the template you want to use, and then click Create.

    ■ Open an existing workbook, choose File ➤ Save As from the menu bar to open the Save As sheet, and then save a copy of the workbook under a different name, in a different location, or both.

2. Name the worksheet on which you'll create the database table. Double-click the worksheet tab, type the name you want (up to 31 characters, including spaces), and then press Return to apply the name.

3. Type the headings for the database table. For example, if the database table will contain customer names and addresses, you type fields such as Last Name, First Name, Middle Initial, Title, Address 1, and so on. Try to get all the fields in place at this point; you can add columns to the table later, but you then need to add extra data to the existing records.

> **Note** Usually, it's easiest to put the headings in the first row of the worksheet, but if you need to have information appear above the database table, leave rows free for that information.

4. Format the headings differently from the rows below them. For example, click the row header for the heading row, and then press Cmd+B to apply boldface.

5. Select the headings and at least one row below them.

6.   Choose Insert ➤ Tables ➤ Table from the Ribbon or Insert ➤ Table from the menu bar to display the Create Table dialog box (see Figure 16-2).

Figure 16-2. In the Create Table dialog box, verify that the "Where is the data for your table?" box shows the correct range and that the "My table has headers" check box is selected before clicking OK

7.   Make sure that the "Where is the data for your table?" box shows the correct range. If not, either type the correct range into the box or click and drag in the worksheet to enter it.

8.   Select the "My table has headers" check box (assuming your table has headers, as in the example).

9.   Click the OK button. Excel closes the Create Table dialog box and makes the following changes:

■   Creates the table.

■   Gives the table a default name, such as Table1 or Table2. This name appears in the Table Name box in the Properties group on the Table tab of the Ribbon.

■   Turns the header row into headers with pop-up buttons.

■   Applies a table style with shading based on the workbook's theme. You can change the style later as needed.

■   Displays the Table tab of the Ribbon, which contains controls for working with tables.

10.   Rename your table by following these steps:

■   Choose Table ➤ Properties ➤ Table Name from the Ribbon, double-clicking in the Table Name text box to select the default name.

■   Type the new name for the table. As with chart names, the database table name must be unique in the workbook, must start with a letter or an underscore, and cannot contain spaces or symbols.

■   Press Return to apply the table name.

Customizing the Database Table's Looks

At this point, you can start entering data in the database table (as discussed next)—but before you do, you may want to change the way it looks. To do so, follow these steps:

1. Click anywhere in the database table.

2. Click the Table tab of the Ribbon if it's not already displayed.

3. If a suitable style appears in the Table Styles box on the Ribbon, click it. If not, hold the pointer over the Table Styles box to display the panel button, and then click the panel button to display the Table Styles panel (see Figure 16-3). Click the style you want to apply.

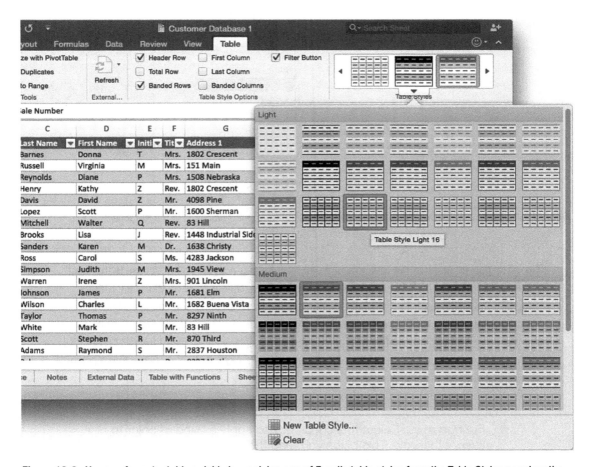

Figure 16-3. You can format a table quickly by applying one of Excel's table styles from the Table Styles panel on the Tables tab of the Ribbon. Scroll down the panel to see the other styles

4. In the Table Style Options group on the Tables tab of the Ribbon, select the check box for each table style option you want to use:

    ■ *Header row*: Select this check box to display the header row. This is almost always useful.

    ■ *Total row*: Select this check box to add a row labeled Total immediately after the database table's last row. This is useful when you need to add a total formula or another formula in the last row. To add a formula, click a cell, click the pop-up button that appears, and then click the formula you want on the pop-up menu (see Figure 16-4).

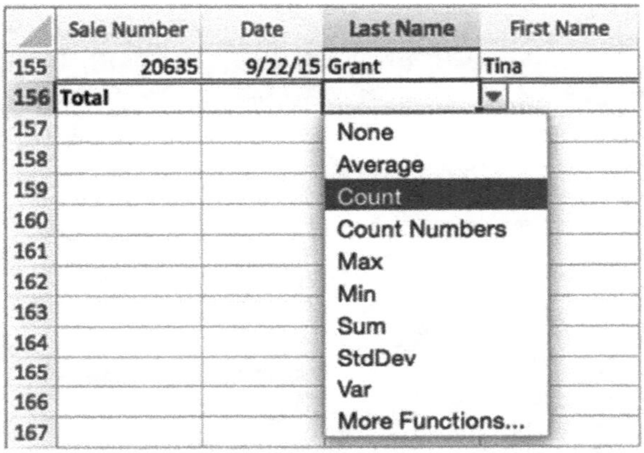

Figure 16-4. Adding a Total row to a database table lets you quickly insert functions in the row's cells

---

Tip   The pop-up menu in the Total row of a database table gives you instant access to the most widely used functions in databases—Average, Count, Count Numbers, Max, Min, Sum, StdDev (Standard Deviation), and Var (calculating variance based on a sample). You can also click the More Functions item at the bottom of the pop-up menu to display the Formula Builder, from which you can access the full range of Excel's functions. For example, you can insert the COUNTBLANK() function to count the number of blank cells in a column. You might do this to ensure that a column of essential data contains no blanks.

    ■ *Banded rows*: Select this check box to apply a band of color to every other row. This helps you read the rows of data without your eyes wandering to another row. Some table styles apply banding to the rows automatically.

    ■ *First column*: Select this check box if you want the first column to have different formatting. You may want to do this if the first column contains the main field for identifying each record (for example, a unique number).

- *Last column*: Select this check box if you want the last column to have different formatting. Usually, you want this only if the last column contains data that is more important in some way than the data in the other columns.

- *Banded columns*: Select this check box to apply a band of color to every other column. This is sometimes helpful but usually less helpful than banded rows. (Don't use both—the effect is seldom useful.)

When you've finished choosing a style and options for the database table, save your work as usual.

Entering Data in a Database Table

A database table is essentially an Excel worksheet at heart, so you can enter data in the database table by using the standard techniques you've learned in the past few chapters. For example, click a cell, and then type data into it; or, if you have the data in another worksheet, copy it and paste it in.

When you enter data in the row immediately after the last row in the database table, Excel automatically expands the database table to include that row. To add a row within the database table, click a cell in the row above which you want to add the new row, and then choose Insert ➤ Rows from the menu bar. Again, Excel automatically expands the database table to include the new row.

To insert a column in the database table, click a cell in the column before which you want to add the new column, and then choose Insert ➤ Columns from the menu bar. Again, Excel automatically expands the database table.

Tip   You can quickly select a row, a column, or an entire database table with the pointing device. To select a row, move the pointer to the left part of a cell in the database table's leftmost column, and then click with the horizontal arrow that appears. To select a column, move the pointer over a column heading, and then click with the downward arrow that appears. To select the whole database table, move the pointer over the upper-left cell in the database table, and then click with the diagonal arrow that appears.

Resizing a Database Table

When you've created a database table, Excel normally resizes it for you automatically when you add or delete rows or columns. Excel also expands the database table automatically if you add data to the row after the current last row in a database table that doesn't have a Total row. Excel calls this feature Table AutoExpansion. If you don't want Excel to do this, click the AutoCorrect actions button that appears below and to the right of the first cell in the added row, and then click Undo Table AutoExpansion (see Figure 16-5). Click the actions button again, and then click Stop Automatically Expanding Tables. The data you entered in the row remains there, but you can use the Undo command to get rid of it if necessary.

Note   When you add a new row to a database table using Table AutoExpansion, Excel makes the change only when you start typing data in the row. When you do, Excel applies the style to the row, and you can see that it's part of the database table. But until you start typing, it's just another plain row.

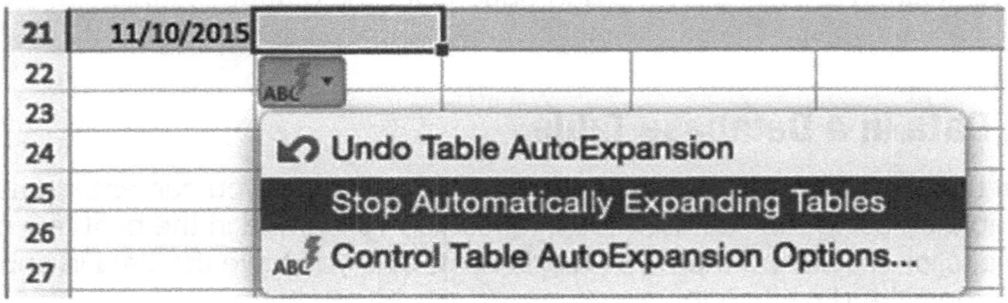

Figure 16-5. *You can use the AutoCorrect actions button both to undo Table AutoExpansion and to turn it off*

Note   The Control Table AutoExpansion Options item on the AutoCorrect actions button gives you quick access to the Tables & Filters preferences pane in the Excel preferences window.

To turn Table AutoExpansion back on, choose Excel ➤ Preferences or press Cmd+, (Cmd and the comma key). In the Excel Preferences window, click the Tables & Filters icon in the Formulas and Lists area to display the Tables preferences pane. Select the Automatically expand tables check box, and then close the Excel Preferences window by clicking the Close button (the red button at the left end of the title bar) or pressing Cmd+W.

Sorting a Database Table by One or More Fields

When you need to examine the data in your database table, it's often useful to sort it. Excel lets you sort a database table either quickly by a single field or by using multiple fields.

Tip   If you need to be able to return a database table to its original order, include a column with sequential numbers in it. These numbers may be part of your records (for example, sequential sales numbers for transactions) or simply ID numbers for the records. In either case, you can use AutoFill to enter them quickly. To return the database table to its original order, you can then sort it by this column.

Sorting Quickly by a Single Field

To sort a database table by a single field, click any cell in the column you want to sort by, and then choose Data ➤ Sort & Filter ➤ Sort A to Z from the Ribbon. This produces a sort in ascending order (A to Z, low values to high values, early dates to later dates, and so on). To reverse the sort to descending order, choose Data ➤ Sort & Filter ➤ Sort Z to A from the Ribbon.

After you sort, the database table remains sorted that way until you change it.

Sorting a Database Table by Multiple Fields

Often, it's useful to sort your database table by two or more fields at the same time. For example, in a customer database, you may need to sort your customers first by state and then by city within the state.

To sort by multiple fields, follow these steps:

1. Click any cell in the database table.

2. Choose Data ➤ Sort & Filter ➤ Sort from the Ribbon or Data ➤ Sort from the menu bar to display the Sort dialog box. Figure 16-6 shows the Sort dialog box with two criteria entered and a third criterion under way.

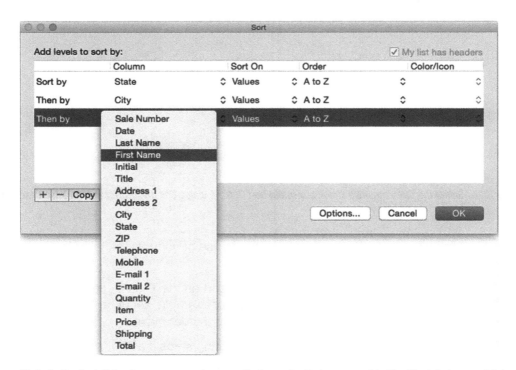

Figure 16-6. In the Sort dialog box, you can set up exactly the sort criteria you need to identify data in your database

3. Set up your first sort criterion using the controls on the first row of
    the main part of the Sort dialog box. Follow these steps:

    ■ Open the Column pop-up menu in the Sort by row, and then click
      the column you want to sort by first. For example, click the State
      column.

    ■ Open the Sort On pop-up menu in the same row, and then click
      what you want to sort by: Values, Cell Color, Font Color, or Cell Icon.
      In most cases, you'll want to use Values, but the other three items
      are useful for tables to which you've applied conditional formatting.

    ■ Open the Order pop-up menu on the same row, and then click the sort
      order you want. If you choose Values in the Sort On pop-up menu, you
      can choose A to Z for an ascending sort, Z to A for a descending sort,
      or Custom List. Choosing Custom List opens the Custom List dialog
      box, in which you can choose a custom list by which to sort the results.
      For example, you could use a custom list of your company's products
      or offices to sort the database into a custom order rather than being
      restricted to ascending or descending order.

    ■ If you need the sort to be case sensitive (so that "smith" appears
      before "Smith," and so on), click the Options button. In the Sort
      Options dialog box (see Figure 16-7), select the Case sensitive
      check box, and then click the OK button.

Figure 16-7. Select the Case sensitive check box in the Sort Options dialog box if you want to treat lowercase letters differently than their uppercase versions

4. Click the Add (+) button to add a second line of controls to the main
    part of the Sort dialog box.

5. Set up the criterion for the second-level sort on the Then by line
    using the same technique as in step 3. For example, set up a
    second-level sort using the City column in the database.

6. Set up any other criteria needed by repeating steps 4 and 5.

7. Click the OK button to close the Sort dialog box. Excel sorts the data
    using the criteria you specified.

> **Note**   When you're sorting data that's not in a database table, there are two main differences. First, the "My list has headers" check box in the Sort dialog box is available, and you must select it if the data range you're sorting includes a header row. (Otherwise, Excel sorts the headers into the data range, which is ugly.) Second, you can select the "Sort left to right" option button in the Sort Options dialog box to sort columns rather than rows, a choice that's not available in a database table.

Identifying and Removing Duplicate Records in a Database Table

When you've created a large database table, you may need to check it for duplicate records and remove those you find. Excel provides a Remove Duplicates feature that saves you having to comb the records by hand.

> **Caution**   Two warnings before removing duplicate values. First, make sure you have a backup copy of your database workbook; for example, use Finder to copy the current version of a file to a safe location. Second, be certain you know which fields in the database table should contain unique values and which can contain duplicate values. For example, a customer ID number field must be unique because each customer has a different ID number, but a customer last name field can't reasonably be unique because many customers will likely share last names. Most databases need a unique ID number or code of this type.

To remove duplicate records from a database table, follow these steps:

1. Click any cell in the database table.

2. Choose Table ➤ Data Tools ➤ Remove Duplicates from the Ribbon or Data ➤ Table Tools ➤ Remove Duplicates from the menu bar to display the window shown in Figure 16-8.

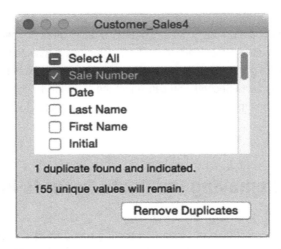

Figure 16-8. Use this window to locate duplicate values in columns that should contain only unique values. The window's title bar shows the name of the database table

3.   If the Select All check box contains a check mark, click the check box to remove the check mark, and clear all the check boxes in the Columns box.

4.   Select the check box for each column you want to check for duplicates. The readout at the bottom of the dialog box shows the number of duplicates.

> **Tip**   Normally, it's best to check a single column for duplicate values at a time. Make sure that the column is one that must contain a unique value.

5.   Click the Remove Duplicates button if you want to remove the duplicates.

6.   Repeat the process with another column if necessary.

7.   When you have finished removing duplicates, click the red Close button at the left end of the title bar to close the window.

Filtering a Database Table

When you need to find records in a database table that match the terms you specify, you can *filter* it. Filtering makes Excel display only the records that match your search terms, hiding all the other records.

> **Note**   You can also search for records by using Excel's Find feature. Choose Edit ➤ Find ➤ Find from the menu bar or press Ctrl+Shift+F to display the Find dialog box, type your search term in the Find What box, and then click the Find Next button. Filtering displays all the matching records together rather than spread out in the database table, so it's often more convenient than using Find.

To make filtering easy, Excel provides a feature named AutoFilter. To use AutoFilter, follow these steps:

1. Click a cell in the database table.

2. Click the Data tab of the Ribbon to display its contents.

3. In the Sort & Filter group, make sure that the Filter button is selected so that it looks pushed in; if not, click the main part of the button. Excel normally selects the Filter button when you create a database table, so this button should be pushed in unless you've turned filtering off. Selecting this button makes Excel display a pop-up button on each column heading in the database table.

4. On the column you want to use for filtering, click the pop-up button to display the AutoFilter window (shown on the left in Figure 16-9). The AutoFilter window's title bar shows the name of the field you clicked.

Figure 16-9. To apply filtering, click the pop-up arrow on a column heading to display the AutoFilter window (left). In the Filter area, open the first pop-up menu, and choose the comparison you want. You can then add further comparisons as needed

5.   Click the type of sorting or filtering you want to apply:

 ■   *Sort*: Click the type of sort you want to apply. Normally, you click either the Ascending button or the Descending button. But if your database table uses colors, you can sort by color instead—just choose the color in the By color pop-up menu in the Sort area.

 ■   *Filter*: If you want to filter the table by color, choose the color in the By color pop-up menu. Otherwise, open the pop-up menu that appears as Choose One in the left part of Figure 16-9, and then choose the comparison from it. For example, choose Equals to set a filter that picks particular states, or choose Begins With to set a filter than selects cities that start with text you specify. Use the fields in the Custom AutoFilter window to set up the rest of the comparison; the right screen in Figure 16-9 shows an example that filters by Equals AK or Equals AL, returning the records that have the state AK or the state AL.

Note   The filter comparisons depend on the contents of the column you selected in the database table. For example, if the column contains numbers, the comparisons include the mathematical comparisons Greater Than, Greater Than or Equal To, Less Than, Less Than or Equal To, Between, Top 10, Bottom 10, Above Average, and Below Average. If the column contains dates, the comparisons include Before, After, Between, Tomorrow, Next Week, Next Month, and Next Year.

When you've specified the details of the filter, Excel applies it to the database table and reduces the display to those rows that match the filter. Excel displays a filter symbol in place of the drop-down button on the column that contains the filtering (as on the State column heading in Figure 16-10).

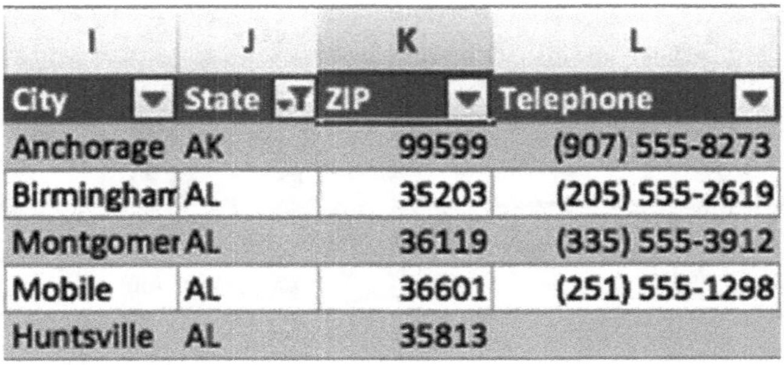

City	State	ZIP	Telephone
Anchorage	AK	99599	(907) 555-8273
Birmingham	AL	35203	(205) 555-2619
Montgomer	AL	36119	(335) 555-3912
Mobile	AL	36601	(251) 555-1298
Huntsville	AL	35813	

Figure 16-10. The filter symbol (shown on the State column heading here) indicates that you're filtering the database table by that column

To remove filtering from a single column, click the filter symbol on the column heading, and then click the Clear Filter button in the AutoFilter window.

To remove filtering from the database table as a whole, choose Data ➤ Sort & Filter ➤ Filter, unpressing the Filter button in the Sort & Filter group.

> **Note**   If AutoFilter doesn't give you the flexibility you need, you can also create custom filters manually. To do this, you insert extra rows above the database table to create a criteria range, enter the criteria in the appropriate columns, choose Data ➤ Sort & Filter ➤ Advanced, and then work in the Advanced Filter dialog box. This topic is beyond the scope of this book, so look it up (online or offline) if you need to perform filtering that AutoFilter can't manage.

Solving Business Problems with Scenarios and Goal Seek

For much of your work with Excel, you probably want to manipulate the hard data you already have, as you've been doing so far in this part of the book. But other times, you may need to ask questions of your data; for example, by how much do you need to raise prices to boost your revenue by a certain amount, or what will happen if you cut 10 percent off your manufacturing costs?

In this section, you'll look at two tools Excel gives you for performing what-if analysis:

- *Scenarios*: Use scenarios when you want to experiment with different data in your worksheet without changing the core data that you already have.

- *Goal Seek*: Use Goal Seek when you need to make one cell's value reach a particular figure by changing one other value.

Examining Different Scenarios in a Worksheet

After you've built a worksheet, you may want to experiment with different data in it. For example, if you're setting budgets, you may need to play around with different figures for the different departments to get the overall balance you require.

You can experiment with different data by changing the values directly in your worksheet—but then you may need to restore your original values afterward. Another approach is to create multiple copies of the worksheet (or of the workbook) and then change the values in the copies, leaving the original untouched. This works fine, but if you then need to change the original worksheet (for example, adding another column of data), the changes quickly become messy.

Instead of working in these awkward ways, you can use Excel's scenarios. A *scenario* is a way of entering different values into a set of cells without changing the underlying values. You can switch from one scenario to another as needed, and you can merge scenarios from different versions of the same worksheet into a single worksheet.

Creating the Worksheet for Your Scenarios

Start by creating the workbook and worksheet you'll use for your scenarios. If you have an existing workbook with the data in it, go ahead and open it. Set up the data and formulas in your worksheet as usual.

> **Tip**   To make your scenarios easy to set up and adjust, define a name for each cell that you will change in the scenario. Click the cell, choose Insert ➤ Name ➤ Define from the menu bar to display the Define Name dialog box, and then work as described in the "Referring to Named Cells and Ranges" section in Chapter 15. For example, type the name in the "Enter a name for the data range" text box, and then click the Add (+) button to add the name and leave the dialog box open so that you can click another cell and define a name for it too.

Figure 16-11 shows the sample worksheet this section uses as an example. The worksheet summarizes the financial returns from a modest portfolio of rental properties.

F9		✕ ✓	*fx*	=D9/D$10			
	A	B	C	D	E	F	G
1	**Financial Scenarios**						
2							
3							
4	**Property Address**	**Monthly Rent**	**Operating Costs**	**Property Profit**	**Property Profitability**	**Financial Contribution**	
5	1860 Lincoln	$1,450	$849	$601	41%	20%	
6	414 Pacific A	$550	$300	$250	45%	8%	
7	414 Pacific B	$650	$0	$650	100%	22%	
8	414 Pacific C	$1,050	$400	$650	62%	22%	
9	2896 Crescent	$2,400	$1,560	$840	35%	28%	
10		$6,100	$3,109	$2,991	57%	100%	

Figure 16-11. To start using scenarios, create a worksheet containing your existing data and the formulas needed

Here's what you see on the worksheet:

- The Property Address column shows each property's address.

- The Monthly Rent column shows each property's monthly rent. Cell B10 contains a SUM() formula to produce the total rent. Each of the cells here has a name to make it easy to recognize: Rent_Lincoln, Rent_Pacific_A, and so on.

- The Operating Costs column shows the monthly operating cost for each property, including all mortgage costs and other financial horrors. Cell C10 uses a SUM() formula to produce the total running cost. The numbers in this column are rounded. Each of these cells has a name: Costs_Lincoln, Costs_Pacific_A, and so forth. Again, this is so that we can refer to the cells easily and clearly.

- The Property Profit column shows how much profit each rental unit returns after subtracting the operating cost from the rent (for example, cell D5 contains the sum =B5-C5). The numbers in this column are rounded. Cell D10 uses a SUM() formula to return the total profit.

- The Property Profitability column shows the property's profitability as a percentage. To produce the profitability figure, divide the Property Profit value by the Monthly Rent value; for example, cell E5 contains the formula = D5/B5. At the bottom of the column, cell E10 uses an AVERAGE() formula to show the average profitability of the properties.

- The Financial Contribution column shows each property's contribution to the total profit as a percentage. To produce the contribution figure, divide each property's profit by the total profit in cell D10. For example, cell F9 contains the formula =D9/D$10, using a mixed reference to keep the row absolute when copying the formula. Cell F10 contains a SUM() formula that adds the percentages, showing that they total 100%.

Times are bad, and the total profit is too low. So let's use scenarios to see how to improve matters by raising rents and shaving costs.

Opening the Scenario Manager Dialog Box

When you're ready to start working with scenarios, choose Data ➤ Data Tools ➤ What-If Analysis ➤ Scenario Manager from the Ribbon or Tools ➤ Scenarios from the menu bar to display the Scenario Manager dialog box. At first, when the workbook contains no scenarios, the Scenario Manager dialog box appears as shown in Figure 16-12.

Figure 16-12. At first, the Scenario Manager dialog box contains nothing but the message "No Scenarios defined."
Click the Add (+) button to get started

Creating Scenarios

After opening the Scenario Manager dialog box, you can create your scenarios.

> **Tip**   First, create a scenario containing your original data. This gives you an easy way to go back to
> the original data when you've finished testing scenarios.

To create a scenario, follow these steps:

1. From the Scenario Manager dialog box, click the Add (+) button to
    display the Add Scenario dialog box (see Figure 16-13).

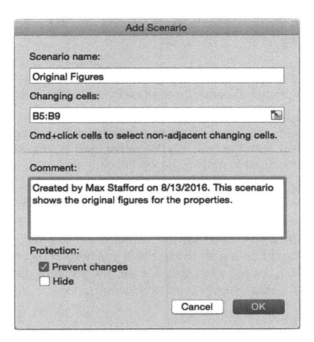

Figure 16-13. *Use the Add Scenario dialog box to set up each scenario. First, create a scenario for your original data so that you can easily return to it*

2. In the Scenario name text box, type a descriptive name for the scenario.

3. Click in the Changing cells text box, and then enter the details of the cells that users of the scenario are allowed to change; for example, cells B5:B9.

   - Click and drag in the worksheet to select a range of contiguous cells. If you need to select noncontiguous cells, click the first, and then Cmd-click each other cell.

   - You can also type the name of a range into the Changing cells text box.

   - There's a Collapse Dialog button to the right of the Changing cells text box, but you don't need to use it because Excel automatically collapses the Add Scenario dialog box when you click and drag in the worksheet. After you've selected the changing cells, Excel expands the dialog box again.

4. In the Comment text box, you can type a comment that explains what the scenario is and how to use it. Excel creates a default comment of *Created by*, your user name (as set in the Office applications), and the date, but a descriptive comment is usually more helpful.

5. Choose settings as needed in the Protection area at the bottom of the dialog box:

    ■ *Prevent changes*: Select this check box when you need to prevent changes to the scenario. To make the protection take effect, you need to protect the worksheet as described in the next section.

    ■ *Hide*: Select this check box when you need to prevent others from seeing this scenario; for example, because you want them to experiment with their own figures rather than looking at your figures. Again, you need to protect the worksheet.

6. Click the OK button to close the Add Scenario dialog box. Excel displays the Scenario Values dialog box (see Figure 16-14). This dialog box shows a list box containing the changing cells in the scenario. Here's where you see the benefit of naming the changing cells—each text box is easy to identify. If you haven't named the changing cells, the cell addresses appear, and you may need to refer to the worksheet to see which cell is which.

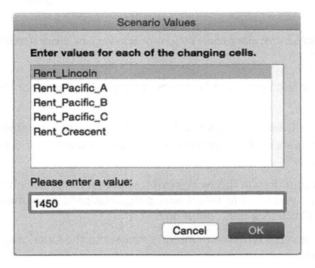

Figure 16-14. In the Scenario Values dialog box, enter the values to use for the new scenario you're creating. The cell names produce the labels (Rent_Lincoln and so on), which are much easier to refer to than cell addresses (for example, B5)

7. Click each changing cell and verify the value in the "Please Enter a Value" box. Normally, you'd be entering values here for the new scenario, but because this scenario is for the original figures, you don't need to change them.

8. Click the OK button to close the Scenario Values dialog box. Excel returns you to the Scenario Manager dialog box, where the scenario now appears in the Scenarios list box.

To add another scenario, click the Add button in the Scenario Manager dialog box, and then repeat the previous process. This time, change the figures for the scenario in step 7.

Applying Protection to Your Scenarios

If you selected either the Prevent changes check box or the Hide check box in the Protection area of the Add Scenario dialog box, you need to protect the worksheet to make the protection take effect.

To protect the worksheet, follow these steps:

1. If the Scenario Manager dialog box is open, click the Close button to close it.

2. Choose Review ➤ Changes ➤ Protect Sheet from the Ribbon or Tools ➤ Protection ➤ Protect Sheet from the menu bar to display the Protect the sheet and contents of locked cells sheet.

3. Type a password in the Password text box and the Verify text box.

4. In the "Allow users of this sheet to" box, make sure the Edit scenarios check box is cleared.

5. Click the OK button to close the dialog box. Excel applies the protection.

6. Save the workbook. For example, press Cmd+S or click the Save button on the title bar.

After protecting the scenarios in the worksheet like this, you need to turn off the protection before you can edit the scenarios. To turn off the protection, choose Review ➤ Changes ➤ Protect Sheet from the Ribbon or Tools ➤ Protection ➤ Unprotect Sheet from the menu bar, type the password in the sheet that Excel displays, and then click the OK button.

Editing and Deleting Scenarios

From the Scenario Manager dialog box, you can quickly edit a scenario by clicking it in the Scenarios list box, clicking the Edit button, and then working in the Edit Scenario dialog box. Excel automatically updates the scenario's comment for you with details of the modification (for example, "Modified by Jack Cunningham on 07/18/2016"), but you may want to type in more details, such as what you're trying to make the scenario show.

When you no longer need a scenario, delete it by clicking the scenario in the Scenarios list box and clicking the Delete button. Excel doesn't confirm the deletion; but if you delete a scenario by mistake, and recovering it is more important than losing any other changes you've made since you last saved the workbook, you can recover the scenario by closing the workbook without saving changes (assuming the scenario was already saved in the workbook). For example, choose File ➤ Close from the menu bar, and then click the Don't Save button in the dialog box that prompts you to save the changes to the file.

Switching Among Your Scenarios

Once you've created multiple scenarios for the same worksheet, you can switch among them by clicking the scenario you want in the Scenarios list box in the Scenario Manager dialog box (see Figure 16-15) and then clicking the Show button. Excel displays the scenario's figures in the worksheet's cells. The Scenario Manager dialog box stays open, so you can quickly switch to another scenario.

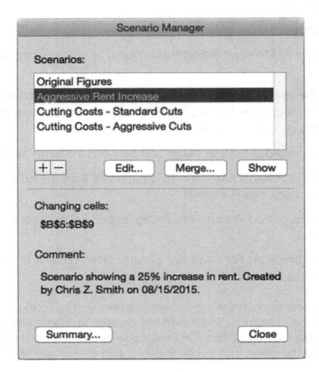

Figure 16-15. To switch to another scenario, click the scenario in the Scenarios list box in the Scenario Manager dialog box, and then click the Show button

Merging Scenarios into a Single Worksheet

If you develop and share your scenarios in a single workbook, you can keep them all together. But other times you may need to develop your scenarios in separate workbooks and then combine them. You can do this easily by using the Merge command in the Scenario Manager dialog box.

To merge scenarios, follow these steps:

1. Open all the workbooks containing the scenarios you will merge.

2. Make active the workbook and worksheet you will merge the scenarios into.

3. Choose Data ➤ Data Tools ➤ What-If Analysis ➤ Scenario Manager from the Ribbon or Tools ➤ Scenarios from the menu bar to display the Scenario Manager dialog box.

4. Click the Merge button to display the Merge Scenarios dialog box (see Figure 16-16).

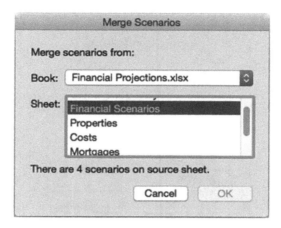

Figure 16-16. In the Merge Scenarios dialog box, choose the workbook and worksheet that contain the scenarios you want to merge into the active workbook

5. Open the Book pop-up menu, and choose the open workbook that contains the scenarios you want to merge in. The Sheet list box shows a list of the worksheets in the workbook.

6. In the Sheet list box, click the worksheet that contains the scenarios. The readout at the bottom of the Merge Scenarios dialog box shows how many scenarios the worksheet contains, which helps you pick the right worksheet.

7. Click the OK button. Excel closes the Merge Scenarios dialog box, merges the scenarios, and then displays the Scenario Manager dialog box again.

Note   If any scenario you merge into the active worksheet has the same name as an existing scenario in the worksheet, Excel adds the current date to the incoming scenario to distinguish it.

Creating Reports from Your Scenarios

Sometimes you can make the decisions you need by simply creating scenarios and looking at them in the worksheet. Other times, it's helpful to create a report from the scenarios so that you can compare them. Excel gives you an easy way to create either a summary report or a PivotTable report straight from the Scenario Manager dialog box.

To create a report from your scenarios, follow these steps:

1. Choose Data ➤ Data Tools ➤ What-If Analysis ➤ Scenario Manager from the Ribbon or Tools ➤ Scenarios from the menu bar to display the Scenario Manager dialog box.

2. Click the Summary button to display the Scenario Summary dialog box (see Figure 16-17).

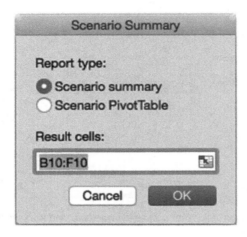

Figure 16-17. In the Scenario Summary dialog box, choose between a scenario summary and a scenario PivotTable, and then select the result cells for the summary

3. In the Report type box, select the Scenario summary option button if you want to create a summary worksheet. If you want to create a scenario PivotTable, select the Scenario PivotTable option button. (Chapter 17 explains what PivotTables are and how you work with them.)

4. Click in the Result cells text box, and then enter the addresses of the cells whose results you want the report or PivotTable to show. You can type in addresses or range names or select the appropriate cells in the worksheet.

5. Click the OK button to close the Scenario Summary dialog box. Excel creates the report or PivotTable. Figure 16-18 shows a sample of a summary report, which Excel places on a new worksheet named Scenario Summary at the beginning of the workbook.

Note If you select the Scenario PivotTable option button in the Scenario Summary dialog box, Excel inserts a new worksheet with a default name (such as Sheet2) containing a PivotTable and displays the PivotTable Builder window so that you can change the PivotTable to suit your needs. See Chapter 17 for information on PivotTables.

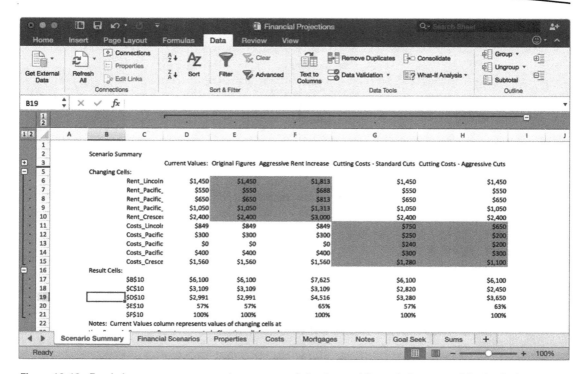

Figure 16-18. Excel places a summary report on a new worksheet named Scenario Summary at the beginning of the workbook

Using Goal Seek

When you're planning or forecasting, you'll often need to work backward from your target to derive the figures you need. For example, when planning your next financial year, you may need to find out how much you need to raise the selling price for your widgets to make an extra $30,000 a year.

To work this out, you can try increasing the unit price for the widgets until your revenue figure is $30,000 higher. But you can save time and effort by using Excel's Goal Seek feature to derive the required price automatically by working backward from the revenue figure.

To derive values using Goal Seek, follow these steps:

1. Open the workbook that contains the data, and navigate to the worksheet that contains the calculation.

2. Make active the cell that contains the formula.

3. Choose Data ➤ Data Tools ➤ What-If Analysis ➤ Goal Seek from the Ribbon or choose Tools ➤ Goal Seek from the menu bar to display the Goal Seek dialog box (shown in Figure 16-19 with settings chosen).

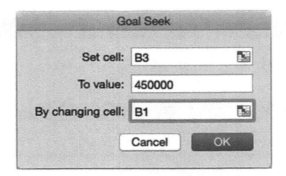

Figure 16-19. Use the Goal Seek dialog box to work backward from your desired result to the figure you need

4. Make sure the Set cell text box contains the cell that contains the formula. (If you selected the cell in Step 2, it will.) If necessary, change the cell either by typing the correct reference or by double-clicking the current contents of the Set cell text box (to select it) and then clicking the right cell in the worksheet. (You can also click the Collapse Dialog button to collapse the Goal Seek dialog box, but the dialog box is so small anyway that it's usually easier to work around it.)

5. In the To value text box, type the value you want to get.

6. In the "By changing cell" text box, enter the cell whose value you want to change; in the example, the cell containing the price of the widgets. Again, you can type the cell reference or simply click the cell in the worksheet.

7. Click the OK button. Goal Seek calculates the answer, enters it in the worksheet, and then displays the Goal Seek Status dialog box (see Figure 16-20).

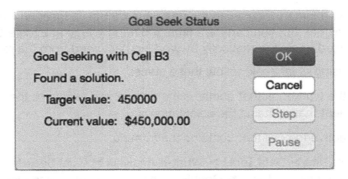

Figure 16-20. When Excel displays the Goal Seek Status dialog box, look at the value in the target cell in the worksheet. Click the OK button if you want to keep the value. Click the Cancel button if you want to revert to the previous value

Note   If the calculation is straightforward, Goal Seek finds a solution quickly. But if the calculation is more complex, Goal Seek may take a while. If this happens, you can click the Pause button in the Goal Seek Status dialog box to pause the calculation to see which value Goal Seek is trying at the moment. If you want to follow the individual values Goal Seek is trying, click the Step button to display the next value but keep the calculation paused; keep clicking the Step button as needed to see further values. Click the Resume button when you want Goal Seek to resume the calculation at full speed.

8. Look at the value in the target cell. Click the OK button if you want to keep it. Click the Cancel button if you want to go back to the previous value.

Tip   If you find Goal Seek useful, take a look at the Solver, which you can download for free from the Solver.com web site (`www.solver.com/mac/`). Whereas Goal Seek lets you change only one variable, the Solver lets you change multiple variables. This enables you to ask more complex questions of your data.

Summary

In this chapter, you learned how to create a database table in Excel—a flat-file database rather than the relational type of database that you create with a database application such as Microsoft Access. You now know how to set up a database table, choose display options for it, format it to look the way you want, and add data to it. You've gained the essential skills of sorting the data into the sort order you need or filtering it to show the records you're interested in.

You also learned how to use Excel's scenarios to explore how different values affect a worksheet and how to use Goal Seek to work backward from a desired result to the value needed to produce it.

Chapter

17

Chapter

Manipulating Data with PivotTables

In this chapter, you'll look at how you can manipulate the data in your worksheets to draw conclusions from it by creating PivotTables. PivotTables are great for asking questions of your data and looking at the data in different ways without having to enter it multiple times in separate worksheets.

You'll start by going over what PivotTables are and what you can do with them. After that, I'll show you how to create a PivotTable either by using Excel's automated tool, which can give you a jump-start by creating a recommended PivotTable that you can adjust as needed, or by placing the fields on the PivotTable framework manually, which gives you total control.

After you build a PivotTable, you may need to change it so that it shows different data or shows the same data differently. I'll show you several examples of the types of changes you can make easily to a PivotTable once you've constructed it.

When the PivotTable is arranged the way you need it, you can format the PivotTable and choose options to control how it appears. And you can sort and filter the data within the PivotTable to show only the information you're after.

Understanding What PivotTables Are and What You Can Do with Them

A PivotTable is a special kind of report that rearranges the fields and records in a table into a different order so that you can examine their relationships. You *pivot* (in other words, rotate) the columns in a PivotTable to display the data summarized in a different way.

© Guy Hart-Davis 2016

G. Hart-Davis, *Learn Office 2016 for Mac*, DOI 10.1007/978-1-4842-2002-3_17

For example, take a look at the worksheet shown in Figure 17-1. This worksheet contains a database table that tracks sales made by a company with four product lines: Hardware, Software, Services, and Supplies. The table uses the following columns:

- *Sale*: A unique sequential number used to identify each sale.

- *Year, Month, and Day*: The year, month, and day of the sale. Having these items in separate columns makes it easier to filter by time; for example, to compare one month against another or to see which salesperson sold what in January.

- *Salesperson*: The name of the sales rep who executed the sale.

- *Line*: The product line of the product sold.

- *Product*: The name of the product sold.

- *Quantity*: The quantity of the product sold.

Sale	Year	Month	Day	Salesperson	Line	Product	Quantity	Price	Total Price	Customer
BD10149	2015	January	2	Lee	Hardware	ThunderPC	2	$499.99	$999.98	Ocean Demographics
BD10150	2015	January	3	Gutierrez	Services	Setup	1	$199.99	$199.99	Novelty Appropriations
BD10151	2015	January	5	Dunne	Software	SmartTax	20	$44.99	$899.80	Industrial Disease Associat
BD10152	2015	January	7	Brenger	Supplies	Photo Paper	40	$8.99	$359.60	Helium Partners
BD10153	2015	January	9	Kim	Services	Malware removal	1	$59.99	$59.99	Planned Senescence Servic
BD10154	2015	January	11	Price	Services	Restore	4	$29.99	$119.96	Pinion Joiners
BD10155	2015	January	14	Lee	Hardware	BlitzScreen	10	$129.99	$1,299.90	Louisiana Jelly Company
BD10156	2015	January	15	Gutierrez	Software	SecureStream	1	$89.99	$89.99	Lost Angels Cleaning
BD10157	2015	January	16	Dunne	Supplies	Printer Paper	100	$3.99	$399.00	Self-Service Meditations
BD10158	2015	January	18	Brenger	Hardware	ThunderPC	3	$499.99	$1,499.97	Petrolia Milk Company
BD10159	2015	January	20	Kim	Services	Setup	3	$199.99	$599.97	Amalgamated Associates
BD10160	2015	January	21	Price	Software	SmartTax	5	$44.99	$224.95	Ocean Demographics
BD10161	2015	January	22	Lee	Supplies	Photo Paper	10	$8.99	$89.90	Novelty Appropriations
BD10162	2015	January	23	Gutierrez	Services	Malware removal	2	$59.99	$119.98	Industrial Disease Associat
BD10163	2015	January	24	Dunne	Services	Restore	2	$29.99	$59.98	Helium Partners
BD10164	2015	January	25	Brenger	Hardware	BlitzScreen	20	$129.99	$2,599.80	Planned Senescence Servic
BD10165	2015	January	26	Kim	Software	SecureStream	2	$89.99	$179.98	Pinion Joiners
BD10166	2015	January	27	Price	Supplies	Printer Paper	50	$3.99	$199.50	Louisiana Jelly Company
BD10167	2015	January	28	Lee	Hardware	ThunderPC	3	$499.99	$1,499.97	Lost Angels Cleaning
BD10168	2015	February	2	Gutierrez	Services	Setup	2	$199.99	$399.98	Self-Service Meditations
BD10169	2015	February	3	Dunne	Software	SmartTax	30	$44.99	$1,349.70	Petrolia Milk Company

Figure 17-1. The sample table you'll use for creating PivotTables in this chapter

- *Price*: The unit price of the product sold.

- *Total Price*: The total price of the products sold (Quantity multiplied by Price).

- *Customer*: The name of the company or organization that bought the products.

This is all straightforward. You can also easily see your sum total of sales (for example, by adding the figures in the Total Price column). But when you need to dig into the details, you need a different tool.

This is where PivotTables come in. By creating a PivotTable from a data table such as this, you can quickly find the answers to questions such as these:

- ■ Which is your best-selling product line? And your best-selling product?
- ■ How do this year's sales stack up against last year's?
- ■ Who was your star salesperson for March? And does another salesperson need a quick application of the spurs?
- ■ Who are your key customers? Who needs more one-on-one attention to bring sales up to where they were last year?

In the following sections, you'll put together a PivotTable with the data in the data table and then manipulate it to see what it shows.

> **Note**   If you want to work through the examples in this chapter, you need a database table like the one shown in the screens. You can either create one yourself or (much easier) download the sample workbook from the book's page on the Apress web site (www.apress.com).

Creating and Laying Out a PivotTable

You can create a PivotTable either from a database table or from a range of data. If you have a database table already, as in the example, you can create the PivotTable from that. Otherwise, create the database table you'll use, or enter the data in a worksheet as usual without creating a database table.

Once your data is ready, you can create a PivotTable either automatically, using the Recommended PivotTables command, or manually. Which works best depends on your data and what you're trying to do with it, but often you can save time by creating a PivotTable automatically and then adjusting it as necessary. If an automatic PivotTable turns out not to be what you need, you can create the PivotTable manually from scratch instead.

Creating a PivotTable Automatically

To create a PivotTable automatically, follow these steps:

1. Open the workbook and display the worksheet that contains the table or data you'll use in the PivotTable.

2. Click in the table that you'll use for the PivotTable. If you'll use a range rather than a named table, select the range.

3. Choose Insert ➤ Tables ➤ Recommended PivotTables from the Ribbon. Excel then does the following:

    ■ Inserts a new worksheet with a default name, such as Sheet5

    ■ Inserts an automatic PivotTable on that worksheet, using a recommended layout

    ■ Displays the PivotTable Builder window

    ■ Adds the PivotTable Analyze tab and the Design tab to the Ribbon, and displays the PivotTable Analyze tab

    ■ Displays some information about PivotTables the first time you create one

Figure 17-2 shows the automatic PivotTable produced from the sample data table, with the PivotTable Builder window positioned in front of the worksheet. You can move the PivotTable Builder window to outside the Excel window if you find that arrangement more convenient.

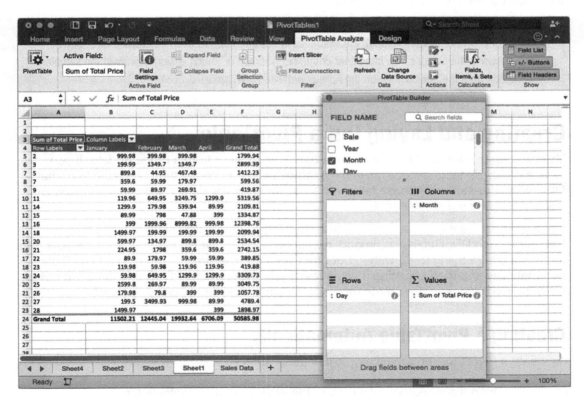

Figure 17-2. *The quickest way to create a PivotTable is to have Excel create a recommended PivotTable automatically. You will usually need to adjust the PivotTable using the PivotTable Builder window to make the PivotTable show the information you want. Depending on the data you're using, the PivotTable may look substantially different from this one*

After creating a PivotTable automatically, you'll normally need to adjust it. This is because Excel seldom guesses exactly which information you need where.

To adjust a PivotTable, use the techniques you'll learn in the next section, which shows you how to build a PivotTable from scratch.

Creating a PivotTable Manually

If creating a recommended PivotTable automatically doesn't give a useful result or if you prefer to do things by hand, you can build the PivotTable manually using the PivotTable Builder.

To create a PivotTable manually, follow these steps:

1. Open the workbook, and display the worksheet that contains the table or data you'll use in the PivotTable.

2. Click in the table that you'll use for the PivotTable. If you'll use a range rather than a named table, select the range.

3. Choose Insert ➤ Tables ➤ PivotTable from the Ribbon or Data ➤ Summarize with PivotTable from the menu bar to display the Create PivotTable dialog box (see Figure 17-3). If you're using a named table, you can also choose Table ➤ Tools ➤ Summarize with PivotTable from the Ribbon; if you're using a range, this command isn't available.

Figure 17-3. In the Create PivotTable dialog box, first choose the table or range of data from which to create the PivotTable. Then choose whether to put the PivotTable on a new worksheet or on an existing worksheet

4. In the "Choose the data that you want to analyze" area at the top of the Create PivotTable dialog box, click the Select a table or a range option button.

Note   Instead of creating a PivotTable from data in a worksheet, you can create a PivotTable from an external data source such as a FileMaker database or Access database. To do so, you select the "Use an external data source" option button in the "Choose the data that you want to analyze" area of the Create PivotTable dialog box, click the Choose Connection button, and then select the data source. Before you can do this, you must install an Open Database Connectivity (ODBC) driver to enable Excel to connect to the data source. To find a suitable driver, search online including the terms *Excel 2016*, *ODBC driver*, and the type of database you need to connect to.

5.   Make sure the Table/Range text box in the "Choose the data that you want to analyze" area shows the table or range you want to use. If you click in the table or select the range in step 2, you'll be all set. If not, type in the table name or click and drag in the worksheet to select the range. If necessary, click the Collapse Dialog button first to get the Create PivotTable dialog box out of the way first.

6.   In the "Choose where to place the PivotTable" area of the Create PivotTable dialog box, choose the appropriate option button:

   ■ *New worksheet*: Select this option button if you want to place the PivotTable on a new worksheet. This is often clearest because it gives you plenty of room for the PivotTable.

   ■ *Existing worksheet*: Select this option button if you want to place the PivotTable on an existing worksheet. Then click in the Table/Range text box, click the worksheet's tab, and then click-drag in the worksheet to enter the location. Again, you can click the Collapse Dialog button to collapse the Create PivotTable dialog box if necessary.

7.   Click the OK button to close the Create PivotTable dialog box. Excel positions a PivotTable framework on a new worksheet or the existing worksheet you chose and displays the PivotTable Builder window. Figure 17-4 shows the PivotTable framework on a new worksheet named Sheet5.

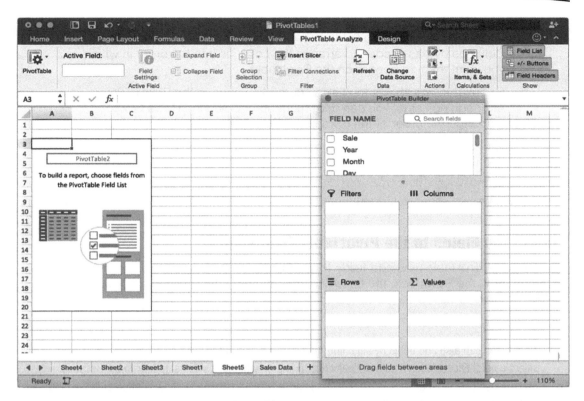

Figure 17-4. When you insert a PivotTable manually, Excel creates an empty framework on which you lay out the PivotTable the way you need it

Now that you've inserted the framework for the PivotTable, you can add fields to it from the Field name list box in the PivotTable Builder window.

Understanding the Contents of the PivotTable Builder Window

Take a moment to look at the PivotTable Builder window. You use this window to set up the fields for your PivotTable. As you do so, Excel adds the fields to the appropriate places on the PivotTable framework.

Here are the essentials you need to know:

- *Field name list box*: This list box in the PivotTable Builder window contains an entry for each of the fields that Excel found in the data table or range you chose. Each item in the list has a check box that you can select to add the field to the PivotTable or clear to remove the field from the PivotTable.

- *Filters*: This box shows the filters you apply to the PivotTable. After applying filters, you can drag them into a different order if necessary.

- *Columns*: This box shows the fields you add as columns to the PivotTable. After adding fields, you can drag them up and down the Columns box as needed to arrange the columns into the order in which you want them to appear on the PivotTable.

- *Rows*: This box shows the fields you add as rows to the PivotTable. After adding fields, you can drag them up or down the Rows box to rearrange the order of the rows in the PivotTable.

- *Values*: This box contains the fields you add as values to the PivotTable and the fields that Excel adds automatically. You can drag the fields up or down the Values box to change their order as needed.

If this doesn't make sense yet, don't worry: you'll see how PivotTables work in just a moment.

Adding the Fields to the PivotTable Framework

To create the PivotTable, you add fields to the PivotTable framework by dragging fields to the Filters box, the Rows box, the Columns box, and the Values box in the PivotTable Builder window.

> **Note**   You can also add fields by selecting their check boxes in the Field name list box. When you select a field, Excel places it automatically depending on what its contents appear to be. Because Excel doesn't know what your data represents and what you're trying to show, it often puts the field in the wrong place. So it's usually best to place the fields yourself by dragging them.

Which fields you need to drag where depends on your data source and what you're trying to make it show. Here's a walk-through using the fields in the data source. If you're using the sample data source, your results should look similar; if your data source is different, they'll look different, but the PivotTable will work in much the same way.

1. In the Field name list box in the PivotTable Builder window, click the Year field and drag it to the Filters box. Excel selects the Year check box, enters Year in cell A2, and creates a pop-up menu for selecting the years in cell B2 (see Figure 17-5).

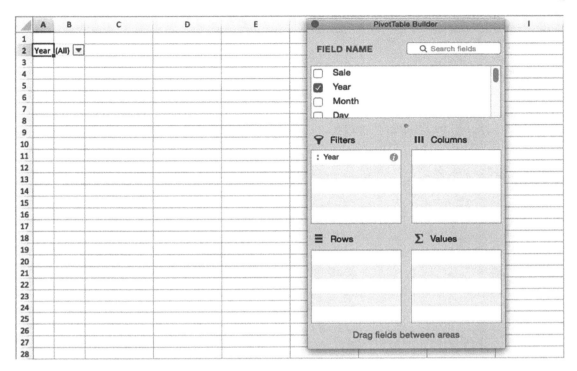

Figure 17-5. Drag the Year button from the Field name box in the PivotTable Builder window to the Filters box to create the Year pop-up menu shown in cell B2 here. Excel selects the (All) item in the pop-up menu at first, making the PivotTable show all the years

2. In the Field Name list box, click the Salesperson field and drag it to the Rows box. Excel selects the Salesperson check box and creates a row label for each salesperson's name (see Figure 17-6).

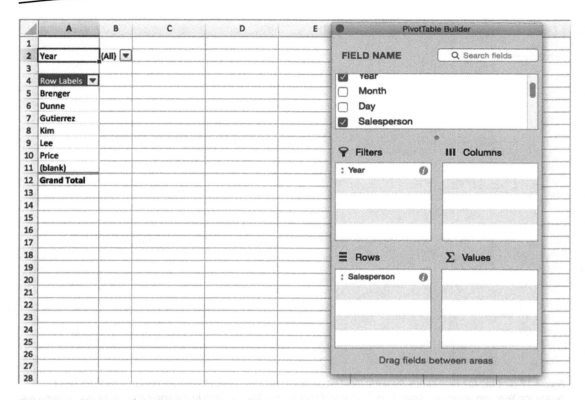

Figure 17-6. Moving the Salesperson button to the Rows box makes Excel create a row label from each salesperson's name

3.   Drag the Line field from the Field name list box in the PivotTable
      Builder window to the Columns box. Excel selects the Line check
      box in the Field name list box and adds the product lines as column
      labels (see Figure 17-7).

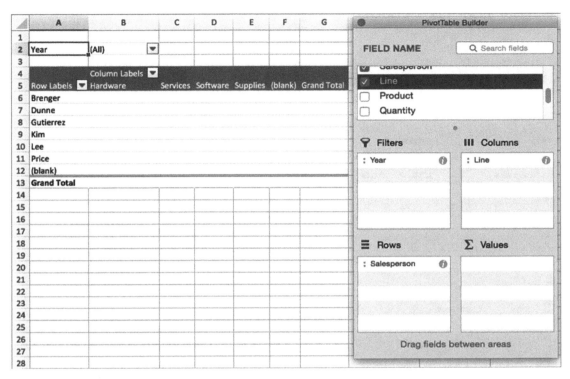

Figure 17-7. Drag the Line item from the Field name list box in the PivotTable Builder window to the Columns box. Excel adds the product lines as column labels and selects the Line check box for you

4. Now click the Total Price field in the Field name list box, and drag it to the Values box in the PivotTable Builder window. Excel adds to the PivotTable the values of the items the salespeople sold (see Figure 17-8).

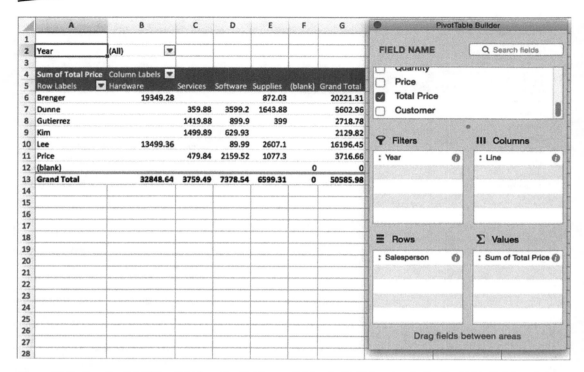

Figure 17-8. Drag the Total Price field from the Field name list box to the Values box in the PivotTable Builder window to add the totals of each salesperson's sales to the PivotTable

This gives you a PivotTable that shows how much of each product line each salesperson sold. At first, the PivotTable shows (All) in the Year pop-up menu in cell B2; to see a breakdown by a year, open the Year pop-up menu, and click the year you want.

This is useful—but it's just the start of what you can do with the PivotTable.

Changing the PivotTable to Show Different Data

The great thing about PivotTables is how easy they are to change to show different data. You can change a PivotTable by adding different fields to it, removing fields it's currently using, or rearranging the fields among the Filters box, the Columns box, the Rows box, and the Values box in the PivotTable Builder window.

> **Note**   If the PivotTable Builder window is not displayed, choose PivotTable Analyze ➤ Show ➤ Field List from the Ribbon to display it.

Here are four examples of how you can change the basic PivotTable created earlier in this chapter. These examples work as a sequence so you need to make each change in turn if you want to work through them.

■ In the Field name list box, click the Product field, and drag it to the Rows box in the PivotTable Builder window. Excel adds a list of the product names of the products each salesperson has sold (see Figure 17-9).

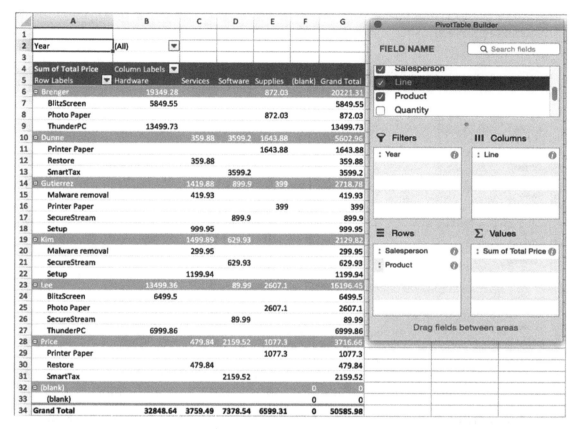

Figure 17-9. Drag the Product field to the Rows box in the PivotTable Builder window to add a list of the products each salesperson has sold. You can collapse any list by clicking the collapse button to the left of the salesperson's name

- In the Rows box in the PivotTable Builder window, drag the Salesperson field below the Product field. The PivotTable then shows each product with a collapsible list of the salespeople who have been selling it (see Figure 17-10).

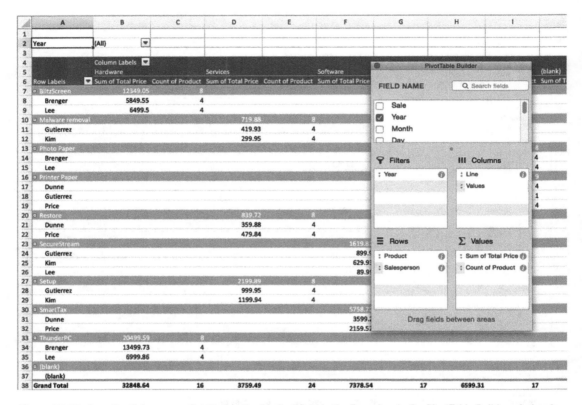

Figure 17-10. *Drag the Salesperson field below the Product field in the Rows box in the PivotTable Builder window to produce a list of products showing the salespeople who have been selling them*

- Drag the Product field from the Rows box in the PivotTable Builder window to the Columns box. Then drag the Line field from the Columns box outside the PivotTable Builder window and drop it, making it disappear from the PivotTable. (You can also clear the Line check box in the Field name list box.) These changes produce a PivotTable showing the salespeople by row and what they've sold of the products in columns (see Figure 17-11).

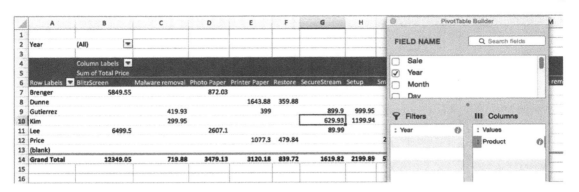

Figure 17-11. Removing the product lines and making column labels of the products produces this PivotTable that shows how much each salesperson has sold of each product

- Make the following changes to see which of your product lines each of your customers bought in a specific period:

  - Drag the Month field from the Field name list box in the PivotTable Builder window to the Filters box, placing it below the Year field. The Month label appears in the cell below the Year label, and the Month pop-up menu appears in the cell below the Year pop-up menu. You can now filter by month as well as by field. For example, you can choose 2015 as the Year filter and then choose January as the Month filter to see only your January 2015 results.

  - In the Field name list box, clear the Salesperson check box to remove the Salesperson field from the Row Labels area. Then drag the Customer field from the Field name list box to the Rows box instead, making the PivotTable show one customer in each row.

  - In the Field name list box, clear the Product check box to remove the Product field from the Column Labels area. Then drag the Line field to the Columns box to make the PivotTable show the product lines in the columns. Figure 17-12 shows the resulting PivotTable.

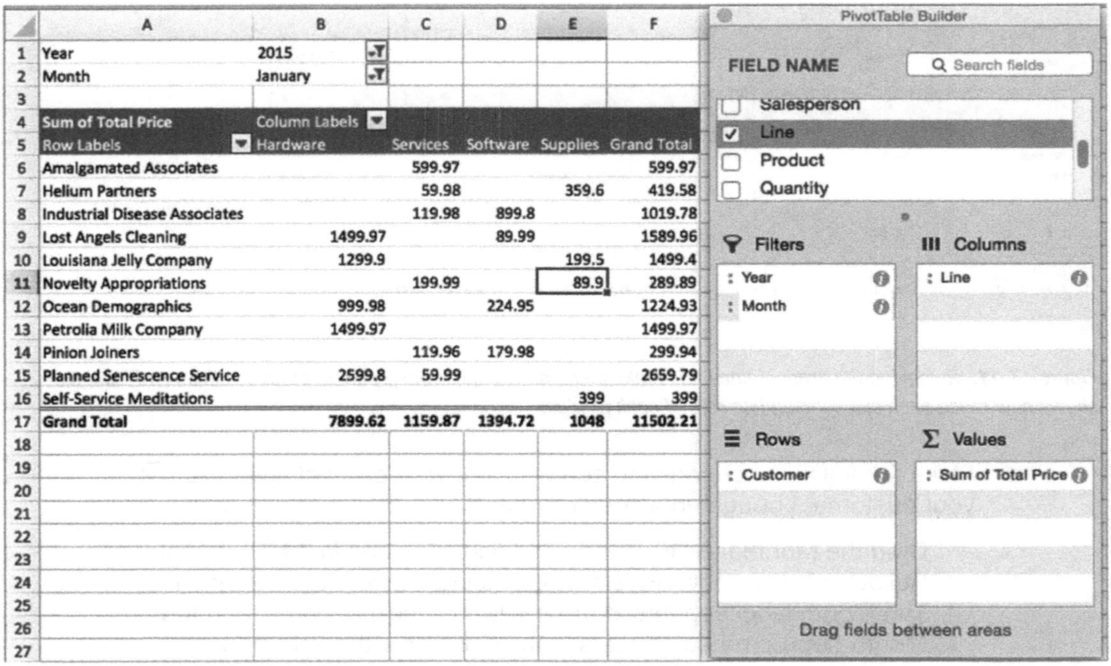

Figure 17-12. You can add the Month field to the Filters box, putting it below the Year field, to filter your PivotTable by first the year (here, 2015) and then the month (here, January). This PivotTable shows how much customers bought from each product line in January 2015

When you've finished working with the PivotTable Builder window, you can close it by clicking the red Close button at the left end of its title bar.

If you need to open the PivotTable Builder window again, choose PivotTable Analyze ➤ Show ➤ Field List from the Ribbon.

Changing the Function Used to Summarize a Field

When you add values to a PivotTable, Excel tries to automatically use the right function for the calculation that type of data needs. For example, when you add a field that shows prices, Excel uses the SUM() function on the assumption that you want to add the values. And if you use nonnumeric data such as names, Excel uses the COUNT() function, giving you the number of different items.

If you need to change a field to a different function, follow these steps:

1.   Click the field or click a cell containing data that the field produces.

> **Tip**   You can also open the PivotTable Field dialog box for a field by clicking the i button to the right of the field's name in the PivotTable Builder window.

2. Choose PivotTable Analyze ➤ Active Field ➤ Field Settings from the Ribbon to display the PivotTable Field dialog box. The main part of this dialog box contains two tabs, the Summarize by tab (shown on the left in Figure 17-13) and the Show data as tab (shown on the right in Figure 17-13). The Summarize by tab is selected at first.

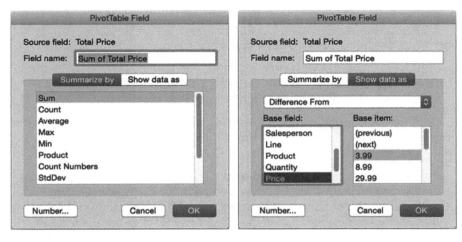

Figure 17-13. In the PivotTable Field dialog box, use the Summarize by tab (left) to change the formula used to summarize the field's data. Use the Show data as tab (right) to change the way the data appears

3. In the list box on the Summarize by tab, click the function you want to use. For example, click the Average function if you want the field to show an average instead of a sum. Excel automatically changes the contents of the Field Name text box to reflect the function you chose; for example, changing the text from Sum of Total Price to Average of Total Price.

4. If you need to present the data in a different format (for example, as the amount of difference from a base value), click the Show data as tab in the PivotTable Field dialog box to display the tab's controls (see the right screen in Figure 17-13). Click the pop-up menu, and then choose the format you want, such as Difference From. Then select the base field in the Base field list box and the base item in the Base item list box.

5. If you want to change the field name, type the change in the Field Name text box.

6. Click the OK button to close the PivotTable Field dialog box.

Controlling the Design of a PivotTable

After setting up the framework for your PivotTable, you can use the tools in the Layout group on the Design tab of the Ribbon to choose where to display subtotals and grand totals, choose among the PivotTable layouts that Excel offers, and decide whether to insert blank rows between items to make the PivotTable more readable. The Design tab appears on the Ribbon when a PivotTable is active, so if you're not seeing the Design tab, click in your PivotTable.

The Design group contains four pop-up menus:

- *Subtotals*: Open this pop-up menu and then specify how to place the subtotals by clicking Show All Subtotals at Bottom of Group, Show All Subtotals at Top of Group, or Don't Show Subtotals.

- *Grand totals*: Open this pop-up menu and then specify how to place the grand totals by clicking On for Rows & Columns, On for Rows Only, On for Columns Only, or Off for Rows & Columns.

- *Report layout*: Open this pop-up menu, and then first choose the layout form you want by clicking Show in Compact Form, Show in Outline Form, or Show in Tabular Form on the upper part of the menu. Figure 17-14 shows the three layouts. Open the Report Layout pop-up menu again, and then click Repeat All Item Labels if you want to repeat item labels or click Don't Repeat Item Labels if you don't want to repeat them.

- *Blank rows*: Open this pop-up menu and specify whether to insert blank rows by clicking Insert Blank Line After Each Item or Remove Blank Line After Each Item.

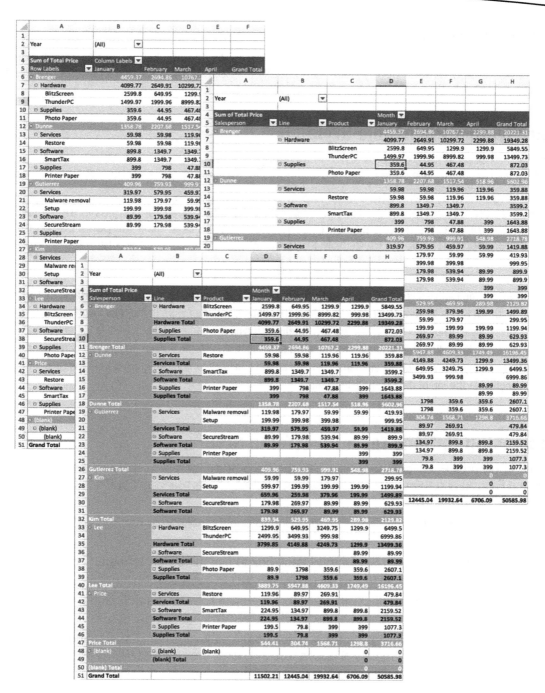

Figure 17-14. *You can choose among three layout forms for your PivotTables. Compact Form (left) is good for presenting data in a small space. Outline Form (right) and Tabular Form (bottom) take up more space but make the data easier to read*

Formatting a PivotTable

To make a PivotTable look good and convey its contents effectively, you can format it. You can apply the formatting at any point, but usually it's best to lay out the framework and fields of the PivotTable first so that you have a fair idea of how it will appear.

Applying a PivotTable Style

As you've seen in the examples so far in this chapter, Excel applies a style to a PivotTable when you create it. The style helps you distinguish the different areas of the PivotTable visually.

To change the way a PivotTable looks, apply a different style to it from the PivotTable Styles group on the Design tab of the Ribbon. You can either click one of the styles in the Quick Styles box or hold the mouse pointer over the Quick Styles box, click the panel button that appears, and then click the PivotTable style you want to the Quick Styles panel.

Note   You can also create your own PivotTable styles. To do so, choose Design ➤ PivotTable Styles ➤ Quick Styles ➤ New PivotTable Style from the Ribbon, and then work in the New PivotTable Quick Style dialog box that Excel displays. Briefly, you type the name for the new style in the Name text box, then click an element in the Table element list box, click the Format button, and choose the formatting you want for the element. After you create a new style, you can apply it from the Custom section at the top of the Quick Styles panel.

Choosing Options for a PivotTable Style

After applying a PivotTable style, you can choose options for it by displaying the Design tab on the Ribbon and then selecting or clearing the four check boxes in the PivotTable Style Options group:

- *Row headers*: Select this check box to use the style's formatting on the row headers.
- *Column headers*: Select this check box to use the style's formatting on the column headers.
- *Banded rows*: Select this check box to make lines or shaded bands (depending on the style) appear along the rows.
- *Banded columns*: Select this check box to make lines or shaded bands (depending on the style) appear up and down the columns.

Naming a PivotTable and Setting Options for It

When you insert a PivotTable, Excel gives it a default name (such as PivotTable1 or PivotTable2) and sets default display options, layout options, and data options. The PivotTable's name appears in the PivotTable Name box in the PivotTable group at the left end of the PivotTable Analyze tab of the Ribbon when the Excel window is moderately wide; when the window is narrower, Excel collapses the PivotTable group into a PivotTable button that you can click to display the group's contents on a pop-up panel.

To rename the PivotTable, go to the PivotTable group if the Excel window is wide enough, or click the PivotTable button if the window is not. Type the new name in the PivotTable Name text box, and then press Return. PivotTable names can include spaces, so you can make them descriptive and readable.

For an alternative way to rename the PivotTable, or to choose different options, choose PivotTable Analyze ➤ PivotTable ➤ Options from the Ribbon to display the PivotTable Options dialog box, and then work with its controls.

Note   When you create a PivotTable on its own worksheet, you should rename the worksheet from its default name (for example, Sheet5) to a descriptive name (for example, Sales PivotTable). Double-click the current name on the worksheet tab, type the new name, and then press Return to apply it.

Figure 17-15 shows the PivotTable Options dialog box with its Display tab at the front.

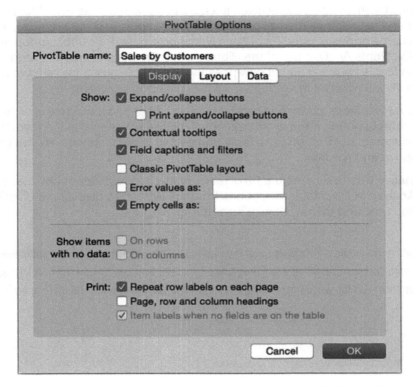

Figure 17-15. *On the Display tab of the PivotTable Options dialog box, choose whether to show items such as expand/collapse triangles and ScreenTips on the PivotTable and whether to print headings and row labels*

Choosing Display Options for a PivotTable

To control how Excel displays a PivotTable, click the Display tab in the PivotTable Options dialog box to display its controls (shown in Figure 17-15), and then choose the options you want.

These are the options you can choose in the Show area:

- *Expand/collapse buttons*: Select this check box if you want to display the expand/collapse buttons you click to expand or collapse row labels or column labels. Usually it's useful to display these expand/collapse buttons, but you can clear this check box if you want to hide them to prevent others from changing the display of a PivotTable.

- *Print expand/collapse buttons*: Select this check box if you want to print the expand/collapse buttons on printouts of the PivotTables. Printing the expand/collapse buttons is often useful for PivotTables you print for your own consumption, but you may prefer not to print the buttons on printouts you produce for other people.

■ *Contextual tooltips*: Select this check box if you want the PivotTable to display tooltips for fields and for values when you hold the mouse pointer over a cell. This option is usually helpful.

Note   Tooltips are the little pop-up messages that appear when you hold the pointer over an item. Many people still refer to tooltips as ScreenTips, which is the name that Microsoft used to use for them.

■ *Field captions and filters*: Select this check box if you want captions to appear at the top of the PivotTable and filter pop-up buttons on column labels and row labels. These are usually helpful.

■ *Classic PivotTable layout*: Select this check box if you want to use the "classic" (in other words, older) style of PivotTable layout, which displays row labels separately from their totals. The classic layout takes up a little more space, but many people find it easier to read.

■ *Error values as*: If you want to display standard text in cells that contain errors rather than displaying error messages, select this check box and type the text in the text box.

■ *Empty cells as*: If you want to display standard text in empty cells instead of having them simply be empty, select this check box and type the text in the text box.

The "Show items with no data" area contains two settings that are available only for PivotTables that use an OLAP (Online Analytical Processing) data source:

■ *On rows*: Select this check box to display row items that have no values.

■ *On columns*: Select this check box to display column items that have no values.

The Print area contains three options for controlling which items print along with the PivotTable:

■ *Repeat row labels on each page*: Select this check box to make Excel print the row labels on each page the PivotTable occupies rather than just on the first page. Repeating the row labels makes the PivotTable easier to read so it's usually a good idea.

■ *Page, row, and column headings*: Select this check box to repeat the page headings, row headings, and column headings. This too is usually helpful.

■ *Item labels when no fields are on the table*: This check box is normally selected but dimmed and unavailable because it applies only to PivotTables created in Excel 2004 (Mac), Excel 2003 (Windows), or earlier versions of Excel. If the check box is available, selecting it makes the PivotTable display item labels even when the Value Area contains no fields.

Choosing Layout Options for a PivotTable

To control the layout of a PivotTable, click the Layout tab in the PivotTable Options dialog box to display its controls (see Figure 17-16) and then choose the settings you want.

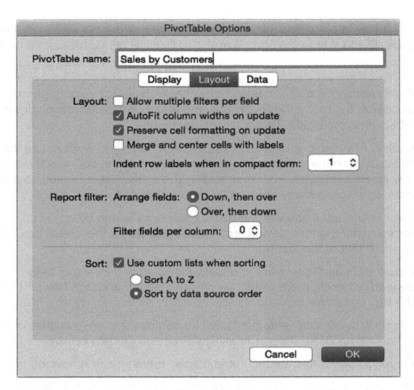

Figure 17-16. On the Layout tab of the PivotTable Options dialog box, you can set options for the layout, for the report filter, and for sorting

These are the settings you can choose in the Layout area of the Layout tab:

- *Allow multiple filters per field*: Select this check box if you want to be able to filter the PivotTable by two or more filters on a single field rather than by just one filter.

- *AutoFit column widths on update*: Select this check box to make Excel automatically resize the column widths to accommodate the data with which you've refreshed the PivotTable. AutoFit is usually helpful.

- *Preserve cell formatting on update*: Select this check box to make Excel retain cell formatting you've applied directly to cells when you update the information in the PivotTable. This option too is usually helpful.

- *Merge and center cells with labels*: Select this check box if you want Excel to merge a label cell with a blank cell next to it and center the label across the cells. Try this look to see whether you prefer it to the regular look.

- *Indent row labels when in compact form*: In this pop-up menu, choose the number of spaces by which you want to indent row labels when using the Compact Layout for a PivotTable.

These are the settings you can choose in the Report filter area of the Layout tab:

- *Arrange fields option buttons*: Select the "Down, then over" option button to have Excel arrange the fields downward first and then across to the right. Select the "Over, then down" option button if you prefer to arrange the fields first to the right and then downward.

- *Filter fields per column*: In this pop-up menu, choose the number of fields to display in the report filter before moving to another column or row.

These are the settings you can choose in the Sort area of the Layout tab:

- *Use custom lists when sorting*: Select this check box if you want Excel to sort by your custom AutoFill lists when it encounters the data in them. For example, if you've created a custom list of your company's offices, select this check box to make Excel sort the PivotTable by the order in that list rather than in ascending order or another standard sort order.

- *Sort A to Z*: Select this option button if you want to sort in ascending order. The alternative is the "Sort by data source order" option button.

- *Sort by data source order*: Select this option button if you want to sort the PivotTable in the same order as the data source. This is the default setting and is useful if you've laid out the data source in your preferred order. If not, select the Sort A to Z option button instead.

Choosing Data Options for a PivotTable

The Data tab of the PivotTable Options dialog box (see Figure 17-17) lets you control how Excel stores the PivotTable's data from an external connection and whether Excel refreshes the data automatically. For a PivotTable connected to an external data source, you can also choose whether to save the connection password with the Excel workbook and whether to run queries in the background.

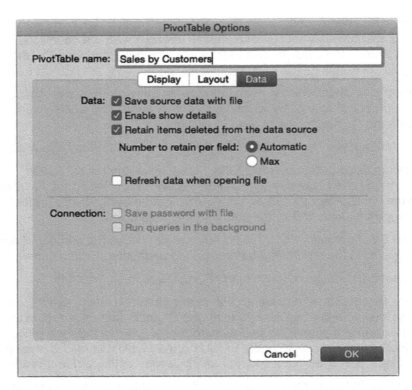

Figure 17-17. *On the Data tab of the PivotTable Options dialog box, choose how to handle the PivotTable's data and connection*

In the Data area of the Data tab, you can choose the following options:

■ *Save source data with file*: Select this check box if you want to store the source data from an external data source in the workbook that contains the PivotTable. This setting has no effect on a PivotTable that contains data drawn from its own workbook because that workbook contains the data already.

■ *Enable show details*: Select this check box if you want to be able to drill down in the PivotTable to show details from the data source.

■ *Retain items deleted from the data source*: Select this check box if you want Excel to store data that has been deleted from the data source. Storing the data is useful if you are working with older data in a data source that's being updated.

■ *Number to retain per field*: These controls are available if you selected the "Retain items deleted from the data source" check box. Select the Automatic option button to have Excel store the default number of items for each field of data. Select the Max option button to store as many items as possible for each field of data.

■ *Refresh data when opening file*: Select this check box if you want Excel to automatically refresh the data in the PivotTable when you open the workbook. Automatic refreshing is useful when you need to make sure you're working with the latest figures.

In the Connection area, you can choose these two options for a PivotTable that connects to external data:

■ *Save password with file*: Select this check box to save the connection's password in the workbook. Saving the password means you don't need to enter it manually on each refresh so you should do this, unless security dictates otherwise.

■ *Run queries in the background*: Select this check box to run queries in the background rather than in the foreground. Running queries in the background typically makes the queries take longer but allows Excel to remain more responsive while a query is running.

When you've finished choosing options in the PivotTable Options dialog box, click the OK button to close the dialog box.

Refreshing the Data in a PivotTable

Even when you create a PivotTable from a data source in the same workbook, the data in a PivotTable remains static rather than updating automatically the way most other Excel objects do. When you want to make sure your PivotTable contains the latest data from the data source, choose PivotTable Analyze ➤ Data ➤ Refresh from the Ribbon, clicking the main part of the Refresh button. To refresh all the PivotTables in a workbook, choose PivotTable Analyze ➤ Data ➤ Refresh ➤ Refresh All from the Ribbon.

If your PivotTable uses an external data source, and you find the refresh operation is taking too long, choose PivotTable Analyze ➤ Data ➤ Refresh ➤ Cancel Refresh to cancel the operation.

Changing the Source of a PivotTable

Sometimes, after building a PivotTable, you may find you need to change its source data. You can do this without deleting the PivotTable and starting again, which is good news.

To change the source data of a PivotTable, follow these steps:

1. From the Ribbon, choose PivotTable Analyze ➤ Data ➤ Change Data Source to display the Change PivotTable Data Source dialog box (see Figure 17-18).

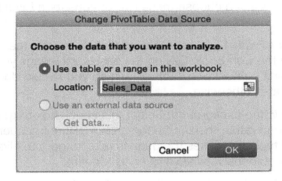

Figure 17-18. Use the Change PivotTable Data Source dialog box when you need to switch the PivotTable to a different data source

2. In the Location text box, enter the range you want to use instead of the current range. You can type in a table name or a range name; type in a range reference; or click the Collapse Dialog button, select the range in the worksheet, and then click the Collapse Dialog button again.

3. Click the OK button to close the Change PivotTable Data Source dialog box. Excel updates the PivotTable with data from the new data source.

Sorting and Filtering a PivotTable

To make a PivotTable show the data you require, you may need to sort it or filter it.

To sort a PivotTable, click the pop-up button on the field by which you want to sort. Excel displays the sorting and filtering window for that field. The window bears the field's name, as you can see in Figure 17-19, which shows the sorting and filtering window for the Product field. You can then click the Ascending button to produce an ascending sort (from A to Z, from small numbers to large numbers, and from early dates and times to later ones) or the Descending button to produce a descending sort (the opposite).

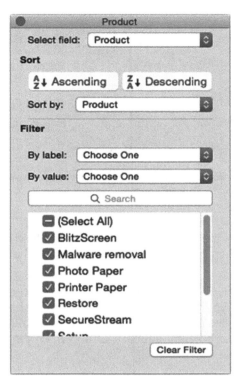

Figure 17-19. To sort or filter a PivotTable, open the sorting and filtering window for the field, and then choose options in the Sort area or the Filter area. The sorting and filtering window's title bar shows the field's name (here, Product)

Note   To control how Excel sorts a PivotTable, choose sorting options in the Sort area of the Layout tab of the PivotTable Options dialog box, as discussed earlier in this chapter.

When you apply sorting to a field, the field name pop-up button changes to show an arrow indicating the direction of the sort. For example, in Figure 17-20, you can see an upward arrow indicating a descending sort on the Salesperson field and a downward arrow indicating an ascending sort on the Product field and the Line field. The Month field shows the regular pop-up button.

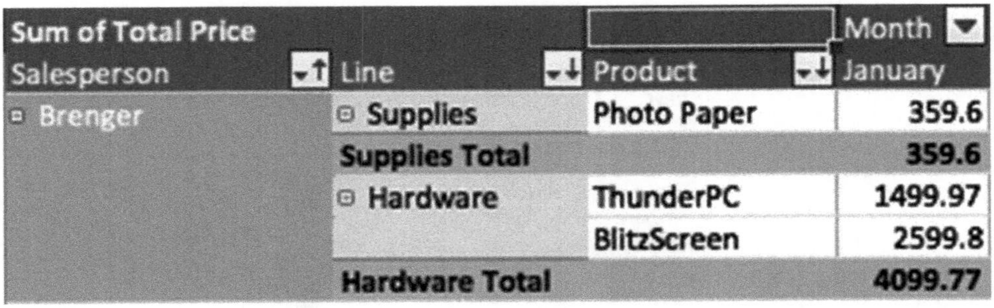

Sum of Total Price				Month ▼
Salesperson ▼↑	Line ▼↓	Product ▼↓		January
▫ Brenger	⊡ Supplies	Photo Paper		359.6
	Supplies Total			359.6
	⊡ Hardware	ThunderPC		1499.97
		BlitzScreen		2599.8
	Hardware Total			4099.77

Figure 17-20. When you sort a PivotTable, the field's pop-up button shows an upward arrow for a descending sort (as on the Salesperson field here) or a downward arrow for an ascending sort (as on the Product field and the Line field here)

To filter the PivotTable, click the pop-up button next to the field's name to display the sorting and filtering window, and then choose the filtering criteria in the Filter area. Here are some examples:

- *Filter by label*: To filter by label, open the By label pop-up menu, choose the comparison type, and then specify the data required. For example, choose the Contains comparison to find labels that match the text string you type in the text box that appears, as shown on the left in Figure 17-21.

Figure 17-21. You can filter a field by its label (as shown on the left here) or by its value (as shown on the right). You can also search in the Search box or clear the check boxes of items you want to exclude

■ *Filter by value*: To filter by value, open the By value pop-up menu, and choose the comparison you want. For example, choose the Top 10 item to create a top-however-many-you-choose filter, and then set the number of items in the left of the two pop-up menus that appears below the By value pop-up menu when it's showing Top 10 (see the right screen in Figure 17-21). In the right of the two pop-up menus, choose Item, Percentage, or Sum as needed for the filtering.

■ *Filter by individual values*: To filter by individual values, clear the (Select All) check box in the lower part of the Filter area, and then select the check box for each item you want to use in the filter. To find only particular items so that you can select or clear their check boxes, click in the Search box, and type the search term.

When you apply a filter, the field's pop-up button displays a funnel-like filter symbol, as you can see on the Price field in Figure 17-22.

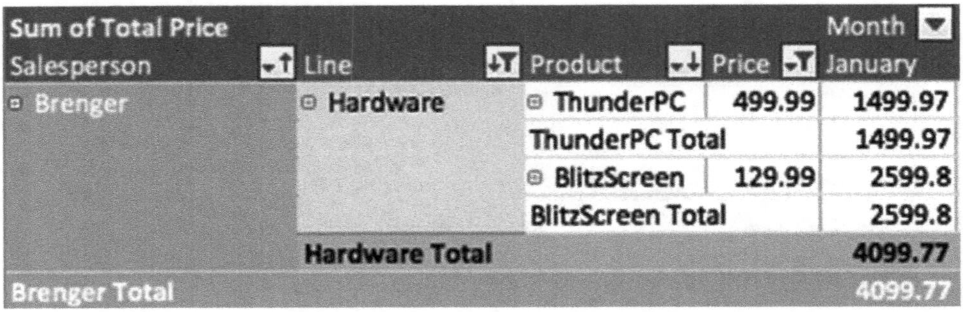

Sum of Total Price				Month ▼
Salesperson 🔽	Line 🔽	Product 🔽	Price 🔽	January
⊟ Brenger	⊟ Hardware	⊟ ThunderPC	499.99	1499.97
		ThunderPC Total		1499.97
		⊟ BlitzScreen	129.99	2599.8
		BlitzScreen Total		2599.8
	Hardware Total			4099.77
Brenger Total				4099.77

Figure 17-22. Excel displays a funnel-like filter on a field's pop-up button to indicate that you've applied filtering to that field

To remove filtering, open the sorting and filtering window again, and then click the Clear Filter button at the bottom.

Summary

In this chapter, you learned what PivotTables are and how to create them from your existing tables or other data sources. You know how to start a PivotTable automatically or build it manually, how to rearrange its fields to change the information it displays and the way it displays the information, and how to design and format the PivotTable. Lastly, you learned how to sort and filter PivotTables to make them show the information you need.

This is the end of the book's coverage of Excel. In the next part of the book, I'll show you how to make the most of PowerPoint.

Part 4

Creating Presentations with Microsoft PowerPoint

In this part of the book, you'll learn how to create compelling presentations using Microsoft PowerPoint and either present them live to an audience or deliver them across the Internet.

In Chapter 18, you'll create a presentation document using either a design template or a content template. You'll then learn how to add, delete, and rearrange slides; how to use PowerPoint's views effectively; how to develop the outline of a presentation; and how to break a presentation into separate sections. You'll also gain the skill of collaborating with your colleagues on creating a presentation.

In Chapter 19, you'll learn how to create slides that convey your meaning clearly and powerfully. You'll plan your presentation, choose suitable slide layouts (or create a custom layout), and add text and other content to your slides.

In Chapter 20, you'll bring your presentation to life by adding graphics, movies, sounds, animations, and transitions. You'll learn how to hide slides to keep them up your sleeve and how to build custom slide shows that enable you to show only part of a larger presentation.

In Chapter 21, you'll master how to deliver the presentation you've created. You can deliver the presentation live in person or create a version of the presentation that you can share via e-mail or in other ways. You'll also learn how to use PowerPoint's Presenter view and how to create a handout for a presentation.

Chapter **18**

Starting to Build a Presentation in PowerPoint

In this chapter, you'll learn how to start building a presentation in PowerPoint.

Your first move is to create the presentation document. PowerPoint gives you a wide range of choices, from colorful design themes to sample templates with content that can give your presentation a kick start. You can change the look, colors, or fonts if you don't like what you have, and you can also customize the slide size and orientation if necessary.

Once you've created the presentation, you add slides to it or customize the sample slides that it contains. A PowerPoint presentation consists of a series of slides that you normally play from start to finish. Each slide can contain any of a wide variety of different types of content, from text titles and bullet points through charts, diagrams, and even movies. You'll look at how to add straightforward content in this chapter and how to add more entertaining content types in the next two chapters.

After making sure you know how to add, delete, and rearrange slides, I'll show you how to use PowerPoint's views to work efficiently on a presentation, how to develop the outline of a presentation quickly, and how to organize a presentation's slides into different sections for convenience. Last, I'll show you how to collaborate with your colleagues on creating a presentation in PowerPoint.

> **Note**   To follow the Ribbon commands easily, please display the group titles on the Ribbon. To do so, choose PowerPoint ➤ Preferences from the menu bar. In the PowerPoint Preferences window, click View to display the View pane. In the Ribbon area, select the Show group titles check box, and then close the PowerPoint Preferences window by clicking the Close button (the red button at the left end of the window's title bar).

© Guy Hart-Davis 2016
G. Hart-Davis, *Learn Office 2016 for Mac*, DOI 10.1007/978-1-4842-2002-3_18

Creating a Presentation

To create a new presentation, you use the New tab of the Microsoft PowerPoint Gallery dialog box (see Figure 18-1). PowerPoint opens this dialog box automatically when you launch the app (unless you've set PowerPoint not to do this), but you can also open it at any time by choosing File ➤ New from Template from the menu bar or pressing Cmd+Shift+P.

> **Note**   A presentation template includes sample content that you can use as the basis of your presentation. A presentation theme is a coordinated look for the slides in a presentation but does not contain sample content.

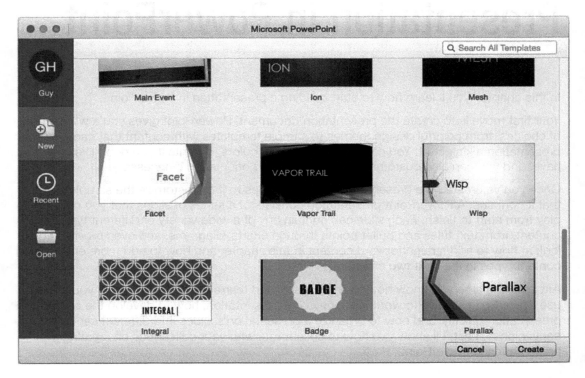

Figure 18-1.   From the Microsoft PowerPoint Gallery dialog box, you can create a blank presentation or a presentation based on a presentation design. You can also search for templates on your Mac or online

> **Note**   If you need to base a new presentation on an existing presentation, click the Recent tab or the Open tab of the Microsoft PowerPoint Gallery dialog box. Select the presentation and click the Open button, and then use the File ➤ Save As command to save a copy of the presentation under a different name, in a different folder, or both.

Changing a Presentation's Theme, Fonts, or Colors

You can change the look of the presentation by applying a different theme to it. A *theme* is an overall look for a presentation, including a slide background design, a set of colors, and a set of fonts.

To change the theme, click the Design tab of the Ribbon, and then use the controls in the Themes group. Click one of the themes displayed in the Themes box or hold the pointer over the Themes box to display the panel button, click the panel button, and then click the theme on the Themes panel (see Figure 18-2).

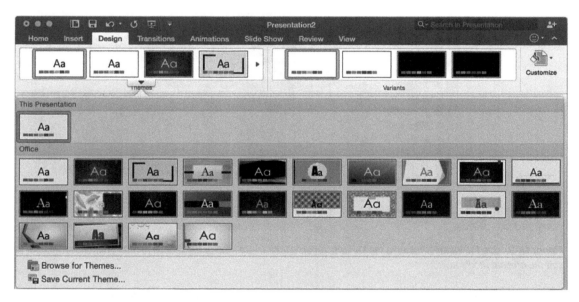

Figure 18-2. Use the Themes panel in the Themes group on the Design tab of the Ribbon to quickly change your presentation's theme

When you've applied the theme you want, choose Design ➤ Variants ➤ Variants from the Ribbon to display the Variants panel (see Figure 18-3). From here, you can make any changes needed to the theme:

Figure 18-3. Use the Variants panel in the Variants group on the Design tab of the Ribbon to alter your chosen theme to suit the presentation's needs

- *Change the colors*: Choose Design ➤ Variants ➤ Variants ➤ Colors from the Ribbon, and then click the color set you want to use. You can click Customize Colors at the bottom of the Colors panel to display the Create Theme Colors dialog box (see Figure 18-4). Change the colors as needed, type a descriptive name for the custom color set, and then click the Save button to save it.

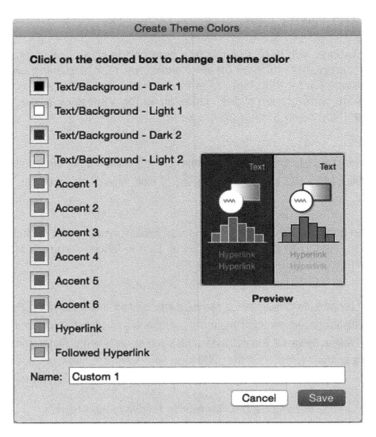

Figure 18-4. Use the Create Theme Colors dialog box to change the colors within the theme or theme variant you've chosen

- *Change the fonts*: Choose Design ➤ Variants ➤ Variants ➤ Fonts from the Ribbon, and then click the fonts set you want.

- *Change the background style*: Choose Design ➤ Variants ➤ Variants ➤ Background from the Ribbon, and then click the appropriate background. To apply custom background formatting, click Format Background at the bottom of the Background panel, use the controls in the Format Background pane to specify the background, and then click the Apply to All button.

Note   After customizing a theme, you can save it for future use. From the Ribbon, choose Design ➤ Themes ➤ Themes (clicking the panel button to open the Themes panel) and then click Save Current Theme. Type a name in the Export As box in the dialog box that opens, and then click the Save button. You can then reuse the theme from the Custom section of the Themes panel.

Changing the Slide Size or Orientation

For some presentations, you may also need to change the size or orientation of the slides. Most PowerPoint templates start you off with slides sized for displaying on a regular-format screen in a landscape (wider than high) orientation, which is what you'll most often need. But if you need to create wide-screen slides, slides sized for printing on paper, or slides in a portrait orientation, you need to change the setup.

> **Note**   Standard slides use a 4:3 aspect ratio: they are four units wide by three units tall. Widescreen slides use a 16:9 aspect ratio: they are 16 units wide by nine units tall.

If you just need to change the slides from the standard format to the widescreen format, or vice versa, choose Design ➤ Customize ➤ Slide Size ➤ Widescreen or Design ➤ Customize ➤ Slide Size ➤ Standard from the Ribbon.

> **Note**   If you change from Widescreen to Standard after adding content to slides, PowerPoint displays a dialog box pointing out that you are converting to a smaller slide size and asking if you want to scale content down. Click the Scale button if you do want to reduce the content size; click the Don't Scale button if you don't. If the slides have no content, this dialog box doesn't appear.

To make other changes to the size or orientation, follow these steps:

1. Choose Design ➤ Customize ➤ Slide Size ➤ Page Setup from the Ribbon or File ➤ Page Setup from the menu bar to display the Page Setup dialog box (see Figure 18-5).

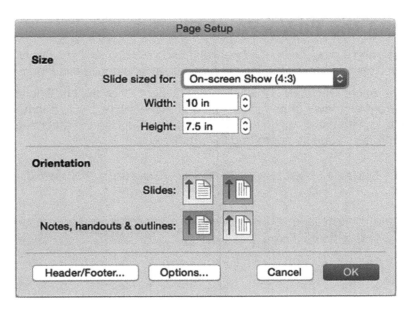

Figure 18-5. Use the Page Setup dialog box to change slide size or orientation. You can also switch the notes, handouts, and outlines from portrait orientation to landscape

2. Open the Slides sized for pop-up menu, and choose the size you need. Here are some examples:

    ■ Choose On-screen Show (4:3) to create slides sized for a standard-dimensions screen (a 4:3 aspect ratio).

    ■ Choose On-screen Show (16:9) to create slides sized for a screen with a 16:9 aspect ratio, or choose On-screen Show (16:10) to use a 16:10 aspect ratio.

    ■ Choose Letter Paper (8.5x11 in) to create slides sized for printing on letter paper.

3. If necessary, change the slide size in the Width box and the Height box. When you do this, PowerPoint changes the selection in the "Slide sized for" pop-up menu to Custom.

4. Choose the slide orientation by clicking the Portrait button or the Landscape button in the Slides section of the Orientation area.

5. Choose the orientation for notes, handouts, and outlines by clicking the Portrait button or the Landscape button in the Notes, handouts, & outlines section of the Orientation area.

6. Click the OK button to close the Page Setup dialog box. PowerPoint applies your choices to the presentation.

Navigating the PowerPoint Window

When you first open a presentation, PowerPoint usually displays it in Normal view. In this view, the PowerPoint window contains three panes, as you can see in Figure 18-6.

- ■ *Slide pane*: This pane shows the current slide. Click the Fit Slide to Current Window button at the right end of the status bar to zoom the slide as large as it will go and still fit in the pane. Use the other zoom controls as usual to zoom to different degrees.

Navigation pane   Slide pane   Notes pane   Placeholder   Status bar   Fit Slide to Current Window button

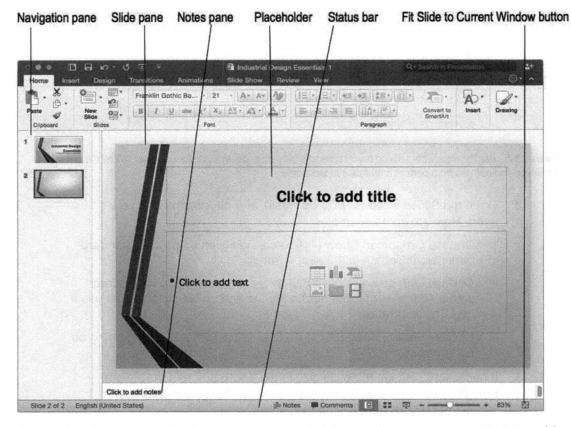

Figure 18-6. In Normal view, the Navigation pane appears on the left and the Notes pane appears at the bottom of the window, leaving the Slide pane taking up most of the space

- ■ *Navigation pane*: This pane appears on the left and enables you to navigate quickly from one slide to another, give commands, and rearrange your slides. In Normal view, the Navigation pane shows a thumbnail picture of each slide that you can click to display the slide in the Slide pane. In Outline view (which you can display by choosing View ➤ Outline View from the menu bar), the Navigation pane displays an outline of the presentation that you can use to quickly develop the presentation's text content. In Outline view too, you click a slide to display it in the Slide pane.

> **Note**   You can resize the Slide pane, Navigation pane, and Notes pane by dragging the borders that separate them. For example, you may want to widen the Navigation pane to make the thumbnail pictures larger so that you can identify the slides more easily.

- *Notes pane*: This pane appears at the bottom of the window, below the Slide pane. This is where you create notes that you want to accompany the slide. These may be notes that you want to view on-screen as you give the presentation to remind you of what to say, notes you plan to print out for yourself or whoever delivers the presentation, or notes that you turn into a handout for the audience.

> **Tip**   If you want more room to work on your slide, close the Navigation pane by dragging its right border all the way to the left side of the window. To display the Navigation pane again, drag the border back to the right. Similarly, you can hide the Notes pane by dragging its border down to the bottom of the window and reveal it again by dragging the border back up.

Add Content to a Slide

Once you've created a slide, you can add content to it. As you'll see in Chapters 19 and 20, PowerPoint slides can contain a wide variety of types of content, from text to audio and movies.

Most slides come with one or more placeholders for adding content. For example, the slide shown in Figure 18-6 has a title placeholder (the upper box that says "Click to add title") and a standard content placeholder for adding text, graphics, tables, or other content. Other slides contain placeholders for other types of content, such as subtitles.

> **Note**   Most themes and templates start you off with one or more slides. If your presentation doesn't have a slide at this point, choose Home ➤ Slides ➤ New Slide from the Ribbon or press Cmd+Shift+N to insert a slide. See the next section for more details on adding slides.

To add text to a text placeholder, click anywhere in the placeholder. PowerPoint hides the "Click to add text" prompt and displays an insertion point. Type the text you want, and then click outside the placeholder to deselect it.

To resize a placeholder, click to select it. You can then

- Drag a corner handle to resize the placeholder in two dimensions freely.
- Drag a side handle to resize the placeholder in only one dimension.
- Shift-drag a corner handle to resize the placeholder in two dimensions but retain its aspect ratio.

■ Option-drag a corner handle or side handle to resize the placeholder symmetrically about its center point.

■ Option-Shift-drag a corner handle to resize the placeholder symmetrically in two dimensions about its center point, retaining its aspect ratio.

> **Note** To reset a slide's placeholders to their defaults, click the slide, and then choose Home ➤ Slides ➤ Reset from the Ribbon. To change the layout of a slide, click the slide, choose Home ➤ Slides ➤ Layout from the Ribbon, and then click the layout you want on the Layout panel.

To move a placeholder, first select it by clicking it. Move the pointer over a border so that the pointer changes to a four-headed arrow. Then drag the placeholder to where you want it to appear.

Adding, Deleting, and Rearranging Slides

If you based your presentation on a theme, you may need to add more slides to it now. If you based the presentation on a sample template or a guided method, you may have the opposite problem—the presentation contains too many slides, and you need to delete some of them. Either way, sooner or later, you will likely need to change the order in which the slides appear in the presentation.

Adding a Slide

To add a new slide, select the slide after which you want to insert the new one. Choose Home ➤ Slides ➤ New Slide from the Ribbon (clicking the drop-down button on the New Slide button), and then click the slide layout on the New Slide panel (see Figure 18-7).

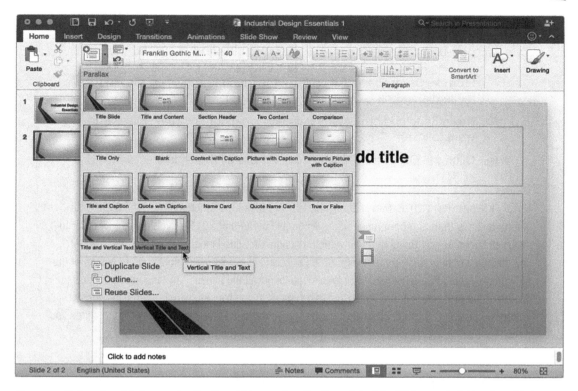

Figure 18-7. *Insert a slide by opening the New Slide panel on the Home tab of the Ribbon and clicking the slide layout you want*

You can also insert slides in a presentation in three other ways:

- *Duplicate slides from the presentation*: To create new slides based on ones already in your presentation, select those slides, and then choose Home ➤ Slides ➤ New Slide ➤ Duplicate Slide from the Ribbon or Insert ➤ Duplicate Slide from the menu bar.

> **Tip**   You can quickly duplicate a slide by Ctrl-clicking or right-clicking it in the Navigation pane or in Slide Sorter view and then clicking Duplicate Slide on the context menu. (You'll meet Slide Sorter view later in this chapter.) Alternatively, select the slide, and then press Cmd+Shift+D. To duplicate multiple slides, select them before giving the command.

- *Copy slides from another presentation*: You can insert all the slides from another presentation; if you need only some of the slides, you can delete those you don't want. Follow these steps:
  - Select the slide after which you want to insert the copied slides.

- Choose Home ➤ Slides ➤ New Slide ➤ Reuse Slides or Insert ➤ Slides ➤ New Slide ➤ Reuse Slides from the Ribbon (clicking the pop-up button on the New Slide button in either case and then clicking Reuse Slides on the New Slide panel) or Insert ➤ Slides From ➤ Other Presentation from the menu bar to open the Choose a File dialog box.

- Navigate to and click the presentation that contains the slides you want to insert.

- Click the OK button. PowerPoint inserts all the slides.

Note   In PowerPoint 2016, Microsoft has severely reduced the functionality of the feature for inserting slides from another presentation. Whereas PowerPoint 2011 let you choose whether to insert all slides or only those that you selected (using the Slide Finder dialog box), and also let you choose whether to keep the design of the original slides instead of applying the design of the new presentation, PowerPoint 2016 only lets you insert all the slides—and the slides pick up the design of the presentation into which you insert them. If you frequently need to reuse slides in your presentations, consider creating separate presentations that contain groups of the slides you need—or even presentations containing individual slides if you need greater flexibility.

- *Insert slides from an outline in a document*: If you've created an outline in a rich text format (RTF) document or a text document, you can create slides based on it. Choose Home ➤ Slides ➤ New Slide ➤ Outline or Insert ➤ Slides ➤ New Slide ➤ Outline from the Ribbon (clicking the pop-up button on the New Slide button in either case and then clicking Outline on the New Slide panel) or Insert ➤ Slides From ➤ Outline from the menu bar to open the Choose a File dialog box, click the document that contains the outline, and then click the Insert button. PowerPoint tries to break up the content to fit the slides by using the heading styles and formatting so you may need to adjust the resulting slides.

Deleting a Slide

You can delete a slide in the Navigation pane in Normal view or Outline view or in the main pane in Slide Sorter view. (You'll learn about Slide Sorter view in a moment.) Use any of these techniques:

- *Context menu*: Ctrl-click or right-click the slide, and then click Delete Slide on the context menu.

- *Delete key*: Click the slide, and then press the Delete key on the keyboard.

- *Menu bar*: Click the slide, and then choose Edit ➤ Delete Slide.

Rearranging Slides

You can change the order of the slides in the presentation in Normal view, Outline view, or Slide Sorter view:

- *Normal view or Outline view*: In the Navigation pane, click the slide you want to move, and then drag it up or down. When the line for the slide appears where you want it, release the button.

- *Slide Sorter view*: Select the slide or slides, and then drag them to the appropriate position. When the slide or slides are where you want them, release the button.

Using Views to Work on Your Presentation

So far in this chapter, you've seen only the Normal view, though I've also mentioned Slide Sorter view and Outline view. Altogether, PowerPoint provides five different views to help you work swiftly and easily on your presentations: Normal view, Outline view, Slide Sorter view, Notes Page view, and Slide Show view. PowerPoint also provides Presenter view, which you use when running a slide show on two screens (one screen for you, the other for your audience).

> **Note**   PowerPoint classes Normal view, Outline view, Slide Sorter view, and Notes Page view as "presentation views" and Slide Show view as something else, but I include Slide Show view here because you'll likely use it while developing a presentation and checking how it looks when running.

You can switch views in any of these ways:

- *Status bar*: Click the appropriate view button in the View Shortcuts group (see Figure 18-8). This group doesn't contain a button for Outline view or Notes Page view.

Normal   Slide sorter   Slide show

Figure 18-8. Click a view button in the View Shortcuts group on the status bar to change views quickly

- *Ribbon*: Choose View ➤ Presentation Views ➤ Normal, View ➤ Presentation Views ➤ Outline View, View ➤ Presentation Views ➤ Slide Sorter, or View ➤ Presentation Views ➤ Notes Page.

- *Menu bar*: Choose View ➤ Normal, View ➤ Slide Sorter, View ➤ Notes Page, View ➤ Outline, or View ➤ Slide Show.

- *Keyboard*: Press Cmd+1 to switch to Normal view, Cmd+2 to switch to Slide Sorter view, Cmd+3 to switch to Notes Page view, Cmd+4 to switch to Outline view, or Cmd+Shift+Return to switch to Slide Show view (and start the slide show). You can exit from Slide Show view by pressing the Esc key.

Creating Your Slides in Normal View

As you've seen already, Normal view is the view you use to create your slides and work on their content. Normal view is the view in which PowerPoint usually opens a presentation, and you can give yourself more space to work on a slide by hiding the Navigation pane and the Notes area.

Developing Your Presentation's Outline in Outline View

Use Outline view when you need to develop the outline of a presentation quickly. Outline view (see Figure 18-9) is similar to Normal view, in that the Navigation pane appears at the left side of the window, the Slide pane appears in the main part of the window, and the Notes pane appears at the bottom of the window (unless you drag its border down to hide it). The difference is that in Outline view the Navigation pane displays the outline, which shows the presentation as a sequence of collapsible slides. Each slide appears as a heading with its ordinal number and the text from the title placeholder (if there is any).

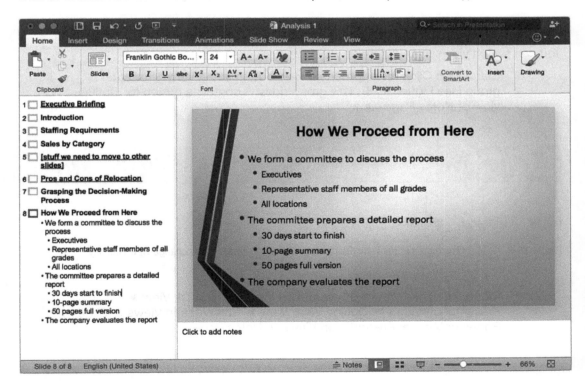

Figure 18-9. Use Outline view to develop the outline of a presentation

You can expand or collapse a slide by double-clicking its icon in the Outline tab. A collapsed slide shows an underline to indicate that material is hidden, as in slides 1, 5, and 6 in Figure 18-9.

Use these techniques for working in Outline view:

- *Create a new slide*: Press Return at the end of a paragraph to start a new paragraph, and then press Shift+Tab one or more times (as needed) to promote the paragraph to a slide title.

- *Create a bulleted paragraph*: After typing a slide title, press Return to start a new paragraph. Then press Tab to demote the paragraph to the first level. You can demote a paragraph to a lower level if needed (for example, to create second-level bulleted paragraphs). The slide in Figure 18-9 shows several second-level bulleted paragraphs.

- *Move a paragraph or selection up or down*: Click at the left end of a paragraph to select it, or click and drag to select multiple paragraphs. You can then drag the paragraph or selection up or down the outline to where you want it to be. For example, you can drag a bulleted paragraph from one slide to another.

- *Paste in text*: You can paste text into the Outline tab, and then promote or demote its paragraphs to the levels at which you want them to appear.

Rearranging Your Slides in Slide Sorter View

When you need to rearrange your slides into a different order, use Slide Sorter view (see Figure 18-10). This view shows a thumbnail picture of each slide laid out in a grid pattern so you can quickly see where each slide appears in relation to the other slides.

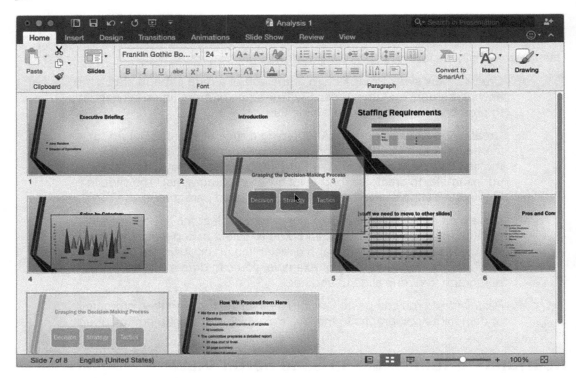

Figure 18-10. In Slide Sorter view, you can quickly drag a slide or a group of slides to a different place in the presentation, as in the middle of the window here. Drag the zoom slider to change the size at which the slide thumbnails appear

Note   To select a slide in Slide Sorter view, click it. To select a range of slides, click the first slide, and then Shift-click the last slide; alternatively, click before the first slide, and drag over the slides you want. To select slides that aren't next to each other, click the first slide, and then Cmd-click each of the others.

Slide Sorter view is most useful for these three purposes:

- *Checking the order of slides*: In Slide Sorter view, you can easily see the order your slides are in and change the order if it's wrong. To move one or more selected slides, drag them to where you want them to appear. PowerPoint moves the other slides out of the way so you can tell where the slides will land when you drop them.

- *Getting an overview of your presentation*: The Navigation pane is good for viewing your presentation as a sequence, but often it's helpful to be able to view all the slides at once.

- *Finding the slide you need to edit*: Once you've located the slide, double-click it to open the slide in Normal view or Outline view (whichever you were using before) so that you can edit it.

Creating Notes Pages in Notes Page View

When you need to add notes to a slide, switch to Notes Page view by choosing View ➤ Notes Page or pressing Cmd+3. In Notes Page view (see Figure 18-11), you can type the notes you need for each slide.

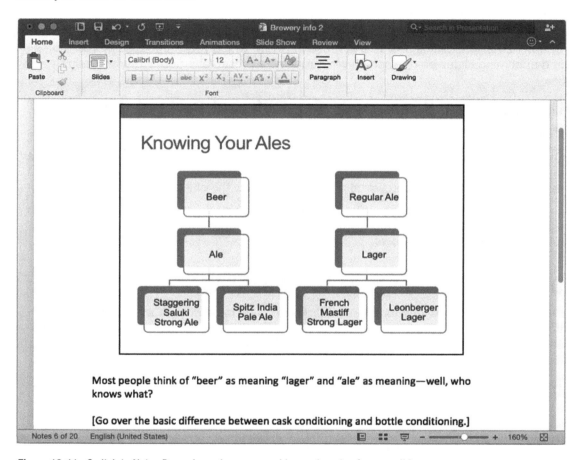

Figure 18-11. Switch to Notes Page view when you need to create notes for your slides

The kind of notes you'll create depends on the presentation and how you'll deliver it, but here are three typical kinds of notes:

- *Notes for viewing on-screen*: If you will use PowerPoint's Presenter view (which you'll learn to use in Chapter 21) when giving the presentation, you can view notes on your screen without the audience seeing them.

- *Notes to print out for the speaker*: If you (or someone else) will need printed notes to deliver the presentation, you can enter the appropriate information in Notes Page view.

- *Notes to include in handouts for the audience*: If you plan to create a handout for the audience, enter any notes you want to include.

Running a Presentation in Slide Show View

Slide Show view is the view you use when running a presentation. Slide Show view displays the current slide full screen on the screen you're using for the presentation. If you have a secondary screen (for example, because you've connected your Mac to a projector), you can choose to show your presenter notes on it to help you with the presentation.

You'll see Slide Show view in action in Chapter 21, which covers running slide shows. Chapter 21 also explains how to use Presenter view, which you use to display your notes and upcoming slides on one screen while running a presentation on another screen.

Opening Extra Windows to See Different Parts of the Presentation

Often, it's useful to be able to see two or more different slides at once so that you can compare them or ensure the ideas flow smoothly from one to the other. The easiest way to do this is to open a new window on the presentation and then display the other slide in that window.

To open a new window, choose Window ➤ New Window from the menu bar. You can then position each window wherever you find most helpful and display different slides—or use different views—in the windows.

Organizing Your Slides into Sections

When you add many slides to a presentation, it can become difficult to navigate through the presentation. To simplify matters, you can divide the presentation up into two or more sections. Each section can contain however many slides you need it to, and you can expand or collapse sections as needed.

To add a section, follow these steps:

1.   Switch to Normal view if you're using any other view. For example, click the Normal view button in the View Shortcuts area of the status bar.

2.   Display the Navigation pane if it's not already displayed.

3.   Click the slide at which you want to start the section.

4.   Choose Home ➤ Slides ➤ Section ➤ Add Section from the Ribbon or Insert ➤ Section from the menu bar. PowerPoint creates a new section, names it Untitled Section on the section bar across the top, and displays the Rename Section dialog box (see Figure 18-12).

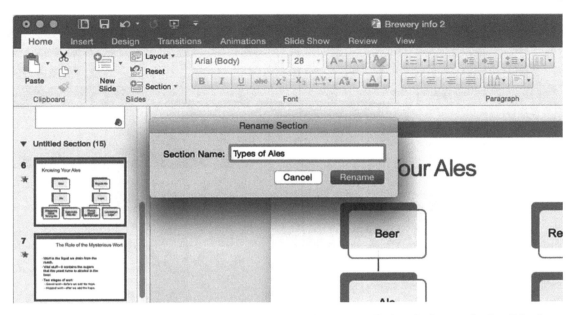

Figure 18-12. PowerPoint creates the section, names it Untitled Section, and displays the Rename Section dialog box so that you can rename it. The number in parentheses after each section name shows how many slides the section contains

5. Type the section name, and then press Return or click the Rename button to close the dialog box and apply the new name.

Note   If the first section you create begins after the first slide, PowerPoint puts the slides before the section into another section named Default Section. Double-click the Default Section heading to display the Rename Section dialog box, type a new name for the section, and then press Return or click the Rename button.

Once you've created your sections, you can manipulate them easily like this:

- *Expand or collapse a section*: Click its disclosure triangle.

- *Expand or collapse all sections*: Ctrl-click or right-click a section heading, and then click Expand All or Collapse All on the context menu.

- *Move a section up or down the list of sections*: Either click the section heading and drag it to where you want the section, or Ctrl-click or right-click the section heading, and then click Move Section Up or Move Section Down on the context menu (see Figure 18-13).

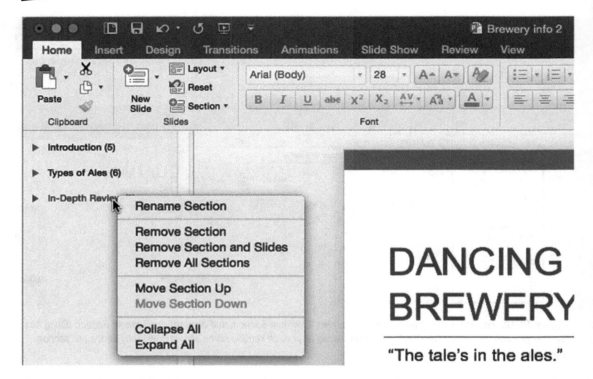

Figure 18-13. After creating sections, you can use the context menu to rename them, rearrange them, or remove them

- *Remove a section but leave its slides*: Ctrl-click or right-click the section heading, and then click Remove Section on the context menu. To remove all sections, click Remove All Sections.

- *Remove a section and its slides*: Ctrl-click or right-click the section heading, and then click Remove Section and Slides on the context menu.

Editing a Presentation Simultaneously with Your Colleagues

When you need to create a presentation quickly, you can edit the presentation simultaneously with your colleagues. As long as you can avoid stepping on each other's toes, coauthoring a presentation is a fast and efficient way to work because you can avoid duplicating effort or working in different directions.

To edit a presentation simultaneously, you must store it on a SharePoint site or on OneDrive. If you have the choice between using a local SharePoint site and using OneDrive, choose the SharePoint site; it'll give much better performance, especially if you create a large and complex presentation.

Note   Instead of editing a presentation simultaneously with your colleagues, you can use PowerPoint's Comments feature to gather input on a presentation. To work with comments, you use the controls in the Comments group on the Review tab of the Ribbon.

Here's how to coauthor a presentation with your colleagues:

- Create the presentation: One of you creates the presentation in the normal way; for example, by basing it on a theme, as described earlier in this chapter, or by cloning an existing presentation (likewise). You save the presentation either to a SharePoint site on your local network or to OneDrive.

Tip   When coauthoring a presentation, either agree beforehand which slides or which section each person will work on or use instant messaging to keep in touch as you work. As far as possible, avoid working on the same slide as one of your coauthors; otherwise, it's all too easy to create conflicting changes that you then need to resolve.

- *Open the presentation*: The first person opens the presentation as usual. Then, whenever another person opens the presentation, PowerPoint displays a pop-up message telling them who else is working on it. The first person also sees a corresponding pop-up message (see Figure 18-14).

Figure 18-14. The Authors readout at the right end of the title bar shows you when another author opens the presentation for editing

- *See the current list of editors*: To see the full list of people editing the presentation, click the Authors readout at the right end of the title bar to display the authors editing this document pop-up menu (see Figure 18-15).

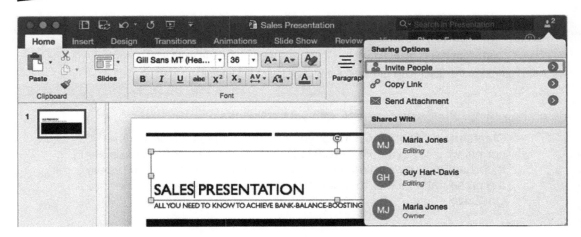

Figure 18-15. Click the Authors readout on the title bar to see the list of people editing the document

- *Edit the presentation*: You can work as normal using almost the full range of PowerPoint's features. The main limitation is that only one person can edit any given element at a time. For this reason, the most practical approach is to work on different slides than your coauthors are editing.

- *Update the presentation*: When you've made changes you want to share with your coauthors or when you're ready to see what changes they've made, click the Save button on the title bar or press Cmd+S to save the presentation. PowerPoint uploads your changes to the document on the SharePoint site or on OneDrive and merges them with your coauthors' changes; if your changes conflict with a coauthor's changes, you need to resolve them, as described next. PowerPoint downloads your coauthors' changes and displays them for you.

- *Resolve conflicts*: If you and another author change the same element at the same time, PowerPoint displays the dialog box shown in Figure 18-16 to whoever saves the document after the other. Click the Review Conflicts button, and then work in the Resolve Conflict dialog box that opens (see Figure 18-17).

Figure 18-16. If PowerPoint displays this dialog box, click the Review Conflicts button, and then use the Resolve Conflict dialog box to work through the conflicting changes

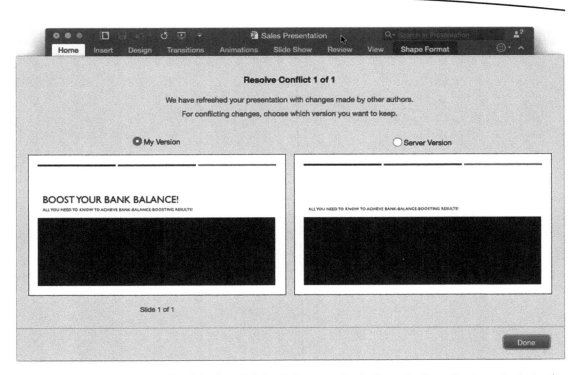

Figure 18-17. *In the Resolve Conflict dialog box, click the My Version option button or the Server Version option button for each change. When you finish deciding which versions of changes to keep, click the Done button to close the dialog box*

- *Close the presentation*: When you have finished working with the presentation, save any unsaved changes that you want to keep. Then close the presentation as usual by choosing File ➤ Close from the menu bar.

Summary

In this chapter, you learned how to create a new PowerPoint presentation by basing it on a sample template, on a design theme, or on an existing presentation. You saw how to add slides to the presentation, rearrange them, and delete ones that aren't needed. You grasped the techniques for adding content to slides, developing the outline of a presentation, and organizing slides into different sections. You also learned how to use PowerPoint's powerful collaboration features to edit a presentation simultaneously with your coworkers.

In the next chapter, you'll look at how to create compelling slides by making the layouts and the content work effectively together.

Chapter 19

Creating Clear and Compelling Slides

In this chapter, I'll show you how to create slides that convey your meaning clearly and powerfully to your audience.

I'll begin where you'll probably want to start your presentation—by looking at how to plan the slides it will contain. Then you'll see which of PowerPoint's built-in slide layouts suits which type of content—and how you can create a custom slide layout when none of the built-in layouts fits the bill.

After that, you'll learn how to add text to your slides and format it to look good. Finally, I'll show you how to add tables, charts, SmartArt graphics, and hyperlinks to your slides.

Planning the Slides in Your Presentation

As you plan your presentation and as you create the slides for it, keep the audience in mind. Whether you'll deliver the presentation in person, via an Internet broadcast, or by distributing digital copies of the presentation, you want to make sure your slides are easy to read, are attractive to look at, and convey your meaning clearly.

For most presentations, follow these general rules when planning and creating your slides:

- *Keep your text concise*: Some presentation experts suggest following the "6×6 rule" for text slides: each slide should have about six bullet points of around six words each. The name is catchy, but the exact numbers are less important than the broader point: it's fine to have anywhere from four to eight bullets, as long as each of them is fairly short and your slide is easy to read.

G. Hart-Davis, *Learn Office 2016 for Mac*, DOI 10.1007/978-1-4842-2002-3_19

> **Note**   For most presentations, you'll have things that you definitely want to say to the audience but that don't fit directly in the text of your slides. Put these items in your notes for the slide. Also put in the notes any things you may need to add, such as statistics to mention if audience members ask questions you've anticipated about the slides.

- *Keep your slides uncluttered*: If you need to choose between fitting in more information on an existing slide and adding a slide, it's usually best to add the extra slide. Don't feel you need to fill up each slide—it's fine to leave blank space on a slide. You're not short-changing the audience by making the presentation easy for them to assimilate.

- *Illustrate your points*: When you make a point, drive it home by illustrating it with an example that catches your audience's imagination. For example, don't just say you're now selling half a million gizmos a year—point out that's enough for everyone in Albuquerque to have one.

- *Use your strongest material—not all your material*: Many presentations suffer from too much detail. Usually, you can convince your audience that you have the facts and figures with just a couple of well-chosen examples; you don't need to numb them with a complete rundown of the data.

> **Tip**   You may find it useful to keep extra material in reserve by using hidden slides or by creating custom slide shows that let you show a series of extra slides when you need to do so. See Chapter 20 for details on both these topics.

- *Provide visual interest—but don't overdo it*: Even with the liveliest presenter, a text-only presentation can be dull as ditch water. As you'll see in this chapter and the next, PowerPoint makes it easy to add tables, charts, graphics, videos, and animations to your slides, so it's a good idea to include visually interesting and relevant information to give the audience something to look at. You can also use audio in your presentations.

- *Put a Welcome slide at the start of the presentation*: Many presentations benefit from having a Welcome slide that gives the audience something to look at on entering the room and waiting for stragglers. A Welcome slide is good for you too because you can see that you have the presentation up and running correctly.

- *Give your presentation a final slide*: Often, when you spend ages creating a presentation, finishing it is such a relief that you don't notice it ends with a bump with the final slideful of content. For many presentations, it's helpful to have a final slide that you can leave on the screen. This slide may be as simple as a single line—for example, "Questions?" or "Coffee and cookies in the lobby"—or even a colored screen with no text at all.

Choosing Slide Layouts to Suit the Contents

To get your material onto a slide and to make it look good, you need to choose a suitable layout. You can either use one of PowerPoint's built-in slide layouts or create a custom layout of your own.

Using PowerPoint's Built-in Slide Layouts

You'll probably want to start by using the standard slide layouts that PowerPoint provides on the New Slide panel, which you open by choosing Home ➤ Slides ➤ New Slide from the Ribbon. The exact list of layouts depends on the theme or template you're using. Table 19-1 lists the most common layouts and explains when to use each.

Table 19-1. PowerPoint's Standard Slide Layouts and When to Use Them

Slide Layout	When to Use It
Title Slide	To start your presentation or to introduce a new section of it.
Title and Content	To display a content item such as a table, chart, or picture.
Section Header	To start a new section of the presentation. In most designs, this slide has a substantially different look from other slides to suggest the change.
Two Content	To display two content items, such as two pictures or two tables, but without necessarily comparing them to each other.
Comparison	To display two content items (for example, two charts) and compare them to each other. The Comparison layout is like the Two Content layout but has an extra text box above each item that you can use to highlight the differences.
Title Only	To add only a title to a slide or to have a title followed by content you place manually.
Blank	To create your own layout or to insert a blank slide as a pause in your presentation.
Content with Caption	To display a content item (such as a table or chart) over most of the slide, with a title and explanatory text alongside it.
Picture with Caption	To display a picture over most of the slide, with a title and explanatory text alongside it. The Picture with Caption layout is almost identical to the Content with Caption layout but is customized for pictures rather than other content types.
Title and Vertical Text	To display a horizontal title (as usual) and then vertical text items. This layout is useful for specialized purposes.
Vertical Text and Title	To display the title vertically on one side of the slide and the text items vertically on the other side. This layout can be useful for highly specialized purposes.
Title, Content and Text	To display a title on the top, content (such as a picture or table) on the left, and explanatory text on the right. This layout is widely useful.
Background Only	To display only a background on the slide. You can add other content as needed or simply show the background as a visual interlude.

You can change a slide's layout at any time by clicking the slide, choosing Home ➤ Slides ➤ Layout from the Ribbon, and then clicking the layout you want. And you can snap a slide's layout back to its default settings by choosing Home ➤ Slides ➤ Reset from the Ribbon.

Note   If you change a slide's layout by applying a layout that has fewer placeholders than the number of placeholders you're currently using, PowerPoint leaves the extra placeholders on the slide so that you can deal with them.

Creating Custom Slide Layouts

When none of PowerPoint's built-in slide layouts is exactly what you want, you can create a custom slide layout in either of these ways:

- Apply the closest slide layout to what you want, and then customize it. For example, you can delete a placeholder by clicking it and then pressing Delete, or you can copy a placeholder by clicking it and then Option-dragging to where you want the copy.

- Start with a blank slide layout, and then add the objects you need.

Tip   After you create a custom slide layout, you can reuse it by selecting the slide and then duplicating it. For example, Ctrl-click or right-click the slide and then click Duplicate Slide on the context menu, press Cmd+Shift+D, or choose Home ➤ Slides ➤ New Slide ➤ Duplicate Slide from the Ribbon.

Formatting Text on Your Slides

You can format text on PowerPoint slides quickly by using the controls in the Font group and the Paragraph group on the Home tab of the Ribbon. You should be familiar with most of these controls from the first part of the book, but Figure 19-1 also points out several key controls and PowerPoint-specific controls that you'll use in this section.

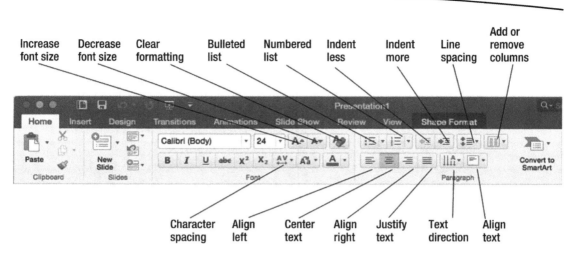

Figure 19-1. You can apply many types of text formatting quickly by using the controls in the Font group and Paragraph group on the Home tab of the Ribbon

> **Note**   To change the formatting of all the text in a placeholder, select the placeholder itself. To change the formatting of just some of the text, select that text.

Changing the Font, Font Size, and Alignment

You can easily change the font, font size, and alignment of text:

- *Change the font size*: Click the placeholder that contains the text, and then click the Increase Font Size button or the Decrease Font Size button in the Font group on the Home tab of the Ribbon.

- *Change the font*: Click the placeholder, open the Font pop-up menu in the Font group on the Home tab of the Ribbon, and then click the font you want. The Theme Headings item and Theme Body item at the top of the list show the primary fonts used for the theme or template, so you may want to use them for consistency.

- *Change the alignment*: Click the placeholder or click in the paragraph you want to affect, and then click the Align Text Left button, the Center button, the Align Text Right button, or the Justify button in the Paragraph group on the Home tab of the Ribbon.

To reach the full range of options for formatting fonts and characters, choose Format ➤ Font from the menu bar. PowerPoint opens the Format Font dialog box with the Font tab displayed (see Figure 19-2). To set widely used font formatting options, work on the Font tab. If you need to space characters farther apart or place them closer together, click the Character Spacing tab to display its controls.

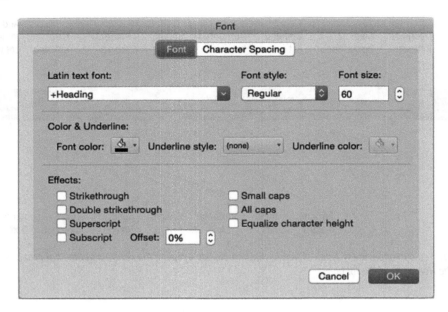

Figure 19-2. When you need full control over text formatting, open the Format Font dialog box, and then work on the Font tab or the Character Spacing tab, as needed

KEEPING YOUR TEXT EASY TO READ

Like most apps, PowerPoint gives you such a wide variety of fonts that it's easy to make poor choices.

When choosing fonts and font sizes for your slides, put clarity foremost. If the audience can't read the text on a slide because you've chosen an unsuitable font or too small a font size, your words of wisdom will be wasted. After creating a slide, make sure that even the smallest text on it will be easy to read from the back of the audience—and by someone with less than perfect eyesight.

Often, it's tempting to use a striking or "designy" font to look different. But in most cases, the best fonts are those that people barely notice because they're simply easy to read, such as the Calibri font used in the Office design. Unless you're presenting to designers, you're usually better off with straightforward fonts rather than fonts that set out to catch the eye.

Above all, keep the number of fonts to a sensible minimum. Using many different fonts can make your presentation look like an old-style ransom note.

Changing the Indentation and Line Spacing of Text

To make text look right on a slide, you may need to adjust its indentation and line spacing. You can change these as follows:

- *Change the indentation*: Click the Indent Less button or the Increase More button in the Paragraph group on the Home tab of the Ribbon. To take direct control, choose Format ➤ Paragraph from the menu bar to display the Paragraph dialog box (see Figure 19-3), and then use the controls in the Indentation area of the Indents and Spacing tab.

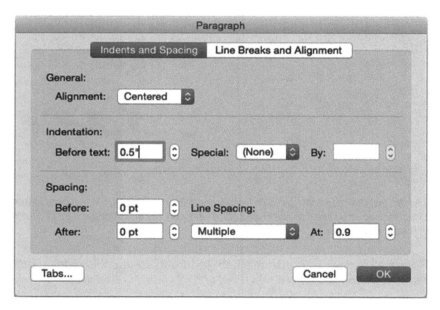

Figure 19-3. Use the Indents and Spacing tab of the Paragraph dialog box when you need close control over the indentation and spacing of paragraphs

- *Change the line spacing*: Click the Line Spacing button in the Paragraph group on the Home tab of the Ribbon, and then make your choice from the pop-up menu, which offers a range of choices from 0.5 lines to 3.0 lines. For greater control, click the Line Spacing Options item on the pop-up menu to display the Paragraph dialog box, and then use the controls in the Spacing area on the Indents and Spacing tab.

Rotating Text

For some slides, you may want to rotate text either in two dimensions or in three dimensions.

To rotate text simply, click the text placeholder, choose Home ➤ Paragraph ➤ Text Direction from the Ribbon, and then click one of the directions on the pop-up menu (see Figure 19-4):

- *Horizontal*: Choose this item to restore text to normal horizontal orientation.

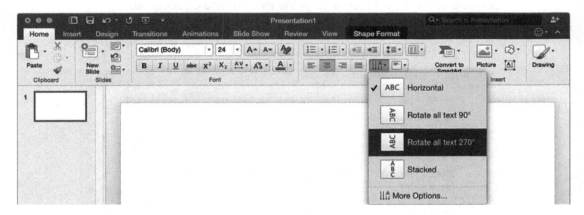

Figure 19-4. Use the Text Direction panel in the Paragraph group on the Home tab of the Ribbon to turn text sideways or make it run in a stack down a slide. For other types of rotation, click the More Options item to open the Text Box category in the Format Text dialog box

- *Rotate all text 90°*: Choose this item to turn the text on its side so that it reads from top to bottom.

> **Note**   To rotate the text box freely rather than in 90-degree increments, click the text box, and then drag the round rotate button above it to the left or right, as for any other graphical object.

- *Rotate all text 270°*: Choose this item to turn the text on its side so that it reads from bottom to top.
- *Stacked*: Choose this item to make the text read from top to bottom but without rotating the letters. This arrangement is good for adding narrow labels to graphical items.

> **Caution**   Use text rotation only for special effects. Don't rely on rotated text to convey important points because the audience may find it difficult to read.

If you need rotate text in other ways, follow these steps:

1. Choose Home ➤ Paragraph ➤ Text Direction ➤ More Options from the Ribbon to display the Text Box subtab on the Text Options tab in the Format Shape pane (see the left screen in Figure 19-5).

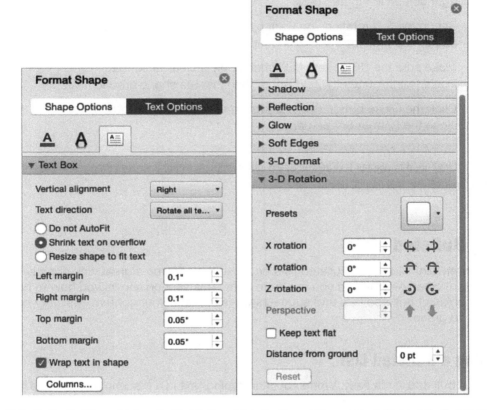

Figure 19-5. On the Text Box subtab on the Text Options tab in the Format Shape pane (left), open the Text direction pop-up menu, and choose the text direction you want. On the Text Effects tab subtab (right), click the 3-D Rotation heading to display the 3-D Rotation controls (right), and then choose the rotation you want

2. In the Text Layout area at the top, open the Vertical alignment pop-up menu, and choose the alignment for the text: Top, Middle, Bottom, Top Centered, Middle Centered, or Bottom Centered.

Note   If you've rotated the text vertically, the Vertical alignment pop-up menu shows the options Right, Left, Center, Right Middle, Center Middle, and Left Middle instead of the options Top, Middle, Bottom, Top Centered, Middle Centered, and Bottom Centered.

3. Open the Text direction pop-up menu and choose the direction for the text: Horizontal, Rotate All Text 90°, Rotate All Text 270°, or Stacked.

4. If you want to apply 3-D rotation, click the Text Effects subtab, and then click the 3-D Rotation heading to expand its contents (see the right screen in Figure 19-5).

5. Set up the 3-D rotation you want by using the Presets pop-up menu and the controls below it. See Chapter 4 for details on rotating shapes.

6. Make sure the "Keep text flat" check box is cleared so that PowerPoint rotates the text rather than just the shape around it.

7. Click the Close button (the X button in the upper-right corner) to close the Format Shape pane.

Tip   If you need to display text upside down, put it in its own container, and then rotate the container so that it is upside down.

Using Bulleted Lists

Many PowerPoint slides use bulleted lists because they can be a great way of presenting your content clearly—provided you get them right. This section shows you how to handle the mechanics of bulleted lists and suggests ways to make your content easy for your audience to grasp.

Creating a Bulleted List

Creating a bulleted list is easy. When you start typing text in a placeholder that has bullets applied, PowerPoint automatically gives the paragraph a bullet. When you press Return to create the next paragraph, PowerPoint displays a bullet for that paragraph too.

To move the current paragraph down to the next lower level of bulleted list, press Tab at the beginning of the paragraph or choose Home ➤ Paragraph ➤ Indent More from the Ribbon. Figure 19-6 shows a slide with three levels of indentation.

To move the current paragraph up to the next higher level, press Shift+Tab at the beginning of the paragraph or choose Home ➤ Paragraph ➤ Indent Less from the Ribbon.

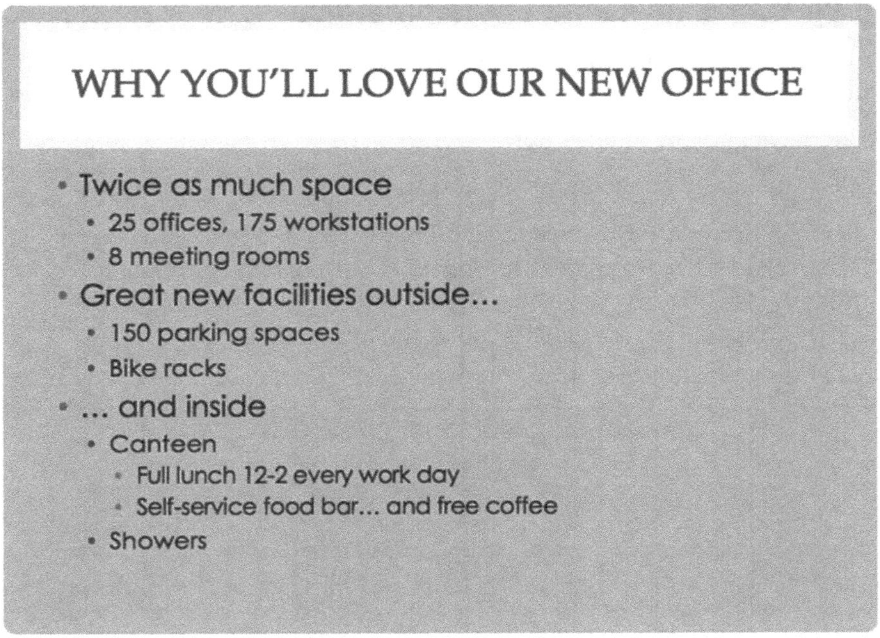

Figure 19-6. You can create a sublist by pressing Tab or by choosing Home ➤ Paragraph ➤ Indent More from the Ribbon

Making Sure Your Bulleted Lists Are Readable

The fonts and font sizes PowerPoint uses for text depend on the slide design. Many bulleted slides start off in a small enough font size to enable you to type five or six bullets of two lines each—so if you have fewer bullets on a slide or if each is less than a single line, it's often a good idea to increase the font size to make the words easy to read.

When you start a bulleted sublist, PowerPoint reduces the font size. This makes the hierarchy of the bullet points clear, but it can easily make the text too small to read. You may need to increase the font size of the bulleted sublist points as well to keep them readable. The extra indentation and different bullets will still indicate the hierarchy.

> **Caution**   PowerPoint lets you create pretty much as many levels of sublist as you want—just keep pressing Tab at the start of a line or clicking the Indent More button to go to the next level. But if you go past two levels of bullets, that should raise a red flag to indicate that your slide is becoming too complex. If some content is that far subordinate, either cut it or break the material up onto several slides.

Livening Up Your Slides with Custom Bullets

One way to make your slides look different is to change from the default bullet characters. PowerPoint provides a wide range of bullet characters, but you can also create your own.

To customize bullets, follow these steps:

1. Click the text placeholder in which you want to use the bullets.

2. Choose Format ➤ Bullets and Numbering from the menu bar, or choose Home ➤ Paragraph ➤ Bullets ➤ Bullets and Numbering from the Ribbon, to display the Bullets and Numbering dialog box. PowerPoint shows the Bullets tab at the front (see Figure 19-7).

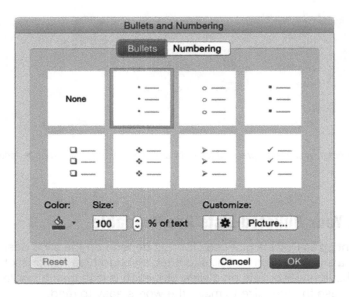

Figure 19-7. Use the Bullets tab in the Bullets and Numbering dialog box to set up custom bullets for a list

1. If you want to create a custom bullet based on an existing bullet, follow these steps:

   ■ Click the bullet style you want to start with.

   ■ Open the Color pop-up palette, and then click the color you want. To choose a color that doesn't appear, click the More Colors button, and then work in the Colors dialog box; click the OK button when you've chosen the color.

   ■ Use the Size box to increase or decrease the bullet's size relative to the text. For example, set the bullet to 150% of text to make the bullet one and a half times the base height of the text.

2. If you want to use a different bullet character, click the Customize pop-up menu to display the Emoji & Symbols panel, and then click the character you want to insert. If you want to use a picture instead, go to step 5.

Tip If you want to be able to reuse a character easily as a bullet, add it to your Frequently Used list in the Emoji & Symbols panel. Look back to the "Inserting a Symbol Using the Emoji & Symbols Panel" section in Chapter 3 for full coverage of the Emoji & Symbols panel.

---

3. To use a picture as a bullet, follow these steps:

    - On the Bullets tab of the Bullets and Numbering dialog box, click the Picture button to display the Choose a Picture dialog box.

    - Navigate to the folder that contains the picture you want to use, and then click the picture file.

    - Click the Insert button. PowerPoint closes the Choose a Picture dialog box.

4. Click the OK button to close the Bullets and Numbering dialog box. PowerPoint applies the bullet you chose to the placeholder.

Adding Tables, SmartArt, Charts, and Hyperlinks to Slides

PowerPoint makes it as easy as possible to add graphical content to your slides. If the slide has a content placeholder (see Figure 19-8), click the appropriate icon in it, and then use the dialog box or pane that PowerPoint opens to identify the item you want. If the slide doesn't have a content placeholder, use the commands on the Ribbon or the menu bar. Here are some examples:

- *Insert a table*: Choose Insert ➤ Tables ➤ Table from the Ribbon or Insert ➤ Table from the menu bar.

- *Insert a picture*: Choose Insert ➤ Pictures ➤ Picture from the Ribbon or Insert ➤ Picture ➤ Picture from File from the menu bar.

- *Insert a chart*: Choose Insert ➤ Illustrations ➤ Chart from the Ribbon, click the chart category, and then click the chart type. Or choose Insert ➤ Chart from the menu bar and then click the chart type on the Chart submenu.

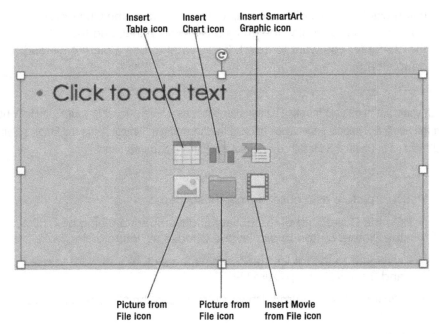

Figure 19-8. Click one of the six icons in a placeholder to start adding that type of content, or click the "Click to add text" prompt to start typing text

Adding Tables to Slides

You can create a new table on a slide, but you can often save time by importing a table from Word or by creating it from cells in an Excel worksheet.

Creating a Table from Scratch

To create a table from scratch, follow these steps:

1. Click the Insert Table icon in a placeholder to display the Insert Table dialog box (see Figure 19-9).

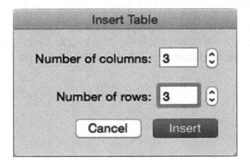

Figure 19-9. To insert a new table, click the Insert table icon in a placeholder, and then specify the number of columns and rows in the Insert Table dialog box

Note   If the slide doesn't have a content placeholder, choose Insert ➤ Table from the menu bar to display the Insert Table dialog box. Alternatively, choose Insert ➤ Tables ➤ Table from the Ribbon, and then choose the table dimensions on the grid.

2. In the Number of columns box, set the number of columns. Unless each data item is very short, you usually need to keep the number low (for example, three or four columns) to make sure the text is readable.

3. In the Number of rows box, set the number of rows. You can add further rows as needed, so it's fine to start with just a few.

4. Click the OK button to close the Insert Table dialog box. PowerPoint inserts the table and gives it a design that works with the presentation's color theme.

5. Type the contents of the table, pressing Tab to move from one cell to the next. Figure 19-10 shows a table with sample data entered.

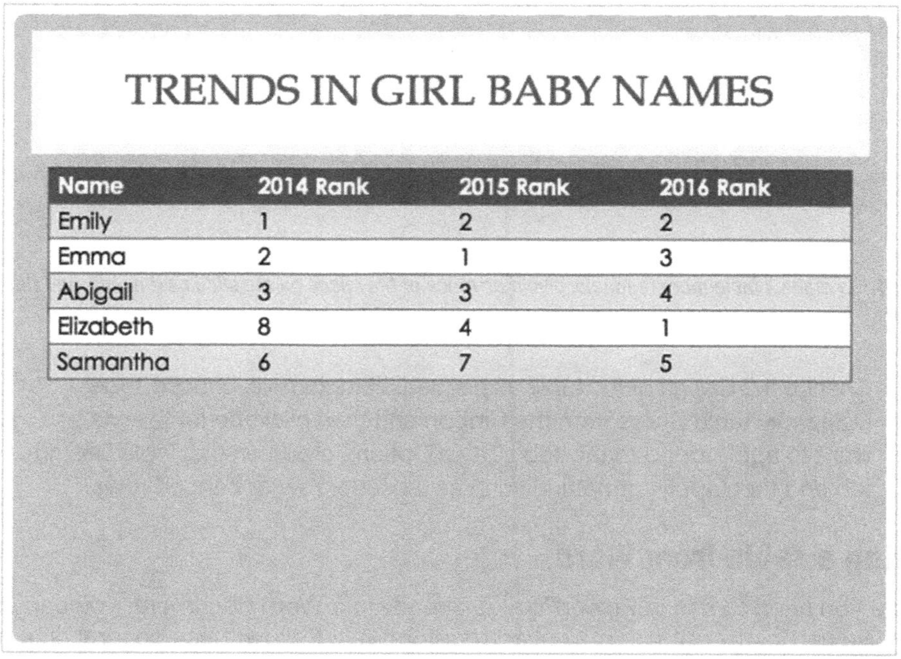

TRENDS IN GIRL BABY NAMES

Name	2014 Rank	2015 Rank	2016 Rank
Emily	1	2	2
Emma	2	1	3
Abigail	3	3	4
Elizabeth	8	4	1
Samantha	6	7	5

Figure 19-10. At its default size, table data is often too small for comfortable reading from a distance

6. Resize the table and its contents as needed; for example,

- If the table occupies only part of the slide, drag the handle at the bottom of its container downward, or drag the lower-right handle down and to the right, to expand the table. PowerPoint increases the row height to take up the extra space.

- With the table container selected, adjust the fonts to make the text easy to read. For example, click the Increase Font Size button a few times to pump up the font size. Figure 19-11 shows the same table taking up the full slide and with the text at a better size.

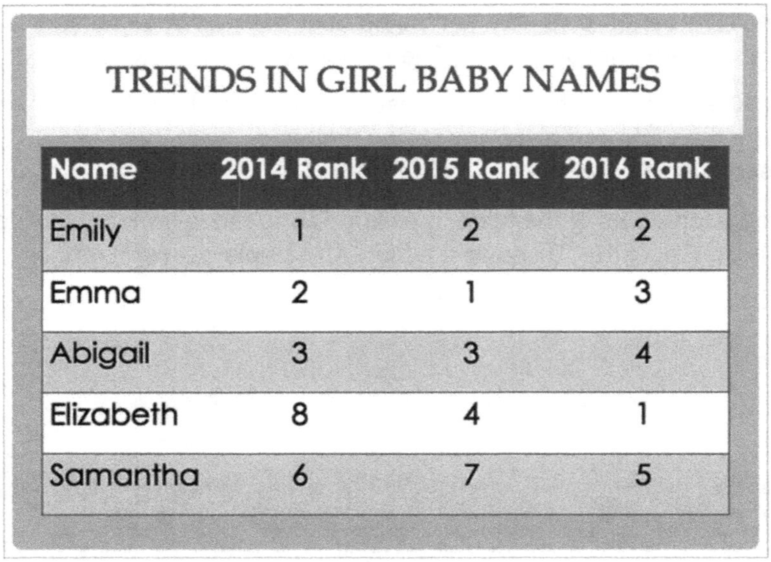

TRENDS IN GIRL BABY NAMES

Name	2014 Rank	2015 Rank	2016 Rank
Emily	1	2	2
Emma	2	1	3
Abigail	3	3	4
Elizabeth	8	4	1
Samantha	6	7	5

Figure 19-11. *To make a table more readable, give it as much of the space on the slide as it needs, and then increase the font sizes*

7. Change the design of the table as needed. For example, choose Table Design ➤ Table Styles from the Ribbon and then click the table style you want to apply, or go to the Table Style Options group on the Table Design tab and then apply formatting such as a header row or banded rows.

Importing a Table from Word

If the table you need to use in PowerPoint is already in a Word document, you can quickly reuse it in PowerPoint—but you may need to reformat it. Follow these general steps:

1. In Word, open the document that contains the table.

2. Select the table, and then copy it to the Clipboard. For example, click in the table, and then choose Layout ➤ Table ➤ Select ➤ Select Table from the Ribbon or Table ➤ Select ➤ Table from the menu bar. Then Ctrl-click or right-click in the selection, and click Copy on the context menu.

3.   In PowerPoint, navigate to the slide on which you want to place the table, and then create a table that has the same number of rows and columns as the table you've copied.

4.   Again in PowerPoint, Ctrl-click or right-click in the table you've just created, and then click Paste on the context menu. PowerPoint pastes the copied data straight into the new table.

5.   Format the table as needed in PowerPoint. Here are some examples:

   ■   Resize the table's container to the size you need.

   ■   Choose Table Design ➤ Table Styles ➤ Table Styles from the Ribbon, and then click the style you want to apply.

   ■   Still on the Table Design tab, choose any options in the Table Style Options group. For instance, select the Total Row check box if the table needs different formatting for a total row at the bottom.

Creating a Table from Excel Worksheet Data

When a PowerPoint slide needs a table of data that you have in an Excel worksheet, copy the data across and paste it in. Don't waste time retyping the data and maybe introducing mistakes into it.

To create a PowerPoint table from Excel worksheet data, follow these steps:

1.   In Excel, select the cells you want, and then copy them. For example, Ctrl-click or right-click in the selection, and then click Copy on the context menu.

2.   In PowerPoint, select the slide on which you want to place the data.

3.   Insert a table in one of these ways:

   ■   If the slide has a placeholder displaying the content icons, click the Insert Table icon. Either set the exact number of rows and columns your Excel selection will occupy or (easier) insert a smaller table of maybe 2 columns by 2 rows. Click the OK button. PowerPoint automatically adjusts the number of columns and rows to fit the data you paste in.

   ■   Choose Insert ➤ Tables ➤ Table from the Ribbon, and then click the table size. Again, either set the right number of rows and columns or create a smaller table.

4.   Click to place the insertion point in the first cell in the table.

5.   Paste in the data. For example, choose Home ➤ Clipboard ➤ Paste from the Ribbon, choose Edit ➤ Paste from the menu bar or press Cmd+V.

6. Format the table as needed in PowerPoint. Here are some examples:

    ■   Resize the table's container to occupy more of the slide.

    ■   Choose Table Design ➤ Table Styles ➤ Table Styles from the Ribbon, and then click the style you want to apply.

    ■   Also on the Table Design tab of the Ribbon, choose options in the Table Style Options group. For instance, select the Header Row check box to add header row formatting.

    ■   Display the Home tab of the Ribbon, and use the controls in the Font group on the Home tab of the Ribbon to change the font sizes as needed. For most slides, you need to increase the font size considerably from the size used in Excel to make the data easy to read in PowerPoint.

Adding SmartArt Graphics to Slides

You can add a SmartArt graphic to a slide by using the techniques explained in Chapter 4. For example, you can add an org chart like this:

1. Select the slide on which you want to add the SmartArt graphic. Create a new slide if necessary.

2. If there's a content placeholder, click the Insert SmartArt Graphic icon to display the SmartArt menu.

3. Click the type of SmartArt item you want to create. The panel for that type of SmartArt appears. For example, click the Hierarchy item to display the Hierarchy panel, which includes organization charts and similar diagrams.

4. On the panel, click the type of graphic, such as Name and Title Organization Chart. PowerPoint inserts the graphic on the slide.

5. If PowerPoint doesn't display the SmartArt Text window, click the SmartArt Text button at the upper-left corner of the SmartArt graphic to display the SmartArt Text window.

6. Type the text for each item in the SmartArt Text window.

7. Drag the sizing handles to resize the SmartArt graphic to suit the slide best. For example, you may want to make it as big as will fit on the slide to enable the audience to read it easily.

Adding Charts to Slides

A chart can be a great way of presenting complex or detailed information in a manner that's instantly clear on a slide. In PowerPoint, you can add a chart to a slide in two ways:

- *Create a chart on an embedded worksheet*: You start the chart from inside PowerPoint, and PowerPoint causes Excel to create a workbook for the chart. The workbook is embedded in the PowerPoint presentation so it becomes part of that file. You don't need to save the chart workbook separately.

- *Copy a chart from an Excel workbook*: Create your chart in Excel using the techniques described in Chapter 14. Then copy the finished chart and paste it into your PowerPoint slide.

Here's how to choose when to create a new embedded workbook, embed an existing workbook, link back to a workbook, or insert a picture:

- *Create a new embedded workbook*: Do this when you don't yet have the data for the chart in Excel and you need to keep the chart's data with the PowerPoint presentation, such as when you're sending the presentation to someone else who will need to work on the chart data too.

- *Embed an existing chart and its data*: Do this when you have the data for the chart or the chart itself in a workbook in Excel and you need to keep the chart's data available in the PowerPoint presentation. After embedding the chart and its data, you can open the chart from PowerPoint in Excel and edit it there. If you open the chart in Excel (outside PowerPoint) and edit the chart, the chart in the presentation doesn't receive the changes.

- *Link back to a workbook*: Do this when you want to be able to change the chart or its source data in Excel and then automatically bring those changes into PowerPoint by updating the chart. Linking requires the workbook to stay in the same relative place in the computer's file system to the presentation so that the presentation can find the updated data. Moving the presentation to a different computer breaks the link.

> **Caution**   Linking a chart can be great when it works—but links can fail at the most awkward times. Before giving a presentation that includes linked charts, double-check that the links are working. That way, you'll have a chance to fix any problems rather than discovering them when your audience sees them.

- *Insert a picture*: Do this when you don't need to keep the connection between the chart and its source data, and you will not need to edit the chart in the presentation.

Creating a Chart in a New Embedded Workbook

To create a chart on a worksheet in a new workbook embedded in your PowerPoint presentation, follow these steps:

1. On the slide where you want to create the chart, click the Insert Chart icon in a placeholder or simply click the Charts tab of the Ribbon. Either way, PowerPoint displays the Charts tab of the Ribbon.

2. In the Insert Chart group, click the pop-up button for the category of chart you want to create. For example, click the Column pop-up button to display the Column panel.

3. On the pop-up panel, click the chart type. PowerPoint creates a chart of that type on the slide and launches Excel, which creates a new workbook, embeds it in the presentation, and gives it a name such as Chart in Microsoft Office PowerPoint.

4. Change the chart range and the sample data (see Figure 19-12) to the data your chart needs. PowerPoint automatically updates the chart to match the data in the Excel worksheet.

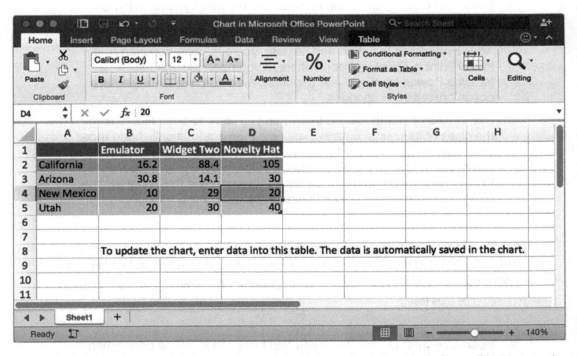

Figure 19-12. Excel enters sample data on the first worksheet in the embedded workbook. Change this data to create your chart

5. When you have finished changing the data, close Excel. For example, click the Close button (the red button at the left end of the title bar) or choose Excel ➤ Quit Excel.

Note   Excel saves the data in the embedded workbook automatically so you don't need to save it while you're working in the Excel window.

6. Use the controls on the Chart Design tab and the Format tab of the Ribbon to format the chart the way you want it. Figure 19-13 shows a slide containing a chart with formatting under way.

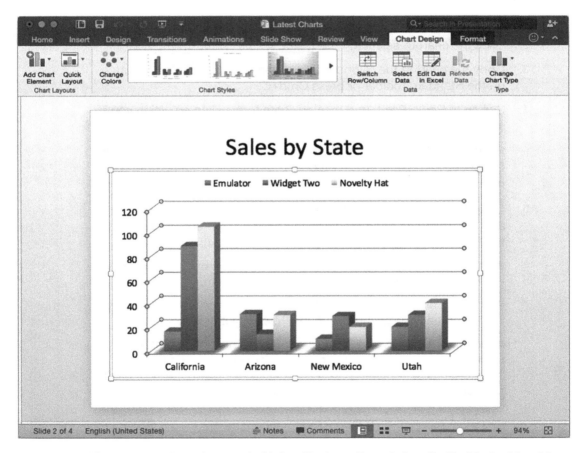

Figure 19-13. After inserting a chart using an embedded workbook, use the controls on the Chart Design tab and the Format tab of the Ribbon to format the chart

7. Save your presentation.

> **Note**   To edit the data on your chart again, click the chart on the slide, and then choose Chart
> Design ➤ Data ➤ Edit Data in Excel from the Ribbon. PowerPoint opens Excel, which displays the
> embedded worksheet.

Pasting a Chart from Excel into a PowerPoint Slide

If you have a chart already created in Excel or if you have a workbook containing the data
from which you will create the chart, you can paste the chart into PowerPoint. Follow these
general steps:

1. Create the chart using the techniques explained in Chapter 14.

2. Click the chart to select it.

3. Copy the chart to the Clipboard. For example, click the Copy button
    on the Standard toolbar or press Cmd+C.

4. Switch to PowerPoint, and then navigate to the slide on which you
    want to insert the chart.

5. Paste in the chart from the Clipboard. For example, choose Home ➤
    Clipboard ➤ Paste from the Ribbon, choose Edit ➤ Paste from the
    menu bar, or press Cmd+V.

6. Click the Paste Options button at the lower-right corner of the chart,
    and then click the appropriate option button in the upper group on
    the Paste Options pop-up menu (see Figure 19-14):

    ■ *Chart (linked to Excel data)*: Select this option button to link the
       chart back to the Excel workbook it came from.

    ■ *Excel Chart (entire workbook)*: Select this option button to embed
       the entire Excel workbook in the PowerPoint presentation.

    ■ *Picture of Chart (smaller file size)*: Select this option button to
       insert a picture of the chart. As the name says, inserting the
       picture helps keep the presentation file size down, but you can't
       edit the picture.

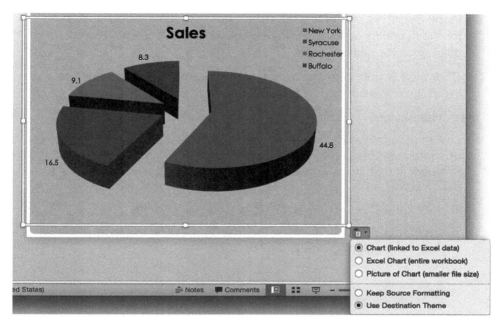

Figure 19-14. When pasting a chart from Excel into a PowerPoint slide, click the Paste Options button, and use the option buttons on the pop-up menu to choose how to paste the chart

7.   If you want the chart on the slide to use the original formatting you gave it in Excel, click the Paste Options button again, and then select the Keep Source Formatting option button. Otherwise, leave the Use Destination Theme option button selected, and the chart will pick up the formatting from the presentation.

8.   Use the controls on the Chart Design tab or the Format tab of the Ribbon to format the chart the way you want it. (If you inserted the chart as a picture, use the controls on the Picture Format tab of the Ribbon.)

9.   Save the presentation.

To edit the data in either an embedded or linked chart, click the chart, and then choose Chart Design ➤ Data from Edit Data in Excel from the Ribbon.

Adding Hyperlinks to Slides

You can add hyperlinks to PowerPoint slides using the standard technique explained in detail in Chapter 3.

1.   Place the insertion point where you want to insert the hyperlink.

2.   Choose Insert ➤ Hyperlink from the menu bar to display the Insert Hyperlink dialog box.

3. In the Select a place in this document box, choose the destination for the hyperlink (see the examples below), and specify the text to display on the slide.

4. Click the OK button to close the Insert Hyperlink dialog box and insert the hyperlink.

In your presentations, you typically use hyperlinks on slides for two purposes:

■ *Link to other slides in the presentation*: To make it easy for the presenter or someone browsing the presentation to move to another slide, add a hyperlink to it. Follow these steps after opening the Insert Hyperlink dialog box:

   ■ Click the This Document tab to display its contents.

   ■ In the Select a place in this document box, click the slide you want the link to display (see Figure 19-15).

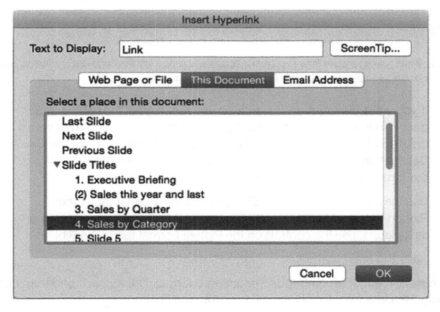

Figure 19-15. Use the Select Place in Document box on the This Document tab of the Insert Hyperlink dialog box to create a link to another slide in the same presentation. This is a great way of enabling the viewer to navigate quickly about the presentation.

   ■ Edit the text in the Text to Display box as needed.

   ■ If you need to provide additional information about the hyperlink, click the ScreenTip button in the Insert Hyperlink dialog box, type ScreenTip text in the Set Hyperlink ScreenTip dialog box, and then click the OK button.

   ■ Click the OK button to close the Insert Hyperlink dialog box and insert the hyperlink.

■ *Link to a web site*: You'll often want to include a link to your web site. In a live presentation, you can click the hyperlink to display your web site directly from a slide. In a presentation you share with others, they can click the hyperlink to go to the web site or to find out how to contact you. Click the Web Page or File tab to display its controls, and then type or paste the address in the Address box.

> **Note**   You can also add a link that starts an e-mail message to a specific address and with a subject line of your choosing. To do so, work on the Email Address tab of the Insert Hyperlink dialog box.

Summary

In this chapter, you learned how to plan and put together attractive and compelling slides. You now know how to use PowerPoint's built-in slide layouts effectively, how to create your own custom layouts, and how to add graphical elements such as table, charts, and SmartArt to your slides.

In the next chapter, I'll show you how to add graphics, movies, and sounds to your presentations; how to animate the objects on a slide; and how to apply transitions between slides.

Chapter **20**

Adding Life and Interest to Your Presentation

In the previous two chapters, you learned how to create a presentation and how to fill it with good-looking slides that convey the message you want. In this chapter, you'll look at how to inject life and interest into a presentation by adding graphics, movies and sounds, animations, and transitions. You'll also learn to hide slides so that they don't appear during a slide show, allowing you to keep them in reserve, and how to create custom slide shows within a presentation so that you can show only specific parts of it.

Adding Pictures to a Presentation

Many slides benefit from having pictures—graphics or photos—to illustrate or offset their text content. You can easily add a picture in these ways:

- *Use a content placeholder*: If the slide includes a content placeholder, click either of the two Picture from File icons to display the Choose a Picture dialog box. Click the picture file, and then click the Insert button.

- *Use the Picture from File command*: If the slide doesn't have a content placeholder, choose Insert ➤ Picture ➤ Pictures ➤ Picture from File from the Ribbon or Insert ➤ Picture ➤ Picture from File from the menu bar to open the Choose a Picture dialog box. Select the picture file you want to add, and then click the Insert button.

- *Drag a photo from the Photo Browser*: If the photo is in the Photos app, choose Insert ➤ Picture ➤ Pictures ➤ Photo Browser from the Ribbon or Insert ➤ Picture ➤ Photo Browser from the menu bar to open the Photo Browser, and then drag the photo to the slide.

- *Drag a picture file from a Finder window*: You can also open a Finder window to the folder that contains the picture file and then drag the picture file to a slide in the PowerPoint window.

© Guy Hart-Davis 2016
G. Hart-Davis, *Learn Office 2016 for Mac*, DOI 10.1007/978-1-4842-2002-3_20

Once you've added a graphic or photo to a slide, you can work with it using the techniques discussed in Chapter 4. For example, you can click the picture and drag it (see Figure 20-1) to where you need it to appear. Or you can use the commands in the Adjust group on the Picture Format tab of the Ribbon to correct the picture's colors, apply filters, or remove the background.

Figure 20-1. The quick way to reposition a picture on a slide is to drag it to where you need it. The ScreenTip shows the details of the picture's position

When you select a picture, PowerPoint adds the Picture Format tab to the Ribbon. You can use the controls on the Picture Format tab to quickly crop and resize the picture as needed. For example, to crop the photo, choose Picture Format ➤ Size ➤ Crop from the Ribbon, and then give the appropriate cropping command on the Crop panel (see Figure 20-2):

- *Crop*: Click this button to display cropping handles around the picture. You can then drag a cropping handle to resize the picture, drag a sizing handle to resize it, or drag the picture to a different position on the slide.

- *Crop to Shape*: Click this item to display the Crop to Shape panel, and then click the shape you want to use. This feature can be great for design effects.

- *Aspect Ratio*: Click this item to display the Aspect Ratio panel, and then click the aspect ratio, such as 3:4 in the Portrait section or 5:3 in the Landscape section.

- *Fill*: Click this item to crop the picture so that it fills the whole placeholder. PowerPoint typically cuts off part of the picture to make it fit, but it doesn't distort the picture. This is usually the best choice for photographs.

- *Fit*: Click this button to resize the picture horizontally, vertically, or both so that the whole picture fits inside the placeholder. Doing this often distorts the picture, so it's not a good choice for most photographs.

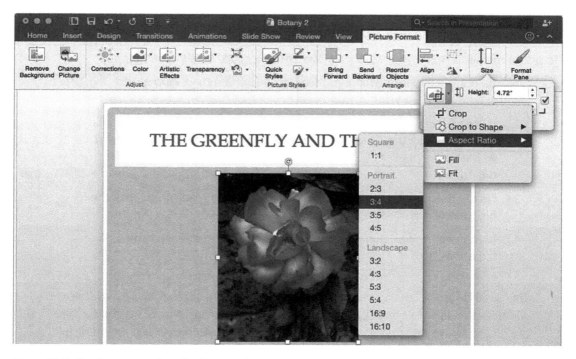

Figure 20-2. Use the commands on the Crop panel to crop a picture the way you want it to appear

Adding Movies and Sounds to a Presentation

Graphics and photos can make a big difference to a presentation, but you may also want to add movies and sounds. This section shows you how to do both.

Adding a Movie to a Slide

You can add a movie file to a slide so that you can play the movie as needed during the presentation. If the movie is in the iMovie app, you can add it by using the Movie Browser. Otherwise, you can add the movie from a file in your Mac's file system.

Adding a Movie from the Movie Browser

To add a movie from the Movie Browser, follow these steps:

1. Choose Insert ➤ Media ➤ Video ➤ Movie Browser from the Ribbon or Insert ➤ Video ➤ Movie Browser from the menu bar to display the Movie Browser.

2. Expand the Movies category, the Photos category, or the iTunes category (as needed) and then navigate to the movie you want to add.

3. Click the movie and drag it to the slide.

Adding a Movie from a File

To add a movie file from your Mac's file system to a slide, follow these steps:

1. Select the slide on which you want to add the movie. Add a new slide if necessary.

2. If the slide has a content placeholder, click the Insert Movie from File icon to display the Choose a Movie dialog box. If not, choose Insert ➤ Media ➤ Video ➤ Movie from File from the Ribbon to open this dialog box.

3. Navigate to the folder that contains the movie file, and then click the file to select it.

4. If you want to link the movie file rather than insert it, select the Link to file check box.

> **Tip**   Linking keeps down the size of the presentation (because the presentation file contains the link rather than the whole movie), but the movie will play only when the movie file is in the same place in the file system as when you created the link. Generally, this means that if you move the presentation to a different Mac, the movie won't play (the exception is if the movie is in exactly the same place in the other Mac's file system, such as on a USB stick or a shared network drive).

5. Click the Insert button. PowerPoint closes the Choose a Movie dialog box and places the movie on the slide.

Making the Movie Look and Play the Way You Want

After inserting a movie, you can change both the way it appears on the slide and how it plays back. To do so, follow these steps:

1. Click the movie to select it. PowerPoint adds the Video Format tab to the Ribbon (see Figure 20-3).

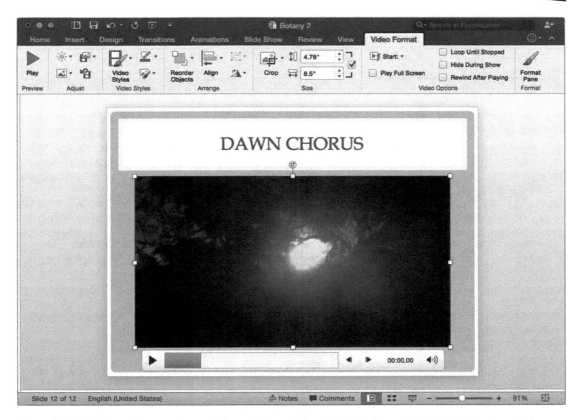

Figure 20-3. After inserting a movie on a slide, use the controls on the Video Format tab of the Ribbon to make it appear the way you want

2. Adjust the movie file's appearance as needed by positioning the movie file and then using the controls on the Video Format tab:

   ■ Click the movie file to select it, and then drag it into the right position on the slide.

   ■ If necessary, resize the movie frame by dragging a corner handle. You can also crop it by choosing Video Format ➤ Size ➤ Crop and then working on the Crop panel.

   ■ To correct the movie's brightness and contrast, choose Video Format ➤ Adjust ➤ Corrections, and then click the balance of brightness and contrast you want.

   ■ To change the movie's color balance, choose Video Format ➤ Adjust ➤ Color, and then click the color option you want. For example, you can apply a sepia hue or make the movie black and white.

   ■ To choose which frame of the movie appears on the slide until you play the movie, use the playback controls to move the movie to the frame you want. Then pause the movie and choose Video Format ➤ Adjust ➤ Poster Frame ➤ Current Frame.

> **Tip** Instead of using a frame from the movie as the poster frame, you can use a still picture. Choose Video Format ➤ Adjust ➤ Poster Frame ➤ Picture from File, select the picture in the Choose a Picture dialog box, and then click the Insert button.

- To put the movie in a frame, choose Video Format ➤ Video Styles and then click the style you want. You can either click one of the styles in the Video Styles box or hold the pointer over the Video Styles box, click the panel button to display the Video Styles panel, and then click the frame you want.

- To crop the movie to a shape, choose Video Format ➤ Size ➤ Crop ➤ Change Shape, and then click the shape on the Change Shape panel.

- To apply effects to the movie, choose Video Format ➤ Video Styles ➤ Video Effects, click the appropriate item on the Effects panel, and then click the effect on the panel that opens. For example, you can apply a shadow, a reflection, or a 3-D rotation.

3. In the Start pop-up menu in the Video Options group on the Video Format tab, choose When Clicked if you want to start the movie playing by clicking it. If you want the movie to start playing automatically, choose Automatically.

4. To control how the movie plays back, use the four check boxes in the Video Options group on the Video Format tab:

   - *Play full screen*: Select this check box to display the movie full screen rather than just in the area it occupies on the slide. This setting is useful for giving the movie full impact without devoting a full slide to it.

   - *Loop until stopped*: Select this check box to make the movie keep playing over and over again until you stop it. Looping the movie can be useful for presentations used at trade shows and the like, but it's cruel and unusual treatment for a regular audience.

   - *Hide during show*: Select this check box to make PowerPoint hide the movie any time it's not playing.

   - *Rewind after playing*: Select this check box to make PowerPoint rewind the movie to the beginning when it reaches the end. Automatic rewinding is useful if you may need to play the movie again.

5. Click the Play button (choose Video Format ➤ Preview ➤ Play) to play the movie and check that everything is how you want it to be.

Adding a Sound to a Slide

Depending on the type of presentation you're creating, you may find it helpful to add sounds to some slides. For example, you can add music that plays automatically when the slide it's on is displayed or insert a sound file that you can play as needed by clicking its icon.

> **Note**   Make sure the audio you add to your slides enhances them rather than distracts the audience. For example, playing background audio when your introductory slide is displayed can help set the scene while your audience is arriving and getting settled, but in a typical spoken presentation, most slides will not need background audio.

You can add a sound to a slide by using the Audio Browser pane, by adding a sound directly from a file, or by recording audio into a slide. The following sections give you the details.

> **Caution**   If you add to a presentation an audio file that you've bought from Apple's iTunes Store in a protected audio format (such as AAC), you'll be able to play the audio back only on computers authorized for your iTunes account. When you move a presentation to a different computer, double-check that your audio files play correctly before you give a presentation.

Adding a Sound from the Audio Browser

If the sound you want to use is in your iTunes library or in GarageBand, you can add it by using the Audio Browser. Choose Insert ➤ Media ➤ Audio ➤ Audio Browser from the Ribbon or Insert ➤ Audio ➤ Audio Browser from the menu bar to display the Audio Browser, locate the sound you want, and then drag it to the slide.

Adding a Sound from a File

If the sound you want to use isn't in your iTunes library or in GarageBand but rather in a file in your Mac's file system, follow these steps to add it to a slide:

1. Select the slide on which you want to add the audio.

2. Choose Insert ➤ Media ➤ Audio ➤ Audio from File from the Ribbon or Insert ➤ Audio ➤ Audio from File from the menu bar to display the Choose Audio dialog box.

3. Navigate to the folder that contains the file you want to insert, and then click the file.

4. If you want to link the audio file rather than embed it, select the Link to file check box. Normally, you want to do this only when you will deliver the presentation on the same Mac you're using to create the presentation.

5. Click the Insert button. PowerPoint adds the sound to the slide.

> **Tip**   You can also add a file from a sound by dragging the sound file from a Finder window to a slide.

Recording Audio into a Slide

Using a prerecorded sound works well for many slides, but you may also want to record custom audio for other slides. PowerPoint's Record Audio feature lets you record audio directly onto a slide using your Mac's microphone or other audio hardware you've connected.

> **Note**   Recording audio via the microphone is fine for adding narration to individual slides. But if you need to create high-quality recorded audio, use an app such as GarageBand to create a sound file and process it as needed. Then add the finished file to the presentation by using the Audio Browser pane.

To record audio onto a slide, follow these steps:

1. Select the slide.

2. Choose Insert ➤ Media ➤ Audio ➤ Record Audio from the Ribbon or Insert ➤ Audio ➤ Record Audio from the menu bar to display the Record Sound dialog box (see Figure 20-4).

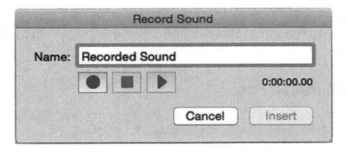

Figure 20-4. Use the Record Sound dialog box when you need to record audio directly onto a slide

3. In the Name text box, type the name you want to give the sound. PowerPoint suggests the generic "Recorded Sound," but a more descriptive name is usually more helpful.

4. Click the Record button (the red circle, as usual) to start the recording. Speak or perform the audio, and then click the Stop button to stop recording.

5. Click the Play button (the black triangle pointing right) to play back the audio and check that it has come out acceptably. Re-record it if necessary.

6. Click the Insert button to save the audio on the slide. PowerPoint closes the Record Sound dialog box and adds the sound to the slide.

Positioning the Sound and Setting Its Volume

Whichever of the previous three ways you use to add the sound to the slide, PowerPoint inserts an audio icon (see Figure 20-5) representing the sound.

Figure 20-5. PowerPoint inserts an audio item as a speaker icon. Click the icon to display controls for testing the audio and setting the volume

Select the icon by clicking it, and then drag it to where you want it to appear. Then, with the icon still selected, use the pop-up controls to test the audio clip and set the volume at which you want it to play.

Adding Transitions to Slides

Instead of having a straightforward switchover from one slide to the next, you can set PowerPoint to play a *transition*, which is an effect that smoothes, animates, or dramatizes the change of slides. You can set a different transition for each side if necessary. You specify the transition by selecting the slide and choosing the transition to play when the slide appears (as opposed to setting the transition for when PowerPoint changes the slide to the next).

PowerPoint provides a wide range of transitions that you can apply from the Transitions tab of the Ribbon (see Figure 20-6).

Figure 20-6. The Transitions tab of the Ribbon gives you one-stop access to the key controls for setting up transitions between slides

> **Note** Depending on the presentation template or design you're using, some or all of the slides in the presentation may already have transitions applied to them.

PowerPoint breaks up the transitions into three categories:

- *Subtle*: Use these transitions when you don't need to draw the audience's attention to the transition. The first transition in the Subtle category is the None transition, which you apply when you don't want a transition effect between slides.

- *Exciting*: Use these transitions when you want to make sure the audience notices the transition. For example, you can use an effect such as Vortex or Shred to dramatize the switchover from one slide to another that uses a similar look and so might be mistaken for the previous slide.

- *Dynamic Content*: Use these transitions when you want to draw attention to the transition. For example, the Ferris Wheel transition makes the incoming slide go around as if it were moving on a Ferris wheel.

Tip   PowerPoint's transitions are easy and fun to apply, but don't go hog wild with them. In a typical presentation, not every slide benefits from a transition; and when you do use a transition, one of the Subtle transitions often gives the best effect. Keep the Exciting and Dynamic Content transitions for those rare occasions when you actually want to draw your audience's attention to the transition rather than to the content of the slides.

To apply a transition, follow these steps:

1. Click the slide to which you want to apply the transition.

2. Click the Transitions tab to display its contents.

3. Apply the transition you want:

    - If the transition appears in the Transitions box in the Transition to This Slide group, click it. You can also scroll the list of transitions to the left or right to make other transitions appear in the box. PowerPoint plays a preview of the transition in the Slide pane.

    - If the transition doesn't appear, hold the pointer over the Transitions box until the panel button appears, and then click the panel button to display the Transitions panel (see Figure 20-7), which lists the transitions in the three categories discussed above. Click the transition you want. Again, PowerPoint plays a preview of the transition in the Slide pane.

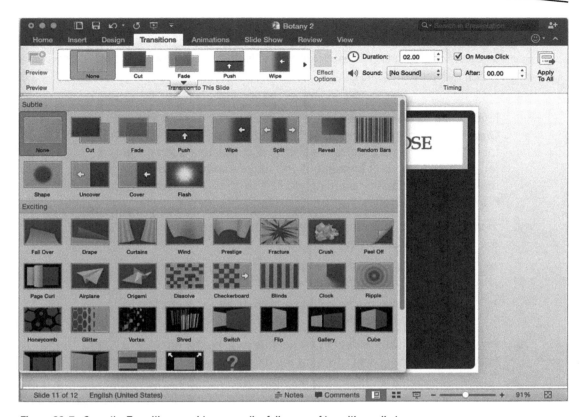

Figure 20-7. Open the Transition panel to access the full range of transitions all at once

4. To choose options for the transition, choose Transitions ➤ Transition to This Slide ➤ Effect Options from the Ribbon, and then click the option you want on the Effect Options panel that opens.

    ■ The choices on the Effect Options panel vary depending on the transition you've selected. For example, the Vortex transition has four directional options (From Left, From Top, From Right, and From Bottom), while the Honeycomb transition has no options.

    ■ PowerPoint plays a preview of the effect after you select it. To preview the transition again, choose Transitions ➤ Preview ➤ Preview from the Ribbon.

5. If you want to add a sound to the transition, choose Transitions ➤ Timing ➤ Sound from the Ribbon, and then click the sound on the pop-up menu. You can make the sound keep playing until the next sound starts (open the Sound pop-up menu, go right to the bottom, and then click the Loop Until Next Sound option to place a check mark next to it), but this is not usually a good idea.

> **Note**   To use a sound other than PowerPoint's built-in sounds, choose Transitions ➤ Timing ➤ Sound ➤ Other Sound from the Ribbon, click the sound file in the "Choose a .wav Sound" dialog box, and then click the Insert button.

6.   If you want to change the duration of the transition, set it in the Duration box in the Transition to This Slide group on the Transitions tab. PowerPoint automatically sets the duration to a suitable length for the transition you choose, but you may need to change it to make your presentation's timing work. The units are seconds and hundredths of seconds.

7.   In the Timing group on the Transitions tab, choose how to advance the slide to the next slide:

   ■   *On Mouse Click*: Select this check box if you want to click the pointing device to move to the next slide.

   ■   *After*: To display the next slide automatically, select this check box, and then set the timing in the text box.

8.   Preview the transition again to make sure it gives the effect you want, and then click the Save button on the title bar to save your changes.

> **Note**   If you want to apply the same transition to all slides, choose the transition and its options, and then choose Transitions ➤ Timing ➤ Apply to All from the Ribbon. You may want to apply the same transition to all slides at first, and then apply a different transition or different effects to a few slides that deserve special attention.

Adding Animations to Slides

When you need to bring a slide to life, you can animate one or more of the objects on it. For example, you may need to make an object appear on a slide, draw attention to itself at a key point, or disappear from view when its role is over—or all three.

You can also use animations to reveal only part of a slide or part of an object at a time, which can help keep the audience focused on your current point rather than reading ahead to the end of the slide.

Understanding the Essentials of Animations

To add an animation to a slide, you apply it to an object on the slide, such as a picture or a text placeholder. Any object can have one or more animations, and you can arrange them into the order you need.

Caution   As with transitions, it's easy to go over the top with animations. Resist the temptation! Animations will have more effect in your slides if you use them sparingly and only at the appropriate times. When you do use animations, make sure the ones you choose work together; PowerPoint provides a wide variety of animations to help you achieve different effects, not to suggest you should use them all in the same presentation—let alone on the same slide.

PowerPoint provides a wide range of animations in four categories:

- *Entrance effects*: These animations bring the object onto the slide. For example, the Appear animation makes the object appear in place, while the Swivel animation makes the object appear and swivel several times.

- *Emphasis effects*: These animations help draw the audience's attention to the object. For example, the Pulse animation makes the object pulse visibly, and the Spin animation makes the object revolve around its axis.

- *Exit effects*: These animations remove the object from the slide. For example, the Disappear animation makes the object vanish, while the Shrink & Turn animation makes the object turn sideways as it disappears into the distance.

- *Path animations*: These animations make the object move around and then return to its original position.

The next section shows you how to add a straightforward animation to an object. The section after that shows you how to create more complex animations.

Adding an Animation to an Object

To add a straightforward animation to an object on a slide, follow these steps:

1. Click the object to select it.

2. Click the Animations tab of the Ribbon to display its controls.

3. Add an Entrance effect, an Emphasis effect, or an Exit effect by following these steps. The example adds an Entrance effect.

   - Hold the pointer over the Entrance Effects box to display the panel button.

   - Click the panel button to display the Entrance Effects panel (see Figure 20-8).

   - Click the effect. PowerPoint applies the effect and plays a preview of it.

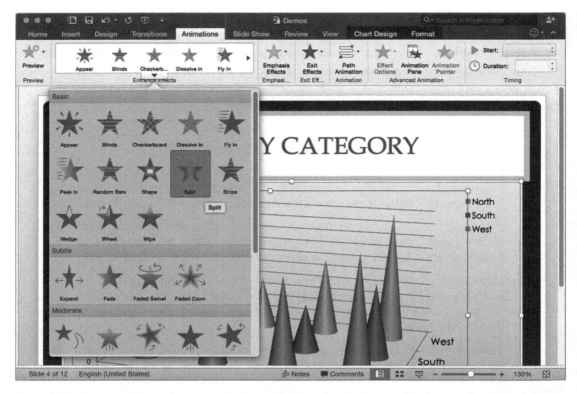

Figure 20-8. You can quickly apply an animation to an object by using the Entrance Effects panel, the Emphasis Effects panel, the Exit Effects panel, or the Path Animation panel on the Animations tab of the Ribbon

■ Apply any options the effect needs by choosing Animations ➤ Advanced Animation ➤ Effect Options from the Ribbon and then clicking the appropriate item on the Effect Options panel. The options available depend on the effect you've chosen; for example, many animations offer direction options such as From Bottom, From Bottom-Left, From Left, From Top-Left, From Top, From Top-Right, From Right, and From Bottom-Right. Some effects have no options.

4. To control when the animation runs, use the controls in the Timing group:

■ Open the Start pop-up menu, and choose when to start the animation: On Click (in other words, when you click the pointing device), With Previous (at the same time as the previous animation), or After Previous (after the previous animation has finished).

■ In the Duration text box, set the number of seconds and hundredths of seconds you want the animation to run, such as 1.50 for one and a half seconds.

5. Repeat steps 3 and 4 to add further animations as needed. For example, if you've already added an Entrance effect to an object, you may want to add an Exit effect as well.

Note   If you need to change the order of animations you've applied to an object, work as described in the next section.

6. Click the Preview button in the Preview group to preview the animation and see whether you need to make further changes.

Changing the Order of Animations

When you apply multiple animations to the same slide, you may need to change the order in which they occur. To do so, choose Animations ➤ Advanced Animation ➤ Animation Pane from the Ribbon to display the Animation pane. Figure 20-9 shows a slide that contains six animations, including all those applied to the text container, with the Animation pane open.

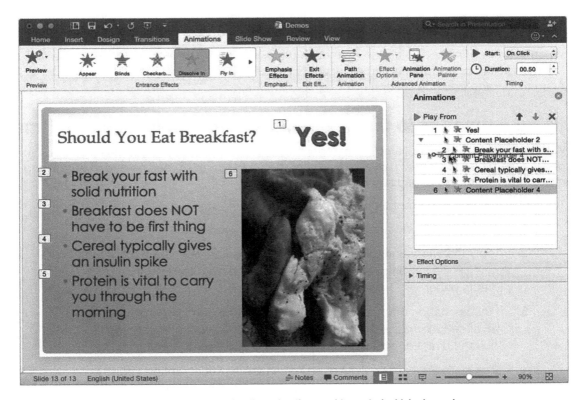

Figure 20-9. Use the Animation pane to examine the animations and to control which plays when

These are the main actions you can take in the Animation pane:

■   *Play an animation*: In the Animation order list box, Ctrl-click or right-click the animation, and then click Play From on the context menu. Alternatively, click the Play From button at the top of the Animations pane.

- *Change the order of the animations*: In the Animation order list box, click an animation to select it, and then click the Up button or the Down button to move it up or down the list. You can also drag an animation up or down the list; drop it when the blue line appears in the right place.

- *Expand or collapse a container's animations*: Click the disclosure triangle to expand or collapse the list of a container's animation. In Figure 20-9, the list for Content Placeholder 2 is expanded.

- *Change an animation's effect options*: Click an animation to select it, click the Effect Options heading in the Animations pane to display the effect options, and then work with the controls. (You can click the disclosure triangle next to the Effect Options heading instead, but clicking the heading is usually easier.)

- *Change an animation's timing*: Click an animation to select it, click the Timing heading in the Animations pane to display the timing options, and then work with the controls. Here, too, you can click the disclosure triangle next to the Timing heading if you prefer.

When you have finished using the Animation pane, close it by clicking its Close button (the X button in its upper-right corner) or by choosing Animations ➤ Advanced Animation ➤ Animation Pane from the Ribbon.

Using Animation to Display Bulleted Paragraphs One at a Time

When you have several bulleted paragraphs in a text placeholder, you can use animation to display them one at a time. This helps prevent the audience from reading ahead of you and missing the point you're explaining.

To display bulleted paragraphs one at a time, follow these steps:

1. Click the container that holds the bulleted paragraphs.

2. Apply the animation to the container from the appropriate Effects panel. For example, apply the Fly In animation from the Entrance Effects panel.

3. If the animation offers different directions, choose Animations ➤ Advanced Animation ➤ Effect Options from the Ribbon, and then click the direction you want. For example, click From Right.

4. Choose Animations ➤ Advanced Animation ➤ Effect Options from the Ribbon again, and this time click the Sequence option you want:

   - *As One Object*: PowerPoint animates the whole object at once.

   - *All at Once*: PowerPoint animates each top-level paragraph separately but runs the animations all at once. Depending on the animation, this can look very similar to As One Object, but it can also look different.

   - *By Paragraph*: PowerPoint animates each top-level paragraph separately. This is usually the most useful setting.

5. Click the Play button (choose Animations ➤ Preview ➤ Preview from the Ribbon) to preview the effect.

6. Click the container that holds the bulleted paragraphs.

7. If the text has different levels, and you need to control their paragraphs separately, click the Text Animations heading in the Animations pane to display the Text Animations controls (see Figure 20-10).

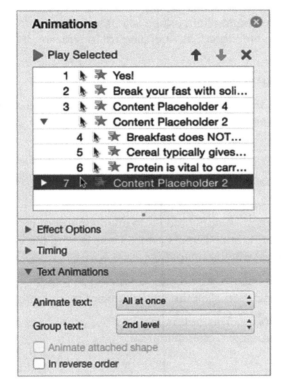

Figure 20-10. In the Group text pop-up menu in the Text Animations section of the Animation pane, choose the level of paragraphs by which you want to animate the object

8. Open the Group text pop-up menu and choose the animation you want: All paragraphs at once, 1st level, 2nd level, 3rd level, 4th level, or 5th level. For example, if the container has two levels of paragraphs, and you want to control both separately, choose 2nd level.

Note   In the Text Animations area of the Animation pane, you can also choose to animate text by word or by letter rather than all at once. Open the Animate text pop-up menu, and then choose By word or By letter, as needed, instead of All at once.

---

9. Select the In reverse order check box if you want to animate the paragraphs in reverse order.

10. Choose Animations ➤ Advanced Animation ➤ Animation Pane from the Ribbon or click the Close (X) button in the upper-right corner of the Animation pane to close the pane.

Animating SmartArt Graphics, Charts, and Tables

You can apply animations to SmartArt graphics, charts, and tables just as you can to other objects in PowerPoint. Animations are especially useful when you want to reveal only part of one of these objects at a time, gradually building up to showing the whole object.

Animating a SmartArt Graphic

PowerPoint enables you to animate the component parts of a SmartArt graphic in sequence, so you can choose between displaying the whole object at once, displaying all the objects at a particular level, or displaying one object at a time.

To choose how to display a SmartArt graphic, follow these steps:

1. Select the SmartArt graphic by clicking it on the slide.

2. Apply the animation to the graphic as a whole from one of the Effects panels. For example, apply the Fade animation from the Subtle section of the Entrance Effects panel. Fade makes the whole graphic appear at once with the animation.

3. Choose Animations ➤ Advanced Animation ➤ Effect Options from the Ribbon, and then click the way you want to animate the graphic:

    ■ *As One Object*: This option displays the graphic as a single object, so it all appears in one animation.

> **Note** The selection of options on the Effect Options pop-up menu depends on the object you're animating. For example, the Level at Once option and the Level One by One option appear only for objects that have levels.

    ■ *All at Once*: This option treats the graphic as separate objects but runs the animation on all the objects at once.

    ■ *One by One*: This option treats each component of the graphic as a separate object. In many cases, this is the most useful option.

    ■ *Level at Once*: This option treats each level of a hierarchical SmartArt graphic as a separate object. Choose this option when you want to display one level of the graphic at a time.

> ■ *Level One by One*: This option treats each level of a hierarchical SmartArt graphic as a separate object and treats each object within the level as a separate object. Choose this option when you want to display the graphic one object of a level at a time.

4. Choose Animations ➤ Preview ➤ Preview to preview the effect.

5. If you need to change the order, choose Animations ➤ Advanced Animation ➤ Animation Pane from the Ribbon. PowerPoint displays the Animation pane.

6. In the list box, click the container that holds the SmartArt object. PowerPoint displays the SmartArt Animation section at the bottom of the Animation pane.

7. Open the Group graphic pop-up menu, and then click the option you want. The options available depend on the type of SmartArt graphic, but these are typical:

> ■ *As one object*: Choose this option to display the whole SmartArt graphic at once.

> ■ *All at once*: Choose this option to display all the components of the SmartArt graphic at once.

> ■ *One by one*: Choose this option to display one component at a time.

> ■ *By branch one by one*: Choose this option to display each branch of a graphic such as an org chart separately, showing one component at a time.

> ■ *By level at once*: Choose this option to display each level of a graphic separately, showing the whole level at once.

> ■ *By level one by one*: Choose this option to display each level of a graphic separately, showing one component at a time.

8. If you want to reveal the SmartArt graphic in reverse order, select the Reverse order check box.

9. Choose Animations ➤ Advanced Animation ➤ Animation Pane from the Ribbon or click the Close (X) button in the upper-right corner of the Animation pane to close the pane.

Animating a Chart

When you're displaying a chart, it's often helpful to use an animation to show part of it at a time rather than displaying the whole chart at once. To do this, follow these steps:

1. Select the chart by clicking it on the slide that contains it.

2. Apply the animation to the chart as a whole from one of the Effects panels. For example, apply the Appear animation.

3. Choose Animations ➤ Advanced Animation ➤ Effect Options from the Ribbon, and then click the way you want to animate the chart:

    ■ *As one object*: This setting displays the chart all at once, so you probably won't want to use it.

    ■ *By series*: This setting displays one full data series at a time and is good for contrasting the data series to each other.

    ■ *By category*: This setting displays one whole category at a time and is good for comparing the categories.

    ■ *By element in series*: This setting displays each element in a series at a time, then the next element in the series, and so on, until the series is finished. This setting is great for focusing on the individual elements in the series.

    ■ *By element in category*: This setting displays each element in a category at a time, then the category's next element, and so on. Use this setting to zero in on the individual elements in the categories.

Note   If you insert a chart as a picture, you can't animate its components.

---

4. If necessary, choose Animations ➤ Advanced Animation ➤ Animation Pane from the Ribbon to display the Animation pane, click the chart's placeholder in the list box, and then adjust the settings. For example, if you've chosen the By Element in Series option, you can set the elements in a series to display automatically one after the other, using a short delay between them (set the delay in the Delay box in the Timing section of the Animations pane).

5. Preview the animation and make sure that the objects appear as you want them to appear.

Animating a Table

When you're displaying a complex table on a slide, it's often helpful to display the rows, columns, or even cells one at a time to keep the audience's attention on the data you're currently talking about. PowerPoint's animations don't work for rows, columns, or cells, so you need to take matters into your own hands.

Here are two approaches you can use:

- *Create two or more separate tables*: Create two or more separate tables and position them next to each other so that they appear to be a single table. You can then animate each of the tables separately, giving the effect of animating different parts of the same table. This approach sounds clumsy, but it's easy to do, and it's effective visually.

- *Hide parts of the table*: Create a single table, and then cover those parts you want to hide with shapes (for example, rectangles) colored the same as the slide's background. You can then reveal a hidden part of the table by running an Exit animation on the shape that's covering it.

Tip   Sometimes you may want to trigger each animation manually so that you can control the timing, but it can be handy to string other animations together so that when one animation ends, the next runs automatically. For example, when you click to display the next bullet point, you can make a picture appear automatically on the slide. To do this, select the animation you want to run automatically, and then choose Animations ➤ Timing ➤ Start ➤ After Previous from the Ribbon. If you want to run an animation simultaneously with the previous one, choose Animations ➤ Timing ➤ Start ➤ With Previous from the Ribbon.

Keeping Extra Information up Your Sleeve with Hidden Slides

In many presentations, it's useful to have extra information that you can summon up to deal with points you don't want to cover unless the audience raises them. To meet this need, PowerPoint lets you hide any slide so that it doesn't appear unless you specifically choose to display it.

To hide a slide, Ctrl-click or right-click the slide in the Slides tab of the Navigation pane or in Slide Sorter view, and then click Hide Slide on the context menu. You can also choose Slide Show ➤ Set Up ➤ Hide Slide from the Ribbon or Slide Show ➤ Hide Slide from the menu bar.

PowerPoint indicates a hidden slide by dimming it and showing a circle with a diagonal line (see Figure 20-11) in the Slides tab in Normal view and in the slides area in Slide Sorter view. On the Go to Slide menu in Slide Show view, a hidden slide appears with parentheses around its slide number.

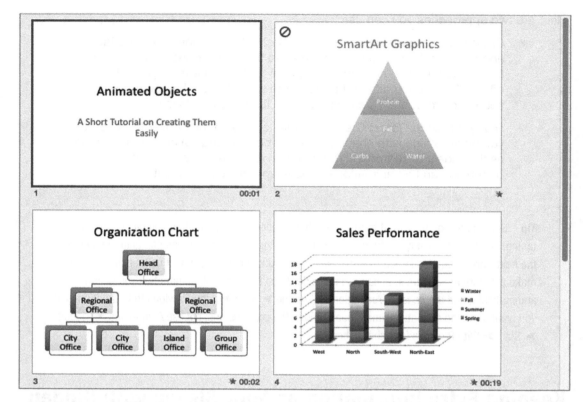

Figure 20-11. *In Slide Sorter view and on the Slides tab of the Navigation pane, a circle with a diagonal strikethrough (as in the upper-left corner of the upper-right slide here) indicates a hidden slide*

To change a slide back from hidden to normal, Ctrl-click or right-click the slide, and then click Hide Slide again, turning off the hiding; PowerPoint removes the check mark from the context menu. You can also choose Slide Show ➤ Set Up ➤ Hide Slide from the Ribbon or Slide Show ➤ Hide Slide from the menu bar.

Creating Custom Slide Shows Within a Presentation

Hidden slides can be great when you want to keep some information in reserve, but if you find yourself hiding many slides within a presentation, you may need to take the next step—creating a custom slide show.

A custom slide show is an arrangement of slides within a presentation. You can choose which of the presentation's slides to include in the custom show, and you can change the order in which they appear. You can create as many custom slide shows within a presentation as you need.

Opening the Custom Shows Dialog Box

To work with custom shows, first open the Custom Shows dialog box by choosing Slide Show ➤ Start Slide Show ➤ Custom Show ➤ Custom Slide Show from the Ribbon or Slide Show ➤ Custom Slide Show ➤ Custom Shows from the menu bar. Figure 20-12 shows the Custom Shows dialog box with three custom shows already created.

Figure 20-12. *From the Custom Shows dialog box, you can create, launch, and manage custom slide shows within a presentation*

Creating a Custom Slide Show

To create a custom slide show, follow these steps:

1. Create all the slides for the presentation or as many of the slides as you can create at this point. (You can add other slides later, but it's easiest to start with all your slides if you've created them.)

2. Choose Slide Show ➤ Start Slide Show ➤ Custom Show ➤ Custom Slide Show from the Ribbon or Slide Show ➤ Custom Slide Show ➤ Custom Shows from the menu bar to display the Custom Shows dialog box.

3. Click the New (+) button to display the Define Custom Show dialog box (shown in Figure 20-13).

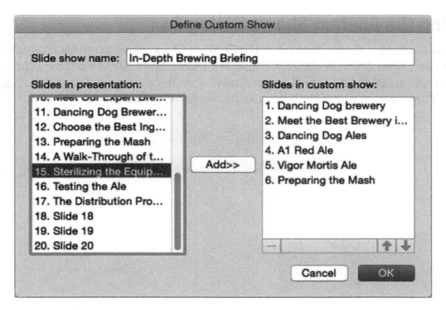

Figure 20-13. Use the Define Custom Show dialog box to name a custom show, add slides to it, and put the slides in the order you want

4. In the Slide show name box, type the name you want to give the custom show. Make the name as descriptive as possible while keeping it short enough to fit fully in the Custom shows box in the Custom Shows dialog box—40 characters or so at most.

5. In the "Slides in presentation" box, click each slide you want to add to the custom show, and then click the Add button.

6. Once you've added the slides you want to the "Slides in custom show" box, rearrange them into the order needed. To move a slide up or down the order, click it, and then click the Up arrow button or the Down arrow button in the lower-right corner of the "Slides in custom show" box, as needed.

7. When you've finished creating the custom show, click the OK button to close the Define Custom Show dialog box. PowerPoint returns you to the Custom Shows dialog box, where the Custom Shows list box includes the custom show you just created.

> **Tip**   To create another show based on a custom show you've created, click the existing show in the Custom Shows dialog box, click the Action button (the gear icon), and then click Copy on the pop-up menu. PowerPoint creates a new custom show called *Copy of* and the existing show's name, such as *Copy of Brewery Introduction*. With the copy still selected, click the Action button and then click Edit on the pop-up menu button to open the copy in the Define Custom Show dialog box. You can then rename the copy and change its contents.

Playing a Custom Slide Show

After you've created a custom slide show, you can play it in either of these ways:

- Choose Slide Show ➤ Start Slide Show ➤ Custom Shows on the Ribbon, and then click the custom show's name on the Custom Shows pop-up menu.

- Open the Custom Shows dialog box, click the show in the Custom Shows list, and then click the Start Show button.

Editing or Deleting a Custom Slide Show

To edit a custom slide show, open the Custom Shows dialog box, click the custom show's name in the Custom Shows list, click the Action button, and then click Edit on the pop-up menu. You can then use the Define Custom Show dialog box to change the selection of slides in the show or alter their order as needed.

To delete a custom show, click its name in the Custom Shows list in the Custom Shows dialog box, and then click the Remove (–) button. PowerPoint removes the show without confirmation.

Summary

In this chapter, you looked at how to add graphics, movies, and sounds to your slides. You also learned how to smooth or dramatize the switchover from one slide to another by choosing a suitable transition to introduce the next slide and how to bring the elements of a slide to life by applying animations and setting them to run the way you want.

You can now also hide slides that you want to keep in reserve and create custom slide shows consisting of only some of the slides from a presentation.

By now, you know how to put together a powerful and convincing presentation. The next stage is to deliver the presentation. You'll learn how to do this in the next chapter.

Chapter 21

Delivering a Presentation Live or Online

By this point, you've created a powerful and compelling presentation stuffed with great content. Now it's time to deliver that presentation.

With PowerPoint, you can deliver a presentation in a handful of ways. The most straightforward way is by giving it live to your audience, showing the slides on a screen. This can be a challenge, but PowerPoint helps greatly by providing Presenter view, which puts your notes and essential controls where you can see them but the audience can't.

To help your audience enjoy your presentation and retain its message, you can print a handout or create a PDF file for distribution. If you need to distribute a presentation rather than deliver it personally, you can record narration to fit the slides.

Later in the chapter, I'll show you how to export and share your presentations. Apart from using means of sharing that you already know, such as e-mailing a presentation or saving a presentation to a SharePoint site or OneDrive, you can save the slides as a series of picture files that you can use separately.

I'll start by going over how to prepare to deliver a presentation—setting up the display, arranging Presenter view, practicing your presentation, and (if you need to) recording automatic timings.

Getting Ready to Deliver a Presentation in Person

Before you deliver a presentation, you need to set up the Mac you'll use with the projector or display on which you'll show the presentation. You will likely want to use PowerPoint's handy Presenter view if possible to keep your notes and controls on-screen. You will almost certainly want to practice your presentation before you actually have to give it. And you may want to record automatic timings for the slides so that the presentation automatically advances itself while you perform.

© Guy Hart-Davis 2016
G. Hart-Davis, *Learn Office 2016 for Mac*, DOI 10.1007/978-1-4842-2002-3_21

Setting Up Your Display and Choosing the Resolution

Start by connecting your Mac to the display or projector on which you'll give the presentation, and then get the displays set up. Here's an example using a MacBook:

1. Connect the display or projector to the MacBook's external display port.

Note   Check the kind of connector cable you need to connect the projector or display to your Mac's external display port. Most current Macs use a Thunderbolt port for output, while older Macs use a Mini DisplayPort, Digital Visual Interface (DVI), or Mini-DVI port; some Macs also have a High-Definition Multimedia Interface (HDMI) port. The 12-inch MacBook has only a USB-C port, so you need to get Apple's USB-C Digital Apple TV Multiport Adapter, which includes an HDMI port. Recent projectors use an HDMI port or DVI port, while many older projectors use a Video Graphics Array (VGA) port; current displays use Thunderbolt, Mini DisplayPort, DVI, or HDMI. Unless your Mac has the same connector type as the projector or display, you need a converter cable such as a Mini DisplayPort to HDMI converter. You can get these from the Apple Store (`http://store.apple.com`) or other online or real-world computer stores.

Thunderbolt and Mini DisplayPort use the same size and shape of connector, but they have different capabilities. Thunderbolt is a multipurpose high-speed technology that includes graphical output capability, whereas Mini DisplayPort is for graphics only. So you can plug a Mini DisplayPort cable into a Mac's Thunderbolt port and get graphical output, but you cannot plug a Thunderbolt cable into a Mini DisplayPort port and get the other Thunderbolt capabilities.

---

2. Turn on the projector or display.

3. Turn on the MacBook and log on.

4. Choose Apple ➤ System Preferences to display the System Preferences window.

5. Choose View ➤ Displays from the menu bar to switch to the Displays preferences pane. OS X shows two Displays windows: one for the MacBook on its screen and one for the projector or external display on the other screen.

6. In the MacBook's Displays window, click the Arrangement tab to display its contents (see Figure 21-1).

Note   If the Arrangement tab doesn't appear in the Displays preferences pane, check the connection of the projector or external display and make sure it is receiving power. If the connection and power are okay, try restarting your Mac.

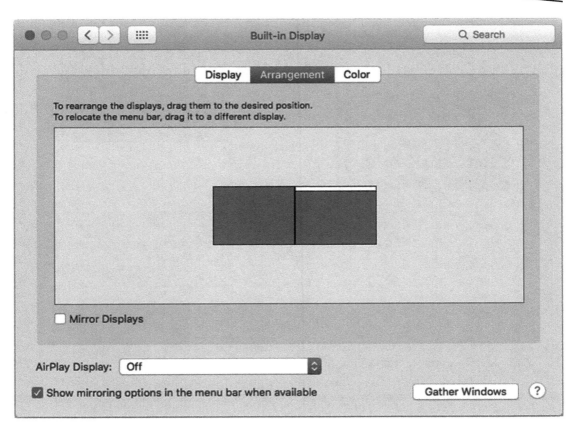

Figure 21-1. Start by setting up the projector or the external display in the Displays pane in System Preferences

7. Drag the display icons to match how the displays are physically positioned. For example, if the projector will be projecting onto a screen that you'll see over the top of your MacBook's display, drag the icon for the projector so that it is above the icon for the MacBook's display. Positioning the displays like this helps you avoid confusing them and enables you to move the pointer accurately from one display to the other.

8. Make sure the Mirror Displays check box is cleared so that you can use Presenter view on the MacBook.

9. If you need to change the resolution for the projector or external display, click the Displays window for that display. On the Display tab (see Figure 21-2), click the Scaled option button, and then choose the resolution in the resolutions list that appears. You can also change the rotation, the refresh rate, and the underscan setting if necessary.

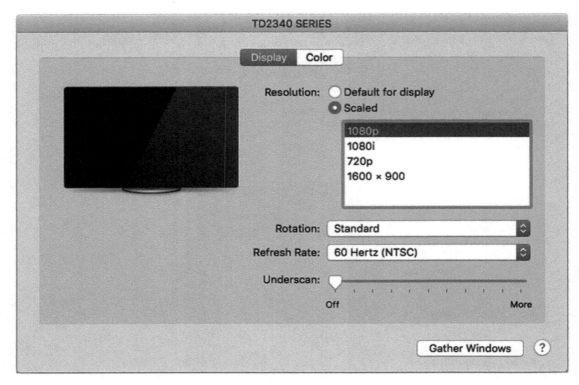

Figure 21-2. You can change the resolution for the projector or external display on the Display tab of the Displays window

10. When you've finished, click the Close button (the red button at the left end of the title bar) on one of the Displays windows or press Cmd+Q to quit System Preferences.

Using Presenter View

The Presenter view is perhaps PowerPoint's biggest aid for giving an effective presentation. While the audience sees only the slide you're currently displaying in Slide Show view, Presenter view (see Figure 21-3) shows your current slide, the next slide or object that will appear, and the slide's notes. Normally, you use Presenter view on your laptop's screen so you're the only one who can see it; you show the slides for the audience on the projector or external monitor.

You can switch to Presenter view in any of these ways:

- ■ *Ribbon*: Choose Slide Show ➤ Start Slide Show ➤ Presenter View.
- ■ *Menu bar*: Choose View ➤ Presenter View.
- ■ *Keyboard*: Press Option + Return.

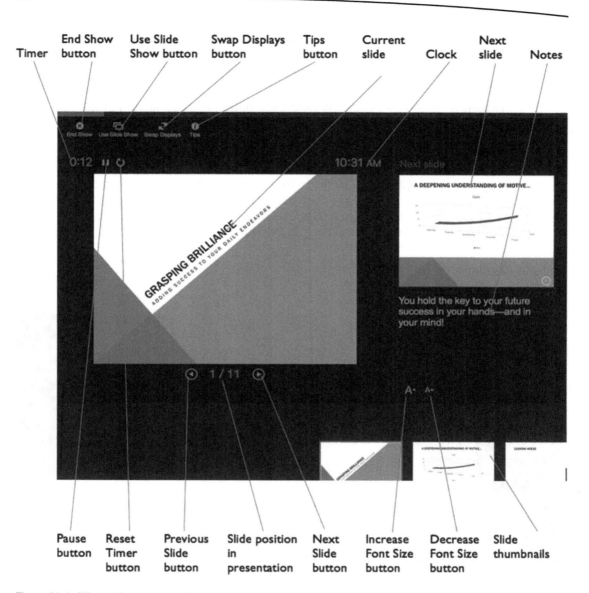

Figure 21-3. When giving a presentation, use Presenter view on a second screen to control the presentation, display your notes, and navigate quickly from slide to slide

In Presenter view, you can take the following actions:

- *View the current slide*: The current slide appears on the left side of the window.

- *View the next slide or object*: The next slide, or the next object that will appear on the current slide, appears in the upper-right corner of Presenter view.

■ *Consult your notes*: The notes for the current slide appear in the Notes pane in the lower-right part of the window. You can click the Increase Font Size button or the Decrease Font Size button to adjust the text to a comfortable size for viewing.

■ *Display another slide*: Click the Next Slide button to move along to the next slide, or click the Previous Slide button to move back to the previous slide. To move in bigger steps, move the pointer over the current slide, making four tiny icons appear in its lower-left corner (you can see three of them in Figure 21-4, but the fourth is obscured by the pop-up menu). Click the Control button to display the control menu, click or highlight By Title, and then click the slide you want on the submenu that appears (see Figure 21-4). You can also click Last Viewed on the control menu to jump back to the last slide viewed.

Control button

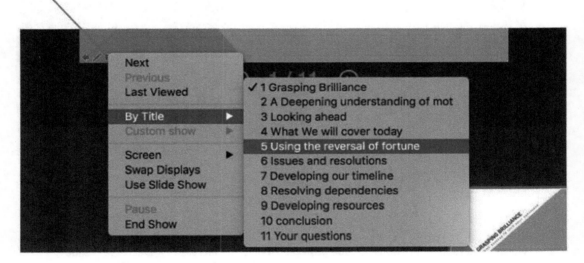

Figure 21-4. Use the control menu to navigate from slide to slide in the presentation

---

Tip   To move to another slide that you identify visually, click the slide in the slide thumbnails bar at the bottom of Presenter view.

■ *End the slide show*: Click the End Show button. You can also press Esc.

Note   If you don't have a second monitor or projector for Presenter view, you need to fall back on traditional means of handling your notes—memorizing them, printing them on cards, or writing them on the palm of your hand or on your cuff.

Practicing Your Presentation

To make sure your presentation goes well on the day, practice it until you're confident you know your material and you can speak fluently from the notes you've given yourself. If you find your notes need more detail, rearranging, or other improvements, work on them too.

Ideally, you will rehearse your presentation in the room in which you will deliver the presentation, using the same equipment. Sometimes you can do this; for example, if you'll be speaking in your company or organization, you may be able to book the conference room for your run-through. But if you will deliver the presentation elsewhere, as is often the case, you will need to practice wherever you find most convenient—preferably somewhere you can speak aloud with interruption or drawing unwelcome attention.

To practice your presentation, use Presenter view (if you'll use it during your presentation) or your notes. You may also want to set timings for slides, as discussed next.

Rehearsing Timings for Slides

For some presentations, you may need to set automatic timings for slides so that you don't need to cue them manually. To set timings, use PowerPoint's Rehearse Timings feature like this:

1. Choose Slide Show ➤ Set Up ➤ Rehearse Timings from the Ribbon or Slide Show ➤ Rehearse Timings from the menu bar. PowerPoint starts the slide show using Presenter view but displays a different timer near the top of the screen (see Figure 21-5).

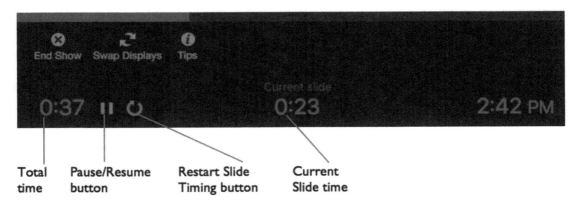

Figure 21-5. Use the controls on the timer to set automatic timings for slides or to control the recording of your narration

2. Go through your presentation, setting the timings like this:

   ■ *Display the next slide*: Click the Next Slide button to display the next slide.

   ■ *Pause and resume the timer*: Click the Pause/Resume button on the timer to pause timing. Click the button again to restart timing.

- *View the time*: The Current Slide readout on the timer displays how long the current slide has been displayed for. The Total readout on the timer shows how long the presentation has been running for.

- *Restart timing for the current slide*: Click the Restart Slide Timing button to start recording the timing for the current slide again.

3. When you finish going through the presentation, PowerPoint displays a dialog box (see Figure 21-6) giving the total show time and asking whether you want to apply the timings to the slide show.

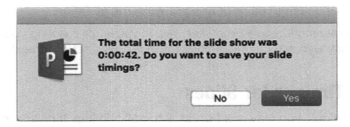

Figure 21-6. Click the Yes button in this dialog box to apply the timings you've recorded to the slide show

4. Click the Yes button to apply the timings to the slide show.

5. Save the presentation. For example, click the Save button on the title bar.

Delivering a Presentation to a Live Audience

When you're ready to deliver the presentation live (or when you're practicing), use the commands and techniques explained in this section to start the presentation and display the slides. If necessary, you can annotate the presentation or display a black screen or white screen instead of your slides. You can also run the presentation from the keyboard rather than using the pointing device.

Starting a Presentation

When you're ready to launch the presentation, choose Slide Show ➤ Start Slide Show ➤ Play from Start from the Ribbon or Slide Show ➤ Play from Start from the menu bar. You can also press Cmd+Shift+Return or click the Slide Show icon on the status bar.

If you need to start from a slide other than the first, select that slide, and then choose Slide Show ➤ Start Slide Show ➤ Play from Current Slide from the Ribbon or Slide Show ➤ Play from Current Slide from the menu bar. You can also press Cmd+Return to start from the current slide.

Displaying the Slides You Need

To give the presentation smoothly and effectively, you need to display slides in the order you want. The most straightforward way is to start at the beginning of the presentation and run straight through to the end, but in many cases, you may need to change the order. For example, you may need to go back to an earlier slide, skip ahead to a particular slide by name or number, or display a hidden slide.

PowerPoint provides plenty of different ways to move from slide to slide. The following ways tend to be the most convenient:

- *Run the next animation or display the next slide*: Click the button on your pointing device or press the spacebar.

> **Note**   You can also move forward or back by holding the pointer over the lower-left corner of the slide and then clicking the Next button or the Previous button on the row of controls that appears.

- *Return to the previous slide*: Press P or click the Previous button in Presenter view.

> **Tip**   In Presenter view, you can use the control menu for quick navigation. Move the pointer over the current slide, click the control icon to display the control menu, and then use its commands to navigate. Look back to Figure 21-4 for an example of navigating with the control menu.

- *Go to a slide by name or number*: Ctrl-click or right-click the current slide, click or highlight Go to Slide on the context menu (see Figure 21-7), and then click the slide on the submenu. PowerPoint truncates long slide names, but it's usually easy enough to identify the slides.

> **Note**   Parentheses around a slide's number on the Go to Slide submenu indicate that the slide is hidden.

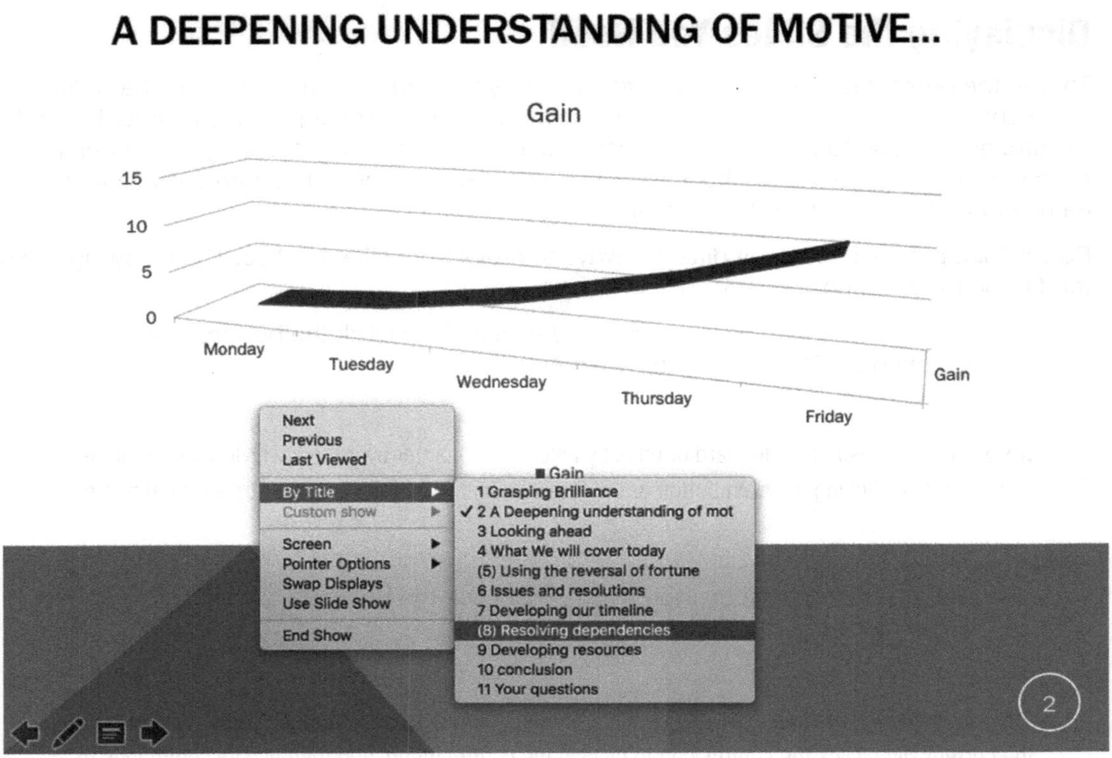

Figure 21-7. The context menu for a presentation includes commands for going quickly to a different slide by name or number, returning to the last slide viewed, or switching to a custom show

- *Return to the last slide viewed*: Ctrl-click or right-click the current slide, and then click Last Viewed on the context menu.

Annotating the Slides

Sometimes you may want to annotate a presentation to make sure your audience grasps your most important points. PowerPoint gives you the following choices on the Pointer Options submenu of the context menu:

- *Automatic*: Choose this item to let PowerPoint change the pointer automatically depending on where you move it.

- *Hidden*: Choose this item when you want to hide the pointer, so that it doesn't distract the audience.

- *Arrow*: Choose this item when you want to restore the pointer to its normal arrow so that you can point to items on slides.

- *Pen*: Choose this item when you want to write or draw on a slide. Figure 21-8 shows an example.

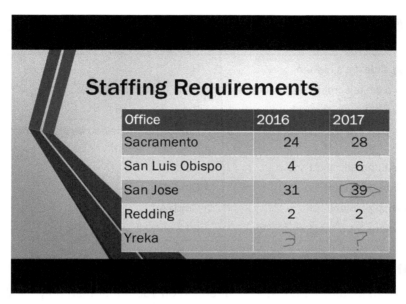

Figure 21-8. You can use PowerPoint's annotation features to mark up slides during a presentation. PowerPoint doesn't save your annotations

■ *Pen Color*: From this submenu, choose the pen color you want, such as red.

Note To erase the annotations from the slide, display the context menu, and choose Screen ➤ Erase Pen.

Controlling a Presentation Using the Keyboard

If you're at your Mac when you're giving the presentation, you can control the presentation by using keyboard shortcuts. Table 21-1 explains the keyboard shortcuts you can use; you'll find the most useful ones explained elsewhere in the text as well. Several of the actions have two or more keyboard shortcuts. Each works the same; the one I listed first is usually the easiest, but try them all, and use whichever you find most convenient.

Table 21-1. Keyboard Shortcuts for Running a Presentation

Action	Keyboard Shortcut
Run the presentation from the first slide	Cmd+Shift+Return
Run the presentation from the current slide	Cmd+Return
End the slide show	Esc or − (numeric keypad)
Display the next slide or trigger the next animation	N, Return, spacebar, Page Down, Down arrow, or Right arrow
Display the previous slide or trigger the previous animation again	P, Backspace, Page Up, Up arrow, or Left arrow

(continued)

Table 21-1. (*continued*)

Action	Keyboard Shortcut
Display the next slide if it's hidden	H
Toggle on or off a white screen with no content	W or , (comma key)
Toggle on or off a black screen with no content	B or . (period key)
Go to a slide by specifying its number	*Number key* followed by Return (for example, 8 and then Return)
Start or stop an automatic slide show	S
Change the pointer to a pen	Cmd+P
Restore the normal pointer	Cmd+A
Erase all annotations from the current slide	E

Displaying a White Screen or Black Screen

When you need to focus your audience's attention on you rather than on your slides, display a white screen or a black screen (whichever best suits the lighting conditions under which you're giving the presentation). To do so, open the context menu, and then choose Screen ➤ Black Screen or Screen ➤ White Screen, as needed.

Press Esc or click to go back from the black screen or white screen to the slides.

Creating a Handout for a Presentation

When you're delivering a presentation live, it's often useful to create a handout that provides your audience with material to browse before you start, to scribble notes on as you proceed, and to take home for further reference afterward.

To create a handout, follow these steps:

1. Open the presentation if it's not already open.

2. Choose File ➤ Print or press Cmd+P to display the Print dialog box.

3. If the Print dialog box opens at its smaller size, click the Show Details button to expand it.

4. Make sure that the PowerPoint item is selected in the unnamed pop-up menu, below the Paper Size pop-up menu and between the upper section and lower section of the Print dialog box. If not, open this pop-up menu and click the PowerPoint item in it.

5. Open the Layout pop-up menu, and choose the Handouts item you want: Handouts (2 slides per page), Handouts (3 slides per page), Handouts (4 slides per page), Handouts (6 slides per page), or Handouts (9 slides per page). PowerPoint displays a quick preview on the left side of the Print dialog box (see Figure 21-9).

Tip   If you want your audience to be able to take notes easily, choose Handouts (3 slides per page). This layout puts the three slides in a vertical stack on the left side of the page, with a lined area to the right of each slide for taking notes, as you can see in the preview in Figure 21-9.

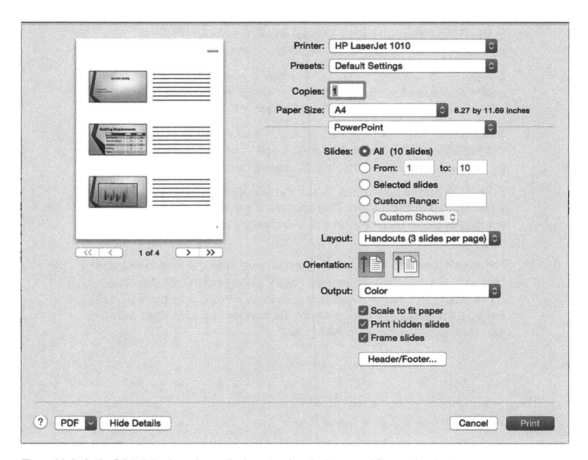

Figure 21-9. In the Print dialog box, choose the layout and content you want for your handout

6. In the Slides area, choose which slides to print handouts for:

    ■ *Print handouts for all slides*: Select the All option button.

    ■ *Print handouts for a range of slides*: Select the From option button, and type the starting number in the text box next to it. Type the ending number in the To text box.

Note   If you need to print a handout for only some of the slides in a presentation but those slides aren't in sequence, select those slides before opening the Print dialog box. You can then select the Selected Slides option button in the Slides area to print handouts for only those slides.

- *Print handouts for slides you identify by number*: Select the Custom Range option button and type the slide numbers in the box separated by commas, using a hyphen to denote a range. For example, you could enter 1, 3-5, 7, 10.

- *Print handouts for a custom show*: Select the custom show by its name in the Custom Shows pop-up menu.

7. In the Output pop-up menu, choose the kind of output for the handouts: Color, Grayscale, or Black and White.

8. Select the "Scale to fit paper" check box if you want PowerPoint to resize the slides to fit the paper better. The preview shows you the effect of this change so you can tell whether it will be helpful.

9. Select the Print hidden slides check box if you want to include hidden slides in the handout. If the selection or presentation contains no hidden slides, this check box is unavailable.

10. Select the Frame slides check box if you want PowerPoint to put a frame around each slide. This is useful if the slides use a light-colored or white background that will disappear on the printout without a frame.

11. To include a header or footer in the handout, click the Header/Footer button to display the Header and Footer dialog box. Click the Notes & Handouts tab button to display the Notes & Handouts pane (see Figure 21-10), specify the details of the header and footer you want, and then click the Apply to All button.

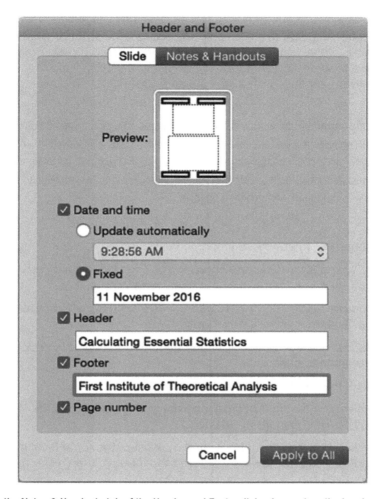

Figure 21-10. On the Notes & Handouts tab of the Header and Footer dialog box, set up the header and footer you want for the handout

12.   If you want to print the handouts, click the Print button. If you want to create a PDF file that you can then print from another computer (or distribute as a PDF), click the PDF pop-up button, and choose click Save as PDF. In the Save dialog box, specify the file name and folder for the PDF, and then click the Save button.

Recording Narration into a Presentation

When you can't deliver a presentation in person, you can record your narration for the presentation and create a file that your audience can play back. This is great for creating a presentation that you will share on the Web or on a CD or DVD.

Unless you're a pro at speaking off the cuff or you can already deliver this presentation in your sleep from relentless practice, you may want to write a script of what you'll say. Having a script helps you avoid the pauses that pass unnoticed in a live presentation but stick out uncomfortably in a recorded presentation. When using a script, avoid the trap of lapsing into a monotone—deliver your lines with all the life and conviction you'd give to a live audience.

> **Note**   To record narration, you need a suitable microphone. In a pinch, you can use the microphone built into your MacBook or iMac, but such a microphone will usually pick up ambient noise (even if you use PowerPoint's noise-cancellation feature). Usually, you're better off using a microphone that you can position freely, such as a handheld microphone or one on a stand, and best off with a noise-canceling microphone mounted on a headset.

To record a presentation, follow these steps:

1. Set up your microphone and check that it's working. What you need to do depends on your setup, but these steps are typical:

   - Choose Apple ➤ System Preferences from the menu bar to open the System Preferences window.

   - Choose View ➤ Sound from the menu bar to display the Sound preferences pane.

   - Click the Input tab if it's not already displayed.

   - Make sure the right microphone or input is selected in the "Select a device for sound input" list box.

   - Speak into the microphone, and make sure the Input level meter shows a suitable level. If not, drag the Input volume slider to set the input volume.

   - Select the "Use ambient noise reduction" check box if you want the Mac to try to tune out as much ambient noise as possible.

   - Click the Close button (the red button at the left end of the title bar) or choose System Preferences ➤ Quit System Preferences to close the System Preferences window and quit System Preferences.

2. In PowerPoint, select the slide from which you want to start recording. For example, if you want to start recording from the beginning, click the first slide.

3. Choose Slide Show ➤ Set Up ➤ Record Slide Show from the Ribbon or Slide Show ➤ Record Slide Show from the menu bar. PowerPoint switches to Presenter view, displays the slide you chose, and starts recording your audio and the timings for moving from slide to slide and from animation to animation.

4. Speak your narration for the presentation, advancing the slides and animations as needed.

> **Note**   If you need to pause the recording, click the Pause/Resume button on the timer; click this button again when you're ready to resume. If you need to start over for the current slide, click the Restart Slide Timing button in the lower-left corner of the timer.

5. When you reach the end of the presentation, PowerPoint automatically stops recording the narration and prompts you to save your timings. Click the Yes button.

Exporting and Sharing a Presentation

Apart from delivering a presentation in person, PowerPoint gives you several ways to get the presentation to other people across the Internet:

- *Send the presentation via e-mail*: The most direct way to get a presentation to somebody else is to e-mail it to them, as discussed in Chapter 2. E-mail works well for small presentations, but many presentation files are too large for mail servers to handle. In this case, you need to use a different means of distribution.

- *Save the presentation to OneDrive*: You can save the presentation to a shared folder on OneDrive, as discussed in Chapter 2. Anyone with permission to view the folder can then download the presentation and view it. This is an effective way to distribute presentations across the Internet.

- *Save the presentation to a SharePoint site*: If you have a SharePoint site, you can save the presentation to it. Anyone with permission to view the folder on the SharePoint site can then view the presentation. In many cases, this is the best way to distribute a presentation within a company or organization that uses SharePoint.

- *Save the presentation as pictures*: If you need to share the presentation with extra comments on a web page or send individual slides to people, you can save it as pictures. When you do this, you lose the transitions and animations so make sure that the slides don't rely on them.

To save a presentation as picture files, follow these steps:

1. Open the presentation if it's not already open.

2. Choose File ➤ Export from the menu bar. PowerPoint displays the Export dialog box and selects the JPEG item in the File Format pop-up menu.

3. If you want, change to a different picture format by opening the File Format pop-up menu and making the appropriate choice:

    - *JPEG*: Joint Photographic Experts Group (JPEG) files are widely used for everything from digital photography to web pages. JPEG files use *lossy* compression—the app that creates a JPEG file discards some of the image data to make the file smaller—so they're not full quality.

- *TIFF*: Tagged Image File Format (TIFF) files are full quality and are widely used in publishing, but they're less good for web pages than PNG. TIFF files usually have a larger file size than JPEG files.

- *PNG*: Portable Network Graphics (PNG) files are full quality and have relatively small file sizes. PNG files are a good choice for most uses.

- *GIF*: Graphics Interchange Format (GIF) is an old file format that uses only 256 colors. GIF files are small, but you lose so much quality that the trade-off is seldom worthwhile.

- *BMP*: Windows Bitmap (BMP) format retains full quality at the expense of a large file size. PNG is usually a better choice.

- *PDF*: The Portable Document Format is extremely widely used and is viewable on most computers and devices. Even so, PNG is usually a better choice.

4. Below the File Format pop-up menu, select the Save Every Slide option button if you want to save every slide as a picture. The alternative is to select the Save Current Slide Only option button, creating a picture file of the current slide.

5. In the Export As text box, type the name of the folder you want PowerPoint to create and put the files in.

6. If you want to put the new folder in a different folder than the current folder, navigate to the folder you want.

7. Click the Save button. PowerPoint exports the slides as pictures, naming them Slide01, Slide02, and so on. It then displays a dialog box telling you which folder to find the files in.

8. Click the OK button. You can now distribute the presentation by zipping the folder and sending it via e-mail or by posting slides on your web site.

Summary

In this chapter, you learned how to deliver a PowerPoint presentation to a live audience in person or to a wider audience by using other means. You now know how to prepare for the presentation by setting up your displays and using Presenter view, and you can record either timings or full-on narration for the presentation's slides. You can also create a handout for your audience and export slides to pictures to use in a slide library for your colleagues.

At this point, you're good to go with PowerPoint. In the next chapter, you'll start exploring Outlook, Office's powerful app for managing e-mail, your schedule, and more.

Part 5

E-Mailing and Organizing with Outlook

In this fifth and final part of the book, you'll learn how to use Outlook to send, receive, and manage your e-mail and to organize your contacts, calendar, and tasks.

In Chapter 22, you'll set up Outlook to work with your ISP or e-mail provider's servers. Once Outlook is working, you'll learn how to get around its complex user interface, how to send and receive e-mail, and how to manage your messages.

In Chapter 23, you'll see how to create contacts either from scratch or by importing them from your address books, spreadsheets, or other sources. You'll also learn how to view and sort your contacts, add or update their contact information, and quickly create communications with your contacts.

In Chapter 24, you'll get up to speed with Outlook's Calendar interface, customize it to suit the way you work, and use its views effectively. After that, you'll learn how to create one-shot appointments and repeating appointments, schedule meetings, and respond to meeting requests.

In Chapter 25, you'll learn how to use Outlook to log the tasks you need to complete and track your progress on completing them. You'll also see how to use Outlook's Notes feature to jot down information as you work.

Chapter **22**

Using E-mail Effectively

In this part of the book, you'll learn how to use Outlook, Office's heavy-duty e-mail and organizer app.

Outlook covers five main areas:

- *Mail*: Outlook calls it Mail, but most of us call it e-mail—and it's the most important part of Outlook. This chapter covers e-mail.

- *People*: Outlook provides a digital address book on steroids for storing the details of your contacts and keeping in touch with them. Chapter 23 explains how to work with contacts in Outlook.

- *Calendar*: Outlook can help you keep tabs on your appointments, whether they occur once only or at regular intervals. Chapter 24 shows you how to manage your calendar with Outlook.

- *Tasks*: Outlook provides a robust task list that you can use not only to track your own commitments but also to offload them onto your colleagues. Chapter 25 teaches you how to organize your life with tasks.

- *Notes*: Outlook provides a straightforward notes capability that you can use for quickly storing information. Chapter 25 shows you how to work with notes in Outlook.

So in this chapter, you'll learn how to use Outlook to send and receive e-mail and attachments.

You'll start by setting up Outlook to work with your e-mail account (or accounts). You'll then take a tour of the Outlook interface because Outlook packs a host of controls into its window in order to handle all of its different roles and tasks.

Once you know what's what, I'll show you how to send and receive messages and attachments; reply to messages and forward them to others; and delete the messages you don't want to keep and file those you do. Then you'll learn how to quickly add standard closings to your messages by creating and using signatures. Finally, you'll learn how to deal with spam, or unwanted e-mail.

© Guy Hart-Davis 2016
G. Hart-Davis, *Learn Office 2016 for Mac*, DOI 10.1007/978-1-4842-2002-3_22

Setting Up Outlook

First, you need to set up Outlook to work with your e-mail account. To do this, you need to know your e-mail address and password. You may also need to know which types of mail servers your ISP uses and their addresses.

If you have your e-mail accounts set up with a different e-mail app already, you can import the accounts into Outlook. You can also choose whether to use Outlook as your primary e-mail app or stick with the app you're currently using.

> **Note**   If you've set up Outlook already, go to the "Meeting the Outlook Interface" section.

Launching Outlook

Start by launching Outlook. The easiest way to launch Outlook is to click the Microsoft Outlook icon on the Dock. If there's no Microsoft Outlook icon on the Dock, click the Launchpad icon on the Dock, and then click the Microsoft Outlook icon on the Launchpad screen.

> **Tip**   If you find Outlook vital to your computing life, add the Microsoft Outlook icon to the Dock. After you've launched Outlook, Ctrl-click or right-click the Outlook icon on the Dock, and then choose Options ➤ Keep in Dock from the context menu. If you want Outlook to start automatically each time you log in, Ctrl-click or right-click the Outlook icon on the Dock, and then choose Options ➤ Open at Login, placing a check mark next to this item.

Going Through the Welcome to Outlook Routine

If this is the first time you've run Outlook, the app displays the Welcome to Outlook window. Click the Next (>) button to move through the screens that introduce the app's main features, and then click the Get Started button. On the You're All Set screen, click the Start Using Outlook button. The Set up my Inbox screen then appears (see Figure 22-1).

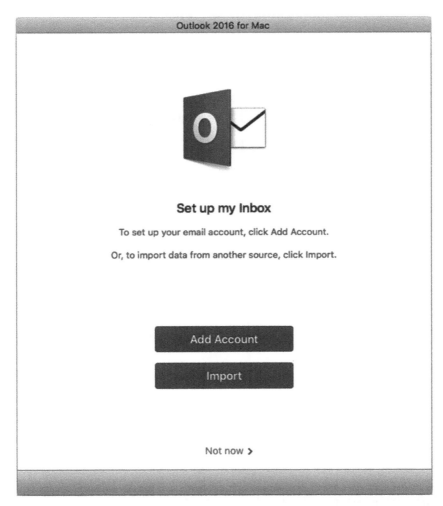

Figure 22-1. *If you haven't yet set up your e-mail account in Outlook, click the Add Account button on the Set up my Inbox screen*

Adding an E-mail Account to Outlook

You can start the process of adding an e-mail account to Outlook in either of these ways:

- *From the Set up my Inbox screen*: Click the Add Account button.

- *Anytime thereafter*: Choose Tools ➤ Accounts from the menu bar.

When you take either of these actions, Outlook displays the Accounts pane in the Outlook Preferences window (see Figure 22-2).

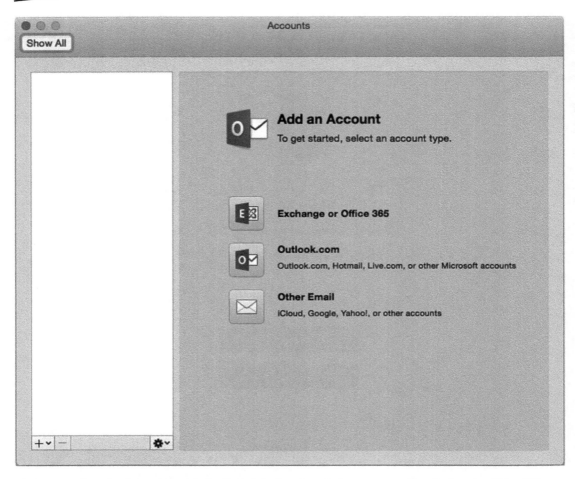

Figure 22-2. From the Accounts pane in the Outlook Preferences window, you can add an Exchange or Office 365 account, an Outlook.com account, or another type of e-mail account

From here, you can add a Microsoft Exchange or Office 365 account, an Outlook.com account, or a regular type of e-mail account (IMAP or POP). I'll start with regular accounts, move on to Outlook.com accounts, and then look at Exchange and Office 365 accounts.

Note   The main difference between an IMAP account and a POP account is that an IMAP account stores your messages on the mail server, while with a POP account your e-mail app (for example, Outlook) keeps your messages on your computer. IMAP is good for when you need to check your e-mail from multiple computers because you see the same inbox and folders from each computer as a result of the folders being on the server. POP usually gives better performance if you use a single computer.

To set up an e-mail account, you need to provide various pieces of information. At the very least, you need to know the e-mail address and password; often, you need to know the e-mail account type as well, and you may need to know the addresses of the incoming server and the outgoing server. You normally get this information from your e-mail provider.

Adding an IMAP or POP E-mail Account to Outlook

If you have an IMAP or POP e-mail account, follow these steps to add the account to Outlook:

1. In the Accounts pane of the Outlook Preferences window, click the Other Email button to display the "Enter your account information" dialog box (see Figure 22-3).

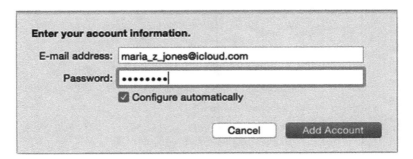

Figure 22-3. *In the "Enter your account information" dialog box, you can set up most IMAP and POP accounts by entering just your e-mail address and password*

2. Type your e-mail address in the E-mail address text box.

3. Type your password in the Password text box.

4. For most accounts, you can simply select the Configure automatically check box and click the Add Account button to have Outlook take care of the configuration details for you. But if you need to enter the details manually, clear the Configure automatically check box. Outlook expands the "Enter your account information" dialog box to show the remaining controls (see Figure 22-4).

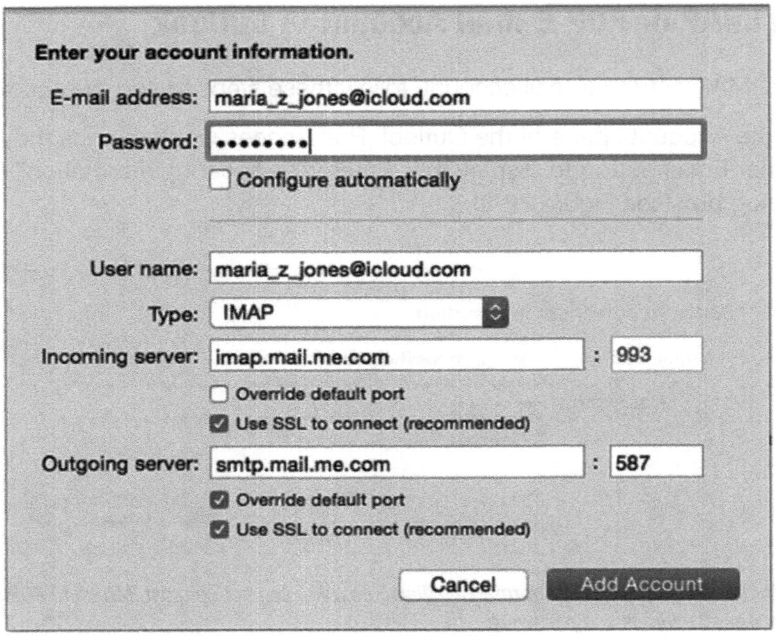

Enter your account information.

E-mail address: maria_z_jones@icloud.com

Password: ••••••••|

☐ Configure automatically

User name: maria_z_jones@icloud.com

Type: IMAP ⌄

Incoming server: imap.mail.me.com : 993

☐ Override default port
☑ Use SSL to connect (recommended)

Outgoing server: smtp.mail.me.com : 587

☑ Override default port
☑ Use SSL to connect (recommended)

Cancel   Add Account

Figure 22-4. If you need to configure e-mail account settings manually, clear the Configure automatically check box, and then work with the extra controls that the "Enter your account information" dialog box displays

5. Change the default settings as needed:

    ■ *User name*: In this text box, type the user name for the e-mail account.

    ■ *Type*: In this pop-up menu, choose IMAP or POP. If you're not sure which type your e-mail account is, contact your e-mail provider.

    ■ *Incoming server*: In the left text box, type the name of the incoming mail server.

    ■ *Override default port*: Select this check box if your e-mail provider has told you to use a specific port for the incoming mail server. Type the port number in the right text box on the Incoming server line.

    ■ *Use SSL to connect*: Select this check box if your e-mail provider provides Secure Sockets Layer (SSL) connections and you want to use a secure connection for incoming mail.

    ■ *Outgoing server*: In the left text box, type the name of the outgoing mail server.

    ■ *Override default port*: Select this check box if your e-mail provider has told you to use a specific port for the outgoing mail server. Type the port number in the right text box on the Outgoing server line.

    ■ *Use SSL to connect*: Select this check box if your e-mail provider provides SSL connections and you want to use a secure connection for outgoing mail.

6. Click the Add Account button. Outlook adds the account and displays it in the Accounts pane (see Figure 22-5).

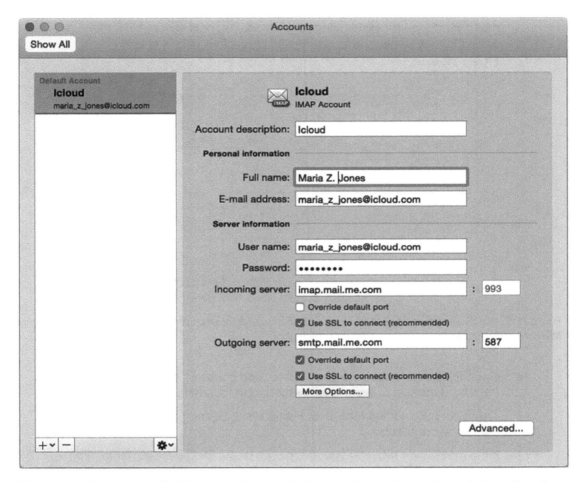

Figure 22-5. After you have added the account, it appears in the Accounts pane. You can change further settings if necessary

7. Change any of the settings needed. These are the settings you're most likely to need to change here:

■ *Account description*: Type the name you want Outlook to show for the account rather than the generic name that Outlook chose.

Note In the Accounts pane of the Outlook Preferences window, you can change many of the same settings as in the expanded version of the "Enter your account information" dialog box. For example, you can enter the name of the incoming mail server or outgoing mail server, override the default mail port on the server, and use SSL to connect.

■ *Full name*: Type your name the way you want Outlook to use it, such as Jack Frederickson or John T. Frederickson.

8. If you need to use different credentials for connecting to the outgoing mail server than for connecting to the incoming mail server, click the More Options button to display the Settings dialog box shown in Figure 22-6.

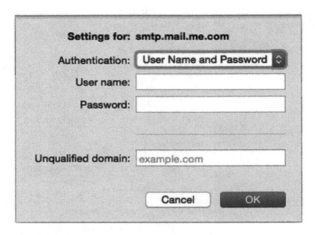

Figure 22-6. *Use the Settings dialog box when you need to provide different credentials for connecting to the outgoing mail server than for connecting to the incoming mail server*

■ Open the Authentication pop-up menu, and choose User Name and Password instead of the default setting, Use Incoming Server Info.

■ Type your user name in the User Name text box and your password in the Password text box.

■ If the mail server requires you to enter an unqualified domain name, type it in the Unqualified domain box.

■ Click the OK button to close the Settings dialog box and return to the Accounts pane.

If you need to set up another e-mail account, click the Add (+) button in the lower-left corner of the Accounts pane, and then click the Exchange item, the Outlook.com item, or the Other Email item on the pop-up menu, depending on the type of account. Outlook displays the "Enter your account information" dialog box, and you can enter the information as discussed in this section.

When you have finished setting up accounts, click the Close button (the red button at the left end of the title bar) to close the Preferences window. You'll then see the main Outlook window, usually with the Inbox displayed. Go on to the "Meeting the Outlook Interface" section later in this chapter.

Adding an Outlook.com Account to Outlook

If you have an Outlook.com account (such as an account with an outlook.com address or a hotmail.com address), you can quickly add it to Outlook. Follow these steps:

1. Click the Outlook.com button in the Accounts pane to display the "Enter your Microsoft account information" dialog box (see Figure 22-7).

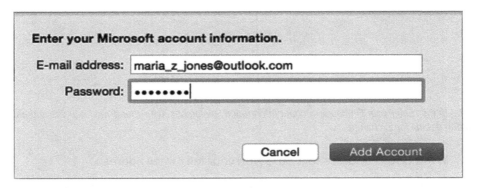

Figure 22-7. In the "Enter your Microsoft account information" dialog box, type your e-mail address and password, and then click the Add Account button

2. Type your e-mail address in the E-mail address box.

3. Type your password in the Password box.

4. Click the Add Account button. Outlook sets up the account, and it appears in the Accounts pane.

Adding a Microsoft Exchange Account or Office 365 Account to Outlook

Microsoft Exchange is a mail server used by many corporations and organizations. Office 365 is an Office-based online service that Microsoft provides.

To add a Microsoft Exchange account or Office 365 account to Outlook, follow these steps:

1. Click the Exchange or Office 365 button in the Accounts pane to display the "Enter your Exchange account information" dialog box (see Figure 22-8).

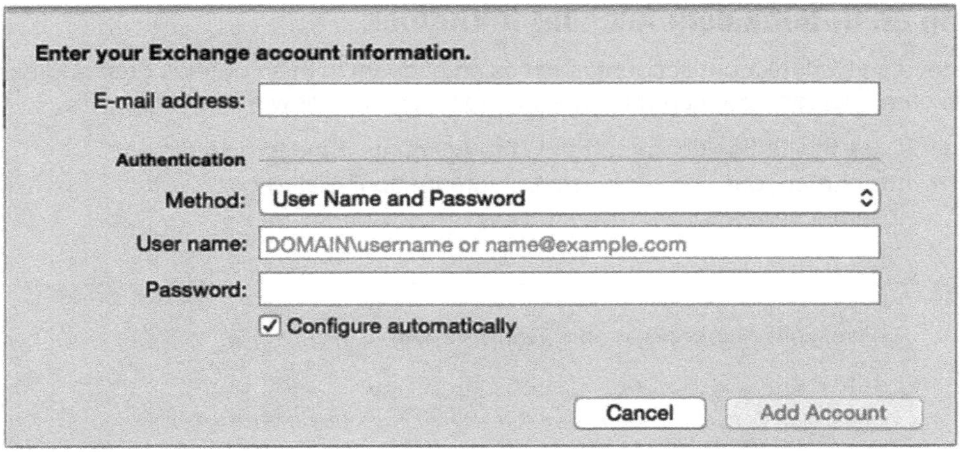

Enter your Exchange account information.

E-mail address: [   ]

Authentication

Method: [User Name and Password   ⌄]

User name: [DOMAIN\username or name@example.com   ]

Password: [   ]

☑ Configure automatically

[Cancel]   [Add Account]

Figure 22-8. In the "Enter your Exchange account information" dialog box, type your e-mail address and enter your authentication details for Exchange

2. In the E-mail address text box, type your full e-mail address.

3. In the Method pop-up menu, choose your authentication method:

   ■ *User Name and Password*: This is the normal choice for most networks. Type your domain and user name (for example, CORP\agreen) in the User name text box and your password in the Password text box.

   ■ *Kerberos*: If your network uses Kerberos for authentication, select Kerberos in the Method pop-up menu, and then open the Kerberos ID pop-up menu (which appears below the Method pop-up menu) and click the Kerberos ID. If Outlook prompts you for your password, type it and click the OK button.

   ■ *Client Certificate Authentication*: If you need to use a digital certificate for authentication, select Client Certificate Authentication in the Method pop-up menu. Then open the Certificate pop-up menu (which appears below the Method pop-up menu) and click the appropriate certificate.

Note   If you're not sure which setting to choose in the Method pop-up menu, ask your network administrator.

---

4. Make sure the Configure automatically check box is selected.

Note   If your network administrator tells you to enter the server name for the Exchange account, clear the Configure automatically check box. The "Enter your Exchange account information" dialog box then displays a Server text box above the two buttons. Type the server's address in this text box.

---

5. Click the Add Account button. Outlook adds the account.

Importing an Existing E-mail Account

Outlook 2016 also enables you to import your existing e-mail account data. This can be from your existing installation of Outlook 2011 on your Mac, from an Outlook for Windows archive file, or from an Outlook for Mac archive file.

> **Note**   An Outlook for Windows archive file uses the Personal Folders File format with the `.pst` file extension. An Outlook for Mac archive file uses the Outlook For Mac Data File format with the `.olm` file extension.

To start importing data, click the Import button on the Set up my Inbox screen or choose File ➤ Import from the menu bar. Either of these commands displays the Import dialog box (see Figure 22-9).

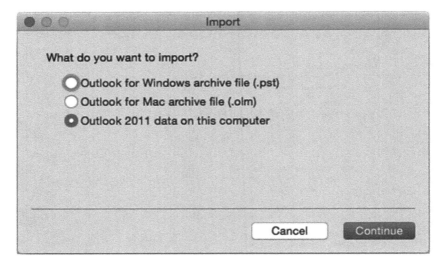

Figure 22-9. Outlook's Import feature enables you to import data from an Outlook for Windows archive file, an Outlook for Mac archive file, or your existing installation of Outlook 2011

Select the Outlook for Windows archive file option button, the Outlook for Mac archive file option button, or the Outlook 2011 data on this computer option button, as appropriate. Click the Continue button, and then follow the prompts in the dialog box that opens. For the first two options, you select the appropriate archive file; for the third option, you select the appropriate identity from your collection of Office 2011 identities.

Meeting the Outlook Interface

When Outlook opens, you'll see a window such as Figure 22-10. Outlook normally displays your Inbox at first, on the basis that you want to start by checking your e-mail. If Outlook is displaying a different item, click the Mail button in the Navigation pane, and then click the Inbox item in the Folder pane.

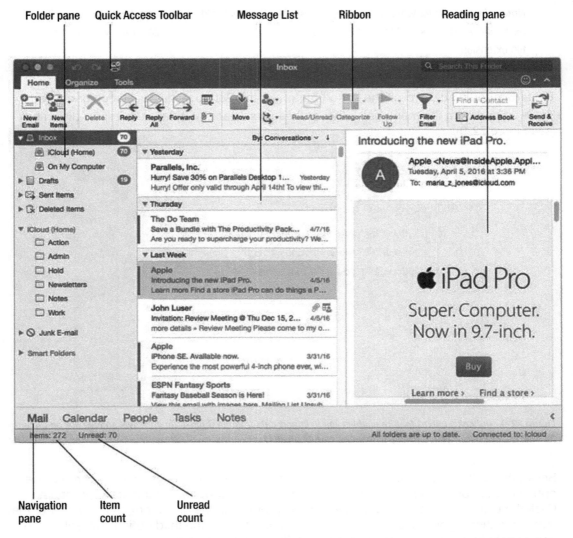

Figure 22-10. Outlook's interface uses many different components to provide access to your information and its features

> **Note**   This chapter introduces you to the Mail aspect of Outlook's interface. The following chapters show you how to use the Calendar aspect, the Contacts aspect, the Tasks aspect, and the Notes aspect.

The following sections explain how to use the main components of the Outlook interface—and how to change those you're most likely to want to change.

Using the Quick Access Toolbar, Ribbon, and Menu Bar

Like the other Office apps, Outlook uses three main means of control: the Quick Access Toolbar on the title bar, the Ribbon below the title bar, and the menu bar across the top of the Mac's display (or primary display if it has more than one).

At this writing, the Quick Access Toolbar in the main Outlook window contains only the Undo button, the Redo/Repeat button, and the Print button, and is not customizable. When you open an item window, the Quick Access Toolbar also has a Save button for saving changes to the item.

The Ribbon for the main Outlook window contains three tabs: the Home tab, the Organize tab, and the Tools tab. Unlike in the other Office apps, Outlook's Ribbon doesn't divide each tab into groups; instead, it has the controls (for example, buttons and pop-up menus) directly on the Ribbon. The contents of the Home tab and the Organize tab change to suit the category of items you're working with; for example, the Home tab contains different controls when you're working with Mail than when you're working with the Calendar. The contents of the Tools tab remain the same.

The menu bar provides access to commands as normal.

Using the Navigation Pane

The Navigation pane is a shallow pane that gives you quick access to Outlook's five main aspects: Mail, Calendar, People, Tasks, and Notes. The Navigation pane can appear either expanded, as a separate pane that extends across the full window of the Outlook window and contains text buttons, as in Figure 22-10; or collapsed, as a part of the Folder pane with graphical buttons (see Figure 22-11). To collapse the Navigation pane, you click the ➤ button at its right end; to expand the Navigation pane again, you click the ➤ button that replaces the ➤ button.

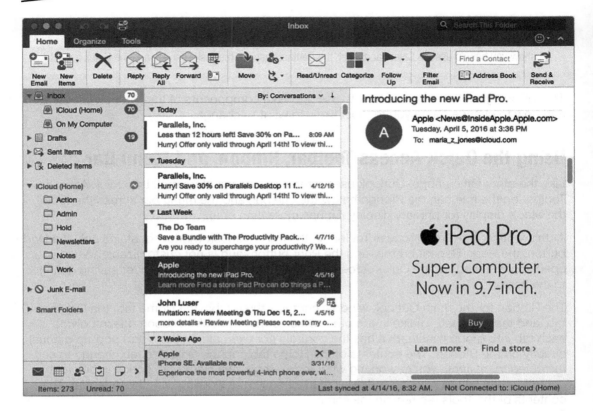

Figure 22-11. You can collapse the Navigation pane to an icon-based bar at the bottom of the Folder pane. Click the ▶ button when you want to expand the Navigation pane again

> **Tip**   You can switch quickly among Outlook's areas by using keyboard shortcuts. Press Cmd+1 to display Mail, Cmd+2 to display Calendar, Cmd+3 to display Contacts, Cmd+4 to display Tasks, or Cmd+5 to display Notes.

Using the Folder Pane

The Folder pane appears on the left side of the Outlook window by default. You use this pane to navigate among different items in the category you've selected in the Navigation pane. For example, after you select Mail in the Navigation pane, the Folder pane displays your mail folders, and you can click the folder whose contents you want to view.

You can change the width of the Folder pane by moving the pointer over its right edge, so that the pointer changes to a two-headed arrow, and then dragging to the left or right.

When you don't need the Folder pane, you can hide it by choosing View ▶ Folder Pane from the menu bar, removing the check mark from the Folder pane item on the menu. Give the same command again when you need the Folder pane once more.

Using and Customizing the Message List and Reading Pane

To the right of the Folder pane is the Message List, which shows the messages in the selected mailbox (for example, the Inbox). To the right of the Message List is the Reading pane, which shows the contents of the selected message (or part of the contents). To view a message in the Reading pane, click it in the Message List.

> **Note**   Outlook provides the Reading pane to help you plow through your messages quickly. But you can also open a message in a separate window if you prefer. To do so, double-click the message in the Message List. Opening a message in a separate window is useful when you need to compare the contents of two or more messages at once.

Arranging and Sorting the Message List

To enable you to quickly find and read the messages you need, Outlook lets you sort the Message List in several different ways. This section runs through the main ways of sorting the Message List, but you will want to spend some time experimenting with the various options to see which types of sorting you find most helpful for the tasks you perform with e-mail and the ways you prefer to approach them.

The easiest way to set up the Message List is to use the By pop-up menu at the top of the Message List (see Figure 22-12). You can also use the View ➤ Arrange By submenu on the menu bar.

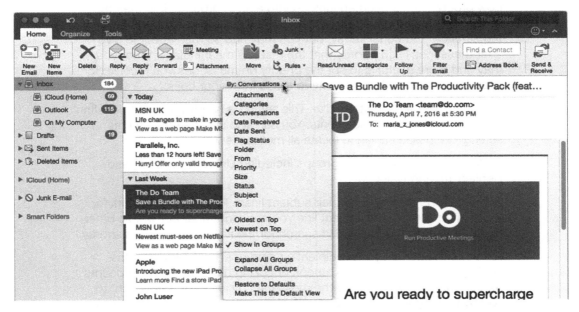

Figure 22-12. Use the By pop-up menu at the top of the Message List to set up the Message List the way you want it. Start by choosing the overall sort order in the top part of the list, such as by Conversations or by Date Received

In the By pop-up menu, choose from the following arrangement settings:

- *Attachments*: Sorts the items into a Has Attachments group and a No Attachments group. This setting is good for locating messages with attachments that you need to deal with.

- *Categories*: Sorts the items into the categories you've applied, such as Manager, Team, and Junk. You can customize the categories that Outlook uses.

- *Conversations*: Sorts the items into conversations by date. (You'll learn about conversations shortly.)

- *Date Received*: Sorts the items by the date and time Outlook received them.

- *Date Sent*: Sorts the items by the date and time the messages indicate they were sent.

- *Flag Status*: Sorts the items into a Flagged group and a No Flag group by the flags you've applied to them. (For example, you can flag a message for follow-up tomorrow.)

- *Folder*: Sorts the items by the folders that contain them. If you're looking at your Inbox, sorting by folders isn't helpful, but if you've searched and found messages in various folders, sorting can be useful.

- *From*: Sorts the items by the sender. This setting is good for locating messages from important people.

- *Priority*: Sorts the items by their Importance tag into High, Normal, and Low groups; items deemed junk go into a Junk group below the Low group. This setting can be useful if your colleagues use the Importance tag sensibly and consistently, but you may find so many people give their messages High priority that the result is meaningless. What you may find more useful is to set the priority on messages you receive; for example, assigning High priority to those from your boss.

- *Size*: Sorts the items by their size. This setting is handy for quickly locating messages with large attachments. You can also use the Attachments setting (discussed earlier) to locate all messages with attachments.

- *Status*: Sorts the items into groups including Unread, Sent or Read, Replied To, and Calendar.

- *Subject*: Sorts the items by their subject lines. This setting is useful for locating an item whose subject line you can remember but whose other details you can't. (You can also search for the item, as described shortly.)

- *To*: Sorts the items by the recipient's name or e-mail address. This setting is useful if you have Outlook checking different e-mail accounts because it lets you separate the messages by account. Items sent to you by name (for example, Chris Smith) appear separately from those sent to the e-mail address.

Changing the Sort Order

Within each arrangement, you can change the sort order by clicking the By pop-up menu in the Message List and then clicking the order you want. For example, if you sort by Date Received, you can choose between Newest on Top and Oldest on Top; if you sort by Subject, you can choose between A on Top and Z on Top; and if you sort by Attachments, you can choose between With on Top and None on Top.

You can quickly reverse the sort order by clicking the Down arrow or Up arrow to the right of the By pop-up menu at the top of the Message List.

Choosing Whether to Group Items

For each arrangement, you can choose whether to show the items in groups or as a series. The groups vary depending on the arrangement. For example, when you sort by Date, Outlook uses groups such as Today, Yesterday, Last Week, and Last Month; when you sort by From, the groups are the senders (by name when it appears and by e-mail address when it doesn't); and when you sort by Size, the groups are Small, Medium, Huge, and Enormous.

To choose whether to group items, open the By pop-up menu, and then click the Show in Groups item. If a check mark appears next to Show in Groups, grouping is on, and you click to turn it off; otherwise, click to place the check mark and turn grouping on.

Viewing Conversations

If you use e-mail to discuss topics with your colleagues, you probably get back-and-forth exchanges of messages about many topics. To view these exchanges easily, open the By pop-up menu at the top of the Message List and click Conversations to arrange the messages by conversations.

When you do this, Outlook presents each exchange of e-mail messages as a separate section, enabling you to see the sequence of messages clearly and to determine who said what when without having to trawl through your Inbox and other mail folders. You can expand a conversation by clicking the horizontal gray disclosure triangle to its left, or you can collapse a conversation by clicking the downward gray disclosure triangle. Figure 22-13 shows a conversation.

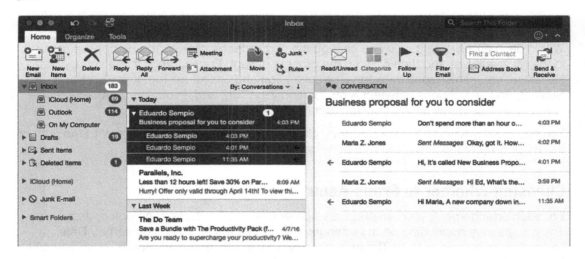

Figure 22-13. When you need to see the sequence of an e-mail exchange, display the messages in conversations

Using and Customizing the Reading Pane

When you click a message in the Message List, Outlook displays the message's contents in the Reading pane so that you can read it.

At first, Outlook displays the Reading pane to the right of the Message List. If you prefer, you can position the Reading pane below the Message List by choosing Organize ➤ Reading Pane ➤ Bottom from the Ribbon. Figure 22-14 shows this arrangement. (To put it back, choose Organize ➤ Reading Pane ➤ Right from the Ribbon.) You may prefer this layout because it gives you a better view of the Message List (but not as much of it).

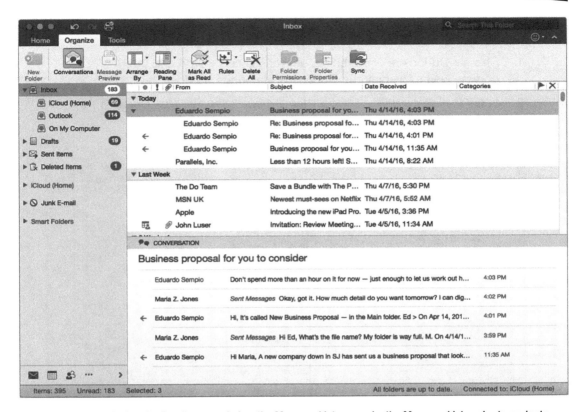

Figure 22-14. Positioning the Reading pane below the Message List can make the Message List easier to navigate

Tip   If your Mac has a small screen or if you need more space for the Message List, you may prefer to hide the Reading pane and read messages in a separate window instead. To hide the Reading pane, choose Organize ➤ Reading Pane ➤ Off from the Ribbon or View ➤ Reading Pane ➤ Hidden from the menu bar. To read a message in a separate window, double-click the message in the Message List.

You can also control the Reading pane from the menu bar or keyboard: choose View ➤ Reading Pane ➤ Right from the menu bar or press Cmd+\ to place the Reading pane on the right; choose View ➤ Reading Pane ➤ Below from the menu bar or press Cmd+Shift+\ to place the Reading pane at the bottom; or choose View ➤ Reading Pane ➤ Hidden from the menu bar or press Cmd+Option+\ to hide the Reading pane.

To control how Outlook interprets your opening a message in the Reading pane, follow these steps:

1. Choose Outlook ➤ Preferences or press Cmd+, (Cmd and the comma key) to display the Outlook Preferences window.

2. In the E-mail section, click the Reading icon to display the Reading preferences pane (see Figure 22-15).

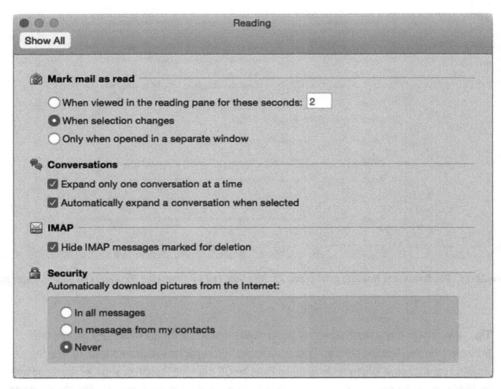

Figure 22-15. In the Reading pane of the Outlook Preferences window, use the options in the "Mark mail as read" area to control when Outlook decides you've read an item

3. In the "Mark mail as read" area, select the appropriate option button:

   ■ *When viewed in the reading pane for these seconds*: Select this option button if you want Outlook to mark a message as read when you open it in the Reading pane and don't move the focus for the number of seconds specified in the text box. The default is two seconds, but you may want to use a longer period so that you can glance through a message without having Outlook mark it as read. If you want Outlook to mark a message as read the instant you open the message, choose 0 (zero) seconds.

- *When selection changes*: Select this option button if you want Outlook to mark an item as read when you display it in the Reading pane and then display another item. In this case, the trigger for marking the item as read is your changing the selection, not the length of time you spend looking at the item.

- *Only when opened in a separate window*: Select this option button if you want Outlook to mark an item as read only after you open the item in its own window.

4. Click the Close button (the red button in the upper-left corner) to close the Reading pane of the Outlook Preferences window.

Sending and Receiving Messages

When you have Outlook set up and working right, you probably want to start by using Mail. This section shows you how to create and send messages, how to receive messages, and how to read your messages.

Sending an E-mail Message

To send an e-mail message, you create a message, address it, and add contents. You may also want to choose options for the message, such as setting its reply-to address to a different e-mail address than the one you're sending from.

Creating a New Message

You can create a new blank message in any of these three ways:

- *Keyboard*: Press Cmd+Option+N.

Note When you've selected the Mail category, you can also press Cmd+N to create a new e-mail message. Cmd+N is the keyboard shortcut for creating a new item of whichever kind you're currently using—for example, when you're using Calendar, pressing Cmd+N creates a new appointment. But you can use the Cmd+Option+N shortcut to create a new e-mail message from anywhere in Outlook.

- *Ribbon*: Choose Home ➤ New Email from the Mail category or Home ➤ New Items ➤ Email from any category.

- *Menu bar*: Choose File ➤ New ➤ Email.

Whichever way you give the command, Outlook opens a new message window. The message window's title bar at first shows Untitled, but then it displays the subject line you give the message. Figure 22-16 shows a message window with a new message open. As you can see, the Ribbon in the message window contains the Message tab and the Options tab.

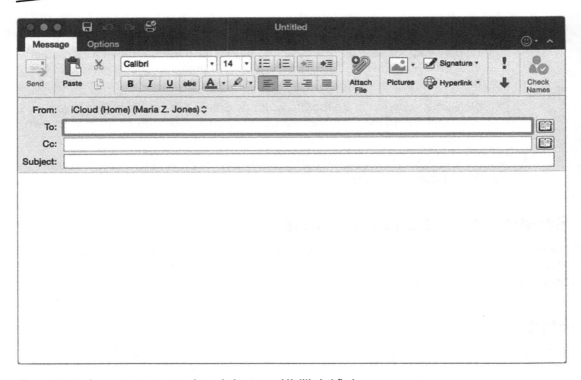

Figure 22-16. A new message opens in a window named Untitled at first

Choosing Which Account to Send the Message From

If you have set up Outlook to use multiple e-mail accounts, check which account appears in the From pop-up menu. Outlook uses the account you're working in, but sometimes you may need to change accounts. To do so, open the From pop-up menu, and then click the account you want to use.

Addressing the Message

You can add the components of a message in any order that suits you, but what you'll usually want to do is address the message first. To do so, you enter the primary recipients in the To box and any Cc (carbon copy) recipients in the Cc box.

You can enter the e-mail addresses in three main ways:

- *Type or paste in an e-mail address*: If you know the e-mail address, you can click in the box (for example, the To box) and simply type it in. Or if you've copied from a document or a web page, you can paste it in.

- *Type the name and have Outlook complete the address for you*: Click in the box and start typing the name. When Outlook suggests a match (see Figure 22-17), press Enter to accept it. If Outlook suggests several matches, click the right address; or move the highlight to the right one by pressing Down arrow or Up arrow, and then press Return.

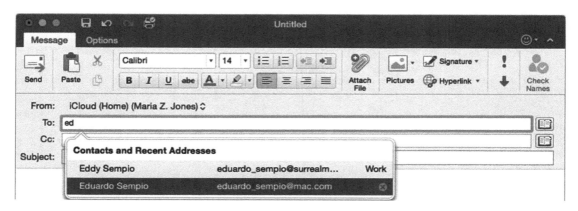

Figure 22-17. Outlook automatically suggests matching contacts for names you start typing

- *Use the Search People window*: Click the button to the right of the To box or the button to the right of the Cc box to display the Search People window (see Figure 22-18), and then work like this:

  - Start typing the search term in the search field at the top of the window. The main part of the window displays matching results.

Figure 22-18. Use the Search People window to select e-mail recipients from your contacts list to a message

■ If you need to restrict the search to just names rather than all fields, open the left pop-up menu, and then click Search Names Only instead of Search All Fields.

■ If you need to restrict the search to a particular address book, click the right pop-up menu, and then choose the address book. For example, choose Address Book in the On My Computer area of the pop-up menu to use your Mac's Address Book.

■ Click the address you want.

■ Click the To button to add the address to the To box, click the Cc button to add it to the Cc box, or click the Bcc button to add it to the Bcc box.

> **Note**   Bcc stands for *blind carbon copy*. You use the Bcc field to add recipients whose names the To recipients and Cc recipients will not be able to see. This is sometimes useful in business situations. It's also useful when you're sending a message to a group of people who may not want to disclose their e-mail addresses to each other—for example, when you send a change-of-address message to your acquaintances. By putting your own address in the To field and all the other recipients' addresses in the Bcc field, you can prevent each recipient from seeing others' addresses.

- When you've chosen all the addresses you want, click the Close button (the red button at the left end of the title bar) to close the Search People window.

Adding the Subject Line and Message Contents

In the Subject box, type the subject of the message. This is the text that appears in the recipient's Inbox to help them identify the message.

> **Tip**   Make your subject lines as clear as possible while keeping them short enough to fit in the narrow columns that appear in a typical e-mail app window. Your message will most likely be competing for the recipient's attention with many other messages, so making the subject clear will help it get read.

In the main box of the message window, enter the text of the message. Many e-mail messages require only plain text, which you can enter by typing as normal (or by using other standard text-entry techniques, such as pasting text or expanding AutoCorrect entries). Other messages need formatted text, pictures, or other graphical items.

> **Note**   Outlook lets you format the message content as plain text or as HTML. To choose which, choose Options ➤ Format Text from the Ribbon in a message window, clicking the Format switch to move it to the HTML position or to the Plain position. You can also choose Draft ➤ HTML Format from the menu bar (clicking to place a check mark next to the HTML Format item or to remove the check mark) or press Cmd+Shift+T. Choose Plain Text when you want the text to have no formatting. Choose HTML when you want to use formatting that is compatible with most e-mail apps.

The easiest way to apply formatting to a message is to use the controls on the Message tab of the Ribbon in a message window. You can also apply formatting from the Format menu and its submenus (on the menu bar or by using keyboard shortcuts (for example, press Cmd+B to apply bold, Cmd++ to increase the font size, or Cmd+– to decrease the font size).

> **Note**   You can mark a message as being important by choosing Message ➤ High Priority from
> the Ribbon in a message window or Draft ➤ Priority ➤ High from the menu bar (or you can choose
> Message ➤ Low Priority from the Ribbon in a message window or Draft ➤ Priority ➤ Low from the
> menu bar to mark a message as being unimportant). But be warned that high importance has been
> so widely abused in e-mail messages that many people ignore it.

Choosing Options for a Message

The Options tab of the Ribbon in a message window (see Figure 22-19) contains a range of
options for making a message look and behave differently from normal.

Figure 22-19. The Options tab of the Ribbon in a message window lets you change the message's look and behavior

Click the Bcc button if you need to add the Bcc field to the message so that you can add
Bcc recipients directly. (You can also add Bcc recipients by using the Select Contacts
window, as discussed earlier.)

To add a background color to the message, click the Background Color button, and then
click the color in the Colors window that opens. To add a background picture, click the
Background Picture button, browse to the picture in the dialog box that opens, and then
click the Open button.

> **Note**   To remove a background picture, choose Options ➤ Background Picture ➤ Remove from
> the Ribbon in a message window, clicking the pop-up button next to the Background Picture button
> and then clicking Remove on the pop-up menu.

The Permissions pop-up menu lets you set restrictions on a message you're sending to
another Outlook user on your e-mail system. For example, you can set the Do Not Forward
restriction on a message to prevent the recipient from forwarding the message. To set up
Outlook to use permissions, choose Options ➤ Permissions ➤ Verify Credentials from the
Ribbon in a message window, enter your credentials in the Login dialog box that opens, and
then click the Sign In button.

Caution   The options on the Permissions pop-up menu work on only some mail servers (such as Microsoft Exchange servers).

The Security pop-up menu contains two commands:

- *Digitally Sign Message*: Use this command to apply a digital signature to the message, proving that the message came from someone who holds the digital certificate you specify. (Normally, you specify your digital certificate so that the recipient can tell the message comes from you.)

- *Encrypt Message*: Use this command to encrypt this message so that it can be decrypted only by someone who holds the appropriate digital certificate.

Note   When you digitally sign a message or encrypt a message, the Information bar appears below the Ribbon in the message window showing a padlock and containing a readout about the security measure, such as "This message will be digitally signed."

SETTING UP DIGITAL CERTIFICATES FOR SIGNING AND ENCRYPTION

Before you can use the Digitally Sign Message command or the Encrypt Message command on the Security pop-up menu on the Options tab of the Ribbon in a message window, you must set Outlook up with the digital certificates it needs for signing and encryption.

To tell Outlook which certificates to use, follow these steps:

1. Choose Tools ➤ Accounts from the menu bar to display the Accounts pane in the Outlook Preferences window.

2. In the Accounts list on the left, click the account for which you want to set up the certificates.

3. Click the Advanced button at the lower-right corner of the account information to display the Advanced dialog box.

4. Click the Security tab to display its contents (see Figure 22-20).

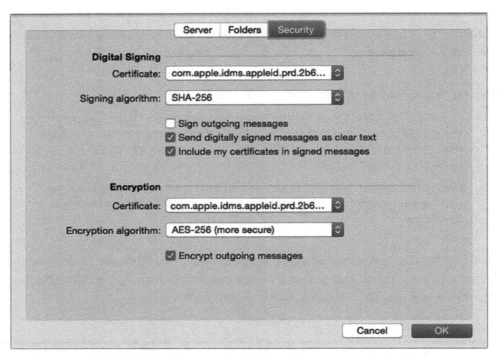

Figure 22-20. If you need to digitally sign and encrypt messages, set up Outlook with digital certificates on the Security tab of the Advanced dialog box for the account

5. In the Digital Signing area, open the Certificate pop-up menu, and then click the certificate you want to use for digital signing.

6. In the Signing algorithm pop-up menu, leave the default selection, SHA-256, selected unless an administrator has told you to use a different signing algorithm.

7. If you need to sign all the messages you send on this account, select the Sign outgoing messages check box. Otherwise, leave this check box cleared, and use the Options ➤ Security pop-up menu on the Ribbon in the message window to sign individual messages as needed.

8. Select the "Send digitally signed messages as clear text" check box if you want to ensure recipients can read your e-mail messages even if they're using a mobile e-mail client or a web-based e-mail service.

9. Select the "Include my certificates in signed messages" check box to make Outlook include your certificate's public key in the messages. Sending the public key enables the recipients to send you encrypted messages, which is usually helpful.

10. In the Encryption area, open the Certificate pop-up menu, and then click the certificate you want to use for encryption.

11. In the Encryption algorithm pop-up menu, leave the default selection, AES-256, selected unless an administrator has told you to use a different encryption algorithm.

12. Select the Encrypt outgoing messages check box only if you want to encrypt every message you send from this account. Otherwise, clear this check box, and then apply encryption from the Options ➤ Security pop-up menu in the message window to individual messages as needed.

13. Click the OK button to close the Advanced dialog box.

14. Click the Close button (the red button at the left end of the title bar) to close the Accounts preferences window.

Checking the Spelling in a Message

Outlook checks spelling and grammar as you type unless you turn off the spelling checker and grammar checker, so you can easily resolve spelling and grammar queries as you create the message.

If you choose not to check spelling and grammar as you work, you can start a check by clicking the Spelling button on the Options tab of the Ribbon in a message window, choosing Edit ➤ Spelling and Grammar ➤ Check Now from the menu bar, or pressing Cmd+; (Cmd and the semicolon key).

> **Note**   To control whether Outlook checks spelling and grammar, choose Edit ➤ Spelling and Grammar from the menu bar, and then place or remove the check mark next to the Check Spelling While Typing command or the Check Grammar With Spelling command on the Spelling and Grammar submenu. To control whether Outlook automatically corrects apparent spelling errors, choose Edit ➤ Spelling and Grammar ➤ Correct Spelling Automatically from the menu bar, either placing or removing a check mark next to the Check Spelling Automatically item on the Spelling and Grammar submenu.

Sending the Message

When you're ready to send the message, click the Send button at the left end of the Message tab on the Ribbon in the message window. Alternatively, choose Draft ➤ Send from the menu bar or press Cmd+Return.

Receiving and Reading Messages

Normally, Outlook automatically checks your incoming mail server for messages and collects those sent to you. You can also force Outlook to check all your accounts for e-mail at any point by clicking the Send/Receive button on the Home tab of the Ribbon or choosing Tools ➤ Send & Receive from the menu bar or pressing Cmd+K.

Once you've received your messages, click the Inbox to display them. You can then read the messages either in the Reading pane or in a separate window. The Reading pane is often easiest because it's designed to enable you to quickly triage your messages. Open a message in a separate window when you need more space to concentrate on it or when you need to compare the contents of two or more messages side by side.

Click the message you want to read, or press the Down arrow or Up arrow to move the highlight to the message so that Outlook displays it in the Reading pane.

> **Tip**   When reading messages in the Reading pane, press the spacebar to display the next screen of the message. When you reach the end of this message, press the spacebar again to display the next message. You can also press Shift+spacebar to display the previous screen of the current message or (from the beginning of the current message) to display the previous message.

To read a message in a separate window, double-click the message in the Message List. In the message window, you can then display the next message by pressing Ctrl+] or display the previous message by pressing Ctrl+[. Alternatively, choose View ➤ Next or View ➤ Previous from the menu bar.

To close a message window, click its Close button (the red button at the left end of the title bar), choose File ➤ Close from the menu bar, or press Cmd+W.

After reading a message, you can reply to it, move it to a folder, or delete it, as discussed later in this chapter.

> **Tip**   As discussed in the "Using and Customizing the Reading Pane" section earlier in this chapter, Outlook normally marks a message as having been read after you view it for two seconds (or the number of seconds you set) in the Reading pane. If you turn off this automatic marking of messages as read, you can manually mark messages as read. From the keyboard, press Cmd+T to mark a message as read or press Cmd+Shift+T to mark a read message as unread. With the pointing device, Ctrl-click or right-click the message in the Message List, and then click Mark as Read on the context menu; to mark a read message as unread, Ctrl-click or right-click the message, and then click Mark as Unread on the context menu.

Sending and Receiving Attachments

E-mail is a great way of sending messages quickly, but it's also useful for transferring files from one computer to another. To send a file via e-mail, you attach it to a message that you then send as usual; and when someone sends you a file, it comes to your Inbox as part of the message that brings it. You then detach the file from the message and store it in a folder.

Sending a File as an Attachment

To send a file as an attachment, start a message as usual. Then choose Message ➤ Attach File from the Ribbon in the message window, choose Draft ➤ Attachments ➤ Add from the menu bar, or press Cmd+E to display a dialog box for selecting the file. Click the file you want, or select multiple files by Shift-clicking or Cmd-clicking, and then click the Choose button. Outlook adds an attachment box below the Subject box in the message window showing the file's name and its size (see Figure 22-21). You can then add other files from other folders by repeating the process.

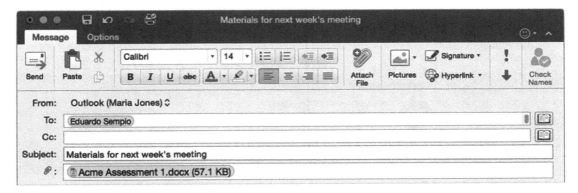

Figure 22-21. Outlook displays the attachment box below the Subject box when you attach one or more files to a message

> **Tip**   You can also attach a file to a message by dragging the file from a Finder window to the message window.

Receiving a File as an Attachment

When you receive a file as an attachment, it arrives in your Inbox with its message. A paperclip icon will appear on the message's listing in the Message List and the attachment's file name will appear at the top of the Reading pane (see Figure 22-22).

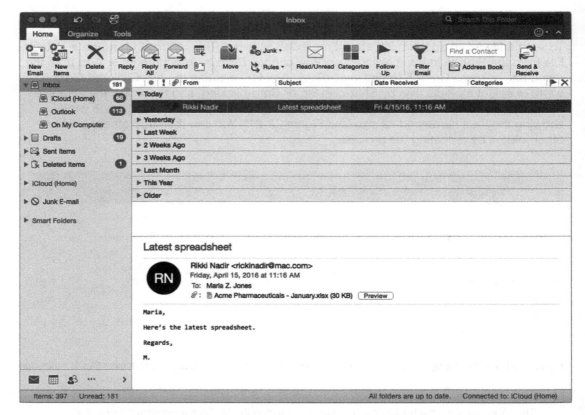

Figure 22-22. *The Message List displays a paperclip icon to indicate that a message has an attachment. The attachment's name appears near the top of the Reading Pane*

To display a preview of the attachment, click the Preview button in the Reading pane. Outlook displays the preview using OS X's Quick Look feature.

To save an attached file to a folder, Ctrl-click or right-click the attachment's name in the Reading pane, and then click Save As on the context menu. In the dialog box that opens, navigate to the folder in which you want to save the file, change the file name if necessary, and then click the Save button. You can then open the file either from a Finder window or from the app you use for that type of file, such as Word for a word processing file or Excel for a spreadsheet file.

Tip   You can also grab an attached file by its name or icon and drag it to a Finder window or to your Desktop to save it there.

Caution   The pop-up menu for dealing with attachments includes an Open item, but don't open an attachment directly from Outlook. This is because the file opens in read-only mode, in which you cannot save changes you make to the file. You then need to use a Save As command to save the file under a different file name or in a different folder. Saving the file from Outlook and then opening it using the appropriate app saves time and avoids confusion.

After you've saved an attachment to a folder, you can either remove it from the message or leave it in the message for reference. Removing attachments is usually a good idea because otherwise your mailbox can become huge, but you may sometimes need to keep attachments in messages as a safety net.

To remove an attachment from a message, Ctrl-click or right-click the attachment icon in the Reading pane, and then click the Remove item on the context menu. In the confirmation dialog box that Outlook displays (see Figure 22-23), click the Delete button.

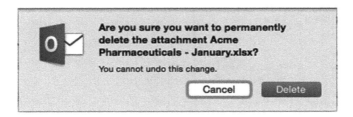

Figure 22-23. *Outlook confirms your removal of an attachment from a message*

> **Tip**   To quickly remove all the attachments from a message, Ctrl-click or right-click one of the attachment icons in the Reading pane, click the Remove All item on the context menu, and then click the Delete button in the confirmation dialog box that opens.

Replying to and Forwarding Messages

To reply to a message you've received, choose Home ➤ Reply from the Ribbon in the main Outlook window, choose Message ➤ Reply from the Ribbon in a message window, choose Message ➤ Reply from the menu bar, or press Cmd+R. To reply to all the recipients of a message you've received, choose Home ➤ Reply All from the Ribbon in the main Outlook window, choose Message ➤ Reply All from the Ribbon in a message window, choose Message ➤ Reply All from the menu bar, or press Cmd+Shift+R.

> **Tip**   To include only part of the message in your reply, select that part of the message before giving the Reply command or Reply All command. This move helps you keep your messages concise and easy to understand.

Outlook opens a message window for the reply, adding "Re:" to the subject line to indicate that it is a reply, and showing the original message and sender information below the insertion point (see Figure 22-24). You can then enter the text of the reply—and any other objects needed—and click the Send button to send it.

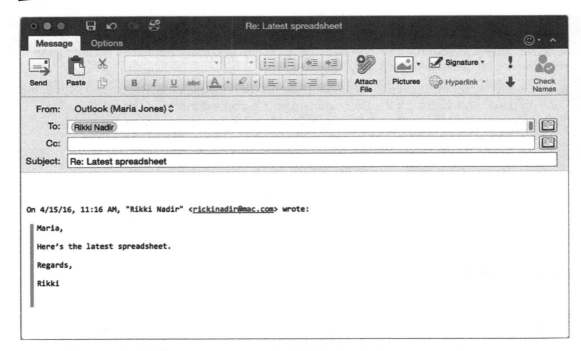

Figure 22-24. Outlook adds "Re:" to the subject of a reply and includes the original message

To send a message you've received to someone else, forward it by choosing Home ➤ Forward from the Ribbon in the main Outlook window, choosing Message ➤ Forward from the Ribbon in a message window, or choosing Message ➤ Forward from the menu bar; from the keyboard, press Cmd+J. Outlook opens a message window containing the forwarded message, adding "FW:" to the subject line to indicate that the message is forwarded, and placing the original message below the insertion point. You can then address the message, type whatever information you need to add to the forwarded message (for example, why you're forwarding it), and then click the Send button.

> **Tip**   To forward only part of a message, select that part of the message before giving the Forward command. If you need to forward several sections of the message, it's usually easier to include the whole message in the forwarded message, and then delete those parts you don't want to send.
>
> Sometimes it's useful to forward a message as an attachment so that the recipient can see it as it originally appeared. To do this, choose Home ➤ Attachment from the Ribbon in the main Outlook window, choose Message ➤ Attachment in a message window, or choose Message ➤ Forward Special ➤ As Attachment from the menu bar. You can also press Cmd+Ctrl+J from the keyboard to forward a message as an attachment.

Deleting, Storing, and Organizing Messages

When you don't need to keep an e-mail message, you can delete it by selecting it and pressing the Delete key on the keyboard, choosing Home ➤ Delete from the Ribbon in the main Outlook window, choose Message ➤ Delete from the Ribbon in a message window, or choosing Edit ➤ Delete from the menu bar. But chances are that you'll need to keep many— perhaps most—of the messages you receive. That means creating a structure of folders in which you can place the messages and then moving each message to the appropriate folder.

Moving a Message to a Mail Folder

The quick way to move a message to a mail folder is to drag the message from the Message List to the folder in the Folder pane. This technique works well when you have few enough folders to fit easily in the Folder pane; if you have a longer list of folders, you can drag down to the bottom of the Folder pane to make it scroll further, but even so, getting to the folder you want can be awkward.

The next way of moving a message is to select it, open the Move pop-up menu on the Home tab of the Ribbon in the main Outlook window or the Message tab of the Ribbon in a message window, and then click the destination folder on the menu (see Figure 22-25).

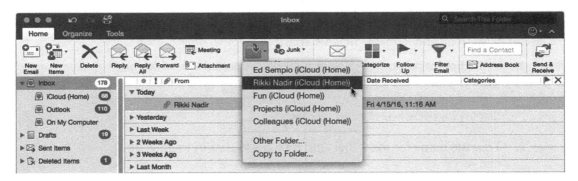

Figure 22-25. You can quickly move the selected message to a folder that appears on the Move pop-up menu. If the folder doesn't appear, click the Other Folder item

> **Tip** You can also move a message to a folder using the menu bar. Select the message, choose Message ➤ Move, and then click the folder on the Move submenu.

If the folder you want doesn't appear on the Move pop-up menu, click the Other Folder item on the Move pop-up menu or choose Message ➤ Move ➤ Choose Folder from the Ribbon to display the Search dialog box (see Figure 22-26). Type the first few letters of the folder name, click the folder in the list of results, and then click the Move button.

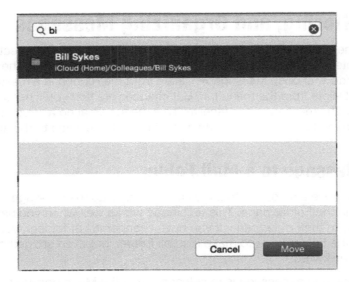

Figure 22-26. When you have many folders, you may find it easier to search for the folder to which you want to move the message

Creating a New Mail Folder

To create a new mail folder, follow these steps:

1. In the Folder pane, Ctrl-click or right-click the folder in which you want to create the new folder, and then click New Folder on the context menu. Outlook adds a new folder named Untitled Folder and displays an edit box around the name.

2. Type the name for the folder, and then press Return to apply the name.

To rename an existing folder, Ctrl-click or right-click it in the Folder pane, and then click Rename Folder on the context menu. Outlook displays an edit box around the name. Type the new name, and then press Return (or click elsewhere) to apply it.

Adding Consistent Closings to Your Messages with Signatures

When you send a message, you often need to let the recipient know standard information about you, such as your name and phone numbers or your company name and address, plus your position in it. To save you having to retype the same information over and over again, Outlook provides a feature called *signatures* that lets you set up one or more standard closings for inserting in your messages.

> **Tip**   If you find signatures awkward, you can create a signature as an AutoCorrect entry and enter it by typing its abbreviation. See Chapter 2 for coverage of AutoCorrect.

To set up your signatures, follow these steps:

1. Choose Outlook ➤ Preferences or press Cmd+, (Cmd and the comma key) to display the Outlook Preferences window.

2. In the E-mail area, click the Signatures icon to display the Signatures pane (shown in Figure 22-27 with a signature being created).

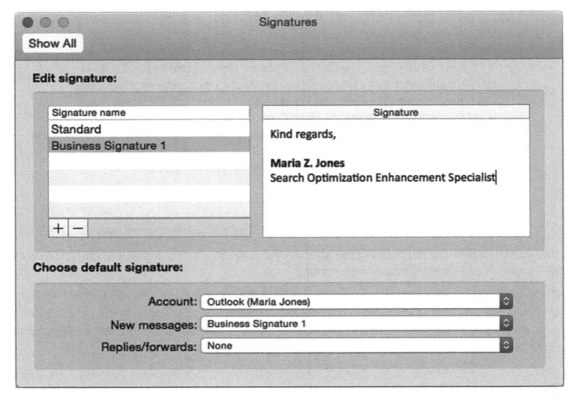

Figure 22-27. Set up one or more standard signatures in the Signatures pane of the Outlook Preferences window

3. To add a signature, click the Add (+) button in the lower-left corner of the Edit signature pane. Outlook adds a new signature named Untitled to the left box. Double-click the Untitled name to display an edit box, type the name for the signature, and then press Return to apply the name.

4. To edit a signature, click it in the left list box. Outlook displays the signature in the box on the right side. You can then edit the existing text, type or paste in additional text, or apply extra content. The Signature pane looks Spartan, but you can apply formatting by using the Format menu on the menu bar or by Ctrl-clicking or right-clicking and then choosing Font ➤ Show Fonts on the context menu.

Tip   You can add a picture to a signature if necessary: choose View ➤ Media Browser ➤ Photo Browser from the menu bar to display the Photos Browser, and then drag the picture you want to the box on the right side of the Signature pane. To keep down the burden on mail servers, it's best to use only small pictures, and even then only when necessary.

---

5. To control which signature Outlook uses by default, use the controls in the Choose default signature area of the Signatures preferences pane. Click the Account pop-up menu and select the account for which you want to configure signatures. Then open the New messages pop-up menu and select the signature you want to use for new messages. After that, open the Replies/forwards pop-up message and select the signature (if any) to use for replies and messages you forward.

6. When you've finished creating signatures, click the Close button (the red button at the left end of the title bar) to close the Outlook Preferences window.

Now create a new message using the account you set up to use a signature, and make sure that Outlook inserts the signature you chose.

If you prefer to insert a signature manually, click in the body area of the e-mail message, choose Message ➤ Signature from the Ribbon in the message window, and then click the signature you want on the Signature pop-up menu. Alternatively, choose Draft ➤ Signatures from the menu bar, and then click the signature on the Signatures submenu.

Dealing with Spam

E-mail monitoring companies report that more than nine out of ten e-mail messages are *spam*, or unsolicited commercial messages. ISPs and e-mail providers generally do a great job of preventing most spam from reaching us, but even so, plenty of spam messages evade the filters and make it to inboxes.

To help you deal with spam, Outlook automatically monitors your incoming mail and puts any suspected spam in the Junk E-Mail folder. It's a good idea to visit this folder every day or two to rescue any messages that Outlook has falsely accused and to get rid of the rest.

Removing Nonspam Messages from the Junk E-Mail Folder

If your Junk E-Mail folder contains a message that's not junk, Ctrl-click or right-click the message in the Message List, and then choose Junk Mail ➤ Mark as Not Junk from the context menu. Outlook moves the message to the Inbox.

After checking that all the messages in your Junk E-Mail folder are spam, Ctrl-click or right-click the Junk E-Mail folder, and then click Empty Folder from the context menu. Alternatively, select the messages in the folder, and then choose Home ➤ Delete from the Ribbon or press the Delete key to delete them.

> **Tip**   If you like using keyboard shortcuts, learn these two: press Ctrl+Shift+J to mark a message as junk, or press Ctrl+Shift+Option+J to mark a message as not junk.

Marking Spam Messages as Junk

If you receive a spam message in your Inbox, Ctrl-click or right-click it, and then choose the appropriate action from the Junk Mail submenu on the context menu:

- *Block Sender*: Outlook adds the sender's name to your Blocked Senders list, but leaves the message in your Inbox.
- *Mark as Junk*: Outlook moves the message to the Junk E-Mail folder.

Creating a List of Safe Senders and Domains for E-Mail

To make sure you receive messages from people you trust, you can create a list of safe senders and safe domains. Safe senders are specific e-mail addresses you judge to be safe. Safe domains are address blocks you tell the junk e-mail filter to treat as being safe. For example, if you want to receive all messages sent from addresses at apple.com, you can add apple.com to the Safe Domains list.

To set up your list of safe senders and safe domains, follow these steps:

1. Choose Tools ➤ Junk E-Mail Protection from the menu bar to display the Junk preferences pane in the Outlook Preferences window.

2. Click the Safe Senders tab to display it (see Figure 22-28).

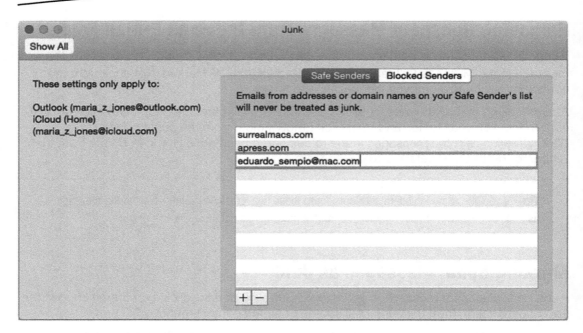

Figure 22-28. Add your safe senders and safe domains to the list on the Safe Senders tab in the Junk preferences pane

3.   Click the Add (+) button below the list box to start a new entry in the list box.

4.   Type the e-mail address or domain.

5.   When you finish adding safe senders and safe domains, close the Preferences window by clicking the Close button (the red button at the left end of the title bar) or pressing Cmd+W.

Removing Senders You've Blocked by Mistake

As you saw earlier in this chapter, Outlook maintains a Blocked Senders list to which you add addresses by blocking individual senders. If you block a sender and then realize you shouldn't have, follow these steps to remove the sender from the Blocked Senders list:

1.   Choose Tools ➤ Junk E-Mail Preferences to display the Junk preferences pane in the Outlook Preferences window.

2.   Click the Blocked Senders tab to bring it to the front (see Figure 22-29).

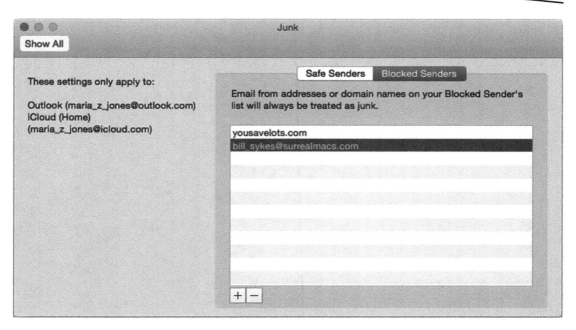

Figure 22-29. On the Blocked Senders tab in the Junk preferences pane, you can remove senders you've blocked by mistake or add entire domains to block

3. In the Blocked Senders list, select the address of the sender you've blocked by mistake, and then click the Remove (–) button to delete it.

4. Add other addresses as needed, separating them with commas. You can add either a specific address (for example, bill@spamming123.com) or the whole domain (for example, spamming123.com).

5. Close the Preferences window by clicking the Close button (the red button at the left end of the title bar) or pressing Cmd+W.

Summary

In this chapter, you learned how to get around the Outlook interface and how to use Outlook's features for managing your e-mail.

You set up Outlook to work with your e-mail account, and you now know how to send and receive e-mail and attachments. You can reply to messages, forward messages to others, delete messages you don't want, and store those you want to keep. You can create and use signatures, and you know how to deal with spam—both identifying messages as spam and recovering those that Outlook has mistakenly sent to the Junk E-Mail folder.

In the next chapter, I'll show you how to use Outlook to organize your contacts.

Chapter 23

Keeping Your Contacts in Order

In this chapter, I'll show you how to use Outlook to keep your contacts in order. I'll start by going through how to create contacts either from scratch or by importing your existing contacts from sources such as address books or spreadsheets. After that, I'll show you how to work with contacts: viewing and arranging your contacts to reveal the ones you need, editing contact information when necessary, and quickly starting communications to your contacts.

Creating Contacts

First, you need to create some contacts in Outlook. You can create contacts by entering the information manually, by merging your OS X contacts with Outlook, or by importing existing contacts from other sources. You'll look at each option in turn.

Creating a Contact from Scratch

If you have a contact's details on a hard copy (for example, a business card or paper) rather than in an electronic form, you need to enter the details manually. To do so, create a contact from scratch by following these steps:

1. Click the People button in the Navigation pane if it's not already selected.

2. Choose Home ➤ New Contact from the Ribbon or File ➤ New ➤ Contact from the menu bar, or press Cmd+N, to open a new contact window. Figure 23-1 shows a contact window with a contact's name entered. Until you enter the name, the window's title bar is blank.

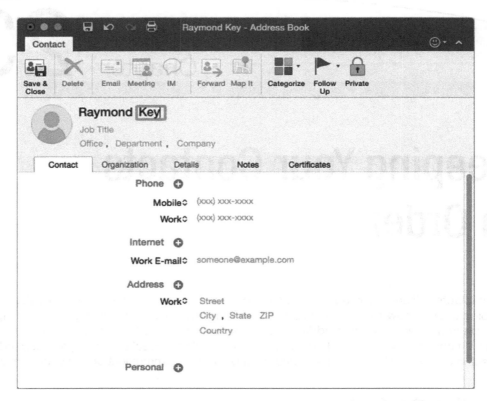

Figure 23-1. When you type in the contact's name, Outlook displays it in the title bar of the contact window

3. Type the contact's first name in the First Name field. Outlook adds the name to the title bar.

4. Press Tab to move to the Last Name field.

5. Type the contact's last name. Outlook adds this to the title bar too.

6. Press Tab to move to the Job Title field, or click in another field to move directly to that field.

7. Continue entering the contact's information. Fill in the Office, Department, and Company fields if you have the relevant data.

8. If you have a photo of the contact, add it like this:

   ■ Double-click the Picture placeholder to display the dialog box shown in Figure 23-2. The empty frame in the middle is the *image well*.

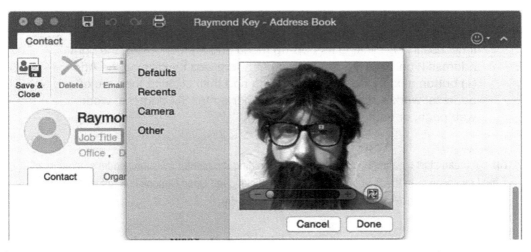

Figure 23-2. Add a photo by dragging it to the image well from a Finder window or by clicking the Other button in the left column and using the Open dialog box. Then use the Size slider to make the photo the right size

- Add a photo by dragging it from a Finder window to the image well or by clicking the Other button in the left column, selecting the photo in the Open dialog box, and then clicking the Open button.

- Click the Zoom In (+) button to zoom in, drag the Zoom Out (–) button to zoom out, or drag the Zoom slider, as needed, to make the face the right size.

- If necessary, click inside the image well and drag the photo so that the face appears in the frame.

- If the photo will benefit from you applying an effect, click the Effect button (the swirly icon above the Done button) and then click the effect you want.

- Click the Done button to close the dialog box and add the photo to the contact record.

9. Enter the contact's phone numbers in the Phone area. Outlook gives you a Mobile entry and a Work entry by default. To change one of these to a different type of entry, click the pop-up button to the right of the name (for example, Mobile), and then click the type you want (for example, Home). You can add other phone numbers by clicking the Add (+) button next to the Phone heading and then clicking the type of number: Work 2, Home, Home 2, Work Fax, Home Fax, Pager, Primary, Assistant, Phone 1, Phone 2, Phone 3, or Phone 4.

10.   Enter the contact's e-mail address or addresses in the Internet area. Outlook displays a work e-mail item at first, but you can change this if necessary by clicking its pop-up menu and then choosing the right address type. You can also add other addresses by clicking the Add (+) button next to the Internet heading and then clicking the type of address: work e-mail, home e-mail, other e-mail, IM address, work web page, or home web page.

Tip   You can start creating a contact quickly by holding the pointer over the sender's name in an e-mail message or in the Reading pane and then clicking the Open Outlook contact icon on the pop-up panel. Figure 23-3 shows an example of this move.

Figure 23-3. In a message window or the Reading pane, hold the pointer over the sender's name, and then click Open Outlook contact on the pop-up panel to start creating a new contact for that person

11.   In the Address area of the contact window, enter the contact's addresses. Outlook displays a work address at first, but you can change this if necessary by clicking its pop-up menu and then clicking Home. Alternatively, you can add home address fields by clicking the Add (+) button next to the Address heading and then clicking Home.

12.   To add personal information, click the Add (+) button next to the Personal heading at the bottom of the General tab, and then click the field you want to add—for example, Middle Name, Spouse/Partner, or Title—on the pop-up menu (see Figure 23-4). Outlook adds the field to the Personal section, and you can type the relevant information in the box.

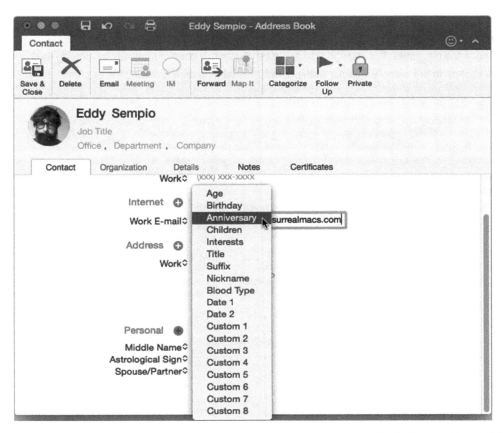

Figure 23-4. The Add (+) pop-up menu in the Personal area provides a wide variety of fields. As you add each field to the Personal area, Outlook removes it from the pop-up menu

13.   On the other four tabs of the Contact window, fill in further information about the contact as needed:

▪ *Organization tab*: If your Mac is connected to a Lightweight Directory Access Protocol (LDAP) server, you can enter organization information here.

▪ *Details tab*: If your Mac is connected to an LDAP server, you can enter details here.

▪ *Notes tab*: This tab contains a text box for entering notes about the contact. You can format the notes by using the commands on the Format menu on the menu bar or on the context menu (Ctrl-click or right-click the selection you want to format).

▪ *Certificates*: On this tab (see Figure 23-5), set up the default certificate you want to use for encrypting e-mail messages to this contact. If a contact has a single certificate, as is often the case, Outlook automatically makes that certificate the default one. If a contact has multiple certificates, and the wrong one is marked Default in the Encryption certificates list, click the certificate you want to use, click the Action button in the lower-right corner, and then click Set as Default on the pop-up menu.

Note   Normally, Outlook acquires digital certificates automatically when your contacts send you encrypted messages. But you can also add a certificate to a contact manually by clicking the Add (+) button in the lower-left corner of the Certificates tab and then following the prompts.

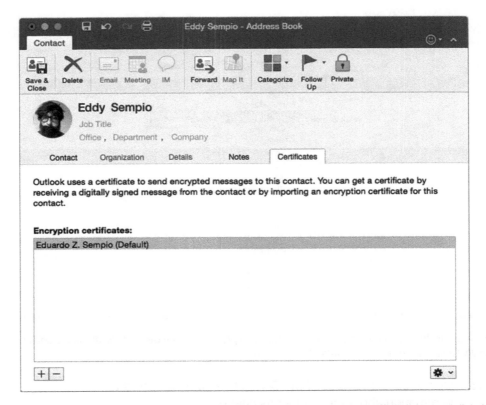

Figure 23-5. On the Certificates tab of the contact window, make sure Outlook has identified the correct digital certificate for encrypting e-mail messages

14.   If you want to assign a contact to a particular category of contacts—for example, Professional, Social, or Family—choose Contact ➤ Categorize from the Ribbon, and then click the appropriate category. Outlook gives the categories generic names, but you can customize the names and colors associated with the categories by choosing Contact ➤ Categorize ➤ Edit Categories from the Ribbon and working in the Categories dialog box.

15.   When you've finished entering the contact's details, choose Contact ➤ Save & Close from the Ribbon to save the contact record and close the window.

Importing Contacts from Other Address Books

Often, you'll have contact data in an address book already, so instead of typing it laboriously into new contacts one by one in Outlook, you can import it. Outlook 2016 gives you only one way to import contacts—as vCard files. A vCard file is a file that contains the virtual address card of one or more contacts. Most address-book and contact-management apps support the vCard standard, making vCards a straightforward way to transfer contact information from one app to another. When importing contact data from vCards, each of the fields is clearly mapped, so there's no confusion about which piece of information goes where.

vCards are great as long as the app that currently contains the contact data can create vCards. In the next subsections, you'll look at how to create vCards from the OS X Contacts app, from Yahoo!'s Contacts feature, and from Google Contacts.

If the app that contains the contact data can't create vCards, you'll need to work around the problem. See the "Getting Contact Data from Excel into a CSV File" section for instructions on getting contact data from an Excel worksheet into a comma-separated values (CSV) file. See the section after that, "Creating vCard Files from a CSV File," for ways to create vCard files from a CSV file.

Creating vCard Files from the OS X Contacts App

If you have been keeping your contact data in OS X's built-in Contacts app, you can create vCard files from the Contacts app and then import those files into Outlook. You can either create a single vCard file that contains all your contacts or pick and choose the contacts you want.

> **Caution**   Outlook 2016 for Mac cannot sync the contacts you import into it with your contacts in OS X's Contacts app and your iCloud account. This is because Outlook 2016 for Mac doesn't support the CardDAV standard for syncing contacts. So after you create vCard files from the Contacts app and import them into Outlook, the contacts in Outlook are separate from those in the Contacts app, and you cannot sync changes back and forth. If you're going to use Outlook extensively, you should commit to keeping your contact data current in Outlook rather than in the Contacts app.

To create vCard files from your contacts in the Contacts app and import them into Outlook, follow these steps:

1. Open the Contacts app. For example, click the Contacts icon on the Dock, or click the Launchpad icon on the Dock and then click the Contacts icon on the Launchpad screen.

2. Select the contacts you want to export as vCards. To select all the contacts, choose Edit ➤ Select All from the menu bar or press Cmd+A.

> **Tip**   If you need only the contacts in a particular group, click the group in the left pane, and then choose Edit ➤ Select All from the menu bar or press Cmd+A to select all the contacts in that group. Alternatively, click the group and then choose individual contacts from it as necessary by clicking the first contact and then Cmd-clicking each of the others.

3. Click anywhere in the selection, and drag the contacts to your desktop or to a Finder window. The Contacts app creates a vCard file containing all the contacts.

> **Note**   Instead of dragging the contacts to your desktop or to a Finder window, you can Ctrl-click or right-click in the selection in the Contacts app and then click Export vCard on the context menu. In the dialog box that opens, choose the folder, specify the file name, and then click the Save button.

Creating vCard Files from Yahoo!'s Contacts Feature

If you use Yahoo! Mail, chances are that you have contact information stored in Yahoo!'s Contacts feature. To get this data into Outlook, export it to a vCard file by following these steps:

1. Sign into Yahoo! and go to Contacts.

2. Select the check box for each contact you want to export. You can click the unnamed check box at the top of the column to select all the check boxes in a single move.

3. Click the Actions button, and then click Export on the pop-up menu to display the Export Contacts dialog box.

4. Select the vCard Single File option button.

> **Note**   The Yahoo! Export screen also offers an option named Outlook for exporting your contacts to a CSV file. You can use this option too for getting the contacts into Outlook, but generally, the vCard file is the easier choice. (The Outlook option is mostly for Windows versions of Outlook, which can handle single-person vCard files but not multi-person vCard files.)

5. Click the Export Now button. Your browser downloads the file, which is called yahoo_contacts.vcf, to your Downloads folder.

> **Note**   If the Contacts app prompts you to add the contacts to its list, click the Cancel button.

Creating vCard Files from Google Contacts

If you use Gmail or Google Mail, you can export your contact data to a vCard file that you can then import into Outlook. Follow these steps:

1. Sign into Gmail or Google Mail, and then go to the Contacts area.

2. If you want to export individual contacts rather than all contacts or a defined group, select the check box for each contact you want to export. You can click the unnamed check box at the top of the column to select all the check boxes in a single move, and then deselect any you don't want. Alternatively, click the pop-up menu to the right of the unnamed check box, and then click the group you want: All, None, Starred, or Unstarred.

3. Click the More button to display the More pop-up menu, and then click Export to display the Export contacts dialog box.

4. In the "Which contacts do you want to export?" area, select the appropriate option button:

    - *Selected contacts*: Select this option button if you selected the contacts you want to export.

    - *All contacts*: Select this option button if you want to export all of your contacts.

    - *The group*: To export a group, select this option button, and then choose the appropriate group in the pop-up menu, such as Friends.

5. In the "Which export format?" area, select the vCard format option button.

6. Click the Export button. Google exports the contacts to a vCard file named contacts.vcf in your Downloads folder.

Getting Contact Data from Excel into a CSV File

If you've created a contact database in Excel, you may need to import contacts from it into Outlook. To do so, you need to save the appropriate worksheet as a CSV file, and then import it.

> **Note**   Comma-separated values, abbreviated to CSV, is a standard format for exchanging data between spreadsheets or databases. The values are separated from each other with commas. When creating vCard files from a CSV file, you may need to adjust the field mapping manually to get each piece of information in the right place.

To save a worksheet as a CSV file, follow these steps:

1. Open the workbook in Excel.

2. Activate the worksheet that contains the addresses. For example, click its sheet tab in the sheet tabs bar.

3. Choose File ➤ Save As from the menu bar to display the Save As dialog box.

4. Open the File Format pop-up menu and click Comma Separated Values (.csv).

5. In the Save As text box, type the name you want to give the CSV file. Excel suggests the workbook's current name, but you'll often want to change it.

6. If necessary, use the Where pop-up menu or the navigation panes to navigate to the folder in which you want to save the CSV file.

7. Click the Save button. Excel displays the dialog box shown in Figure 23-6, telling you that the workbook cannot be saved in the selected file format because it contains multiple sheets. This appears to be a problem, but it's fine and normal.

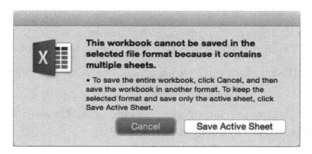

Figure 23-6. If Excel displays this dialog box when you're exporting a spreadsheet page to a CSV file, click the Save Active Sheet button to save just the active sheet

8. Click the Save Active Sheet button. Excel displays the dialog box shown in Figure 23-7, warning you that the workbook contains features that will not work or that may be removed if you use the CSV format. This too is normal.

Figure 23-7. If Excel warns you that the workbook contains features that won't work in the CSV format, click the Continue button

9. Click the Continue button. Excel now saves the active worksheet as a CSV file under the name you chose.

10. Choose File ➤ Close from the menu bar to close the CSV file.

You can now create vCard files from the CSV file using the technique explained in the next section.

Creating vCard Files from a CSV File

If you have a CSV file containing contact data that you want to get into Outlook, you need to create vCard files from the CSV file. Many apps can do this, but usually the easiest option is to use the OS X Contacts app, which is on your Mac and longing for action.

Here's how to create vCard files from a CSV file using the Contacts app:

1. Open the Contacts app. For example, click the Contacts icon on the Dock, or click the Launchpad icon on the Dock and then click the Contacts icon on the Launchpad screen.

2. Choose File ➤ Import from the menu bar to display the Import dialog box.

3. Navigate to the folder that contains the CSV file.

4. Select the CSV file.

5. Click the Open button. The Contacts app displays the Importing dialog box (see Figure 23-8).

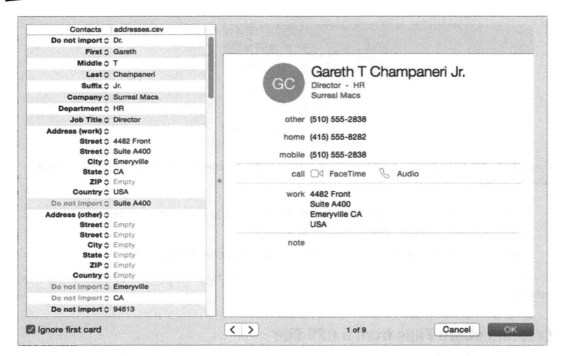

Figure 23-8. In the Importing dialog box in the Contacts app, select the Ignore first card check box if the first row of the CSV file contains field names. You can then use the pop-up menus in the left pane to map the CSV file's fields correctly to the vCard fields. Choose the Do not import setting for any fields you want to omit from the vCard files

6. Select the Ignore first card check box if the first row of the CSV file contains field names. (Otherwise, you'll get a vCard containing the field names.)

Note   If the first row of the CSV file contains descriptive field names, you may want to use the field names rather than the data they contain for reference as you map the fields. If you do this, remember to select the Ignore first card check box before clicking the OK button.

---

7. Use the pop-up menus in the left pane to map the fields in the CSV file to the corresponding fields in the vCard format.

Tip   Several sections of the pop-up menus include a More submenu that contains less-used fields. For example, click the More submenu in the Related Name section to reach fields such as Related Name (spouse), Related Name (assistant), and Related Name (other).

---

8. Click the Next (>) button or Previous (<) button at the bottom of the window to move from one record to another as needed. For example, you may need to view later records that contain data in fields that are blank in the earlier records.

9. When you finish the mapping, click the OK button. The Contacts app imports your data, creating vCard files that you can subsequently add to Outlook.

Importing Contacts from vCard Files

When you create vCard files or receive them from others, you can quickly add them to your contacts list in Outlook. Follow these steps:

1. In Outlook, click the People button on the Navigation bar to display the People area.

2. If the Address Book item in the left pane is collapsed, and you want to assign the incoming contacts to a specific group, click the expansion triangle to the left of the Address Book item to display the groups.

3. Open a Finder window to the folder that contains the vCard file or files.

4. Arrange the windows so that you can see both.

5. Drag the vCard file from the Finder window or the desktop to the left pane in the People area of Outlook. If you want to assign the contacts to a group, drag the file to that group; otherwise, drag the file to the No Category. Outlook adds the contacts from the file.

Working with Contacts

After creating contacts or importing them into Outlook, you can work with them. Outlook makes it easy to view your contacts, sort them in different ways, edit the information in a contact record, organize your contacts into groups, and communicate with them.

Viewing Your Contacts

To view your list of contacts, click the People button in the Navigation Pane. Outlook displays the contacts with the Reading pane on the right of the window at first (see Figure 23-9), showing the details of the selected contact. If you prefer to have the Reading pane at the bottom of the window, choose Organize ➤ Reading Pane ➤ Bottom from the Ribbon or choose View ➤ Reading Pane ➤ Below from the menu bar as usual (or press Cmd+Shift+\).

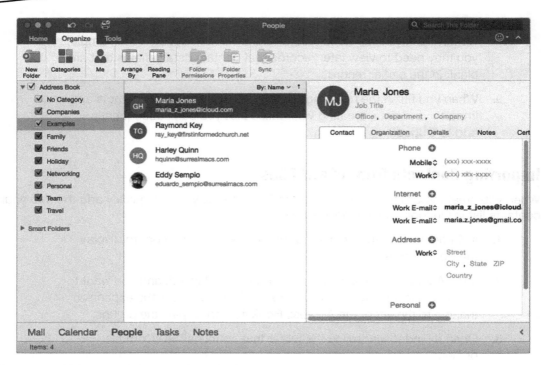

Figure 23-9. Click the People button in the Navigation pane to display your contacts. The Reading pane appears on the right at first, but you can choose Organize ➤ Reading Pane ➤ Bottom to move it to the bottom of the window

Arranging Your Contacts

You can arrange your contacts by whichever field you find most convenient. For example, you can arrange the contact list by First Name or by Last Name; by Work State or Work City; or by Birthday or Job Title.

The easiest way to choose the arrangement is to open the By pop-up menu at the top of the contacts list and then click the field you want. To use this view as the default for your contacts, open the By pop-up menu again, scroll all the way down to the bottom, and then click the Make This the Default View item.

You can also change the arrangement by using the Organize ➤ Arrange By pop-up menu on the Ribbon or the View ➤ Arrange By submenu on the menu bar.

To reverse the sort order, click the arrow button to the right of the By pop-up menu at the top of the contacts list. As you'd imagine, an upward arrow indicates an ascending sort, and a downward arrow indicates a descending sort.

Searching for a Contact

To search for a contact, follow these steps:

1.   Click in the Search box on the toolbar.

2. Start typing your search term. As you type, Outlook opens a pop-up panel to let you choose among matches for the name, for the company, for e-mail addresses, or for the category (see Figure 23-10).

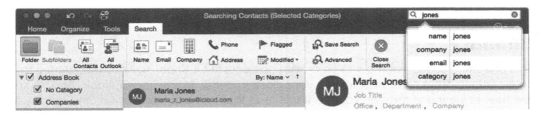

Figure 23-10. Type a search term in the Search box, and then click the category of result you want

3. Click the item you want; for example, click the name item to display name matches.

Editing Contact Information

As you interact with your contacts and learn more about them, you'll often need to take notes, add further details, or change the information you've already entered.

To edit a contact's information, double-click the contact record in the contacts list. Outlook opens the contact in a contact window, where you can edit the information freely.

When you've finished editing a contact record, choose Contact ➤ Save & Close from the Ribbon to save the contact record and close it.

Communicating with Your Contacts

When working in the main Contacts window or an individual contact window, you can quickly start a communication with one of your contacts by giving the appropriate command:

- *E-mail*: Choose Home ➤ E-mail from the Ribbon (in the main Contacts window) or Contact ➤ E-mail from the Ribbon (in an individual contact window) to create a new message to the contact.

- *Meeting*: Choose Home ➤ Meeting from the Ribbon (in the main Contacts window) or Contact ➤ Meeting from the Ribbon (in an individual contact window) to start a meeting invitation to the contact.

- *Instant Message*: Choose Home ➤ IM from the Ribbon (in the main Contacts window) or Contact ➤ IM from the Ribbon (in an individual contact window) to start an instant message to the contact.

> **Note**   You can also start a communication by Ctrl-clicking or right-clicking the contact in the contacts list and then choosing New E-mail to Contact, New Meeting with Contact, or New IM to Contact from the context menu.

Summary

In this chapter, you learned how to work with contacts in Outlook. You now know how to create contacts from scratch or import your existing contact data into Outlook. And you now know how to view and arrange your contacts, edit their contact information, and quickly and easily start communications to them.

In the next chapter, I'll show you how to use Outlook to manage your schedule.

Chapter 24

Managing Your Calendar

In this chapter, you'll look at how to use Outlook to schedule your appointments and keep your calendar in order.

First, you'll meet the Calendar interface, learn to display the dates you want, and customize the calendar settings. I'll discuss the different types of time commitments Outlook uses — appointments, events, and meetings — and then I'll show you how to use the Calendar's different views.

After that, you'll learn how to create one-time appointments (or events) and ones that repeat on a regular schedule. Finally, you'll look at how to use Outlook to schedule meetings and how to respond to meeting invitations you receive.

Meeting the Calendar Interface

To get started working with the Calendar, click the Calendar button in the Navigation pane and choose View ➤ Go To ➤ Calendar from the menu bar or press Cmd+2. The very first time you display the Calendar, Outlook normally uses the Week view, which gives you an overview of the whole calendar week. After that, Outlook displays the Calendar in the last view you used, such as Work Week view (Figure 24-1).

These are the main parts of the Outlook calendar window:

- *Folder pane*: The Folder pane shows the calendar dates for the current month or two, plus your calendar with a list of the categories it contains. You can display the categories by clicking the sideways disclosure triangle or hide the categories by clicking the downward disclosure triangle. You can drag the horizontal dividing line between the monthly calendar area and the list of categories up or down to reallocate the space between the two.

© Guy Hart-Davis 2016
G. Hart-Davis, *Learn Office 2016 for Mac*, DOI 10.1007/978-1-4842-2002-3_24

Note   As usual, you can hide the Folder pane by choosing View ➤ Folder Pane from the menu bar (clicking to remove the check mark from the Folder Pane item on the View menu). Give the command again when you want to restore the Folder pane.

Figure 24-1. Outlook first opens showing the current week's appointments

- *Time bar:* This vertical strip shows the times of day, with the hours marked. You can change the number of hours shown by dragging the Hours slider in the lower-right corner of the window to the left or right. The minimum number of hours you can display is 4; the maximum number is 24.

- *Zoom slider:* Drag this slider to the left to decrease the number of hours shown in the Time bar or to the right to increase the number of hours shown.

- *Previous button:* Click this button to display the previous time unit: the previous day when the Calendar is in Day view, the previous work week when the Calendar is in Work Week view, and so on.

- *Go to Today button*: Click this button to move quickly to the current day without changing the view. For example, if the Calendar is in Week view, clicking the Go to Today button displays the current week with the current day selected.

- *Next button*: Click this button to display the next time unit displayed: the next day, the next work week, the next month or whatever.

Displaying the Dates You Want

After you switch to Outlook to show the Calendar, you'll probably want to first display the dates you need to work with. Make sure the Home tab of the Ribbon is displayed; if not, click the Home tab. Then click the button for the arrangement you want:

- *Day*: Click this button to display a single day at a time. This view gives you an in-depth view of that day.

- *Work Week*: Click this button to display the days of the work week; Monday-to-Friday is the default, but you can change the days as needed, as you'll see in a moment. This view can be highly useful for planning your time at work.

- *Week*: Click this button to display a full week—Sunday through Saturday (you can change the start day of the week as needed).

- *Month*: Click this button to display the full month, including any days from the previous month and next month needed to make up the full weeks.

Customizing the Calendar Settings

Outlook comes with standard calendar settings, but you can often save time and effort by taking a few minutes to customize the settings to suit your work schedule and your needs. For example, you may need to use different start times and end times for work, change the work week to show different days than Monday to Friday, or start the week on a different day than Sunday.

To customize the calendar settings, follow these steps:

1. Choose Outlook ➤ Preferences or press Cmd+, (Cmd and the comma key) to display the Outlook Preferences dialog box.

2. In the Other area, click the Calendar item to display the Calendar preferences pane (see Figure 24-2).

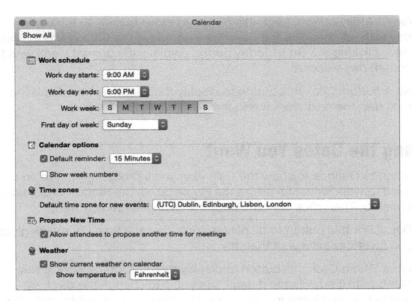

Figure 24-2. In the Calendar pane in the Outlook Preferences window, set your work schedule, reminder interval, and default time zone. You can also choose whether to allow attendees to propose different times for meetings and whether to display the current weather

3. To change your work hours, set the appropriate times in the Work day starts pop-up menu and the Work day ends pop-up menu. In Day view, Work view, and Week view, Outlook shades the hours outside work hours to help you avoid scheduling appointments in them (for example, a 3 a.m. meeting instead of a 3 p.m. meeting).

4. To change the days Outlook displays for your work week, click the buttons in the Work week bar to switch them between dark gray (part of the work week) and light gray (days of freedom). If you set a day within your work week to be a non-workday, Outlook still displays that day in Work view but shades the day to indicate it's not a workday.

5. To set the day Outlook treats as the start of the week, open the "First day of week" pop-up menu and click the day you want. For example, choose Monday to start the week on Monday rather than the default day, Sunday.

6. If you want to use a default reminder interval before appointments, select the Default reminder check box, and then choose the interval in the pop-up menu. Outlook offers intervals ranging from 0 minutes to 2 weeks. Doing this sets a reminder for each new appointment you create, but you can turn off the reminder, or use a different interval, for any appointment.

7. In the "Default time zone for new events" pop-up menu, select the time zone in which most of your events will occur.

8. Select the "Allow attendees to propose another time for meetings" check box if you want to allow attendees to suggest time changes.

9. Select the "Show current weather on calendar" check box if you want the Calendar view to include the current weather. If you select this check box, you can open the "Show temperature in" pop-up menu and choose Fahrenheit or Celsius, as needed.

10. When you've finished choosing calendar settings, click the Close button (the red button at the left end of the title bar) to close the Outlook Preferences window.

Understanding Appointments, Events, and Meetings

Outlook's Calendar uses three different types of time commitments:

- *Appointment*: An appointment is an item on your schedule that requires only you, not other people you need to invite or resources (for example, a conference room or projector) that you need to reserve. The Calendar creates appointments by default unless you choose to create an event or a meeting. An appointment occupies the appropriate time slots in your schedule. For example, if you create a three-hour meeting starting at 10 a.m., Outlook displays the appointment taking up the time slots from 10 a.m. to 1 p.m.

- *Event*: An event is simply an appointment that lasts for 24 hours or more. Instead of taking up all of a day's time slots by displaying an event right across them, Outlook displays events in the banner area at the top of the schedule.

- *Meeting*: A meeting is an appointment to which you invite other people or for which you schedule resources.

Note   You can change any of the three types of time commitments to another type by editing its details. For example, you can change an appointment to a meeting by inviting someone else to it.

Creating Appointments and Events

This section shows you how to create appointments and events. The following section explains how to schedule meetings.

Note   At this writing, you cannot synchronize Outlook's Calendar with other calendars, such as OS X's Calendar app or online calendars such as Google Calendar.

Creating One-Time Appointments

In a typical schedule, many of your appointments will occur only once rather than at regular intervals. You can create such one-time appointments either quickly, providing a minimum amount of information, or by using an Appointment window to enter full details.

Creating a One-Time Appointment Quickly

To create a one-time appointment quickly, follow these steps:

1. Drag through the appropriate slot in the schedule to select it. As you drag, Outlook increases the length of the appointment by a quarter-hour at a time.

2. Type the name of the appointment (or as much detail as you need, but it all goes into a single field). Figure 24-3 shows an example of creating an appointment like this.

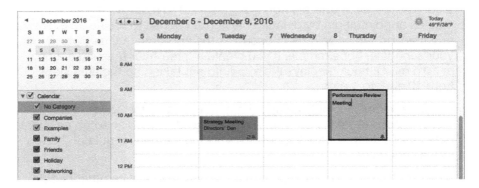

Figure 24-3. You can create a one-time appointment quickly by dragging through the time period and then typing the details into the box that Outlook displays. The bell in the lower-right corner shows that Outlook has added a default reminder, as set in Calendar preferences

3. Press Return to apply the appointment.

Creating a One-Time Appointment or Event with Full Details

Creating a one-time appointment quickly as discussed in the previous section is often handy, but other times you may need to enter full details for a one-time appointment. To do so, follow these steps:

1. Double-click in the schedule at the point where you want the appointment to start. Outlook opens an Appointment window (shown in Figure 24-4 with some settings chosen).

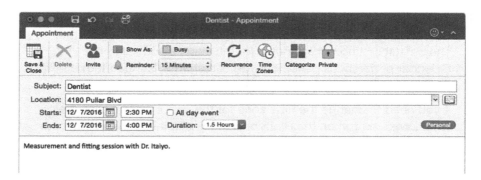

Figure 24-4. *Open an Appointment window when you want to specify the appointment's details beyond the subject and the times*

Note   You can also start an item by Ctrl-clicking or right-clicking the time in the schedule and then clicking the New Meeting item, the New Appointment item, or the New All Day Appointment item on the context menu.

---

2. In the Subject box, type the subject of the appointment or event.

3. In the Location box, type the location for the appointment or event.

4. Use the controls on the Starts line to adjust the date and start time of the appointment if necessary. If you got the date and time right in step 1, these controls will already be set correctly.

5. Use the controls on the Ends line to set the date and end time of the appointment. For most appointments, the easiest way to do this is to open the Duration pop-up menu and choose one of the preset durations. If you need a duration that doesn't appear on the Duration pop-up menu, type the exact end time in the time box on the Ends line.

6. If you want to create an all-day event rather than an appointment, select the All day event check box.

7. Type any notes for the appointment in the box at the bottom of the Appointment window. For example, you may need to prepare materials to take with you.

8. In the Status pop-up menu on the Ribbon, Outlook automatically selects Busy when you create the appointment. Instead, you can choose Out of Office, Tentative, or Free. Outlook displays a shaded bar on the left side of the appointment or event in the Calendar so that you can easily see the status you've set.

9. In the Reminder pop-up menu on the Ribbon, choose whether and when Outlook should play a reminder for you about the appointment. The default setting is 15 minutes (or the interval you set in the Calendar preferences pane), but you can choose None to turn off the reminder or any length of time between 0 minutes and 2 weeks.

10. If you need to change the time zone for the appointment, click the Time Zones button on the Ribbon. Outlook displays a time zone pop-up menu below the Ends time line. Choose the time zone you need.

11. If you need to create a recurring event, click the Recurrence button, and then work as described in the "Creating Repeating Appointments" section later in this chapter.

12. If you need to categorize the appointment, open the Categorize pop-up menu on the Ribbon, and then click the category you want, such as Manager or Team. You can apply multiple categories if you need to do so.

13. If this is a private appointment, click the Private button on the Ribbon to prevent others from seeing the appointment's details when you share your calendar.

14. Click the Save & Close button on the Ribbon to save the details of the appointment and close the window.

Creating Repeating Appointments

If your work life involves repeating appointments, you can set them up easily in Outlook. Follow these steps:

1. Open an Appointment window, and set up the other details of the appointment as described in the previous section. Or, if you've already set up an appointment and now need to change it to a repeating appointment, double-click the appointment to open it in an Appointment window.

2. Click the Recurrence button on the Ribbon to display the Recurrence pop-up menu (see Figure 24-5).

Figure 24-5. You can set up straightforward repeating appointments using the Recurrence pop-up menu. For more options, click the Custom item

3. If you want one of the recurrence types that appears on the pop-up menu, click it—for example, Every Thursday or Day 8 of Every Month—and skip the rest of this list. (The items in the pop-up menu vary depending on the appointment's context.) Otherwise, click the Custom item to display the Recurrence dialog box (see Figure 24-6).

Figure 24-6. Use the Recurrence dialog box when you need to create a repeating appointment

4. Set up the recurrence like this:

    ■   In the Repeats pop-up menu, choose Daily, Weekly, Monthly, or Yearly, as needed. Outlook displays the appropriate controls in the Every area of the dialog box.

    ■   Use the controls in the Every area to set up the recurrence. For example, for a weekly appointment, you can set the number of weeks in the Every *N* week(s) box, and then click the day in the On bar (for instance, click the second T button for Thursday). For a monthly appointment, use the controls in the On line to set the repetition, such as On First Monday or On Day 20.

Tip To set a weekly appointment to recur on multiple days, select those days in the On bar. For example, click the W button and the F button to create an appointment that recurs on Wednesdays and Fridays.

- In the Start box, enter the start date. Outlook uses the date you've specified for the appointment; you can change it if necessary.

- In the End date pop-up menu, choose None, After, or By. For the After option, specify the number of occurrences, such as After 10 occurrences. For the By option, pick the end date.

5. Click the OK button to close the Recurrence dialog box and return to the Appointment window, which is now called Appointment Series. The Recurrence line appears below the other details giving the details of the recurrence (see Figure 24-7).

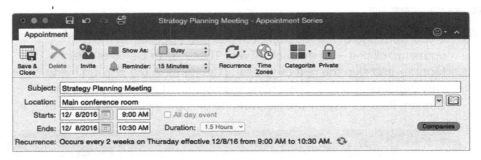

Figure 24-7. When you set up a repeating appointment, Outlook shows the details of the recurrence on the Recurrence line. You can click the rotating arrows icon at the right end of the Recurrence line to display the Recurrence dialog box

6. Click the Save & Close button on the Ribbon to close the window and save the changes.

> **Note**   If you need to stop an appointment from recurring, open the Recurrence pop-up menu, and then click the Once only item.

Scheduling Meetings

As you'll remember from earlier in this chapter, Outlook considers an appointment that involves inviting other people or scheduling resources to be a meeting. Chances are you'll need to schedule meetings of your own and respond to meeting invitations that other people send you.

Setting Up a Meeting

To set up a meeting, follow these steps:

1. Ctrl-click or right-click the meeting time in the schedule, and then click New Meeting on the context menu to open a Meeting window (see Figure 24-8).

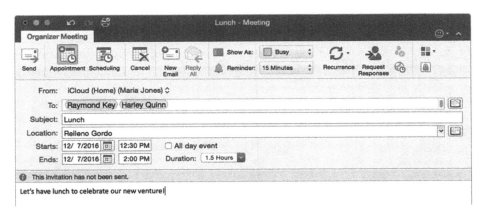

Figure 24-8. In the Meeting window, enter the recipients, the subject, the location, and the date and time for the meeting. In the Message box at the bottom, enter any message needed, and then click the Scheduling button on the Ribbon to display the Scheduling tab

2. In the To box, enter the recipients for the meeting invitations. You can either type in the names (with Outlook suggesting matches) or click the button at the right end of the To box to display the Search People window, and then search as discussed in Chapter 22.

3. Type the subject for the meeting request in the Subject box, such as the name of the meeting.

4. Type the meeting's location in the Location box.

5. Type any message about the meeting in the text box in the Message box at the bottom. For example, you may want to make clear what the meeting will cover, what attendees need to prepare, and so on.

6. If you want to check schedule information, click the Scheduling button on the Ribbon. On the Scheduling tab (see Figure 24-9), you can see the information available about each participant's schedule, which should help you pick a suitable time for the meeting. The information is available only if the participant gives you access to their schedule, such as in a company calendaring system.

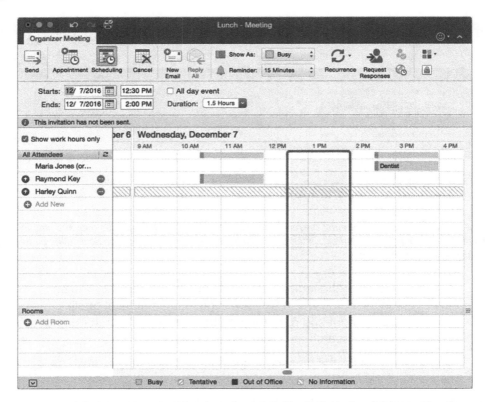

Figure 24-9. Use the Scheduling tab in the Meeting window to identify a suitable time for the meeting. You may be able to access schedule information for only some participants, as in this example

> **Note**   If you need to make changes to the meeting before sending the invitation, click the Appointment button on the Ribbon to display the Appointment tab again.

7. When you've finished setting up the meeting invitation, click the Send button to send the meeting invitation.

Tracking the Status of Meeting Invitations You've Sent

After you send a meeting request, you'll receive the responses that the invitees send. Outlook tallies the acceptances and refusals for you. To see a summary of the responses, double-click the meeting in your calendar to open it in a Meeting window, and then click the Scheduling button on the Ribbon to see the current status of the attendees:

■ A gray circle containing an ellipsis (...) indicates No Response.

■ A green circle containing a check mark indicates Accepted.

■ A blue circle containing a question mark indicates Tentative acceptance.

■ A red circle containing a cross indicates Declined.

Normally, you can let Outlook manage the status for you. But if an invitee gives you a verbal response, you can update the status manually by clicking the button next to the invitee's name and then clicking the appropriate item on the pop-up menu (see Figure 24-10).

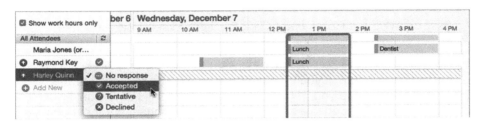

Figure 24-10. You can update the status for an invitee manually if necessary. Click the Refresh button to the right of the All Attendees heading to refresh the information with the latest updates

Dealing with Invitations to Meetings

When someone sends you an invitation to a meeting, you receive an e-mail message with the details of the message and with a built-in mechanism for replying. Double-click the meeting message to open it in a Meeting window (see Figure 24-11).

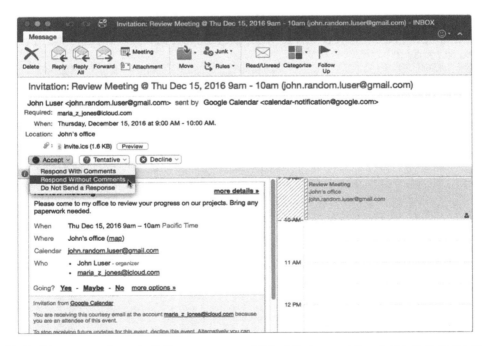

Figure 24-11. When you receive an invitation, you can accept it, tentatively accept it, or decline it. Each pop-up menu lets you choose among responding with comments, responding without comments, and not sending a response

Click the Accept button, the Tentative button, or the Decline button to display the associated pop-up menu, and then click the appropriate command:

- *Respond With Comments*: Click this item to start creating a message to which you can add comments before sending it.

- *Respond Without Comments*: Click this item to send the response without adding comments.

- *Do Not Send a Response*: Click this item to accept, tentatively accept, or decline this item in your calendar but not send a response to the person who invited you to the meeting. This action is occasionally useful for meetings that don't need to receive your response, but most people find it confusing.

Summary

In this chapter, you learned how to use Outlook to schedule your appointments and keep your calendar in order.

You now know how to navigate the Calendar interface and make it show the dates you want in the way you want them to appear. You now know the difference between an appointment and an event, and you know not only what distinguishes a meeting from an appointment but also how to set up meetings and respond to meeting invitations.

In the next chapter, I'll show you how to work with tasks and notes in Outlook. Turn the page when you're ready to start.

Chapter 25

Working with Tasks and Notes

In this chapter, I'll show you how to work with tasks and notes in Outlook.

Outlook's Task feature helps you get organized by defining tasks you need to complete and organizing them by priority, due date, or other criteria. You can create either one-time tasks or recurring tasks, keep notes in them, and mark them as complete when you finish them.

Outlook's Notes feature is useful for jotting down information as you work and then sharing your notes with other apps.

Creating Tasks

In this section, you'll learn how to work with Outlook's Tasks feature. You'll first meet the interface Outlook provides for working with tasks. You'll then create new tasks and manage your tasks.

> **Note** At this writing, you must create each new task in Outlook. You can't import or sync tasks from other sources, such as your To-Do items in OS X's Reminders app or your tasks in Google Tasks.

Meeting the Tasks Interface

To get started with tasks, click the Tasks button in the Navigation pane or press Cmd+4. Outlook displays the Tasks folder (shown in Figure 25-1 with several tasks added).

© Guy Hart-Davis 2016
G. Hart-Davis, *Learn Office 2016 for Mac*, DOI 10.1007/978-1-4842-2002-3_25

Folder   Check box   Task   Priority   Reading   Search
pane   column   list   column   pane   box

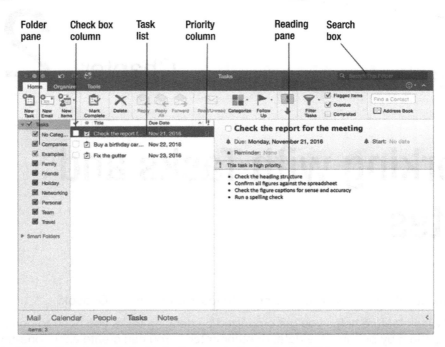

Figure 25-1. Click the Tasks button in the Navigation pane to display the Task List

By default, Outlook displays the Reading pane on the right of the Task List. When you click a task in the Task List, the details of the task appear in the Reading pane. You can move the Reading pane to the bottom of the Outlook window by choosing Organize ➤ Reading Pane ➤ Bottom from the Ribbon, choosing View ➤ Reading Pane ➤ Below from the menu bar, or pressing the Cmd+Shift+\ keyboard shortcut. You can hide the Reading pane by choosing Organize ➤ Reading Pane ➤ Off from the Ribbon, choosing View ➤ Reading Pane ➤ Hidden from the menu bar, or pressing the Cmd+Option+\ keyboard shortcut. When you need to return the Reading pane to the right side, choose Organize ➤ Reading Pane ➤ Right from the Ribbon, choose View ➤ Reading Pane ➤ Right from the menu bar, or press Cmd+\.

Creating One-Time Tasks

Outlook lets you create either one-time tasks—tasks that occur only once—or repeating tasks that recur on a schedule. This section explains how to create one-time tasks; the next section covers creating repeating tasks.

To create a task, you open a Task window and enter the details. Follow these steps:

1. Open a Task window (Figure 25-2 shows an example) in one of the following ways:

   ■ Choose Home ➤ New Task on the Ribbon.

   ■ Choose File ➤ New ➤ Task from the menu bar.

   ■ Press Cmd+N after clicking the Tasks button in the Navigation pane.

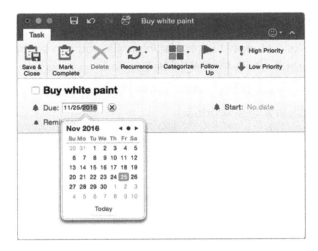

Figure 25-2. Enter the details of the task in the Task window

2. In the upper text box, type the task's subject or description, such as **Buy white paint**.

3. Open the Due pop-up menu, and choose the date the task is due to be completed.

4. If you want to enter a start date, open the Start pop-up menu, and choose the date the task will start. Setting a start date makes Outlook hide the task until the start date, which helps keep your Task List from being overwhelming.

5. If you want to set a reminder for the task, click the Reminder control, and then set the time and date for the reminder.

6. Type any notes about the task in the main box. You can apply formatting by using the context menu (Ctrl-click or right-click in the main box to display the context menu) or by using the Format menu.

7. If you need to create a recurring task, click the Recurrence button, and then work as described in the "Creating Recurring Tasks" section later in this chapter.

8. If necessary, change the task's priority by clicking the High Priority button or the Low Priority button on the Ribbon. If you need to remove the priority you've set, click the button again.

9. If you want to assign the task to one or more categories, click the Categorize button on the Ribbon, and then click the category you want, placing a check mark next to it. Repeat this move to add other categories as needed.

10. Click the Save & Close button on the Ribbon to save the task and close the task window.

Creating Recurring Tasks

If your job includes tasks that repeat at regular intervals, you can set up recurring tasks to have Outlook remind you of them. Follow these steps:

1. Create a task as described earlier in this chapter.

2. Open the task in a Task window.

3. Click the Recurrence button on the Ribbon to display the Recurrence pop-up menu (see Figure 25-3).

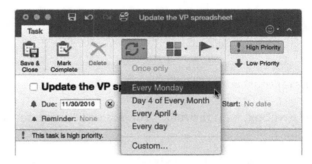

Figure 25-3. You can set up straightforward repeating tasks using the Recurrence pop-up menu. For more options, click the Custom item

4. If you want one of the recurrence types that appears on the pop-up menu, click it—for example, Every Monday or Day 28 of Every Month—and skip the rest of this list. (The items on this pop-up menu vary depending on the context.) Otherwise, click the Custom item to display the Recurrence dialog box (see Figure 25-4).

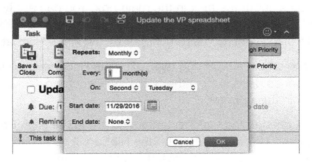

Figure 25-4. Use the Recurrence dialog box to set up the schedule for a repeating task. The options vary depending on the item you choose in the Repeats pop-up menu

5. Set up the recurrence like this:

■ In the Repeats pop-up menu, choose Daily, Weekly, Monthly, or Yearly, as needed. Outlook displays the appropriate controls in the Every area of the dialog box.

■ Use the controls in the Every area to set up the recurrence. For example, for a weekly task, you can set the number of weeks in the Every *N* week(s) box and then click the day in the On bar (for instance, click the second T button for Thursday). For a monthly task, use the controls in the On line to set the repetition, such as On Second Tuesday or On Day 20.

■ In the Start date box, enter the start date. Outlook uses the date you've specified for the task.

■ In the End date pop-up menu, choose None, After, or By. If you choose After, specify the number of occurrences, such as After 10 occurrences. If you choose By, pick the end date.

6. Click the OK button to close the Recurrence dialog box and return to the task window. The Recurrence line appears below the other details giving the information about the recurrence (see Figure 25-5).

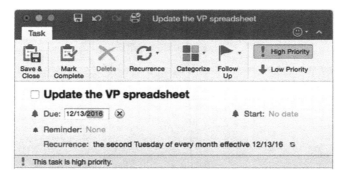

Figure 25-5. Outlook displays the details of a repeating task on the Recurrence line in the task window. To edit the recurrence, click the rotating-arrows icon at the right end of the Recurrence line

7. Click the Save & Close button on the Ribbon to close the window and save the changes.

Now that you've applied recurrence, the task recurs on the schedule you set.

Note   If you need to stop a task from recurring, open the Recurrence pop-up menu, and then click the Once only item.

Viewing, Arranging, and Filtering the Task List

If you have only a handful of tasks in the Task List, you'll probably find it easy enough to view them all at once. But when you have many tasks, you may want to view only particular ones, such as those that are overdue or those you've given high priority.

Choosing Which Columns to Display in the Task List

To work quickly with the Task List, you can choose which columns appear in it. Outlook starts you off with a widely useful set of columns—Completed Status, Due Date, Item Type Icon, Priority, and Title—but you may need to add other columns.

To choose which columns appear, Ctrl-click or right-click any of the column headings displayed in the Task List. The context menu that opens (see Figure 25-6) shows a check mark next to each column that's currently displayed. Click a column that doesn't have a check mark to display that column, or click a column that does have a check mark to remove that column.

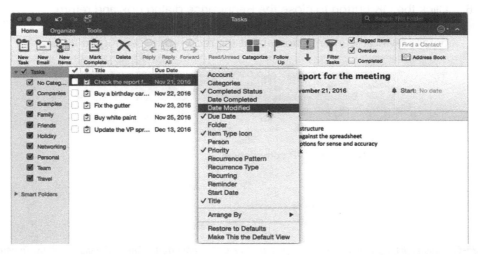

Figure 25-6. You can customize the columns displayed in the Task List by Ctrl-clicking or right-clicking a displayed column heading and then placing or clearing check marks on the context menu of columns

---

Note   You can also choose View ➤ Columns from the menu bar and then click the items on the Columns submenu to add or remove check marks.

Rearranging the Columns

When you've displayed the columns you want to see, you can rearrange the columns into a different order if necessary.

To rearrange the columns, drag a column heading to where you want that column to appear. Outlook moves the other columns out of the way (see Figure 25-7).

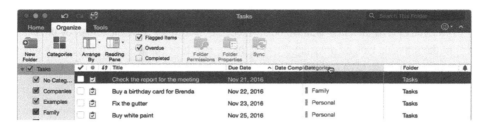

Figure 25-7. You can rearrange the columns by dragging a column heading, such as the Categories column heading shown here, to where you want that column to appear

Filtering Tasks to Show the Ones You're Interested In

To view only the tasks you want to see, you can apply filters. For example, you can display only your High Priority tasks so that you can concentrate on them.

To filter the tasks, choose Home ➤ Filter Tasks to display the Filter Tasks pop-up menu, and then click the filtering you want. For example, choose Due Date ➤ Today (see Figure 25-8) to view tasks whose due date is today, or click the High Priority item on the Filters pop-up menu to display tasks you've flagged with High Priority. You can also use the View ➤ Filters submenu to set filters.

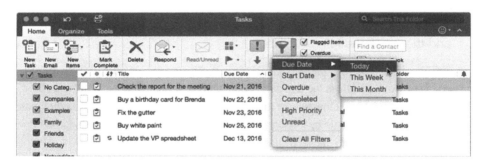

Figure 25-8. To display only particular types of tasks, open the Filter Tasks pop-up menu on the Home tab of the Ribbon, and then choose which tasks you want to see, such as tasks whose due date is today

When you want to see all your tasks again, choose Home ➤ Filter Tasks ➤ Clear All Filters from the Ribbon or View ➤ Filters ➤ Clear All Filters from the menu bar.

> **Note**   Another way to narrow down the list of tasks displayed is to go to the Folder pane and clear the check boxes for the categories you don't want to see.

Managing Your Tasks

To keep your Task List in order, you need to plow through it regularly, adding details to tasks, marking them for follow-up, and—when the time comes—marking them as complete.

> **Tip**   After you open a task in a Task window, you can quickly display the next task by pressing Ctrl+] or the previous task by pressing Ctrl+[. If the current task contains any unsaved changes, Outlook prompts you to save them.

Editing an Existing Task

Often, you may need to edit an existing task—for example, to add further details or to change the due date or priority.

To edit an existing task, either work in the Reading pane or double-click the task in the Task List to open a task window showing the details of the task. You can then change whichever aspects of the task you need to change. When you've finished, click the Save & Close button on the Ribbon to save the changes and close the task window.

Marking a Task for Follow-Up

If a task needs further action, you can mark it for follow-up at the appropriate time. You can quickly mark it for follow-up today, tomorrow, this week, next week, on no due date, or at a custom date of your choosing.

- *Task List*: Click the task, choose Home ➤ Follow Up from the Ribbon, and then click the follow-up date.

> **Caution**   The follow-up date is the due date for the project. If you don't want to change the project's due date, don't mark the task for follow-up; instead, set a reminder to the appropriate time. If you change the due date by marking the task for follow-up, the task moves further down your Task List if you're sorting the list by date.

- *Task window*: Choose Task ➤ Follow Up from the Ribbon, and then click the follow-up date.

> **Tip**   You can also set follow-up for the current task by using the Task ➤ Follow Up submenu on the menu bar.

- *Keyboard*: Press Ctrl+1 to mark the selected task for follow-up today, Ctrl+2 for follow-up tomorrow, Ctrl+3 for follow-up this week, Ctrl+4 for follow-up next week, Ctrl+5 for follow-up with no due date, or Ctrl+6 to open the Dates and Reminder dialog box for setting a custom date for follow-up.

When you need to set a different date than any of the preset buttons offers, click the Custom item, and then use the Dates and Reminder dialog box (see Figure 25-9) to set the details of the follow-up.

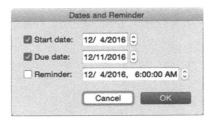

Figure 25-9. Use the Dates and Reminder dialog box to set a follow-up flag using the exact date and time you want

Marking a Finished Task as Complete

When you have finished a task, select its check box in the Task List or in the task window. You can also click the Mark Complete button on the Home tab of the Ribbon for the Task List or on the Task tab of the Ribbon in a task window.

> **Note** You can delete a task by clicking it in the Task List and pressing Delete or choosing Home ➤ Delete from the Ribbon for the Task List or Task ➤ Delete in a task window.

Taking Notes

When you're working in Outlook, you may need to jot down scraps of information that you need to deal with later. To do this, you can use Outlook's Notes feature.

Meeting the Notes Interface

To start using Notes, click the Notes button in the Navigation pane or press Cmd+5. Outlook displays the Notes pane (shown in Figure 25-10 with two notes created).

Figure 25-10. Use Outlook's Notes feature to take quick notes as you work

By default, Outlook displays the Reading pane on the right of the Notes List; the Reading pane displays the text of the current note. You can move the Reading pane to the bottom of the Outlook window by choosing Organize ➤ Reading Pane ➤ Bottom from the Ribbon, choosing View ➤ Reading Pane ➤ Below from the menu bar, or pressing the Cmd+Shift+\ keyboard shortcut. You can hide the Reading pane by choosing Organize ➤ Reading Pane ➤ Hidden from the Ribbon, choosing View ➤ Reading Pane ➤ Off from the menu bar, or pressing the Cmd+Option+\ keyboard shortcut. When you need to return the Reading pane to the right side, choose Organize ➤ Reading Pane ➤ Right from the Ribbon, choose View ➤ Reading Pane ➤ Right from the menu bar, or press Cmd+\.

Creating a Note

To create a new note, follow these steps:

1.   Choose Home ➤ New Note from the Ribbon or press the Cmd+N keyboard shortcut with the Notes List displayed. Outlook creates a new note in a Note window. Figure 25-11 shows a new note with a title and some information entered.

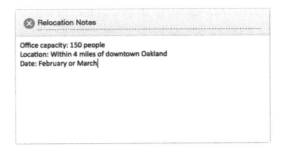

Figure 25-11. Choose Home ➤ Note to create a new note, and then type the information in the note window

2. In the box at the top, type the subject of the note.

3. In the lower box, type the detail of the note.

4. Click the Close button (the × button). Outlook prompts you to save the note (see Figure 25-12).

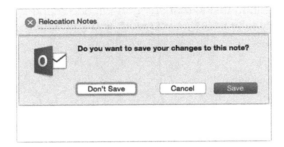

Figure 25-12. Click the Save button in this dialog box to save the note you're closing

5. Click the Save button. Outlook closes the note and adds it to the Note List.

> **Tip** You can also press Cmd+S to save the note as you create it and press Cmd+W to close the Note window when you've finished working with the note.

Editing and Using Your Notes

To edit a note, click it in the Notes List. The note's contents appear in the Reading pane, and you can edit them there.

If you need to edit two or more notes at once, open each in a separate window by double-clicking the note in the Notes List.

You can use the information you've saved in a note in any of these ways:

- *Copy and paste a note's contents*: Copy the contents of the note, and then paste them into whichever app you want to use them in, such as Microsoft Word or Microsoft PowerPoint.

- *Send a note as an e-mail message*: Click a note, and then choose Home ➤ E-mail to create a new e-mail message containing the text of the note. Address and send the message as usual.

- *Forward a note*: Click a note, and then choose Home ➤ Forward to create a new e-mail message with the contents of the note attached as a file in the HTML format. Address the message as usual, type any covering message needed, and then click the Send button to send the message.

Summary

In this chapter, you learned to work with tasks and notes. You now know how to organize your commitments by creating tasks, managing them, and marking them as complete. And you can quickly and easily take notes as you work and share them with other applications.

Index

W, X, Y, Z

Get the eBook for only $5!

Why limit yourself?

Now you can take the weightless companion with you wherever you go and access your content on your PC, phone, tablet, or reader.

Since you've purchased this print book, we're happy to offer you the eBook in all 3 formats for just $5.

Convenient and fully searchable, the PDF version enables you to easily find and copy code—or perform examples by quickly toggling between instructions and applications. The MOBI format is ideal for your Kindle, while the ePUB can be utilized on a variety of mobile devices.

To learn more, go to www.apress.com/companion or contact support@apress.com.